D1612714

THE NEW MPS of '97 - AND RETREADS

Andrew Roth and Byron Criddle

Caricatures by Ed Pentin and Terry Roth

PARLIAMENTARY PROFILES

Address: 34 Somali Road, London NW2 3RL
Telephone: 0171 222 5884 or 0171 435 6673
Fax: 0171 222 5889

ISBN: 0 900582 38 3

Computing Services by Padded Cell Software Ltd, PO Box 1880, London NW6 1BQ

Printed in Great Britain by Unwin Brothers Ltd, The Gresham Press, Woking, Surrey

WHEN THE NEW MPS OF '97 SOUNDED THE DEATHKNELL

Andrew Roth and Byron Criddle

For almost everyone watching on Election Night, it was the new MPs who foretold the deathknell of 18 years of Conservative dominance of the British political scene. It was the very first televised Labour gain - of Birmingham's middle-class Edgbaston seat by Bavarian-born Gisela Stuart, on a swing of 10% - that foretold the average swing and the vulnerability of middle-class seats. When nearly-70-year-old Sir Marcus Fox, Chairman of the 1922 Committee, lost his Shipley lair to nearly-25-year-old Chris Leslie after 27 years, it was clear that the voters were no respecters of enduring prominence. But the defining moment for almost all viewers was the contrast between the near-smirk on the face of Labour's openly-gay, 30-year-old Stephen Twigg and the stoney expression on that of Michael Portillo as he lost his Parliamentary foothold in Enfield-Southgate, until then one of London's safest Conservative seats.

These televised snapshots conveyed instantly the realisation that 1997 was on a par with 1906 and 1945 as an historic floodtide. Of course, in 1906 only three out of five adult males voted. The 1945 general election took place after an interval of ten years, because of World War II. Despite these differences, there was a basic similarity about these floodtides. The winning party roughly doubled its size, while the losing party was halved in strength. What was of concern to Labour leaders, and offered hope to their Tory opponents, was that the two earlier floodtides largely receded in the very next election.

What was special about 1997 was the range of swings and where they impacted. Almost uniformly, the biggest swings were in the most middle-class of seats, previously considered ultra-safe for the Conservatives. In addition to Southgate, there were Wimbledon, Gillingham, Hove, Thanet South, Eastwood, Wirral West, Scarborough, Morecambe and Lunesdale, Shrewsbury and Atcham, Warwick and Leamington, Stroud, Broxtowe - all toppled like ninepins, while changing from blue to pink. A rueful but still witty Tory ex-MP, David Sumberg, commented that he did not mind losing his seat in Bury South because he would no longer be able to recognise anyone in the Commons. Little wonder: in Morecambe and Lunesdale a Guinness heir, Sir Mark Lennox-Boyd, was replaced by a postal clerk, Geraldine Smith.

DEFYING THE CONTROL FREAKS

Although such Conservative losses were greeted with dismay in Smith Square - and mixed dismay and moments of malicious joy in John Major's Huntingdon home - there was not exactly unalloyed pleasure among Labour's 'control freaks'. Unlike the Liberal Democrats' election strategist, Chris Rennard, who spotted in advance almost every possible LibDem win except Rochdale, Labour had at least sixty uncovenanted wins. To be sure of winning a controllable majority of roughly 30, Labour Party strategists aimed at 75 gains on a 7% swing - which would mop up any gap between incumbent Tory MPs and aspirant Labour candidates of up to 14%. This meant that bridging a gap of more than 14% was uncovenanted. The unexpectedly-closed gaps began with No 60, Dr Howard Stoate in Dartford (whose gap was merely 14.7%) and stretched to the No 1 least-expected Labour victor, young Gareth Richard Thomas in Harrow West (whose gap was fully 32.7%!). In descending order they comprise No 2 Michael Jabez Foster, Hastings and Rye (31.9%), No 3 Stephen Twigg, Enfield-Southgate (31.7%), No 4 Christine Butler, Castle Point (31.6%), No 5 Eileen Gordon, Romford (29.8%), No 6 Roger Casale, Wimbledon (29.7%), No 7 Paul Clark, Gillingham (28.1%), joint No 8 Linda Perham, Ilford North and Brian White, Milton Keynes (27.9%), No 10 Barry Gardiner, Brent North (27.1%), No 11 Ivan Henderson, Harwich (27.0%), No 12 Tony Clarke, Northampton South (25.5%), No 13 Derek Wyatt, Sittingbourne and Sheppey (24.9%), joint No 14 Ivor Caplin, Hove and Jonathan Shaw, Chatham and Aylesford (24.5%), No 16 Keith Darvill, Upminster (24.1%), No 17 Geraint Davies, Croydon Central (24%), No 18 Rudi Vis, Finchley and Golders Green (23.9%), No 19 Martin Salter, Reading West (23.7%), No 20 Stephen Ladyman, Thanet South (23.6%), No 21 Alan Hurst, Braintree (23.1%), No 22 Nigel Beard, Bexleyheath and Crayford (22.9%), No 23 Jim Murphy, Eastwood (22.5%), No 24 Christopher Leslie, Shipley (21.9%), joint No 25 Valerie Davey, Bristol West and Paul Hesford, Wirral West (21.7%), No 27 Philip Sawford, Kettering (20.8%), No 28 Kerry Pollard, St Albans (20.7%), No 29 Andy King, Rugby and Kenilworth (20.4%), joint No 30 Jane Griffiths, Reading East and Desmond Turner, Brighton-Kemptown (20.2%), No 32 Andrew Dismore, Hendon (20.1%), No 33 Claire Curtis-Tansley, Crosby, (20.0%), joint No 34 Dan Norris, Wansdyke and Lawrie Quinn, Scarborough (19.9%), joint No 36 Geraldine Smith, Morecambe and Lunesdale, and Paul Marsden, Shrewsbury and Atcham (19.8%), No 38 Paul Stinchcombe, Wellingborough (19.5%), joint No 39 Tony McNulty, Harrow East and Thomas Dawson, Lancaster and Wyre (19.1%), No 41 John Cryer, Hornchurch (19%), No 42 Vernon Coaker, Gedling (18.7%), No 43 George Turner, Norfolk NW (18.5%), No 44 James Plaskitt, Warwick and Leamington (18.3%), No 45 Julia Drown, Swindon South (18.1%), No 46 Joan Ryan, Enfield North (18%), No 47 Robert Marshall-Andrews, Medway (17.7%), No 48 Gareth Thomas, Clwyd West (17.6%), No 49 Syd Rapson, Portsmouth North (17.5%), No 50 Tony McWalter, Hemel Hempstead (17.3%), No 51 David Drew, Stroud 16.9%, No 52 David Lock, Wyre Forest (16.3%), No 53 Nick Palmer, Broxtowe (16.2%), No 54 Peter Bradley, The Wrekin (15.9%), No 55 Harold Best, Leeds NW (15.7%), joint No 56 Tony Colman, Putney and Stephen Pound, Ealing North (15.6%), No 58 John Grogan, Selby (15.5%), No 59 David Borrow, South Ribble (15%). These figures, of course, represent the '92 gaps, not the '97 swing.

UNLIKELY LADS AND LASSES

Because of the unexpectedly broad extent of the swings, two months after the election there was an attempt to set up an "Unlikely Lads and Lasses Club" in the Commons, for those who won not only against the odds but against the limits set by the 'control freaks' in Labour's headquarters in Walworth Road and Millbank. Curiously, they circumscribed their target, to give a new Labour Government a small and controllable majority of 30 or so, as if they had been advised by Francis Pym, the former Chief Whip dismissed by Margaret Thatcher in 1983 for aspiring out loud to only such a manageable majority in a press conference during the 1983 election campaign. To secure this, Labour strategists quite rigorously kept to a swing of 7% and a target list of 75 winnable seats. Whenever Millbank clones were asked the likely size of a Labour victory, they chorused like automatons: "about 30", whatever the opinion polls were saying, no matter how long a much larger Labour lead had been in evidence. Any constituency Labour Party outside their target list which thought it had a chance was brought up short. Spelthorne, last won by Labour in 1945, was warned off trying and told to send its canvassers to marginal Slough, where Fiona Mactaggart, the millionairess daughter of a Scottish Tory, on 1 May won a Labour majority of 13,071 on a swing of 13.7%. In Spelthorne itself, the swing was a mite bigger, at 14.5%, but its Conservative MP, Ulster-fixated David Wilshire survived with a majority of 3,473 (down from 19,843). In some cases, Labour candidates were defiant. Nose-thumbing young Chris Leslie, told to send his activists to marginal Keighley, kept them canvassing in "unwinnable" Shipley, with its 12,362 majority for Sir Marcus Fox. On a swing of 13.8%, young Leslie wound up with a majority of 2,996 over a furious Sir Marcus. This enabled him to become the "Baby of the House".

The wildly unpredictable swings rewarded a number of serious enthusiasts. Computer specialist Dr Nick Palmer flew back almost every weekend from his Ciba-Geigy job in Switzerland to canvass 10,000 potential voters in Broxtowe. This resulted in his unseating its widely-admired Tory MP, Sir Jim Lester. Also swept into Parliament were a handful of what might be called "hobby candidates": men with serious and well-paid professional jobs who enjoyed a three-week stint of heavy political campaigning, usually in "hopeless" seats, without any expectation of winning. One of these was the Netherlands-born economics lecturer, Dr Rudi Vis, who thought he did not have "a hope in hell". His victory over the Rightwing Tory pro-Zionist, John Marshall, in Finchley and Golders Green was accompanied by Dr Vis's mournful complaint that he was booked to see 200 students the next week. Nigel Beard, a senior manager at ICI-Zeneca, had fought four previous "hopeless" seats. He then unexpectedly won Bexleyheath and Crayford. Derek Wyatt, the well-known Rugby player and well-paid Director of the Computer Channel of Rupert Murdoch's BSkyB, volunteered to fight "hopeless" Sittingbourne and Sheppey, against Sir Roger Moate, who had held the seat under various boundaries for 27 years. All were swept into office by the voters on 1 May 1997, some of them silently kicking and screaming to themselves.

IS NEW LABOUR MIDDLE-CLASS?

In the run-up to the election there were a number of surveys of expected victors. On the basis of a few well-publicised selection battles and inadequate candidate biographies, a number of generalisations were propagated. One of the basic ones was that 'New Labour' was fielding a new set of "middle-class" candidates.

One bitter, class-based contest was the failed attempt by the AEEU to keep their union convenor, Jim D'Avila, as the candidate for Swindon North, a fight lost to Michael Wills, a TV producer and friend of Gordon Brown and Peter Mandelson. A slightly less-noticed contest was where a Labour Party organiser and union activist, Eddie Lopez, was shoehorned out of marginal Slough by the imposition of an all-women short-list to the ultimate benefit of Fiona Mactaggart, the very able daughter and heiress of the late Sir Iain Mactaggart Bt, a seriously wealthy Glasgow property developer who was twice a Rightwing Tory candidate. Her mother was the daughter of a Tory MP and baronet.

To extrapolate from such clashes the wholesale transformation of the Parliamentary Labour Party into a middle-class organisation is an overstatement. There have undoubtedly been declines in the representation of particular sets of industrial workers like miners and engineers through falls in their actual strength during the partial de-industrialisaton of the Thatcher years. This was followed by a loss of control by their unions of various seats which they regarded as their fiefs. This has been most dramatic in the case of the miners union which, in 1959, controlled 34 constituencies as "miners' seats" where the NUM felt it had the right to nominate its own members as Labour's candidates. This declined to 21 in 1979 as the number of the country's miners decreased and local parties asserted the rights of the non-NUM majority. But its deathknell was "Scargill's last stand", or the miners' strike of 1984-85. The defeat of the miners and the subsequent decimation of the industry as it lost its preferred position with privatised power stations crippled the NUM and its ability to impose and back its candidates. In 1997 only a dozen NUM nominees remain in the Commons. In only one case was there well-publicised high drama about the loss of such a "miner's seat". In Pontefract and Castleford, one of Labour's safest seats, the very able young woman Blairite journalist, Yvette Cooper, was adopted after its NUM-backed incumbent, former miner and mines manager, Sir Geoffrey Lofthouse, a Deputy Speaker, was squeezed out into the Lords. But even Miss Cooper is the granddaughter of a miner and the daughter of a union chief. In a less-publicised case, former mines electrician Dennis Murphy, the new NUM-backed MP for Wansbeck (in succession to Jack Thompson), won despite being told there was no union money to support him, because of the shutdown of Ashington Colliery, in which he had worked for 30 years.

Other unions also feel they are entitled to certain seats and bridle at their loss. Doug Henderson, Labour's new Minister for Europe, represents Newcastle upon Tyne North, which has long been a "GMB seat" (and before amalgamation, a Plumbers' Union seat). Friction within the Labour movement often centres about changes in such representation owing to the decline in a union's strength, a change in the nature of a seat or the perceived 'voter-unfriendliness' of the man the union wants backed. All of these were elements in the costly and unpleasant fight over the replacement of Jim D'Avila, the AEEU convenor and former candidate, by TV producer Michael Wills in Swindon North. The AEEU was angry enough about that - and two other such perceived snubs - to withhold its promised £250,000 from the Labour Party. The engineering industry has lost a third of its jobs over the past two decades. But this contracting union, even if loyally Blairite, does not give up its Commons representation easily.

Such dramatic clashes tend to encourage over-simplifications, particularly if class definitions are defined simply by blue collars and white collars in a rapidly-evolving and increasingly-complex society with fudged boundaries. The complex job classifications of opinion pollsters tend to assess modern reality better than those of academics. How does one categorise Anthony McWalter, the Principal Lecturer in Philosophy and specialist in Kant, who won Hemel Hempstead from Tory Minister Robert Jones? His pre-election job was certainly that of a white-collar professional. But he started work as a lorry-driver. He also came from a working-class family, his father having been a painter and decorator and his mother an office cleaner. One has a similar problem with Philip Sawford, originally a carpenter, then a steelworker, who was sacked when the Corby steelworks shut down. He retrained at Ruskin College and Leicester University, becoming General Manager of Phoenix, a private training organisation serving Wellingborough Council. That was before he won "hopeless" Kettering from former Cabinet Minister Roger Freeman. The same question about class origins must be asked about Frank Roy, who worked for a dozen years at the Ravenscraig steelworks, before it was closed, blown up and bulldozed into the ground. He worked nights as a barman while studying at Glasgow Caledonian University before becoming Helen Liddell's Personal Assistant, and then the successor to Dr Jeremy Bray as MP for altered Motherwell and Wishaw. Are the above three "middle-class" or "working-class"?

The Blair leadership undoubtedly tried actively to make Labour more accessible to middle-class candidates and succeeded in attracting middle-class voters, among the two million former Tory backers who switched to Labour. In a few dramatic last-minute cases, sitting veteran 'Old Labour' MPs were squeezed out of their seats and into the Lords, to be replaced by more middle-class Blairite professionals. But any serious investigation of all the new Labour MPs will quickly suggest that the big change in the main is the emergence as candidates of the better-educated upwardly-mobile and politically-intense sons and daughters of mainly working-class families. There has never before been a Parliamentary Labour Party which has welcomed over half a dozen PhDs, or a half-dozen widely-recognised scientists or a half-dozen computer specialists at one time. If you investigate a bit, you find that often these are the sons of quarrymen, foundry workers, engineers, chemical process workers, Co-op milkmen, drivers, clerks and such, with the children of middle-class professionals in the minority, even if you include teachers. For every child of a property developer, there are a dozen children of painters and decorators, electricians, carpenters and plumbers. British Rail has left a legacy in Labour MPs who are the children of train-drivers, signalmen, railway clerks and baggage handlers. A fair number are the children of dinner ladies and office cleaners. This we know from those who are not shy about disclosing their family backgrounds, helping make our records more complete. Many are shy. There are all sorts of reasons for reticence, even among Tories. One new Conservative, Owen Paterson, John Biffen's successor at Shropshire North, was somewhat reluctant to disclose that his wife is the daughter of Viscount Ridley, but not about her being the niece of the Viscount's younger brother, the late Nicholas Ridley! Some new Labour MPs plead that they do not want their parents exposed to the relentless scrutiny of tabloid journalists. Some, like Dr Alan Whitehead of Southampton-Test, have been reluctant - despite twenty years of Parliamentary Profiles' probing - to admit that they have middle-class parentage. This is presumably because Labour's basic ethos is still working-class, despite the best efforts of the Millbank repackagers.

PUBLIC SERVICE PROFESSIONALS

The pre-election generalisation which was accurate, was that the victorious incoming Labour MPs would be overwhelmingly from professions in the public services. This is hardly surprising. It has long been observable that the educated children of working-class families tend to go initially into easily-accessible professions like teaching. What has happened recently is that this has broadened into other caring professions in the expanding social services. Labour-controlled urban councils, needing qualified staff, could be expected to be more generous with grants for students seeking such necessary qualifications. Similarly, the burgeoning polytechnics, initially locally controlled and financed, could be expected to produce the courses leading to such qualifications. A close study of the educations and occupations of those new MPs who have provided fuller records reveals that many of them, often starting with unskilled and manual jobs in factories or as drivers, took such paths into the professions, often the caring professions.

Another pre-election generalisation which, in fact, turned out to be an understatement was the dominance of councillors or former councillors among Labour candidates, including Deputy Leaders and Leaders of councils. This is explicable on two grounds. The first is that the Conservatives' electoral dominance of Westminster over nearly two decades very considerably narrowed the opportunities for Labour politicians with Commons aspirations. Even those who were selected often became also-rans on two, three or even four occasions when the election results were announced in 1979, 1983, 1987 and even 1992. For many, election to councils, particularly in Labour-dominated areas, was a softer option. It also often gave them a taste of limited power, when their Westminster colleagues were impotent in Opposition. Some new MPs, like Dr Phyllis Starkey, long tried to tell the Labour Party that MPs had much to learn from Labour-run councils, like the Oxford Council which she led.

FROM COUNCILS TO COMMONS

In the end, this council experience proved useful for moving up the greasy pole into Parliament itself. This was the unexpected result of Labour's adoption of one-member one-vote (OMOV) to choose Parliamentary candidates. In pre-OMOV days, candidates were selected by a tiny minority of party activists, ususally 20 to 40, often late at night when ordinary members had retired, or as a result of a 'fix' among dominant trade unions. The result was usually a union candidate or a cause groupie for whom activists had formed a preference in fringe meetings at party conferences.

The opening out of selection to the party membership has meant that decisions have been made by between 200 and 400 members, not by a score or two of conference-attending activists. The broader selectorate was more likely to opt for local councillors or council leaders whom they knew and trusted, on the basis of more closely observable performance. This has been distorted in a few places like Swindon North and Manchester where the union infrastructure has been exploited to collect postal ballots for union-favoured candidates. OMOV voting explains why the number of councillors or ex-councillors among the 183 new Labour MPs now totals 129, or 70%. These include 23 Leaders of councils. This tendency had already begun to show in 1987 and 1992. But initially it was almost only the Leaders of big-city councils who made it into the Commons for Labour. The full impact of their behind-the-scenes pressure for more expenditure on local education, health and housing remains to be seen.

LIBERAL DEMOCRAT TARGET-HITTERS

Among the Liberal Democrats the most astonishing development has been the fantastic but almost unnoticed benefits of intelligent targeting and tactical voting. Almost no electoral analyst has emphasised the fall in the Liberal Democrat vote from 1992 (6,067,552, or 17.9%) to 1997 (5,243,440, or 16.8%). Despite this, their MPs increased from 20 to 46. This was overwhelmingly the result of the concentrated targeting of some 60 seriously winnable seats and the chasing of tactical votes, masterminded by Chris Rennard. Each of the targeted seats was flooded with leaflets, illustrated with bar graphs, claiming (sometimes dubiously) that only the Liberal Democrat candidate could oust the incumbent Tory. Except for a few cases, including Bristol West and Hastings and Rye, where Labour candidates leapt from third to first place, the strategy worked famously.

CONSERVATIVE EUROSCEPTICS

One of the most striking aspects of the halved Conservative contingent is the way in which it illustrates the historical truism that a defeated ideology often survives a fallen regime. The Thatcherite revolution may have ended in November 1990 with the ouster of Margaret Thatcher, but a substantial number of her most zealous defenders entered or re-entered the Commons in safe seats in May 1997. Some Thatcherite radicals were washed out by the 1997 Labour flood: Nicholas Bennett in Reading West, for example. But others have been exceptionally successful in winning seats on the high ground of very safe-Tory areas, such as Dorset, Hampshire and Buckinghamshire. This has been helped by the recent loss of younger Tory party members, leaving the average age of survivors at 65 or 66, with the patriotic or chauvinist attitudes of that generation. Dr Oliver Letwin, who failed to win his native Hampstead against Glenda Jackson in 1992, has found rural refuge in Dorset West. Buckingham has provided the seat long sought by bustling John

Bercow. His friend, Dr Julian Lewis, scourge of the CND, has bedded down in New Forest East. The Thatcherites' relative success in finding seats has meant that the proportion of Eurosceptics and Europhobes in the shrunken Conservative Parliamentary contingent has increased from roughly two-thirds to more than three-quarters. When the crisis over entry into the single European currency re-ignited in October 1997, it was estimated that there were only 20 to 30 pro-Europeans in the halved Conservative contingent of 165 in the Commons.

This political arithmetic explains why Eurosceptic William Hague was elected over much more widely popular Kenneth Clarke, long known as a Europhile. It also sets the limits of Mr Hague's room for maneuvre. More important, it may help explain how the Hague leadership came to harden its opposition to the Euro from "not in the foreseeable future" at the October 1997 Blackpool conference to "not for a decade at least" by the time the Commons reconvened later that month. This ran contrary to the movement of opinion in big business and the City.

This enabled Chancellor Gordon Brown to run with the tide in placing the new Labour Government in favour of the Euro in principle while holding off a firm decision until after the next general election has consolidated Labour's hold on power. This tactically-clever decision helped precipitate a deep split among the Tories within a week.

This suggests that the influx of Eurosceptics and Europhobes among the Tory 'New Boys of '97' may have a lot to answer for, even if we do not accept the claims of Gordon Brown and Foreign Secretary Robin Cook that the Tories' civil war over Europe will exclude them from power for a generation. But this may be wishful thinking by Cabinet Ministers fully conscious that previous political floodtides have receded almost completely by the very next election. ***

'Gerry' (Gerard) ADAMS **Sinn Fein** **WEST BELFAST '97-, '83-92**

Majority: 7,909 over SDLP 6-way;
Description: The largely-Catholic slums of west Belfast, expanded into Lisburn in '95 to take in almost 10,000 more voters; the UK's most troubled and war-torn constituency, with some of its worst housing, including the Falls Road; much of its population is unemployed; of late it has been a battlefield between the moderate nationalists in the SDLP and the IRA-linked Provisional Sinn Fein;
Position: President '83-, Vice President '79-83 of the Provisional Sinn Fein; Northern Ireland Assemblyman '82-86
Outlook: Is "the driving and controlling force" of the Sinn Fein and IRA (Sir Hugh Annesley, former RUC Chief Constable), having, with Martin McGuinness, ousted the southern old guard fom the leadership of both organisations in the '80s; "the most thoughtful and intelligent person in the Republican leadership", who "turned Sinn Fein from an insignificant and unconvincing IRA front into a serious grassroots political movement" (David McKittrick, INDEPENDENT); a "brave man" (ex-Ulster Secretary Peter Brooke) for bringing about the '94-95 ceasefire; "the most capable person in the [Provisional] movement at thinking simultaneously in political and military terms, as well as its most visible and charismatic figure" (Paul Johnson, GUARDIAN); his voice is that of relative "moderation", in contrast with McGuinness's "hawkishness"; but "Gerry Adams insists that he would not dream of going to the IRA with anything less than their terms for a truce - a British withdrawal and a release of IRA prisoners" (David Hearst, GUARDIAN); has served as an honour guard at over 200 IRA funerals since 1971; allegedly previously the military Chief of the Provisional IRA '76-78; having given up boycotting the Dail, remains shackled to the historic IRA dogma of boycotting Westminster;
History: Joined the Fianna, the IRA's youth wing at 16, "which was a great source of heartbreak to my Da" '64; witnessed the notorious Divis riots, when the RUC brutally broke up the election headquarters of the republican candidate in west Belfast; he joined Sinn Fein '64; was part of the "popular uprising" of the northern Catholic working class from '69; at 20 was "one of the first people to volunteer to join the Provisional IRA after the organisation was set up", splitting from the Orthodox IRA Dec '69; following RUC attacks on nationalist areas in Belfast and Londonderry, allegedly became the commander of the Belfast Brigade's 2nd Battalion '71; was photographed in black jacket and beret as part of a guard of honour at an IRA funeral '71; was missed in the internment scoop, but his father and brother were taken Aug '71; after having been on the run as a wanted man, was arrested and imprisoned, first on the prison ship 'Maidstone' Mar '72; at 24, in response to IRA demands that he be included in the talks, was flown to London for secret negotiations with William Whitelaw, the Northern Ireland Secretary June '72; as 'Brownie' in REPUBLICAN NEWS developed the theory of advancing republicanism on two fronts: "the ballot box and the Armalite" '72; allegedly became Adjutant of IRA's Belfast Brigade; allegedly helped plan 'Bloody Friday' July '72; allegedly became Commander of the IRA's Belfast Brigade Mar '73; was captured by the Army, beaten and reinterned July '73; allegedly became Chief of Staff of the Provisional IRA '76; was jailed on charge of Provisional IRA membership, a charge later dropped '78; was jailed for a further 18 months for trying to escape from the Maze; on his release, he allegedly took command of the IRA's newly-formed 'Northern Command' '80; he and other Northern

Irish 'Young Turks' replaced Southerners in the leadership of the IRA-Sinn Fein; argued that the IRA could not win a purely military victory, therefore a political solution had to be found '80; was elected to Northern Ireland Assembly, topping the poll in West Belfast Oct '82; was banned from the mainland after the Ballykelly bombing Dec '82; said, "assassination of industrialists has been marginally sucessful" Mar '83; was arrested during the election June '83; ousted SDLPer Gerry Fitt from his long-held Belfast West seat June '83; reaffirmed his refusal to take his seat in a "foreign Parliament" July '83; he expected arest after a "supergrass" started spilling the beans Aug '83; placed an IRA beret, belt and gloves on the coffin of an alleged Provo killed by an SASman Dec '83; he denied the veracity of a 'World in Action' telecast accusing him of playing a leading military role in the Belfast Provisional IRA Dec '83; was wounded by a loyalist gunman with three bullets '84; he denied the SUNDAY TIMES' claim that he had taken over as the IRA Chief of Staff Aug '85; he denounced the Anglo-Irish Agreement as containing nothing that would make him urge the IRA to end violence Nov '85; decided on the need for wider support because the IRA alone could not win militarily and Sinn Fein alone could not win politically; he succeeded, at its Dublin conference, in persuading Sinn Fein to end its 60-year-old boycott of the Dail, the Irish Republic's parliament; this change, he claimed, would enable the Provos to cease "being spectators of a struggle in the six counties [of northern Ireland] and become pioneers of republicanism in the 26 counties" of Eire Nov '86; in Oxford Unon debate said, "I have never condemned the IRA and I never will; for me to condemn them would be to say I do not understand them" Mar '87; claimed the Anglo-Irish Agreement had not worked because it had not "removed the causes of alienation" and "will not bring about the isolation of Sinn Fein" Apr '87; defended the IRA killing of an informer Apr '87; was accused of "hypocrisy" by Northern Ireland Secretary Tom King when he desribed the killing of 8 IRAmen in an RUC trap as "murder" May '87; he survived the general election with a halved majority June '87; had a secret meeting with SDLP Leader John Hume Jan '88; tried to calm Catholic youth mobs reacting to cemetery killings of two British corporals, caught by an IRA mob at the funeral of IRA volunteer Kevin Brady, killed by a loyalist Mar '88; after he told a Dublin magazine that another IRA bombing like that at Enniskillen, which killed ll people, would "undermine the validity of the armed struggle", had another secret meeting with John Hume, allegedly to find a peaceful road to Irish unity to "get our people in from the cold"; missing was Martin McGuinness, the Londonderry Provo leader, whom Adams had described as "the head of the IRA" Mar '88; a senior RUC officer salid: "Adams is developing into a poltical figure as distinct from a subversive general; he has distanced himself from the Provisionals to ther extent that he now holds little control over their military activities; Martin McGuinness is the person with the power" Apr '88; he told the OBSERVER that killing British soldiers was "vastly preferable" to killing RUC or UDR members because it yielded more publicity and would "remove the agony" from northern Ireland June '88; the "Adams faction" was said to be urging that "going political" by taking his seat in Parliament would present Britain with bigger problems than continued terrorism July '88; he was forced to withdraw from the talks with John Hume by the IRA hawks who objected to Hume's suggestion of an all-Ireland conference on a peaceful settlement, including Unionists Aug '88; in a US intelligence report 'Terrorist Group Profiles' released by the Pentagon, he was identified, with Martin McGuinness, as the two leaders of the Provisional IRA Jan '89; hit out at IRA killings of civilians "by mistake" Jan '89; at annual conference in Dublin, admitted that IRA and Sinn Fein alone could not win Irish unity Jan '89; the broadcast ban on the Sinn Fein was ended Apr '89; shared a Sheffield platform with Tony Benn who argued the case for British withdrawal from Ulster June '89; his brother, Sean Patrick, was charged with attempting to murder RUCmen Oct '89; in the wake of the killing of 10 Royal Marines at Deal, he defended the IRA's bombing campaign as "legitimate" Oct '89; the new

Northern Ireland Secretary, Peter Brooke, admitted the armed struggle in Ulster was one neither side could win; said there could be talks if the IRA put down its arms Nov '89; described as "cold-blooded murder" the killing of 3 IRA men by an Army under-cover unit Jan '90; blamed "media mischief" for speculating on an IRA cease-fire Mar '90; welcomed the release of the 'Winchester Three' as underlining "how easily and groundlessly Irish people are sentenced to massive terms of imprisonment by the British courts" Apr '90; at the funeral of IRAman Desmond Grew, said: "those of us left to finish the unfinished business, will do so" Oct '90; secret negotiations between the British Government and the Sinn Fein began, at the instigation of MI5 '90; welcomed the IRA's three-day Christmas cease-fire Dec '90; after a fire-bombing campaign, was described by Economy Minister Richard Needham as an "apologist for those who burn jobs" Jan '91; urged Unionists to join in seeking a demilitarised future Feb '92; said, "I regard the IRA as a legitimate organisation, as freedom fighters, but the IRA doesn't tell Sinn Fein what to do and Sinn Fein doesn't tell IRA what to do" Mar '92; was defeated in West Belfast by SDLP's Dr Joe Hendron by 589 votes Apr '92; he briefly shook hands with Irish President Mary Robinson June '93; a grenade attack on his home injured his wife and son June '93; Hume-Adams talks resumed 'in secret', but had apparently been bugged by MI5 Sep '93; was barred from mainland Britain Oct '93; President Clinton initially refused him a visa for being "involved at the highest level" in IRA's terrorist strategy Nov '93; accurately described secret negotiations with the British Government Nov '93; his demand for an amnesty for jailed terrorists was rejected Dec '93; said he was "disappointed" that the Anglo-Irish Downing Street Declaration offered him a place at the negotiating table only if the IRA gave up violence Dec '93; after President Clinton allowed him a visa - to the dismay of John Major and Ulster Unionists -he paid a two-day visit to the USA, during which the President urged him to embrace the Downing Street declaration Feb '94; at the Sinn Fein's annual conference in Dublin, said the mortar bombs at Heathrow showed "the causes of the conflict" still remained Feb '94; was given legal aid to fight his ban from mainland Britain Mar '94; John Hume urged the British Government to resume talks with Adams Mar '94; the IRA called a 72-hour ceasefire Apr '94; he called for a full amnesty for all imprisoned terrorists May '94; after years of his persuasion, the IRA began its ceasefire Aug '94; was welcomed in Dublin by Irish PM Albert Reynolds Sep '94; he demanded British "demilitarisation" and direct talks, insisting the IRA would not disarm before a settlement Oct '94; during his Washington visit, he met President Clinton's security adviser Nov '94; was praised by former Northern Ireland Secretary Peter Brooke as "a brave man" in having urged a ceasefire on the IRA Jan '95; on his St Patrick's Day visit, President Clinton urged the IRA to disarm Mar '95; on the first anniversary of the IRA ceasefire, claimed the British Government was using the decommissioning issue to "try to win a victory through stalemate" Apr '95; visited South Africa to meet President Mandela June '95; accused the UK Government of "strangling the peace process", warning that the IRA "hadn't gone away" Aug '95; said the peace processs was "doomed to collapse" if Britain insisted on IRA disarmament before Sinn Fein could enter the talks Sep '95; called for an independent international judicial investigation into all "disputed killings" by British forces, such as the killing of three IRAmen on the Rock Sep '95; agreed the IRA would not give up arms in advance of a settlement but might gradually decommission some after Sinn Fein had been allowed into talks Jan '96; demanded an unconditional date for talks Feb '96; after he warned the White House it might happen, the IRA cease-fire broke down with a bomb in London's Docklands, which he blamed on the British Government's floundering Feb '96; wrote that the IRA leadership had begun its ceasefire on the basis of a "pan-nationalist alliance" of Dublin, the SDLP, Sinn Fein and Irish America to bring about a settlement; in the absence of the settlement, the IRA might begin "another 25 years of war" Mar '96; there was a breakdown in his relations with SDLP Leader John Hume and Irish PM

John Bruton Apr '96; in the election to all-party talks, he achieved 53.4% of the vote in Belfast West, twice that of the SDLP, with the Sinn Fein collecting 15.4% of the poll in the Province, its best result May '96; said he was "shocked and saddened" by the Manchester bomb June '96; told Irish radio Sinn Fein wanted to "see an end to the armed struggle"; "we're not involved in it and we do not advocate it" June '96; told President Clinton: "don't ask me to push the IRA over a ceasefire - because I cannot deliver" June '96; declared "the peace process is in tatters" after 48 hours of rioting and intimidation visited on Catholic families after the RUC led Orange paraders through Portadown July '96; led Sinn Fein's newly-elected delegates up to the gates of Belfast's Castle Buildings to demand access to talks, despite the IRA's refusal to proclaim a ceasefire July '96; published his autobiography, Before the Dawn Sep '96; the Commons' Serjeant-at-Arms and the Labour Chief Whip Donald Dewar blocked attempts by Jeremy Corbyn and Tony Benn to host an Adams book launch Sep '96; after the Lisburn bombing, Ireland's PM, John Bruton compared the IRA to the Nazis and urged the Sinn Fein to limit itself to the ballot box Oct '96; he rejected angrily SDLP Leader John Hume's conditions for an electoral pact, including "a complete end to violence" by the IRA and his taking a seat in Westminster Oct '96; Australia refused him an entry visa Nov '96; President Clinton refused him an American visa Feb '97; said he was "quite surprised" - when he meant angered - by the proposal that the imprisoned IRA suspect Roisin McAliskey might stand for her mother's old seat of Mid-Ulster, which his partner Martin McGuinness was planning to take Mar '97; showed interest in a "new opportunity for peace" after Labour's 'shadow' Northern Ireland Secretary, Mo Mowlam, promised that if there were an immediate ceasefire, maintained by word and deed, Sinn Fein might enter the multi-party talks in June, Mar '97; the Irish PM, John Bruton, said: "a vote for Sinn Fein is a vote of support for the IRA and the IRA's campaign of killing and murder" Apr '97; he carried the coffin of a Catholic father of 10, murdered by loyalists - as he had done in more than 200 IRA funerals since 1971 Mar '97; he ousted Dr Joe Hendron from altered Belfast West to retake it with a majority of 7,909, a swing of 9.8%, May '97; visited Westminster with fellow SF winner Martin McGuinness, to be told he could have House of Commons stationery, but without pledging allegiance to the Queen, he could not take his seat, speak or vote, despite his election victory May '97; as a reward for the renewed IRA ceasefire, President Clinton granted him a visa Aug '97; he was also invited by Northern Ireland Secretary Mo Mowlam to join the all-party talks Aug '97; in Washington, he promised to "compromise, compromise, compromise, compromise" in all-party talks Sep '97; he accepted the "Mitchell principles", committing Sinn Fein to non-violence, on entering the talks Sep '97; he met PM Tony Blair, the first such meeting in 70 years Oct '97;

Born: 6 October 1948, West Belfast

Family: His maternal grandfather was a personal friend of James Connolly and James Larkin; his paternal grandfather had helped found the Irish Republican Brotherhood, predecessor of the IRA; was the eldest of 10 children of building worker Gerard ("old Gerry") Adams, an IRA veteran of the 1939 campaign who was shot and wounded by the RUC and imprisoned for five years in the troubled '40s; his mother, a Hannaway, came from Belfast's leading Republican family; his cousin, David Adams, was jailed for 25 years for conspiracy to murder '95; m '71 Collette (McArdle); 1s Gearoid '73, who trained as a teacher;

Education: St Mary's Grammar (Christian Brothers); left at 17;

Occupation: Author: Before the Dawn (1996, for which he was alleged to have received £100,000 as an advance), Selected Writings (1994), The Street and Other Stories (1992), Cage Eleven (1990), Politics of Irish Freedom (1988), Falls Memories (1982); was a barman '69-73 in Belfast pubs, since when he has collected unemployed benefit of £53.65;

Traits: Tall; cropped black beard; specs; reconstructed teeth; pipe-smoker; dresses neatly in

dark suits; courteous; polite; wary; "complicated and elusive", "cold-blooded, unemotional, articulate and intelligent" (SUNDAY TELEGRAPH); "hard, cold, cliche-ridden and deep" (Sean O'Callaghan, IRA informer); changes abode almost every night; travels in bullet-proof cars; sometimes wears bullet-proof vests; pious Catholic;
Address: 51-53 Falls Road, Belfast 12;
Telephone: 01232 223214

Richard ALLAN **Liberal Democrat** **SHEFFIELD-HALLAM '97-**

Majority: 8,271 over Conservative 5-way;
Description: Formerly the only Tory seat in Sheffield and south Yorkshire; a leafy, mainly middle-class residential area in the city's southwest, stretching from the university area of Broomhill to the edge of the Peak District; contains Sheffield and Hallam universities and houses much of the city's professional and managerial elite; its latest change, the removal of pro-Labour Nether Edge ward, allegedly made it safer for Conservatives;
Position: On Select Committees: on Home Affairs '97-, on Information '97-; ex: Bath City Councillor '94-95; Avon County Councillor '93-95;
Outlook: Young, locally-born, Leftwing LibDem who won on his first Parliamentary attempt in the party's 1997 mini-landslide; "wary of co-operation with Labour" (NEW STATESMAN); he also won in his first attempts in Bath and Avon; "one of the party's rising stars" (Paddy Ashdown MP); a classless-seeming computer manager; a Leftwing cause groupie: Liberator, ALDC, Green Liberal Democrats, CPRE, Voting Reform Group, Searchlight, World Development Movement; his key political interests are the NHS (its preservation in public service), the social services, civil rights for disabled people: "all are issues on which I have acted or spoken over several years; I am also very supportive of the constitutional reform agenda, especially a legal framework for the relationship between the citizen and the state";
History: At school he was against party politics; he joined the LibDems at 25, Sep '91; successfully contested Avon County Council May '93; successfully contested Bath City Council May '94; was selected as the LibDem candidate for Tory-held Sheffield-Hallam, which had twice been won by Sir Irvine Patnick, in 1992 by a majority of 6,741 over his LibDem opponent Peter Gold '95; won the seat by a majority of 8,271 (18%) on an astonishing swing of 18.53%, making him "the only opposition MP in the whole of south or west Yorkshire" (RA) May '97; in his Maiden speech, emphasised the problem of youth crime in the Low Edges estate and the need to keep a "high-quality urban environment that people will respect" and enough local policemen May '97; asked about compensation for debts of gun clubs June '97; co-sponsored motion urging complete ban on organophosphates June '97; was named to Select Committee on Home Affairs July '97;
Born: 11 February 1966, Sheffield
Family: Son, of John Allan, chauffeur and personnel manager, now retired, and Elizabeth (Beaumont), doctor's receptionist; m '91 Louise (Netley), school supervisory assistant; 1d Rosie '88;
Education: Ecclesall Infants; Ecclesall Junior; Birkdale Prep; Oundle School; Pembroke

College, Cambridge University (BA Hons); Bristol Polytechnic (MSc);
Occupation: Ex: Consultancy and Systems Integration Manager (Information Technology) in NHS's Family Health Systems; previously an archaeologist;
Traits: Oval face, with light tufted fringe beard and thin moustach; holds his head erect; slight Yorkshire brogue;
Address: House of Commons, Westminster, London SW1A 0AA; 99 Clarkehouse Road, Sheffield S10 2LN (constituency office);
Telephone: 0171 219 1104/0941(Fax) (H of C); 0114 249 4775 (Fax); 0410 497095 (mobile); 0114 249 4774 (answering service);

Candy ATHERTON **Labour** **FALMOUTH & CAMBORNE '97-**

Majority: 2,688 over Conservative 9-way;
Description: The unaltered seat in southern Cornwall based on the working port of Falmouth and the former tin-mining centres of Camborne and Redruth; it has the only local Labour tradition, more recently in local councils, since Dr John Dunwoody was ousted by David Mudd in 1970; the difficulty of removing Mudd's successor, Olympic gold medallist Sebastian Coe centred on the rivalry of his Labour and Liberal Democratic would-be ousters;
Position: On the Select Committee on Education and Employment '97-; ex: Islington Borough Councillor (Mayor '89-90)'86-92; on Islington Health Authority '86-90;
Outlook: Proud of being a Labour island in a sea of LibDems; with the Labour tide behind her, managed to overtake the greater, earlier activity of her rival anti-Tory, the LibDems' Terrye Jones, and blocked a LibDem clean sweep in Cornwall; the Blairite former Islington Mayor and journalist who was the first selection from an all-women short-list; won selection and election in a town in which her mother, a former hairdressing salon owner, was the current Mayoress; has fought her corner locally on low wages, unemployment and the high price of water; "a stimulating hybrid of Peter Mandelson and Dawn French" (Robin Stummer, INDEPENDENT ON SUNDAY); as a former researcher for Leftwing MPs Jo Richardson and Judith Hart, may not always have been a moderate;
History: Joined the Labour Party '79; was elected to Islington Borough Council May '86; was made a Freeman of the City of London for her contribution to the reorganisation of local schools '90; selected for hopeless Chesham and Amersham, came 3rd with 10.4% of the vote Apr '92; helped Barbara Follett set up 'Emily's List' to support women politicos in finding seats '93; was the first woman selected from an all-women short-list Dec '94; this selection met with considerable opposition from male aspirants, with three local councillors resigning; Jim Geach, a local county councillor and former Labour candidate for Truro, resigned from the party and threatened a legal action, which collapsed, and then to stand as an Independent candidate; she blamed Conservative policies for the loss of thousands of jobs in the constituency Mar '95; attacked for being a classic example of a shoulder-padded middle-class woman being foisted on a Cornish seat, retorted: "I can speak for the fishermen, the family and economics as well as any former Olympic runner or Labour stalwart; what will make the difference with the [all-women] short-lists is having a mass of women who together can influence the party on

issues like hours in the Commons, civilised debate and childcare" May '95; urged a concerted campaign to restore the lifetime benefit for those injured at work, cut from £38.12 a week to £9.90 June '96; launched a defence of Albert Tong, a Camborne-based illegal immigrant of 17 years standing whom Home Office Minister Ann Widdecombe was trying to deport to Hongkong (an attempt which eventually failed) June '96; when Labour successfully defended a local by-election, she said: "the LibDems are going backwards while Labour surges forward" July '96; told annual conference that Britain was "crying out" for a national minimum wage: "our traditional industries are in decline, so the low-pay merchants have come to town; if we believed the Tories' claim that low pay attracts jobs, we should be knee-deep in Japanese jobs; surprise, surprise, we are not - and unemployment continues to rise in Carnwall, month after month"; "the Tories' idea of the moral high ground is to leave the market free to pay the lowest amount" Sep '96; with 17 other loyal candidates, criticised the INDEPENDENT for seeking divisions among candidates, insisting "the Labour Party is a united dynamic party ready to solve the problems this country faces" Oct '96; opposed a local multi-storey car park "on environmental and social grounds" Feb '97; said "I am not in favour of a federal superstate, but I am not happy with us always being a 'no, no,no' nation" Mar '97; her election efforts were reinforced by the arrival of 20 Labour peers, MEPs and MPs, led by Harriet Harman Apr '97; despite her local Labour rival, Jim Geach, polling 1,691 as 'Independent Labour', she managed to overtake LibDem Terrye Jones and oust the sitting Tory, Olympic champion Seb Coe with a majority of 2,688 , a swing from the Tories of 6.64%; this made her Cornwall's first woman MP since the 1920s May '97; co-sponsored motion applauding restoration of union rights at GCHQ May '97; asked about time taken for breast cancer referrals June '97; complained about rail services to Penzance June '97; in her Maiden raised the crisis in Cornwall Care, the charity to which the LibDem-controlled county council had transferred its homes for the elderly, which had lost its case before the industrial tribunal after trying to cut staff wages sharply June '97; was named to the Select Committee on Education and Employment July '97; she led a delegation to try to stop the closure of South Crofty, the last Cornish tin mine Sep '97; at annual conference fringe complained of the "shameless tactics" of local LibDems, who had called her "that harridan woman from London" Oct '97;

Born: 21 September 1955, Sutton, Surrey

Family: Daughter, of Denis Atherton, ex DAILY MIRROR journalist, and Pamela (Osborn), hairdressing salon owner and Mayoress of Falmouth '96-98; her Partner is Broderick Ross, a Cornishman living in Falmouth;

Education: Sutton High School; Midhurst Grammar School; North London Polytechnic (BA Hons in Applied Social Studies);

Occupation: Free-lance journalist: recently in a Wiltshire-based agency (NUJ); was a co-founder of EVERYWOMAN; a former Probation Officer; a part-time organiser for UNISON; a one-time researcher for Leftwing Labour MPs Judith Hart and Jo Richardson;

Traits: Long straight blonde hair; very chubby; large specs; glider pilot; ornithologist; likes living on narrow-boats (as she did for six years when an Islington councillor);

Address: House of Commons, Westminster, London SW1A 0AA; 4 Webber Hill, Falmouth, Cornwall TR11 2LY (constituency office);

Telephone: 0171 219 3000 (H of C); 01326 314440/314415 (Fax) both in her constituency office;

Charlotte ATKINS **Labour** **STAFFORDSHIRE-MOORLANDS '97-**

Majority: 10,049 over Conservative 4-way;
Description: A lovely north Staffordshire seat changed in all but name by the addition of pro-Labour Kidgrove's 19,000 voters (from Stoke-on-Trent) and the deletion of 27,000 voters from pro-Tory villages; this almost changes it back to the marginal Labour seat of Leek -named after its old textile town - formerly held by the late Harold [later Lord] Davies; it also marks the retirement of Sir David Knox who took it from him; it borders on ten other constituencies; it retains its quota of potteries, but has lost all its pits;
Position: On: Committee of Selection '97-, Select Committee on Education and Employment '97-, Labour Party's National Policy Forum '95-, Women's Committee of Labour's NEC '93-; Wandsworth Borough Councillor (Deputy Leader of its Labour Group '85-86, Chief Whip '83-85) '82-86;
Outlook: Rightward-moving Leftish ex-UNISON lobbyist; after 20 years of working for unions, has been accepted within the party leadership as "quintessentially one of us" (INDEPENDENT); others rate her a "Kinnockite realist" (RED PEPPER) or "Centre-Left" (NEW STATESMAN); has worked her passage partly by helping women aspirants to win selection through the Labour Women's Network; the daughter of Ron Atkins, the former soft-Left Labour MP for Preston North for nine years; a one-time collaborator with Bennite Chris Mullin in instructing activists on how to dump moderate Labour MPs; was in CND and the Labour Co-ordinating Committee, on the editorial board of The CHARTIST and for two years on the Executive of Liberty (formerly National Council for Civil Liberties);
History: Joined the Labour Party when her father won Preston North '66; became COHSE Press Officer '80; collaborated with the leading Bennite, Chris Mullin, in the Leftwing activists' manual, 'How to Select or Reselect Your MP', which made life miserable for scores of moderate Labour MPs for the next decade; her contribution was to analyse how Labour MPs had voted on 12 key Commons divisions; the pamphlet was published by the CLPD and the Institute for Workers' Control Oct '81; was elected to Wandsworth Borough Council May '82; became its Chief Whip May '83; became Deputy Leader of the Labour Group on Wandsworth Borough Council May '85; was imposed by the NEC as the Labour candidate for the Eastbourne by-election, in the wake of Ian Gow's assassination by the IRA; the existing candidate, Peter Day, had refused to pay his poll tax; her Labour vote was squeezed down from 8.8% to 5% (2,308 votes) by the successful Liberal Democrat, David Bellotti Oct '90; as an activist in Labour Women's Network, warned in EMILY NEWS against women aspirants going simply for trade union nominations; she urged women to "get networking" since one-member one-vote required them to "get around the constituency and meet as many members as possible and not rely on trade union nominations, thinking that by just getting on the short-list the union support will lead members to vote for them"; "all the evidence points against this"; "members decide to vote for you on the evidence of their experience of you or their friends' views" Oct '94; her own selection for the favourably redrawn seat of Staffordshire-Moorlands - without the invervention of an all-women short-list - provoked the resignation of some local constituency officers '95; prepared UNISON's evidence for the Nolan Committee into Standards in Public Life '95; in a joint letter with 17 other loyal

candidates, protested to the INDEPENDENT about its search for divisions, insisting "the Labour Party is a dynamic united party, ready to solve the problems this country faces" Oct '96; in a discussion on Parliamentary lobbyists on BBC-TV said that in her role as Parliamentary Officer of UNISON, "we can get to places where we need to get in" Jan '97; her victory, on a notional swing of 8.7%, made her the seat's first Labour MP since the late Harold [Lord] Davies 1945-70, May '97; was named to the prestigious Committee of Selection June '97; was also named to the Select Committee on Education and Employment July '97; in her Maiden, deplored the £2.50 an hour many of her constituents were paid and looked forward to the minimum wage July '97; she ridiculed the "crocodile tears" of Tory MPs deploring the end of tax relief for pensioners taking out health insurance; the £110m spent on this was better used in reducing waiting lists; her own 81-year-old mother, rather than wait a further two years to end "excruciating pain", had to pay to have a hip operation; "my mother did not get any tax relief" July '97; she urged the maintenance of "the principle of free [higher] education for the poorest students" July '97;

Born: 24 September 1950, Chelmsford

Family: Daughter of Welsh-born Ron Atkins, former teacher and further education lecturer and Labour MP for Preston North '74-79 '66-70, and Jessie, "a strong dominant figure"; her twin sister Liz, also a former union and Labour Party officer, recently Head of Policy for the NSPCC, sought the nomination for Gravesham; she has three half-brothers; m Gus Brain, journalist and dealer in 18th century English porcelain; 1d Emma '86;

Education: Colchester County High School; LSE (BSc Econ, MA);

Occupation: Parliamentary Officer, for UNISON '92-97; Press Officer (NUJ), for COHSE/UNISON '80-92; also worked for UCATT and TASS;

Traits: Dark hair in a neat, short practical hair style; straight-faced and serious-looking; has head-prefect good looks; smart; flat classless speech; "brisk to the point of brittleness" (INDEPENDENT ON SUNDAY)

Address: House of Commons, Westminster, London SW1A 0AA; 118 Venner Road, London, SE26 5HR; has moved into the constituency;

Telephone: 0171 219 3591 (H of C); 0181 778 0746 (London home); 01782 517922 (constituency office); 0966 401573 (mobile); 0152 3523523/880068 (pager)

Norman BAKER **Liberal Democrat** **LEWES '97-**

Majority: 1,300 over Conservative 5-way;

Description: The slightly shrunken seat embracing Lewes, the historic East Sussex county town and administrative centre, the ferry port of Newhaven and the resort of Seaford plus many villages, some affluent; the '95 boundary changes decanted to Brighton-Kemptown 16,000 voters including those in Tory-leaning Peacehaven; until the '97 election it had been a Tory seat for 123 years;

Position: On the LibDem Environment team '97-; East Sussex County Councillor '89-; President, Tourism Subcommittee in Assembly of European Regions '95-; Lewes District Councillor (Leader '91-97) '87-97; Director: of Newhaven Economic Partnership;

Outlook: Hyper-active Aberdeen-born East Sussex professional politician who has hit the Parliamentary scene running, spraying questions in all directions; a fiery campaigner who is the first non-Tory MP for Lewes since 1874; a twitchy-nosed hunter of Peter ("Scarlet Pimpernel") Mandelson; in his first three months asked more questions than his predecessor, Tim Rathbone, had asked in 23 years; "any comment I could make on Mr Baker's policies, principles, methods or attitudes would be unprintable" (his defeated opponent, ex-MP Tim Rathbone); a campaigner for the environment, economic regeneration, public transport, tourism, agriculture, constitutional reform; a cause groupie in Greenpeace, Amnesty International, Charter 88, Free Tibet;
History: He has "listened to Queen's speeches since I was in short trousers"; he joined the Liberal Party at 24. '81; was elected to Lewes District Council, ousting the Tory Leader from the previously safe Tory Ouse Valley ward by 524 to 312 votes May '87; against the trend, won the East Sussex County Council seat of Telscombe, held for 22 years by Sir John Lovill May '89; was elected Leader of Lewes District Council May '91; was selected as LibDem candidate for Lewes Jan '90; retained a strong second place (34.5%), but only cut the majority of the sitting Tory MP, Tim Rathbone, by 1,500 to 12,175 Apr '92; challenged Tim Rathbone over his clash of interest between serving as a consultant to Eurotunnel and the vulnerability of the ferry port of Newhaven and a tunnel-linked Downland-despoiling dual carriageway; Rathbone gave up his consultancy '94; apart from boundary changes, was helped in election campaign by local 'Labour Supporters for Tactical Voting' and the anti-European campaigns of the Referendum Party and the UK Independence Party, which mostly hurt pro-European Rathbone Apr '97; won the seat on his second effort, with a majority of 1,300, the two anti-Europe parties having taken 2,481 and 256 votes May '97; Baker promised to "work full-time; there will be no outside interests; I will keep in touch" May '97; in his Maiden speech, said the Blair Government's Queen's Speech was the first one he could largely agree with, although he thought it weak on the environment and lacked a Freedom of Information Bill May '97; in his first fortnight asked questions on legal aid, landfill, BSE, price marking, air pollution, and overseas aid May '97; presented the Public Records (Amendment) Bill to improve public access to public records June '97; backed ban on fox-hunting June '97; sought to amend the Plant Varieties Bill, intervening 24 times to make it more transparent June '97; sought to persuade Peter Mandelson to make himself available for questioning on a regular basis July '97; led a motion opposing the patenting of genetic modifications July '97; led a debate urging a freedom of information Bill July '97; Matthew Parris devoted a whole column to him as a classic reincarnation of what Joseph Chamberlain classified as "the House of Commons bore" July '97; when a local Tory Councillor, Michael Murphy, referred to him as "Storming Norman, a bore of hurricane proportions", Baker dismissed his comments as "sour grapes": "the Tories are still smarting from losing the general election in Lewes" Aug '97; asked for reassurance that the US-controlled listening base at Menwith Hill was "not busying itself with economic sabotage against the UK" Aug '97; at annual conference in Eastbourne, reminded the welcoming Mayor that "here in Sussex we have the first Liberal Democrat MP to be elected since the 1920s" Sep '97;
Born: 26 July 1957, Aberdeen, Scotland
Family: He declines to provide family details;
Education: Royal Liberty School, Romford; Royal Holloway College, University of London (BA in German with History);
Occupation: Teacher of English as a foreign language, Portslade '92-97; Eastbourne-based Researcher for David Bellotti MP '91-92; Westminster-based Environmental campaigner servicing all LibDem MPs '89-90; Manager, of a wine shop in Reigate '84; ran Hornsey railway station '83; London Regional Director, of Our Price record chain '80-83;

Traits: Wide-spaced eyes; dark, receding hair; wily-looking; residual Scots burr; "Stormin' Norman" who "simply crushed the life out of the [Tory] opposition" (SUSSEX EXPRESS); thinks information about his parents is "irrelevant"; also tried to resist inclusion in 1998 WHO'S WHO; collects '60s and '70s rock and roll; enjoys group singing; was originally featured in 'The Gaylords' (along with Archy Kirkwood), half of whom went on to find success in the US as 'The Average White Band';
Address: House of Commons, Westminster, London SW1A 0AA; 2 Railway Cottages, Beddingham, Lewes BN8 6JP;
Telephone: 0171 219 3000 (H of C); 01273 858320; 01273 858013 (Fax);

Mrs 'Jackie' BALLARD **Liberal Democrat** **TAUNTON '97-;**

Majority: 2,443 over Conservative 5-way;
Description: The unaltered seat embracing the large town of Taunton plus four wards of West Somerset District, stretching across Exmoor to the Devon border; there are 1,000 dairy farms in the constituency, with the town increasingly dependent on service jobs from the decline of local manufacture; Taunton's voters have voted for the Liberal Democrats in district, county and Euro elections before;
Position: On Select Committee on Catering '97-; LibDem Spokesman on Women's Issues and on Local Government '97-; Somerset County Councillor (Deputy Leader '93-95) '93-97; ex: South Somerset District Councillor (Leader '90-91, Deputy Leader '88-90) '87-91; on Liberal Democrats' Federal Policy Committee '92-95;
Outlook: The first-ever woman MP for this seat; a strongly-rooted local activist on the radical wing of her party; a promoter of devolution, citizens' participation in local government and an enhanced role for women in politics; a strong opponent of capping; "fiercely anti-hunting" (NEW STATESMAN); a cause-groupie in Charter 88, Liberator, Amnesty International, Friends of the Earth; an opponent of fox-hunting (favoured by Tory-leaning farmers);
History: She was born into a non-political family, although her father's cousin was a long-serving Liberal councillor in Scotland; she spent her first ten years there, arriving in Somerset via Monmouth and LSE at 23, '76; she joined the Liberal Party '85; was elected to South Somerset District Council for Yeovil, Paddy Ashdown's constituency May '87; wrote that the new Liberal Democratic Party should have "a Leader who is committed to the values of Liberalism, justice, freedom and democracy and who can get those values across to the electorate; policy proposals should be formulated by think-tanks and accepted or rejected by the members of the party; the new Leader needs to have the ability to recognise people who are intellectually capable of formulating policy and the commonsense and humility to listen to the grassroots" June '88; became Leader of South Somerset District Council May '90; selected to contest Taunton, polls showed her in the lead right up to the last days, when ex-Tories returned to the fold in fear of a Labour victory nationally; on a 6% swing to the LibDems, she managed to cut the majority of the sitting Conservative MP, David Nicholson, from 10,380 to 3,336, Apr '92; was re-selected to contest Taunton Oct '92; she gave up her post as Deputy

Leader of Somerset County Council May '95; delivered a paper on citizen participation in local government at an international conference in Slovakia Nov '95; at annual conference, expressed her concern about young girls begging on the streets of Taunton and the paradox that one in five under-25s were not registered to vote Sep '96; at the invitation of the British Council, helped in Jordan at a workshop helping potential women Parliamentarians there Nov '96; in the election campaign her leaflets hammered home the need for tactical voting by Labour supporters, who could not win the seat; "only Jackie Ballard or the Conservative can win here"; an OBSERVER-ICM Poll four days before the election was helpful, showing Nicholson on 39%, Ballard on 38% and Labour at 19% Apr '97; won the seat with 43% to Nicholson's 39% and Labour's 13.5% May '97; in her Maiden concentrated on the 2,000 local families in housing need June '97; in the debate on the "fundamentally flawed" Child Support Agency, she concluded that "perhaps the only alternative is to scrap it completely"; she focussed also on the need to assess better the self-employed absent parent June '97; led motion urging a ban on organophosphates June '97; took on her big local hunting lobby: responded to the huge Hyde Park pro-hunting rally by saying, "rural Britain does not need a small minority carrying out a barbaric sport" July '97; asked about "the risk to health from hunt kennels which are assessed to be unsatisfactory under the BSE enforcement programme" July '97; co-sponsored a motion urging a lower council tax banding for mobile homes July '97; with David Heath fought a fruitless battle to reverse capping of Somerset July '97; clashed with pro-hunting lobby when fox-hunting was banned from Exmoor Aug '97; at Eastbourne annual conference, despite backing from Paddy Ashdown, failed to secure adequate backing for allocating to women half the places on all short-lists Sep '97;

Born: 4 January 1953, Dunoon, Scotland

Family: Daughter of Alexander Mackenzie, rtd shopkeeper, and Daisy Margaret (Macdonald), rtd nurse; m '75 Derek Ballard, quantity surveyor; 1d, Christine '79; divorced '89;

Education: Varous Scottish state primary schools; Monmouth School for Girls (where she started a debating society and was "generally rebellious" and "a trouble-maker" (JB); LSE (BSc in Social Psychology);

Occupation: Local Government Adviser with the Association of Liberal Democratic Counciillors (ALDC) (advising LibDem councillors across the country) '94-; Author: 'Beyond Public Question Time' (1995), 'On The Council' (ALDC 1993); ex: Lecturer in Psychology, Computing and Communications in Further Education colleges '81-93, Social Worker in London's East End '74-76;

Traits: Large, square, with no neck; wears her hair short; unphotogenic; likes Cajun music; is sensitive to the problem of leukaemia (her godson, Harry Burden, died of it at seven);

Address: House of Commons, Westminster, London SW1A 0AA; 71 Greenway Crescent, Taunton, Somerset TA2 6NH;

Telephone: 0171 219 6247 (H of C); 01823 324512 (home); 01823 337874 (constituency); 01823 323075 (Fax);

EXPLOSIONS:

Sometimes an explosion unveils those who rely on our volumes. After the 1994 explosion damaged the Israeli Embassy in London, an eagle-eyed Welsh fan of ours scanned one of the pictures of its damaged interior and spotted a set of these volumes. A similar photograph of the interiors of other embassies would often show the same - foreign diplomats have been among the most enthusiastic about our interest in the positions of MPs on crises abroad, such as the deep split in the Commons over former Yugoslavia.

(Christopher) Nigel BEARD FRSA Labour BEXLEYHEATH & CRAYFORD '97-

Majority: 3,415 over Conservative 6-way;
Description: A new seat combining parts of old safe-Tory Bexleyheath and marginal old Erith & Crayford; it is the London constituency that is the furthest east on the south bank of the Thames; it was considered safe enough for Tories for ex-Tory MP David Evennett to fight to represent it; on a '92-type division of the vote, it was expected to provide a 12,000 Conservative majority;
Position: On the Select Committee on Science and Technology '97-; ex: Chairman, Woking Constituency Labour Party '81-82; on Board, Royal Marsden Hospital '82-90, SW Thames Regional Health Authority '78-86; on the Political Committee of CWS, Labour's Southern Region Executive;
Outlook: The seniormost member of Labour's 1997 intake, a former election-time "hobby politician" who was unexpectedly successful on his fourth effort; self-described as "fairly consistently New Labour"; a top planner, originally for the MoD, then GLC, recently for R & D at ICI-Zeneca; apart from his Maiden, initially played a minimal role in the Commons, while extricating himself from his ICI-Zeneca commitments; a Fabian who wants wider and deeper industrial democracy, Government support in establishing high-technology industries, Marshall-Plan-type economic aid for the ex-USSR, EU control of the arms trade, legal and electoral reform;
History: His family background was Tory, although his father, a BR goods porter, was an NUR activist; he joined the Labour Party '63; campaigned for consistent and predictable levels of Government funding for inner-city renewal, especially in the East End '74-79; contested hopeless Woking May '79; was selected for Portsmouth North by 15 to 10 from a short-list of four Oct '82; spoke at a meeting with Ken Livingstone and Ted Knight sponsored by their Trotkyist LABOUR HERALD Feb '83; unsuccessfully fought Portsmouth North June '83; as a Co-op nominee, was beaten by Russsell Profitt in selection for marginal Lewisham East, when its constituency party defied the NEC and held an unofficial selection conference with the participation of an illicit 'black caucus' May '85; was selected to retake Tory-held marginal Erith & Crayford Feb '90; backed higher pensions Dec '90; complained of an 48% increase in unemployment in the constituency in the previous year Mar '91; increased the Labour vote by 6,000, but lost by 2,339 votes (5%) Apr '92; was re-selected for overlapping Bexleyheath and Crayford July '95; quite unexpectedly won the seat, by a majority of 3,415 after a notional swing to Labour of 15%, ending the 14-year Commons career of David Evennett May '97; in his impressive Maiden underlined the loss of his seat's engineering industries during the two previous decades, emphasizing: "we have to regenerate opportunities for people to use their skills and talents to the full; unless we do that, we shall not raise the long-term rate of economic growth of the country as a whole"; "a greater proportion of small and medium-sized companies need to be based on high technology so that they can compete internationally" July '97; was named to the Select Committee on Science and Technology July '97; ridiculed the idea that Britain could usefully use "even half of the 232 [Eurofighter] aircraft that we are committed to purchase" Oct '97;
Born: 10 October 1936, Leeds
Family: Only son of Albert Leonard Beard, BR goods porter and NUR activist, and Irene

(Bowes); m '69 Jennifer Anne (Cotton), teacher; 1s Daniel '71, 1d Jessica '73;
Education: Temple Street Junior, Castleford; Castleford Grammar School, York; University College, London University (BSc [Hons] in Special Physics); London Business School;
Occupation: Senior Manager, for Research and Development, of ICI-Zeneca (pharmaceuticals) (GMB) '93-; Author: The Practical Use of Linear Planning in Planning and Analysis (HMSO 1974); Senior Consultant, to ICI, on New Business and New Technology '79-93; Director, of London Docklands Development Team '74-79; Chief Planner, for Strategy, GLC '73-74; Superintendent of Studies, Army Land Operations in the Defence of Europe '68-72; Scientific Officer, later Principal Scientific Officer, in the Defence Operational Analysis Establishment '61-68; Market Researcher, Esso Petroleum '61; Physicist, with English Electric's Atomic Power Division, working on design of Hinckley Point '59-61; Assistant Mathematics Master, Tadcaster Grammar School '58-61;
Traits: Serious-looking; high forehead; parted hair; hooded eyes; enjoys sailing, theatre, music;
Address: House of Commons, Westminster, London SW1A 0AA; Lanquhart, The Ridgeway, Pyrford, Woking, Surrey GU22 8PW
Telephone: 0171 219 3000 (H of C); 01932 348630 (home);

Anne BEGG **Labour** **ABERDEEN SOUTH '97-**

Majority: 3,365 over Liberal Democrat 5-way;
Description: A completely redrawn three-way marginal on both sides of the Dee; made up of half of old Aberdeen South, a Con-Lab marginal, and 27,000 voters from old Kincardine & Deeside, a Con-LibDem marginal; "a beautiful city: when the sun shines, it positively sparkles with the light reflected off the grey granite" (AB)
Position: On the Select Committee on Scottish Affairs '97-; Teacher Member of General Teaching Council '95-97; on Board of Scottish PHAB (Physically Handicapped, Able-Bodied) '94-97; on National Council of Educational Institute of Scotland '90-95;
Outlook: Britain's first permanently wheelchair-bound MP; a Blair-loyal, Left-inclined teacher; a strong home-ruler who also overcame the electoral disability of starting from third place; she sees herself as "a role model for disabled people"; the only MP who knew her wheelchair would place her at the front bench if elected;
History: When an impoverished student she was helped by her Tory constituency MP, Iain Sproat, with an enormous 'phone bill unfairly assigned to her and other poor students '70; despite this, she joined the Labour Party '83; was named the 'Disabled Scot of the Year' '88; was selected from an all-women short-list to contest redrawn Aberdeen South, joking to her selection meeting that, with her wheelchair, she would go straight to the front bench if Labour won '95; at Labour's annual conference in Brighton, she was warmly applauded when introduced as "the next MP for Aberdeen South"; in her speech, she deplored people having to sleep rough in Aberdeen Oct '96; was included in Tony Blair's cavalcade during his visit to the constituency Mar '97; in the election campaign complained her Tory opponent, Scottish Minister Raymond Robertson, always dodged any head-to-head debate, warning him: "you can

run, but you can't hide!" Apr '97; was helped electorally by the OBSERVER-ICM poll which showed her ahead of the LibDem as well as the Conservative four days before polling: Labour 35%, Tory 27%, LibDem 24%, Apr '97; with a majority of 3,365, defeated the LibDem and the Scottish Tory Minister Raymond Robertson, who was pushed into third place May '97; supported Scottish devolution in a charming Maiden speech May '97; was named to Select Committee on Scottish Affairs July '97; applauded the fact that the Scottish Parliament would be "elected by a form of proportional representation, which is of supreme importance to people in the northeast of Scotland" July '97; led a motion criticising Air UK for its "discriminatory and insulting" behaviour toward disabled passengers July '97;

Born: 16 December 1955, Brechin

Family: Daughter, of David Begg, ortnotist (rtd), and Margaret Catherine (Ross) nurse (rtd); unmarried ("too independent" [AB])

Education: Brechin High School; Aberdeen University; Aberdeen College of Education;

Occupation: Principal Teacher of English, in Arbroath Academy '91-97; Teacher in comprehensive '78-91 (EIS); she had to fight for three years before she was allowed to teach because it was claimed that it was against the General Teaching Council's medical regulations to have a wheelchair-bound teacher;

Traits: Pretty; longish dark-brown centre-parted hair; toothy; alternately smiling or serious-looking; dogged ("when somebody says 'no' it spurs me on"; optimistic ("I always see the glass as half-full"); "an attractive woman" who "radiates confidence" and "describes her life philosophy as eternally optimistic" (Sarah Villiers, MAIL ON SUNDAY); has Gaucher's Disease, an enzyme deficiency in the blood, making her bones soft and easily broken;

Address: House of Commons, Westminster, London SW1A 0AA; 5 Boyd-Orr Avenue, Brechin, Angus DD9 6YH;

Telephone: 0171 219 3000 (H of C); 01224 658881 (constituency);

Martin BELL **Independent** **TATTON '97-**

Majority: 11,077 over Conservative 10-way;

Description: Until the '97 election, was rated the fifth safest Conservative seat, after the '95 removal of Labour-leaning industrial Northwich and the addition of Alderley Edge, a favourite Cheshire commuting area for well-off executives;

Outlook: The first Independent MP since 1950, trying to maintain that status after the accidental fusion of the election; this was created by the impact of his own first-rate reputation as a shrapnel-wounded BBC-TV war correspondent on local disgust with the lying, sleaze-ridden sitting Tory MP, Neil Hamilton; an un-saintly idealist ("I wear an OFF-white suit because I am NOT a saint"); was more a Labour-supported candidate than initially admitted; thinks he still "has a chance to make a difference"; is a mild Eurosceptic who doesn't disagree with the single European currency in principle; his desire to carve out a new role may be motivated in part by his aversion to being squeezed out of the Birtian BBC into unproductive premature retirement; "a loner" (BBC producer David Akerman);

History: He joined Cambridge University's Marxist Society "to find out what was like"; "I seemed to be the only one at King's College who was not a member" '60; joined the Young Liberals '60; quit the Young Liberals on joining the BBC '62; spent 30 years developing his reputation as an honest BBC-TV reporter/war correspondent, culminating in his being wounded by shrapnel in Sarajevo, while reporting the Bosnian civil war Aug '92; blamed the civil war on the British Government for having traded opt-outs on Maastricht for German-desired recognition of breakaway ex-Yugoslav republic of Croatia in Dec '91; was one of two war correspondents to testify to the War Crimes Tribunal in Brussels; came into conflict with the BBC over its requirement for neutral reporting: "you don't report genocide in the same terms as a flower show" July '96; initially at the suggestion of photographer Tom Stoddart, partner of Labour MP Kate Hoey, emerged as the all-party Independent anti-sleaze candidate to oppose the discredited Tory MP Neil Hamilton, with Labour and LibDem candidates standing down in his favour Apr '97; his first press conference was aggressively gate-crashed by Neil Hamilton and his formidable wife, Christine Apr '97; virtually all Conservative newspapers and journalists were hostile to Bell's candidacy Apr '97; gave his opponent, Neil Hamilton, a detailed list of the lies and corruption to which he had already confessed Apr '97; had to drop "Anti-Corruption" from his nomination papers to avoid a legal challenge from Neil Hamilton Apr '97; his campaign was helped by the OBSERVER-ICM Poll which predicted he would take 50% and Hamilton 39%, Apr '97; won the seat by a sensational majority of ll,077 May '97; in his Maiden speech, paid tribute to Neil Hamilton "for the effect that he had, whether deliberately or not, in reviving the spirit of democracy in Tatton"; insisted: "good and evil are not abstractions, but actual forces in the world, and that the difference that an individual can make is greater now than it was in the more predictable world of the old cold war"; he called for the banning of anti-personnel mines, duly announced by PM Tony Blair the next day May '97; in his first constituency problem-visit, backed the right of protesters against Manchester Airport's second runway to protest peacefully and also the right of bailiffs to evict peacefully May '97; as a member of the all-party Land Mines Group, regretted Princess Diana's withdrawal from a planned Commons meeting, forced by Conservative criticism June '97; he criticised the 20% pay rise of John Birt as damaging BBC staff morale July '97; in his Maiden, urged a "clear-eyed as well as compassionate" approach to foreign aid; "never again must we push food aid into an active war zone where we and the agencies associated with us do not control the secondary distribution" because "we prolong rather than shorten the conflict because we are feeding the front-line troops" July '97; when Sir Gordon Downey's report concluded that Neil Hamilton had "received cash payments directly from [Mohamed] al-Fayed", Bell said this vindicated his decision to stand in Tatton July '97; again sided with protesters against a second runway for Manchester Airport July '97; admitted that Alastair Campbell had composed much of his first election address Sep '97;

Born: 31 August 1938, Beccles, Suffolk

Family: Grandson, of Robert Bell, News Editor of the OBSERVER; son, of Adrian Hanbury Bell, farmer and novelist who was the compiler of the first TIMES crossword, and Marjorie (Gibson); m 1st '71 Nelly Lucienne (Gourdon); 2d: Melissa, his campaign manager (who later married Peter Bracken, a Labour helper) '72, Catherine '74; divorced '81; m 2nd '85 Rebecca Sobel, American TV reporter; this marriage was "four years of pure disaster"; divorced '88;

Education: The Leys School, Cambridge; King's College, Cambridge University (First Class Hons in English);

Occupation: Author: In Harms Way (1995); ex: BBC-TV Newsman '62-97, successively as Trainee '62-65, Reporter, '65-77, Diplomatic Correspondent '77-78, Chief Washington Correspondent '78-89, Berlin Correspondent '89-93; Bosnian and East European Correspondent '93-94, Pool TV Reporter with 7th Armoured Brigade in Gulf War '91; honoured as Royal Television Reporter of the Year '77, TV Journalist of the Year '92, OBE

'92;
Traits: Medium height; grey hair; deep-set eyes; staccato speech; a crumpled face like a middle-aged Russian; has a bear-like shambling gate; walks with a limp from his shrapnel wound; dour; dogged; no small talk; self-consciously righteous; wears crumpled off-white or cream suits as a uniform; "stands around looking lugubrious like a little boy lost" (disaffected campaign helper); "that rare breed, an old-fashioned patriot, the sort of person whose eyes would go moist at the sound of Elgar" (former war correspondent colleague); "the trouble with you, Corporal Bell," said Captain Pat Hopper, during his National Service, "is that you think too much"; in Bosnia "he was never the kind of person who would send his cameraman where he was not prepared to go himself" (fellow TV newsman); his toothbrushes are always yellow and his socks are always green; likes to dine at Hampstead's La Gaffe which he describes as "like a home from home"; there he always eats either the scampi al funghetto or the fegato alla Veneziano; as a young man he swam for Suffolk;
Address: House of Commons, Westminster, London SW1A 0AA; he lives in Hampstead Garden Suburb;
Telephone: 0171 219 3000 (H of C);

John BERCOW **Conservative** **BUCKINGHAM '97-**

Majority: 12,386 over Labour 4-way;
Description: A solidly Conservative county seat, including Buckinghamshire's small county town and a large tract of the county south of Milton Keynes; part agricultural, part affluent suburbia; in the '90 split of MK into two constituencies, the new town took away bits around the pro-Labour old railway town of Wolverton; in the '95 boundary revision Buckingham acquired Aston Clinton ward from Aylesbury; the seat attracts oddities: the country's first private university, Robert Maxwell and George Walden;
Position: On Select Committee on Welsh Affairs '97-; ex: Special Adviser: to Virginia Bottomley '95-96, to Jonathan Aitken '95; Lambeth Borough Councillor (Deputy Leader of Conservative Group '87-89) '86-90; National Chairman, Federation of Conservative Students '86-87; Chairman, Essex University Conservatives '84-85; former Secretary of the Monday Club's Race and Repatriation Committee '81-83;
Outlook: A Thatcherite Right Europhobic replacement for quirky 'One Nation' Tory MP George Walden; the political son Norman Tebbit never had; only his hair is parted in the centre; one of the ambitious, driven Rightwing figures, formerly floating between the "barmy Right" (initially in the Monday Club) and the acceptable face of the Tebbit-Thatcher Right; admits to having been the beneficiary of a network of ex-FCS activists; an "elegant master of intrigue and Thatcherite phrase-maker" (TATLER); has a talent for abandoning sinking ships in favour of others floating in his desired direction; formerly dependent on the tolerance of big names, he has - after many disappointments -successfully found a safe Tory seat; "a tremendous street fighter" (Lord [Cecil] Parkinson); with "the oratorical equipment to be the Tories' answer to Arthur Scargill" (TODAY); in the Thatcherite 'Conservative Way Forward', Freedom Association;
History: He became consciously a Conservative at 15, '78; joined Hendon YCs and Finchley

YCs '80; became Secretary of the Monday Club at 18, Sep '81; became Secretary of its Immigration and Repatriation Committee, run by Powellite Tory MP, Harvey Proctor; recorded its minutes which, according to PRIVATE EYE, read: "it was formally agreed that the policy of the Committee should be an end to New Commonwealth and Pakistani immigration; a properly financed scheme of voluntary repatriation, the repeal of the Race Relations Act, and the abolition of the Commission for Racial Equality; particular emphasis on repatriation" '83; he resigned as Secretary of the Monday Club at 20, Feb '83; resigned from the Monday Club because the views of its racialists were "unpalatable" Feb '84; became Chairman of the Essex University Conservative Association '84; was elected to Lambeth Borough Council at 23, May '86; became National Chairman of the ultra-Right-dominated Federation of Conservative Students, a year after it had disgraced itself by riotous vandalism at Loughborough Apr '86; was outvoted by 16 to 1 when, in a damage limitation exercise, he atempted to censure Harry Phibbs, editor of its NEW AGENDA, for having published an interview with Count Nicolai Tolstoy stigmatising Harold Macmillan as a "war criminal" Sep '86; after the disbandment of the FCS by the Chairman of the Conservative Party, Norman Tebbit, became his National Student Director of its sanitised replacement, the Conservative Collegiate Forum, to which a £30,000 subsidy was transferred Oct '86; he became the youngest-ever Deputy Leader of Lambeth's Conservative Group Oct '87; contested the hopeless seat of Motherwell South against Labour's Dr Jeremy Bray, reducing the Tories' vote from 20% to 14.5% and their position from second to third June '87; he did not contest his seat on Lambeth Borough Council May '90; he organised 125 Conservative candidates in support of embattled Margaret Thatcher, then backed John Major Nov '90; said he found Edward Heath's pro-European views "irritating, not to say obnoxious" Oct '91; contested the Labour marginal of Bristol South against Dawn Primarolo, whom he denounced as "an extremist implanted by the Labour Left"; her majority went up from 1,500 to 9,000 Apr '92; after working as a lobbyist, became Special Adviser to Jonathan Aitken, Chief Secretary to the Treasury Mar '95; on Aitken's forced resignation from the Cabinet, became Special Adviser to Virginia Bottomley, National Heritage Secretary Aug '95; having failed in a hopeless and a marginal seat, he pursued safe ones, at first unavailingly: Bedfordshire North East (close runner-up to Attorney General Sir Nicholas Lyell Sep '95), Hampshire North West, Worthing West (pipped by Peter Bottomley Feb '96); dramatically, he commuted by helicopter between two occurring on the same day: Surrey Heath and Buckingham where, he recalled: "I rushed onto the stage with seconds to spare and made a joke about how I had arrived; I don't think it did me any harm; I had put my money where my mouth is; I hope people think of me as resourceful and not as someone who is enormously wealthy and flash"; even before he had been selected over David Rutley and Howard Flight, he told fellow helicopter-traveller, friend Julian Lewis, that hiring the helicopter was "the best £1,000 I've ever spent" Feb '96; replied to call from Brian Wilson for him to apologise for the abuse heaped on "Communist terrorist" Nelson Mandela by the FCS when he was its Chairman by demanding Wilson apologise for his "support for the Marxist government of Nicaragua and the pro-Castro UK-Cuba Association and unilateral nuclear disarmament" July '96; backed nursery school and university vouchers Sep '96; named as one of 16 prospective Tory candidates working for lobbying companies, insisted: "I intend to take a Parliamentary salary and no consultancies and directorships whatsoever" Oct '96; replying to the DAILY TELEGRAPH's inquiry, said he would put his opposition to a single European currency in his election manifesto Dec '96; retained Buckingham with a majority of 12,386, down 8,000 after an anti-Conservative swing of 10.58%, May '97; defending quangos, claimed that "election is not the only source of legitimacy" May '97; dubbed Labour and LibDem MPs as "abstract rationalists who want to meddle with Parliamentary practice" May '97; in the Tory Leadership contest, first joined the campaign team of Peter Lilley May '97; after John Redwood's defeat, said he would consult him before deciding between Clarke and Hague June '97; his Maiden was mainly a panegyric to Baroness Thatcher July '97; was named to the Select Committee on Welsh Affairs July '97; with the support of 52 Tory colleagues, called for the resignation of Lord Simon, the European Competitiveness Minister, over his alleged failure to disclose his interest in BP shares July '97; was part of the Redwood-inspired pack in hot pursuit of Lord Simon for not divesting himself of BP shares July '97; was warned by Speaker Boothroyd that he would "be out in a moment" if he continued his boisterous behaviour July '97;

Born: 19 January 1963, Edgware

Family: Son, of late Charles Bercow, car salesman and minicab driver, and Brenda (Bailey), formerly a legal secretary, recently a mature student at Middlesex University; has a girlfriend, Sally Illman;

Education: Finchley Manorhill School '74-81; Essex University (BA Hons First in Politics) '82-85;

Occupation: Free-lance Political Consultant (worked with Westminster Strategy) '96-97; Public Affairs Consultant '88-95 with Rowland Sallingbury Casey (a subsidiary of Saatchi & Saatchi); he was a Director '94-95; he acquired a redundancy package from this firm although he quickly become Special Adviser to Jonathan Aitken; he repaid 10% of his redundancy package '95; Credit Analyst, Hambros Bank '87-88;

Traits: Shortish ("just because I am a little chap, it doesn't mean I haven't got a big ambition"); upturned head; centrally-parted spikey hair; mobile mouth; clear deliberate enunciation; confident; fluent; sallow-skinned; Mediterranean appearance; Jewish; combative ("a tub-thumping public speaker"; "he's quick, he's sharp, he's bright and he knows his own mind" (Lord [Norman] Tebbit); driven; well-networked; tennis coach; "charming but scary" (NEW STATESMAN);

Address: House of Commons, Westminster, London SW1A 0AA; 31 Marsham Court, Marsham Street, London SW1P 4JY;

Telephone: 0171 219 3000/0981(Fax) (H of C); 0171 828 5620 (home)

Harold BEST **Labour** **LEEDS NORTH WEST '97-**

Majority: 3,844 over Conservative 7-way;

Description: The unaltered major middle-class residential area in West Yorkshire's principal city; its safety for the Tories was helped in '83 by the inclusion of commuting villages and in '92 by the even split between their rival opponents; the Tories' disadvantage lay in the very large number - fully 35,000 - of university students within its boundaries, leading to its former Tory MP, Dr Keith Hampson, advocating an election during their absence at Christmas or Easter;

Position: Chairman, of Leeds North West Constituency Labour Party '91-95; West Yorkshire County Councillor '81-86; formerly on National Executive Committee of National Council for Civil Liberties (later called Liberty);

Outlook: A traditional Left working-class ex-councillor, who succeeded in the task of ousting Keith Hampson from the Tories' safest seat in Leeds; a life-long political activist, he was a friend of the late Marxist historian, E P Thomson, with whom he was linked in the emergence of the New Left in the '60s; was active in CND, anti-racist groups and Humanist organisations; is now in the Campaign Group; is said to work on two levels: as an ideological near-Marxist, or a practical political fixer who could chair effectively the Police Committee on West Yorkshire County Council; an ethical socialist; as a 59-year-old grandfather, is somewhat old-fashioned; he is the second oldest of the candidates fielded and, unexpectedly, elected by Labour;

History: As a young electrician he joined the old Electrical Trades Union (ETU) '50; as a non-Communist Leftwinger, resisted the ballot-rigging of its Communist leadership; joined the Labour Party '60; when the ETU's Communist leadership was replaced by by that of the authoritarian Rightwinger, Frank Chapple, in '66, he was equally out of favour; he stood for election as General Secretary of the EETPU against Frank Chapple '77; was then blacklisted by the EETPU, compelling him to work for Leeds City Council; was elected to West Yorkshire County Council May '81; as Chairman of West Yorkshire's Police Committee visited 113 picket lines during the miners' strike '84-85; was elected Chairman of the Leeds North West Constituency Labour Party '91; was selected to contest "hopeless" Leeds North West, the city's safest Tory seat '95; unexpectedly won the seat -moving from third place to first - with a majority of 3,844 over Keith Hampson, a Tory MP for 23 years, as a result of an 11.77 swing to Labour May '97; he joined the hard-Left Campaign Group May '97; in his Maiden, emphasised how difficult it had been to ascertain the fate of threatened Wharfedale Hospital June '97; was a co-sponsor of a Campaign Group motion opposing any cut in lone-parent benefit July '97;

Born: 18 December 1937, Leeds

Family: Son, of Fred Best, lorry driver, and Marie (Hogg); m Mary (Glyn); 2s; 2d; 7 grandchildren;

Education: Meanwood County Secondary School; a Technical College;

Occupation: Electrical Technician, recently at Leeds Education Craft Centre; formerly a full-time trade union official for 13 years and an electrician from youth; UNISON/TGWU/EPIU;

Traits: Bald; grizzled grey beard; an active Humanist who has officiated at weddings, naming ceremonies and funerals;

Address: House of Commons, Westminster, London SW1A 0AA; 63 St Michael's Lane, Leeds LS6 3BR;

Telephone: 0171 219 3000 (H of C); 0113 275 5692 (home);

'Liz' (Elizabeth) BLACKMAN **Labour** **EREWASH '97-**

Majority: 9,135 over Conservative 5-way;
Description: A very slightly altered Derbyshire seat between Derby and Nottingham, better known earlier as South East Derbyshire and Ilkeston; the increase in owner-occupied estates and the decline of mining have changed it from the native area written about by D H Lawrence, who restyled Ilkeston as 'Keston';
Position: On the Select Committee on Treasury Affairs '97-; Broxtowe Borough Councillor (Deputy Leader '95-97) '91-;
Outlook: A fast-climbing woman professional; after loyal back bench support for Gordon Brown's Budget strategy, was rewarded with a place on the Treasury Select Committee; was a first-time candidate from an all-women short-list who was able to capitalise on her status as Deputy Leader of Broxtowe Council and head of the upper school of a highly-regarded local comprehensive; "I try to give my best in all areas of my life - as a parent, [and formerly] as a full-time teacher, Deputy Leader of the council and as a candidate; I believe in full commitment"; had the experience of negotiating a private-public regeneration of a local former mining community; thinks women MPs can stop male MPs "behaving like a bunch of badly-behaved schoolboys"; a member of the Fabians, the Socialist Environmental Association and NASUWT;
History: She joined the Labour Party at 39, '89; was elected to Broxtowe Borough Council, becoming Deputy Leader of its Labour Group May '91; became Deputy Leader of Broxtowe Borough Council when it was won by Labour May '95; was selected from an all-women short-list to contest Erewash against its sitting Tory MP -Minister Angela Knight - before the practice was ruled illegal in Jan '96; emphasised education during the campaign: "I'd like to see a tangible improvement in education, with support staff to help deliver the best standards" Apr '97; won the seat from Angela Knight with a majority of 9,135 (15.14%) as the result of a pro-Labour swing of 12.08%, May '97; asked Education Secretary David Blunkett how he proposed to help teachers "confronted by persistent poor behaviour on the part of a small number of pupils" June '97; urged Lottery distribution be made more widely acceptable to her region June '97; complained about inadequate payout by Nationwide to shareholders with learning difficulties June '97; urged women be encouraged more to have breasts screened for cancer June '97; urged police grants be more fairly distributed June '97; urged lorry drivers be banned immediately from driving if they exceeded permitted driving hours July '97; led motion urging the Government to be "tough on road crime" July '97; co-sponsored motion attacking mis-selling of pensions under the Tories July '97; urged care in expanding membership of NATO July '97; repeatedly and vehemently defended the Budget changes as underpinned by Labour values on fairness July '97; emphasised that while the welfare-to-work programme might be temporary, the working skills imparted had an "air of permanence" July '97; objected to majority of taxpayers having to pay twice, once for their own NHS care and again for tax relief for those pensioners who took out private medical insurance July '97; was named to the Select Committee on Treasury Affairs, while Diana Abbott was transferred out July '97;
Born: 28 September 1948, Carlisle
Family: She is married, with two children;
Education: Carlisle County High School for Girls; Prince Henry's Grammar School, Otley; Clifton College of Further Education, Nottingham (B Ed);

Occupation: Teacher '72-97; her last post was as Head of the Upper School of Bramcote Park Comprehensive School ("which achieves some of the best results in Derbyshire" [EB])
Traits: Dark hair with front-combed fringe; hollow cheeks; pleasant-looking; energetic; fully-committed;
Address: House of Commons, Westminster, London SW1A 0AA;
Telephone: 0171 219 3000 (H of C); 0115 922 3602 (home);

Hazel (Anne) BLEARS **Labour** **SALFORD '97-**

Majority: 17,069 over Conservative 5-way;
Description: Manchester's shrinking Siamese twin city beyond the Irwell; a solidly working-class, Labour-voting area; the home of 'Coronation Street' and its begetter, Granada TV;
Position: On Executive, North West Regional Labour Party '91-; North West representative on National Policy Forum '93-; ex: Chairman, Salford Community Health Council '93-97; Salford City Councillor '84-92; Chairman, Bury & Radcliffe CLP, Vice Chairman, Eccles CLP, Campaigns Co-ordinator for Salford CLP;
Outlook: The first woman MP for the city in which she was "born and bred"; an ambitious woman, formerly close to John Prescott and the TGWU, which used to sponsor her; a hyper-intense formerly-Left activist with roots in almost every Left, libertarian or working-class organisation in the area and nationally: Society of Labour Lawyers, NCCL (now Liberty), Legal Action Group, Co-operative Party, Amnesty International, Salford Relate, Greater Manchester Low Pay Unit; Trustee of the Working Class Museum and Library; was in CND; initially moved from hard-Left to Kinnockite; was still Left enough to have opposed the revision of Clause IV; is deviant as a Leftist as a "passionate adherent of constitutional reform" (HB) - including 'Partnership in Power' - and a believer in the practical improvements to be gained from closer European integration; would like to see herself as an "intensely practical person rather than an organisational apparatchik" (HB) which is her image; favours use of art in industry;
History: She joined the Labour Party '78; was elected to Salford City Council May '84; was selected from a short-list of two women to fight the then-safe Tory seat of Tatton against Neil Hamilton Nov '85; she came 3rd in Tatton, but upped the Labour vote by 3%, from 18% in '83 to 21%, June '87; was selected to contest key marginal, Bury South Feb '90; was accused of leaking details of possible routes of the M62 through the constituency Dec '90; unexpectedly failed to win Bury South from David Sumberg by 788 votes on a low swing of 1.8%, perhaps because her Tory opponent frightened its large Jewish minority with the allegation that her support of CND aligned her with opponents of the Gulf War and so threatened Israel May '92; was selected for Salford, to follow retiring Stan Orme, first from an all-women short-list, then - after the court ruled all-women short-lists illegal - from a mixed short-list; she was supported by the local "TGWU Mafia", other unions, 7 out of 8 party branches and 75% of the votes Mar'96; opposed the revision of Clause IV '95; was elected with a majority of 17,069 (51.53%), a notional swing to Labour of 9.45%, May '97; in her over-loaded Maiden speech welcomed the radical overhaul of the youth justice system May '97; spoke loyally in favour of the Blairite reconstruction, 'Partnership in Power' at Brighton conference Sep '97;

Born: 14 May 1956, Salford
Family: Daughter of Arthur Blears, maintenance fitter and AEU shop steward, and Dorothy (Leighton), secretary; m '89 Michael Halsall, solicitor;
Education: Cromwell Road Junior School, Swinton; Wardley Grammar; Eccles VIth Form College; Trent Polytechnic (2:1 BA Law Hons); Chester College of Law (Law Society Finals);
Occupation: Solicitor '85-: Principal Solicitor with Manchester City Council '85-97; was initially in private practice, and then with Wigan and Rossendale Council '80-81;
Traits: Puckish-looking; brown hair, frequently restyled; small eyes; "snappily dressed" (ECONOMIST); cheerful; vivacious; perky; good sense of humour; fast-talker; gets high on attending small political meetings; loves cats (Russian blues); fell-walker; won a gold medal for tap-dancing; was also a ballerina; enjoys cinema and motor cycling; repeats, "I have to say";
Address: House of Commons, Westminster, London SWIA 0AA; Dolphin Square; 46 Victoria Road, Salford M6 8EY;
Telephone: 0171 219 6595 (H of C);

'Bob' (Robert) BLIZZARD **Labour** **WAVENEY '97-**

Majority: 12,453 over Conservative 4-way;
Description: Now largely the Suffolk fishing, cargo and industrial port of Lowestoft - its former name - and the market towns of Beccles and Bungay and their rural hinterlands, on Britain's most easterly coast; Lowestoft suffers from heavy unemployment and the deterioration of its guest-houses into DSS hostels; the seat's loss of 10,000 Tory-leaning voters in Halesworth and Southwold in the '95 boundary change was thought to make it marginal;
Position: Waveney District Councillor (Leader '91-) '87-; Vice Chairman, Standing Conference of East Anglian Local Authorities;
Outlook: An extremely practical local improver; a typical class-of-'97 beneficiary of Labour's one-member one-vote system of selection: a local council leader and teacher; is more pro-European than his anti-Maastricht predecessor, Tory David Porter, having secured access to European structural funds for job creation; also set up 'Lowestoft 2000', a partnership with town businesses to promote Lowestoft for inward investment and tourism; interested in education, health, employment and local government;
History: He joined the Labour Party '83; was elected to Waveney District Council May '87; was elected Leader of the Council after Labour had climbed from four councillors to 40, May '91; was selected to contest Waveney as the Labour candidate '95; at annual conference, spoke out for cuts in administration in NHS trusts Sep '96; retook Waveney for Labour after 38 years, with a 12,453 majority over the Tory Maastricht critic David Porter, as a result of a pro-Labour notional swing of 14.63%, May '97; made a good-natured Maiden, in which he emphasised that, after 25 years of teaching, he was convinced that class size was crucial June '97; expressed solidarity with jailed Indonesian union leader June '97; urged inclusion of those recovering from mental illness in Labour's welfare-to-work programme June '97; urged changes in law to prevent gazumping June '97; complained to Tory MP wanting only non-council housing initiatives that his council had built its own houses while working with the

private sector; "for ever £1m released under this [Local Government Finance] Bill, about 250 of those homes [with] no central heating [and double glazing] can be fitted with double glazing and central heating; that will be good for energy efficiency, jobs and business" June '97; expressed concern that BSE incinerators would "destroy business confidence" locally" June '97; in an adjounment debate complained convincingly that his area was starved of economic development because of its horrendously inadequate transport infrastructure June '97; applauded the end of two-tier access to NHS hospitals July '97; co-sponsored motion applauding patenting of genetic advances July '97; backed action against quota-hoppers, complaining: "in Lowestoft, there is a trawler - which is a Lowestoft trawler with a Lowestoft company -that purely and simply is a quota-hopper; it does not land any fish in the port of Lowestoft, although it is registered there" July '97; criticised excessive paperwork in benefits system, including the "33-page questionnaire" that the disabled had to complete July '97;
Born: 31 May 1950, Bury St Edmunds
Family: Son of a sign-writer; married, with two children;
Education: Culford School, Bury St Edmunds; Birmingham University (BA Hons 2:1);
Occupation: Formerly Head of English, at a Norfolk high school, which had 70% A-C passes in English and 80% in English literature) (NUT) '86-97; taught elsewhere '72-86;
Traits: Burly; portly; protruding chin; light-brown greying parted hair; a vigorous speaker; "perky and confident", "big", "malco-ordinated", "gallops awkwardly" "like a day-old heifer bumping into things" (A A Gill, SUNDAY TIMES); enjoys walking and skiiing;
Address: House of Commons, Westminster, London SW1A 0AA; 619 London Road South, Lowestoft, Suffolk NR33 0BA;
Telephone: 0171 219 3000 (H of C); 01502 514913;

Crispin BLUNT **Conservative** **REIGATE '97-**

Majority: 7,741 over Labour 6-way;
Description: The safely-Tory commuter conurbation of Reigate-Redhill which in '95 lost Horley to East Surrey but gained Banstead from Epsom and Ewell; its more dramatic '97 loss was the premature political suicide of its sitting Thatcherite Tory MP, Sir George Gardiner, sacked by his long-suffering constituency association for intemperate and disloyal remarks about John Major;
Position: On Select Committee on Defence '97-; ex: Special Adviser to Malcolm Rifkind as Defence Secretary '93-95 and Foreign Secretary '95-97;
Outlook: Well-connected mainstream Right-moving loyalist; a General's son and former Captain in the Royal Hussars, he treats Labour Ministers as though they are muddled-brained Other Ranks who mistakenly think they are in command; still believes Britain can again become "the richest major nation in the world" through "policies that encourage wealth creation, free trade, strong defence, a Europe of nation states, continuing reduction of the public sector" (CB); initially considered pro-European as a Heseltine supporter, he has become "a latter-day Eurosceptic" (Simon Sebag Montefiore, SUNDAY TIMES) with his former boss, Malcolm Rifkind;
History: He gave in his resignation notice from the Army July '89; was selected from 65 candidates to fight the Labour-held marginal of West Bromwich East against Peter Snape Aug

'89; backed Michael Heseltine in his Leadership bid Nov '90; Peter Snape's majority trebled from 983 in '87 to 2,813, Apr '92; was named Special Adviser to Defence Secretary Malcolm Rifkind Feb '93; continued this role when Malcolm Rifkind transferred to the Foreign Office July '95; in the wake of the de-selection of Reigate's Europhobic Thatcherite Sir George Gardiner for his disloyal - "get off the fence" - remarks about PM John Major, was selected over former Tory MPs Tony Favell and Chris Butler as Sir George's replacement, despite his remark that "if you put up a donkey as a Conservative in Reigate it would win" Feb '97; Sir George followed up by announcing he would contest the seat as a Referendum Party candidate Mar '97; when polled by the DAILY TELEGRAPH, said he was against a single European currency Apr '97; retained Reigate for the Conservatives with a shrunken majority of 7,741 (down from 16,940); this came partly from a swing to Labour of 11.98%; Sir George came fourth with 3,352 (6.9%) May '97; asked about minimum mandatory sentences for career burglars and dealers in hard drugs May '97; warned about the dangers of a minimum wage for the tourist industry June '97; complained about Clare Short's "complete fixation with the eradication of poverty" at the expense of sustainable economic development and in isolation from other Government departments July '97; backed the amendment of Julian Lewis that nuclear disarmament could only work if accompanied by conventional disarmament July '97; attacked the Budget's "smash and grab raid on private pensions" July '97; was named to the Select Committee on Defence July '97;

Born: 15 July 1960,

Family: Son, of Major General Peter Blunt, retired soldier and company director, and Adrienne (Richardson); m '90 Victoria (Jenkins); 1s 'Freddie'/Frederick '94, 1d Claudia '92;

Education: Wellington College '73-78; Royal Military Academy, Sandhurst (Queen's Medal) '79-80; Durham University (in-Service degree of BA in Politics; President of the Union) '81-84; Cranfield School of Management (MBA) '90-91;

Occupation: Formerly Special Adviser to Malcolm Rifkind, when Foreign Secretary '95-97, Defence Secretary '93-95; Political Consultant: with PI Political Consultants '93, self-employed '91-92; Army Officer '79-90, reaching the rank of Captain in the Armoured Reconnaissance Regiment, 13th/18th Royal Hussars (Queen Mary's Own), serving in Cyprus and Germany;

Traits: Slim; dark receding parted hair; bulging forehead; good teeth; gently-spoken; "crisply-suited" (TIMES); "charming and decent" but "not universally loved by civil servants, hence the FCO nickname 'Blunt, Whitehall's best-known typographical error'" (SUNDAY TELEGRAPH); "his nickname as Crippen need not be taken too seriously" (Kenneth Rose, SUNDAY TELEGRAPH); "confident, erudite, expert and incisive" (David Davis MP); "cannot hear or his brain is unable to receive information"; "out of tune with the mood of the country" (Clare Short MP); enjoys bridge and cricket (was the captain of his side in the Army) and historical novels;

Address: House of Commons, Westminster, London SW1A 0AA; 35 Fernhurst Road, Fulham, London SW6 7JN;

Telephone: 0171 219 3000 (H of C); 0171 731 1785 (home)

David BORROW **Labour** **SOUTH RIBBLE '97-**

Majority: 5,084 over Conservative 6-way;
Description: Altered marginal seat hugging the south bank of the River Ribble, over the water from Preston; contains the Labour-leaning town of Leyland (Leyland Trucks) and the Tory-leaning suburbs southwest of Preston; bits and pieces have been traded to Preston and from West Lancashire, without altering the assessment of this constituency as a Tory marginal which, after all, they had held since its creation in '83;
Position: Preston Borough Councillor (Leader '95-97, '92-94) '87-; Chairman, Preston Constituency Labour Party '90-97;
Outlook: The replacement candidate who unexpectedly defeated John Major's friend and former Minister, the jaunty lightweight Robert Atkins; a strong backer of locally-produced Eurofighter; a mainstream Labour type who has had to battle with the hard-Left dominating Preston Council; was ousted by Valerie Wise in '94, but returned in '95; is interested in electoral and constitutional reform, British Aerospace, local government finance; a member of the Fabian Society, the Co-operative Party and the Labour Campaign for Electoral Reform;
History: Joined the Labour Party at 18, '70; became Secretary, Treasurer and Chairman of the Labour Club at Lanchester Poly '70-73; was elected to Preston Borough Council May '87; was elected Chairman of Preston CLP '90; became Leader of Preston Borough Council May '92; was ousted from the Leadership by hard-Leftwinger Valerie Wise May '94; was restored to the Leadership Nov '95; was runner-up to Dennis Golden when the latter was selected as the Labour candidate for South Ribble Jan '96; was selected to replace Dennis Golden - who was dying of a brain tumour - to oppose the sitting Tory MP, Robert Atkins Feb '97; having seen the Labour victory in the Wirral South by-election, was reassured that his victory at South Ribble was likely; was elected with a majority of 5,084 after a pro-Labour notional swing of 12.11% May '97; backed outlawing of fox-hunting June '97; expressed solidarity with jailed Indonesian union leader June '97; in his Maiden welcomed the Budget as possibly ending the contrast between the ability of his generation to walk into secure jobs and the stark prospects of the young in the '90s, July '97; urged crime prevention be based on more accurate crime statistics July '97; strongly defended the commitment to the Eurofighter produced locally at Warton: "it is essential that Britain retains the capability to produce defence equipment at the cutting edge of technology, rather than becoming entirely dependent on the United States as a monopoly supplier" July '97; led the motion which erroneously criticised John Redwood for having dealt with matters involving BA while a Minister when his wife was BA's Company Secretary July '97;
Born: 2 August 1952, Huddersfield
Family: Son, of James Borrow, ICI fitter, then training manager, and Nancy (Crawshaw), shorthand typist;
Education: Mirfield Grammar School; Lanchester Polytechnic (BA); Coventry Polytechnic; IRVTech;
Occupation: Ex: Clerk to Merseyside Valuation Tribunal (UNISON) '83-97;
Traits: Square-faced; good looking; shrewd; can speak without notes;
Address: House of Commons, Westminster, London SW1A 0AA; 117 Garstang Road,

Preston PR2 3EB;
Telephone: 0171 219 4126 (H of C); 0181 345 6789; 8800 35 (pager); 01772 787792 (home); 01772 454727 (constituency office);

Peter BRADLEY **Labour** **THE WREKIN '97-**

Majority: 3,025 over Conservative 3-way;
Description: The name remained the same after the removal of much of Telford new town to a seat named Telford; the remains, the northern part of Telford , plus bits of Ludlow and North Shropshire, were thought to mean a new Conservative seat and the return of a former Conservative MP; the voters thought otherwise;
Position: On Select Committee on Public Administration '97-; ex: Westminster City Councillor (Deputy Leader its Labour Group '90-96) '86-96; Political Secretary, Paole Zion '81-83;
Outlook: The political affairs consultant who removed the threat of the "Return of the Hangman", Peter Bruinvels, to the Commons; as a Westminster Councillor was a leader of the campaign to force the Council to re-acquire its three cemeteries sold for 15p and a leader of the Westminster Objectors who insisted in '93 on an investigation into political corruption there, particularly the 'homes for votes' plot to sell council houses in marginal wards to presumed Tories; he was "staggered" at the "stench of corruption" uncovered;
History: His father was (and is) "staunch Labour"; he himself supported Labour in his public school and joined the Labour Party at 26, '79; was elected to Westminster City Council May '86; as a leader of the Westminster Objectors, urged the Auditor to investigate a Tory 'homes for votes' plot '89; was elected Deputy Leader of the Labour Group on Westminster City Council May '90; supported all-women short-lists as he could see no better way of getting more women into Parliament Apr '95; was selected for the revised version of The Wrekin, when the sitting Labour MP, Bruce Grocott, was selected for the new and safer Telford, formed of the bulk of the old Wrekin constituencyu; The Wrekin, as redrawn, was considered as likely to be a Tory seat, to be won by ultra-Right ex-Tory MP Peter Bruinvels; Labour did not agree; when the Magill Report into Westminster's 'homes for votes' conspiracy was published, Bradley was made the subject of a sustained and scurrilous muck-raking attack by Tory MP David Shaw, alleging he had not disclosed the clients of his PR firm in the Westminster Council's register of interests; Bradley had already received libel recompense for similar charges planted in the TIMES; Bruce Grocott challenged Shaw to repeat his charges outside the House May '96; Bradley won The Wrekin by a majority of 3,025 over Peter Bruinvels, on a pro-Labour notional swing of 11.27% May '97; in his Maiden, welcomed the phased release of council funds to help ease "a housing crisis of monumental proportions"; it was particularly difficult in his constituency "because The Wrekin is the nation's low-pay capital", with 3,500 earning under £2 an hour June '97; co-sponsored motion urging a public inquiry into the functionig of Westminster City Council June '97; was named to Select Committee on Public Administration July '97; criticised Lord Rees-Mogg for his "black propaganda" in favour of Dame Shirley Porter Sep '97;
Born: 12 April 1953, Birmingham

Family: Son, of Fred Bradley, technical translator, and Gertrude (Zunz); his partner is Annie Hart, nursery school teacher; twin sons, Tom and Jess '97;
Education: New College Prep School, Oxford; Abingdon School; Sussex University (BA Hons); Occidental College, Los Angeles;
Occupation: Ex: Director: of Millbank Consultants (public affairs consultants) '93-97; previously of Good Relations (PR) '85-93; Research Director, for Centre for Contemporary Studies '79-83 (MSF);
Traits: Thinning light brown hair; specs; keen sportsman, especially cricket (member of Warwickshire CCC); Aston Villa supporter; Jewish by origin;
Address: House of Commons, Westminster, London SW1A 0AA; 80 Cambridge Street, London SW1V 4QQW
Telephone: 0171 219 4112 (H of C); 01952 240010 (constituency);

Ben(jamin) BRADSHAW **Labour** **EXETER '97-**

Majority: 11,705 over Conservative 7-way;
Description: Devon's still unaltered historic county town and commercial centre; it leans to the Conservatives but goes Labour at its high tides, as in '66 and '97; initially the latter seemed unlikely in view of furious controvery among local Labour activists about the culpability in a South African resistance tragedy of their then candidate; curiously, afterwards the tide probably may have risen higher in '97 because of the clash between an attractive self-proclaimed homosexual and an unpleasant homophobe;
Position: On Select Committee on European Legislation '97-; Secretary all-party Cycling Group '97-;
Outlook: Loyal young Blairite regionalist and pro-European; a bit self-absorbed in his determination not to be pigeon-holed as a gay crusader; otherwise an assiduous self-publicist; the former local reporter and rising star of the BBC who was the hands-down election victor despite two obstacles: he was chosen belatedly after the previous veteran Labour candidate, John Lloyd, was forced to step down after late revelations about his role in refusing to try to save the life of a friend in the South African resistance movement; his other alleged disability was that he was openly gay and was opposed by a primitive Rightwing 'Christian' Tory doctor and homophobe, Dr Adrian Rogers, who described homosexuality as "sterile, God-forsaken and disease-ridden"; Bradshaw preferred to campaign on the NHS, jobs and the environment: "Exeter is a nice, clean, green place; my ambition is to make it greener still and for it to become the green capital of Britain"; in Christian Socialist Movement, Labour Campaign for Electoral Reform, Amnesty, Campaign for Real Ale;
History: After reporting a speech by John Lloyd, a local Labour barrister-councillor, he joined the Labour Party '84; Lloyd succeeded in making Exeter a Con-Lab marginal, losing to its popular Tory MP, Sir John Hannam, by only 3,045 votes (4.9%) Apr '92; Bradshaw was selected from a short-list of five as the replacement for John Lloyd as candidate for Exeter after the latter was disqualified by Labour's NEC in the light of fuller information from his executed friend's widow; Bradshaw had told his selection conference he was gay but would not make a big thing of it Sep '96; his strange Tory opponent, Dr Adrian Rogers, leader of the

one-man Conservative Family Campaign, insisted on making an issue of it, referring to him as "Bent Ben"; Bradshaw admitted Dr Rogers was "my greatest asset"; Bradshaw urged local LibDems to accept Lord [Bill] Rogers' suggestion that they vote tactically in such Con-Lab marginals Sep '96; the complaint of the Exeter Labour Party about John Lloyd's de-selection was kept off the agenda at annual conference; Bradshaw loyally hailed Tony Blair's conference speech as "the speech of the next Prime Minister - one of the greatest Prime Ministers this country has ever seen" Oct '96; urged a more pro-European policy, to the benefit of the south west and Exeter Mar '97; urged a seven-county south west regional development body, with a Devon-Cornwall sub-region within that Apr '97; regained marginal Exeter for Labour by the massive majority of 11,705 after a swing to Labour of 11.91%; Dr Rogers lost 8,000 of the '92 Tory vote; the LibDems, otherwise strong in the southwest, lost 1,000 of theirs to tactical voting May '97; introduced Pesticides Bill June '97; co-sponsored motion backing fight against prescription fraud June '97; his Maiden, was a model of loyal support for the Budget July '97; was elected Secretary of the all-party Cycling Group July '97; was named to the Select Committee on European Legislation July '97; obtained a Commons' spouse's pass for his male partner, Neal Dalgleish July '97; counter-attacked against Roy Hattersley's diatribe against pious cyclists, insisting cyclists "cut congestion, cut pollution and cut costs to the NHS by staying fit" July '97; avoided attending 'Gay Night' at Labour's annual conference because "to allow myself to become appropriated as a gay crusader would lessen my effectiveness as an MP" Sep '97; enthused about Chancellor's declaration in principle for entering the single European currency Oct '97;

Born: 30 August 1960, London

Family: Son, of late Rev Peter Bradshaw, Anglican vicar and Daphne (Murphy); his Partner is Neal Dalgleish;

Education: Thorpe St Andrew School, Norwich; Sussex University (BA Hons);

Occupation: Journalist: on BBC 86-97: BBC Radio Devon (three years), 'The World at One', 'The World This Weekend'; awards as 'Consumer Journalist of the Year, for coverage of the East German revolution, the fall of the Berlin Wall; EXETER EXPRESS & ECHO (NUJ) '84-86;

Traits: Good-looking ("a veritable Hugh Grant look-alike" -Clare Garner, INDEPENDENT; blond; centre-parted hair; bags under his eyes; pointed chin; "a leggy, fresh-faced, floppy-haired young man with a quick mind, a pleasant manner, a ready smile, a vaunting ambition, unlimited energy, a merry laugh and a strategic sense of humour-failure whenever humour looks risky" (Matthew Parris, TIMES); a "fairly devout" [BB] practicing Anglican who has preached in Westminster Abbey; considers himself a Labour MP, not a gay MP; has refused a substantial sum from HELLO!. enjoys cooking, tennis, music, the theatre and cycling;

Address: House of Commons, Westminster, London SW1A 0AA;

Telephone: 0171 219 6597 (H of C); 01392 275004 (constituency office);

AN EXTENSION OF MPS

MPs have developed an added dimension, called researchers. Until recently only more sophisticated MPs used them. Or were used by them. One former Northwest MP, suddenly seemed fascinated with by Trans-Pacific trade, according to questions in his name. These were planted by his research assistant, an American PhD-aspirant, writing his dissertation with the help of answers provided by UK civil servants. Recently the number of questions has increased by a third, as researchers vie with lobbyists and cause groupies. One now has to distinguish between MPs' questions and those planted on them. Our monitoring does so.

Graham (Stuart) BRADY **Conservative** **ALTRINCHAM & SALE WEST '97-**

Majority: 1,505 over Labour 7-way;
Description: A redrawn seat in the southern Manchester suburbs; with Cheadle is one of the two in the Greater Manchester area to remain Tory, as part of Cheshire's middle-class suburban belt; it has lost eastern Sale to Wythenshawe but gained the equivalent from former Davyhulme;
Position: On Select Committee on Education and Employment '97-; ex: Vice Chairman, East Berkshire Conservative Association '92-95; Chairman, Northern Area Conservative Collegiate Forum '88-89; Chairman, Durham University Conservative Association '87-88;
Outlook: At almost 30 he was the Tories' youngest new MP, as the successor to retiring Sir Fergus Montgomery; a lucky middle-brow PRman selected and elected for one of the few remaining safeish Tory seats in the north; a locally-born and locally-raised Rightish Eurosceptic who finds it "hard to stomach that the European Court can overturn democratic decisions taken by a British Government"; an obsessed defender of his local grammar schools, gramt-maintained schools and the Assisted Places; favours: employee share ownership, town centre residential development and tough sentencing; is hostile to collective bargaining and public sector strikes;
History: He came from a Conservative but politically inactive family; he joined the Conservatives in Timperley at 16 to defend the status of his own threatened Altrincham Grammar School '83; was elected Chairman of the Durham University Conservative Association, following Piers Merchant '87; became Chairman of the Northern Area of Norman Tebbit's neutered Collegiate Forum '88; was an unsuccessful candidate for Bowburn and Coxhoe, in the Durham County Council election May '89; published a Centre for Policy Studies pamphlet 'Towards an Employees' Charter and Away from Collective Bargaining', which opposed public sector strikes '91; made a "well-received" (GB) speech on Ulster at annual conference Oct '94; although expected, because part of Davyhulme went into redrawn Altrincham and Sale West, Winston Churchill MP did not apply for selection; Brady was chosen as a local son in his first contest to replace retiring Sir Fergus Montgomery in redrawn Altrincham & Sale West, making him one of the youngest candidates for a winnable seat Oct '95; was one of the 14 candidates for winnable seats who declared in a DAILY TELEGRAPH poll that he would say in his election address that he opposed Britain ever joining a single European currency Dec '96; retained Altrincham & Sale West by 1,505 votes, a tenth of the majority expected in terms of the previous general election May '97; in the Tory Leadership contest, joined the campaign team of Michael Howard May-June '97; urged Education Secretary David Blunkett to "approve outstanding applications for grant-maintained status" May '97; his Maiden was in defence of the threatened Assisted Places Scheme June '97; warned that subsidised jobs for the young unemployed would displace others June '97; asked Minister to "join me in applauding North West Water for its investment in combating leaks" and to cancel the windfall tax of that wildly profitable and unpopular company July '97; urged "a guarantee that my grammar schools are safe" July '97; was named to Select Committee on Education and Employment July '97;
Born: 20 May 1967, Salford, Manchester
Family: Son, of John Brady, accountant, and Maureen (Birch), medical secretary; m '92

Victoria (Lowther), TV reporter; 1d Catherine '93;
Education: Heyes Lane Primary School, Timperley, Cheshire; Altrincham Grammar School (Deputy Head Boy); Durham University (BA Law);
Occupation: Public Affairs Director, of Waterfront Partnership (a transport and strategic PR consultacy) '92-97; ex: Assistant Director of Publications, Centre for Policy Studies '90-92; Trainee, with Shandwick Plc (public relations; a source there says he was sacked as unpromising; he insists he left "from choice")'89-90;
Traits: Very tall; boyish-looking; toothy smile; dark brown parted hair; his "irresistible combination of hair, muscles and teeth puts one in mind of Prince Andrew at his most virile" (David Aaronovitch, INDEPENDENT); "my family resembles a circus trekking up and down the M6 with child and dog and luggage; it is quite a show to keep on the road" (GB);
Address: House of Commons, Westminster, London SW1A 0AA; Thatcher House, Delahays Farm, Green Lane, Timperley, Altrincham, Cheshire WA15 8QW (constituency office);
Telephone: 0171 219 3000 (H of C); 0161 904 8828 (constituency phone); 0161 904 8868 (constituency Fax);

'Tom' (Thomas) BRAKE **Liberal Democrat** **CARSHALTON & WALLINGTON '97-**

Majority: 2,267 over Conservative 7-way;
Description: A previously safe-Tory seat in the LibDem-controlled borough of Sutton, despite the 40,000 houses in the St Helier estate, built as a garden city in the '30s; before '97 it had never before been out of Conservative hands in this century; the '97 result was anticipated by the May '94 local council elections, when the Tories lost every council seat in this constituency;
Position: On the Select Committee on Environment, Transport and Regional Affairs '97-; on LibDem MPs' Environment Team '97-; on the Transport, Environment and Strategic Planning Team of London LibDem MPs '97-; Sutton Borough Councillor (Vice Chairman, Policy Committee) '94-; ex: Hackney Borough Councillor '88-90; was on the LibDem Environment Working Group;
Outlook: One of the six thoughtful and enthusiastic new LibDem "thirty-something" MPs; a young computer buff who loves fighting elections and won at his second attempt at this Tory stronghold; backs most LibDem policies (pro: Europe, market economy and positive action to improve the environment) but opposes their decision to allow non-elected representatives in a reformed second Chamber; is a member of Greenpeace, Friends of the Earth, Oxfam, Amnesty International;
History: His family was non-political; he joined the Liberals '83; was elected to Hackney Borough Council Feb '88; left Hackney for Carshalton after he had been selected to contest the latter, giving up his Hackney Council seat Nov '90; he cut the 14,000 majority of Carshalton's 'One Nation' Tory MP, Nigel Forman, by 4,500 votes Apr '92; was elected to Sutton Borough Council May '94; at annual conference endorsed the importance of closed-circuit TV on local estates Sep '96; again contested Carshalton and, to the surprise of Nigel Forman, ousted him by a majority of 2,267 on a 11.76 swing, part of a LibDem sweep

through London's southwestern suburbs from Carshalton to Twickenham May '97; was named to the LibDems' Environment Team May '97; in his Maiden did not see how the £100m supposed to be saved by the abolition of the Assisted Places Scheme could do enough for the massive needs of education, on which the LibDems had pledged an extra £2b each year June '97; in the debate on the London Underground urged the Labour Government to "consider setting up a public interest company which would be free to borrow money on the markets", "outside PSBR" as in the USA; he also suggested "the option of a tax on non-residential parking spaces in London" and road-pricing June '97; co-sponsored motion urging the saving of network cards for rail users July '97; co-sponsored motion urging UK exploitation of "substantial world-wide market opportunities" for "environmental technologies and services" July '97; co-sponsored motion urging patenting of genetic advances July '97; sought to protect the Accident and Emergency unit at St Helier, "the local hospital at which our first child was born two weeks ago" July '97; called for curbs on domestic air travel in favour of rail travel Sep '97;

Born: 6 May 1962, Melton Mowbray

Family: Son, of Michael Brake, IT Manager, and Judith (Pape) teacher; separated; his Partner is Candida Goulden; 1c '97;

Education: Lycee International (for ten years), Paris; Imperial College, London (BSc Physics);

Occupation: Computer software consultant (worked for ICI Paints in Slough);

Traits: Tall; lean; young-looking; thin face; brown hair; dark eyebrows; straight-faced good looks; London accent; cyclist; runner; French-speaker;

Address: House of Commons, Westminster, London SW1A 0AA; 62 Gordon Road, Carshalton, Surrey SM5 3RE;

Telephone: 0171 219 3000 (H of C); 0181 647 9329 (home);

Dr Peter BRAND **Liberal Democrat** **ISLE OF WIGHT '97-**

Majority: 6,406 over Conservative 9-way;

Description: The longtime Con-LibDem marginal, with a tradition of long stints: Stephen Ross '74-87, Barry Field '87-97; a quiet south coast holiday and retirement island; has 100,000 electors and sixty miles of coastline; is only reachable by ferry, whose delays impede further development of its industry, now including helicopters (Westland) and electronics (Plessey); Parkhurst and two other prisons also provide jobs; has lowest average GDP of any county;

Position: On Select Committee on Health '97-; on LibDem Health team '97-; Isle of Wight Unitary Councillor '95-; ex: Isle of Wight Councillor (Deputy Leader '89-93) '85-95; Chairman: Isle of Wight Liberal Democrat Political Committee, LibDems' Health Policy Working Group '94-95, Community Care Working Group '93-94; Chairman, British Medical Association for Isle of Wight '80-84;

Outlook: Witty, intelligent, socially-conscious local GP, LibDem policy formulator and former local BMA Chairman; has long targeted this seat; on the Isle of Wight Health Authority he opposed the setting up of competing health trusts; pushed hard for the

integration of health authorities and the maintenance of community hospitals; also for better provision for community care, to allow the elderly and disabled to lead a fuller life in their homes; opposed compulsory water metering without protection for large families living on state benefits; before reaching the Commons had a leading role in formulating LibDems' health and community care policies; with many elderly patients, tends to concentrate on their nursing needs and opposes the concentration of the NHS on acute care; has long campaigned against dumping sewage off the coast; in Amnesty International;
History: He came from a Left-of Centre Dutch family; at school as Captain, he avoided politics, but successfully bet the local South Gloucestershire Tory MP, Fred Corfield, his majority would fall Oct '64; was elected for Brading to the Isle of Wight County Council as an Independent May '85, joining the Liberals Nov '85 ; became Deputy Leader of the LibDem Group May '89; contested Isle of Wight - one of the LibDems' target Parliamentary seats -against Barry Field, cutting the majority from 6,442 but losing by 1,827 (2.3%) Apr '92; became a member of the LibDems' Community Care Working Party '93; became a member of the LibDems' Health Policy Group '94; was elected to the Isle of Wight Unitary Authority May '95; at annual LibDem conference, insisted on people getting "their medical and nursing needs free of charge"; warned against the NHS over-concentrating on acute care Sep '96; was criticised by PRIVATE EYE for having been Chairman of IsleCare, which had been found guilty by local magistrates of "a very serious breach" of regulations by failing to provide adequate night staff; said: "we have sacked the manager" Oct'96; was elected by a majority of 6,406 over Andrew Turner, the Tory candidate who replaced ailing Barry Field May '97; denounced the "insanitary" Commons voting conditions June '97; co-sponsored motion urging improved procedure for complaints against solicitors July '97; was named to Select Committee on Health July '97; having had experience in buying in private services for his surgeries, was unhappy about the unclear definitions in Labour's Bill to reactivate PFI for hospitals, fearing "a form of cosy commissioning and delivery by favoured friends" July '97; co-sponsored motion urging a sympathetic review of laws on gays and lesbians July '97; in humorous LibDem conference speech said, that since wombs were no longer necessarily involved, clinical care should be from "the sperm to the worm" instead of from "the womb to the tomb" Sep '97;
Born: 16 May 1947, Zaandam, Netherlands
Family: Son, of Louis Brand, shipbuilder, and Ans (Fredericks), teacher; m '72 Jane (Attlee, great niece of Clement Attlee, PM '45-51) GP; 2s: Edmund '76, Jonathan '78;
Education: Thornbury Grammar School, Gloucestershire (School Captain); Birmingham University Medical School; MRCS, LRCP, DObst,RCOG, MRCGP;
Occupation: General Practitioner '71-: ex: Chairman of IsleCare (a non-profit company set up to run 21 residential old people's homes formerly owned by the council; unpaid) '93-96; Director, The Mount, Wadhurst, East Sussex (special needs school) '70-76;
Traits: Greying blond parted hair; intelligent; witty; Dutch-speaking; enjoys sailing (Brading Haven Yacht Club, Island Sailing Club, Royal Yacht Association);
Address: House of Commons, Westminster, London SW1A 0AA; Beechgrove, The Mall, Brading, Isle of Wight PO36 0DE;
Telephone: 0171 219 4404 (H of C); 01983 407368 (home); 01983 406277 (Fax);

WE'RE GETTING FATTER

MPs profiles tend to get fatter, like the papier mache masks we made in our youth by adding to a clay portrait model soggy strips of newsprint soaked in flour and water. Just as you can build up a strong papier mache mask, so too we hope we have transformed a dimly lit outline form into sharp features plus a few warts.

Colin BREED **Liberal Democrat** **CORNWALL SOUTH EAST '97-**

Majority: 6,480 over Conservative 7-way;
Description: A traditional Tory-LibDem marginal which, after '74, remained in Tory hands so long as its MP was the 'One Nation' regionalist Tory, Sir Robert Hicks, who retired in '97; just over the dividing line of the Tamar from Plymouth, it embraces Liskeard, seaside resorts like Polperro, Fowey, Lostwithiel and East and West Looe plus Saltash and Torpoint;
Position: Spokesman on Competition '97-; Saltash Town Councillor (Mayor '95-96, '89-90) '82-; Caradon District Councillor '82-93;
Outlook: An agreeable London-born conservative businessman who has retaken the seat after 23 years; a local Saltash-based councillor who has campaigned against Cornwall's neglect and opposed a second Tamar bridge; has benefited from the retirement of Sir Robert Hicks, his replacement by a typically unsuitable Tory succcessor and the general rise of the LibDem tide in the Westcountry; crusades against high and unfair water charges;
History: Joined the Liberal Party '66; was elected to both Caradon District Council and Saltash Town Council May '82; became Mayor of Saltash May '89; became Agent to the LibDem candidate for Cornwall South East, Robin Teverson (later an MEP), who made no headway against the sitting Tory MP Robert Hicks Mar-Apr '92; was selected as the LibDem candidate for Cornwall South East Mar '94; again became Mayor of Saltash May '95; opposed the conversion of a store in Saltash to a JobCentre June '96; campaigned against reducing help for the elderly in local hospital July '96; urged the renationalisation of Devonport naval dockyard July '96; attacked Government delay in deciding to set up a business and science park in Saltash July '96; said Olympics sportsmen needed professional-level support instead of competing as "brave amateurs" Aug '96; at annual conference emphasised the problems of youth offenders in small towns Sep '96; campaigned on the neglect of Cornwall, including tourism, cost of water, poor road and rail links, high unemployment Apr '97; opposed any further reduction in the age of consent for homosexuals or same-sex marriages Apr '97; to squeeze the Labour vote, his literature said, "Only local man Colin Breed or the Conservative from London can win this election" Apr '97; was backed by the actor Edward Woodward Apr'97; captured the seat by a majority of 6,480 on the biggest Cornish swing to the LibDems (12%), May '97; complained about security restrictions at the Liskeard count May '97; co-sponsored motion celebrating the 500th anniversary of the rebellious Cornish march on the London of Henry VII June '97; co-sponsored motion urging a development agency for Cornwall, to block the poaching of jobs from those for Wales, Scotland and the north June '97; in his Maiden welcomed the £40m in Lottery money for the creation of the Eden Botanical Institute in his constituency June '97; expressed solidarity with jailed Indonesian union leader June '97; complained of the decline in small shops in Cornwall under pressure from out-of-town shopping centres and tax-favoured charity shops July '97; introduced a Bill to prohibit the use by water companies of rateable values as the basis of their charges July '97;
Born: 4 May 1947, London
Family: Son, of Alfred Breed, chef, and Edith (Smith); m '68 Janet (Courtiour) bank official; 1s Matthew '75, 1d Esther '72;
Education: Primary school in Wandsworth; Torquay Grammar School; Associate, Chartered

Institute of Bankers (ACIB);
Occupation: Owner-Director, of Gemini Abrasives Ltd (regional distribution company) '92-; Chairman, Wesley Housing and Benevolent Trust; ex: Stockbroker '91-92; Managing Director, of Dartington & Company Group Plc (regional merchant bank) '81-91; Midland Bank employee '64-81;
Traits: Chubby; greying light brown front-combed hair; trim beard; mild-looking; Methodist lay preacher; golfer;
Address: House of Commons, Westminster, London SW1A 0AA; 10 Dunheved Road, Saltash, Cornwall PL12 4BW;
Telephone: 0171 219 4594 (H of C); 01752 845516 (home); 01752 840820 (Fax);

Helen (Rosemary) BRINTON **Labour** **PETERBOROUGH '97-**

Majority: 7,323 over Conservative 7-way;
Description: A cathedral city on the edge of the Fens, swollen by accepting London overspill; a once-marginal seat - held by Tories by 3 votes in '66, then held by Labour '74-79; was made marginal again in '83 and '95, causing Dr Brian Mawhinney to flee, just in time;
Position: Secretary, Full Employment Forum (Gouldite pro-Keynesian body) '93-; ex: Secretary: Kent County Labour Party '89-95, Chairman, North Yorkshire County Labour Party '85-88;
Outlook: Outspoken and controversial former Centre-Left Eurosceptic Keynesian, transformed into a Blair-Mandelson super-loyalist; "I am certainly 'New Labour' but certainly NOT a 'luvvie'"; the first new MP to become the butt of newspapeer diarists' vicious humour: Paul Routledge of the INDEPENDENT ON SUNDAY describes her as belonging to the "I Ring the Local Paper Three Times a Day Tendency"; now insists she is "totally without ideological baggage"; but in '92 ran 'Women for Gould' and the next year became National Secretary of his Full Employment Forum; is still strong on animal welfare, particularly against fox-hunting; belongs to the Co-operative Party, Fabian Society, Labour Women's Network, Labour Housing Group, Labour Economic Strategy Group, Labour Planning Group, Socialist Health Association, World Disarmament Campaign, Labour Action for Peace,
History: Both her parents were Labour Party members; she joined the Harrogate Labour Party '84; as Labour's Faversham candidate, campaigned against under-priced sale of local houses by London Residuary Body June '91; defended the singing of 'We Are the Champions' as showing John Smith and company "letting their hair down" at the end of Labour's annual conference Oct '91; attacked TRIBUNE for giving space to Lindi St Clair of the sado-masochist 'Corrective Party' instead of an explanation of Maastricht opt-outs Dec '91; campaigned for Kevin McNamara's Wild Mammals Protection Bill to ban fox-hunting Feb '92; succeeded in over-taking the LibDems in coming second in Faversham Apr '92; complained that "Labour has lost touch and we cannot go forward unless we recognise this"; objected to Labour's failed use of a local NHS inadequacy (the 'War of Jennifer's Ear'), without consulting her or the local party about a case which "should not have been touched with a bargepole" May '92; with Leftwingers Dr Roger Berry and Dr Lynne Jones, was a co-founder of Bryan

Gould's Keynesian 'Full Employment Forum', which was implicitly critical of shadow Chancellor Gordon Brown's monetarism Mar '93; unexpectedly, became Kent Co-ordinator for Blair's Leadership campaign (four years after Blair had said to her in '90: "it is so great to meet a PPC of such QUALITY") June '94; was selected from an all-women's short-list for the altered key marginal of Peterborough, from which the Conservative Party Chairman, Dr Brian Mawhinney, had fled July '95; did not oppose Blair's abandonment of all-women's short-lists, even before it was declared illegal, insisting "it is not a talking point" Aug '95; won Peterborough with a majority of 7,323 over Jacqueline Foster, a notional swing of 13.41%; "she thought she had won because she was such a wonderful person; most normal people would realise that Tony Blair and the Labour Party had won" (her agent, Mary Rainey) May '97; in her Maiden, enthused about Peterborough's efforts to improve its environment May '97; on her 'Newsnight' debut she wound up with "we're all speaking with one voice, and that is Peter Mandelson's great achievement" May '97; "the degree of Blair worship is now measured in 'Brintons'" wrote the FINANCIAL TIMES Diary, quoting a backbencher: "Helen, who has a Mandelsonian chip wired into her brain, is the sole 10-carat Brinton" June '97; the GUARDIAN Diarist, Matthew Norman, took to referring to her as an "android" June '97; she fell out with her local Agent, Mary Rainey June '97; the SUNDAY TIMES quoted her as telling a local paper that it "would be nice to have a valet", then itself added: "whoever heard of an android that needed a valet" July '97; co-sponsored a motion urging better protection of water meadows July '97;

Born: 23 December 1947, Derby

Family: Daughter, of George Henry Dyche, teacher, and Phyllis May (James) teacher; m '79, Ian Richard Thomas Brinton, teacher; "I wouldn't have married him if he'd been into politics, for God's sake"; "he enjoys doing his own thing - he digs the allotment"; 1s Hal Ian '85; 1d Gwendolen '82;

Education: Avalton and Boulton County Primary School, Derby; Spondon Park Grammar Scchool; Bristol University (BA Hons English Literature, MA in Medieval Literature; PGCE)

Occupation: Ex: Teacher of English in Rochester Girls' Grammar School '93-97; Free-lance Examiner for GCE and A-level English with Cambridge Board and others; (NUT/TGWU)

Traits: Straight blonde hair and fringe (shortened from shoulder-length); thin face; toothy; abrasive (has a "vigorous approach to matters about which she feels strongly" - John Prescott MP); "hyper-active, with an annoyingly earnest manner" (Leftwing journalist); "spine-chilling" (GUARDIAN diarist); can show "rudeness" and "arrogance" (her former Agent, Mary Rainey); her favourite phrase: "I have a job to do";

Address: House of Commons, Westminster, London SW1A 0AA; 48B Newton Road, Faversham, Kent ME13 8DZ;

Telephone: 0171 219 3000 (H of C); 01795 530860 (home)

KEEPING PARLIAMENTARY SECRETS

A rueful MP claimed, with some truth, that the best way to keep something secret is to make a speech about it in the Palace of Westminster. He was commenting on the emptiness of the Press Gallery (except for HANSARD writers and the Press Association). Long gone are the days when serious newspapers carried a full or half-page summarising Parliamentary debate. Of late, Westminster has been used as a source of news stories. In our old-fashioned way, we read HANSARD daily and watch the Commons and Lords on the Parliamentary Channel. Parliamentary debaters are very self-revealing in debate. And we don't mean only Kerry Pollard MP, in whose Maiden he disclosed that until 12 he had to drop his trousers regularly to prove that Kerry was not a girl's name.

Russell BROWN **Labour** **DUMFRIES '97-**

Majority: 9,643 over Conservative 6-way;
Description: Previously one of the two safest Conservative seats in Scotland, with Sir Hector Monro retaining it by 6,415 in '92; apart from Dumfries itself it embraces mostly small towns - including Lockerbie - and rural areas, spreading over nearly 2,500 square miles; it contains plants of ICI, BNFL, and the boiler-making subsidiary of Rolls-Royce; Robert Burns is buried there; its former mining areas were moved into Galloway in '83;
Position: Dumfries and Galloway Unitary Councillor (Labour Group Leader '95-) '95-; ex: Dumfries & Galloway Regional Councillor '86-96; Chairman, Public Protection Committee '90-94; Annandale & Eskdale District Councillor '88-96; "I served as a member of the Dumfries and Galloway Police Authority for 11 years, four of which were as its Chairman";
Outlook: A long-established locally-born local government stalwart who, on his first Parliamentary attempt, rode the anti-Conservative tide into a hitherto unbreachable fortress; he had pioneered local improvements like free travel for senior citizens on public transport, in partnership with private companies; one of Labour's few working-class members in the 'Class of '97';
History: He joined the Labour party '78; he was elected to Dumfries and Galloway Regional Council May '86; was elected to Dumfries and Galloway Unitary Council, becoming its Labour Group Leader May '95; was selected for Dumfries, made more vulnerable by the retirement of the sitting Tory MP Sir Hector Monro, after three decades Oct '96; claimed the Dumfries area had the second lowest average wage levels in Scotland Apr '97; became the first Labour MP for Dumfries, winning by 9,643 over the veteran Tory candidate Struan Stevenson on a near-record swing of 16.49%; "even in our wildest dreams, we had never contemplated the size of the eventual majority" May '97; asked International Development Secretary Clare Short how many refugees had returned to Rwanda, Burundi and Zaire May '97; asked the Scottish Secretary about his plans to improve Scottish food standards June '97; urged the amalgamation of the NHS trusts in sparsely-populated areas like his July '97; urged a further detailed survey of offshore Beaufort's Dyke and a public inquiry into the dumping there July '97; his Maiden, in loyal support of Chancellor Brown's Budget, was largely a recital of all the advances which had first taken place in Dumfries July '97; was given a brief walk-on part in Tam Dalyell's enormously lengthy new adjournment debate on Lockerbie because he had "served on the Dumfries and Galloway Police Authority for 11 years, four of which were as its Chairman"; he was sure the two Libyan accused could receive a "fair trial" and was opposed to the trial being handed over to a "third party" as desired by Dalyell July '97;
Born: 17 September 1951, Annan, Dumfriesshire
Family: Son, of late Howard Russell Brown and Muriel (Anderson); married Christine Margaret (Calvert); 3d;
Education: Annan Academy;
Occupation: Former Plant Operative, in ICI Films, Dumfries '92-97; previously Production Supervisor, in ICI Explosives, Dumfries '74-92 (TGWU);
Traits: Slim face; short dark brown greying hair and beard; enjoys sport, particularly foootball (runs a local primary school football team);

Address: House of Commons, Westminster, London SW1A 0AA; 56 Wood Avenue, Annan, Dumfriesshire DG1 6DE;
Telephone: 0171 219 3000 (H of C); 01461 205365 (home);

Des(mond) BROWNE QC **Labour** **KILMARNOCK & LOUDOUN '97-**

Majority: 7,256 over SNP 6-way;
Description: The unaltered seat embracing the proud and independent town of Kilmarnock and smaller towns and communities; it contains the major bottling plant of Johnnie Walker whisky; in '92 the SNP became the leading challenger to Labour supremacy;
Position: On: Scottish Catholic Bishops' Conference Working Party on Child Sexual Abuse '95-, Scottish Council for Civil Liberties '76-, Scottish Office Consultative Committee on Child Law '92-94; Chairman, Children's Rights Group '81-86;
Outlook: Able, well-connected party loyalist and top Scots Catholic advocate, specialising in family law; was parachuted in as the last-minute replacement candidate for this SNP-threatened seat; formerly a local solicitor, he more than held the SNP at bay; is linked with Scottish Secretary Donald Dewar through the Glasgow law firm of Ross Harper and Murphy; also was "Gordon Brown's preferred candidate for the seat" (NEW STATESMAN);
History: Following an upbringing on a council estate at Steventon, as the son of an ICI process worker, joined the Labour Party at 23, '75; contested LibDem-held Argyll & Bute, running in Labour's traditional fourth place Apr '92; represented Labour in court, preventing a 'Panorama' interview with PM John Major being shown in Scotland on the eve of local elections May '95; was selected over eight others within 20 days of the election by Labour's NEC when the Labour MP-candidate, Leftwinger Willie McKelvey, had to stand down due to a slight stroke Apr '97; derided the policies of his main challenger, the SNP, as "dangerous pie in the sky"; rejected the claims of his SNP opponent, Alex Neil, saying "no one in the party believed a Blairite had been deliberately imposed on them", noting that "Willie McKelvey hasn't disappeared; he is here to help me"; claimed the main issue was job creation to ease the unemployment "epidemic" in certain housing estates and the extension of the M77 to Fenwick Apr '97; retained the seat with a majority over the SNP of 7,256, a slight (0.62%) swing from SNP to Labour May '97; led a motion congratulating Knockentiber Amateur Football Club for their victory in the Scottish Amateur Club Final May '97; expressed solidarity with jailed Indonesian union leader June '97; pressed PM Tony Blair to take measures against "the threat of organised crime emanating from Russia and eastern Europe" June '97; asked for encouragement for a local heritage facility training the young in old lacemaking skills June '97; his Maiden, understandably for an advocate specialising in child law, was on the Child Support Agency; he urged a £15 disregard and warned about the CSA's possible challenge to the European Convention on European Rights June '97; asked when Britain would incorporate into British law the European Convention on Human Rights July '97; urged a level playing field for Scotch whisky exports, particularly in India July '97; made one of the best contributions to the debate on the Social Security Bill, emphasising the need for the system's complete overhaul July '97;

Born: 22 March 1952, Steventon, Ayrshire
Family: Son of an ICI process worker; married; 2s: Daniel '85, Samuel '88;
Education: St Michael's Academy (RC), Kilwinning '64-70; Glasgow University (LLB) '70-74;
Occupation: Advocate, called to the Bar '93, specialising in child law; on Deans' Council, Faculty of Advocates '94-; Clerk to the Human Rights Committee, Faculty of Advocates '94-; formerly a Solicitor '76-92: Senior Partner, in McCluskey, Browne, Kilmarnock '85-92, Partner, in Ross Harper & Murphy, Glasgow '80-85; on Council of Law Society of Scotland '88-91;
Traits: Stocky; small, bird-like features; square face; speckled greying dark swept-back full head of hair; moderate in tone; Roman Catholic of working class origins;
Address: House of Commons, Westminster, London SW1A 0AA; 20 Glenlockhart Road, Edinburgh EH14 1BN;
Telephone: 0171 219 3000 (H of C); 0131 443 5439;

Karen BUCK **Labour** **REGENT'S PARK & KENSINGTON NORTH '97-**

Majority: 14,657 over Conservative 6-way;
Description: A new seat, a gift to Labour from the Boundary Commission: a combination of safe-Tory St John's Wood, with mixed Little Venice and Maida Vale and strongly-Labour Queen's Park, Harrow Road, Westbourne and Notting Hill; "we have the liveliest markets and hippest bars in town; we host the Notting Hill carnival", "the largest and most successful street festival in Europe" (KB);
Position: On the Select Committee on Social Security '97-; Westminster City Councillor (Chairwoman, Labour Group '95-; previously Chairwoman of Social Services, Housing, Social Services) '90-; on Queens Park Single Regeneration Budget Board '95-; ex: Chairwoman, of Westminster North CLP '88-90; on Paddington and North Kensington Health Authority '87-88;
Outlook: One of Labour's brightest Centre-Left feminist insiders: from Walworth Road and the Conservatives' sleaze-ridden Westminster Council; a potential minister with a very good ability to grasp detailed briefs; as Chairwoman of the Westminster Objectors Trust was "disgusted" by the 'homes for votes' scandal; an "inner-party hackette, though friendly to everyone" (RED PEPPER); a key advocate and final beneficiary of all-women short-lists; believes that "the House of Commons is terribly out of touch on so many issues because it is run by an oligarchy of middle-aged men", adding, "when we get more women in, the Tories will suddenly look terribly old-fashioned"; is in Grenpeace and Amnesty International, formerly in CND;
History: Joined the Labour Party at 20, '78; was elected to Wesminster City Council May '90; she wrote to Peter Brooke MP to urge him to vote for full disclosure of MPs' interests in the Nolan debate Nov '95; was selected from an all-woman short-list for the new safe-Labour seat of Regent's Park and Kensington North Nov '95; this precipitated a legal challenge from thwarted aspirant Peter Jepson, a part-time law lecturer who secured a legal decision declaring such short-lists illegal Jan '96; the Labour Party decided to suspend further all-women

short-lists but to retain the 38 already consummated Jan '96; won the new seat with a majority of 14,657, a notional swing to Labour of 11.84% May '97; co-sponsored motion urging a public inquiry into the functioning of Westminster City Council June '97; in her Maiden contrasted the surface luxury of the affluent part of her seat with deprivation and squalor in its worst back streets June '97; was named to the Select Committee on Social Security July '97; co-criticised Lord Rees-Mogg for his "black propaganda" in favour of Dame Shirley Porter before her court hearing Sep '97;
Born: 30 August 1958, Castlederg, County Tyrone;
Family: Daughter of Pat Buck; her Partner is Barrie Taylor; 1s;
Education: Chelmsford County High School for Girls; LSE (BSc in Economics, History and Politics; MSc Econ, plus MSc in Social Policy and Administration);
Occupation: The Labour Party's Acting Head of Campaigns and Elections '94-95, Campaign Strategy Co-ordinator '92-97, Health Policy Officer '87-92 (TGWU); Public Health Officer, Hackney '86-87 (NALGO); Specialist Officer in Disabled Employment, Hackney '83-86, Research and Development worker at Outset '79-83 (ASTMS);
Traits: Light brown hair; fringe; attractive; diligent; "steely-tongued" EVENING STANDARD); a rapid speaker; has great mastery of '60s trivia, including the names of obscure groups; good sense of humour; enjoys music, cinema and squash;
Address: House of Commons, Westminster, London SW1A 0AA; 254 Ashmore Road, London W9 3DD;
Telephone: 0171 219 3000 (H of C); 0181 960 1119 (home/Fax); 0171 286 9692 (constituency office);

Colin BURGON **Labour** **ELMET '97-**

Majority: 8,779 over Conservative 4-way;
Description: The unaltered marginal seat named after the last Celtic kingdom in England; it actually embraces the furthest eastern wards of Leeds; although it has some Labour wards, these are normally outweighed by the heavily-Conservative market town of Wetherby; this provided the incumbent Conservative MP with a majority of over 3,000 in '92;
Position: On Joint Committee on Statutory Instruments '97-; ex: Chairman and Secretary of Elmet CLP; on Labour's Yorkshire Regional Executive for six years; Chairman, Leeds Euro-CLP;
Outlook: A slow-starting, steady-as-she-goes newcomer; a locally-based teacher-turned-local-government-officer who was third time lucky in the same seat, on what he thought was his last chance, at 49; has campaigned against opencast mining in Elmet; is in Amnesty International and Friends of the Earth;
History: Joined the Labour Party '79; as Labour's election agent in Elmet later described the campaign as a "shambles", "we never even had a map of the constituency" May '83; was selected as Labour's candidate for Elmet by 40 votes to 7, Dec '85; expressed admiration for "the way Neil Kinnock has transformed the Labour Party since the last election, and his hold on the party is absolute" June '87; despite a 2.9% pro-Labour swing failed to unseat Tory MP Spencer Batiste by 5,356 votes June '87; was the Labour Agent in the Leeds Euro-election

June '89; was re-selected for Elmet June '90; found it "extremely strange" that thieves broke into the regional HQ of his then union, NUPE, taking sensitive political documents but leaving valuables behind Apr '91; achieved only a 2.1% swing, failing to unseat Tory MP Spencer Batiste by 3,261 votes Apr '92; was again selected for Elment, by then seen as a key marginal '95; Labour scored a clean sweep in Elmet district elections, May '95 and May '96; ousted Spencer Batiste with a majority of 8,779 on a swing of 10.91% May '97; led a motion calling for electoral registration officers to allow voters to cast ballots after "a genuine adminstrative mistake" May '97; in his humorous Maiden thanked Elmet's voters for "finally recognising my worth before it was too late", "given my advancing years"; he also criticised the social security system as "complex, inefficient and unfair"; "I especially welcome new criminal penalties for serious cases of deliberate evasion and fraud" July '97;
Born: 22 April 1948, Leeds
Family: Son of Thomas Burgon, tailoring worker, and Winifred (Feeley); m Kathy, health visitor; 1d Maria '91; now separated;
Education: St Charles RC Junior School; St Michael's College, Leeds; Becketts Park Carnegie College, Leeds (B Ed Hons) '70-74; Huddersfield Polytechnic (part-time study for MA in History):
Occupation: Local Government Policy and Research Officer for Wakefield Metropolitan Borough Council (GMB); previously a secondary school teacher at Foxwood School, Leeds, for 16 years; before that was a Clerical Officer in the CEGB, a Driver, and a Warehouseman;
Traits: Back-brushed light-brown wig-like hair; strong chin; good sense of humour; RC by education; interested in most sports, especially football (a Leeds United supporter); football coach (Leeds City Boys under 19s); youth club leader; enjoys music and the countryside;
Address: House of Commons, Westminster, London SW1A 0AA; 16 St John's Court, Thorner, Leeds LS14 3AX
Telephone: 0171 219 3000 (H of C); 0113 2893011;

John (Patrick) BURNETT **Liberal Democrat** **DEVON WEST & TORRIDGE '97-**

Majority: 1,957 over Conservative 6-way;
Description: Devon's largest seat, a sprawling, rural, largely inland seat, despite its shipbuilding port of Appledore; it embraces much of Dartmoor, including bleak Princetown with its fearsome prison; it has had a strong Liberal tradition, including the '58 victory of Mark Bonham-Carter in its previous incarnation as Torrington;
Position: Spokesman on Legal Affairs '97-; on Council of the Devon Cattle Breeders Association, the Law Society's Revenue (Tax) Committee '84-96;
Outlook: A widely-based conservative LibDem victor interested in helping small local businesses and beef farmers; a rooted local solicitor and farmer; was able to capitalise on the rising tide of LibDem support in the Westcountry and the turmoil in Tory ranks after Emma Nicholson's defection in this seat;
History: Joined the Liberal Party; defended the decision of the Liberal-SDP Alliance group on the Devon County Council to raise rates by 19.8% against the criticisms of local Tory MP Sir Peter Mills, pointing out that almost all the increase was caused by the net cut in the Rate

Support Grant by the Thatcher Government, the rest by increased spending on education Mar '86; was selected to contest Devon West and Torridge against the new Tory candidate Emma Nicholson May '86; at annual Liberal Assembly spoke of the "insolvency and misery" for many small farmers, urging an agricultural bank, an independent version of the Agricultural Mortgage Corporation, saying it would help farmers who were on the "interest rate treadmill" and enable new entrants to get into farming Sep '86; halved the Tory majority June '87; did not contest the seat in '92; was re-selected to fight it in Feb '96, following the withdrawal of the LibDem candidate, Matthew Owen, and the sensational defection to the LibDems of the sitting Tory MP Emma Nicholson in Dec '95; won the seat on a notional swing of 4.4% by a majority of 1,957 against a weak outside Tory candidate Ian Liddell-Grainger May '97; urged extra NHS funds for sparsely-populated areas like his June '97; urged the extension of the 30-month cull of beef cattle to 36 months for cattle farmers "using traditional extensive grass-based systems" June '97; having come sixth in the ballot for Private Members Bills, introduced his Energy Efficiency Bill with all-party support June '97; asked for statistics on imprisoned young offenders and on mandatory drug-testing July '97; in his Maiden gave qualified support to the Budget's attempt to end the boom-and-bust cycle, from which the southwest suffered particularly: "the brakes get put on the economy by dramatic increases in interest rates when overheating in the southeast demands it, which is usually just before the recovery reaches us" July '97; made a strong appeal to keep open Winsford, a local rural hospital July '97; as a former Marine, deplored the rumoured merger between the Royal Marines and the Parachute Regiment; pressed for two new replacement landing ships Oct '97;
Born: 19 September 1945, Oswestry, Shropshire
Family: Son of Anbowe Burnett, solicitor, and Joan (Bolt); m '71 'Billie'/Elizabeth (Sherwood de la Mare); 2s Robert '78, George '79; 2d Alice '72, Laura '76;
Education: Ampleforth College, York; Royal Marines Commando Training Centre, Britannia Royal Naval College, Dartmouth; College of Law, London;
Occupation: Solicitor '72-: Senior Partner, in Burd Pearse (offices in Okehampton, Tavistock, Torrington and Hatherleigh); Cattle Farmer at Petrockstowe, near Oakhampton; ex: Royal Marines Officer '64-70
Traits: Tall; parted longish dark blond hair; snub nose; Roman Catholic (active in Torrington RC Church); personable, confident;
Address: House of Commons, Westminster, London SW1A 0AA; Allisland, Petrockstowe, Okehampton, Devon EX20 3EY;
Telephone: 0171 219 3000 (H of C);

WELCOME WORDS

One of the MPs' bouquets most welcome among the occasional brickbats is the frequent refrain: "Thanks for recalling that speech! I had completely forgotten ever making it...."

PROSPECTIVES SATISFACTION

The 1 May 1997 general election increase in the number of Labour and Liberal Democrat MPs provided what might be called "archive satisfaction". In a fair number of cases we have been tracking such candidates as "possible" victors for as many as four or five contests, badgering them for information and writing up their profiles, just in case. In their cases - as in the case of the 17 'retreads' - there was the satisfaction of knowing that the previous efforts were not wasted.

Paul BURSTOW **Liberal Democrat** **SUTTON & CHEAM '97-**

Majority: 2,097 over Conservative 6-way;

Description: The unaltered seat on the edge of the North Downs which has reverted to what was seen as the "false dawn" of a Liberal victory when Graham (now Lord) Tope won the '72 by-election there; over the next quarter century, it seemed to underline the observation that no matter how firmly local people trusted Liberal or LibDem councillors, they did not want them as MPs; this has been reversed dramatically, in a band of five seats in London's southwestern suburbs, not merely because of the local "Olga Maitland experience";

Position: Spokesman on Disability Rights and Social Services and LibDems' team leader on Local Government '97-; Sutton Borough Councillor (Deputy Leader '94-97, Chairman, of Environmental Services '93-96, '88-91) '86-; Political Secretary '96-97, Campaigns Officer '87-96, of Association of Liberal Democrat Councillors; on Liberal Democrats' London Regional Executives; ex: on LibDem Federal Policy Committee '88-90;

Outlook: A leading young LibDem local government apparatchik who joined their '97 phalanx of five MPs from London's southwestern suburbs; in his case he had extra multi-party thanks for ending the shrill career of the Rightwing Serbo-Scottish aristocrat, Lady Olga Maitland; very active on behalf of the blind and the disabled; a hyper-active member of the social-democratic wing of his party inclined to sympathetic but firm pressure on Labour; "constructive and sensible" (Nick Raynsford MP); a member of Charter 88; "I believe passionately in the need for decentralisation, which is vital for renewing our democratic life and for rebuilding a sense of community";

History: Joined the SDP '82; was elected to Sutton Borough Council May '86; joined the Liberal Democrats from the SDP '88; on Sutton Council was responsible for local Agenda 21 and for sustainability and disability issues; he also led the council's development of award-winning environmental programmes; only dented the majority of Lady Olga with a swing of 5.4% which shaved 30% off her 16,000 majority Apr '92; finished the job with a massive 13% swing, giving him a majority of 2,097 over Lady Olga May '97; in his Maiden, emphasised the need for more opportunities for the disabled; also said, "I look forward to the creation of a new strategic authority for London" May '97; launching a debate on 'Youth Crime', urged "a sophisticated, well-researched and successfully-implemented strategy to tackle crime" such as carried out in Sutton and Cheam's "Youth Awareness Programme" June '97; backed ban on fox-hunting June '97; welcomed the £5b in phased release of housing receipts, but insisted it no more than scratched the surface of housing need, including a £20b housing repair backlog June '97; urged "a national strategy on dementia care" June '97; warned against the centralising tendency of new Labour Government June '97; was active on the Local Government (Contracts) Bill, trying to secure more power and discretion for local authorities June-July '97; was critical of the Budget because of the Government's "self-imposed straitjacket" which would bring "another winter of crisis and chaos" in the NHS and elsewhere July '97; repeatedly urged improved facilities for blind and near-blind voters July '97; led motion urging retention of rail travellers' network cards July '97; introduced his Elections (Visually Impaired Voters) Bill July '97; co-sponsored motion complaining of polls' inaccessibility for the disabled July '97;

Born: 13 May 1962, Carshalton
Family: Son of Brian Burstow, tailor, and Sheila (Edmond); married to Mary (Kemm);
Education: Glastonbury High School, Carshalton; Carshalton College of Further Education; South Bank Polytechnic;
Occupation: Director: Business Ecologic, Business Link London South (local government organisation) '96-97; previously ALDC Campaigns Officer, '87-96;
Traits: Front-combed hair; specs; small-featured; hyper-assiduous; "constructive and positive" (Alun Michael MP);
Address: House of Commons, Westminster, London SW1A 0AA;
Telephone: 0171 219 3000 (H of C); 0181 643 9904;

Christine BUTLER **Labour** **CASTLE POINT '97-**

Majority: 1,116 over Conservative 5-way;
Description: The unaltered, '83-created Essex seat consisting of Benfleet and refinery-dominated Canvey Island; nine out of ten electors are owner-occupiers; until '97 this was the 77th safest Tory seat, providing its former Tory MP, Dr Robert Spink, with a majority of almost 16,000 in '92;
Position: On Select Committee on Environment, Transport and Regional Affairs '97-; Essex County Councillor '93-; Chairman, of the Essex Co-operative Development Agency;
Outlook: The local county councillor who delivered Labour's fourth most unexpected gain on a near-record swing of 16.94%, ousting the sitting Tory MP, Dr Robert Spink; "in this new optimistic era, I'd like to make sure all of Labour's policies are implemented, tackling unemployment first" (CB); was slow at first in mastering Parliamentary skills, concentrating on local issues; is in the Co-operative Society, Fabian Society, Greenpeace;
History: She joined the Labour Party '73; was elected to Essex County Council for Castle Point May '93; Labour representation on the Castle Point Borough Council, which has the same boundaries as the Parliamentary seat, moved from a minority of four to full control May '95; ousted the sitting Tory MP, Dr Robert Spink, with a majority of 1,116, on a massive swing of 16.94% May '97; co-sponsored motion attacking the BBC for showing "a self-confessed paedophile" on the 'Kilroy' programme June '97; expressed solidarity with jailed Indonesian union leader June '97; asked about prospecting for sand and gravel in the Thames estuary July '97; co-sponsored motion warning of dangers of reduced use of pilots in the Thames July '97; was named to the Select Committee on Environment, Transport and Regional Affairs July '97;
Born: 14 December 1943, Lancashire
Family: Married to a teacher; has three sons and two small grandchildren;
Education: State primary and grammar schools; Middlesex Polytechnic (BA);
Occupation: Former Research Assistant: in the pharmaceutical industry and in the NHS (MSF);
Traits: Short red hair; gap-toothed; lived-in face;
Address: House of Commons, Westminster, London SW1A 0AA; 38 Second Avenue,

Canvey Island, Essex SS8 9LL;
Telephone: 0171 219 3000 (H of C); 01268 684722 (home)

Dr Vincent CABLE **Liberal Democrat** **TWICKENHAM '97-**

Majority: 4,281 over Conservative 6-way;
Description: The long-Conservative affluent middle-class suburban seat across the Thames from the main local Liberal Democrat threat in Richmond; in the end, Tories were ousted on both sides, here ditching the quirky veteran Toby Jessel; the seat contains Hampton Court Palace and is the home of Rugby Union; was only slightly changed in '95, with the return of East Twickenham; contains four Twickenham town wards plus Teddington, Whitton and the various Hamptons;
Position: Finance Spokesman on LibDems' Economics team '97-; Glasgow City Councillor '71-74 (as Labour);
Outlook: A "thoughtful intellectual" (NEW STATESMAN) who seemed initially a leading LibDem advocate of collaboration with Labour to keep the Tories in the wilderness for a decade at least; this changed from the '97 Eastbourne conference when LibDems took fright at losing their identity in a Blairite takeover; a fierce opponent of inflation, partly because its main victims are the poor; a political and geographic nomad: a former Labour Councillor in Glasgow, and former Special Adviser to John Smith who - via the SDP - has wound up as a Liberal Democrat MP for Twickenham; an academic economist specialising in international trade who became Chief Economist to Shell; a pro-European opponent of import controls; racial egalitarian;
History: His father was an active Tory; at school he was Liberal-inclined; at Cambridge he was Chairman of the Liberal Club while President of the Union; joined the Labour Party to work for a "more egalitarian, fairer society" '64; wrote a Fabian pamphlet on Kenya Asians '68; at 27 contested Glasgow Hillhead for Labour, gaining half as many votes as Tory MP Thomas Galbraith June '70; while a graduate student at Glasgow University won a seat on Glasgow City Council May '71; wrote Fabian pamphlet 'The Case Against Import Controls'; became Special Adviser to John Smith, Labour's Trade Secretary '79; joined the SDP, having become concerned about Labour's drift to Left extremism '82; contested York for the SDP, coming 3rd with 23%, enough to unseat its Labour MP, Alex Lyon, and giving the seat to Tory Conal Gregory June '83; was re-selected for York '86; polled a reduced vote of 16%, just enough to allow the sitting Tory MP to retain his seat June '87; selected for Twickenham, initially managed only to reduce Toby Jessel's Conservative majority from 7,000 to 5,700 Apr '92; at annual conference attacked the accuracy of the Government's economic statistics, which included the costs of divorces and stolen goods in GDP Sep '96; in the NEW STATESMAN urged the need for practical co-operation between LibDems and Labour even before an election to inflict a lengthy defeat on the Tories Dec '96; worried by evidence of a rise in the Labour vote in a local by-election, concentrated his campaign on the need for tactical voting Apr '97; ousted Twickenham's Tory MP Toby Jessel, who had served 27 years, by a majority of 4,281, on a notional swing of 8.8%, May '97; endorsed Gordon Brown's giving the Bank of England US-style control over inflation to avoid political delays June '97; said it was

"outrageous that world airlines should land at [Heathrow] one of the busiest and most congested airports [and] pay nothing to the taxpayer for the right to land and pay landing charges that are way below the economic and environmental cost that they cause" July '97; urged chess be encouraged by the Sports Council June '97; after trying to amend the Finance Bill, opposed curbing the Budget debate because its full impact was not understood: "local authority budgets are still capped despite the need to top up pension funds following the loss of tax credits on A[dvance] C[orporation] T[ax]" July '97; co-sponsored motion opposing a 12-lane super-highway to Heathrow July '97; tried to modify Labour's PFI Bill to ensure more adequate consultation with the public and the NHS professionals July '97; at LibDems' annual conference was scathing about Labour's Budget, attacking its new imposts along Tory lines Sep '97;

Born: 9 May 1943, York

Family: Son, of late John Leonard Cable, a Tory joiner and fitter who became a technical lecturer, and Edith Pinkney; m '68 Maria Olympia (Rebelo), musician, teacher and historian with a PhD from Glasgow University; 2s: Paul '69, Hugo '79; 1d: Aloa '72;

Education: Poppleton Road Primary School, York; Nunthorpe Grammar School, York; Fitzwilliam College, Cambridge University; Glasgow University (PhD);

Occupation: Chief Economist, Shell International til '97; Author: Protectionism and Industrial Decline; former Head of Economics, Royal Institute of International Affairs; Director of Economic Division, Commonwealth Secretariat (ASTMS) '83-??; Deputy Director, Overseas Deelopment Institute '76-83; in the Diplomatic Service '74-76; Lecturer, in Economics at Glasgow University '68-74; Treasury Finance Officer, Government of Kenya '66-68; Special Professor of Economics, Nottingham University;

Traits: Bald; grey fringe and sideburns; oval face; enjoys ballroom and Latin dancing, classical music;

Address: House of Commons, Westminster, London SW1A 0AA; 102 Whitton Road, Twickenham TW1 1BS;

Telephone: 0171 219 3000 (H of C); 0181 892 3212 (home);

Alan CAMPBELL **Labour** **TYNEMOUTH '97-**

Majority: 11,273 over Conservative 5-way;

Description: The northeast's former last-remaining Tory seat, previously held by Labour only in '45-50; its alleged Tory leanings were not helped by the removal of rock-solid Labour Riverside ward in '95; a mainly coastal seat containing middle-class Tynemouth itself, North Shields, Cullercoats, Monkseaton and Whitley Bay;

Position: Former Secretary and Campaigns Co-ordinator of Tynemouth Constituency Labour Party;

Outlook: Another Labour recruit from the chalk-face; a pro-European; "every inch the New Labour man" (Neil Sears, NEWCASTLE EVENING NEWS); won with a huge swing (14%) on his first attempt, making him the seat's first Labour MP in half a century; the size of his majority astonished even his faithful supporters; rather unusually for a Labour teacher, was in the NAS-UWT; interested in education and

constitutional reform;
History: Joined the Labour Party at 30, '87; was selected for Tynemouth, where its long-sitting Tory MP, Neville ('Globe') Trotter, was retiring '95; gave the Conservative Government credit for attracting Siemens to the Tyneside; while local Tories were claiming they were "neck and neck" with Labour, he was helped by a NEWCASTLE JOURNAL poll which accurately predicted Labour would have a 21% lead; he pledged he would be "a local MP for local people and not a paid mouthpiece for a few wealthy interests", like the outgoing Tory Apr '97; won the seat by an unexpectedly large 11,273 majority, a notional swing of 14.19%, May '97; in his Maiden emphasised that Siemens' investment of £1b in a microchip plant in his constituency was a tribute both to local people and "an acknowledgement of Britain's key role in Europe; we meddle with that at our peril" June '97; backed ban on fox-hunting June '97; co-sponsored motion backing comprehensives as "the foremost and most efficient way to provide secondary education" June '97;
Born: 8 July 1957, Consett, County Durham
Family: Married Jayne, a former student; 1s 1d;
Education: Blackfyne Secondary School, Consett, Co Durham; Lancaster University (BA Hons); Leeds University (PGCE); Newcastle University (MA);
Occupation: Ex: Teacher '80-96: former Head of 6th Form at a comprehensive where, in '96, two-thirds of the sixth formers went to university ("among the highest recorded levels" (AC) (NAS-UWT);
Traits: Dark brown hair; square face; good-looking; well-paced speaker; shy about revealing family information;
Address: House of Commons, Westminster, London SW1A 0AA; 19 Sandringham Avenue, North Shields NE29 9AX;
Telephone: 0171 219 3000 (H of C); 0191 296 1318 (home); 01426 2033757 (pager);

Ivor CAPLIN **Labour** **HOVE '97-**

Majority: 3,959 over Conservative 7-way;
Description: Brighton's smaller but more staid Siamese twin, with elegant Regency homes at the seafront, but seedier streets behind; has a significant Jewish minority and council estates at Portslade; until '97 it was considered a traditionally safe Conservative seat;
Position: Brighton and Hove Unitary Councillor (Deputy Leader '96-) '96-; ex: Hove Borough Councillor (Leader '95-97) '91-97; Chairman, Hove Constituency Labour Party '85-91;
Outlook: A Blairite local Deputy Council Leader, unexpectedly catapulted into Parliament as Hove's first-ever Labour MP; one of the three - with David Lepper and Des Turner - providing Labour with a first-ever clean sweep of the Brighton-Hove conurbation, on the back of prior victories in local government; a supporter of electoral reform; a member of the Co-operative Party, the League Against Cruel Sports and the Labour Friends of Israel; in Campaign for Ending Animal Exports; as a (non-practicing) Jew is opposed to the campaign against religious slaughter promoted by the locally-based animal welfare group, VIVA;

History: Joined the Labour Party '79; was elected to Hove Borough Council May '91; became Leader of Hove Borough Council when Labour won the local election in May '95, giving it "a two-year opportunity to prove that Labour could deliver what it promised"; "during those two years we put in place plans to rehouse the residents of a decaying block of flats called Portland Gate"; "we also cut the price of bus passes for Hove pensioners, as we pledged we would"(IC); after selection as a candidate, considered himself "clearly the only candidate local enough to deal with the very difficult issues affecting Hove and Portslade", particularly the fact that "Brighton Health Care Trust is at breaking point"; contesting Hove against Robert Guy, the Tory replacement for Sir Tim Sainsbury, retiring after 24 years, Caplin won by 3,959, securing an almost record-breaking 16% swing to Labour, with the LibDem vote cut in half May '97; decided to combine continued Deputy Leadership of Brighton and Hove Unitary Council with being Hove's new MP May '97; said his first priority would be to see the new Health Secretary, Frank Dobson, to seek help for Brighton Health Care Trust, which was "at breaking point" May '97; in Maiden expressed his support for a ban on export of live animals, not merely from nearby Shoreham; praised the Chancellor's decision to transfer control of interest rates to the Bank of England as having "generated confidence" in the financial services sector in which he had worked for 20 years June '97; urged a bar on EU subsidies being used to grow fibre flax on land of environmental importance June '97; co-sponsored motion urging ban on fox-hunting June '97; baited Peter Lilley on why he had left uncompensated 500,000 who had been mis-sold pensions July '97; recounted to Labour's annual conference at Brighton the secret of his success at Hove in the general election: the public-private rebuilding of decaying Portland Gate to time and to budget Oct '97;
Born: 8 November 1958, Brighton
Family: Son of late Len Caplin, accountant and a member of the Management Board of Brighton's Middle Steet Synagogue, and Alma, a market researcher living in Hove; married to Maureen (Whelan); 1s 1d;
Education: King Edward's School, Witley; Brighton College of Technology;
Occupation: Sales and Marketing Quality Manager, Legal and General Assurance Society (MSF) '78-97;
Traits: Dark, receding hair; full-lipped; able speaker; an accomplished club cricketer (batsman/wicket-keeper); "he gets what he wants" (sporting colleague); from childhood a supporter of troubled, locally-based Brighton & Hove Albion Football Club; animal lover (Executive Treasurer of AP - animal welfare group); enjoys music; a non-practicing Jew who is keenly aware of his background;
Address: House of Commons, Westminster, London SW1A 0AA; 31 Elder Road, Portslade, Hove BN41 2ER;
Telephone: 0171 219 3414 (H of C); 01273 382 868 (home);

ANOREXIA OR OBESITY

Profiles, like politicians, can be very slim or very full-bodied. This can depend on how varied and colourful is the past of the MP concerned, or the quality of the newspapers reporting them. Some politicians are paranoid about disclosing anything beyond the bare minimum and then complain if second-hand information beyond the bare essentials turns out to be less than accurate. Others turn to their libel lawyers as an expensive threat. We adhere to the quaint idea that if people have decided to plunge into the glass fishbowl of politics they are not entitled to wear wetsuits. After all, most wrongdoing has been exposed by the media's investigative journalists, very little by politicians themselves.

Roger (Mark) CASALE **Labour** **WIMBLEDON '97-**

Majority: 2,980 over Conservative 8-way;
Description: The affluent southwest London seat which is the home of lawn tennis and many desirable residences rented out to tennis buffs; until '97 was considered ultra-safe Conservative territory -their 95th safest seat - with only patches of Labour support around Haydons Road and South Wimbledon station; has recently become the site of the national headquarters of the GMB;
Position: On Select Committee on European Legislation '97-; Co-Chairman of all-party Future of Europe Trust '97-; Chairman of the Party of European Socialists (London Association); Co-ordinator of Wimbledon Labour Party Regeneration Project; President, of Wimbledon Council of Christians and Jews; ex: Vice Chairman and Secretary of Wimbledon Labour Party;
Outlook: A locally-active Europhile and idealistic internationalist; an enthusiast for open government; a former special adviser to Larry Whitty and policy adviser to Tony Blair and John Prescott; has taken long to recover from his surprise at capturing, so handsomely, a seat which is a by-word for suburban affluence; a Founder-Co-ordinator of European Socialist Initiative (ESI); a member of the Fabian Society, Labour Movement in Europe, Labour Finance and Industry Group;
History: Joined the Labour Party '84; was selected for Wimbledon, which he did not regard as hopeless; what surprised him was the extent of his victory when he defeated its two-term Tory MP, Dr Charles Goodson-Wickes by 2,980 votes on an exceptional 17.94% swing, the country's fifth highest to Labour May '97; backed ban on fox-hunting June '97; with Derek Wyatt, tried to start an "Unlikely Lads and Lasses Club" for over 80 new Labour MPs who succeeded despite being outside Labour's target seats; he said it would be to help such new MPs who had found entry "like going to a new school, only to find that there aren't any classes or teachers and that you have to find your own way" July '97;
Born: 22 May 1960, London
Family: Son, of Edward Casale, teacher at a Wimbledon school for 30 years, and Jean (Robins) occupational therapist; m '97 Fernanda (Miucci);
Education: Hurstpierpoint College; Brasenose College, Oxford University (BA); Ludwig Maximilians University, Munich; Johns Hopkins University, Bologna Centre(MA); LSE (PhD candidate);
Occupation: Lecturer in European Studies, Greenwich University; ex: Policy Adviser, to Tony Blair and John Prescott (GMB); previously head of a training institute in Germany;
Traits: Dark, parted, front-falling hair; multilingual (German, Italian); supports Wimbledon FC; enjoys playing tennis, happily; also cooking, art and the theatre;
Address: House of Commons, Westminster, London SW1A 0AA; 17 Lingfield Road, Wimbledon SW19 4QD;
Telephone: 0171 219 4565/0789 (Fax) (H of C); 0181 540 1012; 0181 946 2462 (Fax) (constituency office);

Martin CATON **Labour** **GOWER '97-**

Majority: 13,007 over Conservative 6-way;
Description: "It snuggles around the southwest and north of Dylan Thomas's 'ugly, lovely town of Swansea'" (MT); it is a mixture of the seaside holiday resort and affluent homes for Swansea commuters on the Gower peninsula and its industrial working class hinterland of Gorseinon, Pontardulais and Pontardawe;
Position: On Select Committees: on Welsh Affairs '97-, on Broadcasting '97-; Swansea Unitary Authority Councillor '95-; on Welsh Labour Party Executive '95-; ex: Swansea City Councillor '88-95;
Outlook: A pleasant, articulate Swansea councillor from "away", into whose lap a safe Welsh seat has fallen after a rapid rise within Welsh Labour ranks; has served loyally as a Labour Agent in local and Parliamentary elections; a member of the Socialist Environmental Resources Association (SERA), Socialist Health Association; another example of Welsh Labour's willingness to select non-Welsh-born MPs, like Hain, Hanson, Ainger, Marek, Lawrence and Alan Howarth;
History: Joined the Labour Party at 24, '75; became Political Assistant to David Morris, MEP for South Wales West June '84; was elected to Swansea City Council May '88; was elected to Swansea Unitary Council May '95; on the announced retirement of David Wardell, was selected for Gower '96; raised the scare of possible VAT on food if the Tories returned to power Apr '97; claimed the Conservatives had "insulted" Gorseinon by putting up a "Britain is Booming" poster only yards from nine empty shops and three charity shops in a run-down part of town Apr '97 was elected with a majority of 13,007, a swing of 7.5% May '97; his Maiden speech was widely appreciated because he managed to mention and pronounce almost every village, correctly; this was considered very clever for a non-Welshman June '97; complained about Welsh Development Agency's favouring the southeast of Wales at the expense of the southwest June '97; expressed solidarity with jailed Indonesian union leader June '97; complained that the Development Board for Rural Wales had only served mid-Wales, not his patch July '97; was named to the Select Committee on Welsh Affairs July '97; pointed out that only 6 of the 34 Welsh Labour MPs were unenthusiastic about a Welsh Assembly July '97;
Born: 15 June 1951, Bishops Stortford
Family: Son, of John Caton, grocer, and 'Jim'/Pauline (Gardner); married to Bethan (Evans); 2 stepchildren;
Education: Newport Grammar School, Essex; Norfolk School of Agriculture; Aberystwyth College of Further Education (HNC in Applied Biology);
Occupation: Political Assistant, to David Morris MEP for South Wales West '84-97; previously Scientific Officer, at Welsh Plant Breeding Station, Aberystwyth '74-84;
Traits: Brown, parted hair and beard; specs; loud voice; witty (in his Maiden disclosed his constituents were tagged "Jerks" because they were halfway between Llanelli (called "Turks") and Swansea (nicknamed "Jacks");
Address: House of Commons, Westminster, London SW1A 0AA; West Cross Avenue, West Cross, Swansea SA3 5TX;
Telephone: 0171 219 5111 (H of C); 01792 892100 (constituency);

Ian (Arthur) CAWSEY **Labour** **BRIGG & GOOLE '97-**

Majority: 6,389 over Conservative 4-way;
Description: The north Lincolnshire market town of Brigg now linked with the larger, more pro-Labour port town of Goole, set amidst pro-Tory flatlands; as the home of John and Charles Wesley, was the birth-place of Methodism; until 1 May '97 it was seen as a Tory marginal;
Position: North Lincolnshire Unitary Authority Councillor (Leader '95-) '95-; ex: Humberside County Councillor (Chairman, Humberside Police Authority '93-96) '89-96; Director, Humberside International Airport;
Outlook: Blairite locally-rooted council leader who captured a new seat largely overlapping with his municipal domain; his rise has been helped by his prominence as chairman of the local police authority and his work for neighbouring Scunthorpe MP, Elliot Morley;
History: He joined the Labour Party '77; contested Grimsby council seats in May '83, May '84, May '85; moved to Scunthorpe, becoming Personal Assistant to the new Labour MP, Elliot Morley June '87; was elected for Ashby ward in Scunthorpe to Humberside County Council May '89; contested Conservative-held Brigg & Cleethorpe against Michael Brown, registering a 5.8% swing to Labour, recovering 2nd place from the LibDems Apr '92; was elected Chairman of Humberside Police Authority May '93; was elected Leader of the North Lincolnshire Shadow Unitary Authority May '95; was selected for new Brigg & Goole, overlapping his previously-fought seat, again against Michael Brown Apr '95; protested against the closure of local Binns, a House of Fraser department store Jan '97; had the advantage of publicity surrounding the involvement of his opponent, Michael Brown, in payments from lobbyist Ian Greer Feb '97; defeated Brown by a majority of 6,389, on a notional swing of 13.90% May '97; in his Maiden, backed Labour's attempt to further control handguns, as former Chairman of the Humberside Police Authority June '97; welcomed impending new measures to arm councils with powers to curb anti-social behaviour July '97; co-sponsored motion urging Government to be "tough on road crime" July '97;
Born: 14 April 1960, Grimsby
Family: Son, of Arthur Henry Causey, fitter, and Edith (Shaw), clerk; m '87 Linda Mary (Kirman), child minder; 1s Jacob '93; 1d Hannah '88;
Education: Wintringham School;
Occupation: Political Assistant, to Elliot Morley MP for Glanford & Scunthorpe '87-97; Computer Systems Analyst, with Imperial Foods, in Grimsby and Hull (Seven Seas Healthcare) til 87;
Traits: Spikey, greying, light-brown centre-parted hair; chubby heart-shaped face; strong chin; slightly skewed mouth; a local musician who performed with the '60s group 'The Moggies'; Methodist; an enthusiastic sportsman who has made appearances for the local Labour Club on cold, wet Sunday mornings;
Address: House of Commons, Westminster, London, SW1A 0AA; 10 Glover Road, Scunthorpe DN17 1AS;
Telephone: 0171 219 3000 (H of C); 01724 872560/296060 (home); 01724 276242 (Fax);

David CHAYTOR **Labour** **BURY NORTH '97-**

Majority: 7,866 over Conservative 4-way;
Description: Prosperous Lancashire textile town made more so as a Manchester commuter suburb via the M66; four-fifths are owner-occupiers; is famous for its black puddings, its football club and as the birth-place of Sir Robert Peel; a long-standing marginal which, until '97, resisted the pro-Labour trend with the help of an attractive Tory MP, Alistair Burt, and the help of its strongly pro-Tory town of Ramsbottom;
Position: On the Deregulation Committee '97-; Calderdale Borough Councillor (Chairman of its Labour Group) '82-;
Outlook: Third-time-lucky aspirant who finally won in his home town; a "Left-leaning" (NEW STATESMAN) "Old Labour" (SUNDAY TIMES) lecturer-councillor forced to shift from Yorkshire back to Lancashire by the imposition of an all-women short-list on the Calder Valley, which he had fought twice before; a "smoothie who won't cause Blair any trouble, though not a true believer; aspires to office but unlikely to get there" (RED PEPPER); a member of the Full Employment Forum, Amnesty International, Greenpeace, Labour Campaign for Electoral Reform, SERA, the Campaign for Press and Broadcasting Freedom, formerly of Anti-Apartheid; as a Calderdale councillor, he helped secure a multi-million pound flood protection scheme for Todmorden;
History: He joined the Labour Party at the time of the miners' strike and the three-day week "because of what Heath was doing to British industry" '73; was elected to Calderdale Borough Council May '82; was selected to fight Calder Valley, where Labour had been pushed into 3rd place in the previous election Jan '86; insisted that "Mrs Thatcher's criminal record is the real issue" May '87; failed to oust the sitting Tory MP, Donald Thompson, but restored Labour to 2nd place, 6,045 votes behind June '87; was re-selected to fight Calder Valley Sep '90; securing a swing of only 1%, left Donald Thompson still almost 5,000 votes ahead Apr '92; Calder Valley was designated an all-women's contest; his wife stood instead but failed to be selected Feb '95; he was selected instead for his home town, the key marginal of Bury North, occupied by the barnacle-like Tory Minister Alistair Burt '95; said, "we're good at educating the elite, hopeless in developing the potential of the majority...which doesn't come cheap"; said he backed Blair's "fair tax" strategy but he could "live with" an increase in the top rate of tax Mar '97; said he thought the monarchy was "slowly destroying itself" and would "wither away into one of those [Scandinavian-style] bicycle monarchies" Mar '97; ousted Burt by a majority of 7,866 on a swing of 11.19%, May '97; in his lengthy Maiden complained against discrimination in funding: "why is Bury allowed to spend only £79 per person on capital expenditure when Bolton is allowed to spend £118, Rochdale £120, Trafford £175 and Oldham £219?" June '97; backed ban on fox-hunting June '97; asked about strengthening democracy in Albania June '97; asked about costs of alcohol abuse June '97; urged encouragement of cycling June '97; protested under-financing of further education colleges June '97; pressed for help for smaller professional football clubs June '97; urged inspection of private nurseries June '97; urged the Government to undertake strategic planning in further education colleges, instead of the existing "shambles of the internal market", if it wished to avoid "a series of bankruptcies and closures" June '97; asked about the cost of expanding NATO June '97; expressed solidarity with jailed Indonesian union leader June '97; asked about

control of air rifles July '97; asked about abuse of ground rents July '97; was named to the Deregulation Committee Aug '97;
Born: 3 August 1949, Bury
Family: He is married, with three children;
Education: Bury Grammar School; Huddersfield Polytechnic (BA); London University (M Phil); Bradford University (PGCE);
Occupation: Senior Tutor and Head of Continuing Education at Manchester College of Arts and Technology '93-97; Lecturer in Adult Education (helping adults who failed the 11-plus to secure university entrance) '73-93; (NATFHE/TGWU)
Traits: Centre-parted hair; lantern-jawed; craggy; handsome; "a fluent pavement performer" (Andrew Rawnsley, GUARDIAN); cyclist and walker;
Address: House of Commons, Westminster, London SW1A 0AA; 7 Rock Rimmy, Lumbutts, Todmorden, OL14 6JE;
Telephone: 0171 219 3000 (H of C); 0161 812052 (home);

Christopher CHOPE OBE  **Conservative** **CHRISTCHURCH '97-**

Majority: 2,165 over Liberal Democrat 5-way;
Description: A seat north and east of Bournemouth - with the UK's highest proportion of detached homes (55%) - recently famed for its dramatic swings: was the Tories' 10th safest seat, which provided the late Robert Adley with a 23,000 majority in 1992, it registered the 3rd biggest swing in recent history (35%) when it returned Liberal Democrat Diana Maddock with a 16,000 majority in the July '93 by-election; although it reverted narrowly to the Tories in '97, even this represented a notional swing of 18.28% from the previous general election;
Former Seat: Southampton-Itchen '83-92
Position: Spokesman, on Local Government '97-; ex: Chairman, Conservative Parliamentary Candidates Association '93-97; on DTI Deregulation Task Force on Transport and Communications '93-97; on Local Government Commission for England '94-95; on Health & Safety Commission '93-97; Under Secretary, for Transport '90-92, for Environment '86-90; Vice President, of Selsdon Group; PPS, to Peter Brooke '85-86; on Select Committee on Procedure '84-86; Secretary, Conservative MPs' Environment Committee '83-86, Shipping and Shipbuilding Subcommittee '85-86; on Executive Committee of Society of Conservative Lawyers '83-86; Leader of Wandsworth Council '79-83;
Outlook: The return of the ultimate ideologue of the hard-Right; formerly a Cromwellian company commander in the Tories' onslaught on Labour's town halls; a fervent advocate of the poll tax and compulsory tendering; a Rightwing scion of St Andrews and the Adam Smith Institute, later in the 'No Turning Back' group of Thatcherites; "specifically dry" with "hard economic liberal convictions" (Edward Pearce, SUNDAY TELEGRAPH); long part of "the St Andrews privatisation Mafia" (PRIVATE EYE); formerly London's leading privatiser of public services and proselytiser for standing up to the public service unions from his one-time Wandsworth base; "a man conscious that local government finance is the crucible, the cauldron, the cockpit" (Frank Johnson, TIMES):

History: An acolyte of Dr Madsen Pirie at St Andrews, was in the Federation of Conservative Students in the late '60s; with Harvey Proctor and Piers Merchant, was a member of the Universities Group of the Rightwing 'Monday Club' Dec '69; was elected to Wandsworth Borough Council May '74; became Leader of Wandsworth Borough Council May '79; steamrollering his opponents, cut Wandsworth's costs by selling its properties; boasted he had cut 2,000 employees (20%), had cut rates but increased expenditure June '82; was awarded an OBE for his services to local government June '82; was selected for Itchen, which 'Bob' Mitchell had narrowly won for Labour before defecting to the SDP Dec '82; campaigned against Labour's defence policy as likely to lose jobs at Vosper-Thorneycroft; won Itchen, with a majority of 5,290 over the sitting SDP MP 'Bob' Mitchell, with Labour's John Denham coming 3rd June '83; he made his Maiden speech against any MPs' pay rise beyond 4%, saying "we must set an example" July '83; voted for the restoration of death penalty for all categories July '83; took on controversial far-Right Harry Phibbs as his researcher Aug '83; attacked the "complacent cabal" of local government officers for "pulling the wool over the eyes of elected councillors" instead of "cutting out waste" Jan '84; visited South Africa, as a guest of its government Jan-Feb '84; backed playing Rugby with South Africa, and increased trade with it Feb '84; claimed ILEA was "systematiclly wrecking education in inner London" in preparation for a "Leftist takeover" Feb '84; criticised building societies for not giving mortgages on system-built homes Mar '84; was one of five Tories seeking to make it mandatory for employers to get employees' permission before deducting political levy Apr '84; headed a motion urging action against misuse of student funds for political purposes June '84; he asked Mrs Thatcher to appeal to the TGWU to end the "pointless" dock strike in Southampton July '84; visited the USA as a guest of the State Department Sep '84; called for advertising on BBC and the fading out of license fees Nov '84; criticised the Government for delaying orders for Type 22 frigates, causing unemployment in his constituency Nov '84; co-signed a letter, claiming pre-Thatcher full employment was really over-manning Dec '84; voted against fluoridation Jan '85; had an adjournment debate on the black economy and shoddy work in the building trade Jan '85; initiated a debate urging the abolition of "outdated" wages councils Feb '85; at his behest, the Government dropped a clause from the Transport Bill to allow representations on the unroadworthiness of applicants (later restored in the Lords) Apr '85; was one of two Tory members of the Procedure Committee who favoured time-tabling all Bills May '85; introduced a Bill to transfer sub post offices to an independent licensing body, instead of "bribing" some of them to close down by "spurious financial targets" June '85; in an adjournment debate attacked local authorities (like Southampton) which set up "fraudulent sham" companies with ratepayers' and taxpayers' money and without accountability June '85; was one of the 13 authors of the super-Thatcherite 'No Turning Back' pamphlet rejecting caution Nov '85; elicited from the Attorney General that Lord Kagan's firm had been given 7 years to pay its fine Feb '86; asked about police powers to deal with witchcraft Feb '86; again urged time-tabling of Bills, clashing with Leader of the Commons John Biffen Feb '86; complained that supplementary benefits failed to keep up with rising costs, compelling rest-home owners to waive charges for elderly residents Mar '86; sought reassurance that the local Vosper-Thorneycroft shipyard would not face unfair competition Mar '86; complained that some petrol stations were charging 10p more than necessary Apr '86; asked how many cleaning contracts had been kept in-house despite lower tenders from outside June '86; expressed fears that Vosper-Thorneycroft might lose experienced teams through loss of orders June '86; was promoted Under Secretary for the Environment Sep '86; announced he would stop "propaganda on the rates" Nov '86; caused consternation when he suggested an Ealing Labour councillor convicted of indecency should resign, just when the House was agog with similar rumours about a leading Tory MP Nov '86;

announced his support for a Whitehall reorganisation which would end the £2.8b Property Services Agency Jan '87; announced ILEA members would be subject to disqualification in cases of surcharges Jan '87; defended retrospective clauses in the Local Government Finance Bill Jan '87; denounced a Labour council which advertised for a Director of Social Services in LABOUR WEEKLY Feb '87; made concesssions to Toby Jessel in latter's opposition to wildlife-destroying Government plans to clear Thames river banks up to Hampton Court Mar '87; voted to restore hanging for "evil" murders Apr '87; refused Tony Banks' request for an independent audit of the savings the Government claimed would come from abolishing the GLC Apr '87; he increased his majority by 1,500, with SDPer 'Bob' Mitchell being forced into 3rd place by Labour June '87; became responsible to Environment Secretary Nicholas Ridley for PSA affairs and to Minister of State Michael Howard for poll tax and compulsory competitive tendering June '87; despite three negative reports, asked for further investigation of the possiblity of private provision of MPs' new offices July '87; claimed the poll tax was the last chance to save local government finances from "an advanced state of senility and decay" July '87; despite Treasury caution because of falling Stock Market, urged quick privatisation of Crown Suppliers Nov '87; claimed local councils could save a further £600m through compulsory tendering Jan '88; admitted the poll tax would cost twice as much to collect but denied the need for a national identity number system Feb '88; denied misleading the Commons by refusing to admit that the PSA could have valued DHSS headquarters at Richmond Terrace for £1,500 instead of the £40,000 charged by Cluttons Apr '88; investigated transferring Crown Suppliers' civil servants to the private sector without their agreement or legislation May '88; curbed local government publicity considered propaganda by Government July '88; voted against ordination of divorced men July '89; denied security would be endangered by privatisation of Defence bases Sep '89; claimed Bill ending council house rent subsidies would establish a truthful rent pattern Nov '89; was jeered at AMA conference when he alleged bad management over escalating rent arrears Feb '90; sought to embarrass non-poll-tax-paying Militant MP David Nellist in disclosing he had registered for the poll tax in low-tax Wandsworth rather than high-tax Coventry Feb '90; saw no prospect of reversing poll tax, insisting he had experienced worse resistance when privatising the Wandsworth dustmen Mar '90; announced cash incentives to lure council tenants into private dwellings Mar '90; voted against embryo research Apr '90; after rumours held that Mrs Thatcher was unhappy about his privatisation of PSA and Crown Suppliers, was moved sideways into Transport as Under Secretary for Roads and Traffic July '90; announced compulsory seatbelts Nov '90; through his boss, Cecil Parkinson, urged Mrs Thatcher to contest the 2nd round of the Leadership contest Nov '90; announced 20 mph speed limits near schools Dec '90; announced introduction of speed limiters on all heavy goods vehicles Feb '91; with fellow Thatcherite Michael Forsyth, tried to persuade Michael Heseltine not to abolish the poll tax Mar '91; was named as one of the Selsdon Group favouring privatising the NHS Oct '91; announced regulations curbing car alarms July '91; defended screen-washing gangs lurking at lights July '91; with Thatcherites Eric Forth and Edward Leigh was listed as considering resignations over the Maastricht summit Dec '91; was punched in the face while canvassing; lost his seat to Labour's John Denham by 551 votes Apr '92; admitted the market-testing of civil service departments was pointless in view of EU regulations on retaining the same pay and conditions May '93; unsuccessfully sought candidacy for Eastleigh, lost to LibDems at by-election June '94; was selected for Christchurch, which had been lost to LibDem Diana Maddock in the 3rd biggest by-election swing '94; recaptured Christchurch from Diana Maddock with the reduced majority of 2,165, which represented an 18.28% notional swing from '92; it was the only Tory reversal of a by-election loss May '97; in the Tory Leadership contest, joined the campaign team backing Michael Howard May-June '97;

led the attempt to deny a second reading to the Labour Government's Firearms (Amendment) Bill to ban most handguns June '97; asked the Attorney General whether he was "aware that many persistent burglars on their seventh conviction are not even being sent to prison?" June '97; the new Tory Leader, William Hague, named him Local Government Spokesman July '97;
Born: 19 May 1947, Eastbourne
Family: Son, of late His Honour Robert Charles Chope, retired Circuit Judge, and Pamela (Durell); m '87 'Christo'/Christine (Hutchinson), fine arts archivist who worked as his secretary; 1s 1d;
Education: St Andrew's School, Eastbourne; Marlborough College; Dundee University; St Andrews University (LLB Hons) where he was a contemporary of Michael Fallon and Michael Forsyth, and was influenced by Dr Madsen Pirie;
Occupation: Barrister, Inner Temple, '72-; in Lord (Peter) Rawlinson's chambers; ex: on DTI Deregulation Task Force on Transport and Communications '93-97; Special Adviser, Ernst & Young (accountants and management consultants) '92-97; on Local Government Commission for England '94-95; on Health & Safety Commission '93-97;
Traits: Tall; blond; specs; angular features; Boy Scout manner; exhibits a studied greyness; as a minister was "an inveterate droner", "one of the most insufferably boring fellows in the House" (Stuart Wavell, GUARDIAN); in local government was considered brave to the point of foolhardiness by his Tory friends; by his opponents was known as "Chopper" Chope, "unscrupulous and crude", "rasping and aggressive, willing to break all the rules" (a Labour opponent, quoted in GUARDIAN; "pitiless" (Frank Johnson, TIMES): Rottweiler owner;
Address: House of Commons, Westminster, London SW1A 0AA; 63 Roupell Street, Waterloo SE1 8SS;
Telephone: 0171 219 3000 (H of C); 0171 633 9129;

Rt Hon Alan (Kenneth McKenzie) CLARK **Conservative** **KENSINGTON & CHELSEA '97-**

Majority: 9,519 over Labour 9-way;
Description: The new seat whose concentration of wealth makes it the second safest in the country for a Tory candidate; the habitat of the mythical 'Sloane Ranger'; contains many of London's famous institutions, set in exclusive residential areas;
Former Seat: Sutton, Plymouth '74-92;
Position: Vice Chairman, of 1922 Committee '97-; ex: Minister of State, for Defence '89-92, for Trade '86-89; Under Secretary, for Employment '83-86; Secretary, Conservative MPs' Home Affairs Committee '82-83, '76-81; Vice Chairman '80-83, Secretary '79, their Defence Committtee; on Select Committee on Sound Broadcasting '76-83;
Outlook: The dashing, cynical, wealthy Renaissance Prince of the chauvinist hard-Right; "I'm a political junkie; I couldn't stay away from it"; believes "it is natural to be proud of your race and your country"; a maverick who is cynical about everything but his Thatcher-worship (until recently); exposed this and many other personal and political secrets in his fabulously popular diaries; a blurter of the needs of realpolitik, like the need for an overnight slaughter of 600 IRAmen; "Mr Clark is terrific at thinking the unthinkable; what he just can't do is think the

thinkable" (Simon Hoggart, GUARDIAN); like many Rightwing nationalists, is anti-German and anti-American but pro-Russian; is deeply suspicious of the EU, thinks NATO has outlived its usefulness; is deeply suspicious of pro-European Tories like Michael Heseltine and Kenneth ("puffball") Clarke; a believer in 'Fortress Britain' who would have struck a peace deal with Hitler in 1940; self-described as "romantic and reactionary"; "I am a reactionary populist Tory, [a] hanger but not a flogger", "like Gengis Khan, only richer" - with £28m at last count; is against cruel sports except for Europhile-baiting; was an open opponent of Devonport dockyard privatisation; "the first Tory Minister to resign to spend more time with other people's families" (Labour MP John Reid);

History: He decided he wanted to be a politician at Eton; he joined the Conservative Party '58; joined the Rightwing, pro-Empire Monday Club; rejected as unwinnable the candidacy offered for the Swindon by-election '69; was banned from the Tories' candidates' list as too reactionary, on the orders of Ted Heath '69; was adopted as candidate for Sutton, Plymouth Sep '72; said Uganda Asian immigrants should be told: "you cannot come into the country because you are not white" '72; won Sutton Feb '74; urged Ted Heath be dropped as Leader Mar '74; opposed Channel Tunnel, though it would benefit his Kent landholding, because "the English Channel has always protected us from invasion" Apr '74; supported a part-elected Tory Shadow Cabinet July '74; opposed sanctions against Ian Smith's Rhodesia Nov '74; opposed talk of coalition May '75; attacked Plymouth's Workers' Education Association as a "school for scroungers" Sep '75; was among 28 Tory MPs who voted against devolution after being asked by the Whips to abstain Jan '76; warned that the Tories were losing their working-class base Dec '76; opposed Hitachi being allowed to build TVs in the UK Apr '77; backed SPUC May '77; warned against banning National Front march in Manchester in response to the "insatiable" hunger of the "extreme Left" Sep '77; rebelled against sanctions against Rhodesia Nov '78; opposed sale of Harriers to China Dec '78; talked out Ethnic Groups Grant Bill Mar '79; opposed fluoridation of water Aug '79; opposed Cruise deterrent Nov '79; was named Chairman of committee to investigate Britain's civil defence May '80; opposed interfering with wage levels June '80; warned that UK civil defence was inadequate and run by those "ignorant of their task" July '80; warned against further cutbacks in British defence spending Dec '80; urged defence cuts be made in Rhine Army, not in the Navy May '81; urged a referendum on capital punishment Nov '81; backed Keith Speed in his resignation from office over Royal Navy cuts May '81; opposed judicial whipping Mar '82; suspected collusion over Argentine landings in the Falklands; warned against betrayal of the Falklands Apr '82; insisted UK had no nuclear independence since US permission was needed to launch US-provided missiles Jan '83; expressed sympathy for the police in shooting of innocent Stephen Waldorf, alleging his companions in the car were "tainted with criminality" Jan '83; said Government's subliminal approach in anti-CND advertising was demeaning Feb '83; was appointed Under Secretary for Employment June '83; although a non-drinker was accused of being "incapable" by Clare Short, when he mocked a statement on equal pay for women by reading it slowly July '83; launched the start-your-own-business Enterprise Scheme for the unemployed Aug '83; resigned as Patron of the Anti-Hunt Council because the Government announced it did not intend to legislate against hunting Aug '83; attacked Esperanto, saying, "if you want an international language, it should be English" Sep '83; urged the rejection of Jo Richardson's Sex Equality Bill, insisting it would inhibit the employment of women Dec '83; survived Michael Heseltine's demand he be sacked for "slightly treasonable" remark on the BBC, admitting Ministers had given in to admirals in placing Harpoon missiles in the USA, instead of the UK, giving Americans "a tremendous vested interest...against arms control" Apr '84; was accused of having made a remark about "Bongo-Bongo Land" Oct '84; nodded in agreement with Teddy Taylor's anti-EEC remarks while on the Front Bench Jan '85; admitted he was "totally ashamed" of the Government's decision to privatise the Devonport dockyard July '85; with Lord Young's backing, he opposed Home Office plans to introduce US-style contract compliance Oct '85; avoided voting for the Government's Dockyards Bill by arranging an out-of-town engagement Dec '85; revealed massive dole frauds in 25 towns Dec '85; was promoted Minister of State for Trade at DTI in Paul Channon's place as part of reshuffle after Leon Brittan's resignation over Westland Feb '86; defended Multi-Fibre Agreement because "free trade, like unilateral nuclear disarmament, is fine only as long as everyone is doing it" Feb '86; admitted it was unlikely International Tin Council could be rescued Mar '86; was again pointedly absent on the dockyard privatisation vote Mar '86; in a letter to Frank Field, he admitted job losses from South African sanctions could not be quantified June '86; warned GATT against a flood of protectionist measures which could cause a world trade collapse Sep '86; announced he favoured US consultants for Devonport dockyard rather than a management buy-out Oct '86; although not consulted, opposed Paul Channon's refusal to refer to the MMC the BTR bid for Pilkington Jan '87; voted for Geoffrey Dickens' Bill to hang child murderers Jan '87; voted for Sir Ian Percival's Bill to restore hanging for "evil" murderers Apr '87; threatened retaliatory action unless the Japanese stopped import discrimination Apr '87; again declared his opposition to the Channel Tunnel June '87; lost two-thirds of his majority, largely due to job losses from dockyard privatisation June '87; the Japanese congratulated him on his reappointment as Trade Minister June '87; backed David Alton's abortion-curbing Bill Nov '87, Jan '88; privately gave ambiguous advice to Matrix-Churchill executives about exports of arms-making equipment to Iraq Jan '88; opposed the "protectionist" EEC's effort to limit non-EEC TV programmes to 40% of transmissions Mar '88; urged "real teeth" for GATT Mar '88; opposed plans for a nuclear waste store in Devonport dockyard Apr '88; his effort to label some furs as caught by leghold traps was opposed by Canadian Indians May '88; was reshuffled sideways as Minister of State for Defence Procurement July '89; a leak of his defence cuts, reducing the Navy from 48 to 32 destroyers and infantry battalions from 55 to 32, put him at odds with Defence Secreraty Tom King and defence chiefs May '90; Tom King's 18% cuts were less swingeing July '90; was sent by Mrs Thatcher as her emissary to bolster Arab support for the multinational military force in the Gulf Aug '90; horrified by Mrs Thatcher's fall - for which he would never forgive Michael Heseltine - backed John Major as her successor Nov '90; the SUNDAY TIMES disclosed the ambiguous advice he had given to Matrix-Churchill Dec '90; announced NATO was obsolete Dec '90; became a Privy Councillor Jan '91; claimed Britain's European partners "ran for their cellars" on the Iraqi invasion of Kuwait Jan '91; was quoted as saying, "what we need now is the ability to create an alliance with Russia against the Japanese" Jan '91; claimed one of his last acts as Defence Minister was to try to persuade Mrs Thatcher to authorise the sale of Hawks to the Iraqis Mar '91; as a landowner in Scotland was described by Scots Labour MP Brian Wilson as "a parasite on the people of the Highlands and Islands" Apr '91; HM Customs investigators indicated their intention of interviewing him and Lord Trefgarne over the sale of munition-making tools to Iraq Apr '91; was attacked in a GUARDIAN letter for attending a party hosted by the far-Right historian, Hitler-apologist David Irvine Dec '91; fined for doing 99 mph in his Porsche on the M5 in Somerset, said he thought the police car pursuing him was his personal escort Jan '92; voted for the anti-hare-coursing Bill of Labour MP Kevin McNamara Feb '92; before the Commons Trade and Industry Select Committee claimed the first he knew about the Iraqi 'supergun' was when it was seized by Customs in April '90 at Teesport Feb '92; at the last minute, he decided not to contest his seat again Mar '92; at the Old Bailey trial of Matrix-Churchill executives, caused the collapse of the trial when he admitted he had been "economical with the actualite" in telling executives to emphasise the likely peaceful use of their machine tools when Whitehall knew they were destined for Iraq's arms factories Nov '92;

the Crown Prosecution Service decided not to prosecute him over the export of arms-making equipment to Iraq Mar '93; admitting the drug of politics was too strong for him, put his name forward for the Newbury by-election Mar '93; revealed that Government ministers' phones were routinely tapped by MI5 May '93; claiming that no British interests were at stake, urged withdrawal from ex-Yugoslavia May '93; his frank 'Diaries' were hailed as unequalled since those of 'Chips' Channon June '93; was arrested in London for driving through a police bomb cordon Feb '94; was accused by South-Africa-based Judge Harkness of having had intercourse with his wife and daughters '94; claimed the Cabinet was "top-heavy with federalists - Hurd, Clarke, Heseltine and Hunt - who were all turnoffs and Heathite groupies who should have been consigned to the knackers' yard years ago" Dec '94; attended the Coventry Cathedral funeral of the animal rights activist, Jill Phipps, who had been run over Feb '95; claimed that 'New Labour" were no more than "a bunch of people in suits who want to win an election" Mar '95; joined animal rights protesters at Dover docks to oppose the export of live sheep and calves, accusing police of "pushing up the profits of a load of thugs in the haulage industry" Apr '95; it was rumoured he was taking instruction in the Catholic faith May '95; a leak from the Scott Report named him and two other ministers who had deliberately failed to inform Parliament of the decision to relax the guidelines on defence sales to Iraq from Dec '88, Nov '95; having admitted his decision not to stand again was an error, sought selection for the new safe seat of Kensington and Chelsea, along with John Maples and Michael Fallon, but they lost out to Chelsea's sitting MP, Sir Nicholas Scott Nov '95; sought unsuccessfully to be selected for Sevenoaks, Dorset North and Tunbridge Wells '95-96; in a rerun of Kensington & Chelsea after Sir Nicholas Scott had been found drunk on a pavement, Clark was successful in being chosen from a short-list of four on the third ballot Jan '97; Elizabeth Peacock MP - about whom he had been rude in his 'Diaries' - wondered how Kensington & Chelsea could choose a "self-confessed philanderer, reprobate and adulterer who has been extremely rude about people in trade yet is no aristocrat himself, his family having made their money in the cotton trade" Feb '97; campaigned as an opponent of the single European currency Apr '97; won the seat by 9,519, despite a notional swing to Labour of 12.93%, at 69 the oldest member of the '97 intake May '97; was elected a Vice Chairman of the 1922 Committee May '97; in the Leadership contest, joined the campaign team of Michael Howard May-June '97; deplored as a "tragedy" the collapse of the libel trial against the GUARDIAN of his close friend Jonathan Aitken June '97; asked Scottish Secretary Donald Dewar if the cost of getting the Hyundai factory for Fife would cost the taxpayer £120,000 per job June '97; said, "I do not hunt and I do not permit hunts to cross land that I own" but urged opponents of fox-hunting to make some concessions to countrymen July '97; welcomed Labour's defence review because it would be policy-driven, not Treasury-driven, but was hostile to the Eurofighter project July '97; blamed journalists for suicide of Gordon McMaster, citing the remorseless hunting of his own wife and family Aug '97; objected in a letter to The TIMES to balloting Tories to endorse William Hague and his reform principles as a single question; Hague just wanted Tories to sign a "blank cheque on a small coterie of management consultants" Sep '97; in his BBC TV 'History of the Conservative Party' blamed the Tory election defeat on Mrs Thatcher's "ruthless economic Darwinism" which damaged "the fabric of the British nation state" Oct '97; at a fringe meeting at the Blackpool annual Conservative conference suggested "the only solution for dealing with the IRA is to kill 600 in one night" Oct '97;

Born: 13 April 1928, London

Family: Descendant of wealthy Paisley thread manufacturers; son of the late multi-millionaire Lord (Kenneth)) Clark, OM. CH, famous art expert, collector, lecturer ('Civilisation') and writer, and the late Elizabeth (Martin), "remarkable but alcoholic" (David Piper, GUARDIAN); m '58 Caroline Jane (Beuttler), whom he courted at 14 and married at 16, and

who still says, "I know he is a S-H-one-T, but I love him"; 2s James '60, helicopter pilot, and Andrew '62, former Captain in the Life Guards;
Education: Eton College ("an early introduction to human cruelty, treachery and extreme physical hardship"); Christ Church, Oxford University ("a complete waste of time" until he became a star pupil of Hugh Trevor-Roper; MA); Inner Temple;
Occupation: Military Historian who worked under Sir Basil Liddell-Hart; Author: BBC TV series, "Alan Clark's History of the Tory Party" (1997), The Donkeys, A History of the BEF in 1915 (1961), The Fall of Crete (1963), Barbarossa, The Russo-German Conflict, 1941-45 (1965), Aces High (1973), A Good Innings, Viscount Lee of Fareham (1974), Diaries (1993); Owner: of a fabulous collection of inherited paintings worth £12m, despite transfers in lieu of tax; of Saltwood Castle (50-roomed 14th Century castle acquired from father of Lord ('Bill') Deedes after the '29 crash); Broomhayes Farm, Wiltshire; Town Farm, Bratton-Clovelly, Devon; Eriboli Estate (27,000 acres) and harbour in Sutherland, bought for £425,000 in '84 and kept undeveloped; Shareholder, with six $10,000 (nominal) shares in Woods Petroleum field in Brunei; Barrister (non-practicing); Marshall of the Southeast Assize '53-??; ex: Lecturer, Services Division, Department of Extra-Mural Studies, Oxford University;
Traits: Aquilinely handsome, despite age lines; rakish look; permanent sneer; a cynical realist; has "an aggressive contempt for hypocrisy" (George Hill, TIMES); couldn't-care-less cavalier style (claims to have urinated out of his ministerial window on passers-by); elitist ("I believe in privilege"); "I have no guilt about being rich"; "an old-fashioned combination of hauteur and noblesse oblige" (GUARDIAN); gamey; witty; a pithy dispatcher of his contemporaries (asked which great figure from the past he would like to lunch with, he replied "Sir Geoffrey Howe"); non-drinker; engagingly frank about his own faults (admitted "I deserve to be horse-whipped" for his philandering); a genuine animal lover (almost went to war with the BBC because of the threat to have Hannah, his pet rottweiler, put down in the wake of its biting a litigious BBC cameraman);
Address: House of Commons, Westminster, SW1A 0AA; Saltwood Castle, Hythe, Kent CT21 4QU;
Telephone: 0171 219 3000 (H of C); 01303 265 445 (home);

Dr Lynda CLARK QC **Labour** **EDINBURGH-PENTLANDS '97-**

Majority: 4,862 over Conservative 7-way;
Description: The perennially-marginal southwestern Edinburgh suburbs, capped by the beautiful Pentland hills; until '97 it remained stubbornly Tory with Conservative-leaning Colinton and Balerno outvoting the Labour-leaning estates of Wester Hailes and Sighthll;
Position: On Edinburgh University Court '95-; on Scottish Legal Aid Board '91-94;
Outlook: The most senior woman Advocate practicing at the Scottish Bar, who collected the most senior Tory scalp at the election, that of the former Foreign Secretary, Malcolm Rifkind; a confirmed homeruler: "as a Scots lawyer with more than 20 years' experience, I know that Scots law and development have suffered badly from the present [pre-devolution] system"; a successful professional - one of only seven women QCs in

Scotland - from a poor working-class Dundonian background, brought up in an inner city tenement and then in a council flat; she prospered in the conservative climate of the Scottish Bar, despite a reputation as a Leftwing feminist; "a true Blairite in the English mould; an example of Scottish sovereignty residing with Tony Blair as far as New Labour is concerned; she mouthes Blairite cliches with the passion of a senior QC" (RED PEPPER); formerly on the Scotttish Council for Civil Liberties; UNISON (ex-NUPE);

History: She joined the Labour Party at 36, out of concern at the state of the party '83; was selected to fight the hopeless seat of North East Fife, held by Liberal Democrat Menzies Campbell '91; narrowly retained her deposit, as the Labour vote was squeezed from 6.6% to 5.5% by Menzies Campbell Apr '92; emphasised her sex in seeking selection for Pentlands, claiming she would attract media attention as a woman standing against a Cabinet Minister Oct '95; "I have benefited from years of free education, good NHS care, local authority housing and a Labour-inspired system which has encouraged equal opportunity; I am shocked and angry at the results of 16 years of Tory policies and legislation" Oct '95; criticised as inexperienced Scotland's first woman judge, Sheriff Hazel Aronson, and was accused of sour grapes July '96; ; an ICM poll in the OBSERVER four days before polling put her ahead with 42%, Rifkind trailing on 34%, the SNP at 15% and LibDems at 7% Apr '97; she ousted Malcolm Rifkind with a majority of 4,862, with similar percentages: Labour (43%) Conservative (32%), SNP (13%), LibDems (10%), May '97; made her witty Maiden speech in support of Scottish devolution May '97; co-sponsored motion deploring Air UK's "discriminatory and insulting" treatment of disabled passengers July '97; insisted that "the British Parliament has never been an exercise in academic logic"; "in our system, the Queen in Parliament is sovereign; any legislation approved by the Queen in Parliament is legal and constitutional"; implied that the 'West Lothian question' was one of many anomalies; "no other country that claims to be a democracy has hereditary peers voting on legislation; Conservative Members have lived with that anomaly for many years" July '97;

Born: 26 February 1949, Dundee

Family: Daughter of a van driver and worker at National Cash Registers, Dundee; her mother was a shop assistant for 40 years; she is married;

Education: Lawside Academy, Dundee; St Andrews University (LLB Hons '70); Edinburgh University (PhD '75);

Occupation: Advocate at the Scottish Bar '77-, QC '89-; member of the English Bar '88-; ex: on the Scottish Legal Aid Board '91-94; Law Lecturer, Dundee University '73-76; has special expertise in medical law;

Traits: Dark shoulder-length hair; snub-nosed; toothy smile; "smart, confident" (Greg Neale, SUNDAY TELEGRAPH);

Address: House of Commons, Westminster, London SW1A 0AA; 7 Regent Terrace, Edinburgh EH7 5BN

Telephone: 0171 219 3000 (H of C); 0131 558 9154 (home);

LAW OF UNEVEN DEVELOPMENT

One cannot impose pure egalitarian standards on MPs' profiles. One MP's file will be anorexia-slim, another's as overstuffed as that of former MP Sir Cyril Smith. This is not merely a difference of talent or attainment. A rent-a-quote backbencher with a flow of vivid views can mop up more publicity than a squad of Parliamentary Secretaries answering boring questions with more boring answers. Some MPs retire from controversy into being chairmen of committees. Others go into the Whips' Office, where they tear off strips in private. These strain our effort at equal treatment.

Paul (Gordon) CLARK **Labour** **GILLINGHAM '97-**

Majority: 1,980 over Conservative 8-way;
Description: The north Kent seat which is the largest of the three Medway towns, with the onetime role of housing those working in the now defunct Chatham Navy Dockyard; until '97 was rated the Tories' 107th safest seat; it is over 80% owner-occupied, with only 10% in council housing; it remained in the hands of Tory MP James Counchman from '83 to '97, partly because of the previous neck-and-neck position of his LibDem and Labour opponents;
Position: Gillingham Borough Councillor (Labour Group Leader '89-90, Deputy Group Leader '83-89) '82-90;
Outlook: A locally-born and locally-resident TUC administrator and ex-councillor who was one of the most unexpected '97 victors; slow-starting "New Labour" (NEW STATESMAN);
History: He joined the Labour Party '75; was elected to Gillingham Borough Council May '82; became Deputy Leader of the Labour Group on Gillingham Borough Council May '83; became Leader of the Labour Group on Gillingham Borough Council May '89; contested Gillingham, narrowly moving Labour from 3rd to 2nd place; this neck-and-neck place of his opponents enlarged Jim Couchman's majority to 16,638, Apr '92; re-selected for the seat, won it by a majority of 1,980, on a near-record notional swing of 16.02%; he was helped by a squeeze on the LibDem vote and by a combined vote for the Referendum and UK Independence parties larger than his majority May '97; backed ban on fox-hunting June '97; opposed Eurotunnel's open lattice goods wagons as unsafe June '97; co-sponsored motion attacking Tory-controlled Kent County Council for its moratorium on capital expenditure on schools June '97;
Born: 29 April 1957, Gillingham
Family: Son, of Gordon Clark, rtd journalist, and Avo Sheila (Warner) Gillingham Councillor '84-, Mayor '94-95; m '80 Julie (Hendrick); 2c;
Education: Gillingham Grammar School; Keele University (BA in Economics and Politics); University of Derby (DMS '96)
Occupation: Manager: of the TUC'S National Education Centre, of the TUC (AEEU) '86-97;
Traits: Parted dark hair; retreating forehead; heart-shaped face; specs; estuarial cockney speech;
Address: House of Commons, Westminster, London SW1A 0AA; 50 Maidstone Road, Bounds Green, London N11 2JR;
Telephone: 0171 219 5207/2545(Fax) (H of C); 0181 361 8382 (home);

BULGING EX-MP FILES
Because of the unprecedented retirements before the 1 May 1997 election and the major massacre of Conservative MPs on the day, our computer and paper files on former MPs are bulging to an unprecedented degree. These are kept up to date, partly because defeated ex-MPs may come back. We also update these files as the base of the obituaries in at least two of the broadsheets.

'Tony' (Anthony) CLARKE **Labour** **NORTHAMPTON SOUTH '97-**

Majority: 744 over Conservative 6-way;
Description: A populous seat which, as the Tories' 131st safest, until '97 was thought the fief of the former Tory Deputy Speaker, Michael Morris, and possibly beyond Labour's grasp; it contains half of Northampton and affluent commuter suburbs to the south, some of which were removed in '95; it houses Church's shoes, Carlsberg, Barclaycard, and MFI;
Position: Northampton Borough Councillor (Chairman of Environment Services '94-97) '91-
Outlook: A young, locally-born, locally-based councillor who unseated Deputy Speaker Michael Morris after a 23-year stint; as Chairman of Environment Services and a committed environmentalist, led many local green initiatives; a football enthusiast and social work trainer; a Leftwinger formerly in the the local Campaign Group;
History: Joined the Labour Party '89; was elected to Northampton Borough Council at 28, May '91; at 32, was selected to contest almost out-of-reach Northampton South '95; Northampton was visited during the election campaign by Tony Blair and John Prescott, mainly to support the capture of more-vulnerable Northampton North, where Tory rebel Tony Marlow was vulnerable to a 3.6% swing Apr '97; Tony Clarke was elected for Northampton South, on a 13.38% notional swing, securing a majority of 744; this was half of the 1,405 votes cast for the Referendum Party candidate; the UKIP candidate, also called Clark, won 1,159 votes, taking votes from Tony Clarke May '97; asked the Home Secretary what proportion of crime he estimated to be linked to drug abuse May '97; co-sponsored motion urging the Nationwide to remain a mutual building society June '97; co-sponsored motion urging more care in extraction of coal and aggregates July '97; in his Maiden showed pride in being "the first member of the town for many years to serve the place of my birth"; he also celebrated the victory at Wembley of his team, Northampton Town, as showing "that anything is possible under a Labour Government" July '97;
Born: 6 September 1963, Northampton
Family: Son of Walter Arthur Clarke, engineer (rtd), and Joan Ada Iris Clarke; divorced; is married with two children;
Education: Lings Upper School, Northampton; Institute of Training and Development (Certificate of the Institute of Safety and Health);
Occupation: Social Work Trainer (Disability), with the Northamptonshire County Council (GMB) '84-97;
Traits: Burly; bearded; straight-talking; local football enthusiast (Vice Chairman of the Northampton Town Football Club Supporters' Trust; Manager and Coach of the Northampton Labour Club football team);
Address: House of Commons, Westminster, London SW1A 0AA; 30 Ethel Street, Northampton NN1 5ES;
Telephone: 0171 219 4469 (H of C);

Charles CLARKE **Labour** **NORWICH SOUTH '97-**

Majority: 14,239 over Conservative 7-way;
Description: The centre of historic Norwich, including the cathedral close and the University of East Anglia; it has been the classic Labour marginal, sometimes its only East Anglian seat; curiously, the inclusion of some Tory-leaning suburbs was thought to endanger Labour's hold;
Position: On Select Committee on Treasury Affairs '97-; ex: Chief of Staff to Labour Leader Neil Kinnock '83-92; Hackney Borough Councillor (Chairman of Housing, Vice Chairman of Economic Development) '81-86; President, of the National Union of Students '75-77;
Outlook: The shrewd and able politician who has finally come out of the backroom; an "effective fixer, talented and ambitious, but his historic connections with Kinnock could hold him back" (NEW STATESMAN); still "too closely tied to the Kinnock era for full Blairification" (RED PEPPER); a mandarin's son who was first a Marxist student radical ("further to the Left than Wedgwood Benn"), then a Kinnock intimate but who has recently sounded mildly Blairite; was the last-minute replacement for ailing ex-MP John Garrett, which made him one of the few high-flying metropolitan staffers to come through the localising grid of Labour's OMOV (one-member, one-vote);
History: He became the sabbatical President of the Cambridge University Students Union '72; called for the nationalisation of Oxbridge; was elected to the National Executive of the National Union of Students '73; joined the Labour Party '74; was elected President of the NUS '75; was accused by Conservatives in the NUS of "peddling the Moscow line" during a fraternal visit to Bucharest; spent a year in Cuba organising for its World Youth Festival also attended by Peter Mandelson, Paul Boateng, Fiona Mactaggart and Nigel Evans; all worked to block pro-Communist motions '78; was elected to Hackney Borough Council May '81; joined Neil Kinnock's staff as a Researcher '81; followed Kinnock to the office of Leader of the Opposition as his Chief of Staff after Kinnock replaced Michael Foot as Labour Leader June '83; with Patricia Hewitt, helped write Kinnock's conference speech attacking Derek Hatton and the Liverpool Militants Oct '85; "was swiftly marginalised after Kinnock's departure" from office; after the death of Ron Leighton MP, was short-listed for Newham North East but not selected; complained about irregularities, with two other candidates, Charlotte Atkins (later MP for Staffordshire-Moorlands) and Claude Moraes Apr '94; these irregularities were put right before the selection of Stephen Timms; beating TRIBUNE editor Mark Seddon among others, Clarke was selected for Norwich South, "without assistance from the leadership" (RED PEPPER) Oct '96; in an article for the NEW STATESMAN, warned against believing in poll predictions of a massive Labour majority because the fickle voting public, spurred on by a hostile press, might turn on Labour, as in '92, Jan '97; warned that "the millions of Labour Party [supporters] who believe the party's job is to offer hope to those who now have little are asking...whether New Labour is committed to change at all" Apr '97; retained Norwich South with a majority of 14,239, a swing to Labour of 10.10% which more than doubled the majority May '97; in his Maiden, urged rapid passage of promised Bill to put Private Finance Initiative into action, to enable the construction of the delayed Norfolk and Norwich Hospital May '97; came reluctantly to the conclusion that the new PFI-built hospital would be erected at Colney, a few miles outside the city and inaccessible to those without cars: "it's fundamentally

unsatisfactory, but our hands are tied; to try to cancel the PFI contract would cost tens or even hundreds of millions of pounds, which would have to come out of the health service budget" June '97; co-sponsored motion approving of advances by Anglia Water and Cambridge Water Company July '97; was named to Select Committee on Treasury Affairs July '97;
Born: 21 September 1950, London
Family: Son, of Sir Richard Clarke, KCB, former Permanent Secretary at the Ministry of Technology, and Brenda (Skinner) psychologist; m '83 Carol Marina (Pearson) researcher; 2s Christopher '87, Matthew '90;
Education: Highgate School; King's College, Cambridge '69-73 (BA in Maths and Economics);
Occupation: Chief Executive, QPA (public affairs management consultancy which advised the Association of District Councils, among many others) '92-97; Chief of Staff, to Labour Leader Neil Kinnock '83-92; Researcher, to Neil Kinnock as Education Spokesman (TGWU) '81-83; Lecturer, in Maths (part-time), City Literary Institute '81-83; Organiser, Hackney People in Partnership '78-80; President, of the NUS '75-77;
Traits: Burly; shortish blond beard, once much longer ("I have no plans to shave it off"); matey beer drinker; elusive;
Address: House of Commons, Westminster, London SW1A 0AA; has moved to Norwich;
Telephone: 0171 219 3000 (H of C);

Vernon COAKER **Labour** **GEDLING '97-**

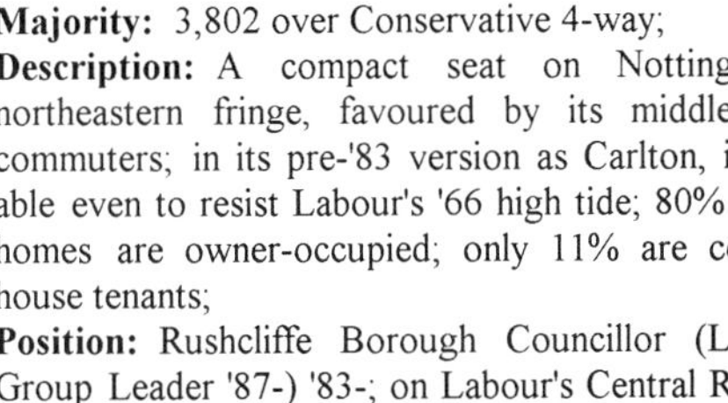

Majority: 3,802 over Conservative 4-way;
Description: A compact seat on Nottingham's northeastern fringe, favoured by its middle-class commuters; in its pre-'83 version as Carlton, it was able even to resist Labour's '66 high tide; 80% of its homes are owner-occupied; only 11% are council house tenants;
Position: Rushcliffe Borough Councillor (Labour Group Leader '87-) '83-; on Labour's Central Region Executive; on Labour's National Policy Forum '93-;

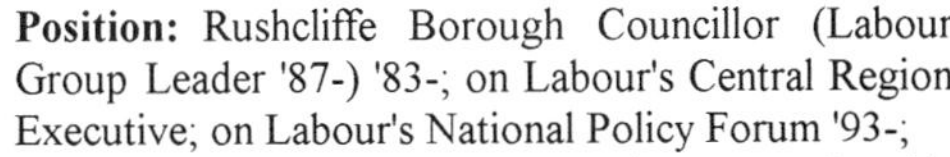

Outlook: The loyal first-ever Labour MP for this seat; an archetypal teacher-councillor who beat an able young Minister; has been third-time lucky, having fought the same seat twice before; was a Leftwinger in the '60s, '70s and '80s as a unilateralist, opponent of the Vietnam War and an opponent of EEC entry; his causes reflect his preoccupations: Socialist Educational Association, League Against Cruel Sports;
History: At school he opposed the US war in Vietnam '68; opposed UK's entry into the EEC '72; joined the Labour Party at 25, '78; was elected to Rushcliffe Borough Council May '83; contested Rushcliffe against Kenneth Clarke, coming 3rd, June '83; was selected for Gedling Nov '85; first fought Gedling, restoring Labour to 2nd place above the SDP June '87; contested the seat again, raising the Labour vote from 24% to 34% and reducing Tory MP Andrew Mitchell's majority from 16,539 to 10,637 Apr '92; raised with minister Andrew Mitchell the MRC report on the Institute of Hearing, alleging that new government guidelines would effectively deprive veterans with war-damaged hearing of their war pensions Dec '96;

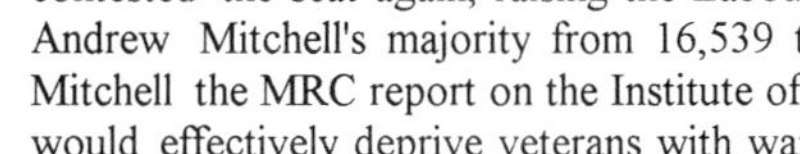

although 108th on Labour's target list, he decided "we can win Gedling" Apr '97; on a swing of 13%, ousted Andrew Mitchell by a majority of 3,802 May '97; asked about raising the basic state pension May '97; made a generous tribute to Andrew Mitchell in his Maiden, which concentrated on securing smaller classes, a higher status for teachers and ending pupil alienation June '97; pressed for action "to stop the illegal trade in wild animals and plants" June '97; co-enthused about comprehensive education "as the foremost and most efficient way to provide secondary education" June '87; backed expansion of school sports June '97; co-urged ban on fox-hunting June '97; urged the need for education about international development July '97; helped press the Government to be "tough on road crime" July '97; backed curbs on detention of asylum seekers July '97; backed focus groups as "the way forward for the Government that will be welcomed by most people" July '97; loyally supported the Finance Bill against Tory scoffers July '97; insisted that people did not claim benefits to which they were entitled because "the Conservative Pary created a culture in which people believe that anyone who claims benfit is a scrounger" July '97; enthused about the chance of England hosting the soccer World Cup in 2006, July '97; urged debate on the "dramatic increase in the number of permanent exclusion from our schools" Oct '97;
Born: 17 June 1953, London
Family: Son, of Edwin Coaker, policeman, and (he doesn't know his mother's maiden name); m '78 Jacqueline (Heaton), teacher; 1s Matthew William '86, 1d Laura Clare '84;
Education: Oaklands Primary School; Drayton Manor Grammar School, Hanwell, London; Warwick University; Trent Polytechnic (BA Hons);
Occupation: Deputy Head Teacher, of Nottingham's Big Wood Comprehensive '95-97; Teacher, ("the best teacher I ever had" (local voter) (NUT) '76-95;
Traits: Tall; burly; flat hair with deep widows peaks; small moustache; London accent; was the manager of Nottingham Academicals Football Club;
Address: House of Commons, Westminster, London SW1A 0AA; 6 Ingleby Close, Cotgrave, Nottinghamshire;
Telephone: 0171 219 3000 (H of C); 0115 989 2721 (home);

Iain COLEMAN **Labour** **HAMMERSMITH & FULHAM '97-**

Majority: 3,842 over Conservative 9-way;
Description: The home of both Fulham FC and Chelsea FC; a '95 amalgam of the evenly-balanced five most southerly parts of Hammersmith merged with partly-yuppified Fulham; despite such infiltration, it is the UK's 16th poorest borough; 35% of the constituency's households are on benefit, with 53% of its schoolchildren entitled to free school meals; nevertheless until May '97 this seat was expected to be held by the Conservatives;
Position: On the Deregulation Committee '97-; Hammersmith and Fulham Councillor (its Leader '91-) '91-; ex: Hammersmith Borough Councillor (Chief Whip til '86) til 91;
Outlook: The Leftish Leader of Hammersmith & Fulham Council who unexpectedly captured its new Parliamentary seat; a "principled and hard-working 'Hain-ite', sympathetic to the Left" (RED PEPPER);
History: He came from a Labour family, his psychologist mother becoming Mayor of Barnet

and his brother, Neale, becoming a leading objector to the Conservatives' 'homes for votes' ramp on Westminster Council; Iain joined the Labour Party '78; elected to Hammersmith Borough Council, became its Chief Whip; resigned as Chief Whip on Hammersmith Council, in protest against service cuts '86; became Leader of Hammersmith and Fulham Borough Council May '91; when Westminster City Council's misdeeds were under attack in Parliament, the then Tory MP for Dover, the widely-criticised David Shaw, made libel-proof attacks in the Commons against the whole Coleman family, against Iain's brother Neale, as well as his mother and father; his father was erroneously accused of having run "the Ann Summers chain of sex shops"; his brother was misleadingly accused of causing the suicide of the Tory councillor Dr Michael Dutt by raising the 'homes for votes' scandal in which Dr Dutt was involved; Shaw refused to repeat the charges outside Parliament, where he could have been sued for libel May '96; unexpectedly, Iain won the Hammersmith & Fulham seat, defeating Fulham's former Tory MP, Matthew Carrington by 3,842 votes, on a notional swing of 10.06%, May '97; in his Maiden welcomed the Bill offering a phased release of council housing funds; in his constituency, 6,000 families were on the housing register, 2,724 were on the housing transfer list; social housing was desperately needed "with a three-bedroom flat in South Fulham costing an average of £200,000" June '97; was named to the Deregulation Committee Aug '97;

Born: 18 January 1958, London

Family: His father worked in the '70s for the same company that owned the Ann Summers shops; his mother, Pamela, Mayor of Barnet '95-96, was an NHS psychologist for 30 years; his brother, Neale, was a Westminster Labour Councillor for 8 years;

Education: Tonbridge School;

Occupation: Leader, of Hammersmith and Fulham Borough Council (UNISON, ex-MSF) '91-; previously a local government administrator in Ealing and Islington;

Traits: Full-faced; parted thinning hair; retreating hairline; specs; worried expression; has been an Arsenal FC season ticket-holder for over 20 years and very rarely misses a match, home or away;

Address: House of Commons, Westminster, London SW1A 0AA;

Telephone: 0171 219 3000 (H of C); 0181 749 1043 (home); 0171 736 3045; 0181 741 8119 (Council Leader's Office);

Tim(othy) COLLINS CBE Conservative WESTMORLAND & LONSDALE '97-

Majority: 4,521 over Liberal Democrat 4-way;

Description: The slightly altered sprawling eastern Cumbria seat; largely agricultural and Tory but also a tourist haven, taking in the southern Lake District; has some light industry in Kendal; a "curious mixture of farmers in tweeds and sprightly geriatrics in spotless Barbours" (INDEPENDENT);

Position: On Select Committee on Agriculture '97-; ex: Media Consultant, to Conservative Party Chairman Dr Brian Mawhinney '96-97; in Prime Minister John Major's Policy Unit '95;

Outlook: The ultimate former back-room "whizz-kid" who made a delayed start as an able counter-propagandist - due to his father's accidental death - but began by backing his old boss Michael Howard for the Tory Leadership; the highly-regarded former party press apparatchik who won with this safe seat in the wake of his services to former PM John Major; "razor-sharp" (James Blitz, FINANCIAL TIMES); "the finest communications chief since Michael Dobbs 10 years ago" (Peter Oborne, EVENING STANDARD); thought likely to be "his generation's Norman Tebbit, but with gentler manners" ('Quidnunc', SUNDAY TIMES); has a "good feeling for politics and a passionate loathing of Labour"; "he has developed a formidable political brain which can come up wih a counter-offensive at speed; after a political controversy has died down, it is often his sulphurous words, whispered anonymously by Mr Collins, that stick in the mind" (Russell Jenkins, TIMES); the former "Conservative Central Office media guru who claimed the credit for John Major's victory at the [1992] general election" (Paul Routledge, INDEPENDENT ON SUNDAY); spent his whole previous career in Westminster, whether Smith Square or Downing Street; a cautious Eurosceptic who has remained apart from the near-religious war over Europe which has raged in the columns of the DAILY TELEGRAPH;

History: Was born into a family of Essex Conservatives, active mainly as councillors; his mother has been Chairman of the Epping Forest Conservative Association; he joined Conservative Central Office after university '86; festooned his Pimlico flat with photographs of Margaret Thatcher; worked as a ministerial aide to Cabinet Ministers David Hunt and Michael Howard, and as speech-writer to Prime Ministers Margaret Thatcher and John Major; protested against the dropping of his heroine, Margaret Thatcher Nov '90; reappeared as a Major loyalist Dec '90; was with John Major "throughout the historic [and victorious] day and night of 9th April 1992" (TC); in briefing the press, claimed that Major's "Back to Basics" speech was aimed at "rolling back the permissive society" Oct '93; was there to brief the press when John Major defeated John Redwood, describing it as a "crushing, clear-cut victory" although 109 Tory MPs failed to support Major; described some of Redwood's suporters as a "swivel-eyed barmy army from Ward 8 at Broadmoor" July '95; he denies that he was recommended by John Major or Central Office for selection to follow Michael Jopling at Westmorland and Lonsdale; he was able to reassure local selectors about his Rightwing roots; his selection made him one of only two bachelors picked for safe Tory seats July '95; on his selection, retired from Central Office but was re-appointed as a Media Adviser by Dr Mawhinney Nov '95; was rewarded with a CBE June '96; with five other loyal Tory candidates for safe seats, wrote to the DAILY TELEGRAPH stating that "the Prime Minister must be prepared to put Britain's interest first in negotiations with Europe even if this means standing alone" but that "Britain is right to make a full and constructive contribution to the debate within Europe before any decisions are taken on a single currency" Dec '96; was drafted in by Dr Brian Mawhinney to be the party's media guru at the Wirral South by-election; "Mr Collins' job is to harry and harass Labour at every turn to ensure that it does not inflict such a humiliating defeat that voters go to the polls in the general election with a stirring victory for Labour still fresh in their minds" (Russell Jenkins, TIMES) Feb '97; he blamed the disastrous result at Wirral South on the media not getting the Government's message Feb '97; retained Westmorland with a shrunken majority of 4,521 over the Liberal Democrat challenger, after a swing from the Conservatives of 10.26% May '97; backed his former boss, Michael Howard, for the Tory leadership May-June '97; in his Maiden admitted that since his constituency stretched from Yorkshire into Lancashire, it was unwise to comment on the War of the Roses or test cricketers Mike Atherton and Geoff Boycott June '97; accused some Labour local authorities of "blackmail" over early education June '97; objected to curbing the Budget debate July '97; urged US-style repositioning of lorry exhausts July '97; urged extra subsidies for sheep farmers since "much of the beauty of areas such as the Lake District depends on the hard work of hill farmers" July '97; was named to the Select Committee on Agriculture July

'97; made a powerful speech at the Tories' annual conference at Blackpool Oct '97;
Born: 7 May 1964, Epping, Essex
Family: Son, of late William Collins, Conservative dairy farmer who died from the electrification of his farm pond in June '97, and Di(ana) (May), Chairman of Epping Conservative Association; acquired a Lake District fiancee, teacher Clare Benson, following his selection;
Education: Chigwell School; LSE (BSc in International Relations); King's College, London University (MA in War Studies);
Occupation: Senior Strategy Consultant to WCT Live Communication and Media Adviser, to Conservative Party Chairman '95-97; in Prime Minister's Policy Unit, 10 Downing Street, '95; Director of Communications, Conservative Central Office '92-95; Founding Chairman, of CCO Conferences Ltd, a company which contracted for services for Central Office, with a turnover of £1m) '94-95; Press Secretary to PM John Major during election campaign Mar-Apr '92; Special Advisor, to Michael Howard at Employment (where he helped campaign against the minimum wage, '90-92; Special Adviser, to Michael Howard and David Hunt, at Environment '89-90; Staffer at Conservative Research Department '86-89;
Traits: Boyish-looking; fresh-faced; front-combed hair; "amiable, mild-mannered" (Chris Moncrieff, HOUSE MAGAZINE): "self-esteeming" (Paul Routledge, INDEPENDENT ON SUNDAY); "looks like Harry Enfield playing a computer nerd"; "he does not drink" (Russell Jenkins, TIMES); "a dead ringer for those chilling Hitler clones, The Boys from Brazil" (MAIL ON SUNDAY); "Trekkie" (a fan of Star Trek, Dr Who and Thunderbird); a Fanta-quaffing junk-food addict; dislikes exercise; "something of a split personality - quiet to the point of gaucheness, but also capable of being uproariously funny"; his Commons speaking style can be boring in tone;
Address: House of Commons, Westminster, London SW1A 0AA; Flat E, 62 St George's Square, London SW1V 3QT;
Telephone: 0171 219 3000 (H of C);

Anthony ('Tony') COLMAN **Labour** **PUTNEY '97-**

Majority: 2,976 over Conservative 10-way;
Description: The leafy, affluent, middle-class seat on the south bank of the Thames which seemed to have become safely Conservative, partly due to the 'Wandsworth effect' of low rates set by its efficient Tory local government; these assumptions were upset by the adverse reactions evoked by its high-profile former Tory MP, David Mellor; despite his many talents, he attracted criticism for his sexual activities, his many partly-declared business interests, and his pro-Europeanism, which made him a target for his Referendum Party opponent, Sir James Goldsmith, since deceased;
Position: On Select Committee on Treasury Affairs '97-; Merton Borough Councillor (Leader '91-97) '90-; Chairman: Low Pay Unit '90-, Public-Private Partnership Scheme, Labour London Research Centre '94-, UK Steering Committee on Local Government Superannuation, Local Authorities Mutual Investment Trust; ex: an Executive member of Labour Finance and Industry Group '70-92; a member of

the Prices Commission '77-79;

Outlook: A major new figure at the interface between the Blair leadership and local government; an extremely rare example of a wealthy former captain of industry transformed into a Labour borough chieftain; "everyone's favourite to be the first of the new intake for promotion" (TIMES); has an "obsession with local government finance" (Robert Hardman, DAILY TELEGRAPH); "the archetypal Christian Socialist Blairite" (Simon Sebag Montefiore, SUNDAY TIMES); "a moderniser" who "favours PR" (NEW STATESMAN); has quoted Thomas Rainborowe, leader of the Levellers, in support of a London mayor and strategic authority elected by PR; a leading member of London Agenda 21 and also a member of the Fabians, the Christian Socialist Movement, Labour Finance and Industry Group;

History: He joined the Labour Party at 29, '72; was named to the Prices Commission by the Labour Government '77; contested hopeless South West Hertfordshire against Geoffrey Dodsworth, coming 2nd with 28%, a 5% drop from the previous contest May '79; was elected to Merton Borough Council May '90; became Leader of Merton Borough Council May '91; was selected to contest Putney against David Mellor July '95; like David Mellor and the Referendum Party leader and Putney candidate, Sir James Goldsmith, suffered a break-in, concluding: "someone is clearly trying to undermine the democratic process" Nov '96; after his police constable brother had to face, unarmed, a criminal with a .22, "as a local government leader, I led the movement within London borough councils to pass resolutions proposing a total handgun ban, which were adopted by UK local government associations"; avoided attacking David Mellor for his steamy personal life: "I'm on my third marriage, so I can't talk" Apr '97; admitted that, unlike himself, most local Labour authority leaders preferred London's mayor to be selected from the majority group on any strategic London authority Apr '97; the former Liberal Democrat candidate said, "given the electoral arithmetic in Putney, the only candidate who can beat David Mellor is Tony Colman" Apr '97; won the seat by a majority of 2,976, by London standards a moderate 11.18% swing to Labour; the count was disfigured by extreme taunting between Goldsmith and Mellor May '97; in his Maiden promised to fight his constituency's NHS hospital cuts, air and noise pollution and unemployment but concentrated on economic regeneration, as Chairman of the widely-supported consortium London Agenda 21 Initiative; he also pledged his support for a mayor and London strategic authority, elected by proportional representation June '97; strongly supported the Government's Bill virtually banning handguns, citing his police constable brother's experience with a criminal armed with a .22 and the derisory demonstration (by 78) and vote (90) for the Sportsmen's Alliance candidate in the Putney contest June '97; strongly supported the Government Bill for phased release of housing receipts to increase social housing; he contrasted the behaviour of Merton, the council he had led, in building 3,000 social housing units, and that of Conservative-led Wandsworth which had emphasised selling off its housing stock, often unsuitably; he cited a constituent who, at 78, had had to buy her council flat with a 25-year-long mortgage; "now at the age of 86, she faces huge bills, large service charges and large capital charges amounting to more than £10,000" June '97; urged reversal of severe pre-election cuts imposed on local Queen Mary's University Hospital in Roehampton June '97; as head of the local authorities' pension group, wrote privately to Chancellor Gordon Brown warning that the planned Budget abolition of Advance Corporation Tax "would add at least 3% - or £300m to [local authority] employers' pension costs and compensation would be needed, otherwise there would be further cuts in local services unless there was an increase in the revenue support grant" June '97; when this letter was quoted by a Tory MP, he was compelled to disclose in the Commons that he had received a letter from the Minister for Local Government, Hilary Armstrong, "which plainly states that when the actuarial figures are given following revaluation or the fresh look in 1998 and if it is found that there is a problem, the Govrnment will take such

factors into account in determining local authority provision for 1999-2000 and subsequent years" July '97; congratulated Government on closing two meat plants violating anti-BSE rules July '97; was named to the Select Committee on Treasury Affairs July '97; he asked, successfully, for a "pathfinder project for the use of PFI in social housing" July '97; as "a humble back-bencher" took pride in the Local Government (Contracts) Bill, quickly worked out between the new Government and his Public-Private Partnership July '97; strongly criticised the Multilater Agreement on Investment reached at Earth Summit 2 for its restrictions on hiring local personnel and on use of local materials in manufacturing, pointing out he was the former manager of a multinational (the United Africa Company) July '97; in a letter to the GUARDIAN on vitamin B6 wrote: "I hope the Government will take the initiative if it emerges a mistake has been made in deciding to change the regulation of this vitamin" Aug '97; deplored the "noise pollution" of 1,200 daily flights into Heathrow, largely over Putney Oct '97; emphasised the importance of proper management of the radio spectrum for radio-controlled taxis and fishermen at sea Oct '97;
Born: 24 July 1943, Upper Sheringham, Norfolk
Family: Son, of William Benjamin Colman and Beatrice (Hudson); his police constable brother Ronald won the British Empire Medal for disarming a criminal; "a cousin of mine fishes for crab and lobster in the North Sea"; m 3rd Juliet, personnel executive; 5s, 1d, 2 stepc;
Education: Paston Grammar School, North Walsham; Magdalene College, Cambridge; University of East Africa; LSE;
Occupation: Leader, Merton Borough Council '91-97; Chairman, of venture capital company '90-; ex: Director, Burton Plc '81-90, Chief Executive, for Development and Concessions for Burton: Top Shop (which he helped Ralph Halpern set up), Top Man, Dorothy Perkins and Evans '69-90; he received a £750,000 payoff from the Burton Group; United Africa Company '64-69;
Traits: Long, narrow face; pinched nose; large spectacles; neat coiffure; hard corporate-man mien; "mellifluous" (Piers Merchant MP); "a prissy, keen man of good works and public service"; his "dapperness is high game-show camp; his hair has tinges of a red-blonde colour" (Simon Sebag Montefiore, SUNDAY TIMES); "can lapse into worthy boffinry" (Robert Hardman, DAILY TELEGRAPH); a Wimbledon FC fan; enjoys swimming and the theatre;
Address: House of Commons, Westminster, London SW1A 0AA; 'Phoebus', 14 Lambourne Avenue, London, SW19 7DW;
Telephone: 0171 219 3000 (H of C); 0181 879 0045 (home);

Yvette COOPER **Labour** **PONTEFRACT & CASTLEFORD '97-;**

Majority: 25,725 over Conservative 4-way;
Description: A West Yorkshire Labour stronghold, previously largely based on now-shut coalmines; still retains factories in Pontefract, potteries in Castleford, a power station at Ferrybridge, glassworks and chemical works at Knottingley and Castleford, plus liquorice fields;
Position: On Select Committees: on Education and Employment '97-, Intelligence and Security '97-;
Outlook: "One to watch" (NEW STATESMAN): the "dazzling star of the Blairite nomenklatura" (Simon Sebag Montefiore, SUNDAY TIMES); a young journalist on the INDEPENDENT shoehorned into a super-safe West Yorkshire seat after Sir Geoffrey Lofthouse had been squeezed out; "no doubt talented, she has nonetheless benefited from leadership patronage because of close links to senior Blairites" (TRIBUNE); was an adviser to late John Smith and Gordon Brown and is the partner of Brown's adviser, Ed Balls; is also the grand-daughter of a miner and the daughter of a union leader; whatever the origins of her talents, she soon showed them by seeming to reply ably for the Government in economic debates soon after her Maiden;
History: She joined the Labour Party '87; advised Labour Leader John Smith '91-92; she worked on Bill Clinton's staff in Arkansas '92; she advised the team of Labour's 'Shadow Chancellor' Gordon Brown '93-94; was short-listed for the safe seats of Wentworth Dec '96 and the all-woman contest at Warrington North, where she competed with Valerie Vaz, Valerie Shawcross and winner Helen Jones Mar '97; having failed on these occasions, Sir Geoffrey Lofthouse was squeezed out of Pontrefract and Castleford by the carrot of a life peerage and the stick of not being allowed to continue as Deputy Speaker; she was fielded with four other NEC nominees: Tony Benn's son Hilary, Blair adviser and ex-SDPer Derek Scott, Kirklees Council Leader, John Harman, AEEU convenor Cath Ashton, none from the constituency; she won, after a "virtuoso performance", winning the selection conference over with "a combination of research and pep" (Martin Wainwright, GUARDIAN) Apr '97; retained the seat with a majority of 25,725, on a 6.6% swing May '97; in her Maiden enthused about Gordon Brown's "wise and radical" "people's Budget" because of its help in curbing youth unemployment July '97; backed curb on detention of asylum-seekers July '97; made impressive, economically-literate speeches defending the Government in its pensions policy July '97; was named to the Select Committees on Education and Employment, and on Intelligence and Security July '97;
Born: 20 March 1969, Inverness
Family: Her grandfather "began his working life in pits as a teen-ager"; daughter, of Tony Cooper, General Secretary, Engineers and Managers Association, and June (Iley); is the partner of Ed Balls, adviser to Gordon Brown;
Education: Eggars Comprehensive School, Alton, Hants; Alton Sixth Form College; Balliol College, Oxford University (1st in PPE); Harvard University (Kennedy Scholar '91-92); LSE (MSc Econ);
Occupation: Journalist, on the INDEPENDENT (leader-writer and economics columnist) '95-97; Research Associate, Centre for Economic Performance, LSE '94-95; Adviser, on Youth Unemployment, to Labour's Treasury team, led by Gordon Brown '93-94; Staffer, in

Bill Clinton's 'War Room' in Arkansas '92; Economic Researcher, to Shadow Chancellor John Smith '91-92;
Traits: Short; elfin look; short brown hair; heart-shaped face; brainy; articulate; a sense of humour: as "a Finance Bill virgin, friends and family asked, 'how was it for you?'; I have to say that it was a strange experience";
Address: House of Commons, Westminster, London SW1A 0AA;
Telephone: 0171 219 5080 (H of C); 01459 106 221 (pager);

Brian COTTER **Liberal Democrat** **WESTON-SUPER-MARE '97-**

Majority: 1,274 over Conservative 4-way;
Description: The large, mostly traditional Bristol Channel resort town in the North Somerset estuary whose Tory majorities were slipping even before the '97 election;
Position: Small Business Spokesman '97-; on the Deregulation Committee '97-; on National Executive of Liberal Democrat Parliamentary Candidates Association; ex: Woking District Councillor '86-90;
Outlook: A small manfacturer in the LibDem's conservative wing; interested in small business's role in job creation; won on his second try by exploiting the tactical vote; in Charter 88, Amnesty International, Green Liberal Democrats;
History: He joined the Liberals '83; was elected to Woking District Council May '86; selected to contest Weston-super-Mare, he cut Tory MP Jerry Wiggin's majority from 7,998 to 5,342 Apr '92; was re-selected; Jerry Wiggin stepped down, as did the local Green candidate, who moved to adjoining Woodspring; at annual LibDem conference, backed 5% VAT on tourism; complained that for every £1 spent in the Westcountry on tourism, £40 was spent in Scotland Sep '96; in the election campaign concentrated wholly on tactical voting, with a former Chairman of the local Labour Party helping with "we must not let wasted votes for Labour let the Tory scrape in"; Cotter's election literature emphasised a bar chart illustrating how this had happened previously Apr '97; managed to defeat by 1,274 votes the able new pro-European Tory candidate and former MEP for the area, Margaret Daly, helped by a Referendum Party vote of 2,280 May '97; urged better monitoring and regulation of shipping in Bristol Channel June '97; asked Minister to "reduce the regulatory burden on small businesses" June '97; pressed for cuts in business rates June '97; urged a review of credit reference agencies June '97; in his Maiden emphasised his role as the LibDems' Small Business Spokesman, saying, "if just one job were to be created in every small business, it would solve the employment problem in this country"; he endorsed the planned late-payment Bill and regional development agencies; he also called for a "fairer rating system" and warned that the windfall tax "will inevitably hit consumers and pension fund holders" July '97; he urged a reassessment of the "deregulation initiative" July '97; was named to the Deregulation Committee Aug '97;
Born: 24 August 1938, Ealing
Family: Son, of Dr Michael Cotter, GP, and Mary (Nugent); m Eyleen (Wode); 2s, 1d;
Education: St Benedict's School, Ealing; Downside School, Bath;
Occupation: Managing Director, of Plasticable Plc (plastics manufacturing company employing 27 people); was previously unemployed for a year;

Traits: A de Gaulle look-alike; long face; beaky nose; crooked smile; receding grey straggling parted hair; educated in Benedictine public schools; enjoys reading, films, gardening, walking;
Address: House of Commons, Westminster, London SW1A 0AA; Belmont House, Brinsea Road, Congresbury, Bristol BS19 5JF;
Telephone: 0171 219 3000 (H of C); 01934 832755 (home); 01934 876919 (Fax);

Dr Ross CRANSTON **Labour** **DUDLEY NORTH '97-**

Majority: 9,467 over Conservative 7-way;
Description: The historic iron-working Black Country town newly divided on a different axis, with both halves being considered marginal -until '97;
Position: On Select Committee on Home Affairs '97-; Chairman, Board of Trustees, Public Concern at Work (the whistleblowers' charity) '96-97;
Outlook: The highly-intelligent, loyal Blairite implanted into a seat from which Labour veteran Dr John (later Lord) Gilbert was squeezed out; a stonewalling Labour loyalist, but not an exciting Commons debater; a respected Australian-born Barrister-Recorder, formerly Professor of Commercial Law at LSE and an authoritative and prolific legal author; a former Labour candidate against William Hague for hopeless Richmond, Yorkshire; a member of the Society of Labour Lawyers and the Labour Finance and Industry Group;
History: He arrived in Britain in '73, joining the Labour Party '74; contested hopeless Richmond, Yorkshire against William Hague, retaining Labour's traditional 3rd place, with an almost identical percentage of votes Apr '92; three weeks before the '97 election, after 70-year-old Dr Gilbert had been squeezed out by the offer of a peerage and a ministerial post in Defence, he was selected in London, and finally in Edinburgh, by an NEC committee from its list of seven candidates, without the involvement of the Dudley constituency; this procedure was apparently devised to select, instead, Tony Blair's friend and former flatmate, Charles Falconer QC, due to become Solicitor General; he was allegedly ruled out because his children attended private schools; Falconer was therefore made a peer to become Solicitor General; when Cranston was selected, it only required endorsement by his constituency association; he was "unanimously endorsed by all members present" according to the CLP Chairman, Alan Harvey; a former MP and continual aspirant, Geoff Edge, complained: "the issue is not whether Ross Cranston is an able candidate; it is that we know nothing about him and have had no say in his selection" Apr '97; Cranston was elected by a majority of 9,547, a notional swing of 9%, whereas the swing to Labour in Dudley South was 11%; Mark Atherton, a Scargillite 'Socialist Labour' candidate who was top of the ballot paper, attracted 2,155 votes (4%) May '97; urged more use of local museum to encourage culture and economic regeneration May '97; expressed solidarity with jailed Indonesian union leader June '97; blamed the windfall tax on the Conservatives' lax price controls in the early '90s July '97; was named to Select Committee on Home Affairs July '97; ridiculed the Tories' continued commitment to tax relief on pensioners' BUPA payments July '97; loyally backed Gordon Brown's removal of tax relief on dividend payments to pension funds, despite former Labour

Treasury Minister Denzil Davies' pointing out that, under the previous Labour regime, "pension funds used not to pay tax on dividends, rent from property developments and gilts" July '97; at Law Society fringe meeting in Brighton claimed Labour policy on youth crime was based on empirical evidence while Tory policy had been based on populism Oct '97;
Born: 23 July 1948, Brisbane, Australia
Family: Son, of Frederick Hugh Cranston, clerk/paint salesman, and Edna Elizabeth (Davis); m '88; 1d; separated '94;;
Education: University of Queensland, Australia; Harvard University; Wolfson College, Oxford University (DPhil);
Occupation: Professor of Commercial Law, LSE '93-97; Barrister '74-; Recorder '97-; Author: Consumers and the Law (1997), Principles of Banking Law (1997), Principles of Banking Law (1997), Legal Ethics and Professional Responsibility (1995), Law, Government, and Public Policy (1987), Legal Foundations of the Welfare State (1985), Regulating Business (1979); ; ex: Assistant Recorder '91-97; Law Lecturer, at Warwick University '75; Consultant: to the Commonwealth Secretariat '94-95, to the World Bank '92, to IMF '91-92, to the UN '91-93; he "worked [with] the West Midlands County Council's Trading Standards Department for 3 months in the 1970s" (BIRMINGHAM POST):
Traits: Neat, close-cropped dark receding hair with bald pate; intelligent; careful; articulate; soft-spoken; residual Australian accent; reads his speeches like a law lecturer with students who are compelled to listen;
Address: House of Commons, Westminster, London SW1A 0AA; lives in Lewisham, London;
Telephone: 0171 219 3000 (H of C);

David CRAUSBY **Labour** **BOLTON NORTH EAST '97-**

Majority: 12,669 over Conservative 5-way;
Description: Part of the former pioneering cotton-spinning town - the birth-place of Samuel Crompton - that turned to initially-prosperous engineering; a former knife-edge marginal embracing depressed inner-city and middle-class suburbs; it was tipped toward Labour by the '95 addition of inner-city Halliwell;
Position: On Select Committee on Administration '97-; ex: Bury Metropolitan District Councillor (Chairman of Housing '85-92) '79-92; Chairman, Bury North Constituency Labour Party '87;
Outlook: The well-rooted, quiet but sharp local politician and trade unionist (AEEU); was second-time lucky in this seat, where he has long worked as an engineer and AEEU trade unionist; this came after an earlier failure in Bury North, his home town; one of the few skilled engineers in Labour's '97 entry; he backs proportional representation;
History: He joined the Labour Party '74; was elected in his home town to Bury Metropolitan District Council May '79; was selected 43-24-7-1 to contest marginal, Tory-held Bury North Oct '85; protested to local MEP Barbara Castle against the impact of bus deregulation on Ramsbottom, in particular Jan '86; despite a national swing to Labour, he suffered a 3.5% swing to the Conservatives, with Bury North's sitting Tory MP, Alistair Burt, increasing his

majority from under 3,000 to almost 7,000 June '87; after Ann Taylor had failed to win the seat in '84 and Frank White had failed to take it in '87, was selected for Bolton North East Mar '90; warned that the seat was "not typically northern" and that in a region of marginal seats "we're not going to get much help from other constituencies"; pointed out that the sitting Tory MP, Peter Thurnham, "plays to people's prejudices quite well and [even if] he's not a sparkling character, he has won twice"; he failed to take the seat, despite cutting Thurnham's majority from 813 to 185, Apr '92; stayed on to fight the seat again, helped by the boundary revision which made it a Labour marginal and caused Thurnham to announce he would not fight it again '95; Thurnham later left the Conservatives for the Liberal Democrats Feb '96; Crausby claimed, "Conservatives are coming over to us in droves"; "I've never met that throughout my political career" Apr '97; he won the seat with a majority of 12,669 after a pro-Labour swing of 10.17% May '97; co-sponsored motion urging better funding for further education colleges June '97; backed ban on fox-hunting June '97; urged trying to persuade the USA that "our common policy on Bosnia should be 'in together, out together'" June '97; in his Maiden urged the rebuilding of Bolton's engineering base and the conversion to a university of the Bolton Institute of Higher Education July '97; co-sponsored motion congratulating Bolton Wanderers on their promotion to the Premier League July '97;
Born: 17 June 1946, Bury
Family: Son of Thomas Crausby, industrial labourer/club steward, and Kathleen (Lavin); m '65 Enid (Neen), who was also active in the AEEU; 2s both of whom attended university;
Education: Bury primary; Derby Grammar School, Bury;
Occupation: Engineering Turner: former full-time Shop Steward and Works Convenor at Beloit Walmsely (Bolton engineering works) for 18 years; previously an Engineering Turner (AEEU);
Traits: Dark, receding hair; broad forehead; medium build; Mediterranean appearance; persistent; quiet-spoken; earnest; a football enthusiast (Bury FC and Bolton Wanderers);
Address: House of Commons, Westminster, London SW1A 0AA; 139 Reel Lane, Bolton;
Telephone: 0171 219 3000 (H of C);

(Constance) Ann CRYER **Labour** 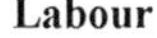 **KEIGHLEY '97-**

Majority: 7,132 over Conservative 4-way;
Description: The loveliest and most northerly part of Bradford metropolitan district, including the Bronte country and Haworth as well as the textile town of Keighley, with its possibly 10,000 Asians and heavy unemployment; unaltered in '95, but in '83 Ilkley Moor, predominantly-Tory Ilkley and Addingham's 10,000 electors were added from Ripon and Skipton;
Position: Vice President, Keighley and Worth Valley Railway Preservation Society '94-; JP Bradford; ex: on Social Security Appeals Tribunal '87-96; Darwen Borough Councllor '62-65;
Outlook: A more restrained version of her widely-popular hard-Left late husband, Bob; is in the Campaign Group; opposed poll tax payment and the wars in Vietnam, the Falklands and the Gulf; backed the '84-85 miners' strike and opposed subsequent pit closures; strongly anti-EU (in Common Market Safeguards; CND;

"as an MP, I'll inevitably think to myself, what would Bob have done in my position? But at the end of the day, I'll make my own decisions; I'm not a continuation of him, not Bob Cryer Mark Two"; "she's seen as a decent, honest person who brought up her family in Yorkshire; she's trustworthy" (local party member);

History: Joined the Labour Party at 18, '58, CND '60, the Co-operative Party '65; was elected to Darwen Borough Council May '62; after her husband's death, refused to enter the selection contest as his successor at Bradford South ("it was too soon, I wasn't up to it") June '94; urged on by her daughter Jane ("you've virtually done the job for years"), agreed to enter the all-women's short-list to contest Keighley - once held by her late husband - against its Tory incumbent, Gary Waller, rather than see the seat go to a 'Blairite moderniser'; she won selection July '95; campaigned against rail privatisation from '95; campaigned against green belt erosion and in favour of retaining the Carlisle-Settle rail link and for a tougher line against crime ("Keighley people are frightened in their homes") Apr '97; Lord Attenborough campaigned for her Apr '97; won the seat, ousting Gary Waller, with a majority of 7,132 on a pro-Labour swing of 10.21% - with her son John winning Hornchurch May '97; in her Maiden speech, in which she was very cautious about referring to her late husband, she backed the Labour Government's priority for "human rights, world-wide; I trust that that commitment will extend not only to the Muslims in Kashmir but to the long-suffering women in Afghanistan" May '97; she joined the Campaign Group, but not necessarily the same wing as her son John May '97; backed ban on fox-hunting June '97; led motion urging elimination of all nuclear weapons, with strict and effective international control July '97; led motion attacking 40% bonuses self-awarded by Yorkshire Water directors July '97; co-sponsored motion deploring BA's selling off of its catering division July '97; co-sponsored motion deploring police attacks on peaceful demonstrators in Kenya July '97; co-sponsored motion to print out a consolidated version of the principal treaties of the European Union July '97; co-sponsored motion opposing any cut in lone parent child benefit July '97; had an adjournment debate on Bronte-sanctified Top Withens in her constituency July '97; was one of the Leftwing MPs who urged the Government to "negotiate away" its nuclear weapons, ditch NATO expansion and scrap the Eurofighter project Aug '97;

Born: 14 December 1939, St Annes-on-Sea, Lancashire

Family: Her grandmother Dinah Place was a leading suffragette and an ILP activist; daughter of Allen Place, shoemaker, then labourer and ILP and Labour activist, and Margaret Ann (Ratcliffe), "a very skilled producer of soft furnishings" (AC); m '63 Robert Cryer, teacher and lecturer, MP for Keighley '74-83, MEP for Sheffield & North Derbyshire '84-89, and MP for Bradford South '87-94 (when he was killed in a motor accident which she survived); 1s John '64, Labour MP for Hornchurch '97-; 1d Jan '65; 5 grandchildren;

Education: Highfield Infants, St John's Junior, Darwen; Spring Bank Secondary Modern, Darwen; Bolton Technical College (secretarial diploma); Keighley Technical College (O-lvels);

Occupation: Writer, Boldness Be My Friend (a memoir to her late husband); Personal Assistant, part-time to her husband, as MP and MEP '74-94 (TGWU); Researcher, part-time for Essex University '69-70; Clerk, at ICI and GPO '55-64;

Traits: Handsome; acquiline features; white hair; suffered from post-traumatic stress disorder for a long time after she and her husband were involved in their '94 car crash;

Address: House of Commons, Westminster, London SW1A 0AA; 28 Kendall Avenue, Shipley, Yorks BD18 4LY;

Telephone: 0171 219 3000 (H of C); 01274 584701 (home & Fax);

John CRYER **Labour** **HORNCHURCH '97-**

Majority: 5,680 over Conservative 6-way;
Description: An unchanged suburban seat on London's Essex fringe; three-quarters owner-occupied, often by skilled workers; 15% of them work at Ford's Dagenham plant; until '97 this was considered safe for Conservatives;
Position: On Deregulation Committee '97-
Outlook: "A rising star of the Left" (TIMES) and one of the worries of the Blairites: a hard-Left journalist who claims to share "the ideals and beliefs" of his late father, the widely-admired Bob Cryer; but there is a much harder edge to his political position, illustrated by his refusal to pay the normal tribute in his Maiden to his predecessor, Robin Squire, generally regarded as a decent Centre-Left Tory; "I don't want to be pally with the Tories, I want to grind them into the dirt" (JC); this 'class war' approach is more in line with the Trotskyist LABOUR BRIEFING and Communist MORNING STAR for which he worked than with his late father's good-humoured application of his Leftwing views; strongly anti-European ("when I was canvassing in Hornchurch, I hardly met anybody who was in favour of a single currency"); favours renationalisation of all the public utilities; proclaims his links with Tony Benn and Jeremy Corbyn, as well as his father's friend and collaborator, Dennis Skinner; with his mother, Ann, is the first Commons mother-and-son pair since the Oppenheims in '83-87; in the Campaign Group, the Labour Euro-Safeguards Committee and the First-Past-the-Post Group;
History: He was raised in a very Leftwing family, his father becoming the MP for Keighley when he was 9, Feb '74; joined the Labour Party at 15, '79; after his father's death in a car crash, sought to follow him at Bradford South, but the choice fell to Gerry Sutcliffe, Leader of Bradford City Council May '94; claimed that Labour was trying to fudge its commitment to renationalise Britain's railway system Jan '95; in TRIBUNE hailed the achievements of Jeremy Corbyn Jan '95; in TRIBUNE claimed Labour's NEC was being sidelined or used as a rubber stamp by the Blair leadership July '95; was selected for Hornchurch, thought "hopeless" by the Labour leadership, since it required a 9.5% swing to capture it Sep '95; in TRIBUNE cited criticisms of the redrafting of Clause Four because of the "absence of specifics and a general acceptance of the economic status quo" Nov '95; was attacked in TRIBUNE by Stephen Twigg, Islington Councillor and candidate for Southgate, for his inaccurate criticisms of Islington's poor education record Feb '96; in TRIBUNE predicted that Labour was in for a "summer of discontent" over the Blair leadership's plans to provide only minimal rights at work and social security protection, while retaining much of the Conservative's trade union legislation June '96; somewhat unexpectedly captured Hornchurch from its incumbent Tory MP Robin Squire by a majority of 5,680, on a pro-Labour swing of 15.95%, one of London's highest; this made him Labour's 41st least-expected victor May '97; in his Maiden he paid homage to Tony Benn, Jeremy Corbyn and Dennis Skinner, but said of his predecessor only "the constituency elected a Conservative Member of Parliament for 18 years"; emphasised, "I was elected to this Chamber to defend universal benefits, free and universal health care, jobs and living standards" May '97; raised the threat of closure for Romford's Oldchurch Hospital May '97; asked for a review of the Child Support Agency May '97; called for the scrapping of the CSA June '97; complained that further education colleges were "marked by gross

under-funding, anarchic organisation and an almost complete lack of strategic planning" June '97; backed Labour Government's halt in sales of Forestry Commission land June '97; urged the creation of Grand Committee for London June '97; co-sponsored his mother's motion to abolish nuclear weapons under strict and effective international controls July '97; criticised Labour leadership for dropping plans to renationalise railways July '97; urged a debate to show the dangers of PR July '97; attacked the Tories for their mis-selling of pensions, with "25,000 miners being conned out of their occupational schemes" July '97; co-sponsored Campaign Group motion protesting refusal of entry clearance for Nigerian Abdul Onibuyo July '97; called for the restoration of the earnings link with state pensions and the rebuilding of SERPS July '97; was named to Deregulation Committee Aug '97; was one of the Leftwing MPs who urged the Government to "negotiate away" its nuclear weapons, ditch NATO expansion and scrap the Eurofighter project Aug '97; urged a delay in consideration of the Labour leadership's 'Partnership in Power' "because there hasn't been enough time to debate it" Sep '97; complained that the planned cut in single parents' benefit failed "to deliver hope and sustenance to the socially excluded but could make their lives even worse" Oct '97;
Born: 11 April 1964, Darwen, Lancashire
Family: Son, of late Robert ('Bob') Cryer, teacher and lecturer, MP for Keighley '74-83, MEP for Sheffield & Derbyshire North '84-89, MP for Bradford South '87-94 and Ann Cryer, MP for Keighley '97-; m Narindar (Batas); 1s, ld ;
Education: Oakbank School, Keighley; Hatfield Polytechnic (BA in Literature and History); London College of Printing;
Occupation: Journalist '88-: on Lloyds List '96-97, TRIBUNE '93-96, LABOUR BRIEFING (where he "personally penned several of the more fascinating profiles in the popular series, 'Class Traitor of the Month' - PRIVATE EYE) '96-97, MORNING STAR ("he is fondly remembered as a colleague; he was a sub-editor working in news and features; he wasn't penning 3000-word pieces on Kim Il Sung and he didn't come to work in a tank", Deputy Editor Paul Corry); Insurance Underwriter ("it may surprise Hon Members to learn that a raving firebrand like me was a yuppie for a few years; I worked as an underwriter - but I could not get out fast enough") '86-88;
Traits: Young; reddish hair; specs; likes railways, architecture, old sport cars; a "voracious reader" (JC);
Address: House of Commons, Westminster, London SW1A 0AA; 65 Haverhill Road, Balham, London SW11;
Telephone: 0171 219 3000 (H of C); 0181 673 2124 (home);

Claire CURTIS-TANSLEY **Labour** **CROSBY '97-**

Majority: 7,182 over Conservative 6-way;
Description: The largely middle-class north-of-Merseyside commuter seat which now also embraces the heart of Liverpool's docklands; it was made famous by Shirley Williams' '81 capture of it for the SDP, interrupting its semi-permanent stay in Conservative hands; its '97 fall to Labour was due partly to the removal of Maghull from the communities of Crosby and Formby and the addition of two Labour-leaning wards from Bootle;
Position: On Select Committee on Science and Technology '97-; Crewe & Nantwich Borough Councillor '95-
Outlook: A Leftwing Welsh chartered engineer, feminist and animal-lover who took this seat from a highly-respected Tory on swing of over 18%; a rare woman chartered mechanical engineer who held top jobs in industry (including Shell); the first Labour MP for Crosby and the first female chartered engineer to enter the Commons; says, "I want to promote manufacturing science and technology to girls in school and women returners" (CC-T) she used both 'Emily's List' and the Labour Women's Network to ensure her candidacy; an active animal rights defender, in the League Against Cruel Sports and the Whale and Dolphin Society; also in the Fabian Society, Co-operative Society;
History: She joined the Labour Party; was elected to Crewe and Nantwich Borough Council May '95; sought selection in the all-women contest for Chester '95; was selected for Crosby '96; complained about the sex discrimination she had suffered as a woman as a fitter and mechanical engineer, in a BBC phone-in May '96; was named by anti-abortion Tory MPs Ann Winterton and Elizabeth Peacock as a beneficiary of 'Emily's List' which helped Labour women candidates financially in return for a commitment to a 'woman's right to choose' stance if elected; this was calculated to damage her, since a quarter of her electors were Catholics Mar '97; was supported during the campaign by John Moores Jr, a deviant Littlewoods Pools heir Apr '97; although her seat was 120th on Labour's target list, on the eve of poll a LIVERPOOL DAILY POST head-count predicted it would fall to her Apr '97; captured the seat from its widely-respected incumbent Tory MP, Sir Malcolm Thornton, by a majority of 7,182, on a near-record pro-Labour notional swing of 18.15%; this made her the 33rd least-expected Labour victor May '97; expressed solidarity with jailed Indonesian union leader June '97; urged primary school teachers be qualified to teach science to 5-to-8-year-olds July '97; asked whether industrialists would be consulted over the proposal for a European patent system based on a single patent application July '97; in her Maiden, complained that, as a chartered engineer, her profession was very under-represented in the Commons, although engineering "is probably the most innovative and exciting profession" July '97; was named to the Select Committee on Science and Technology July '97;
Born: 30 April 1958, Neath, Glamorgan
Family: She is married with two children;
Education: Mynyddbach Comprehensive School for Girls, Swansea; University College, Cardiff, University of Wales (BSc in Mechanical Engineering); Aston University (MBA); "I am researching the ethical framework of the private and public sector for a PhD" (CC-T):
Occupation: Chartered Mechanical Engineer; Partner, in Business Services for Industry (TGWU); previously Head of Strategic Planning, for Birmingham City Council, Head of

Environmental Affairs, Shell Chemicals, Head of UK Distribution, Shell Chemicals; initially a Fitter;
Traits: Tall; has short, bobbed hair; since only 3% of engineers are women, initially felt "very lonely"; early on in the Commons, she was said to be a "candidate for the 'Don't You Know Who I Am?' Trophy", mythically awarded by Commons staff (Paul Routledge, INDEPENDENT ON SUNDAY);
Address: House of Commons, Westminster, London SW1A 0AA; 30 Elmstead Crescent, Leighton, Crewe CW1 3PX
Telephone: 0171 219 3000 (H of C);

Keith DARVILL **Labour** **UPMINSTER '97-**

Majority: 2,770 over Conservative 4-way;
Description: The long, thin constituency on London's eastern fringe, on the Essex border at the end of the District Line; in its northern part is the giant Harold Hill council estate, in its southern part are the middle class suburbs of Cranham and Emerson Park; in '95 it lost Conservative-leaning Ardleigh Green ward; "most of the residents of this seat have come from the inner part of east London or are members of families born there", "part of the well-known eastward drift that has taken place since the 1920s" (KD);
Position: Chairman, Upminster Constituency Labour Party '94-97;
Outlook: The "charismatic" (Patrick Hennessy, EVENING STANDARD) local self-made solicitor who ousted the former Foreign Office Minister, Sir Nicholas Bonsor Bt, like all but one of the Tories in the near-Essex suburbs; the first-ever Labour MP for this seat; as a school governor for over 15 years has an involved nonpartisan appoach to improving education; is in the Fabian Society, Co-operative Party, the Society of Labour Lawyers;
History: He joined the Labour Party '71; was selected to contest Upminster '95; helped by almost half of the LibDem vote, unexpectedly ousted Sir Nicholas Bonsor Bt by a majority of 2,770 votes, with a pro-Labour swing of 15.38%, May '97; backed outlawing of fox-hunting June '97; expressed solidarity with jailed Indonesian union leader June '97; in his Maiden attributed his victory to the fact that Upminster voters, mostly immigrants from east London, had "returned to Labour"; he loyally supported the Budget proposals July '97; in the Schools debate, speaking as a school governor for over 15 years, warned against overloading governors, or undervaluing local education authorities' expertise or undermining teachers' morale; he also supported early testing to detect dyslexia July '97; backed curbs on detention of asylum-seekers July '97;
Born: 28 May 1948, Forest Gate, London
Family: Son, of Ernest Arthur Darvill, docker, and Ellen May (Carke); m Julia (de Saren); 2s, 1d;
Education: Norlington Secondary Modern, Leyton E10; East Ham Technical College; Thurrock College of Further Education; Polytechnic of Central London; College of Law, Chester;
Occupation: Solicitor '82-; deals largely with property (TGWU)

Traits: Blond, parted hair; heart-shaped face; youthful looking; "charismatic" (Patrick Hennessy, EVENING STANDARD); enjoys tennis, badminton, sports generally and gardening;
Address: House of Commons, Westminster, London SW1A 0AA; 54 Park Drive, Upminster, Essex RM14 3AR (constituency);
Telephone: 0171 219 3000 (H of C); 01708 250514 (constituency);

Edward DAVEY **Liberal Democrat** **KINGSTON & SURBITON '97-**

Majority: 56 over Conservative 7-way;
Description: A merger of two formerly Conservative seats in London's southwestern suburbs: former Surbiton linked to that part of Kingston-upon-Thames south of the main railway into London; what remained unsure until the '97 general election was the extent to which Liberal Democrat victories on Kingston council would be translated into a Parliamentary seat;
Position: Public Spending and Taxation Spokesman on LibDems' Treasury team '97-; ex: on Liberal Democrat Federal Policy Committee '94-95; Chairman, of the Costing Group on the LibDem Manifesto '94-97; on LibDem Policy Groups on Economics, Tax and Benefits, Transport;
Outlook: The first MP for this new seat; one of the clever young backroom boys transmuted into a rising star on the LibDems' front bench; was one of those insiders instrumental in forming the policy for a penny on income tax to pay for education; is respected by Labour Ministers for his economic expertise, if not his patronising whiplashing ("I always enjoy his speeches" -Helen Liddell MP); wants a strategic authority for London, elected by PR, but is opposed to a separate directly-elected mayor; a former Senior Economics Adviser to LibDem MPs; one of the young LibDem apparatchiks who secured their five-seat sweep in the southwestern London suburbs; "conservation is his big issue" (INDEPENDENT ON SUNDAY);
History: He was active at Oxford "discussing the minutiae of energy conservation and green economics" (ED) '86; he joined the Liberal Democrats '89; was selected for the new Kingston and Surbiton seat following the abolition of the old Kingston seat Mar '95; at annual conference argued against demands from Scottish LibDems for a cut in VAT on hotel services as "incredibly inefficient and costly" at a time when the party was calling for a tax increase to fund education Sep '96; captured Kingston and Surbiton from Tory MP Dick Tracey by 56 - the third smallest majority - on the basis of a 13.6% swing May '97; in his Maiden complained about the punishing cuts imposed on education in Kingston June '97; tried to save Thames Ditton Lawn Tennis Club from demolition June '97; backed motion favouring abolition of hunting with hounds June '97; in the debate on exchange rate, insisted that Austin Mitchell always argued for devaluation, "a recipe for inflation"; an independent central bank was better July '97; criticised the rapid passage of the Finance Bill, because it contained "a dramatic change in fiscal policy" not foreshadowed in Labour's manifesto; the Budget was "designed for political considerations, not economic ones, and aimed at fulfilling a political project and bulding a war chest for the next election", "that is why Liberal Democrat Members will vote

against the Second Reading"; he described Chancellor Brown's willingness to accept Kenneth Clarke's ceilings as "Clownism" July '97;
Born: 25 December 1965, Annesley-Woodhouse, Nottinghamshire
Family: Son of late John George Davey, solicitor, and late Joan (Stanbrook) teacher;
Education: Nottingham High School (head boy); Jesus College, Oxford University (BA in PPE, First Class Hons); Birkbeck College, London University (MSc Econ);
Occupation: Management Consultant, with Omega Partners '93-97; Director, of Omega Partners Postal (specialising in new markets for post offices) '96-97; Senior Economic Adviser to the LibDems in Parliament '89-93;
Traits: Parted light-brown hair; long jaw; cleancut; very bright; can seem self-satisfied and patronising; received a Chief Constable's Certificate and an award from the Royal Humane Society for rescuing a woman who had fallen onto the track at Clapham Junction station;
Address: House of Commons, Westminster, London SW1A 0AA;
Telephone: 0171 219 3152 (H of C); 0181 399 3774;

Mrs Valerie DAVEY **Labour** **BRISTOL WEST '97-**

Majority: 1,493 over Conservative 7-way;
Description: The city's formerly-Conservative heartland, including the University and the more fashionable residential slopes of Clifton and Redland, as well as troubled, multiracial St Paul's; the addition of Tory-leaning Westbury-on-Trym was thought likely to save the seat for William Waldegrave;
Position: On Select Committee on Education and Employment '97-; ex: Avon County Councillor (Leader of its majority Labour Group '92-96) '81-96;
Outlook: The education-preoccupied former Avon Council Leader and ex-teacher who ended William Waldegrave's Commons career and the Tories' long-standing hold on the seat by exploiting tactical voting; a Methodist who taught in Tanzania; in Amnesty and Action for South Africa; favours electoral reform;
History: She formed her convictions when she worked among the poor in Tanzania in the '60s; she joined the Labour Party '70; was elected to Avon County Council May '81; became Leader of the Labour Group on Avon County Council May '92; was selected for Bristol West, in the knowledge that Labour had come 3rd with 24.8% in '92, with her LibDem opponent having come 2nd with 30.7%, '95; expressed her concern about homelessness and sleeping rough in Bristol on BBC TV's 'Midnight Hour' Jan '97; she concentrated her campaign on getting back from the LibDems the tactical votes which had gone to them in '92, when they were best-placed to oust William Waldegrave; she argued bitterly with their "dishonest" bar graphs which portrayed Bristol West as a two-horse (LibDem v Tory) contest, ignoring pro-Labour local and Euro elections after '92; her case was helped considerably by the publication, four days before polling, of an ICM poll - confirmed by canvassing returns - which showed her ahead of Waldegrave by 39% to 31% with the Liberal Democrat, Charles Boney, trailing badly with 24%; she sent an eve of poll leaflet on this to every household Apr '97; won the seat, ousting William Waldegrave by a majority of 1,493, a notional swing to Labour of 12.08%, May '97; in her Maiden complained about the past under-funding of Bristol, including

an allocation of only £17,500 for repairing its schools; she also complained of inadequate funds for curbing growing homelessness June '97; urged a review of "the role and function of the Equal Opportunities Commission" June '97; supported the outlawing of fox-hunting June '97; expressed solidarity with jailed Indonesian union leader June '97; urged increased concentration on children with special educational needs July '97; was named to Select Committee on Education and Employment July '97; co-expressed concern about injured employees whose companies had gone into liquidation July '97;
Born: 16 April 1940, Sutton, Surrey
Family: Daughter, of Mr Corbett, roving branch manager for W H Smith; is married to Mr Davey; they have three children;
Education: Attended three different state primary schools; attended three different state secondary schools; Birmingham University (MA); London University (PGCE);
Occupation: Full-time Councillor '82-; ex-teacher (in Tanzania in the '60s) (NUT);
Traits: Short, light brown straight hair; metal-framed specs; snub nose; blue-stocking school-teacher look; "sartorially the model 'New Labour Woman'" (David Hill, OBSERVER); Methodist; a forceful and accomplished speaker, not needing notes; enjoys homely pursuits (gardening, making marmalade);
Address: House of Commons, Westminster, London SW1A 0AA; 29 Norton Road, Knowle, Bristol BS4 2 EZ;
Telephone: 0171 219 3000 (H of C); 0117 909 3491 (home);

Geraint (Richard) DAVIES **Labour** **CROYDON CENTRAL '97-**

Majority: 3,897 over Conservative 6-way;
Description: Croydon's skyscraper-dominated commercial and shopping centre, embracing New Addington council estate; Croydon is "the largest London borough" and it "commands one-fifth of the capital's economy" (GD)
Position: Croydon Borough Councillor (Leader '94-, previously its Housing Chairman) '86-;
Outlook: The third-time-lucky Croydon Council Leader who ousted his former council sparring partner, ex-MP David Congdon; "I am a committed supporter of New Labour" (GD); "he will be a real asset to the Labour Whips" (Michael Jack MP); one of Labour's few new recruits from the private sector ("my background is in multinational marketing and in running my own small business"); on the Executive of Labour Finance & Industry Group; in Croydon Co-operative Party, SERA;
History: He joined the Labour Party '82; became Assistant Secretary of the Croydon North East CLP '83; was elected to the Executive of the Croydon Central CLP Feb '84; was elected to Croydon Council for New Addington May '86; contested the very safe Tory seat of Croydon South against Sir William Clark, coming 3rd with 10%, June '87; fought Croydon Central against Sir Paul Beresford, increasing Labour's vote from 9,516 to 12,518, largely at the expense of the Alliance Apr '92; became Leader of Croydon Council when Labour secured a majority May '94; denied TIMES report that his new Leadership represented a "Leftwing takeover" May '96; was re-selected to contest Croydon Central, expected to provide a Conservative majority of almost 10,000 on '92 projections '95; won Croydon Central by 3,897

over former Tory MP David Congdon, on a notional swing of 15.48% to Labour May '97; in his Maiden, apart from enthusing about Gordon Brown's masterly Budget, boasted about the regeneration of Croydon as "an emerging European city" with its new cultural centres and tram system in whose creation he had participated as Council Leader June '97;
Born: 3 May 1960, Dorking, Surrey
Family: Son of David Thomas Davies, senior civil servant, and Betty (Ferrer); m '93 Dr Vanessa (Fry); 2d Angharad Mair '94, Meiriam Sien '97;
Education: Birchgrove Junior School (where Ted Rowlands gave him an Investiture Mug in '69); Llanishen Comprehensive, Cardiff; Jesus College, Oxford University (MA PPE);
Occupation: Tour Operator: Managing Partner, Pure Crete (specialist green travel company) and Managing Director, Pure Aviation Ltd (GMB) '90-; previously Marketing Manager, Colgate Palmolive Ltd (MSF) til '82;
Traits: Broad face; broad retreating forehead; Cardiff-educated; sense of humour; enjoys partisan politics, hill-walking, particularly in Wales, and community singing;
Address: House of Commons, Westminster, London SW1A 0AA; 3 Mulgrave Road, Croydon CRO 1BL;
Telephone: 0171 219 3000 (H of C); 0181 680 5877 (home); 0181 680 5833 (constituency);

(Thomas) Hilton DAWSON **Labour** **LANCASTER & WYRE '97-**

Majority: 1,295 over Conservative 6-way;
Description: The marginal but Tory-leaning seat of historic Lancaster, combined in '95 with the Tory-leaning small town of Poulton le Fylde and its rural hinterland; until the '97 election, it was expected - on '92 projections - to produce an 11,000-plus Conservative majority;
Position: On the Select Committee on Administration '97-; Lancaster City Councillor (its Deputy Leader '91-95) '87-;
Outlook: The social services manager and Deputy Leader who became the seat's first Labour MP in 27 years; a supporter of Charter 88 and backer of PR; a rebel on gun law;
History: He joined the Labour Party '78; was the Labour Agent for Morecambe and Lonsdale in the general election June '83, and for Lancaster June '87; became Deputy Leader of Lancaster City Council May '91; was selected to contest the new Lancaster and Wyre seat '95; won the seat by 1,295, defeating the former Tory MP for Wyre, Keith Mans, on a notional swing of 10.6%; his majority was exceeded by the Referendum Party vote of 1,516, May '97; in his Maiden enthused about his beautiful and historic constituency but deplored its rendering plant which "blights the future and must go"; he also warned against being stampeded by the Dunblane tragedy into violating the rights of "law-abiding individuals" to do target-shooting June '97; voted with five other Labour MPs against a ban on all handguns June '97; expressed solidarity with jailed Indonesian union leader June '97; asked about BSE and landfill June '97; asked about protection for children threatened by domestic violence June '97; asked about hundreds of thousands of tons of life-threatening waste products from BSE rendering June '97; urged cancellation of the debts of poor countries July '97; asked about end of beef ban June '97; led motion urging a Children's Rights Commissioner July '97;

Born: 30 September 1953, Stannington, Northumberland
Family: Son of Harry Dawson, teacher, and Sally (Renner) teacher; m '73 Sue (Williams); 2d: Charlotte '77, Helen '81;
Education: Ashington Grammar School, Northumberland; Warwick University (BA in Philosophy and Politics); Lancaster University (Social Work Diploma);
Occupation: Social Services Manager (UNISON, ex NALGO/NUPE) '79-97
Traits: Parted dark hair; good-looking;
Address: House of Commons, Westminster, London SW1A 0AA; 1 Malham Close, Lancaster LA1 2SU;
Telephone: 0171 219 4207 (H of C); 01253 899847 (constituency);

Mrs Janet (Elizabeth Ann) DEAN **Labour** **BURTON '97-**

Majority: 6,330 over Conservative 4-way;
Description: The brewing town which was Conservative 1950-97 because pro-Labour Burton and Uttoxeter were outvoted by their pro-Tory rural hinterlands; even before the election, this balance was tilted in '95 when it lost two strong Tory wards;
Position: On Catering Select Committee '97-; Staffordshire County Councillor '81-97; East Staffordshire Borough Councillor (Mayor '96-97) '91-97; Uttoxeter Town Councillor (Vice Chairman: Social Services '93-96, Highways '85-93)'95-; Founder-Member of Uttoxeter Crime Prevential Panel, Chairwoman, of Uttoxeter Citizens' Advice Bureau; on Arthritis and Rheumatism Council;
Outlook: The ultra-busy three-level local government activist who ousted barrister-MP Sir Ivan Lawrence QC, the one-man fan club of Michael Howard; she was previously active on local issues like fighting, successfully, for the Uttoxeter bypass and against the closure of the local magistrates' court; "known to favour traditional Labour values, [she] did not receive a visit from Mr Blair"; local journalists described Mrs Dean, a former Mayor of East Staffordshire, as a John Prescott fan who "could not really be described as New Labour" (Job Rabkin, INDEPENDENT);
History: She joined the Labour Party '71; was elected to Staffordshire County Council May '81; was elected to East Staffordshire Borough Council May '91; was elected to Uttoxeter Town Council May '95; was selected from an all-women short-list to fight Burton July '95; her constituency's JCB plant was visited by Tony Blair Oct '96; campaigned that the Tories had "betrayed" homeowners; they "lied about mortgage tax relief, cutting it two years running" Apr '97; won the seat, ousting Sir Ivan Lawrence by a majority of 6,330 on a swing of 9.30%, May '97; asked Chancellor Gordon Brown about his discussions with business about his welfare-to-work proposals since, having "six of the poorest wards in the West Midlands", they could help her constituency July '97;
Born: 28 January 1949, Crewe
Family: Daughter, of late Harry Gibson, farmer, and late Mary Elizabeth (Walley); m '68 late Alan Dean, railway clerk and town and borough councillor who died in '94; 2d: Carol Ann '70, Sandra Marie '72;
Education: Elworth Primary School, Cheshire; Winsford Verdin County Grammar School,

Cheshire;
Occupation: Bank Clerk, at Barclays Bank '65-69; Clerical Worker, at Bass Charrington, Burton '69-70 ("before raising a family")
Traits: Blonde; broad face; seamstress (made wedding dresses for both daughters and nine bridesmaids in the same year);
Address: House of Commons, Westminster, London SW1A 0AA; 53 Carter Street, Uttoxeter, Staffs ST14 8EY;
Telephone: 0171 219 3000 (H of C); 01889 565835 (home);

Andrew DISMORE **Labour** **HENDON '97-**

Majority: 6,155 over Conservative 6-way;
Description: The '95 merger of old Hendon North with two wards of old Hendon South in northwest London; a multi-class seat with upper-middle-class Mill Hill (including the public school), middle-class Edgware, and the vast council estate of Burnt Oak; it is also multi-ethnic with a fifth of non-white residents and a sizeable Jewish minority;
Position: Westminster City Councillor (Leader of its Labour Group '90-, their Whip til '90) '82-;
Outlook: The Leader of the minority Labour Group on embattled Westminster City Council who won an unexpected victory in Hendon, ousting the veteran Tory MP and PRman, Sir John Gorst; the first Labour MP there since 1950; a very hardworking, dogged campaigner with a bright legal mind; resourceful and hard-hitting but not overly charming or charismatic; on Westminster Council was better as Labour's Whip than as the Leader of the minority Labour Group; a Left-of-Centre solicitor interested in the rights of accident victims; in CND, the Fabian Society, Co-operative Party, Action for Southern Africa, and the Society of Labour Lawyers;
History: He joined the Labour Party '74; was elected to Westminster City Council May '82; became Whip of its minority Labour Group May '8?; became Leader of its minority Labour Group May '90; he agreed with the thesis that Westminster Council Tories had deliberately waived millions of pounds of repair bills to encourage Tory supporters to buy flats to increase the Tory vote in marginal wards; said "I would be extremely surprised, given the importance of the home-for-votes sales drive, if the associated problem of the high leaseholders' bills were not brought to the attention of the leading members running the council at that time" Jan '95; was selected to contest Hendon against Sir John Gorst, who had been active in defending Edgware Hospital '95; unexpectedly won Hendon from Sir John Gorst, by a majority of 6,155 on a pro-Labour notional swing of 16.21% May '97; in a meeting with new Minister Alan Milburn, learned that it was considered a waste of money and would raise false expectations to promise to save the Accident and Emergency department of Edgware Hospital May '97; asked about an enhanced Rough Sleepers' Initiative June '97; asked about statutory bereavement payment under the Fatal Accidents Acts June '97; in his Maiden, backed a London-wide authority and emphasised that in Hendon "5,000 families - almost one in four households of working age - have no breadwinner" June '97; backed outlawing of fox-hunting June '97; expressed solidarity with jailed Indonesian union leader June '97; "as a personal injury lawyer" complained that a the life of a child killed in an accident - perhaps mown down by a drunken

driver - was "worth practically nothing" June '97; asked a brace of questions on the Criminal Injuries Compensation Scheme June '97; complained about "the previous Government's education policy, which turned out illiterate and semi-literate pupils from primary school" June '97; led motion calling for a public inquiry into the running of Westmister City Council; this was signed by over 100 MPs, but was brought to a halt by the lawyers for Dame Shirley Porter who pointed out there was a court action pending June-July '97; asked about regulation of immigration advisers July '97; led a motion in praise Boosey and Hawkes July '97; co-wrote a letter to TIMES deploring Lord Rees-Mogg's "black propaganda" defence of Dame Shirley Porter Sep '97;
Born: 2 September 1954, Bridlington, Yorkshire
Family: Son, of Brenda and Ian Dismore, hotelier;
Education: Bridlington Grammar School; Warwick University (LLB); LSE (LLM);
Occupation: Solicitor: Partner, in Russell Jones, Walker, working largely "as a personal injury lawyer" (AD) '95-; ex: Partner in another firm '78-95; previously was an Employee of GMBU;
Traits: Parted dark hair; thick specs; dimpled chin; sharp nose; is interested in modern Greek history;
Address: House of Commons, Westminster, London SW1A 0AA; 6 Leamington Road Villas, London W11 7HS;
Telephone: 0171 219 3000 (H of C); 0171 221 4720 (home);

'Jim' (James) DOBBIN **Labour & Co-operative** **HEYWOOD & MIDDLETON '97-**

Majority: 17,542 over Conservative 5-way;
Description: These two Labour-leaning towns from Rochdale borough in Greater Manchester had a further 17,000 LibDem/Tory-leaning voters added from Rochdale itself in '95; it was expected to show a Labour majority of 8,000 on '92 projections;
Position: Rochdale Metropolitan Borough Councillor (Leader '96-Deputy Leader '90-92) '94-'83-92; Chairman, Rochdale District Labour Party; Chairman, Rochdale Credit Union; Alternate Director, of Manchester Airport '96-97; on Community Health Council; on Rochdale Health Authority;
Outlook: Scottish-born local political fixer; self-effacing, but "doesn't miss a trick" (Rochdale colleague): a former NHS microbiologist and manager; is an enthusiast for decentralisation; RC anti-abortionist (in Labour Life); in Amnesty International; ex-Fabian;
History: He was born into a Fife mining family; has been a Labour supporter from school days; joined the Labour Party '75; was elected to Rochdale Borough Council May '83; was elected Deputy Leader of the Labour Group on Rochdale Council May '90; was selected to contest Bury North May '90; was congratulated by Labour MPs "for his forethought and concern in taking up the plight of the employees of Stormseal UPVC" which went into receivership, after failing to pay wages and refusing its employees the protection of a union Feb '91; lost Bury North to Alistair Burt by 4,764 votes on a 2.1% pro-Labour swing Apr '92;

disputed Paddy Ashdown's statement that he would not prop up the Tories, since "that is what they are doing in Rochdale" where the LibDems were in alliance with the Conservatives to control the council June '95; was selected to contest Heywood and Middleton in successon to retiring Jim Callaghan, with the backing of the local "T&G Mafia" Feb '96; remained on the Rochdale Council "to maintain continuity", after 10 local Labour gains ousted the Tory-LibDem alliance, with him becoming the new council Leader May '96; retained Heywood and Middleton with a majority doubled to 17,542 on a notional swing of 9.9% May '97; expressed solidarity with jailed Indonesian union leader June '97;
Born: 26 May 1941, Kincardine, Fife
Family: Son, of late William Dobbin, ex-miner, and Catherine (McCabe); m '64 Patricia Mary Duffy (Russell) teacher; 2s Barry Liam '71, Patrick '75; 2d Mary Louise '65 clinical psychologist, Kerry Jane '69;
Education: Holy Name Primary, Oakley, Fife; St Columba's High School, Fife; St Andrew's High, Kirkcaldy, Fife; Napier College, Edinburgh; Fellow of Institute of Medical Laboratory in Microbiology;
Occupation: NHS Medical Scientist at Royal Oldham Hospital (MSF) '73-94; Alternate Director, of Manchester Airport '96-97; ex: NHS Microbiologist '61-94: worked for two Scottish Regional Health Authorities and one in Oldham;
Traits: Balding; grey beard; steel-rimmed spectacles; self-effacing; behind-the-scenes manipulator/fixer; RC; Celtic football fan;
Address: House of Commons, Westminster, London SW1A 0AA; 43 Stonehill Drive, Rochdale OL12 7JN;
Telephone: 0171 219 3000 (H of C); 01706 342632 (home); 0589 519215 (pager);

Jeffrey (Mark) DONALDSON **Ulster Unionist** **LAGAN VALLEY '97-**

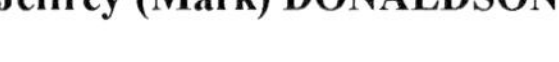

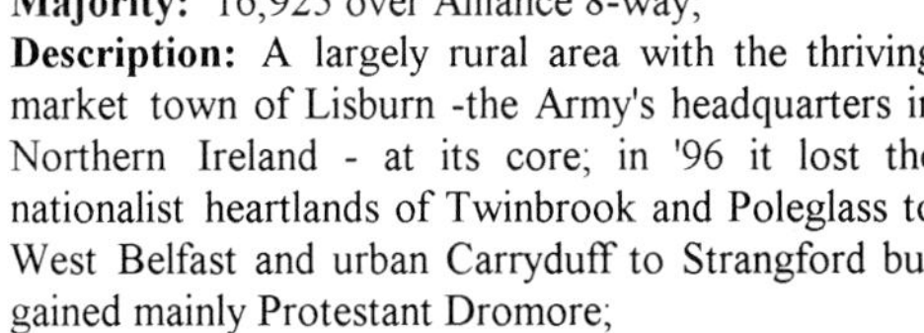

Majority: 16,925 over Alliance 8-way;
Description: A largely rural area with the thriving market town of Lisburn -the Army's headquarters in Northern Ireland - at its core; in '96 it lost the nationalist heartlands of Twinbrook and Poleglass to West Belfast and urban Carryduff to Strangford but gained mainly Protestant Dromore;
Position: Vice Chairman, Standing Committeee on Public Order, Northern Ireland Forum '96-; Assistant Grand Master of the Orange Order '94-; Secretary, Ulster Unionist Council '88-; ex: Chairman, Ulster Young Unionist Council '85-86; Northern Ireland Assemblyman '85-86;
Outlook: "The rising star of the Ulster Unionist Party" (Mark Simpson, BELFAST TELEGRAPH); "a strong public defender of the Orange Order, but seen as a political moderate" (NEW STATESMAN); young Lisburn businessman, Ulster Unionist apparatchik and No 2 in the Orange Order who inherited the well-worn shoes of retired James Molyneaux;
History: The baby of the Ulster Unonists, he joined the Young Unionists at 18, '81; became Election Agent to Enoch Powell in South Down Apr '83; was elected Chairman of the Ulster Young Unionist Council '85; was elected at 22 as the youngest member ever to the Northern Ireland Assembly May '85; was elected Secretary of the Ulster Unionist Council '88; was part

of the Ulster Unionist negotiating team in the Northern Ireland constitutional talks '91; was elected Assistant Grand Master of the Orange Order '94; was elected to the Northern Ireland Forum at the top of the poll May '96; was selected as the Ulster Unionist candidate to succeed retiring James Molyneaux by over two-thirds of the vote Jan '97; pledged his constituents to remedy the "democratic deficit", help local business development and secure enough resources for health and education Mar '97; after the DUP decided to contest Lagan Valley for the first time since '83, said "I'm disappointed at the decision of the DUP to oppose me; I've long been a supporter of Unionist unity; I was brought up to believe that unity is strength, division is weakness" Apr '97; retained Lagan Valley by a majority of 16,925, despite a notional 8.5% swing to the Alliance Party May '97; in his Maiden speech urged more inward investment, particularly in the Lagan Valley - rather than West Belfast - and "a real peace that recognises the rights of the people of Northern Ireland to determine their own political future, free from the threat of terrorist violence and political interference" May '97; led motion urging PM Tony Blair to urge President Yeltsin to veto Duma's "draconian law" curbing religions July '97; insisted the Ulster Unionists would still "confront the Sinn Fein as appropriate" Sep '97;
Born: 7 December 1962, Kilkeel, Co Down
Family: Son, of James Donaldson, civil servant, and Sarah Anne (Charleton); m '87 Eleanor; 2d Claire '90, Laura '92;
Education: Kilkeel High School, Co Down; Castlereagh College, Belfast (Diploma in Electrical Engineering);
Occupation: Partner, in a financial services and estate agents' business in Lisburn and Dromore;
Traits: Youthful-looking; centre-parted short dark hair; full face; Celtic good looks; impassive expression; bright;
Address: House of Commons, Westminster, London SW1A 0AA;
Telephone: 0171 219 3000 (H of C);

Frank DORAN **Labour** **ABERDEEN CENTRAL '97-**

Majority: 10,801 over Conservative 5-way;
Description: A '95-new seat embracing the city centre and made up of equal bits of Aberdeen North and South, with pro-Labour council estates from the north and some Tory-leaning areas from the south; on a projection from '92, it was expected to go Labour by 5,000-plus votes;
Former Seat: Aberdeen South '87-92;
Position: Ex: Assistant Spokesman, on Energy (under Tony Blair) '88-92;
Outlook: Cautious Rightward-moving former semi-hard Leftwinger; was in the 'Supper Club' and opposed the Gulf War; has recently been described as part of the pro-Blair 'Network' in the Scottish Labour Party; in '87 won former Aberdeen South from Gerald Malone, but was the only Labour MP to lose his seat in '92 - after personal and professional problems; is not universally popular locally; formerly sponsored by GMB;
History: He joined the Labour Party '76; fought district and regional council elections in '80 and '82; contested the Euro-constituency of North East Scotland, calling for reform of the

CAP June '84; was selected for Tory-held Aberdeen South from a short-list of six on the fourth ballot by 25 to 24, Sep '85; won the seat from Gerald Malone June '87; in his Maiden complained that while the Scottish Development Agency was trying to create jobs in Aberdeen, Government policies were creating unemployment in its university and shipyards Oct '87; with five other new Labour MPs, sponsored a Bill urging a Peace-Building Fund to "encourage and initiate non-military peace-building initiatives" Oct '87; he and three other Labour MPs involved (George Galloway, William McKelvey, Ernie Ross) submitted a lengthy complaint to the IBA about the Channel 4 and Scottish TV programmes on the Dundee Labour Club Nov '87; claimed that the Government had been unable to put down the necessary secondary legislation for the "regressive" poll tax because "they cannot work out what to put into them, so hastily prepared and ill-thought-out is the measure" Dec '87; put down a motion condemning the SNP "calling for a campaign of non-registration for and non-payment of the poll tax" without warnings about the penalties Jan '88; co-sponsored a motion attacking the arrest in East Germany of nuclear disarmers Feb '88; supported much more generous funding for Aberdeen University, which was losing 500 jobs Mar '88; co-urged selective economic sanctions against Israel for the death of Abu Jihad, Deputy Leader of the PLO Apr '88; rushed back from a "magnificent victory" in Aberdeen's local elections to speak against David Alton's Abortion (Amendment) Bill, urging an appeal system for a woman who had been denied an abortion May '88; backed improved procedures in child sexual abuse, which had long been under-reported May '88; opposed privatising St Andrews' golf course, long run successfully by the local authority July '88; after the local Piper Alpha disaster, killing 167, urged a wider inquiry than allowed under Scots fatal accident law July '88; protested against an exodus of workers because of low wages and dangerous oil rig practices Aug '88; the press reported a legal action by his brother-in-law, Graham Lamont, demanding repayment of a £15,000 loan and a Law Society investigation of Doran's law firm's financial transactions Sep '88; claimed the Government had failed to carry out its statutory responsibilities on oil rig safety before the Piper Alpha disaster Oct '88; was named an Assistant Spokesman on Energy (Oil and Gas), under Energy Spokesman Tony Blair Nov '88; urged faster compensation for Piper Alpha victims Dec '88; reported sacking of oil worker for reporting safety violations Jan '89; backed confidentiality of social work records Jan '89; praised Scotttish Secretary Malcolm Rifkind for saving 400 jobs by subsidising the building of a ferry at local Hall Russell shipyard Feb '89; failed to secure debate on delayed report into the '87 Chinook helicopter disaster Apr '89; claimed loss of 40% of North Sea oil production through accumulated shutdowns Apr '89; introduced Employers' Liability Bill to require provision of death-in-service insurance benefits Apr '89; tried to mediate with Thomson Newspapers in strike at Aberdeen Journals over NUJ recognition Aug '89; urged Government to support local Raeden Centre for severely handicapped children rather than Budapest's Peto Institute Oct '89; protested Government's failure to release report on previous year's Ocean Odyssey explosion Oct '89; was criticised by Law Society of Scotland's disciplinary tribunal Jan '90; urged expansion of compulsory no-fault compensaton to cover all oil-rig workers Mar '90; sought unsuccessfully to exempt Scotland from lowered limit for abortions, claiming existing Scottish practice was more flexible Apr '90; claimed macho management threats had provoked offshore strikes Sep '90; welcomed support of Cullen Report into Piper Alpha tragedy for union safety representation Nov '90; opposed opt-out of Aberdeen Royal Infirmary from health board control Dec '90; co-opposed military action against Iraq until sanctions had operated longer Jan '91; Dundee Procurator Fiscal submitted a report on his business dealings in Dundee and Edinburgh Jan '91; underlined risk of Aberdeen port privatisation under the Ports Bill Jan '91; urged a no-fault liability scheme to avoid long delays in hospital negligence cases Feb '91; was named as a member of the semi-hard Left 'Supper Club', along with John Prescott, Margaret Beckett and Michael Meacher Feb '91; urged a tougher Health and Safety regime, with its headquarters moved to Aberdeen Mar '91; press reports claimed he had moved in with Joan Ruddock, who had left her husband Mar '91; he sought to keep secret the £2,500 fine of the Scottish Law Society for his professional misconduct over money borrowed from his brother-in-law June '91; complained about cancelled operations caused by underfunding of Aberdeen Royal Infirmary Oct '91; asked why a helicopter flew in a snowstorm, killing 11 oil-rig workers in resultant crash Mar '92; was the only Labour MP to lose his seat - to Raymond Robertson - on a pro-Tory swing of 3. 3% Apr '92; worked for Trade Union Co-ordinating Committee on campaign for political fund ballots which enabled unions to fund Labour Party; also worked as Researcher for Joan Ruddock; seeking selection for the new Aberdeen Central seat, stressed his local campaigning record; defeated veteran Aberdeen North MP, Bob Hughes, by one vote, forcing latter's retirement Oct '95; with five other Labour candidates, was identified by the SCOTSMAN as part of a pro-Blair 'Network" in the Scottish Labour Party Jan '97; after a low-key campaign, won Aberdeen Central by a majority of 10,801, a pro-Labour swing of 8.02% May '97; complained about Aberdeen's 1,500 unemployed under-25s June '97; urged more expenditure on drug abuse in Scotland June '97; asked about 'black' fish July '97; complained about insufficient action on fishing problems July '97;

Born: 13 April 1949, Edinburgh

Family: Son, Francis Anthony Doran, painter and decorator, and Betty (Hedges); m '67 Patricia Ann (Govan), former community worker, later Tayside Regional Councillor; 2s Francis Richard '69, Adrian '71; separated '91; has been close to Joan Ruddock, according to press reports;

Education: Ainslie Park Secondary; Leith Academy; Dundee University (LLB Hons)

Occupation: Researcher, for Joan Ruddock '92-97; Scottish Organiser, for Trade Union Co-ordinating Commitee on Political Fund Ballots (GMB) '92-96; Solicitor, in Dundee and Edinburgh, (specialising in family law and mental health '77-87; no longer practicing) Assistant Editor, Scottish Legal Action Group Bulletin '75-78;

Traits: Slightly-built; dark, receding hair; snub nose; canny-looking; guarded;

Address: House of Commons, Westminster, London SW1A 0AA;

Telephone: 0171 219 3000 (H of C);

David DREW **Labour & Co-operative** **STROUD '97-**

Majority: 2,910 over Conservative 4-way;

Description: The beautiful, slightly-altered Cotswold seat south of Gloucester and north of Bristol, stretching down to the Severn; this sprawling seat is mainly rural, with Stroud as its main town; "some 40% of the work force are still involved in manufacturing" (DD); in '95 it lost Tetbury to the new seat of Cotswold and picked up two wards from Gloucester; until the '97 election it was considered safely Conservative, with Roger Knapman twice registering majorities of about 13,000;

Position: Gloucestershire County Councillor '93-97; ex: Stroud District Councillor '87-95; Stevenage Borough Councillor '81-82; Treasurer, Gloucester CLP; on Executive, of Stroud CLP;

Outlook: An idealistic Christian Socialist lecturer who won a seat only won before by Labour in '45; "an example of Old Labour" (Paul Routledge, INDEPENDENT ON SUNDAY) another of Labour's incoming teacher-councillors; multiple cause groupie: Christian Socialist Movement, Labour Campaign for Electoral Reform, Charter 88, Socialist Educational Association, Labour Party Rural Revival. formerly Anti-Apartheid; National Officer of Economics Association;
History: He joined the Labour Party at 17, '69; was elected to Stevenage Borough Council May '81; was elected to Stroud District Council May '87; campaigned for public housing and to keep open Standish Hospital '91; contested the Stroud Parliamentary seat against incumbent MP Roger Knapman, picking up 4,500 votes to recover second place from the Liberal Democrat but still 13,405 votes behind Knapman Apr '92; was elected to Gloucestershire County Council May '93; was re-selected for Stroud Mar '95; captured the seat for Labour for the first time since 1945, by a majority of 2,910 on a notional swing of 11%, May '97; when he won, Peter Mandelson was said to say, "I never thought he'd win, so I didn't bother to get his name off the [candidates] list" May '97; asked Home Secretary what plans he had to incorporate the European Convention on Human Rights into domestic law May '97; co-congratulated Government on restoring trade union rights to GCHQ May '97; in his Maiden backed the phased release of housing receipts but attacked developers seeking to exploit greenfield sites June '97; asked the Chancellor of the Exchequer if he would review the proposal to end tax relief on profit-related pay, particularly for the first £1,000 of income June '97; urged further compensation for former prisoners of war in Japanee prison camps June '97; co-sponsored motion urging compulsory sprinkler syatems for single-storey supermarkets and superstores July '97; co-sponsored motion deploring difficulties for injured employees of liquidated companies July '97; said on TV that he was "very unhappy" about new tuition burdens on university students and its special impact on those from poorer families Sep '97; urged a debate on how to improve relations between the NHS and local community services Oct '97;
Born: 13 April 1952, South Gloucestershire
Family: Son, of Ronald Montague Drew, company accountant, and Maisie Jean (Elliott), health worker; m 1st Olga (Samson); divorced '89; m 2nd '91 Ann Hilary (Baker) teacher; 2s: Laurence '84, Christopher '91; 2d Amy '82, Esther '92;
Education: Downend C of E Primary; Kingsfield School, Kingswood, Bristol; Nottingham University (BA in Economics); Birmingham University (PGCE); Bristol Polytechnic (MA in Business History, M Ed);
Occupation: Senior Lecturer, in Education, University of the West of England (formerly Bristol Polytechnic) '86-97 (NATFHE); Author, The Electronic Office (1989); previously a school teacher in Stevenage '76-86;
Traits: Parted dark hair; chubby face; moustache; sporty; deeply involved in church affairs; enjoys cycling, Rugby and cricket
Address: House of Commons, Westminster, London SW1A 0AA; 17 Quietways, Stonehouse, Gloucestershire GL10 2NW;
Telephone: 0171 219 6479 (H of C); 01453 825603 (home);

With all the destabilizing constituency changes, we think it necessary to try to have accurate seat descriptions. Some newspapers (like the SCOTSMAN and GLASGOW HERALD), some MPs, and especially The Almanac of British Politics by Robert Waller and Byron Criddle (Routledge), have been particularly helpful.

Julia DROWN **Labour** **SWINDON SOUTH '97-**

Majority: 5,645 over Conservative 6-way;

Description: The more Tory-leaning half of Wiltshire's premier industrial town just off the M4; initially based on the GWR's massive locomotive works, that works' decline has been compensated for by new industries, with a burgeoning population; the '95 split put Swindon's city centre and middle-class housing in this new seat, along with villages from former Devizes; the ex-Tory MP for unified Swindon, Simon Coombs, chose this as more likely to enable him to survive;

Position: On Select Committee on Health '97-; ex: Oxfordshire County Councillor (Vice Chairwoman, its Labour Group and Spokesperson on Social Services) '89-96;

Outlook: "A National Health Service high-flyer before leaving [her job as Finance Director of Radcliffe Infirmary] NHS Trust" (Clare Longrigg, GUARDIAN) in protest against its two-tier state; her aims remain unchanged: "I want to see the restoration of the Health Service and patients seen according to need - not how rich or poor they are" (JD); was a founder-member of of the Campaign to Close Campsfield Detention Centre in Kidlington (her ward as a county councillor); multiple cause groupie: was on Executive of World Development Movement, in Labour Women's Network; Amnesty International, Greenpeace, Friends of the Earth, CND; with Swindon North's Labour MP, Michael Wills, supports a University for Industry, located in Swindon;

History: She joined the Labour Party '86; was elected for Kidlington to Oxfordshire County Council May '89; was selected for the new seat of Swindon South Sep '95; resigned as Finance Director of Radcliffe Infirmary over cuts Apr '96; won Swindon South, ousting Tory MP Simon Coombs by a majority of 5,645, a pro-Labour notional swing of 14.57% May '97; in her Maiden, urged the redevelopment of Princess Margaret Hospital May '97; led a Parliamentary motion calling for the retention of the mutual building society status of Nationwide, based in Swindon June '97; urged drastic overhaul of the "Tories' CSA", to "make the agency foster co-operation between the agency and parents and between parents and children, that it should provide support to families rather than pulling them further apart and be fair to both partners and that it should give proper incentives for people to go to work and to co-operate with the agency" June '97; co-sponsored motion opposing exports of arms to Indonesia July '97; co-sponsored motion to compel installation of sprinkler systems in single-story supermarkets and superstores July '97; was named to the Select Committee on Health July '97; again urged ring-fencing of mutual building societies Aug '97;

Born: 23 August 1962, London

Family: Daughter, of David Drown, picture restorer, and Audrey (Harris) nurse;

Education: Hampstead Comprehensive '73-80; University College, Oxford University (BA in PPE, after starting in Physics); CIPFA;

Occupation: Public Service Accountant (CIPFA): worked for NHS '85-96: as Director of Contracts, Finance and Information at Radcliffe Infirmary (UNISON)'90-96;

Traits: Long straight brown hair; long neck; pleasant-looking; two-dimensional head; a very serious lady; enjoys cinema, music;

Address: House of Commons, Westminster, London SW1A 0AA; 76 York Road, Swindon

SN1 2JU
Telephone: 0171 219 2392 (H of C); 01793 610644 (home); 01793 615444 (constituency);

Maria EAGLE **Labour** **LIVERPOOL-GARSTON '97-**

Majority: 18,417 over Liberal Democrat 7-way;
Description: Southeast Liverpool's most middle-class housing in Woolton and Atherton, out-voted by the poor terraced centre of Garston, the largely-abandoned tower blocks of Netherley and the massive peripheral council estate near Speke airport; it was Conservative-held until 1979, but has registered bigger and bigger Labour majorities, due partly to "the slow death of the Tory party in Liverpool" (ME);
Position: Ex: Chairman, Formby Constituency Labour Party, Secretary, its Women's Section;
Outlook: Energetic Left-of-Centre Merseyside-bred Oxford-educated solicitor; the latest Eagle twin to land, virtually indistinguishable from sister Angela when they wear the same hairstyle; is considered more radical, more heterosexual, less cautious and more witty; with a safe seat, has made up for failing to take Crosby in '92, when her twin took Wallasey; they are the first known set of twins ("we're not identical twins" [ME]) in Parliamentary history; in the Society of Labour Lawyers, Nicaragua Solidarity; in GMB, formerly in TGWU;
History: With her twin sister Angela, was prominent in the Oxford Labour Club, joining the Labour Party '79; became Deputy Co-ordinator of the Capital Transport Campaign under hard-Left activist Jon Lansman '87;; became Secretary of its Women's Section, then Chairman of Formby Labour Party; contesting Conservative-held Crosby - the seat held by Shirley Williams '81-83 - she overtook the LibDem to take 2nd place for Labour, still 14,408 votes behind the Tory incumbent, Sir Malcolm Thornton Apr '92; was selected from an all-women short-list to contest safe Garston to replace its retiring hard-Left MP Eddie Loyden May '95; there was talk of a legal challenge from a local activist who claimed her activities as a local solicitor advising on housing repairs disqualified her Jan '96; she was also attacked by the Liverpool housing chairman, Margaret Clarke, who dubbed such solicitors "piranhas and parasites"; a Militant Labour councillor, George Knibb, brandished a letter signed by Eagle urging council tenants to sue to enforce their rights Feb '96; won the seat with a majority of 18,417, representing a notional swing from the LibDems to Labour of 6.45%; "my dear sister got more votes than me, a higher swing than me, and a bigger majority than me" (ME) May '97; urged women's inclusion in poverty elimination strategies May '97; asked about plans to curb housing fraud May '97; in her witty and articulate Maiden backed the Government's efforts to overcome her constituency's dire housing needs June '97; expressed solidarity with jailed Indonesian union leader June '97; asked about Government's plans to curb housing benefit fraud June '97; urged legal aid for Hillsborough relatives June '97; complained about sportswomen being treated as "second class" and inadequate status for chess, although "Britain is recognised as the best chess-playing nation in the world outside the nations of the former Soviet Union" June '97; co-sponsored motion on the sunken bulk carrier 'MV Derbyshire', one of Eddie Loyden's causes July '97;
Born: 17 February 1961, Bridlington

Family: Younger twin daughter of Andre Eagle, printer, and Shirley (Kirk);
Education: Formby High School; Pembroke College (her sister was at St John's), Oxford University (BA in PPE); Lancaster Gate College of Law (CPE and Law Society Finals);
Occupation: Solicitor. with Stephen Irving & Co (specialising in housing and employment law); formerly with Goldsmith, Williams and Brian Thompson & Partners; previously Press Officer, for Ken Stewart MEP;
Traits: Blonde hair, alternately curled and straight; "I haven't padded my shoulders or practiced shouting or anything" (ME); "I am a lot more cautious, whereas Maria goes flying in, boots first, if she sees an injustice; I like to calculate a bit more first" - Angela; cricketer (represented Lancashire with sister); chess prodigy (played for Lancashire and England; "I have played chess since the age of eight"; "I no longer compete, but I spent 10 to 12 years of my youth competing seriously" [ME]); enjoys weight-training; a rock music fan (her favourite used to be 'Chrissie Hynde and the Pretenders'); more humourous than her strait-laced sister;
Address: House of Commons, Westminster, London SW1A 0AA; 4, Gable Mews, 75 Liverpool Road, Formby, Merseyside L37 6BU;
Telephone: 1017 219 3000 (H of C); 01704 871796 (home):

Huw (William Edmund) EDWARDS **Labour** **MONMOUTH '97-, '91-92**

Majority: 4,178 over Conservative 5-way;
Description: The unaltered seat embracing the soft and fertile green farmland of the Usk and Wye valleys on the Welsh Border; despite the resemblance to South Wales' industrial culture of the former mining valleys of Ebbw Vale, Abertillery and Pontypool, only three per cent of its voters speak Welsh; before the '97 election, it went Labour only twice before: in '66, when Peter Thorneycroft was ousted; Labour's Huw Edwards also won in the May '91 by-election which followed the death of John Stradling Thomas; Edwards defeated Roger Evans then but was ousted by Evans in '92;
Position: On Select Committees: on the Moderisation of the House of Commons '97-, on Welsh Affairs '91-92; on Commons Information Committee '91-92; President, Chepstow Mencap '92-; on Executive of Shelter Cymru '88-91;
Outlook: The return of a low-profile London Welsh Christian Fabian loyalist; a University lecturer specialising in low pay (and part of the Frank Field fan club); in Parliament for Wales Campaign '92-, Labour Campaign for Electoral Reform '91-, Fabian Society '92-;
History: As a student, was influenced by the researches of Frank Field; joined the Labour Party in the '70s; was selected for the impending Monmouth by-election Nov '90; won the seat in the by-election caused by the death of the incumbent Tory, John Stradling Thomas, with the help of a NHS privatisation scare organised by Peter Mandelson; he stuck doggedly to Mandelson's briefs; "at his worst he could be so doggedly determined not to offend the party hierarchy that he would do himself a disservice - his refusal for instance to express his belief in electoral reform for fear it might upset the apple cart, made him look foolish, even if it stemmed from loyal and modest motives" (Patrick Wintour, GUARDIAN); he defeated Roger Evans by 2,406 votes May '91; took his oath in Welsh as well as in English May '91; in his

Maiden said he was "proud to be a Welshman", "born and brought up in a fine Welsh community - the Welsh community in London" and high-lighted the plight of the low-paid June '91; urged a democratically-elected Welsh Assembly June '91; again complained about low pay in Wales July '91; was named to the Select Committee on Welsh Affairs '91; attacked EU Commissioner MacSharry's proposal to cut aid to small farmers in Britain while protecting smaller farmers on the Continent Dec '91; welcomed removal of binary line in higher education, converting the polytechnics into universities Feb '92; was defeated by Roger Evans in the general election by 5,209 votes Apr '92; was re-selected for Monmouth '96; Labour's local popularity was allegedly damaged by the introduction of car-parking permits in Abergavenny, Chepstow and Monmouth by the Labour-dominated Monmouthshire County Council Apr '97; Tony Blair's visit to the constituency was marred by an attempted clownish intervention by the defending Tory incumbent Roger Evans Apr '97; Edwards urged the abolition of school transport charges Apr '97; in their 3rd confrontation, he ousted Roger Evans from Monmouth by a majority of 4,178, on a 7.4% swing May '97; expressed solidarity with jailed Indonesian union leader June '97; asked for official recognition of the Prison Service Union June '97; protested the closure of the Abergavenny Slaughterhouse June '97; asked about safety of bus safety belts June '97; was named to the Select Committee on the Modernisation of the House of Commons July '97; backed element of PR in Welsh Assembly as helping the Welsh Tory Party "which secured no seats but received 20% of the votes at the general election" July '97;

Born: 12 April 1953, London (in the same hospital as John Major)

Family: Son, of Esme and Rev Dr Ifor Edwards; he lives with his sister, a nurse, in Brighton;

Education: Eastfields High School, Mitcham (after 11+ failure); Manchester Polytechnic ("such is his passion for Manchester United that he turned down offers of places at other universities to be near Old Trafford" - Patrick Wintour, GUARDIAN; BA); York University (MA in Social Policy, MPhil);

Occupation: Author: Low Pay in South Wales (1989), Wales in the 1990s, Land of Low Pay (1994); Lecturer in Social Policy: University of Brighton (NATFHE) '92-97, '88-91, Manchester Polytechnic '85-88; Polytechnic of the South Bank '84-85, Sheffield University '83-84, Coventry Polytechnic '80-81; Tutor with the Open University '87-??; Research Associate, Low Pay Unit '85-??;

Traits: Dark; retreating hair; rounded face; "I was very much a son of the Manse and brought up in the London Welsh community" (HE); "handsome looks, youthful energy and informal jacket over the shoulder"; "approachable", likeable and genial", "astonishingly equable temperament", "a mischievous sense of humour" (Patrick Wintour, GUARDIAN); "not a man given to excesses; immensely loyal; a good companion" (friend Keiith Bradley MP); Welsh Congregationalist (in Borough Welsh Congregational Chapel, London, where his father was Minister); Welsh choral singer (in Gwalia Male Voice Choir); sportsman: football (in London Welsh Veterans Football Club; plays striker on the 3rd team of London Welsh), Rugby, tennis, cricket;

Address: House of Commons, Westminster, London SW1A 0AA; 8 College Street, Kemptown, Brighton, East Sussex BN2 1JG;

Telephone: 0171 219 3000 (H of C); 01273 625125 (home);

Clive EFFORD **Labour** **ELTHAM '97-**

Majority: 10,182 over Conservative 6-way;
Description: The long-marginal southern half of southeastern London's borough of Greenwich; the birthplace of Bob Hope, Frankie Howerd, Herbert Morrison and Denis Healey; previously known as Woolwich West, it was held from '75 until '97 by Peter Bottomley; it is a mixture of Tory-leaning middle-class owner-occupier areas plus former local authority council estates like Shooters Hill; although the '95 changes were neutral in effect, Bottomley was shrewd enough to do a 'chicken run' to safety in true-blue Worthing West;
Position: Greenwich Borough Councillor (Chief Whip '90-91, Group Secretary '86-87) '86-
Outlook: Probably the Commons' first cab-driver, he is an advocate of a co-ordinated transport strategy; a local municipal politician with a long record as a caring campaigner: against the privatising of Queen Elizabeth Hospital, for the Greenwich Community Alarm (a scheme providing security for the old at home) for a Job Club (which he ran, to help youong people find work); a proponent of public-private collaboration in the 'Town Centre Manager' scheme in Eltham;
History: He joined the Labour Party '77; set up the Job Club to help young people into employment '80; was elected to Greenwich Borough Council May '86; was elected its Chief Whip May '90; opposed privatisation of services for local royal parks -Eltham Palace and Greenwich Park Aug '91; accused Peter Bottomley of not backing a campaign against building a relief road through Oxleas Wood Oct '91; contested Eltham against Peter Bottomley, cutting his majority from 6,460 to 1,666, with the help of LibDem tactical voters Apr '92; was re-selected to contest Eltham '95; Peter Bottomley did a 'chicken run' to Worthing West Feb '96; won by a majority of 10,182 over his new Conservative opponent, Clive Blackwood May '97; in the first Labour MPs' meeting with the new PM Tony Blair, he demanded urgent moves to stop hospitals running out of beds in winter May '97; called for a public inquiry into the case of Stephen Lawrence, the black youngster murdered by young white thugs May '97; in his Maiden, pointed out that the London Underground would first reach Greenwich in time for the Millenium celebrations; he urged that all local authorities be compelled to participate in a London-wide taxi card scheme but opposed road-pricing as "a poll tax on wheels" June '97; expressed solidarity with jailed Indonesian union leader June '97; introduced his Energy Conservation (Housing) Bill June '97; co-sponsored motion criticising BA for its "intimidatory tactics" against its employees July '97;
Born: 10 July 1958, London
Family: Son, of Stanley Efford, civil servant, and Maureen (Caldwell); is married with two daughters, one of them Alice;
Education: Walworth Comprehensive School;
Occupation: Taxi Driver '86-97 (TGWU: on its Cab Trade Committee; represents the TGWU on the London Taxi Board);
Traits: Dark; full head of hair; bearded; canvassed in "a shiny suit and comfortable shoes" (TIMES); football coach (has a preliminary Football Association Coach's Badge); a lifelong Millwall supporter;
Address: House Commons, Westminster, London SW1A 0AA; 110 Earlshall Road, Eltham,

London SE9
Telephone: 0171 219 3000 (H of C); 0181 850 5744 (home);

Mrs Louise (Joyce) ELLMAN Labour & Co-operative LIVERPOOL-RIVERSIDE '97-

Majority: 21,799 over Liberal Democrat 9-way;
Description: The enlarged Merseyside dockland heart of the hard-hit former premier port city, containing some of its poorest and most deprived areas, with the second highest unemployment rate in the country; it is an amalgamation of former Scotland-Exchange and Toxteth; in the north it embraces both the old dockside Irish Catholic ghetto and the Orangemen of Everton; in the south, multi-racial Toxteth saw the '81 riots; it embraces the Royal Liverpool Philharmonic and Liverpool Institute of Performing Arts;
Position: On the Select Committee on Environment, Transport and Regional Affairs '97-; on Local Government Advisory Committee of Labour's NEC '77-; on Executive, Northwest Regional Labour Party (Chairman '93-) '85-; ex: Lancashire County Councillor (Leader '81-97, Chairman '81-85, Leader, Labour Group '77-97) '70-97; Vice Chairman: of Lancashire Enterprises '83-97, of Leyland Trucks (which saved jobs after Leyland DAF went into receivership); Chairman, Fair Play (Lancashire) '94-97; West Lancashire District Councillor '74-87; Founder member of North West Partnership '92-97;
Outlook: The most experienced of Labour's local government supremos in the '97 intake; a pioneer of public-private collaboration in regional economic development, having set up Lancashire Enterprises as Lancashire County Council's economic regeneration agency; is enthusiastic about European help in economic regeneration in her new constituency; clashed with Jack Straw over abolition of the County Council; self-described as "mainstream"; "always loyal to her leaders, be they Blairite, Smithite or Kinnockite" (RED PEPPER); has taken "the first step towards eventually joining a Blair Government" (David Rose, LIVERPOOL DAILY POST); "tipped for rapid promotion" (JEWISH CHRONICLE); a believer in the thesis that women in politics are different; benefited from one of the few all-women short-lists in a safe Labour seat;
History: She joined the Labour Party at 18, '63; was elected to Lancashire County Council May '70; was elected to West Lancashire District Council May '74; was in the "radical Left, non-Zionist Jewish Socialists' Group" (RED PEPPER); was elected Leader of the Labour Group on Lancashire County Council May '77; she joined the Co-operative Party '78; contested Darwen against Charles Fletcher-Cooke, losing by 13,026 Apr '79; was elected Leader of Lancashire County Council May '81; set up Lancashire Enterprises as Lancashire County Council's economic regeneration agency '82; went on the Executive of the North West Regional Labour Party '85; became Chairman of the North West Regional Labour Party '93; was attacked by Blackpool North's Tory MP, Harold Elletson, for her refusal to contract out residential care services to the private sector '95; was selected over a local candidate from an all-women's short-list to follow Robert Parry in Riverside, Labour's 17th safest seat July '95; was shocked when a jury jailed for rape Owen Oyston, the Labour-supporting millionaire with

a £2.5m holding in Lancashire Enterprises, of which she was Vice Chairman June '96; said, "women are saying to me, 'it's great to see a woman'; they think there's someone who will understand us" Apr '97; retained Riverside, with a majority increased to 21,799 on a notional swing from the LibDems of 3.58% May '97; in her Maiden speech emphasised the continuing need for EU funding to help regenerate the economy of her constituency, with the second highest unemployment in the country June '97; co-sponsored motion criticising Eurotunnel's unsafe open lattice goods wagons June '97; co-sponsored motion congratulating Co-ops for banning alcopops June '97; complained against the removal from Liverpool of its blood centre July '97; was named to the Select Committee on Environment, Transport and Regional Affairs July '97; urged recognition of the North-West Regional Association and the North-West Patnership "which have brought public, private and voluntary sectors together to develop strategies for the region" July '97; the SUNDAY TIMES insinuated that investigations were being considered into the relations between the Lancashire County Council and the training company, Lancashire Enterprise, which had received £30m in contracts, without competitive tendering; she pointed out that her relations with the company had been "at all times non-pecuniary" Oct '97;

Born: 14 November 1945, Manchester

Family: Daughter, of late Harold Rosenberg, and Annie (Goodenday); m '67 Geoffrey David Ellman, pharmacist and District Councillor; 1s, 1d;

Education: Manchester High School for Girls; Hull University (BA Hons); York University (MPhil in Social Administration);

Occupation: Fulltime Leader of Lancashire County Council '81-97; as such held 23 unpaid Directorships in joint public-private companies, including Lancashire Enterprises (restructured and renamed Lancashire County Enterprises in '89), some of which make money from contracts with Lancashire County Council); previously Lecturer in Further Education and Open University Counsellor (NATFHE) '70-76;

Traits: Dark hair; austerely attractive; blue-stocking look; lectures like a severe schoolmistress; "formidable" (FINANCIAL TIMES); she arrives home "too tired to say what she's been doing" (her husband, Geoff); she admits "the house is in a better state than it was when I was here"; Jewish;

Address: House of Commons, Westminster, London SW1A 0AA; 40 Elmers Green, Skelmersdale, Lancashire WN8 6SB;

Telephone: 0171 219 3000 (H of C); 01695 723 669 (home);

TRACKING SCANDALS

By noting the warts in our portraits of MPs, we have long tracked their scandals. Sometimes we have been the first to notice a wart. In the Profumo scandal, we were the first to publish, in 1963, his letter to Christine Keeler in our newsletter, WESTMINSTER CONFIDENTIAL. We pushed another hole in the dam holding back disclosure about the corrupt lobbying activities of the Ian Greer organisation when, in 1989, our PARLIAMENTARY PROFILES volume published, in its profile of Michael Grylls, the fact that he was accepting from Ian Greer an unregistered percentage of all the business referred to Greer's firm. Press Gallery colleagues declined to report this disclosure after Grylls pretended that he was going to sue us for libel. The story seemed to die for a long time until Greer and Neil Hamilton, with the full support of the Major Government, threatened to sue the GUARDIAN. In the preparation for that trial-which-never-happened, it was discovered that Ian Greer changed his whole accounting system when faced with our publication of his secret relationship with Grylls, giving the game away to the GUARDIAN lawyers.

Michael FALLON **Conservative** **SEVENOAKS '97-**

Majority: 10,461 over Labour 7-way;
Description: One of the safest Tory seats, with the highest proportion of professionals and managers in Kent, the largest amount of detached homes and the smallest proportion of council tenants; affluent villages like Westerham feed sleek commuters into London; it is the site of Winston Churchill's former Chartwell home and, until the '95 changes, Hever Castle as well; the seat then lost 10,000 voters to Tonbridge and Malling;
Former Seat: Darlington '83-92
Position: Deputy Spokesman, on Trade and Industry '97-; on Higher Education Funding Council '93-; ex: Under Secretary, for Education '90-92; Whip '90, Assistant Whip '88-90; PPS, to Cecil Parkinson '87-88; Secretary: Conservative Northern Members' Group '83-88, British-Turkish Parliamentary Group '88; Treasurer, Conservative Group for Europe '80-82;
Outlook: The return of a leading innovative intellectual of the Thatcherite hard-Right, welcomed back by William Hague, after shedding his early Europhilism; he finally found a safe seat after more than 15 tries; with Michael Forsyth, he was one of the 'St Andrews Mafia' and a co-founder of the Thatcherite 'No Turning Back' group; he might well have climbed into the Cabinet with his equals and contemporaries, Michael Forsyth and Michal Portillo, had he not lost marginal Darlington to Alan Milburn in '92; he had made his mark as the Thatcher-appointed Minister for Schools '90-92; while pretending to be a 'traditionalist' -extolling the teaching of Latin - his main crusade was to cut the umbilical cord between schools and the LEAs, dominated by the educational Establishment and, often, by Labour-controlled councils; he spent his political interregnum chasing a safe seat while employed part-time on the Higher Education Founding Council; he also wrote Rightwing pamphlets, including one urging decrepit schools to lease new premises from private 'education parks'; he was also a Director of Quality Care Home Plc; he was considered a "splendid fellow" by Alan Clark, not least for saying of the supergun barred from export to Iraq, "we should be making them and selling them to everyone";
History: At St Andrews he was in the Federation of Conservative Students, identified with Dr Madsen Pirie, later Director of the Adam Smith Institute '72-73; went to work assisting Tory peers, assisting at the politicisation of the Lords '75; co-wrote 'The Quango Explosion' '78; wrote 'Sovereign Members?' '82; was selected for marginal Darlington July '82; at Durham University debate in support of Michael Heseltine was very hostile to unions Feb '83; was telephoned by Mrs Thatcher after he narrowly lost the Darlington by-election to Labour's Ossie O'Brien to congratulate him on a good fight without false promises Mar '83; won Darlington at the general election June '83; voted to restore capital punishment for all categories of killings July '83; on MPs' pay increases, was one of only two MPs to vote against the complete package July '83; urged diversion of money from 'sunset' industries in Darlington to small-scale 'sunrise' industries July '83; urged northeast be guaranteed 30% of regional development grants July '83; backed US intervention in Grenada Oct '83; urged cuts in business rates and index-linked pensions with proceeds to go to 'sunrise' industries Oct '83; backed import of cheap coal for CEGB Nov '83; opposed nuclear dumping at Billingham Nov '83; backed Newcastle-London BR electrification Nov '83; attacked "whingeing pessimism" of

union-dominated northeastern Labour MPs Dec '83; backed forcing councils to release lands for factories to create jobs Dec '83; urged incentives to encourage firms in assisted areas with spare cash to invest in small new local companies Feb '84; was one of 40 Tory MPs to rebel against a Government deal to allow the contracting out system for the unions' political levy to continue Apr '84; forced a debate on increases in Northumbrian water charges May '84; announced a monthly 'Golden Fleece' award for misuse of public funds -starting with Tyne Council fund for striking miners June '84; backed Edward Leigh's amendment to Trade Union Bill to bar ballot-rigging July '84; visited USA as its Government's guest Sep '84; urged a break-up of the NCB, not the NUM, since most miners were "hard-working, patriotic and law-abiding to a fault" Oct '84; led a Parliamentary motion urging the BBC's license fees be replaced by advertising Nov '84; urged sale of poorer polys to save the rest Nov '84; opposed Sir Keith Joseph's attempt to increase parental contributions to grants, preferring loans Nov '84; co-urged end of closed shop, scrapping of works councils and pruning of health and safety measures to mop up the 3m unemployed Dec '84; voted against fluoridation Jan '85; with Piers Merchant, wrote that the northeast lacked private not public investment, therefore it had to be made more attractive by low wages and an end to restrictive practices Feb '85; his local party, disagreeing with his opposition to regional aid, urged Government to reconsider "savage" regional aid cuts Mar '85; complained that his local firm, Cleveland Bridges, had lost its bid for the Bosphorus Bridge because its Japanese competitor had offered softer credit terms May '85; urged legislation to curb unemployment benefit in the south, using the money to generate work in the north July '85; co-authored 'No Turning Back', the manifesto of the Thatcherite hard-Right, urging privatisation of hospitals and schools Nov '85; denying anti-Thatcher plots, insisted "I am a fully paid-up supporter of the PM" Feb '86; urged increased funding for Marriage Guidance Council Mar '86; warned Minister of "strong resentment" in northeast if Belfast's Harland & Wolff secured £240m destroyer contract instead of Swan-Hunter Mar '86; urged cut in more generous Scottish teachers' pay Apr '86; complained that Ministers were blocking Mrs Thatcher's radical reforms, with some Whips regarding Thatcherism as "a political craze like skateboarding whose time will pass" Aug '86; backed Edwina Currie's criticisms of northern eating and drinking habits Sep '86; was the only Tory backbencher to rebel openly against the Chancellor's Autumn Statement, complaining that the Star Chamber had become "the school tuck shop" Nov '86; demanded an end to subsidies for Southern Rail Jan '87; tried to amend the Coal Industry Bill to end the NCB monopoly Jan '87; attacked Leyland Truck-DAF deal as handing the Dutch firm a major share of the UK component market Feb '87; urged privatisation of 10,000 empty council houses in the northeast Mar '87; voted to restore capital punishment Apr '87; retained seat with a drop of over 500 in his majority June '87; backed poll tax but urged single-tier local government July '87; became PPS to Cecil Parkinson '87; urged lower government spending, including cuts in "our well-appointed encampment on the Rhine" Sep '87; criticised the Government's sale of part of a northeast new town to a London property company rather than allow a local management buy-out Oct '87; defended teaching of Latin in schools Nov '87; signed motion congratulating Turkey on free elections Dec '87; urged a debate on "secretive" allocation by Liaison Committee of £300,000 a year for foreign trips by select committees Jan '88; opposed Scottish Assembly as entrenching public ownership Jan '88; visited Paris as guest of Air Europe Feb '88; pressed for abolition of Dock Labour Scheme Mar '88; visited Turkey as guest of its National Assembly Apr '88; was named an Assistant Whip '88; was promoted Government Whip '90; was named Under Secretary for Education '90; led efforts to detach primary and secondary schools from LEA control; he gave 24,000 schools their own budgets '90-92; lost Darlington to Labour's Alan Milburn by 2,798 votes Apr '92; in a paper for the Social Market Foundation, 'Brighter Schools', urged they be allowed to borrow money from the private sector for capital spending, an idea later taken up by Education Secretary John Patten Nov '93; was appointed, with Francis Maude, to the Deregulation Task Force July '94; in an article in the INDEPENDENT he urged that private caring companies, like the one of which he was a Director, be allowed to run entire hospitals June '95; in his long search for a safe seat, was pipped at Woking by Humfrey Malins Sep '95; failed to be selected for Kensington and Chelsea Nov '95; also failed to be chosen for Bromley, Horsham and Runnymede Nov '95; failed to be selected for Worthing West, where he was beaten by Peter Bottomley Jan '96; finally - after more than 15 tries - was selected for safe Sevenoaks, on the retirement of Mark Wolfson '96; although previously pro-European, opposed a single European currency in his election address Apr '97; won Sevenoaks by 10,461 - down from 19,154 - a swing from the Conservatives of 10.33% May '97; in his second Maiden speech, deplored the "social authoritarianism" of the Blair Government; also deeply deplored the proposal to incorporate the European Convention on Human Rights into UK's legal system May '97; urged that, in Leadership contests, Tory MPs' votes should be recorded along with ballots from their constituency parties May '97; in a barrage of questions, urged that Scottish servicemen and other Scots outside Scotland be allowed to vote in the devolution referendum June '97; spoke twice against the Referendum Bill June '97; was named a Deputy Spokesman on Trade and Industry in the Shadow Cabinet of the new Leader, William Hague June '97; asked David Blunkett whether fair funding meant that "Kent's existing grammar schools could face suden death if there were local ballots?" July '97; attacked Labour's policies on the Information Society July '97;

Born: 14 May 1952, Perth

Family: Son, Martin Fallon, OBE, FRCSI, convivial Perth-based Irish surgeon, and Hazel, former almoner of Inchture, Perthshire; his parents separated; his two brothers are farmers; m '86 Wendy Elizabeth (Payne), former Assistant Group Secretary to Darlington NFU; 2s;

Education: Epsom College; St Andrews University (BA Hons in Classics and Ancient History);

Occupation: Director: of Just Learning Ltd '96-, Quality Care Homes Plc '92-; on Higher Education Funding Council '93-, on Advisory Council of Social Market Foundation '94-; on Government's Deregulation Task Force '94-97; Author: Brighter Schools (1993), The Rise of Euroquango (1992), Sovereign Members? (1982), The Quango Explosion (1978; jointly); ex: Adviser, to Jepson & Co '87-88; Lecturer, on Public Sector Policy Making '81-83; Joint Managing Director, CSM European Consultants Ltd '79-81; Assistant, to Baroness Elles '79-83; EEC Officer, Conservative Research Department '77-79; Secretary, Lord Home's Committee on Future of the Lords '77-78; Assistant, in Conservative Whips' Office '75-77; Assistant to Lord Carrington '74-77;

Traits: Tall, dark, thin, boyish; "coolly cerebral" (Robin Oakley); "cool and serious, not a man to readily engage in small talk" (INDEPENDENT); "fluent", "patronising" (Peter Riddell, FINANCIAL TIMES); "being clever, sarcastic and abrasive, he is not the most popular MP" (Simon Heffer, DAILY TELEGRAPH); "opponents see him as crashingly ambitious, patronising and arrogant" (NEWCASTLE JOURNAL); "snide, bitter, sneering, cynical" (Tory colleague); "unimaginably unpopular" (Edward Pearce, SUNDAY TELEGRAPH); squash player; swimmer; convivial; litigious (won substantial damages from PRIVATE EYE);

Address: House of Commons, Westminster, London SW1A 0AA;

Telephone: 0171 219 3000 (H of C);

'Ronnie' (Ronald Cyril) FEARN OBE **Liberal Democrat** **SOUTHPORT '97-, '87-92**

Majority: 6,160 over Conservative 7-way;
Description: Attractive, genteel, upmarket Merseyside seaside resort from which the sea has retreated; it retains its shrimp industry, but has become mainly a commuting base for affluent Merseysiders; long a Liberal-Tory seesaw seat, the tide came in again in '97 for the Liberals' seven-time candidate 'Ronnie' Fearn;
Position: On the Select Committee on National Heritage '97-; LibDem Spokesman on Tourism '97-, '88-92; Sefton Metropolitan Borough Councillor '74-; ex: on Select Committee on Parliamentary Commissioner for Administration '87-92; Spokesman: on Local Government, Housing, Transport '89-92, Health and Social Security '87-89; Deputy Whip '87-88;
Outlook: The popular local councillor and "Comeback Kid" who became an able Commons Spokesman; a veteran local bank manager, pantomime Dame and multi-councillor, who was brought back to provide 'one last heave' successfully in '87, a feat he repeated a decade later; a progressive on almost everything but abortion;
History: He joined the Liberal Party '60; was elected to Sefton Borough Council May '63; won a seat on Merseyside County Council May '73; contested Southport in June '70, February and October 1974, and May '79, when he took 38%; having been replaced by Ian Brodie-Brown for the June '83 general election, he was selected by STV on the first count at a crowded joint Liberal-SDP meeting of 200, July '84; campaigned as 'Mr Southport', capturing the seat on a pro-Liberal swing of 6.7%, June '87; urged profit-sharing for beauty contestants June '87; opposed abortion on demand July '87; urged control of embryo research July '87; warned that sewage privatisation would threaten UK beaches and tourism July '87; disagreed with Cyril Smith on Liberals' intention of obliterating the breakaway SDP Aug '87; warned that the poll tax would involve gangs of "snoopers" Sep '87; was named Deputy Whip Oct '87; backed Bill to make obligatory rear seatbelts for children Oct '87; asked about possible link between local child leukaemia and Sellafield's nuclear contamination of beaches Nov '87; attacked decision to charge for dental and optical tests Nov '87; unsuccessfully asked Mrs Thatcher to smile Jan '88; voted for 2nd Reading of David Alton's abortion-curbing Bill Jan '88; again urged caution on embryo research Feb '88; opposed the new Social Fund as a "bureaucratic nightmare destined to cause chaos" Feb '88; urged Government to match private money in fighting AIDS Feb '88; urged uprating of child benefit Mar '88; gave qualified approval to Government fund for haemophiliac AIDS sufferers Mar '88; condemned TV failure to broadcast Mother Teresa's anti-abortion statements Apr '88; urged Government to allow additional time for abortion debate May '88; backed Ashdown against Beith in LibDem Leadership contest May '88; backed free optical and dental checkups July '88; urged inquiry into selective prosecution of drug cases Aug '88; was named Health and Tourism Spokesman by the new Leader, Paddy Ashdown Sep '88; in debate on 'Care in Community' urged "a genuine partnership between clients, carers, the state and the voluntary and private sectors" Apr '89; urged a unified family court system Apr '89; said neglect of mentally ill was "an appalling indictment for a country" Apr '89; attacked smoking in public May '89; attacked Government's failure on food research as having "put the botch into botulism" June '89;

attacked use of controversial cyclotron machine to treat cancer June '89; urged condoms be provided for prison inmates June '89; proposed NHS funding of 2% above inflation July '89; at annual LibDem conference, presented party policy of ban on tobacco and alcohol advertising Sep '89; again attacked Government's dental test charges Oct '89; was replaced as Health Spokesman by Charles Kennedy, becoming Spokesman on Local Government, Housing, Transport and Tourism Oct '89; revealed his membership of the National Union of Seamen Nov '89; said, "our streets and alleyways have become living testimony to the indifference and harshness marking the Thatcher decade" Nov '89; in '88-89, was rated the 21st most assiduous questioner among MPs Nov '89; insisted the country was too small to allow the population to own and travel in cars unhampered Nov '89; urged curbs on use of firearms by private security guards at ports Jan '90; backed Michael Mates' Bill to ensure prompt payment of bills Feb '90; urged resignation of disgraced Tory MP John Browne Mar '90; backed LibDem local income tax against poll tax Apr '90; joined London homeless for a night Nov '90; backed random breath-testing Dec '90; urged an end to badger-baiting Feb '91; called for the voters of Walton to give Labour "a boot up the arse" in the pending by-election Jan '91; attacked use of Vagrancy Act as "turning the homeless into criminals" Nov '91; pressed for owner-occupiers to be allowed to convert mortgages into rental to avoid repossession Feb '92; predicted the victory of 45 LibDem MPs, who would have to be consulted over how "to play a hung Parliament" Apr '92; lost his seat to his Tory opponent Matthew Banks by 3,063 votes, on a pro-Tory swing of 4.5%, allegedly due to a fears of a Labour victory nationally Apr '92; re-selected for Southport, his campaign was marred by Tory and Labour charges that leaflets urging tactical voting for him did not come from legitimate Labour Party supporters Apr '97; was elected with a majority of 6,160, on a swing of 8.85%, May '97; urged better access to museums for the disabled May '97; urged limits on transmitter masts for cellular phones June '97; as a member of Sefton's Sports Council, urge help in financing a new running track for the Merseyside June '97; co-sponsored motion urging settlement of claims of nuclear test victims June '97; co-sponsored motion attacking over-medication of the elderly June '97; urged exhuming of local authorities' artworks "many of which have not come out for 50 years" July '97; was named to Select Committee on National Heritage July '97;

Born: 8 February 1931, Southport

Family: Son, late James Fearn, master decorator, and Martha Ellen (Hodge); m '55 Joyce Edna (Dugan), salaries clerk with Sefton Health Authority, later his Personal Assistant; 1s, Martin John '62, 1d Susan Lynn '59;

Education: Norwood Road County Primary School, Southport; King George V Grammar Shool, Southport (where Kenneth Baker was a classmate); FCIB;

Occupation: Director, of Merseyside Enterprise Board Ltd; retired Assistant Bank Manager, with William Deacons Bank, Williams & Glyn's Bank, Royal Bank of Scotland (NUBE/BIFU) '50-87; ex-Chairman, Southport Area Institute of Bankers;

Traits: Dark banker's clothes in the Commons, colourful clothes at leisure; rugged good looks; greying dark hair; former "part-time panto turn" starring as a Dame in '86; camp style: "a voice and manner heavily reminiscent of John Inman in 'Are You Being Served' (Edward Pearce, DAILY TELEGRAPH); "that's right, Ronnie, hit 'em with your handbag!" (Norman Tebbit MP); "the Larry Grayson of the House" (Andrew Rawnsley, GUARDIAN); gives a "vocal impersonation of the late Gracie Fields' hairdresser" (Simon Heffer, DAILY TELEGRAPH); long-winded ("most interventions... are several hours long and in a language most of us don't speak" (INDEPENDENT);

Address: House of Commons, Westminster, London SW1A 0AA; 56 Northwood Avenue, Southport, Merseyside PR9 7EQ;

Telephone: 0171 219 3000 (H of C); 01704 28577;

'Jim' (James) FITZPATRICK **Labour** **POPLAR & CANNING TOWN '97-**

Majority: 18,915 over Conservative 6-way;
Description: A new seat in London's East End dockland, made up of wards from former Newham South and Bow and Poplar; for the first time it crosses the age-old boundary between Middlesex and Essex to cover an area separated by the River Lea; mainly a working-class seat, with some yuppified London Docklands developments; it has a large Bangladeshi minority; Poplar includes the Isle of Dogs, in whose Millwall ward a BNP candidate won a by-election in '93, reversed by Labour in '94;
Position: Chairman, Greater London Labour Party '91-; on Executive Council, of Fire Brigades Union '88-; ex: Parliamentary Agent, to Jo Richardson MP '86-91;
Outlook: Low-profiled Scots-born ex-Trotskyist, most of whose political and working life has been spent in the Left-dominated Fire Brigades Unon; has recently been seen as "an ally of Tony Blair" (TIMES); an "accomplished compromiser who keeps his options open - feared to lack strength of personality to retain political independence and may fall at first offer of patronage" (RED PEPPER); an internationally-focussed multi-cause groupie: Amnesty International, War on Want, Action in Southern Africa, El Salvador Solidarity Campaign, Nicaragua Solidarity Campaign, Greenpeace; in the Co-operative Party as well as the FBU;
History: Was active in the Fire Brigades Union, from '74; joined the Labour Party '76; was in the Socialist Workers Party '78-79; rejoined the Labour Party '82; became Parliamentary Agent for Labour MP, Jo Richardson '86; was elected to Executive of Greater London Labour Party '88; was elected Chairman of Greater London Labour Party '91; "was gazumped for inheritance [of Barking from Jo Richardson] by Margaret Hodge" (RED PEPPER) '94; was selected for merged Poplar and Canning Town, defeating both incumbent MPs, Mildred Gordon and Nigel Spearing, resulting in both retiring from the Commons Aug '95; with other loyal candidates, insisted Labour was a "united dynamic party ready to solve the problems this country faces" Oct '96; was elected, with a majority of 18,915 on a pro-Labour notional swing of 11.33% May '97; in closed initial meeting of new PLP, asked about timetable for legislation to create a new-style GLC for London May '97; co-sponsored motion deploring the sale by London Docklands Development Corporation of land planned for use by the Civilians Remembered Campaign to honour the sacrifices of London's civilian population during the 2nd World War May '97; expressed solidarity with jailed Indonesian union leader June '97; congratulated Peabody Trust for introducing solar power in Silvertown June '97; co-sponsored motion calling for the "immediate outlawing of hunting animals with hounds" June '97; in his Maiden concentrated on sports for all June '97; co-sponsored motion urging a public inquiry into Westminster City Council June '97; co-sponsored motion backing compulsory fire sprinklers in single-storey supermarkets and superstores July '97;
Born: 4 April 1952, Glasgow
Family: Son, of James Fitzpatrick, driver, and Jean (Stones), secretary; m '80 Jane (Lowe) teacher; 1s James '81, 1d Helen '82;
Education: Holy Cross School, Daisy Street, Glasgow; Holyrood Secondary School, Glasgow;
Occupation: Fireman ("mostly at Battersea fire station" [JF]) and lay FBU official '74-97; ex:

Driver, in London '73-74, Trainee, in motor component company, in Glasgow '70-"73;
Traits: Parted greying brown hair; poker-faced; clean-cut; neatly groomed; serious-minded; introverted; RC origins; enjoys soccer, golf and cycling; on the Parliamentarians' football team; is a West Ham season ticket-holder;
Address: House of Commons, Westminster, London SW1A 0AA; 71 Shirley Gardens, Barking, Essex IG11 9XB;
Telephone: 0171 219 5085 (H of C); 0850 764022 (mobile);

Lorna FITZSIMONS **Labour** **ROCHDALE '97-**

Majority: 4,545 over Liberal Democrat 5-way;
Description: Greater Manchester's former textile town, long a battleground between Labour and Liberal Democrats, with most local Tories voting tactically to keep Labour out of office; for 20 years the Conservatives kept in power the massive figure of Liberal Cyril Smith, indisputably working-class by origin and Labour in his first loyalty; although his successor became increasingly virulently anti-Labour, she failed to breast '97's pro-Labour tide; although Rochdale lost two wards and gained two wards in the '95 changes, the overall effect appeared to be neutral;
Position: On Executive of Labour Co-ordinating Committee '95-; ex: President, National Union of Students '92-94;
Outlook: A young, very ambitious home town girl who broke the LibDems' quarter-century hold on her first try; a lobbyist who made her name first as an NUS President; very flexible: in 'Women for Gould' in '92, but a Blairite by '94; "very much a member of Labour's new model army" (INDEPENDENT ON SUNDAY); "I am a moderniser firmly in the Blair wing of the party, and I suppose I embody New Labour" (LF); is impressed by Blair's "huge presence"; a supporter of electoral reform; "a power-mad parasite, a supreme factionalist" with "an embarrassing penchant for power-dressing"; "intellectual debate is not her forte"; "laughable self-importance is inevitably underscored by a strong streak of paranoia"; "transparently and justifiably insecure" ('Class Traitor of the Month', Trotskyist LABOUR BRIEFING); in the Labour Industry Forum, the Fabian Society, Labour Women's Network, and the Co-operative Party;
History: She joined the Labour Party at 18, '85; was in the 'Democratic Left' caucus of the National Organisation of Labour Students (NOLS) '85-94; in succession to Stephen Twigg, she was elected President of the National Union of Students '92; she was re-elected despite the stiff opposition of student Trotskyists, who dismissed her as a "bourgeois bitch" Apr '93; introduced a Students' Charter and backed a Graduate Tax; denies she ever said, "John Patten is a man I can do business with"; this certainly became impossible when he targeted the NUS; her proud boast was that she fought off the '94 effort of the Education Secretary to shut down the NUS by ending its closed-shop status; "we opted for being unconventional and threw the traditional image of 1968 out of the window"; "they tried to shut us down and we were the only Labour-led collective organisation to defeat them in seventeen years"; was selected as Labour's candidate for her home town of Rochdale, to oust the LibDem incumbent, Liz Lynne, successor to Cyril Smith Apr '96; after her selection, PR WEEK misquoted her as saying the

reason she wanted to be an MP was to help her lobbying company's clients: "the value to Rowland's clients is that they've got one more person in the House who really understands them" June '96; she then rejected the implications of this misquoting, saying "if elected, I plan to drop all consultancy work (because), as the practices of the few have shown, paid consultancies devalue Parliament" Oct '96; co-signed letter of loyalist Labour candidates insisting Labour was a "united dynamic party ready to solve the problems this country faces" Oct '96; in the election campaign defended her smart dressing as part of the working-class ethic: "where I come from, putting your best clothes on - your Sunday best - is what you do when you want to make an effort for people you respect, as I do the people of Rochdale" Apr '97; was elected as Rochdale's first Labour MP in 25 years by a majority of 4,545 votes over Liz Lynne, a notional swing of 4.8% May '97; in her Maiden, emphasised Rochdale's high youth unemployment May '97; backed a ban on fox-hunting June '97; loyally defended the Government's Finance Bill, insisting that, from her work as a lobbyist, she knew the utilities could easily cope with the windfall tax July '97; favoured lowering the age of gay consent to 16 July '97; pointed out that free universal higher education did not exist because 2m "Open University students, part-time students and further education students have always paid fees" July '97;

Born: 6 August 1967, Wardle, Rochdale

Family: Daughter, of Derek Fitzsimons. millworker, and Barbara (Taylor), who "works at a garage called Grimes Motor Bodies";

Education: Wardle High School; Rochdale College of Art; Loughborough College of Art and Design (textile design);

Occupation: Political Consultant, with Rowland Sallingbury Casey (PR subsidiary of Saatchi and Saatchi, whose Chairman was Tory MP John Maples) (MSF) '94-97; on Quality Committee of Further Education Funding Council '93-94; previously NUS President '92-94;

Traits: Very short ("my mum's smaller and my gran's even smaller"); loud ("although I am only 5 feet tall, I do not need a microphone"); parted red hair; short back and sides; freckled; chubby face; big specs; broad-smiling; flirtatious ("I'm an immensely sexual person but you do have to be careful these days as you don't want to be exploited for the wrong reasons; I realise that I can't do the things I used to do; I can't have alfresco sex, three-in-a-bed or get totally out of it on drugs -not that I did"; "generally if I want to go to bed with somebody I tell them; if I want to do something particularly gross with them, I tell them; if I don't, I tell them" (LF in NEWS OF THE WORLD); bouncy; "Rochdale's Mrs Merton" (PRIVATE EYE): dyslexic; clothes-conscious power-dresser; talks very fast (200 wpm: "John Prescott on acid" - a contemporary); local accent ("you can call me dead northern"); enjoys hill-walking, playing the horn ("I am a secret horn player"), listening to jazz, classical and modern music;

Address: House of Commons, Westminster, London SW1A 0AA; 310 Ramsden Road, Rochdale, OL12 9NJ; London flat;

Telephone: 0171 219 3000 (H of C); 018442 8289 (Home); 0171 323 0221 (work);

Howard (Emerson) FLIGHT Conservative ARUNDEL & SOUTH DOWNS '97-

Majority: 14,035 over Liberal Democrat 4-way;
Description: A new West Sussex seat comprised of a ragbag from five previous constituencies; a collection of Arundel and other affluent small Tory towns and villages lying behind the urbanised coastal strip; Arundel is dominated by the great castle of the loyally Conservative Duke of Norfolk, the premier Catholic peer;
Position: On the Select Committee on Environment, Transport and Regional Affairs '97-; ex: Chairman, Putney Conservative Political Centre '84-94; Vice Chairman, Thamesfield ward, Putney Conservative Association '79-82; Vice Chairman and CPC Organiser, Vauxhall Conservative Association '74-77; Vice Chairman, Federation of Conservative Students '69; Chairman, Cambridge University Conservative Association '68-69; Vice Chairman of Little Waltham and Great Leighs Young Conservatives '64-65;
Outlook: Self-described "Essex man": extrovert, Rightwing and ambitious ("I'd like to be Chancellor of the Exchequer"); a Eurosceptic investment manager; "I've always been a passionate believer in capitalism; to me it is like a Bach fugue - a wonderfully complicated thing which has come about naturally and works" (HF); "has never experienced a moment of self-doubt"; has "incredible confidence in his own abilities" (Judi Bevan, DAILY TELEGRAPH); "a genuine English eccentric with the capacity to come up with big ideas; he has stamina and courage, but he is not a quiet or restful soul" (Sir Alastair Morton); a supporter of Conservative Family Campaign, Freedom Association, Selsdon Group; has former links to Lord (Norman) Tebbit; backed John Redford for the Leadership; believes in privatising most social services; self-described "a specialist in the history and theory of exchange rates" (HF) and an advocate of radical tax and spending cuts;
History: He was politically active from his school days, becoming Vice Chairman of the Little Waltham and Great Leighs Young Conservatives at 16, '64; was elected Chairman of Cambridge University Conservative Association, with David Mellor, Richard Ryder, Roger Evans, John Watts and William Powell on his Committee '68; became Vice Chairman of the Federation of Conservative Students '69; helped Norman Tebbit in the general election in Epping June '70; became Vice Chairman of the Vauxhall Conservative Association '74; fought against Bob Mellish for hopeless Bermondsey, gaining 17% and 14% of the vote, Feb and Oct '74; helped candidate William Powell win the new seat of Corby June '83; became Personal Consultant to Norman Tebbit at DTI 83; became Chairman of the Putney CPC '84; assisted John Maples in Lewisham West June '87; was on Tax Consultative Committee at Treasury from '88; again assisted John Maples in Lewisham West in lost campaign of Apr '92; was selected for new safe seat of Arundel and South Downs, the Tories' 33rd safest Mar '96; urged Tories to cut the Government's percentage of GDP spending from 40% to 35% to "give the economy a vital shot in the arm"; "state pensions should be privatised"; "sickness and unemployment benefit should be transferred to the private sector" Sep '96; was among the Tories' most Eurosceptic candidates, telling the DAILY TELEGRAPH his manifesto would oppose ever joining a single European currency Dec '96; urged a 20% top tax rate Mar '97; said, "a common currency would be a disaster on a huge scale; it would be like Italy on a large scale...imagine it!" "I do not wish to become part of a United States of Europe" Mar '97; said,

"if there are 25 Conservative MPs after the election, I should be one of them" Mar '97; after his handsome victory, said "I would have thought that Redwood is the best candidate" and served on his campaign team May '97; after Redwood was defeated, voted for Ken Clarke June '97; asked how HMG would obtain "the balance of compensation owed by Iraq to former British hostages held in Kuwait, following the Iraqi invasion in 1990" June '97; introduced his Bill to exempt the 75-plus from paying for TV licenses July '97; like all other Tory MPs, criticised the abolition of ACT refunds in the Budget July '97; was named to the Select Committee on Environment, Transport and Regional Affairs July '97;

Born: 16 June 1948, Romford

Family: "My father's father was a rampant socialist and I would argue furiously with him; I thought it was all rubbish from an early age" (HF); son, of late Bernard Thomas Flight, head of Westminster Bank's Trustee Department for East Anglia, and Doris Mildred Emerald (Parker); m '73 Christabel Diana (Norbury), Sotheby cataloguer; "we are both Gemini and it works extremely well; we fight like cat and dog when required but are all friends again in no time"; "her mother was an enormous Prussian opera singer while her father was a delightful Worcestershire fruit farmer" (HF); 1s, Thomas '78, 3d: Catherine '75, Josephine '86, Mary Anne '88;

Education: Brentwood School, Essex '59-66; Magdalene College, Cambridge University '66-69 (MA History & Economics); Michigan University '69-71(Power Scholar; MBA);

Occupation: Deputy Chairman, of Guinness Flight Hambro Asset Management '97-; Author: All You Need to Know About Exchange Rates (Sidgwick & Jackson; 1988)); ex: Managing Director, of Guinness Flight Global Asset Management Ltd (set up with Tim Guinness; 63% owned by merchant bank Guinness Mahon; acquired the fund management business of Hambros to create a group with £9.3b under management) '86-97; Director, of Guinness Mahon '79-87; Investment Adviser: to Hongkong & Shanghai Bank, in Hongkong and India '77-79, to Cayzer '73-76, N M Rothschilds & Sons '70-73;

Traits: Tall; thinning hair; long oval face; big cheery grin; plummy voice; "Paisley braces and hitched-up pin-striped trousers"; "exudes huge amounts of energy"; "his energy is possibly his greatest strength; he can happily work 15 hours a day as long as he has his weekends with the family in the Worcester farm Christabel inherited"; "his voice is a cross between a Hooray Henry bray and a klaxon, effortlessly running up and down the octaves and carrying well above the rowdiest of gatherings"; "he likes running things, possessing the kind of confident energy that makes people gratefully hand over responsibility"; "he owes his dark, exotic looks to Welsh blood" (Judi Bevan, DAILY TELEGRAPH); a 40-a-day smoker; almost died from typhoid in India in '78; collects Flight and Barr Worcester china; enjoys skiing, classical music and architecture; has a liking for vivid phraseology: he described his negotiations with Hambros: "we smelt each other's bottoms and decided that we fit together quite well" (HF);

Address: House of Commons, Westminster, London SW1A 0AA; 6 Ruvigny Gardens, Putney London SW15 1JR;

Telephone: 0171 219 3000 (H of C); 0171 522 2112 (work); 0181 789 0923 (home); 0181 787 0723 (Home Fax);

UNEXPECTED REACTIONS

One can never predict the reaction of MPs to recording what they disclose about themselves to a lightly-attended House, forgetting about HANSARD reporters and TV cameras. We wrote sympathetically about two former Conservative MPs, one of whom overcame congenital deafness and the other born spastic. To our double astonishment, the first cursed us out to local TV reporters, the other enthused about the sympathy expressed.

Caroline (Louise) FLINT **Labour** **DON VALLEY '97-**

Majority: 14,659 over Conservative 7-way;
Description: A kidney-shaped seat curling around the south side of Doncaster, embracing mainly the former pit villages in the dying Yorkshire coalfield; still safely Labour despite the '83 changes and the '95 loss of Labour-voting Mexborough, which was expected to produce a 7,000 majority on '92 projections; one of its two castles is Conisbrough, the Saxon setting for 'Ivanhoe', penned locally by Sir Walter Scott;
Position: On Select Committee on Education and Employment '97-; Chairman: Working for Childcare '91-95, Brentford and Isleworth CLP '91-95; National Women's Officer, National Organisation of Labour Students '83-85;
Outlook: Youngish Londoner and GMB staffer who stole a march on others and won a former Yorkshire NUM seat, becoming its first woman and non-miner; Blairite ("Associate Editor of Blairite in-house journal RENEWAL" - NEW STATESMAN); in the Fabian Society;
History: She joined the Labour Party at 17, '78; she was elected Head of the Women's Unit of the National Union of Students '83; was short-listed for the Barnsley East by-election following the death of its Labour MP Terry Patchett Dec '96; "I put in for Don Valley at the outset of the selection process when Martin Redmond announced his retirement in November 1996, cold-calling on party and branch officers and members; as a result, unlike most outside candidates, I was invited to half the branches; as the situation developed following Martin's death and the publicity caused by the District Auditor's report concerning councillors' expenses and trips, more outside candidates threw their hats in the ring; at the NEC short-listing, I had the second largest number of nominations (4); by the time of the hustings, I had spoken to over 300 members - three-quarters of the eligible members"; the NEC imposed a short-list of four (others: displaced Glasgow MP Mike Watson, RMT official Mark Walker and AEEU Convenor Cath Ashton; a popular local councillor was excluded because of his foreign free-tripping); "I won on the first ballot with over 50% of the vote, 70 votes ahead of the second-placed candidate" Feb '97; won the seat with a majority of 14,659, twice that expected, on a swing of 9.91%, despite 1,000 votes going to a Scargillite May '97; urged discounts for people going to national museums, and local ones like Don Valley's Earth Centre June '97; in her Maiden speech strongly supported improved education standards June '97; asked about tackling "anti-social behaviour within neighborhoods" June '97; asked that convicted child sex offenders "are not placed on community work programmmes which bring them into direct contact with children" June '97; asked about wolf hybrids July '97; complained that "it still takes up to two years to remove an incompetent teacher from the classroom" July '97; was named to the Select Committee on Education and Employment July '97; endorsed Home Secretary Jack Straw's stricter approach after an evening with the local police; "what emerged from that evening was the fear among my constituents of people who have stolen from their homes yet who then come out into the streets and walk around bold as brass, as if they had got away with it" July '97;
Born: 20 September 1961, St John's Wood, London
Family: Daughter, of Mr Flint and the late Wendy (Beasley), a clerk and shopworker; was

married and divorced; lives with her partner, Phil Cole; 1s Karim '87, 1d Hanna '89, 1 stepson Nicholas '85; all are in "state education" (CF);
Education: Twickenham Girls School; Richmond Tertiary College (3 A-levels); University of East Anglia (BA Hons in American History, Literature and Film Studies);
Occupation: Senior Researcher and Political Officer of the GMBU (MSF) '94-97; previously Welfare and Staff Development Officer, Lambeth Council '91-93; Equal Opportunities Officer, Lambeth Council (GMB shop steward) '89-91; Head of Women's Unit, National Union of Students '87-88; Policy Officer, ILEA '85-89; Management Trainee, GLC/ILEA (NALGO shop steward) '84-85;
Traits: Dark, parted hair; heart-shaped face; dimples; striking; vivacious; twisted mouth; brave (with her partner, Phil Cole, helped stop an armed bank raid which resulted in the raider being jailed for ten years and Cole getting the Sheriff of London's Bravery Award Sep '94); she has wiped out her father's existence;
Address: House of Commons, Westminster, London SW1A 0AA; 114 Ridgeway Road, Isleworth, Mddx TW7 5LN
Telephone: 0171 219 4407 (H of C);

(Daphne) Barbara FOLLETT **Labour** **STEVENAGE '97-;**

Majority: 11,582 over Conservative 6-way;
Description: Britain's first-ever New Town, deprived in '95 of 4,000 voters in its Tory-leaning rural hinterland; the other factor which kept it in Tory hands was the survival of an SDP-LibDem vote after the '79 defeat of Shirley Williams; on a '92 projection, it was expected to produce a slim, 3,000-vote Labour majority;
Position: On the Select Committee on International Development '97-; ex: on Labour's Southern Regional Executive; Branch Secretary, Farnham CLP;
Outlook: A Left-of-Centre Kinnockite over-publicised as "the First Lady of the Luvvie Tendency" (MAIL ON SUNDAY) for her roles as a political feminist who led 'Emily's List' (Early Money Is Like Yeast) to promote female candidates, or as the fund-raising wife of millionaire novelist Ken Follett, or as the style guru credited with the 'Folletting' of Labour politicians like Robin Cook; "I share the suspicions of others that she is not a political heavyweight" (Professor Anthony King); in fact, she is more interesting as a returned radical colonial, born in Jamaica, who lived in Ethiopia, and developed politically as a fellow-traveller in Apartheid South Africa, where her Leftwing anti-Apartheid first husband was banned and then killed by the police; recently has been a multi-cause groupie: Fabians, Greenpeace, Friends of the Earth, Charter 88, One World Action, Liberty, Co-operative Party, Friends of Southern Africa, formerly CND;
History: She was born in Jamaica to a Tory-leaning colonial family; was raised in Jersey and Essex, and from 7, in Ethiopia; from 15 she lived in South Africa, where she married lecturer Richard Turner, a radical anti-Apartheid activist; she helped to found multi-party South African Women for Peace and helped form the black Domestic Workers Union, the brainchild of Bishop's wife, Leah Tutu, but widely regarded as fronts for the banned South African Communist Party; she returned to Britain shortly after her husband was murdered by the

security forces '78; settling in Farnham, she joined the local Labour Party in '79, where she met Ken Follett; as Barbara Broer, contested hopeless Woking against Cranley Onslow, coming third June '83; as Daphne Follett, contested hopeless Epsom and Ewell against Archie Hamilton, coming third June '87; co-founded Labour Women's Network, to encourage the selection of women candidates '87; was narrowly beaten by Tessa Jowell for selection for key marginal of Dulwich Mar '90; revisited South Africa with fellow Anti-Apartheid activist Glenys Kinnock, meeting Nelson Mandela Mar '92; established US-emulating Emily's List UK, helping raise £60,000 in its first year to ease women into winnable seats, providing they agreed to "a woman's right to choose" whether she wanted an abortion Mar '93; with her husband, Ken, helped raise £80,000 for the Blair leadership campaign June '94; she flew to Washington with her husband, Patricia Hewitt and John Carr to investigate securing an advanced computer (Excalibur) for Labour Dec '94; the project was set back by the DAILY MAIL's splashing photos (BAMBI IN LUVVIELAND) of Blair and wealthy guests, including Lord Attenborough, arriving at the Follett home to discuss funding Excalibur; Tony Blair's spin-doctors distanced him from the "luvvies", almost killing the project until millionaire Philip Jeffrey, then proprietor of the NEW STATESMAN, agreed to find £500,000 to finance Excalibur; she was selected from an open short-list for Stevenage, Labour's 37th target seat Mar '95; after four years, Ken Follett ceased being chairman of the celebrity '£1,000 Club', a Labour fund-raising effort allegedly disliked by Tony Blair Apr '95; she met resistance in Stevenage with an application to enclose a plot of land next to her £100,000 listed cottage Feb '96; her 'Emily's List' came under attack from the anti-abortionist Tory MP Ann Winterton for only backing pro-choice women candidates Apr '96; she and her husband won undisclosed libel damages from Ann Robinson and TODAY for challenging their political sincerity Apr '96; gave evidence to South Africa's Truth and Reconciliation Commission about her first husband's murder Oct '96; hostile publicity featured a local Catholic schoolgirl who refused to accept a prize from her because of her pro-choice posture Nov '96; anti-abortion Tory MPs Ann Winterton and Elizabeth Peacock attacked Labour women candidates for being helped by pro-choice 'Emily's List' Mar '97; was elected by an unexpectedly large majority of 11,582 over the incumbent Tory MP Tim Wood, on a 13.93% notional swing May '97; urged help for British film industry June '97; in her Maiden pleaded for the young unemployed in Stevenage June '97; after another Ulster bombing, insisted "the lack of a political settlement was at the heart of the tragic events of last weekend" July '97; asked about curbs on women's human rights in Nicaragua July '97; co-sponsored motion urging curbs on detention of asylum-seekers July '97; in International Development debate recalled her moving experiences as a young health worker in South Africa, where illiteracy helped kill black babies by misfeeding July '97; was named to Select Committee on International Development July '97; her husband, Ken, disclosed how angry he was that the Labour Party had abandoned the £1m Excalibur on winning power Sep '97;

Born: 25 December 1942, Kingston, Jamaica

Family: Daughter, of William Vernon Hubbard, peripatetic insurance expert, and Charlotte (Goulding), shop assistant; m 1st '63 Richard Turner, philosophy lecturer at Natal university; 2d: Jann '64, Kim '68, in whose presence Turner was shot in '78; divorced '71; m 2nd '71 Gerald Stonestreet, clinical psychologist, with whom she and four other couples set up the 'Leaderless Couples Encounter Group', "an experiment in group dynamics and not a free love commune" (BF); divorced '74; m 3rd '74 Les Broer, architect; 1s Adam '75; divorced '85; m 4th '85 Ken Follett (after having lived with him '83-85); 1 steps, Emanuele '68, 1 stepd Marie-Claire '73; l grand-daughter, Alexandra '94, daughter of Kim;

Education: Junior schools in Jersey; Sandford School, Addis Adaba, Ethiopia; Ellerslie Girls High School, Sea Point, Cape Town, South Africa; University of Cape Town (left after one

year to support family when father became ill '61-62); Open University '80-85; LSE (BSc in Economic History);
Occupation: Visiting Research Fellow, Institute for Public Policy Research (researching 'The British Woman: A Status Report') '93-; Director, 'Emily's List UK '92-; ex: Lecturer, in 'Cross Cultural Communication', at the Farnham Centre for International Briefing, Henley Management College '85-87; Assistant Course Organiser, Centre for International Briefing, British Council, Farnham '80-84; National Director, of Health Education for Kupugani (a charity set up to combat black malnutrition) '75-78; Regional Manager, for Kupugani '71-74; Acting Regional Secretary, South African Institute of Race Relations, Cape Town '70-71; Joint Manager, of her first mother-in-law's fruit farm, Stellenbosch '66-70; English as Foreign Language teacher, in Berlitz School of Languages, Paris '64-66; Ledger Clerk, Barclay's Bank of South Africa Ltd "62-63; Saleswoman: at Woolworth's, Cape Town '61-62, Barnes Shoe Store, Cape Town '60-61;
Traits: Small; shoulder-length dark hair and fringe; Betty Boop good looks; toothy; wide-eyed girlishness; heavily made-up; very quiet voice; style-conscious wearer of red jackets, gold buttons and shoulder pads; "vexatiously young-looking" (Mary Kenny); "neat and petite, driven and self-possessed" (Geraldine Bedell, INDEPENDENT ON SUNDAY); not a "champagne socialist" ("I never even drink champagne; I can't drink - it makes me ill; I'm more a cappucino socialist"; "I hate being trivialised as a poor little rich girl;" "I am very impatient" and "obsessional about tidiness" (BF); "voice low and emphatic, hands folded in her lap like a convent girl to rivet attention on her face, there is a bugger-them-all enthusiasm about her that is wholly likeable" (INDEPENDENT); an adroit self-publicist; "quite a man-eater" (Jane Turner, her first mother-in-law); Jewish; plays Scrabble on her time off;
Address: House of Commons, Westminster, London SW1A 0AA; 92 Cheyne Walk, London SW10 0DQ; Rose Cottage, 1 Bowling Green, Stevenage SG1 3BH; houses in Cannes and Antigua;
Telephone: 0171 219 3000 (H of C); 01438 361133 (Stevenage office);

Michael (Jabez) FOSTER DL **Labour** **HASTINGS & RYE '97-**

Majority: 2,560 over Conservative 7-way;
Description: The unaltered, most easterly seaside seat in East Sussex, stretching to the Kent border; it contains the old Cinque Ports of Rye and Winchelsea and the new beach resort of Camber Sands; its largely run-down seaside town of Hastings has a high proportion of elderly voters and many unemployed youths; safely Tory since 1906, the seat's curious aspect was that the Tories, with 48% in '92, were thought to be vulnerable only to the Liberal Democrats, who then lagged over 12% behind; in '92 Labour was a further 10% behind, and thought to be almost a non-runner; 1997's phenomenal swing of 18.5% to Labour changed all that;
Position: Hastings Borough Councillor (Leader, Labour Group '73-76) '71-; East Sussex County Councillor '71-; Deputy Lieutenant, East Sussex '93-;
Outlook: A Christian Socialist veteran local councillor and solicitor who leap-frogged over both the LibDem challenger and the incumbent Tory MP with a massive, near-record swing of

18.5% in his fourth attempt at the seat, making him the second least-expected Labour victor; a consumer-protector; in the Fabian Society and the Society of Labour Lawyers;
History: He joined the Labour Party '65; was elected to Hastings Borough Council and East Sussex County Council May '71; contested Hastings against Kenneth Warren for the first time, taking second place with 29% Feb '74; fought Kenneth Warren again, increasing the Labour vote to 33.5%, Oct '74; contested the seat for the 3rd time, with the Labour vote falling to 30% May '79; did not contest the redrawn seat, embracing affluent Tory-leaning Rye and affluent villages, enabling the Liberals to overtake Labour '83 and '87; was again selected as the candidate for Hastings; defended the TUC demand for a minimum wage pf £4.26 as a negotiating position and not a snub to Tony Blair Sep '96; in the run-up to the election, a crucial ICM poll in the OBSERVER predicted his victory, with the LibDem challenger, Monroe Palmer, coming 2nd and Tory incumbent, Jacqui Lait MP, coming in third: 34%, 29%, 28% Apr '97; in the actual election, he won 34%, Lait 29% and Palmer 28%, giving him a 2,560 majority on a huge swing of 18.5%, May '97; he told cheering supporters: "I am surprised; we must have picked up an awful lot of new friends, and these are people who want to see a decent society" May '97; supported the end of fox-hunting; his namesake, 'Mike' Foster, the new Labour MP for Worcester, as the sponsor of the anti-fox-hunting Bill, was threatened with having his house burned June '97; asked whether the public were "properly informed of the results of food chemical surveys" by MAFF July '97; complained about computer sellers falsely claimed their machines were millenium-compliant July '97;
Born: February 1946, Hastings
Family: Married to Rosemary, with two sons born '74 and '78;
Education: Hastings Secondary School for Boys; Hastings Grammar School; Leicester University (LLB); also has a Master's degree in Employment Law;
Occupation: Solicitor, in private practice, specialising in employment law; ex: Solicitor's Managing Clerk (GMB);
Traits: Slim; grey-haired; Methodist; qualified footbhall referee; enjoys tennis and table tennis;
Address: House of Commons, Westminster, London SW1A 0AA; 202 Wishing Tree Road, St Leonards-on-Sea, Sussex TN38 9LB;
Telephone: 0171 219 3000 (H of C)

'Mike' (Michael John) FOSTER  **Labour**  **WORCESTER '97-**

Majority: 7,425 over Conservative 4-way;
Description: This county town and cathedral city was not won by Labour even in '45 or '66; but in '83 it lost Droitwich and in '95 it lost 10,000 voters in Tory-leaning villages in its hinterland; on a '92 projection it was expected to give the Tories a 6,000 majority; this was considered inadequate by Tory incumbent Peter Luff, Peter Walker's succcessor, who sensibly did a "chicken run" to safer Mid-Worcestershire;
Position: Secretary, Worcester Constituency Labour Party '92-95;
Outlook: Worcester's first-ever Labour MP, "tipped to be a rising star" (BIRMINGHAM POST); another

Labour recruit from the chalkface, unusually a lecturer in accountancy; unusual too is his experience in the private sector, as an accountant at Jaguar Cars; hates "barbaric" fox-hunting but enjoys fishing; in Labour Finance and Industry Group, as well as the Co-operative Party; GMB-endorsed;
History: Joined the Labour Party at 17, '80; was agent to Jacqui Smith when she contested Mid-Worcestershire Apr '92; was selected for redrawn Worcester over Blairite Derek Scott, former defector to the SDP Sep '95; was one of 16 GMB members backed by the union during the election Apr '97; found "patronising and offensive" the pollsters' definition of 'Worcester Women' as the key swing voters Apr '97; conducted a US-style 'blitz' campaign, promising to end fox-hunting Apr '97; won the seat with a majority of 7,425 over Peter Luff's hapless successor, Nicholas Bourne, on a swing of 10% May '97; won top position in the Private Members' Ballot May '97; in his Maiden joked that it was lucky for the Tories that they picked 'Worcester Woman' as their switch voters rather than 'West Bromwich Wench' June '97; after polling his constituents and despite warnings from Labour Whips decided to present a controversial Private Member's Bill - Wild Mammals (Hunting with Dogs) Bill - to outlaw fox-hunting with hounds June '97; on the eve of a massive meeting of 100,000 pro-hunters in Hyde Park, Labour Whips were said to be inclined not to force a vote on his Bill if it proved too controversial July '97; urged a reduction in court fees impose by the previous Government July '97;
Born: 14 March 1963, Great Wyrley, Staffs
Family: Grandson of a miner; son, of a former shop steward who still works on the Jaguar production line at Castle Bromwich; is married to Shauna, with three children;
Education: Great Wyrley High School, Walsall; Wolverhampton Polytechnic (BA Economics, PGCE); University of Central England; Associate of the Chartered Institute of Management Accountancy;
Occupation: Lecturer, in Accountancy, Worcester College of Technology (NATFHE)'91-96; ex: Management Consultant, Jaguar Cars '84-91;
Traits: Tall; slim; light brown hair, front-combed; youthful looks; long slender face; heavy eyebrows; spruce; fluent; "articulate and photogenic" (Charles Clover, DAILY TELEGRAPH); nice sense of humour; has a black labrador and two cats (Jasper and Carrot); enjoys angling: was a competition angler until 28;
Address: House of Commons, Westminster, London SW1 0AA; 1 Cromwell Crescent, Worcester WR5 3JW;
Telephone: 0171 219 3000 (H of C); 01905 763775 (home);

WELCOME WORDS

One of the MPs' bouquets most welcome among the occasional brickbats is the frequent refrain: "Thanks for recalling that speech! I had completely forgotten ever making it...."

PROSPECTIVES SATISFACTION

The 1 May 1997 general election increase in the number of Labour and Liberal Democrat MPs provided what might be called "archive satisfaction". In a fair number of cases we have been tracking such candidates as "possible" victors for as many as four or five contests, badgering them for information and writing up their profiles, just in case. In their cases - as in the case of the 17 'retreads' - there was the satisfaction of knowing that the previous efforts were not wasted.

Christopher (James) FRASER **Conservative** **DORSET MID & POOLE NORTH '97-**

Majority: 681 over Liberal Democrat 4-way;
Description: A new, affluent, fairly compact semi-suburban and rural seat curling around the north and west of Poole; made up of parts of Poole, Bournemouth West and Dorset North and Dorset South; it has a fairly strong LibDem presence in local government;
Position: On Select Committee on National Heritage '97-; ex: Three Rivers District Councillor (on Resources Committee) '92-96; Editor, TORY INSIGHT, the publication of SW Hertfordshire Conservative Association '92-96;
Outlook: A formerly mainstream Hertfordshire party activist who has re-positioned himself geographically and politically; on the Centre-Right, he became a Michael Howard campaigner by May '97; with two generations of his family in Dorset, now claims his seat is "the enterprise centre of Dorset"; pro-hunting;
History: Joined the Conservative Party in his late teens; unsuccessfully contested Leavesden Ward on Three Rivers District Council May '91; was personal assistant to Richard Page in the general election Apr '92; won Ashridge ward on Three Rivers District Council, Hertfordshire May '92; was selected for new Dorset Mid and Poole North seat Nov '95; at annual conference praised the "resolute consistency" of the beleaguered Chancellor, Kenneth Clarke, adding, "this party believes in low taxes, but not as a dogma, never as a bribe"; as a small businessman, starting his own business, wanted to be "free from all the job-destroying measures so beloved of Brussels" and warned "never to be led into a Brussels cul-de-sac" Oct '96; in election campaign narrowly fended off strong challenge from the top LibDem strategist Alan Leaman Apr '97; his manifesto opposed joining a single European currency in '99, Apr '97; resisting the West Country's LibDem high tide, won the seat by a narrow 681 votes, on an anti-Tory swing of 5.4% May '97; was part of team supporting Michael Howard for the Tory leadership May '97; after his constituency experienced the birth of a child to 12-year-old schoolgirl, asked about "the quality and implementation of sex education in secondary schools" July '97; also asked about children turning to crime July '97; in Maiden called attention to Dorset's very exceptional record: "before the general election, there were six Tory-held seats in Dorset; on 2 May there were eight" July '97; urged a higher fee for digital television than for terrestrial July '97; was named to Select Committee on Culture, the Media and Sport July '97; enthusiastically backed hunting as essential to rural life and employment Oct '97;
Born: 25 October 1962, Bushey, Hertfordshire
Family: Son, of R A Fraser, retired company chairman, and D (Hutchinson); m '87 Lisa Margaret (Norman); 2c;
Education: Hertfordshire primary schools; Harrow College; Regent Street Poly (later Westminster University);
Occupation: Chairman/Managing Director, of marketing and communications group founded by him '85-
Traits: Young-looking; dark centre-parted hair; chubby face; droopy nose; middle-class accent; perfectionist; reads speeches;
Address: House of Commons, Westminster, London SW1A 0AA; 38 Sandbanks Road,

Poole, Dorset BH14 8BX;
Telephone: 0171 219 6569 (H of C); 0171 219 4499 (Fax); 01202 718080;

Barry GARDINER **Labour** **BRENT NORTH '97-**

Majority: 4,019 over Conservative 5-way;
Description: A slightly-altered northwest London middle-class residential suburb, better known as Wembley because it grew out of the Wembley Empire exhibition; it includes two-fifths of upwardly mobile ethnic minorities, largely entrepreneurial East African Asians; this was a freak seat in its continuing loyalty to the quirky Dickensian Rightwing Tory, Sir Rhodes Boyson, an active constituency MP; he had a 10,000 majority in '92; this was wiped out in a near-record swing of 18.8%;
Position: Cambridge City Councillor (Mayor '92-93) '88-94; Treasurer, Cambridge Constituency Labour Party '88-89;
Outlook: One of the best-educated newcomers, who has achieved a historic 18.8% swing, ousting Sir Rhodes Boyson, partly from his persuasive preoccupation with local health and education; as an outsider, from Scotland and Cambridge, he was able to overcome latent suspicions of the 'Loony Left' which had dominated Brent Town Hall; in the Fabians and Co-operative Party; GMB and MSF;
History: Joined the Labour Party at 24, '81; was elected Treasurer of the Cambridge CLP '88; was elected to Cambridge City Council May '88; became Mayor of Cambridge May '92; pioneered an anti-crime initiative that cut the Cambridge crime rate by over 10% in one year from '93; was selected for safe-Tory Brent North, against Sir Rhodes Boyson, its Tory incumbent since Feb '74, who had a 10,000 majority '95; Brent Town Hall was evacuated in the midst of a transfer of power back to Labour because of a suspect bag, which he sheepishly admitted was his Apr '96; at annual conference complained that taxes were inadequately linked to earnings Oct '96; campaigned actively for the retention of the Accident and Emergency facilities of Edgeware Hospital Apr '97; unexpectedly, won the seat on a massive 18.8% swing, ousting Sir Rhodes by a majority of 4,019 (making him the 10th least-expected Labour victor) May '97; after intense private, largely fruitless talks to the Labour Minister for Health, Alan Milburn, about the Accident and Emergency facilities at Edgware Hospital, welcomed Government's additional funds for the NHS in general June '97; his wife gave birth to another son while he made his Maiden speech; in his Maiden he expressed concern "that there is no clearly articulated mechanism of quality control" for the young people the Labour Government was trying to place in jobs July '97;
Born: 10 March 1957, Glasgow
Family: Is married to Caroline; they have three sons, including Jesse and Cameron, and a daughter Bethany;
Education: Glasgow High School; Haileybury College; St Andrews University; Harvard University (Kennedy Scholarship); Corpus Christi, Cambridge University;
Occupation: Arbitrator of Maritime Casualties: Senior Partner, in an international company of shipping arbitrators; travels widely in Eastern Europe, where he lectures annually at Moscow's Academy of National Economy;
Traits: Parted dark brown hair and dark beard; clever, articulate; bird-watcher;

Address: House of Commons, Westminster, London SW1A 0AA; Pump Lodge, 406 Cherryhinton Road, Cambridge, CB1 4BA;
Telephone: 0171 219 3000 (H of C);

Andrew GEORGE **Liberal Democrat** **ST IVES '97-**

Majority: 7,170 over Conservative 8-way;
Description: The unaltered Cornish seat in the mainland's far southwest, comprising Land's End, the Lizard peninsula, the Scilly Isles and beautiful St Ives itself; the dropping Tory vote parallels the decline of its troubled fishing industry; the industry's strong defender, its Tory ex-MP David Harris, formerly a DAILY TELEGRAPH Political Correspondent, decided not to stand here again in '97 but sought unsuccessfully to fight elsewhere;
Position: Spokesman on Fishing '97-; Vice Chairman, Cornwall Racial Equality Council;
Outlook: The first non-Tory MP for St Ives since the '30s: a Cornish nationalist thinly disguised as a classical LibDem community politician; bills himself as "a local man who is committed to Cornwall"; a campaigner for devolution to Cornwall, the environment, fishing, housing, poverty, small business, a Cornish Development Agency, a Cornish Assembly, and a Cornish university; in Friends of the Earth, World Development Movement, Cornish Social and Economic Research Group, Cornwall Racial Equality Council, Celtic League, Mebyon Kernow;
History: He joined the Liberal Democrats; wrote 'Cornwall at the Crossroads', warning against planning decisions being decided by the developers '89; was selected to contest St Ives; opposed the replacement of the poll tax by a council tax "because a mismatch between high prices and low incomes would work against local people on Cornish incomes" Nov '91; called for more council house building Mar '92; reduced incumbent Tory MP David Harris' majority from 7,555 to 1,645 Apr '92; claimed the Government spent less per head on education in Cornwall than the English average Mar '95; his call for a Cornish Development Agency was backed by his constituent, Sir John Banham Oct '95; backed the campaign against the deportation of a long locally-resident illegal Hongkong immigrant who had taken sanctuary in a local church July '96; greeted John Major's visit to St Ives as proof that local Tories were running scared July '96; backed LibDem proposal to scrap the Common Fisheries Policy, to give local boats sole access to local waters Aug '96; urged compensation for local residents affect by jet aircraft noise near Culdrose RAF base Dec '96; opposed joining Devon to Cornwall in a development agency; insisted 88% of Cornish businesses backed a Cornwall Development Agency Apr '97; campaigned hard for Labour tactical votes as "the only Cornishman standing for election here" who could defeat the Tory candidate with "only an 8% swing to win"; actually it only needed 1.5% Apr '97; on a swing of 8.09%, won St Ives by a majority of 7,170 over Conservative William Rogers, who replaced departed David Harris; it was the first time the constituency had not returned a Tory MP in 66 years May '97; his Maiden, begun in Cornish, celebrated the march on London of 15,000 Cornishmen in 1497; he deplored the "poverty and deprivation" in his beautiful constituency, with "the lowest wages in the country and among the highest levels of unemployment anywhere"; claimed Cornwall had

its version of the West Lothian question, the Trelawny question: "And shall Trelawny live or shall Trelawny die, there's 20,000 Cornish folk who'll know the reason why" May '97; backed ban on arms for Indonesia June '97; urged overseas aid go to the poorest people in less developed countries June '97; urged placing mobile homes in a council tax band "related to their real market value" June '97; urged Government to place Cornwall at the top of the queue for European Union structural funds June '97; hailed the march to London of Cornish nationalists backing a Cornish Assembly, a Cornish university college and an economic development body June '97; urged more leniency for illegal immigrants with children born in Britain July '97; claimed the latest economic blow, the closure of the St Ivel creamery, clinched the case for Cornwall's top claim for EU funds July '97; called for renegotiation of the Common Fisheries Policy after the European Court ruled that Spanish fishermen be compensated for exclusion from UK waters July '97; lead a motion calling for a university college in Cornwall July '97;

Born: 2 December 1958, Mullion, Cornwall

Family: Son, of Hugh George, horticulturist, later unemployed, and Diana May (Petherick), music teacher; m '87 Jill (Marshall), St Ives-born nurse-midwife; 1s Davy '90, 1d Morvah '87;

Education: Council schools in Mullion, Cury; Helston Grammar School; Helston School; University College, Oxford University; Sussex University (Agricultural Economics);

Occupation: Deputy Director '95-, Field Officer '81-95 Cornwall Rural Development Council (community work, pre-school care for under-5s, housing);

Traits: Strong-jawed rugged face; pleasant-looking; "lugubrious speaker" (Quentin Letts, DAILY TELEGRAPH); astigmatic; intelligent; cautious; athletic; Cornish-speaking unegomaniac ("in the race for...attention, you will find me keen to stand back and observe from a repectable distance" (AG); like other Cornishmen, displays "self-mocking irony and a dry sense of humour" (AG));

Address: House of Commons, Westminster, London SW1A 0AA; 10 Tremeadow Terrrace, Hayle, Cornwall TR27 4AF;

Telephone: 071 219 3000 (H of C); 01736 757070 (home);

Nicholas ('Nick') GIBB **Conservative** **BOGNOR REGIS & LITTLEHAMPTON '97-**

Majority: 7,321 over Labour 4-way;

Description: A new, ultra-Tory seat containing the named coastal resorts; it comprises most of the former Arundel constituency minus the town of Arundel itself; its third of pensioners are stiff with the affluent; there is some industry around Littlehampton; on a '92 projection, it was expected to produce a majority of over 15,000 for the Conservative candidate in '97;

Position: On the Select Committee on Social Security '97-; ex: in Conservative Social Security Manifesto Policy Group '95-96; Chairman '89-90, Treasurer '88-89, Bethnal Green & Stepney Conservative Association; Chairman, Northern Region Conservative Students '80-81; Chairman, Durham University Conservative Association '79-80;

Outlook: An arch-Rightwing Tory tax accountant and pamphleteer linked to the Adam Smith Institute and Peter Lilley; an assiduous Commons defender of the Tory record on taxation and social security; a crusader for privatisation and lower taxes, expecially on inheritance and capital gains; previously close to fellow-acountant Lord (Cecil) Parkinson, Peter Lilley and Michael Portillo; "arch-Rightwinger" (Julie Kirkbride, DAILY TELEGRAPH); has been a Rightwing activist since student days, when in the Federation of Conservative Students (dissolved in '86 by Norman Tebbit);

History: He was elected Chairman of Durham University Conservative Association '79; was elected Chairman of Northern Region Student Conservatives '80; wrote 'The Forgotten Closed Shop', urging the abolition of compulsory membership of the National Union of Students '82; was elected to Executive of the Hackney and Shoreditch Conservative Association '85; served as aide to Tory Chairman Cecil Parkinson during the general election June '87; in 'Simplifying Taxes' published by the Adam Smith Institute, proposed lowering income tax, national insurance and corporation tax and abolition of stamp duty, capital gains tax and inheritance tax Nov '87; in 'Budget Forecast', published by the Adam Smith Institute, predicted a 40% top rate of income tax and 25% basic rate Feb '88; was elected Treasurer of Bethnal Green Conservative Association '88; contested by-election for Tower Hamlets council seat Sep '88; at annual conference called for privatisation of London Transport, British Rail and private funding of road-building Oct '88; was elected Chairman of Bethnal Green Conservative Association '89; in 'The College Closed Shop', in the GUARDIAN, urged the abolition of compulsory membership of student unions May '89; in 'Duty to Repeal', published by Adam Smith Institute, called for abolition of stamp duty Oct '89; at annual conference, called for legislation to compel councils to sell derelict land, calling attention to the "disastrous effect" of LibDem control of Tower Hamlets Oct '89; was selected as candidate for hopeless Stoke on Trent Central Mar '90; in 'Bucking the Market' published by the Adam Smith Institute, opposed Britain's membership of the Exchange Rate Mechanism June '90; at annual conference condemned Labour's "knocking attitude" to country's transport infrastructure Oct '90; co-signed Eurosceptic letter in DAILY TELEGRAPH opposing single European currency and political union Nov '91; in 'Maintaining Momentum' called for lower capital gains tax and abolition of inheritance tax Feb '92; during campaign, attacked "corruption" of Labour-controlled local Stoke council Mar '92; suffered a 4.3% swing to Labour in general election Apr '92; urged Conservative Government not to increase income tax Oct '93; was selected to fight hopeless by-election in Rotherham Mar '94; in by-election received only 9.9% May '94; at annual conference backed Michael Howard's tough Criminal Justice and Public Order Bill, attacking the liberal "soft-on-crime Establishment" Oct '94; was short-listed for selection for Dorset West, emerging as runner-up Nov '94; was named as Adviser to Social Security Secretary Peter Lilley Mar '95; was short-listed for Selby, emerging as runner-up Mar '95; was selected for Bognor Regis and Littlehampton Nov '95; favoured traditional education, with a grammar school in every town, formal teaching methods, streaming and restored discipline Oct '96; favoured abolition of top 40% rate of income tax Mar '97; ruled out a single European currency in his manifesto Apr '97; in a swing to Labour of 13.82%, won Bognor Regis and Littlehampton by only 7,321 over Labour May '97; asked about impact of differential stamp duties on the competitiveness of the City of London June '97; asked about viral monitoring of sea water June '97; was on Peter Lilley's leadership campaign team June '97; co-sponsored Early Day Motion amendment which warned that nuclear disarmament would "make the world safe, once again, for full-scale conventional warfare" July '97; in the Finance Bill Standing Committee, opposed Government's plans to abolish ACT credits and Foreign Income Dividends July '97; sought fruitlessly to save tax relief on BUPA payments for the over-60s July '97; elicited figures showing slow growth of NHS expenditure under the

Tories July '97; his "expertise" was derided by Economic Secretary Helen Liddell July '97;
Born: 3 Sepember 1960, Amersham
Family: Son, of late John Gibb, civil engineer, and Eileen (Quayle) retired teacher;
Education: Maidstone Grammar School; Roundhay School (9 O-levels), Leeds; Thornes House School, Wakefield (4 A-levels); Durham University '78-81 (BA in Law);
Occupation: Chartered Accountant and Senior Manager, with KPMG Peat Marwick, specialising in corporate tax '84-97; National Westminster Bank '82-83;
Traits: Lean; retreating hair; earnest, frantic look; articulate in tax consultants' gobbledegook; twice a competitor in London Marathon;
Address: House of Commons, Westminster, London SW1A 0AA;
Telephone: 0171 219 3000;

Dr Ian GIBSON **Labour** **NORWICH NORTH '97-**

Majority: 9,470 over Conservative 7-way;
Description: The once-safe half of a pro-Labour city made safer for the Tories by adding Broadland suburbs in '83 and '95; on '92 projections it was still expected to provide a small Tory majority in '97, even if the retiring incumbent Tory MP, Patrick Thompson, did not believe it;
Position: On Select Committee on Science and Technology '97-; Vice Chairman, of Health and Food Forum; on the Ministry of Science Task Force; ex: on Grants Committees of Medical Research Council '82-90, and Cancer Research Campaign; on Executive, of ASTMS (later MSF) '72-96;
Outlook: Distinguished Scots-born academic biologist with a radical approach to biotechnological advance; a moderniser and electoral reformer; in maturity - at 58 one of the oldest entrants - is a pragmatic politician, responding to his constituents' desire for Labour to win on a realistic programme; was one of 16 Labour candidates backed by the GMB; this recent moderation has overridden his '70s dalliance with Trotskyism in the International Socialists and Socialist Workers Party; a recent critic of women-only short-lists;
History: Joined ASTMS (later MSF) '65; in the '70s was active in International Socialists and its successor the Socialist Workers Party; "he masterminded factory sit-ins in the town; he also made two visits to Moscow to the General Assembly of the World Federation of Scientific Workers - a Soviet propaganda tool considered by the Labour Party too dangerous for members to become involved with"; "also headed the Norwich Anti-Nuclear Campaign against the Sizewell B power station and [was] a member of Scientists Against Nuclear Armaments; he was [Hon Treasurer] of the former scientific staff union ASTMS but was given a three-year suspension for atacking its leadership" (SUNDAY EXPRESS); joined the Labour Party at 45, '83; "in the late 1980s, Gibson was still claiming that 'capitalism must be superseded, with no place for a mixed economy' because 'reforms are not going to change and make a better system'" (SUNDAY TIMES); was selected to fight Norwich North, being described by Neil Kinnock as "a marvellous candidate" Apr '90; told the SUNDAY EXPRESS that he had "rejected SWP policies and favoured democratic ballot-box decisions; he was in favour of retaining a nuclear deterrent but added, 'science should develop towards peaceful ends and not

the development of nuclear weapons'; he described himself as a 'radical' rather than a hard-line Marxist" Mar '92; narrowly failed, by 266 votes, to oust incumbent Tory MP Patrick Thompson, despite a high anti-Tory swing of 7.6% Apr '92; warned against Labour's Rightward swing: "You have got to be very careful; if you dilute your policies so much, what have you got left?" Sep '94; was again selected to contest Norwich North Dec '95; was forced to defend Labour's plans for student loans at a heated meeting with local sixth-formers June '96; admitted it was "much more difficult being a candidate this time" July '96; favoured collaboration with voluntary organisations: "Labour sees the voluntary sector as a source of creativity and innovation and will work with it in the public interest" July '96; won the seat on a swing of 10.56%, winning a 9,470 majority May '97; urged more research on organophosphates June '97; asked the Agriculture Minister "what research his department has commissioned and evaluated into the hazards of bio-aerosol production in and around commercial compost-making facilities" June '97; asked the Health Secretary "what research he has evaluated on the change in incidence of the new variant form of CJD" June '97; asked the Agriculture Minister "what criteria will be used to determine the location of the Food Standards Agency" June '97; in his Maiden emphasised that "the recession came late to Norwich, but it certainly came"; he boasted of a native son "who can teach the Chancellor of the Exchequer to understand and talk with authority about post-neoclassical endogenous growth theories"; he also boasted of its large research park, "where science and technology will flourish; we are trying to build on a model similar to the research triangle park in North Carolina, where massive private sector investment associates with a dynamic public sector grouping of research establishments" June '97; led a motion sending greetings to a cancer-afflicted imprisoned Indonesian trade union leader June '97; had an adjournment debate on the 'Gulf War Syndrome' June '97; co-protested the BBC's interviewing a self-confessed paedophile on the 'Kilroy' programme June '97; in another adjournment debate, predicted that "biotechnology" "will be the most important science for the next millenium" and urged it be made possible to patent scientific methodology in the field; the alternative was to allow US domination to continue and grow July '97; led a motion backing the patenting of biotechnological advances July '97; was named to the Select Committee on Science and Technology July '97; urged the Agriculture Minister to consider the Institute of Food Research in Norwich as the basis of the planned Food Standards Agency to ensure "world-class research into food science" July '97; protested the Government's "red meat cancer" scare, as launched without adequate scientific backing Sep '97; made a scientific analysis of hunting sports and their myths Oct '97;

Born: 26 September 1938, Dumfries

Family: Son of Willie John Gibson, clerk, and Winifred (Kerr), clerk; he married in '37 and has three children;

Education: Local state schools; Dumfries Academy; Edinburgh University (BSc; PhD); College of Education; Indiana University; University of Washington;

Occupation: Biologist: Professor and Dean of Biological Sciences, University of East Anglia (with a staff of 1,700 manning research laboratories on cancer, leukaemia and Aids) '91-97; Governor, of John Innes Centre (world-clas biotechnology centre) '91-97;

Traits: Tall; balding egghead; intelligent-looking; residual Scots burr; has recently had a moderate and pragmatic approach; founder and coach of Red Rose Football Club, financed by local trade union, for local 8-to-11-year-old children; he is Joint Manager of the MPs' Football Club;

Address: House of Commons, Westminster, London SW1A; 220 College Road, Norwich NR2 3JA;

Telephone: 0171 219 1265 (H of C); 01603 455277 (home);

Linda GILROY **Labour & Co-operative** **PLYMOUTH-SUTTON '97-;**

Majority: 9,440 over Conservative 7-way;
Description: A continuing name for an almost wholly changed seat; in fact, it is mostly the old marginal Plymouth-Drake, from which Dame Janet Fookes fled, plus two of the three remaining wards of old Plymouth-Sutton west of the Plym; on a '92 projection, it was expected to provide the Tories with a 2,000 majority; not believing it, Gary Streeter fled to safer Devon South West;
Position: Chairman, Cornwall County Labour Party '90-94; Vice Chairman, Cornwall and Devon Area Committee of the National Association of Citizens Advice Bureaux '86-90; Secretary, Plymouth-Drake Constituency Labour Party '87-88;
Outlook: An ambitious Scots-born, Plymouth-based Labour activist who is its first Labour and Co-operative Member; was one of the first beneficiaries of all-women short-lists; "I want to see a reduction in the waiting list for breast cancer patients and unnecessary waits for surgery"
History: She became Deputy Director of Age Concern in Scotland '72; she joined the Labour Party '74; became Regional Manager of the Gas Consumers Council for the southwest, joining NALGO '79; was selected as candidate for Cornwall SE July '90; at annual conference complained about Cornwall's low-pay economy Oct '90; contested Cornwall South East against incumbent Tory Robert Hicks; she came third, behind LibDem Robin Teverson, with 9.2% Apr '92; contested the Devon and East Plymouth Euro-seat, winning 20% of the vote June '94; was short-listed for the Christchurch by-election, but was beaten by Nigel Lickey June '93; was selected from an all-women's short-list for extensively redrawn Plymouth-Sutton, from which both Gary Streeter and Dame Janet Fookes fled '95; reacted against the decision of the industrial tribunal making illegal all-women short-lists by saying, "the key question is how far do you see the previous situation as fair?; and if we don't do it this way, can somebody came up with a better scheme?" Jan '96; at annual conference praised Tony Blair's promise to link schools to the information super highway Oct '96; won the seat by a majority of 9,440; she said, "I did not dare to dream of a result like this; I am very pleasantly surprised at the depth of trust that the people of Plymouth have put in New Labour" May '97; backed outlawing of fox-hunting June '97; introduced Private Members Bill to control sale of fireworks June '97; made her Maiden in the Defence debate, extolling Plymouth's lengthy defence history and her predecessors as its women-MPs Oct '97;
Born: 19 July 1949, Moffat, Scotland
Family: Daughter of William Jervie, engineer, and Gwendoline (Grey), telephone operator; m '86 Councillor Benny Gilroy, her Agent;
Education: Maynard School, Exeter; Stirling High School; Edinburgh University (MA Hons in History); Strathclyde University; Diploma in Consumer Affairs from Institute of Trading Standards Administration; Diploma in Seceretarial Studies;
Occupation: South West Regional Manager, Gas Consumers' Council (NALGO, Chairman its staff branch '89-90) '79-96; Deputy Director, Age Concern, Scotland (TGWU) '72-79;
Traits: Brown, curly hair; glasses; beaky features; middle-aged, clumsy walk;
Address: House of Commons, Westminster, London SW1A 0AA; 21 Harbourside Court, Hawkers Avenue, Plymouth PL4 0QT;

Telephone: 0171 219 4740 (H of C); 01752 276626 (home);

Paul GOGGINS **Labour** **WYTHENSHAWE & SALE EAST '97-**

Majority: 15,019 over Conservative 5-way;
Description: Altered but still a mainly working-class council-estate seat south of Manchester, a development of the first municipal garden city in Britain; it takes in Manchester's Ringway Airport, now Manchester International Airport, including half of Runway Two;
Position: Salford City Councillor (Chairman, Community Strategy Committee) '90-; Chairman, UK Poverty Coalition '96; ex: Chairman, Manchester Labour Party;
Outlook: TGWU-backed longtime social worker who has recently been National Director of Church Action on Poverty, succeeding John Battle MP; is concerned to improve the social security system which "is failing the taxpayer, and most importantly, failing those who rely on it for their income"; is in Oxfam, Christian Aid, the Christian Socialist Movement and Greenpeace;
History: He joined the Labour Party '75; was elected a Salford District Councillor May '90; became Chairman of 140-strong UK Poverty Coalition formed to mark 1996 as the international year for the eradication of poverty Jan '96; on announcement of imminent retirement of Alf Morris, threw his hat in the ring, with two other councillors plus Bryan Davies MP and ex-MP Frank White Apr '96; asked of Labour's social policy statement, 'Welfare to Work', "will this new flexibilily lead to lower social security payments?", "will Labour abolish the Jobseekers' Allowance and restore entitlement to unemployment benefit for a full year?; the ultimate success of these policies depends entirely on creating new jobs for people to move into; this would lead to savings and extra revenue in the long run, but requires a huge level of public investment in the short run" June '96; was selected for revised Wythenshawe and Sale East, with support from local TGWU July '96; retained the seat by a majority of 15,019, on a pro-Labour swing of 9.2% May '97; asked a series of questions on low pay and housing benefits June '97; backed abolition of fox-hunting June '97; led Parliamentary motion congratulating Manchester on its rebuilding in the wake of the '96 IRA bomb June '97; backed protest against imprisonment of Indonesian trade union leader June '97; on 'Thought for the Day' said that at "the heart of religion is a concern for justice" June '97; urged importance of parents listening to their children reading July '97; complained about local loss of water through leakage July '97; urged close monitoring of the 14 NHS PFI projects, "I am happy to say that one is in my constituency" July '97; pointed out to objector Martin Bell MP that "half of Runway Two will be in my constituency" but that most of its businessmen and residents backed the airport's expansion; "some 2,000 of my constituents, who live barely a mile from Manchester Airport, are out of work; some of the young people in Wythenshawe...are third generation unemployed; they have given up hope of ever finding a job" July '97; in the debate on the Social Security Bill pointed out that "the experience of those who claim benefit is frequently appalling, with long and complex claim forms, lengthy delays in appeals, and inaccurate calculations; it is a bureaucratic nightmare that compounds the sense of rejection and exclusion that many claimants feel" July '97;

Born: 16 October 1953, Manchester
Family: Son, of John Goggins, headteacher, and Rita (Froggatt) medical secretary; m Wyn (Bartley); 2s: Matthew '80, Dominic '85; 1d Theresa '82;
Education: St Bede's RC Grammar School, Manchester; Manchester Polytechnic (CQSW -Certificate of Qualification in Social Work);
Occupation: National Director, Church Action on Poverty '89-97; ex: Social Worker for 15 years '74-89;
Traits: Retreating hair; specs; bearded; "attractive and pleasant" (Assistant Editor, MANCHESTER EVENING NEWS); enjoys swimming, walking and watching Manchester City;
Address: House of Commons, Westminster, London SW1A 0AA; 153 Leigh Road, Worsley, M28 1LG (home);
Telephone: 0171 219 5865 (H of C); 0161 790 1854 (home); 0161 499 7900 (constituency);

Eileen GORDON **Labour** **ROMFORD '97-**

Majority: 649 over Conservative 6-way;
Description: A 750-year-old Essex market town, formerly solidly Conservative suburbia - their 94th safest seat until '97; three-quarter owner-occupied, a mixture of skilled working class and lower middle class; made safer for the Tories by excluding, in '83, the GLC's gigantic Harolds Hill housing estate and including, in '95, Tory-leaning Ardleigh Green ward; all this was narrowly wiped out by a pro-Labour swing of 15.6% in '97;
Position: On the Select Committee on Broadcasting '97-; on Greater London Labour Party Regional Executive; Vice Chairman, Romford Constituency Labour Party;
Outlook: Low-profiled local Leftwinger linked to Tony Banks who quite unexpectedly ended the 23-year local reign of Sir Michael Neubert, chalking up Labour's fifth least-expected victory; in the Campaign Group, League Against Cruel Sports;
History: She joined the Labour Party '64; selected to fight Sir Michael Neubert in Romford, she lifted the Labour vote from 22.8% to 29.5% Apr '92; re-selected for Romford, won it by a narrow majority of 649 - less than half the Referendum Party vote - on a near-record pro-Labour notional swing of 15.6% May '97; was one of half a dozen of the 183 new Labour MPs who joined the hard-Left Campaign Group May '97; said, "if I were lucky with the Private Member's ballot, I'd go for banning blood sports; I think it's long overdue" May '97; urged that all listed sporting events be shown on TV without payment May '97; made her Maiden on London, urging the recreation of a strategic authority June '97; strongly criticised the Child Support Agency, which she said had an "immediate and devastating" impact on her previous job as a case-worker for Tony Banks MP when introduced: "partners who had previously had amicable arrangements with ex-partners and who had felt settled were immediately thrown into turmoil"; "the agency became notorious for its incompetence" June '97; asked about the advantages and disadvantages of school league tables July '97; was named to the Select Committee on Broadcasting July '97;
Born: 22 October 1946, London

Family: Is married to Mr Gordon, with a son born in '75, and a daughter born in '78;
Education: Harold Hill Grammar School; Shoreditch Comprehensive; Westminster College of Education (Cert Ed);
Occupation: Constituency case-worker for Tony Banks MP (TGWU)til '97; previously a teacher;
Traits: Short; chubby face; heavy owlish horned rims; canny-looking; short hair; "politics has always been part of my life, so this is an ideal job for me" (EG);
Address: House of Commons, Westminster, London SW1A 0AA; 2 Dorset Avenue, Romford RM1 4LP;
Telephone: 0171 219 3000 (H of C); 01708 727918 (home);

Donald GORRIE OBE **Liberal Democrat** **EDINBURGH WEST '97-**

Majority: 7,253 over Conservative 7-way;
Description: Formerly the country's tightest Tory-LibDem marginal, until Lord James Douglas-Hamilton finally failed to perform his normal Houdini-like escape from defeat; mostly the affluent parts of the city, with its best schools; in '95 it was extended into SNP-leaning Queensferry and Labour-leaning Muirhouse;
Position: On Liberal Democrats' Parliamentary Scottish team '97-; Edinburgh Unitary Councillor (Leader, Liberal Democrat Group) '95-; Edinburgh District Councillor (Liberal and Liberal Democrat Group Leader) '80-96 ; Lothian Regional Councillor (Leader, Liberal and Liberal Democrat Group) '74-95; Edinburgh Town Councillor '71-75; Chairman: Edinburgh City Youth Cafes Ltd, Diverse Attractions;
Outlook: A worthy veteran; belatedly-rewarded high-scoring local Edinburgh-Lothian councillor; a Left-of-Centre LibDem (in Liberator); also in Amnesty International, Charter 88; he has been fifth-time lucky after 25 years of local activism and many local achievements: a new suburban station, youth cafes, a community arts venue, a sports centre and after-school care centres; is a Director of many local institutions: the Edinburgh Festival Theatre Trust, Royal Lyceum Theatre, Queen's Hall, Lothian Enterprise;
History: Following a family precedent - a relative was Agent to Liberal PM Sir Henry Campbell-Bannerman - he joined the Liberal Party '61; first fought Edinburgh West against incumbent Tory James Stoddart, coming a poor third behind George Foulkes, with 8.2%, June '70; was elected to Edinburgh Town Council for Corstorphine May '71; again fought Edinburgh West, again coming 3rd but with a vote increased to 21.5%, Feb '74; was elected to Lothian Regional Council May '74; for the 3rd time fought Edinburgh West, but came 4th behind the SNP with 16.4% Oct '74; was elected to Edinburgh District Council May '80; campaigned to keep open the casualty department of Western General Hospital May '91; his petition forced Scottish Health Minister Michael Forsyth to set up a review of Edinburgh Royal Infirmary's Accident and Emergency unit Nov '91; insisted savings from closing small schools were "small and often disappear completely" Dec '91; fighting Edinburgh West for the 4th time, came within 879 votes of ousting Lord James Douglas-Hamilton, its incumbent MP and Scottish Officer Minister Apr '92; again insisted that if the Government pushed a unitary

system for local government, Edinburgh should form one of its councils Aug '93; at annual conference warned that Tony Blair could become a dictator unless a written constitution vested sovereignty in the people, not in Parliament Sep '96; admitted to Nolan Committee on Standards in Public Life that his suspicions of corruption by local planning committees were unprovable because they received "a brown envelope full of notes from a developer" Dec '96; with the help of tactical voting, won Edinburgh West by 7,253 votes over Lord Douglas-Hamilton May '97; was named to LibDems' Scottish team, under Jim Wallace May '97; in his Maiden said his constituents would benefit from a Scottish Parliament, insisting that English Conservatives displayed toward Scotland "the sort of arrogance that previous British people perhaps displayed to some of their colonies" May '97; opposed a referendum on home rule in Scotland, a proposal he blamed on Labour's "panic"; if it were held, he opposed its second question, on taxation June '97; opposed inclusion of Conservatives on Scottish Grand Committee June '97; accused the Conservatives of having shown "the flattest learning curve in history" on Scottish home rule July '97; asked for public bodies to be encouraged to commission tapestries for their buildings July '97; worried that paying for university tuition costs would discriminate against Scottish students, with their four-year courses July '97; led motion urging more ecumenical prayers in the Commons July '97; urged the public be consulted in NHS PFI projects, to curb the "strong Napoleonic tendencies" of some consultants July '97;

Born: 2 April 1933, Dehra Dun, India

Family: Son, of Robert Maclagan Gorrie, forest officer and soil erosion consultant, and Sydney Grace (Easterbrook); m '57 Astrid Margaret (Salvesen), housing officer; 2s: Robert '59, Euan '62;

Education: Hurst Grange School, Stirling; Oundle School; Corpus Christi College, Oxford University (Classical Mods and Modern History); Edinburgh University;

Occupation: Fulltime Councillor '95-97; ex: Administrative Director/Research Director, Scottish Liberals and Liberal Democrats; started a small business in '77; was initially a schoolmaster at Gordonstoun and Marlborough College for 9 years;

Traits: Balding; grey; long-headed; glasses; dour; lugubrious; hound-dog expression; Scots burr; former Scottish 800m record-holder; Elder of the Church of Scotland;

Address: House of Commons, Westminster, London SW1A 0AA; 9 Garscube Terrace, Edinburgh EH12 6BW;

Telephone: 0171 219 3000 (H of C); 0131 337 2077 (home);

James (Whiteside) GRAY **Conservative** **WILTSHIRE NORTH '97-**

Majority: 3,475 over over Liberal Democrat 6-way; **Description:** Largely renamed old Chippenham plus the rolling countryside and beautiful villages of northwest Wiltshire, which straddles the M4 industrial corridor; the market town of Malmesbury houses the fast-growing Dyson vacuum cleaner factory; the seat was deprived in '95 of Cricklade and Calne; on a projection from '92, it was expected to provide the Tories with a majority of almost 15,000;
Position: On Select Committee on Environment, Transport and Regional Affairs '97-; Secretary, Conservative MPs' Agriculture Committee '97-; in Parliamentary Maritime Group '97-; ex: Deputy Chairman, Tooting Conservative Association '94-96; in Conservative Foreign Affairs Forum, Parliamentary Maritime Group; Associate of the Centre for Policy Studies;
Outlook: A not-overly-partisan mainstream loyalist stepping queasily into ex-MP Richard Needham's 'wet' shoes; a self-described "Dunblane boy" who opposed Labour's Firearms (Amendment) Bill; a former futures broker turned political adviser and lobbyist; a former Special Adviser and lobbyist who claims "British politics is the cleanest in the world"; therefore considered ""Tim-nice-but-dim" by some former lobbying colleagues; a Eurosceptic and a counter-devolutionary Scot who was one of the first to jump on the Hague bandwagon;
History: He came from a Conservative family, and supported the Tories in Glasgow High School and Glasgow University; joined the Conservative Party at 16, '70; at Glasgow University became the Arts Faculty Representative on the Students Representative Council '73; became a branch chairman of the Wandsworth Tooting Conservative Association '89; was selected to fight Charles Kennedy in Ross, Cromarty and Skye Mar '91; with other Tory candidates, co-signed a letter to DAILY TELEGRAPH expressing "scepticism about both a single European currency and political union" Oct '91; admitted the Tory loss of the Kincardine and Deeside by-election was a "trouncing" but ascribed it to protests against regimental mergers and unpopular trust hospitals; he denied it reflected a demand for a tax-raising Scottish Assembly; independence would convert Scotland into an offshore Cuba Nov '91; insisted the Skye bridge could only be financed by tolls Jan '92; after suffering thousands of pounds of damage to his car from an acid attack, said "this kind of viciousness has no place in Highland politics" Feb '92; secured a 5.6% swing against Charles Kennedy, cutting almost 4,000 off his previous 11,000-plus majority Apr '92; was named Political Adviser to Environment Secretaries Michael Howard '92, and John Gummer '93; while advising Gummer, he was approached by Brent's then Tory Council Leader Bob Blackman to help secure an increase in Brent's rate support grant, at the instigation of lobbyists Westminster Strategy, to whom Brent's Tories were then paying £30,000 a year (according to Labour MP Ken Livingstone, who secured access to the files when Brent went Labour again); later on, in Gummer's reign at Environment, a proposal emerged to remove the duty of local authorities to put homeless families at the top of the council house waiting list; this provoked a campaign by Shelter; he tried to discredit this campaign by Shelter by hostile briefings to Tory councillors but was curbed; he then joined lobbyists Westminster Strategy, one of whose clients (Shelter) immediately departed '95; was selected for safe Wiltshire North, to replace Richard Needham who had announced his early retirement to return to his business career Jan

'95; came under "huge pressure from the gun lobby" (JG) in North Wiltshire, but backed Michael Howard's Firearms Act '96; was listed in the DAILY TELEGRAPH as planning to rule out in his election address ever joining a single European currency; he was also listed with mainstreamers Shaun Woodward and Damian Green as favouring a "full constructive contribution to the debate within Europe before any decisions are taken on a single currency" Dec '96; told the SUNDAY TIMES he was "deeply concerned about the way we are thundering down a path controlled by Europe"; he saw "no economic advantage" in a single currency and believed the Tory government's pledge to hold a referendum if it decided to join was not enough; "it should be supported by the will of the people in a free referendum" Mar '97; retained Wiltshire North on a majority shrunken to a quarter, by a 9.3% swing to the Liberal Democrats May '97; claimed his local employers would "lay off workers the morning after [Blair] brings in the minimum wage" May '97; was an early Hague supporter June '97; in his Maiden, urged the Government to ban quickly beef from Europe's "dodgy abattoirs"; also supported fox-hunting and opposed Labour's Firearms (Amendment) Bill, although his mother was one of the local doctors "who took part in the counselling in the aftermath of the tragedy" in Dunblane, where he grew up June '97; urged a comprehensive review of service pensions June '97; urged extension of closed circuit TV July '97; asked a brace of questions on Wiltshire care homes July '97;

Born: 7 November 1954, Glasgow

Family: Son, of late Very Rev Dr John R Gray, former Moderator of the General Assembly of the Church of Scotland and Minister of Dunblane Cathedral, and Dr Sheila (Whiteside) GP, who helped counsel the young survivors in the aftermath of the Dunblane tragedy; m '80 Sarah Ann (Beale); 2s John '84, William '91; 1d Olivia '86;

Education: Hillhead Primary; Glasgow High School '66-71; Glasgow University '71-75 (MA Hons); Christ Church, Oxford '75-77 (Postgraduate research)

Occupation: Author: Shipping Futures (1990), Futures and Options for Shipping (1987; winner of Lloyds of London book prize), Financial Risk Management (1985); ex: Director, Westminster Strategy (lobbyists) '95-97; Political Adviser, to Environment Secretary John Gummer '93-95, Environment Secretary Michael Howard '92-93; Director, Baltic Futures Exchange '89-91; Managing Director, GNI Freight Futures Ltd '85-92; Senior Manager, GNI Ltd (futures brokers) '89-92; Shipbroker and Department Manager, with Anderson Hughes Ltd '78-84; Trainee, then Shipbroker, with P&O '77-78;

Traits: Tall; handsome; sleeked-back dark brown retreating hair; long, oval face; long nose; "grim-looking" (OBSERVER); statesmanlike mien; urbane, Anglicised product of the Scottish church Establishment; retains only the faintest Scottish burr; enjoys riding in the Honourable Artillery Company's Saddle Club;

Address: House of Commons, Westminster, London SW1A 0AA; Rosewood Cottage, Slaughterford, Chippenham, Wilts SN14 8RF

Telephone: 0171 219 6237 (H of C); 01249 782378 (home);

PROFILERS AS BARBERS

When we started illustrating our volumes, we never anticipated outdated MPs' photographs would force us to double as barbers. In every volume ever published we have incurred cries of "I no longer have a moustache!" or "I have shaved my beard" or "I haven't worn my hair that long for five years". There is nothing more dismaying than telling your artist how good his sketch was and then seeing the woman MP portrayed with hair five inches shorter two hours later.

Damian GREEN **Conservative** **ASHFORD '97-**

Majority: 5,355 over Labour 6-way;
Description: The south Kent seat increasingly known for its Channel Tunnel terminus; politically it is dominated by its Tory-leaning rural southern hinterland - 'Darling Buds of May' territory -stretching to Tenterden, near the Sussex border; these areas more than compensate for the Labour-voters on the London overspill estate around Stanhope in west Ashford, or the LibDem voters in the private housing estates in Willesborough on its southern borders; on '92 projections it was expected to produce a Tory majority of 17,000-plus;
Position: On the Select Committee on Culture, the Media and Sports '87-; ex: in John Major's Downing Street Policy Unit '92-94; Treasurer, Hammersmith Conservative Association '88-91; Vice Chairman, National Association of Conservative Graduates '80-82; President of the Oxford Union '77; Chairman, Oxford's Tory Reform Group '76-77;
Outlook: The 'One Nation' pro-European who seems to be shedding his Centre-Left credentials, in the wake of campaigning for Ken Clarke; has already lapsed his Tory Reform Group membership but claims he is still a supporter of electoral reform; retains his concern that the potential impact of the digital revolution may damage public service broadcasting; initially turned out to be a strongly partisan Labour Budget-basher in competition with his predominantly Rightwing colleagues; his 15 years as a financial journalist made him resemble them more closely; superimposed on those years were his six years as John Major's speech-writer and as a member of the Downing Street Policy Unit;
History: He joined the Conservative Party '75; he joined the executive committee of the Oxford University Conservative Association '76; he becamer Chairman of Oxford's Tory Reform Group '76; he became Chairman of the Oxford Union '77; he became Vice Chairman of the National Association of Conservative Graduates '80; contested council seat in Hammersmith May '86; wrote speeches for John Major as Treasury's Chief Secretary '88; was selected as Ken Livingstone's opponent in Brent East Sep '89; again constested a council seat in Hammersmith May '90; backed licence fees as least worst alternative for funding BBC Mar '91; at annual conference, said he didn't mind that "the Church of England is no longer the Tory Party at prayer, but wished it was sometimes the Church of England at prayer" Oct '91; contested Brent East against Ken Livingstone, suffering one of the biggest (6%) swings to Labour Apr '92; joined John Major's Downing Street Policy Unit '92; at annual conference, called for a Grand Committee of London MPs, to co-ordinate policy for the capital Oct '92; in pursuit of selection for Dorset West was beaten by Thatcherite Oliver Letwin Nov '94; won selection on the first ballot for Ashford against the unmarried Rightwing Lamont adviser David Cameron Dec '94; as a candidate had to resign from the Downing Street Policy Unit Dec '94; was active in John Major's contest against John Redwood for the Leadership June '95; warned that digital TV could mean the end of public service broadcasting Apr '96; was listed among the minority of Tory candidates loyal to John Major and willing to negotiate to enter a single European currency Dec '96; retained Ashford with a shrunken majority of 5,355 after a pro-Labour swing of 12.5% May '97; urged that the Monetary Policy Committee be vetted by the Treasury Select Committee May '97; urged school students previously helped by the phased-out Assisted Places Scheme be allowed to stay on until 18, June '97; was on

Kenneth Clarke's campaign team June '97; claimed there had been a generation shift among Tory MPs, with new MPs deciding not to behave as "our elders and supposed betters behaved in the last Parliament" June '97; urged minimum mandatory sentences for "persistent burglars and dealers in hard drugs" July '97; said Chancellor Gordon Brown' Budget had "put a massive time bomb under the British economy; when it goes off, it will blow up the Chancellor's reputation and, more important, it will cause enormous damage to the prosperity of the British people and the prospects of job creation"; "his actions on Advance Corporation Tax, which will damage pension funds, and on removing tax relief on health care insurance for the elderly go against all the nostrums propounded" by Frank Field July '97; was named to the Select Committee on Culture, the Media and Sports July '97;

Born: 17 January 1958, Barry, Glamorgan

Family: Son, of Howard Green, journalist and company director, and Audrey Edith (Lyons) teacher; m '88 Alicia (Collinson), barrister (who does not like being called just 'Mrs Green'); 2d Felicity '90, Verity;

Education: St Helen's RC School, Barry; Alfred Sutton School, Reading; Reading School; Balliol College, Oxford University (MA 1st Class Hons in PPE; President of the Union '77);

Occupation: Public Afairs Consultant '94-; Policy Director: European Media Forum (think tank) '95-; Author: 'Communities in the Countryside' (1996 Social Market Foundation), 'The Cross-Media Revolution' (1995), 'Freedom of the Airways' (Conservative Political Centre, 1990), 'A Better BBC' (Centre for Policy Studies 1991); 'ITN Budget Factbook' (1986, 1985 1984); ex: on Downing Street Policy Unit '92-94; Speechwriter, to John Major '88-92; Financial Journalist '74-92: Presenter and City Editor, Business Daily, Channel 4 '87-92, Business Editor, Channel 4 '85-87, News Editor, Business News, TIMES '82-84, Producer of financial news programme, BBC Radio 4 '78-82;

Traits: Retreating mousey light brown hair; broad nose; plain-looking; cocked left eyebrow; awkward; financial journalist type; "a nice guy" (OBSERVER); cricket enthusiast (MCC and Surrey); member of 'The Fowlers' football team (named after Sir Norman Fowler);

Address: House of Commons, Westminster, London SW1A 0AA;

Telephone: 0171 219 3911 (H of C); 01233 820911 (constituency);

Dominic (Charles Roberts) GRIEVE Conservative BEACONSFIELD '97-

Majority: 13,987 over Liberal Democrat 9-way;

Description: One of London's most affluent suburbs, the Tories' 3rd safest pre-'97 seat; it is in South Bucks, the most Tory part of that most Tory county; it contains affluent Stoke Poges, Gerrards Cross and Burnham Beeches as well as Beaconsfield itself; Disraeli took his title from it because of his nearby Hughenden home; it was made even safer in '83 by losing its near-Slough council houses; in '95 it acquired a ward from Wycombe; much more exciting was the last- minute departure of its former Tory MP, Tim Smith, who very belatedly resigned for concealing his acceptance of £25,000 in used notes from Harrods owner Mohammed al-Fayed; on a '92-style division of the vote, the seat was expected to produce a Tory majority of over 23,000;

Position: On Joint Committee on Statutory Instruments '97-; Secretary of Conservative MPs' Constitutional, Legal and Northern Ireland Committees '97-; ex: Hammersmith and Fulham Councillor (Chairman Housing) '82-86; Vice Chairman, Fulham Conservative Association '88-91; Chairman of the Research Committee of the Society of Conservative Lawyers; President, of Oxford University Conservative Association '77;

Outlook: The churchy barrister son of a former churchy barrister Tory MP; not overly partisan; a bilingual Francophile with a French mother; a descendant of Roxburghshire cattle thieves who opposes devolution: "I do not want to follow the English nationalist road; my ancestors come from every corner of the UK and I see myself as British through and through" (DG); favours incorporating the European Convention on Human Rights into UK law;

History: Claims to have been in politics since 1962 when, at 6, he distributed leaflets for his father, who became MP for Solihull two years later '64; he helped in all subsequent elections until his father retired; he himself was elected President of the Oxford University Conservative Association '77; was elected to Hammersmith and Fulham Council May '82; was selected to contest Labour-held Norwood against John Fraser '85; suffered a higher than average anti-Tory swing of 2.3% in Norwood June '87; following the last-minute resignation of the incumbent cash-for-questions MP, Tim Smith, he was unexpectedly selected for super-safe Beaconsfield, because of his "intellectual approach", defeating better-known MPs David Harris and Dame Janet Fookes, who had both decided to quit their threatened marginal West country seats, and Martin Howe QC the Eurosceptic nephew of Geoffrey Howe; he was the last candidate to be selected Apr '97; retained the seat with a halved majority of 13,987, after an anti-Tory swing of 8.2%, May '97; in his anti-devolution Maiden told how the Union had benefited his family, who had started as "cattle and sheep thieves" in Roxburghshire; said it was "desirable" to incorporate into UK law the European Convention on Human Rights May '97; opposed the handgun ban in the Labour Government's Firearms (Amendment) Bill, insisting that .22 calibre handguns were almost never used in crimes (despite the murders of Robert Kennedy and Yitzak Rabin) June '97; was named to the Joint Committee on Statutory Instruments June '97; co-sponsored motion attacking the Labour Minister, Lord Simon of Highbury, for having failed to sell his £2m of BP shares July '97; worried about Commons supervision of the Welsh Assembly's power to issue secondary legislation (or statutory instruments) July '97; urged a "twin-track approach" to early detection and cure since "the seeds of delinquency are sown in early childhood" July '97;

Born: 24 May 1956, London

Family: Son, of Percy Grieve QC and MP for Solihull '64-83, and Evelyn Raymonde Louise (Mijouain) of Paris; m '90 Caroline (Hutton), barrister; 2s: James '94, Hugo '95;

Education: Colet Court (where he won a speaking competition on the subject of de Gaulle); Westminster School; Magdalen College, Oxford University (MA in Modern History); called to the Bar for Middle Temple '80;

Occupation: Barrister '81- ; ex-Director, of Hutton-Rostron (unremunerated; it is his father-in-law's firm) '96;

Traits: Parted short plastered-down hair; beaky nose; crooked smile; bilingual (French mother); "I hope I came into politics intending to conduct myself with integrity and courtesy" (DG); a hill-walker; on Church of England London Diocesan Synod; a Lay Visitor to police stations;

Address: House of Commons, Westminster, London SW1A 0AA; 1 Temple Gardens, Temple, EC4Y 9BB; 38 Gunterstone Road, London W14 9BC

Telephone: 0171 219 3000 (H of C); 0171 353 0407 (chambers); 0171 602 4257 (home);

Jane GRIFFITHS **Labour** **READING EAST '97-**

Majority: 3,795 over Conservative 7-way;
Description: One of the seats seemingly put outside Labour's reach by dividing the Labour-leaning town in half and adding to each half Tory-leaning suburban and rural areas; this enabled its previous Tory MP, Dr Sir Gerard Vaughan to survive for a quarter century mainly on his bedside manner; when John Watts became the Tory candidate, in flight from marginal Slough, he was entitled to expect, on projections from '92, a majority close to 15,000, because the '95 changes had been limited to the exchange of two pro-Labour wards within the town and the exchange of five pro-Tory rural wards for four pro-Tory suburban wards;
Position: Reading Borough Councillor (Chairman, of Arts and Leisure) '84-;
Outlook: One of the '97 election's biggest surprises, who won on a 14% swing, despite not being in one of Labour's well-supported target seats; hopes such "unlikely" newcomers can help reform the Commons "before we become institutionalised"; she won without the help of an all-women's short-list but is still a feminist ("by changing the atmosphere of Parliament we can send a message to women that they can do anything they want to"); a local woman councillor and linguist-translator, who has an international outlook; in Transport 2000, Greenpeace and Charter 88;
History: She joined the Labour Party at 29, '83; was elected to Reading Borough Council May '89; was selected to contest Reading East Oct '95; found out the possible date of the election by 'phoning Conservative Central Office to ask when their election manifesto would be available Jan '97; on a swing of 14%, won the seat with a majority of 3,795 over Transport Minister John Watts, who thought he had found a seat safer than Slough; with Martin Salter's win in Reading West, she helped capture the town for Labour for the first time since '70, May '97; urged a speedy phasing out of the Assisted Places Scheme May '97; in her Maiden disclosed that both her daughter and her mother were currently university students June '97; co-sponsored motion applauding the Labour Government for stripping out the bureaucracy from the NHS June '97; backed outlawing of fox-hunting June '97; backed motion supporting a jailed Indonesian trade union leader June '97; urged the reinstatement of benefits for asylum seekers June '97; asked about subsidies for Gallagher's tobacco company in Northern Ireland July '97; co-sponsored motion deploring loss of insurance access for injured employees of companies in liquidation July '97; led motion urging further protection of water meadows July '97;
Born: 17 April 1954, West London
Family: Daughter, of late John Griffiths, advertising agent, and Pat (Thomas), who became a university student in her late 60s; m '75 Ralph Spearpoint; 1s Toby '81, aspiring actor; 1d Martha '76, student; divorced '94; her "live-in partner" (PRIVATE EYE) is Andrew Tattersall, her Researcher and a fellow Reading Councillor; of working-class parentage and Welsh and Scottish heritage; distantly related to Dylan Thomas on her mother's side;
Education: Cedars Grammar School, Leighton Buzzard; Durham University (BA in Russian);
Occupation: Translator/Journalist: Asia Editor, BBC Monitoring, Caversham, Reading (NUJ) '84-97; ex: Translator from Russian and Japanese at GCHQ Cheltenham '77-84;

Traits: Tall; rangy; auburn hair; cafe au lait colouring; "sometimes I see myself on television and think I look terminally ill"; subtle; thoughtful; speaks without notes; enjoys cycling, the cinema and the theatre;
Address: House of Commons, Westminster, London SW1A 0AA; 21 Gane Wharf, Reading RG1 3AY;
Telephone: 0171 219 5079 (H of C);

John GROGAN **Labour** **SELBY '97-**

Majority: 3,836 over Conservative 5-way;
Description: The flat countryside south of York, containing York University, the two towns of Selby and Tadcaster (beer), Drax power station, the massive new Selby coalfield and many farms; solidly Tory since its creation in '83, it was the safe pulpit for the 2nd Church Commissioner, Sir Michael Alison, who bequeathed it to ex-Tory MP Kenneth Hind; he had the right to expect a Tory majority of 9,000, if voters behaved as in '92;
Position: President, Oxford University Students Union '82-83;
Outlook: A third-time-lucky witty young political staffer rewarded for his patience by becoming the first-ever Labour MP for this seat; in his three tries he hacked away at a Tory majority initially standing at 16,000; "New Labour" (NEW STATESMAN); pro-Europe; favours electoral reform; his previous big win was to become the first Labour President of Oxford's Student Union; formerly in CND;
History: He joined the Labour Party at 15, '76; initially in CND, he was the first Labour man to be elected President of the Oxford University Students Union '82; contested "hopeless" Selby against incumbent Tory MP Michael Alison, increasing the Labour vote from 3rd place with 20.5% to second place with 26.7%, June '87; as a Yorkshire candidate in the Euro-election, campaigned against privatisation of Yorkshire water, because of its threat to access to 17,000 acrea of recreational land June '89; was re-selected for Selby July '90; again contested Selby against Michael Alison, improving Labour's vote from 26.7% to 34.8%, Apr '92; on an 11.1% swing, defeated Michael Alison's would-be Tory successor, ex-MP Kenneth Hind by a majority of 3,836; said: "I won because of the Blair effect and the modernisation of the Labour Party" May '97; was asked by a Whip whether he would accept Michael Alison's job as 2nd Church Commissioner, but had to demur as a Roman Catholic May '97; asked about risks from disposal of BSE carcasses in landfill sites May '97; in a witty Maiden, he disclosed he was an Oxford contemporary of William Hague; he had become President of the Oxford Students' Union, while Hague had become President of the Oxford Union; Hague's career had soared higher, he admitted, but "I have retained just a little bit more of my hair" July '97;
Born: 24 February 1961, Halifax
Family: Son, of John Martin Grogan, teacher (rtd), and late Mauren (Jennings);
Education: St Michael's (RC) College, Leeds; St John's College, Oxford University (MA in Modern History and Economics);
Occupation: Director, Yorkshire Business Forum '95-; ex: Director, of his own business

event management consultancy which "probably owed as much to the business techniques of Arthur Daley as to those of ICI" '94-97; ex: Communications Co-ordinator, of Leeds City Council (GMB) '87-94; Personal Assistant, to Leader of Wolverhampton Council '85-87; Personal Assistant, to Barry Seal, MEP for Yorkshire West '84;
Traits: Dark; square face; tousled Irish look; witty; Roman Catholic; supporter of Yorkshire County Cricket Club and Bradford City Football Club;
Address: House of Commons, Westminster, London SW1A 0AA; 141 St Johns Terrace, Leeds LS3 1DU;
Telephone: 0171 219 4043 (H of C); 01937 531830 (constituency);

Patrick HALL **Labour** **BEDFORD '97-**

Majority: 8,300 over Conservative 5-way;
Description: The former North Bedfordshire seat made marginal in '95 by stripping out its rural hinterland, reducing it to its urban core; it is a thousand-year-old town with industries (including brewing) and a large Italian minority, attracted by its surrounding brickfields; there is also a non-white minority of around 15%; on its '95 boundaries, the '92 election would have produced a roughly 4,500 Tory majority;
Position: Bedfordshire County Councillor '89-; on North Bedfordshire Community Health Council; Chairman, Bedfordshire Door-to-Door Dial-a-Ride;
Outlook: A low-profiled second-time-lucky moderate Blairite town planner and county politician; believes in a "fair society", "balancing rights and responsibilities" in a "one-nation society"; in Greenpeace, Friends of the Earth, Amnesty International, the Co-operative Party;
History: He joined the Labour Party at 23, '74; initiated local political education social-political evenings in the early '80s; was elected to Bedfordshire County Council May '89; contested Bedordshire North against Sir Trevor Skeet, moving Labour from 3rd place with 23.2% to 2nd place with 31%, Apr '92; accused those favouring women-only short-lists of using "a strong element of moral blackmail" Oct '94; was re-selected for the renamed, favourably redistributed seat Apr '95; was criticised at a local 'What's Left' meeting addressed by pro-Trotskyists, Labour MP Jeremy Corbyn and the barred Leeds NE candidate, Liz Davies Nov '95; won the seat with a swing of 13% providing a majority of 8,300 over Sir Trevor Skeet's successor, Robert Blackman May '97; urged a reform of the distribution of the proceeds of the National Lottery May '97; urged Government to carry out its manifesto promise to incorporate the European Convention on Human Rights into domestic law June '97; in his wide-ranging Maiden emphasised Bedford's cultural diversity, with people from "more than 50 different countries of origin", many suffering from a shortage of affordable housing and the "bureaucratic nightmare which is the Child Support Agency" July '97
Born: 20 October 1951, Birmingham
Family: His mother is Belgian;
Education: Bedford Modern School; Birmingham University (BA in Geography); Oxford Polytechnic (Post-Graduate Diploma in Town Planning); in Chartered Institute of Public Finance and Accountancy;

Occupation: Town Planner: Planning Officer and Town Centre Co-ordinator for Bedford (introduced its town centre CCTV and retailers' radio communications link to the police) (NALGO/UNISON);
Traits: Youthful-looking; parted brown hair; high forehead; enjoys squash, gardening, photography;
Address: House of Commons, Westminster, London SW1A 0AA; 12 Cowper Road, Bedford MK40 2AU;
Telephone: 0171 219 3000 (H of C);

Fabian HAMILTON **Labour** **LEEDS NORTH EAST '97-**

Majority: 6,959 over Conservative 5-way;
Description: The unaltered former Tory stronghold in Leeds - for 31 years the base of Sir Keith Joseph; it stretches from inner city multi-ethnic Chapeltown to the affluent suburbs and the stately home of Harewood House; it has become increasingly marginal as more of its large older houses in the inner city have been taken over by students and non-white immigrants; its Moortown and Allerton wards house the third largest Jewish settlement in Britain;
Position: On the Select Committee on Administration '97-; Chairman, Leeds Racial Equality Committee '88-; ex: Leeds City Councillor (Chairman, Education) '87-97; Chairman, Leeds West Constituency Labour Party '87-88;
Outlook: Blairite 'New Labour' newcomer who supplanted as the candidate the NEC-barred semi-Trotskyist, Liz Davies, after a bitter local battle; unpopular with partisans of Ms Davies, who have publicised his business failures; "to some an affable loyalist, to others a ruthless opportunist in benign disguise" (RED PEPPER); "a brilliant speaker but a terrible businessman; he will make a wonderful MP" (fellow Leeds Labour MP); in the Co-operative Party, formerly in Anti-Apartheid;
History: He joined the Labour Party at 24, '79; was elected to Leeds City Council May '87; became Chairman of the Leeds Racial Equality Committee '88; contested Leeds North East against Tim Kirkhope, pushing Labour from 3rd place with 25.3% to 2nd place with 36.8%, Apr '92; selection for Leeds North East, designated as an all-women's short-list, was won by Islington councillor Liz Davies, whose candidacy was disallowed by Labour's NEC for her semi-Trotskyist sympathies and connections and her initial refusal to pay poll tax Sep '95; the subsequent selection contest was opened to all, as a result of the court ruling against all-women short-lists; despite wide publicity given by Leftwingers to his business failures - the liquidation of two graphic design companies and seven court orders against him for personal debts -Hamilton won selection by 165 to 141 over 'Bennite' Pam Tatlow Sep '96; he was summoned to appear before Leeds magistrates in a private prosecution said to have been brought by Leftwing opponents alleging 17 breaches of the Companies Act, Jan '97; this was quashed, with heavy costs against Hamilton's persecutors Apr '97; Labour's NEC suspended Leeds NE CLP after a failed attempt to oust Leftwing office holders at the AGM and a dispute about the eligibility of some of the delegates Feb '97; unprecedentedly the NEC barred four named local activists from representing the Labour Party in the election campaign Feb '97; in

the campaign backed plan to relocate in Leeds the Jewish public school, Carmel College Apr '97; won the seat on a swing of 11.9%, ousting Home Office Minister Tim Kirkhope by a majority of 6,959, making him the seat's first Labour MP since Alice Bacon ('45-55) May '97; told the JEWISH CHRONICLE he would continue to back Carmel College as a Jewish high school in Leeds May '97; backed motion supporting a jailed Indonesian union leader June '97; in his Maiden claimed Leeds had "one of the fastest growing economies of any city in Great Britain" partly because of "the partnership between the Labour-controlled local authority and the business community" June '97; pointed out that £100m in prescription frauds would finance 14,500 heart operations June '97; in the wake of a bomb in Jerusalem, urged PM Tony Blair to encourage the Middle East peace process July '97; asked about chemical contamination of food July '97; asked for a reduction in "the bureaucracy connected with the regulation of small businesses" July '97; was named to the Select Committee on Administration July '97;

Born: 12 April 1955, London

Family: Son, of John Hamilton, circuit judge, and Patricia (Henman); is married, with three children;

Education: Brentwood School, Essex; York University (BA Hons in Social Sciences);

Occupation: Full-time Leeds City Councillor til '97; Systems Consultant; former Graphic Designer: Director, of Crypticks Graphic Design Ltd (wound-up voluntarily '91), Serif Typesetting Ltd (ceased trading '94); these resulted in seven county court judgements against him, all of which were paid off in full; two other companies of his were struck off the Register for failing to lodge annual returns; was a Taxi Driver at one time;

Traits: Tall; black beard; "his arguments and affability are impressive" (Anne Simpson, GLASGOW HERALD); Jewish; enjoys swimming, music, cars and computers;

Address: House of Commons, Westminster, London SW1A 0AA; 22 Occupation Lane, Pudsey, Leeds LS 28 8HL;

Telephone: 0171 219 3000 (H of C);

Philip HAMMOND **Conservative** **RUNNYMEDE & WEYBRIDGE '97-**

Majority: 9,875 over Labour 6-way;

Description: A new seat, based mainly on former Chertsey and Walton plus a bit of Surrey NW; it includes not only the historic field on which Magna Carta was signed, but also some of the most sumptuous recent suburbs, like Virginia Water; this makes it about the sixteenth safest Tory seat; if voters had reacted as in '92, it would have provided a Conservative majority of over 22,000;

Position: Chairman, Lewisham East Conservative Association '89-96; on Conservative Greater London Area Executive Council '89-96;

Outlook: A mainstream, Bow Group management consultant and small manufacturer of medical equipment; "Centre" (Julie Kirkbride, DAILY TELEGRAPH); opposed to "knee jerk" complete privatisation; inherited a blue chip seat after a by-election blooding at Newham NE;

History: He joined the Oxford University Conservative Association '77; his first active political involvement was in support of Sir John Wheeler in Westminster North June '79;

campaigned for Colin Moynihan in Lewisham East June '83; at annual conference, opened the Health debate Oct '90; at annual conference spoke in Law and Order debate Oct '93; contested a seat on Southwark Borough Council May '94; fought by-election in hopeless Newham NE, retaining 2nd place for the Tories June '94; was short-listed for Maidenhead, but lost to Theresa May Nov '95; was selected for the new, super-safe seat of Runnymede and Weybridge Nov '95; in his election address, opposed a single European currency Dec '96; in the campaign, insisted: "in all areas of public spending we need to look at where we can introduce private provision; the question is who can deliver a given level of cover most efficiently; we don't want to knee-jerk and privatise everything" Mar '97; won the seat by a 9,875 majority, despite a swing to Labour of 13.1% May '97; was on Peter Lilley's campaign team (later switching to William Hague) June '97; in his Maiden, paid a fulsome tribute to his predecessor, Sir Geoffrey Pattie, but only passing acknowledgement to Ian Greer's accomplice, Sir Michael Grylls June '97; asked about the frequency of ministerial overseas trips to promote British exports July '97; asked about days lost from strikes July '97; boasted that Conservative Runnymede had switched on "a splendid CCTV" which made "a significant contribution to controllIng local crime" while Elmbridge "controlled by a coalition of Liberal Democrats and Ratepayers" had rejected CCTV for "rather spurious libertarian arguments" July '97; asked whether "the estate of the late Frederick West is now solvent" July '97;

Born: 4 December 1955, Epping, Essex

Family: Son of Bernard Lawrence Hammond, civil engineer and local government officer, and Doris Rose (Clarkson); m '91 Susan (Williams-Walker), former Researcher to Richard Ottoway MP; 2d: Amy '94, Sophie '96;

Education: Brookfield County Primary School, Hutton, Essex; Shenfield School, Brentwood; University College, Oxford University (MA, 1st Class Hons in PPE);

Occupation: Managing Director and Majority Shareholder, of Castlemead Homes Ltd (a small housebuilding company) '84-; ex: Co-Founder, of Castlemead Ltd (a business development consultancy with blue-chip clients in the oil and gas, engineering and brewing industries) '92-95; Director, of Speywood Medical Ltd, Arbo GmbH and Meditech Sri Lothers (firms of medical equipment manufacturers '87-95; Director & Shareholder, of a firm of medical equipment manufacturers '81-86; Personal Assistant to Chairman, of Speywood Laboratories Ltd '77-81;

Traits: Brown, parted hair; lean face; cadaverous look; bags under eyes; lop-sided mouth; enjoys hill-walking in Scotland; a non-golfer, although his seat "stretches from the Wentworth golf course in the west to the St George's Hill golf course in the east, by way of another five first-class courses" (PH);

Address: House of Commons, Westminster, London SW1A 0AA;

Telephone: 0171 219 4055/5851(Fax) (H of C);

KEEPING PARLIAMENTARY SECRETS

A rueful MP claimed, with some truth, that the best way to keep something secret is to make a speech about it in the Palace of Westminster. He was commenting on the emptiness of the Press Gallery (except for HANSARD writers and the Press Association). Long gone are the days when serious newspapers carried a full or half-page summarising Parliamentary debate. Of late, Westminster has been used as a source of news stories. In our old-fashioned way, we read HANSARD daily and watch the Commons and Lords on the Parliamentary Channel. Parliamentary debaters are very self-revealing in debate. And we don't mean only Kerry Pollard MP, in whose Maiden he disclosed that until 12 he had to drop his trousers regularly to prove that Kerry was not a girl's name.

'Mike' (Michael Thomas) HANCOCK CBE **Liberal Democrat** **PORTSMOUTH SOUTH '97-, '84-87**

Majority: 4,327 over Conservative 7-way;
Description: An unaltered seat including the city centre, the ferry port, the former Royal Navy base with the more conservative seaside resort of Southsea; it has normally been a Conservative seat, perhaps because of its 30,000 workers employed in defence-related industries such as Vosper-Thorneycroft and Marconi Space and Defence Systems; the earlier exception was when the then SDPer Mike Hancock won the June '84 by-election; although he kept his base as a county councillor and city counillor, as a Liberal Democrat he was narrowly defeated by Conservative David Martin in '87 and '92; as an unaltered seat, had the '92 voting pattern remained, David Martin could have narrowly won in '97;
Position: Spokesman on Defence '97-, on Education Training and Employment '84-87; Portsmouth City Councillor (ex: Leader, its Labour Group '76-81) '71-; Hampshire County Councillor (Leader of the Lab-LibDem-controlled council '93-; sat as Labour '73-81, SDP '81-88, LibDem '89-) '73-;
Outlook: One of the most persistent candidates, who has fought the seat five times; won it the second time for the SDP, the fifth time for the Liberal Democrats; a deeply-rooted working-class type with union roots unusual for a LibDem; as Leader since '93 of the Hampshire County Counciil - controlled jointly by the LibDems and Labour - is a genuine Lib-Lab; an energetic middle-brow with a commonsensical approach; pours forth questions as if trying to make up for his decade out of the Commons; orthodox on defence: pro-NATO but anti-Trident; hostile to abortion, animal experiments, live animal exports and drug abuse;
History: His early roots were in the Labour Party which he joined at 18, '64; he became an AUEW shop steward at 21, '67; at 25, was elected for Labour to Portsmouth City Council May '71; came under the influence of the local Labour MP, Frank (later Lord) Judd; was elected to Hampshire County Council May '73; became Leader of the Labour Group on Hampshire County Council '76; left the Labour Party for the SDP "largely because of the lack of tolerance and understanding"; "I saw friends and colleagues torn limb from limb and realised there was no future for me in the party" June '81; contested Portsmouth South for the SDP, pushing Labour into 3rd place June '83; with the death of Bonner Pink, Portsmouth South's sitting Tory MP, was selected to fight the Portsmouth South by-election in preference to Bob Mitchell, after Shirley Williams had declined May '84; narrowly won the seat, overturning a 12,335 Tory majority, scoring the first by-election gain of any party in that Parliament June '84; urged the SDP to become more local, less smooth and not allow big names to be foisted on local parties June '84; in Maiden reaffirmed the Alliance's loyalty to NATO and US bases, but sought assurance that Portsmouth would remain the country's premier naval base June '84; urged prompt and positive action for drug abuse problems July '84; proposed raising dog licenses to £5, July '84; supported remaining in UNESCO Nov '84; favoured retaining the one-pound note Nov '84; worried about the use of live animals for research Nov '84; attacked Merrell Pharmaceutical for paying less compensation in UK than in USA for children damaged by Debendox Nov '84; supported the inclusion of homeopathy within the NHS Nov '84; co-sponsored Robin Squire's Local Government (Access to

Information) Bill Dec '84; voted against fluoridation Jan '85; supported Enoch Powell's Unborn Children (Protection) Bill Feb '85; favoured turning polytechnics into universities Feb '85; urged ballots for unions' political funds Mar '85; urged a new TGWU election, emphasising the "dangers of abuse inherent in work-place ballots" Apr '85; Labour refused to support him as Chairman of Hampshire County Council June '85; complained that Tory withdrawal of Wage Council protection for under-21s would "lead to the re-emergence of the sweatshops of 19th century" Aug '85; signed pro-Zionist motions Nov '96; after shutdown of Vosper-Thorneycroft, urged restoration of shipbuilding in Portsmouth Dec '86; opposed giving free TV licenses to all pensioners Jan '87; was named Alliance Spokesman on planning Jan '87; sponsored ban on crossbow sales Feb '87; lost the seat to Tory David Martin by 205 votes June '87; he sharply criticised Dr David Owen for not abiding by the SDP's democratic vote for merger Sep '87; was re-selected as the Liberal Democrat candidate for Portsmouth South; he again lost the seat, by 242 votes Apr '92; became Leader of Hampshire County Council with joint Labour and LibDem support May '93; was narrowly defeated by a Conservative in the Wight and Hampshire South Euro-seat, following lurid tabloid coverage of his private life June '94; again won Portsmouth South on a swing of 4.4%, ousting incumbent Tory MP David Martin by a majority of 4,327 May '97; was named the LibDems' Spokesman on Defence May '97; co-sponsored motion attacking the over-medication of the elderly June '97; backed motion expressing solidarity with jailed Indonesian union leader June '97; backed Labour's legislation to ban handguns, accepting the compensation as fair June '97; urged ban on white asbestos July '97; led motion urging ban on export of live animals July '97; opposed class and ethnic discrimination in the Forces but worried that recruitment of the homeless might turn into "new-style press gangs" Oct '97;

Born: 9 April 1946, Portsmouth

Family: Son, of Thomas Hancock, Royal Navy, and Eva (John); m '67 Jacqueline (Elliott); 1s Dean '76; 1d Jodi '73;

Education: Copnor and Portsea School;

Occupation: District Officer for MENCAP '89-; Engineer, in Portsmouth plant '75-84;

Traits: Greying dark mop of hair with greyed beard; chubby face; energetic; "I have a good basis of common sense"; Salvationist (on their Board of Management); "I have a firearms certificate, and have had one for a long time; I have fired pistols and rifles for nearly two decades";

Address: House of Commons, Westminster, London SW1A 0AA;

Telephone: 0171 219 3000 (H of C); 01329 287340 (home)

Dr Evan HARRIS **Liberal Democrat** **OXFORD WEST & ABINGDON '97-**

Majority: 6,285 over Conservative 9-way;
Description: Those six wards west of the Cherwell and Thames containing the whole of the historic walled city - including the bulk of the university, the main shopping centre and the town and county halls - plus the less cerebral town of Abingdon; this has been a Conservative-Liberal marginal since its creation in '83; its previous Tory occupant, former Education Secretary Dr John Patten, decided not to contest it after having won a majority of only 3,539 in '92;
Position: On the Liberal Democrats' parliamentary Health team '97-; on the National Council of British Medical Association (representing junior doctors in the southeast) '91-;
Outlook: A young Leftish medical trade unionist who chalked up one of the greatest LibDem successes in ousting his Tory opponent by tactical voting in Britain's most intellectual electorate; post-election, he has emerged as the scourge of Health Secretary Frank Dobson for inadequate funding for the NHS; an Oxford-trained medic who was the BMA's spokesman for young doctors in the southeast; very loyal to the NHS, has campaigned especially against long working hours of junior doctors; in Stonewall, Searchlight, ASH, Green Liberal Democrats;
History: He joined the SDP '85, Liberals '86, becoming President of the Oxford University Alliance Society '86; he switched to the Liberal Democrats '88; was selected as candidate for Oxford West in preference to Paddy Ashdown's favoured aide Alan Leaman and ethnic minorities campaigner Zerbanoo Gifford Mar '94; was denied the possibility of targeting the abrasive, sacked Education Secretary, John Patten, by the latter's announcement he would not stand again '95; at the annual LibDem conference, urged the retention within the NHS of nursing care for the elderly Sep '96; won Oxford West on an anti-Tory swing of 10.3%, giving him a 6,285 majority over his new Tory opponent, Laurence Harris May '97; in his Maiden, rattled off the names of all the Oxford colleges; expressed concern that higher education might well be denied to the less well-off May '97; actively campaigned for an improvement in the position of asylum-seekers June '97; co-sponsored motion to scale down council tax for mobile homes July '97; he defended his amendment to Government's PFI legislation, barring privatisation of any clinical services, as a defence of health teams in the NHS; his amendment was accused by Labour Health Minister Alan Milburn of wrecking the chance of hospitals being built under PFI at Dartford and Norwich July '97; co-sponsored motion welcoming the Blair Government's review of the detention of asylum seekers July '97; welcomed Labour's abolition of the two-tier system in NHS hospitals but retailed doctors' concern about "another two-tier system - those people on long waiting-lists who can afford to go privately can jump the queue, leaving those without means to wait even longer" July '97; at the Eastbourne annual conference of the LibDems was enthusiastically applauded for his vitriolic attack on Labour's inadequate funding of the NHS Sep '97;
Born: 21 October 1965, Liverpool
Family: He discloses no family details; divorced;
Education: Blue Coat School, a Liverpool comprehensive; Wadham College, Oxford University (BA Hons in Physiology, BM, BCh);
Occupation: Doctor and Public Health Registrar of Oxford Health Authority '94-97; ex: Junior Hospital Doctor, in Oxford hospitals '91-94, previously in Liverpool hospitals '88-91;

Traits: Young; handsome; dark, parted hair; long oval face; very articulate orator; Jewish;
Address: House of Common, Westminster, London SW1A 0AA; 32A North Hinksey Village, Oxford OX2 0NA;
Telephone: 0171 219 3000 (H of C); 01865 250424 (home);

John HAYES **Conservative** **SOUTH HOLLAND & THE DEEPINGS '97-**

Majority: 7,991 over Labour 4-way;
Description: The new seat covering the southeastern corner of Lincolnshire, surrounding its main market town of Spalding; mostly flat drained Fens fringing the Wash, between the Rivers Nene and Welland; prosperously agricultural and strongly Conservative; on its '92 showing, was expected to produce a 16,000 Tory majority;
Position: On the Select Committee on Agriculture '97-; Nottinghamshire County Councillor (Tory spokesman on Education) '85-; ex: Chairman, Aspley Ward, Conservative Association '80-83; on National Committee, Federation of Conservative Students '82-84; Chairman of Nottingham University Conservative Association '81;
Outlook: Bright but patronising hardline Rightwing Eurosceptic; rewarded with a safe seat after twice fighting Harry Barnes in NE Derbyshire; a former Nottingham University FCS activist recalled for "his tracts supporting Apartheid and his McCarthyite attacks on university staff" and "ardent strident feminists" (PRIVATE EYE);
History: He joined the Young Conservatives at 15, chairing a YC branch in Eltham '73; an FCS activist, he became Chairman of the Nottingham University Conservative Association '81; his dislike of "ardent, strident feminists" left him with few friends at university: "you could have counted the people on campus more unpopular than myself on the fingers of a thalidomide's hand" (JH); won a Nottinghamshire County Council seat May '85; fought NE Derbyshire against incumbent Labour MP Harry Barnes, slightly increasing the Tory vote, but seeing a larger Labour majority June '87; again slightly increased the Tory vote in NE Derbyshire, only to see Harry Barnes increase his majority Apr '92; having claimed "one of the best results in the Midlands", was selected for safe South Holland and The Deepings '95; wrote to the DAILY TELEGRAPH asking to be added to the list of Tory candidates opposed to Britain ever joining a European single currency Dec '96; retained the seat, despite a pro-Labour swing of 8.5%, securing a majority of 7,991 May '97; in his "noncontroversial" Maiden, attacked Labour's long predicted Bill to phase out the Assisted Places scheme as "an attack on poor people" forced into "dull egalitarian mediocrity" June '97; was mistakenly reported as being on Michael Howard's campaign committee; in fact he voted for John Redwood and then William Hague June '97; welcomed the Plant Varieties Bill June '97; was named to Select Committee on Agriculture June '97; attacked Gordon Brown's Budget for its windfall tax on utilities and tax on pension funds July '97;
Born: 23 June 1958, Woolwich, South London
Family: Son, of Harry Hayes; m 1st Alison, a former Nottinghamshire County Counciillor; divorced; m 2nd July '97 Susan (Hopewell);
Education: Colfe's Grammar School, Lewisham (school captain); Nottingham University

(BA Hons in Politics and History; PGCE); on its University Challenge team '79;
Occupation: Sales Director, of The Data Base Ltd, (two-man computer company, "with offices in Nottingham, Manchester and Wolverhampton employing 150+ staff with an annual turnover of over £20m" (JH) '85-; Management Consultant/Advisor, "to schools, colleges nd universities" (JH);
Traits: Dark; now clean-shaven but formerly bearded, unusually for a Conservative; chubby face; heavy; "a committed Christian" (LINCOLNSHIRE FREE PRESS); "I combine passionate beliefs, values and loyalties with an ability to laugh - even at myself - a combination which in my experience is unique" (JH): tends to exaggerate to his local paper the hours he spends in the Chamber, including Prayers; interested in antiques, painting and local history;
Address: House of Commons, Westminster, London SW1A 0AA; 23 Middleton Crescent, Beeston, Nottingham NG9 2TH
Telephone: 0171 219 3000 (H of C); 0115 9256808 (home):

Mrs Sylvia (Lloyd) HEAL Labour HALESOWEN & ROWLEY REGIS '97-

Majority: 10,337 over Conservative 6-way;
Description: The '95-new West Midlands marginal twinning Tory-leaning Halesowen with Labour-voting Rowley Regis;
Former Seat: Mid-Staffordshire '90-92;
Position: Ex: Assistant Spokesman, on Health and Women '91-92; on Select Committee on Education '90-92;
Outlook: The most attractive woman 'retread'; the return of a loyal former Kinnockite, at the same time as her sister, Ann Keen, who joined her husband, Alan Keen; the former miraculous winner of the Mid-Staffordshire by-election in '90, who narrowly lost it to Michael Fabricant in '92; an attractive lady with the externals of a Surrey magistrate: "an impressive opponent with that slightly intimidating manner that says 'magistrate' a mile off" (Jon Hibbs, DAILY TELEGRAPH); despite this, has the concerns of a social worker and the foreign and defence views of a Welsh Leftwinger: was in CND until '88 and initially opposed the Gulf War in '91;
History: She was born into the actively pro-Labour family of a Shotton steel worker and Labour councillor; from the age of eight was involved in distributing leaflets and helping to man the family's committee room '50; joined the Labour Party at 16 '58; her speaking ability attracted the attention of the local Labour MP, Eirene (later Baroness) White, who encouraged her to attend Coleg Harlech; at 17 she was the Welsh representative on the National Council of Young Socialists '59; she met Neil Kinnock as a member of the Socialist Society at Swansea University '67; when she settled in Egham, Surrey, she became a local teller at elections and CND activist from '70; she became a local magistrate '73; she helped campaign for her nurse sister Ann Keen, an even closer friend of the Kinnocks, and Labour candidate for Brentford and Isleworth May-June '87; she gave up her CND membership Dec '88; she made a splash at Labour's annual conference at a crucial time in the debate on unilateralism; she persuasively urged new thinking as a lapsed CND member: "I am not prepared to put the election of a Labour government at risk by clinging on to a unilateralist policy"; but she also backed a CND-supported motion for a £5b cut in defence spending Oct

'89; on the death by suicide of John Heddle, the sitting Tory MP for Mid-Staffordshire, she won selection to contest the seemingly safe-Tory seat against five other candidates Jan '90; she fought such a carefully scripted campaign that Paddy Ashdown dismissed her as a 'Barbie Doll', she overturned a 14,654 majority to win the seat by 9,449, a swing of 21%, helped by Labour's nationwide poll lead of 20%, due to the poll tax and high mortgage rates Mar '90; she said her victory marked the deathknell of "the dark age of Thatcherism"; she took her seat, swearing by affirmation, after Tory Whips managed to delay her triumph with three ministerial statements Mar '90; in her Maiden complained about the "chaotic and unjust" benefit scheme for the disabled May '90; had to cope with the aftermath of the shooting of three soldiers on Lichfield station June '90; was named to the Education Select Committee Dec '90; initially opposed Gulf War in a motion Jan '91, but then supported it Feb '91; complained about hardships among poor families and underfunding of NHS hospitals Mar '91; in reshuffle, was named an Assistant Spokesman on Health under Robin Cook and on Women under Jo Richardson Oct '91; was given a prominent role in Labour's national election campaign Mar-Apr '92; lost Mid-Staffordshire to Tory Michael Fabricant by 6,236 votes Apr '92; was selected for West Midlands' new marginal, Halesowen and Rowley Regis '95; was singled out as one of 16 GMB members to be backed in key seats Apr '97; won the seat on an 11% swing, beating Serb-connected John Kennedy, while her sister Ann Keen won Brentford and Isleworth; they joined the twin sisters Angela and Maria Eagle, May '97; loyally supported Tony Blair's change of PM's Questions to one thirty-minute session a week May '97;

Born: 20 July 1942, Ewloe, Clwyd

Family: Granddaughter of a Shotton steelworker, daughter of John Lloyd Fox, Shotton steelworker and local Labour councillor, and Ruby, a Labour Party member from 1936; her sister, Ann Keen, became a Labour candidate and MP for Brentford & Isleworth '97-; her brother, Malcolm, became a Labour councillor; m '65 Keith Heal, personnel manager, whom she met at Coleg Harlech; ls Gareth Aneurin '73, 1d Joanne Sian '70;

Education: Ewloe Green County Primary School (failed the 11-plus); Elfed Secondary Modern, Buckley; Coleg Harlech; Swansea University (BSc Econ '68);

Occupation: National Young Carers Officer, Carers' National Association (GMB) '92-; Social Worker at Department of Employment's Egham residential rehabilitation centre for mentally and physically disabled '80-90; Social Worker, in the NHS and Department of Employment '68-70; Medical Records Clerk, Chester Royal Infirmary '57-63;

Traits: "She is always immaculatedly dressed; her hair, blue-grey, is perfectly coiffeured, with nothing out of place; she wears tailored suits, cream blouses, a pearl necklace"; she "actually looks like a Tory" (George Gale, DAILY MAIL); "has a strong facial resemblance to Lady (Janet) Young, the former [Tory] Leader of the House of Lords" (Bruce Anderson, SUNDAY TELEGRAPH); "has lovely grey hair which seems to have been put on with a spray gun" (Alan Watkins, OBSERVER): "an earnest, smartly dressed, grey-haired social worker whose benevolent concern and persuasive ways used to be the hallmark of Tory women" (Nicholas Wapshott, OBSERVER); "articulate, approachable", "with something of the style of Glenys Kinnock" (Robin Oakley, TIMES); soft North Wales accent; "brisk manner...always ready with an anecdote" (DAILY TELEGRAPH); "ultra-respectable" (GUARDIAN); enjoys walking, the theatre, and listening to male voice choirs;

Address: House of Commons, Westminster, London SW!A 0AA; Meadlake, 15 Vicarage Avenue, Egham, Surrey TW20 8NW;

Telephone: 0171 219 3000 (H of C); 01784 435423 (home);

John HEALEY **Labour** **WENTWORTH '97-**

Majority: 23,959 over Conservative 4-way;
Description: Unaltered impregnable Labour seat in the Rother and Dearne valleys in the heart of the former South Yorkshire coalfield, which has lost its last pit; curiously, the seat takes its name from the home of the 1st Marquis of Rockingham on its far western edge;
Position: On Select Committee on Education and Employment '97-; Administrator: all-party Parliamentary Disablement Group, Job Creation Group '97-; ex: TUC Campaigns Director '94-97; Treasurer, NUJ Parliamentary branch '83-86;
Outlook: Pro-European Centre-Left modernising Yorkshireman who managed to win an ultra-safe seat into which the Labour leadership wanted to parachute Alan Howarth or other Blair favourites; in Amnesty, Liberty, Child Poverty Action Group;
History: He joined the Labour Party at 23, 1983; was selected for Tory-safe Ryedale, where he grew up Oct '90; contested Ryedale coming 3rd behind the LibDem ex-MP Elizabeth Shields, but nearly doubled Labour vote to 9,812 Apr '92; as Head of Communications at MSF ensured succession of moderate Roger Lyons to become its General Secretary against the resistance of Stalinists still loyal to predecessor Ken Gill '92-94; was head-hunted by pro-European TUC General Secretary John Monks to become TUC's chief of media operations July '94; after the announced resignation of its incumbent MP, Peter Hardy, was unexpectedly selected for Wentworth, one of Labour's safest seats, which Walworth Road wanted for one of Mr Blair's favourites, even after it had rejected Conservative defector, Alan Howarth; he defeated Yvette Cooper Dec '96; showed that he was essentially a Blairite in his reaction to the Labour victory at the Wirral South by-election: "the promises Labour are making are popular and believed"; "we're not going to get a Labour government doing things to please the unions"; "there is no appetite among union members for confrontation with a Labour government"; "in the public sector it's more than just about pay"; "the mood and morale among public sector workers will be drastically different under Labour" Mar '97; retained Wentworth with a majority of 23,959, on a pro-Labour swing of 5.3%, May '97; made his Maiden on an adjournment debate opposing local opencast mining May '97; urged support for young unemployed in his constituency July '97; backed support for West Indian banana imports July '97; co-sponsored motion supporting EU Biotechnology Patenting Directive July '97; asked whether compulsory competitive tendering could be replaced by "a duty of best value" in local government July '97; complained that "urban authorities outside London have been sytematically short-changed by Government grant settlements under the Tories" Oct '97;
Born: 13 February 1960, Wakefield, Yorkshire
Family: Son, Aiden Healey, head of PE branch of Prison Service, and Jean (Leiper), teacher; m '93 Jackie (Bate), Labour's head of Exhibitions and Events at Millbank Tower Media Centre; 1s Alex '95;
Education: Lady Lumley's Comprehensive, Pickering; St Peter's School (public school), York; Christ's College, Cambridge University (Scholar);
Occupation: Campaigns Director, TUC '94-97; ex: Head of Communications MSF '92-94; Tutor (Part-Time), at Open University's Business School '91-94; Campaigns Consultant, at

Issue Communications (a PR consultancy for public sector and voluntary organisations): worked for: National Carers Association, GMB, Hertfordshire County Council '90-92; Disability Campaigner, working for Royal National Institute for the Deaf (RNID), Royal Association for Disability and Rehabilitation (RADAR) and MIND. co-ordinating campaigns in support of Private Members Bills (Disabled Persons Act 1986, Hearing Aid Council Act 1988) '84-90; Deputy Editor, HOUSE MAGAZINE (NUJ) '83-84;
Traits: Heart-shaped slim long face; retreating blond hair; wide forehead; long sharp nose; prominent ears; quiet; cerebral; friendly; direct; a reputation for preferring beer to white wine;
Address: House of Commons, Westminster, London SW1A 0AA; 119 High Street, Wath upon Deane, Rotherham S63 7PX; 6 Archbishop's Place, London SW2 2AJ
Telephone: 0171 219 5170 (H of C); 01709 872618 (constituency);

David HEATH CBE **Liberal Democrat** **SOMERTON & FROME '97-**

Majority: 130 over Conservative 5-way;
Description: A scarcely altered marginal seat in eastern Somerset carved out of Yeovil and Wells in '83; it is based on a number of small semi-industrialised towns: Frome, Castle Cary, Wincanton, Langport, and Somerton; the growth of Liberal Democratic support has steadily eroded its Conservative leanings;
Position: Spokesman on Europe '97-; ex: Somerset County Councillor (Chairman, its Education Committee '96-97, Leader of the Opposition '89-91, Leader of the Council '85-89) '85-97; Vice Chairman, Association of County Councils and Committee of Local Police Authorities '94-97; Chairman, Avon and Somerset Police Authority '93-96; on Liberal Democrats Federal Executive '89-92, Liberal Party Executive '86-88;
Outlook: One of the West Country's most impressive former county leaders; has made an impact of substance since reaching the Commons; at 31 was the youngest-ever county council Leader; opposed Hinckley 'C' PWR nuclear power station, use of BST; was among the first to recognise and call for action against BSE; has "commonsense and prudence" (WESTERN DAILY PRESS); a traditional West Country radical Liberal; a former hereditary optician;
History: His family was Liberal and Nonconformist; he joined the Liberal Party at 16, '70; was elected to Somerset County Council for Frome North, becoming its Leader at the same time May '85; switched to the Liberal Democrats '88; ceased being Leader when the LibDems lost control of Somerset County Council, becoming Leader of the Opposition instead May '89; was awarded a CBE (on LibDem nomination) June '89; fought Somerton and Frome, securing one of the biggest swings (5.1 %) and halving the former Tory majority to 4,341, Apr '92; became Chairman of the Police Authority when LibDems recaptured control of Somerset County Council May '93; was the first Liberal Democrat named to the Audit Commission '94; gave evidence to the Nolan Committee on Standards in Public Life '95-96; re-selected to fight Somerton and Frome, called for a regionally variable minimum wage and higher taxes on incomes over £100,000 ("Why should they not pay more so that people at the bottom can have a better life?"), "genuine care in the community" and a retained NHS ("I don't want a privatised Health Service") Apr '97; won the seat by a slim 130 majority after three counts, on

a derisory 4% swing, due to the growth of the Labour vote May '97; attacked Labour's retention of "the iniquitous Conservative capping proposals" on education May '97; urged ban on organophosphates June '97; urged more opening time for local job clubs June '97; co-urged retention of Network Card benefits July '97; co-urged more ecumenical Prayers in the Commons July '97; sharply criticised the Labour Government for capping Somerset, resulting in a loss of 90 teachers, although Bridgewater Tory MP Tom King insisted he had voted to exceed the cap knowing Labour's intentions July '97; made a witty attack on Tory Europhobia at the LibDem conference at Eastbourne Sep '97;
Born: 16 March 1954, Westbury-sub-Mendip
Family: Son, of Eric Heath, registered optician, and Pamela (Bennett); m '87, Caroline (Netherton), accountant; 1s Thomas '91, 1d Bethany '88;
Education: St Thomas's Junior School, Wells; Millfield School (Scholarship); St John's College, Oxford (contemporary of Tony Blair; MA in Physiological Sciences); City University (Opthalmic Optics; President of Students' Union);
Occupation: Consultant, Worldwide Fund for Nature (WWF) '90-91; Registered Optician, no longer in practice, Director, E W Heath Ltd, his family's opticians business) '79-89;
Traits: Stocky; black beard; retreating hair; panda-like rings around eyes; serious; authoritative; can make witty speeches; fluent; soft-spoken; former breeder of Tamworth pigs; enjoys cricket and Rugby;
Address: House of Commons, Westminster, London SW1A 0AA; 34, The Yard, Witham Friary, Frome, Somerset BA11 5HF;
Telephone: 0171 219 6245 (H of C); 01749 850458 (home); 0385 294623 (mobile);

Ivan HENDERSON **Labour** HARWICH '97-

Majority: 1,216 over Conservative 5-way;
Description: The ferry port of Harwich, with the seaside resorts of Clacton, Frinton-on-Sea and Walton-on-the-Naze; in '95 it was deprived of 6,700 electors in its rural hinterland, but was still thought to be the Tories' 122nd safest seat, with an estimated 15,000-plus majority if it had voted on '92 lines;
Position: Harwich District Councillor '95-; Harwich Town Councillor '86-; President, Clacton and District Chamber of Trade and Commerce;
Outlook: Labour's eleventh least-expected victor: a locally-born dockworker, union official, councillor and sportsman who unseated the Scots carpet-bagger, Iain Sproat, who had become an unexpectedly successful Minister; "the first native-born MP for Harwich since Sir Anthony Deane in 1784" (IH); Henderson won a seat never before held by Labour, becoming one of the shrinking minority of working-class MPs in a party increasingly dominated by professionals; "although I have a strong trade union background, I cannot be tagged with the 'Old Labour' label; it was vital for the Labour Party to modernise and reflect the needs of our country as we approach the millennium; I don't believe in the Old Labour/New Labour business; there is only one Labour Party and that is the one that John Smith and now Tony Blair have shaped and moulded into a party ready for government" (IH);
History: He was in the Young Socialists until he joined the Labour Party at 18, '76; he was

elected to Harwich Town Council May '86; was elected to Harwich District Council May '95; was selected to contest Harwich '95; received a curt reply from the abrasive incumbent MP, Iain Sproat, when he called for the defence of Harwich's dying maritime industry when unions feared loss of 200 jobs if Stena Sealink Ferries hired an all-Dutch crew for a new ferry Dec '95; exploited press reorts that Iain Sproat had recommended a CBE for Tory party fund-raiser, millionaire property developer John Beckwith Apr '97; unexpectedly took the seat and ended Iain Sproat's one-term revival of his political career on a 15% swing and a squeeze on the LibDem vote, leapfrogging from 3rd place to first with a majority of 1,216, May '97; backed barring fox-hunting June '97; led motion urging privatised water companies to repair householders' leaking pipes June '97; led a motion urging protection of local hospital services against being "sacrificed to the financial short-falls from the bureaucratic excesses of the NHS internal market created by the previous Government" July '97; co-sponsored motion deploring the inaccessibility for the disabled of polling stations July '97; co-sponsored motion paying tribute to retiring cricketer Graham Gooch July '97; co-sponsored motion criticising Port of London Authority for curbing use of pilots July '97;

Born: 17 June 1958, Harwich

Family: From his first marriage: 1s Stuart '82, 1d Melissa '84; divorced; m 2nd '92 Jo(anne) (Atkinson);

Education: Sir Anthony Deane Comprehensive School, Harwich;

Occupation: Union Organiser, for RMT '91-94; on RMT Executive '91-94; ex: President RMT Anglia District Council; Dock Operator and Stevedore for Stena Line, Harwich International Port;

Traits: Short; long straight poker face; small down-turned mouth; swept-back receding short back-and-sides hair; reads speeches; amateur footballer with Clacton and District Sunday League; Vice President, Harwich and Dovercourt Cricket Club; also enjoys golf and sailing;

Address: House of Commons, Westminster, London SW1A 0AA; 41 Portland Crescent, Dovercourt, Essex CO12 3QH;

Telephone: 0171 219 3434 (H of C); 01255 552859 (home); 01255 552859/556771(Fax) (constituency);

Stephen HEPBURN **Labour** **JARROW '97-**

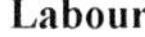

Majority: 21,933 over Conservative 6-way;

Description: The shipbuilding town on the south bank of the Tyne, east of Newcastle, whose name is synonomous with high unemployment; it became world famous through its 1936 hunger march; heavy unemployment returned in the early '80s because "the last coalfield has closed as have the steel industry and most of the shipping industry" (SH); its boundary was changed in '95 by giving up one council estate to South Shields, while acquiring another from Gateshead East, but its nature as an impregnable Labour fortress remained unchallenged;

Position: On the Select Committee on Administration '97-; South Tyneside Metropolitan Borough Councillor (Deputy Leader '90-) '85-; Chairman, Tyne & Wear Pensions Committee '89-96; President, Jarrow Branch of UCATT;

Outlook: Don Dixon's handpicked successor; a former building worker promoted his Research Assistant then selected by the compliant Jarrow party to succeed Labour's forceful former Deputy Chief Whip; one of the shrinking minority of former manual workers in a 'New Labour' party dominated by professionals; a loyal local son; in the Co-operative Party and Association of Labour Councillors;
History: He joined the Labour Party at 23, '80; was elected to South Tyneside Metropolitan Borough Council at 27, May '85; became Deputy Leader of South Tyneside Council May '90; became Research Assistant to Don Dixon, MP for Jarrow and Labour's Deputy Chief Whip; in rivalry between factions representing Jarrow and South Shields on the South Tyneside Council, he objected to a page of jokes by rival councillor Iain Malcolm and punched him in the head; after being convicted for assault, fined £75 and ordered to pay costs and compensation, he was asked by Labour's NEC to consider his position; he resigned as Deputy Leader but was re-elected within less than a year '94-95; was selected as the candidate to succeed Don Dixon for Jarrow Nov '95; during the election campaign favoured funding a second Tyne tunnel from the Private Finance Initiative, was agreeable to a North East regional assembly if it had public approval Apr '97; was elected for Jarrow with an enhanced majority of 21,933 on a pro-Labour swing of 5.43% May '97; in his Maiden he told of a new Jarrow march of the unemployed to Europe; he also urged a reform of the Commons voting system May '97; urged companies to move to Jarrow, which had "some of the highest unemployment figures in the country, but there has not been the social breakdown that has afflicted other areas"; also raised the future of the Benefits Agency in Jarrow, and the Appeals venue in South Tyneside July '97; was named to the Select Committee on Administration July '97;
Born: 6 December 1957, Jarrow
Family: Son, of a former Tyneside shipbuilding buddy of Don Dixon;
Education: Springfield Comprehensive School, Jarrow; Newcastle University (BA in Politics);
Occupation: Research Assistant, to Don Dixon, previous MP for Jarrow; previously a Building Worker;
Traits: Heart-shaped face with broad forehead; thinning flat hair; short-tempered (convicted in '95 for assaulting a fellow councillor after a row in the South Tyneside Council chamber); enjoys football, Rugby and the classical guitar;
Address: House of Commons, Westminster, London SW1A 0AA; 38 Stirling Avenue, Jarrow, Tyne & Wear NE32 4JT
Telephone: 0171 219 3000 (H of C);

Stephen HESFORD **Labour** **WIRRAL WEST '97-**

Majority: 2,738 over Conservative 4-way;
Description: The most affluent middle class residential areas of the Wirral peninsula, largely inhabited by commuters from Liverpool and Birkenhead; it has the UK's third-largest proportion of pensioners; before, Labour voters were almost only to be found on the Woodchurch council estate; with a majority in '92 of 11,064 ((21.7%), David Hunt was thought to be unchallengeable in this unaltered seat - until the last-minute by-election loss of similar Wirral South next door;
Position: Ex: Chairman, Altrincham Branch Labour Party '94-97; Vice Chairman, Manchester North Community Health Council '95-97, on National Executive Committee of Socialist Educational Association '95-97, on Executive of Village Aid; Regional Organiser of Child Poverty Action Group '89;
Outlook: The unexpectedly successful vanquisher of David Hunt: a caring, mildly-Left barrister, formerly employed by unions and overseas charities; an electoral reformer; in Greenpeace, Amnesty International, Fabian Society;
History: He joined the Labour Party '83; represented miners and their wives during Scargill's strike '84; contested safe-Tory South Suffolk against Tim Yeo, increasing Labour vote from 19% to 24%, while still remaining in third place April '92; was selected for "hopeless" Wirral West against longtime Tory incumbent David Hunt Nov '95; during the election campaign, he was alleged by local Tories to be sending his sons to Birkenhead School, the nearby public school; infuriated at having his children dragged into the public arena, insisted his sons went to a state-supported Catholic primary in Altrincham Apr '97; on a 14% swing, ousted former Cabinet Minister David Hunt from Wirral West, ending all Tory representation on the Merseyside, achieving a majority of 2,738 May '97; backed ban on fox-hunting June '97; opposed export of arms to Indonesia July '97; in his Maiden, strongly supported a minimum wage which would help 6,000 in his constituency, "mainly women part-time workers who currently earn, disgracefully and unacceptably, less than £2.50 an hour" July '97; expressed concern that vulnerable pensioners might run afoul of provisions of the new Social Security Act because they were incapable of providing the information that might be required July '97;
Born: 27 May 1957, Lowton, Lancashire
Family: His paternal grandfather was a miner; son of Bernard Hesford, small businessman, and Nellie (Haworth); m '84 'Liz' (Henshall); 2s: John '86, David '88, who have attended a state-supported RC school in Altrincham;
Education: Urmston Grammar School; Bradford University (BSc in Social Science); Regent Street/Central London Polytechnic (Post-Graduate Diploma in Law); Inns of Court School of Law;
Occupation: Barrister '81- specialising in crime; ex: Equal Opportunities Officer with GMB '95-96; Assistant (unpaid), to Joan Lestor MP '93-94;
Traits: Dark; good-looking; he likes watching Manchester United, cricket, collecting antiquarian books, Russian novels and biographies;
Address: House of Commons, Westminster, London SW1A 0AA;
Telephone: 0171 219 6227 (H of C); 0151 522 0531 (constituency);

Patricia HEWITT FRSA **Labour** **LEICESTER WEST '97-**

Majority: 12,884 over Conservative 9-way;
Description: An unaltered traditional East Midlands Labour seat, in a strip wriggling down the west side of the city; long the fiefdom of the Janners; ethnically mixed but more preponderantly white than the mainly-Asian and more pro-Labour other Leicester seats; its one-third of voters in council housing, being largely white and thinking Labour too pro-ethnic, are not necessarily supportive of Labour;
Position: On Select Committee on Social Security '97-; Deputy Chairman of Commission on Social Justice '93-; on Board of International League for Human Rights '84-; Trustee, IPPR '94-; ex: Policy Co-ordinator '88-89, Press Secretary '83-88 to Labour Leader Neil Kinnock; on Labour Women's Committee '79-83; Secretary, of Advisory Commitee on the Employment of Women '77-84; on Council of the Campaign for Freedom of Information '83-89; on Labour Party Enquiry into the Security Services '80-81; on Executive Committee of the Fabian Society '88-93; Co-Chairman, of Human Rights Network '79-81; Vice Chairman, of Healthcare 2000, '95-96; General Secretary, of National Council for Civil Liberties (NCCL, now Liberty) '74-83;
Outlook: "One of the brightest of the 101 Labour women MPs" (INDEPENDENT); "she can be abrasive but she is one of the cleverest people in the Labour Party and her opinion is always worth listening to" (Ken Follett, OBSERVER, attributing the idea for the 'Excalibur' rapid-response computer to her); the highly talented and ambitious longtime party insider who has been near the top of almost every Left libertarian group for a quarter century; she suffered the disadvantage of arriving on the Parliamentary scene later than her network of metropolitan women contemporaries: Harman (in the NCCL they were known as the "Hattie and Pattie show"), Jowell and Hodge; her arrival was delayed in part by her observation in '87 that Labour had been made unelectable by the behaviour of London's loony Left; while waiting for entry, she had the compensation of being well-rewarded ("six-figure salary" - MAIL ON SUNDAY) as research chief at Andersen Consulting; has given the impression of conforming with the dominant Labour creed of each era; "Labour's great 'chameleon'", "has successfully made the switch from Kinnockism to Blairism" (RED PEPPER); "Neil Kinnock's former press officer" who was "a fiery Leftist when she ran the NCCL in the 1970s and early '80s, who transformed herself into a passionate Centrist when Kinnock became Leader, and now under the Blair regime she is a born-again Rightwinger" (PRIVATE EYE); one of two Australians in the '97 intake;
History: She joined the Labour Party at 22, '70, while remaining hostile to most of its MPs; while General Secretary of NCCL, she and her subordinate, Harriet Harman, attracted the attention of MI5; vigorously attacked the recently-defeated Callaghan Government Oct '79; fought Labour-held Leicester East following the defection of Tom Bradley to the SDP; lost the seat to Rightwing Tory, Peter Bruinvels, because Bradley's continued vote diminished Labour support June '83; then realised "that if we went on losing touch with traditional Labour voters, we would never be able to put our principles into practice"; she wrote several memoranda for Neil Kinnock about party reorganisation July-Aug '83; with Charles Clarke, helped write Kinnock's conference speech attacking Derek Hatton and the Liverpool Militants Oct '85; as Neil Kinnock's Press Secretary, attacked Labour councils' support for gay and

Lesbian rights, following Labour's loss of the Greenwich by-election Feb '87; helped write Labour's manifesto for the election of June '87; with two small children decided not to contest the next election, although she helped write its manifesto Apr '92; lunching with Ken Follett at the Savoy Grill, he asked her: "is there anything the Blair team should be doing that they aren't?"; "she did not hesitate; 'Rapid response' she said" July '94; she flew to Washington with Ken Follett, Barbara Follett and John Carr and decided that the 'Excalibur' computer would be best Dec '94; became Vice Chairman of Healthcare 2000, under Sir Duncan Nichol, Thatcher's former Chief Executive of the NHS, where he introduced elements of privatisation and then moved on to run BUPA: Health 2000 recommended increased private expenditure in the NHS through the extension of user charges and partial co-payments Sep '95; in 'Men and Their Children' called for unmarried fathers to have the "same rights and responsibilities in respect of their children as fathers who have tied the legal knot; rather than focussing on relationships between parents, the law needs to focus on relationships betwen children and parents" May '96; on the retirement of Greville Janner, who had inherited the seat from his father, but could not pass it on to his defector son, was selected to fight Leicester West; she denied she was a carpet-bagger "shoehorned" in by Walworth Road, pointing out that her husband's family had many local connections June '96; predicted a new political culture with the expected increase in women MPs Apr '97; retained the seat with a majority of 12,864 on a pro-Labour swing of 11.6% May '97; complained that the Commons was designed "to suit the working patterns of a Victorian man" June '97; congratulated Leicester on the Millennium Commission award for its Space Science Centre June '97; opposed the sale of arms to Indonesia June '97; wanted small and medium-sized businesses in her constituency to be able to participate in the welfare-to-work programme June '97; her Maiden was a classic, explaining the Budget's impact wholly in terms of her constituency July '97; urged police be given the right to be able to notify the authorities of the existence of somebody with a previous paedophile conviction July '97; was named to Select Committee on Social Security with the task of riding herd on the department of her old friend, Harriet Harman July '97;

Born: 2 December 1948, Canberra, Australia

Family: Daughter, of Sir Lenox Hewitt, Australian civil servant, economist and businessman (formerly the first Permanent Secretary of the Australian PM's department, Chairman of Qantas and of mining companies), and Alison (Hope); m 1st '70 Julian Gibson-Watt; separated '74; twice won damages from the DAILY MAIL on their references to her first marriage; m 2nd '81 Bill Birtles, barrister and Labour councillor; ls, 1d;

Education: Church of England Girls Grammar School, Canberra; Australian National University, Canberra; Newnham College, Cambridge University (MA);

Occupation: Head of Research, Andersen Consulting (at £90,000 salary - RED PEPPER)(MSF) '94-; Visiting Fellow, Nuffield College, Oxford University '92-; Author: About Time: the Revolution in Work and Female Life (1993), Your Second Baby (co-author; 1990), The Abuse of Power (1981), Your Rights At Work (1978), Civil Liberties (1977), Rights for Women (1975), Your Rights (1973); ex: Deputy Director, Institute for Public Policy Research (IPPR; set up to rival dominance of Rightwing think-tanks) '89-94; Policy Co-ordinator '88-89, Press Secretary '83-88 to Labour Leader Neil Kinnock; General Secretary, NCCL '74-83; Women's Rights Officer, NCCL '73; Age Concern '72;

Traits: Small and attractive; bird-like; big eyes and mouth; toothy smile; laughter lines; fluent; earnest; "intense, quick to smile and to flare; both impulsively abrasive and impulsively diplomatic at once" (NEW STATESMAN); an "enthusiastic gardener and horse-rider" (PH);

Address: House of Commons, Westminster, London SW1A 0AA; 21 Rochester Square, London NW1 9SA;

Telephone: 0171 219 3000 (H of C); 0171 267 2567;

Phil(ip Ian) HOPE **Labour & Co-operative** **CORBY '97-**

Majority: 11,860 over Conservative 6-way;
Description: The East Midland new town seat, previously Conservative-held by William Powell from when it acquired its own name in '83; this was largely because the urban town's Labour leanings were counter-balanced by the Conservative hinterland of small towns and villages, including prosperous Oundle; its steel industry core, lost except for steel tube-making, has been replaced by other industries, thanks partly to generous EU funding;
Position: Northamptonshire County Councillor '93-; ex: Kettering Borough Councillor (Deputy Leader, Labour Group '86-87, Chairman its Equal Opportunities Committee) '83-87;
Outlook: A local teacher-councillor with voter appeal; a reforming do-gooder and party loyalist; a critic of poverty pay and child labour; an advocate of strong family policies; proudly pro-European because of the help received from the EU over Corby's '80s steel closure; moderate, low-profile management consultant and youth policy adviser; author of a range of documents, including a curriculum pack on parenthood education, as piloted in Manchester schools;
History: He joined the Labour Party at 23, '78; was elected a Kettering Borough Councillor May '83; became Deputy Leader of the Labour Group on Kettering Council May '86; contested Kettering, recapturing 2nd place from the LibDems on a pro-Labour swing of 5.7% but still left incumbent Tory MP Roger Freeeman with a majority of 11,154 Apr '92; was elected a Northamptonshire County Councillor May '93; was selected to contest Tory-held marginal Corby, one of Labour's targeted seats, against William Powell MP May '96; at annual conference, spoke of the dangers of child labour and deplored conditions of casual labour Sep '96; won Corby, ousting William Powell by a majority of 11,860, on a swing of 11% May '97; in his Maiden deplored loss of jobs in Corby's remaining steel tube-making plant May '97; told Eurosceptic Tory MP Bill Cash that in Corby the EU had operated in Britain's interest: "in the 1980s, during the closure of our steelworks, Corby benefited from the European Regional Development Fund to the tune of £30m, and we benefited from iron and steel contributions and from loans and grants; without Europe, Corby town and the Corby constituency would not be flourishing" May '97; complained that local employment agencies in Corby were placing people in illegal child labour and "zero-hour contracts, which mean that they can be told that they have a job one day but no job the next" May '97; asked the PM about progress "on the refusal of the United States to pay its contribution to the UN" June '97; urged Clare Short to "raise young people's awareness of the globalised world and its effect on their lives" June '97; asked for improved animal transport June '97; co-sponsored motion congratulating the Co-ops for banning alcopops June '97; co-urged Government to be tough on road crime July '97; co-urged investigation of complaints against solicitors July '97; backed the Government's new Social Security Bill as a "first step" to "reduce the compexity, inefficiency and unfairness in the present [Social Security] system" July '97;
Born: 19 April 1955, Battersea, London
Family: Son, of Commander Bob Hope, of the Metropolitan Police and Grace (Thorogood); m '80 Alison (Butt), Kettering Labour Councillor and Lecturer in Economics; 1s Nicholas '84, 1d Anna '87; both in local LEA schools;

Education: Wandsworth Comprehensive; St Luke's College, Exeter (BEd Hons);
Occupation: Management and Community Work Consultant (MSF); Author: Analysis and Action on Youth Health (1995), Performance Appraisal (1995), Education for Parenthood (1994), Making the Best Use of Consultants (1993); ex: Community Worker; former Director of Framework in Print (a publishing co-operative); previously Secondary School Teacher at Kettering School for Boys;
Traits: Dark brown bush-combed hair; helps care for his two children; enjoys tennis and juggling with burning clubs; formerly a tap-dancer; once appeared in 'Z Cars';
Address: House of Commons, Westminster, London SW1A 0AA; Gaywood Cottage, Oakley Road, Pipewell, Northants NN14 1 QY
Telephone: 0171 219 4075/2673(Fax) (H of C); 01536 763580 (home); 01536 443325 (constituency); 037 800 5226 (mobile); 01523 184 186 (pager)

Kelvin (Peter) HOPKINS **Labour** **LUTON NORTH '97-**

Majority: 9,626 over Conservative 5-way;
Description: The seat which radically changed its representation, partly by being stripped of its hinterland of Tory-leaning villages in '95; it remains less industrial, with fewer non-white voters and with better residential areas than Luton South; but its shrewd incumbent Rightwing Tory MP, John Carlisle, could read the boundary revisions and the opinion polls and decamped before the '97 contest; this resulted in its being captured by a Leftwing Labour MP;
Position: Former Luton District Councillor '73-76, Luton County Borough Councillor '72-74;
Outlook: Low-profiled Leftwing economist and statistician in the hard-Left Campaign Group; previously Policy and Research Officer for UNISON/NALGO; before that was on the economic staff of the TUC;
History: He joined the Labour Party at 19, '60; contested Luton North, narowly keeping the SDP out of 2nd place June '83; was again selected for Luton North June '95; as its Chairman of Governors, campaigned for recognition of the Luton College of Higher Education by the Polytechnic Central Funding Council; this enabled it to be recreated as the University of Luton '96; was one of the 16 Labour candidates supported by the GMB in key target seats Apr '97; won Luton North by a majority of 9,626, on a big notional swing of 17.2% May '97; was one of only six of the new Labour MPs who joined the hard-Left Campaign Group May '97; opposed export of arms to Indonesia June '97; co-deplored attacks of Kenyan police on peaceful demonstrators July '97; co-sponsored motion urging better protection of water meadows July '97;
Born: 22 August 1941,
Family: He has not provided family information;
Education: Queen Elizabeth's Boys' Grammar School, Barnet; Nottingham University (BA in Politics, Economics and Mathematics-with-Statistics);
Occupation: Economist and Statistician (free-lance) '94-; Policy and Research Officer at UNISON/NALGO (GMB) '77-94; previously in the Economic Department of the TUC; Further Education Lecturer at Luton College of Higher Education;

Traits: Balding, with grey fringe and trim beard; secretive;
Address: House of Commons, Westminsters, London SW1A 0AA; 1 Alexander Avenue, Luton, Bedfordshire LU3 1HE;
Telephone: 0171 219 3000 (H of C); 01582 229113 (home);

(James) Gerald (Douglas) HOWARTH **Conservative** **ALDERSHOT '97-**

Majority: 6,621 over Liberal Democrat 6-way;
Description: The Army's town in northwestern Hampshire, including the air research base of Farnborough, plus the major commuting area of Yately, near the M3; it lost some rural bits around Eversley in '95;
Former Seat: CANNOCK & BURNTWOOD '83-92
Position: On Home Affairs Select Committee '97-; ex: PPS: to Margaret Thatcher '91-92, Sir George Young '90-91, Michael Spicer 87-90; Secretary, No Turning Back Group '90-92; on Select Committee on Sound Broadcasting '86-87; Secretary, Conservative MPs' Aviation Committee '83-88; on the Council of the Monday Club '71;
Outlook: Hard-Right radical; Neil Hamilton's most loyal and publicly most uncritical friend; in the Thatcherite 'No Turning Back' group of Rightwing radicals; backed Americans in Vietnam, Nicaragua's 'Contras', UK cricketers in 'Apartheid' South Africa; pro: capital punishment and birching; "although slightly deranged...is no racist" (PRIVATE EYE); Aldershot's U-turn choice after the 'One Nation' Tory, Sir Julian Critchley; "a fierce anti-federalist, anti-immigration hardliner, supporter of the birch and devotee of Mary Whitehouse, his speeches have often reduced the House to embarassed silence" (OBSERVER);
History: His mother, originally in the Liberals, had a brief flirtation with the National Front and then was a foundation member of the Immigration Control Association; he joined the Young Conservatives in Maidenhead at 17, '64; at the Vietnam demonstration in Grosvenor Square carried "the only banner in support of the Americans - I took the precaution of ensuring that there was a thin blue line of men from the Metropolitan Police between me and the hordes" Mar '68; at Southampton University, tried to organise a meeting for Enoch Powell for its Conservative Association Apr-May '68; became General Secretary of the Society for Individual Freedom under Sir Iain Mactaggart Bt (father of Slough's Labour MP Fiona) Sep '69; demonstrated outside the Bank of England with a placard demanding the end of exchange controls '70; with Lord Arran, promoted the adoption of a Bill of Rights '70; with Ross McWhirter, ran the Peter Hain Prosecution Fund to block the latter's efforts to interfere with the South African cricket tour '70; became a Council member of the Monday Club '71; on the (anti-) Immigration Committee of the Monday Club with G K Young, former Deputy Director of MI6, wrote: "while the Committee is and will remain a purely Conservative organisation, it is felt that opposition to coloured immigration and lack of proper repatriation arrangements also exercise many of other political views who should be encouraged to lend their support" '71-72; in the split in the Monday Club, sided with G K Young '73; became Director of Francis Bennion's Freedom Under Law organisation '74; with Dr Rhodes Boyson founded the Dicey

Trust to teach the young the rule of law '75; was elected to Hounslow Borough Council May '82; was selected for Cannock Mar '83; defeated Gwilym Roberts, incumbent Labour MP for the changed constituency June '83; condemned Arthur Scargill for his challenge to the rule of law by his extra-Parliamentary opposition July '83; visited Berlin Aug '83; attended a Commons meeting of the extreme Rightwing organisation, Tory Action, run by his former boss, G K Young Sep '83; denied charge that he was a Rightwing infiltrator, as claimed in a Young Conservative report: "I have never belonged to any party apart from the Conservatives" Oct '83; backed US invasion of Grenada Oct '83; rebelled in favour of House Buyers Bill to legalise conveyancers Dec '83; backed businessmen's veto on business rates Jan '84; opposed indoctrination of children Jan '84; backed playing Rugby with South Africa Feb '84; with Neil Hamilton, sued BBC over implication they were semi-fascists in 'Maggie's Militant Tendency' Feb '84; urged clemency for Soviet-held refusenik Zionist, Anatole Shcharansky Mar '84; was one of 40 Tory MPs who rebelled against Government's deal with the TUC to retain contracting out from the political levy Apr '84; backed 15% VAT on fish and chip takeaways Apr '84; visited Chicago and Atlanta as guest of BA Sep '84; criticised Bishop of Durham for his pro-NUM enthronement speech Oct '84; voted against Aviation Bill because of its knock-on effect on Birmingham's feeder lines Nov '84; opposed Water (Fluoridation) Bill Jan '85; urged tax cuts to create jobs Jan '85; opposed any further concession to NUM Feb '85; visited Munich as guest of Panavia Mar '85; visited US as guest of British Caledonian Mar '85; visited Paris Air Show as guest of British Aerospace May '85; voted against more money for EEC June '85; opposed electric cable makers being made liable for defective products July '85; with 12 other Rightwingers in 'No Turning Back' pamphlet, urged more radical measures Nov '85; opposed televising the Commons Nov '85; rebelled to provide more funds for MPs' researchers and secretaries Jan '86; co-sponsored Right to be Self-Employed Bill Feb '86; urged restoration of military conscription Mar '86; supported US bombing of Libya from UK bases Apr '86; voted against Single European Act July '86; collected £20,000 plus costs from BBC for its 'Maggie's Militant Tendency' programme, a libel action backed by Sir James Goldsmith Oct '86; complained about defective local systems-built homes Oct '86; co-sponsored motion alleging passive smoking was no danger Oct '86; with Mrs Thatcher's backing, secured 2nd Reading of his Obscene Publications Bill, which added "gross offensiveness" to the "deprave or corrupt" definition of obscenity Apr '87; in debate on Consumer Protection Bill, backed existing origin-marking system in support of the Electric Cable Makers Confederation, which he served as a Consultant Apr '87; withdrew his Obscene Publications Bill May '87; increased his narrow majority by 600-plus votes June '87; opposed sale of Midland Red North, a subsidiary of National Express, to British expatriate, for fear of a monopoly Oct '87; when he tried to bar from Channel 4 an allegedly obscene poem by Tony Harrison as "another, probably bolshie poet seeking to impose his frustrations on the rest of us", Harrison responded by describing him as "another idiot MP trying to impose his intellectual limitations on the rest of us" Oct '87; defended the right of Nicaraguan Contra leader, Dr Catero, to visit Britain Nov '87; backed reintroduction of corporal punishment Mar '88; defended Budget against Bishop of Durham's charge that the rich would become richer and the poor poorer Mar '88; defended Mary Whitehouse as "best suited" for Broadcasting Standards Council May '88; co-sponsored motion attacking BBC's broadcast of Mandela concert June '88; tried to amend Finance Bill to exempt entertainment expenses of directors and higher-paid employees July '88; co-sponsored motion urging prosecution of doctors in Cleveland child sex abuse scandal July '88; deplored exclusion of cricketers who had played or coached in 'Apartheid' South Africa Jan '89; voted against ordination of divorced clergy July '89; backed recognition of Turkish-occupied North Cyprus Nov '89; co-attacked Granada TV's "massive deception" in programme on Peter Hain's return to South Africa Jan '90; was listed as one of the 30 Tory MPs in the Conservative Family Campaign favouring restoration of the married man's tax allowance Jan '90; was 'minder' to Tory candidate Charles Prior, devastatingly defeated in a safe Tory seat in Mid-Staffordshire by-election Mar '90; accused Edward Heath of "appeasement" for calling for concessions to Saddam Hussein Sep '90; as its Secretary, described the 'No Turning Back' group as the "conscience of Thatcherism" Sep '90; backed amendment to Broadcasting Bill to impose impartiality on TV companies Sep '90; attacked Sir Geoffrey Howe's resignation speech as "an open incitement to rebellion, born of thwarted ambition" Nov '90; left the Commons committee room in which the votes for Leader were cast proclaiming: "I voted for Thatcher, I voted for Thatcher" Nov '90; defended subsidies for hill farmers Feb '91; praised Peter Lilley for accusing Brian Redhead in broadcast of having voted Labour Mar '91; attacked Jeremy Corbyn's Asylum Seekers and Refugees Bill for trying to "make it easier for yet more foreigners to be admitted for settlement to our overcrowded kingdom" May '91; abstained with 8 other Tory MPs, including Mrs Thatcher, over endorsing Maastricht treaty Dec '91; was named as Mrs Thatcher's PPS Dec '91; lost his Cannock seat to Labour's Dr Tony Wright Apr '92; on the impending retirement of Julian Critchley, was selected for Aldershot, defeating Keith Simpson June '93; publicly supported the need for a referendum on a single European currency called for by Sir James Goldsmith, a client of his lobbying firm, Taskforce Communications Feb '96; defended Pakistan's embattled PM, Benazir Bhutto Sep '96; was listed in the DAILY TELEGRAPH as one of the Tory candidates who would never agree to join a single European currency Dec '96; on Central TV wholeheartedly defended his longtime friend Neil Hamilton against all the GUARDIAN's charges Apr '97; retained Aldershot, despite a 9.7% anti-Tory swing and a majority cut to a third, from 18,716 to 6,621 May '97; was on Peter Lilley's campaign team May '97; complained that Martin Bell, the vanquisher of his soul-mate Neil Hamilton, had been "unfairly ungracious" about his friend, who had "made a significant contribution to the quality of our debates" June '97; complained about the composition of the new Select Committee on Standards and Privileges (which would judge Neil Hamilton among others) June '97; was accused in a motion by Labour MPs of "ignorance and prejudice" in his critical remarks about Liverpool June '97; led a motion enthusing about departing Governor Chris Patten's "distinguished service" in Hongkong July '90; rushed into the Commons to complain the Labour Government was having a conference to discuss banning tobacco advertising but had unaccountably neglected to invite the tobacco companies July '97; urged unhampered defence exports July '97; was named to Home Affairs Select Committee July '97;

Born: 12 September 1947, Guildford, Surrey

Family: "I come from a long line of rapers and pillagers" on the Borders; his grandfather, in his first foray south of the Borders, found an English wife in Cheshire; son, of James Howarth, RAF liaison officer, company director and Conservative Councillor in Windsor, and Ada Mary (Douglas), founder member of the Immigration Control Association; m '73 Elizabeth (Squibb) picture framer; 2s: Alexander '78, Charles Robert Richard '85; 1d Emily '76;

Education: Haileybury and Imperial Service College Junior School, Windsor; Bloxham School, Banbury; Southampton University (on its Student Representative Council);

Occupation: Lobbyist: Joint Managing Director, Taskforce Communications (lobbying company set up with Cecil Parkinson and Patrick Robertson in '93) '93-96; ex: UK Adviser, to Sukhoi Design Bureau, Moscow (aerospace designers; "I spent a year..."); Consultant, to Standard Chartered Bank (its Manager of Loan Syndication '81-83) '87-92, Astra Holdings Plc (fireworks and armaments) '87-92; Trade Indemnity Plc (credit insurers owned by major insurance companies) '87-92, British Cablemakers Confederation '85-??; Director, Richard Unwin International (fireworks) '84-87; Manager, European Arab Banks '77-81; Employee, Bank of America Ltd '71-77; General Secretary, Society for Individual Freedom '69-71;

Traits: Lean; small; dark; forelock; hooded staring eyes; strong chin; "mild-mannered" (PRIVATE EYE); earnest; "nervous, angst-stricken manner" (Andrew Rawnsley, GUARDIAN); "Biggles" (longtime flying enthusiast, since Southampton University days; has a private pilot's licence; was an acting Pilot Officer in the RAF Volunteer Reserve; "I suffer from periodonsis....a dental disease"; scans his newsagents displays because "I resent paying any money to line the pockets of newpaper proprietors";
Address: House of Commons, Westminster, London SW1A 0AA
Telephone: 0171 219 3000 (H of C);

Lindsay HOYLE **Labour** **CHORLEY '97-**

Majority: 9,870 over Conservative 5-way;
Description: A traditionally marginal Lancashire seat; its Labour-supporting town of Chorley is counter-balanced by its pro-Conservative hinterland; this hinterland was reduced slightly in '95; on '92's figures, this should have given its incumbent Tory MP, Den Dover, a 2,500 majority;
Position: Chorley Borough Councillor (Deputy Leader til '97, Chairman of Economic Development) '80-
Outlook: Another Labour Deputy Leader of a local council; this time the pragmatic, entrepreneurial son of soft-Left Doug Hoyle, who left the Commons for the Lords just as his son arrived; Lindsay was the favourite son of Chorley's apolitical party cabal for his job-creating talents in the face of massive job losses at Royal Ordnance;
History: Was born into the family of a Leftwing Lancashire engineer and trade unionist Doug Hoyle and his wife Pauline; when he was one, his father attended his first Labour Party conference; when he was seven, his father contested Clitheroe; he was 13 when his father first contested marginal Nelson and Colne June '70, 17 when his father first won it from David Waddington, narrowly Oct '74; his father lost it in May '79; Lindsay himself won a seat on Chorley District Council at 23, May '80; "I was Chairman of Chorley Borough Council's Economic Development and Tourism Committee, and I helped to bring investment to Chorley, by working with businesses and showing them the attractions and benefits of what we have to offer"; "I also helped to found the Chorley Partnership, to join businesses and community leaders in working together in the town's social and economic development"; became Deputy Leader of Chorley Borough Council; in that capacity he won kudos for winning EC aid to redevelop 800 acres of land formerly held by Royal Ordnance; in talks with receivers, he also supported the management buy-out of the local Multipart car parts business, and negotiated with British Coal to develop 300 acres as a permanent site for the Lancashire Agricultural Show; as the favourite son of a local apolitical party cabal, was selected to contest Chorley against Den Dover, its Tory incumbent since '74, '96; won the seat by 9,870 votes, on a pro-Labour swing of 10.6% May '97; asked about the British Academy of Sport May '97; in his Maiden, admitted local unemployment was low (4%) because "more than 50% of the working population travels outside Chorley to work, as most of our manufacturing has been destroyed"; "the Royal Ordnance site, which is now essentially derelict, once employed 30,000 people"; urged a regional development agency backed by a "progressive" central government

able to exploit funds from the EU; "I hope that the Royal Ordnance site will become a flagship for the whole of the northwest" May '97; backed bar on fox-hunting June '97; asked PM Tony Blair about his success in lobbying Chancellor Kohl about the Eurofighter June '97; pushed the application of Southlands School as a future technological college, with "the support of good business interests and fine financial support from the whole community" June '97; initiated adjournment debate in support of the European Fighter Aircraft, a major project for local British Aerospace and Royal Ordnance; "Aerospace is a major employer in Lancashire, where it forms the backbone of the county's economy; Lancashire represents the largest concentration of aerospace production in the UK"; "in Lancashire last year 13,000 people, or 10% of the county's total manufacturing work force, were employed directly by the industry in more than 40 different establishments; Lancashire also accounts for 13% of the national total employment in the industry"; "in addition to the main contractors involved in the Eurofighter programme - British Aerospace, Rolls-Royce and GEC-Marconi - there are 32 major equipment suppliers and 60 sub-suppliers involved in contracts for the manufacture of the airframe, equipment and engine accessories"; "so far, 11,000 people have been employed in the development phase, and estimates from the industry suggest that the peak of production could provide 16,000 jobs directly and another 16,000 among suppliers of goods and services"; he sharply attacked those who would abandon the potential "world-beater" EFA for the American F22, which would cause massive unemployment in the aerospace industry; "we have sold off our motor industry and run down our shipbuilding industry; during the past 18 years, our heavy engineering and manufacturing industry has fallen to a third of its previous capacity; yet in aerospace we remain a world leader" July '97; urged renaming Heathrow Airport after Diana, Princess of Wales Sep '97;

Born: 10 June 1957, Chorley

Family: Only son, of (Eric) Doug(las Harvey) Hoyle. MP '74-79, '81-97 and Baron Hoyle since '97, and Pauline (Spencer);

Education: Bolton School; Horwich College of Further Education;

Occupation: Director, of a printing company (MSF); Founder-Director, of Chorley Rugby League Club (sold as a limited company '96) '92-96;

Traits: Oval face; short hair; longish sharp nose; plummy voice; Rugby League enthusiast (apart from founding Chorley Rugby League Club, set up a junior Rugby League for schools; is irritated that his father's cricket enthusiasm, especially for the '50s Australian cricket captain Lindsay Hassett, led him to give him an ambivalent name, particularly when mispelled as 'Lindsey', which led to attempts to recruit him for 'Emily's List';

Address: House of Commons, Westminster, London SW1A 0AA; 30 Ashfield Road, Anderton, Chorley PR6 9PN;

Telephone: 0171 219 3000 (H of C); 01257 481999 (home);

REWRITING HISTORY

Some MPs have an amazing capacity for trying to rewrite their own histories. The late Robert Adley tried to excise the fact that he had supported Enoch Powell's tirade against coloured immigration in 1968, protesting: "But that was before I was an MP!" A Labour MP repeatedly denied a line in her profile that she had refused to applaud an acclaimed Kinnock speech at conference, until the message was passed via her husband that this was observed first-hand at a distance of twenty feet.

Beverley HUGHES **Labour** **STRETFORD & URMSTON '97-**

Majority: 13,640 over Conservative 4-way;
Description: Greater Manchester's newly-combined seat in Trafford which helped squeeze out Winston Churchill; it is just to the west of Manchester's city centre and sports Manchester United, the Lancashire County Cricket Club and the new Trafford Centre; the Stretford half, which stretches into the inner-city with its multiply deprived and depressed Moss Side, has long favoured Labour; the formerly Tory-supporting Urmston half is the northwestern end of the Cheshire belt favoured by middle-class commuters and suburban home-owners; it was expected, on '92 figures, to produce a Labour majority of roughly 4,500;
Position: On the Select Committee on Home Affairs '97-; ex: Trafford Councillor (Leader '95-97) '86-97;
Outlook: Another of Labour's local-rooted public sector workers and municipal politicians; Trafford's ex-Leader of the council: "this is my local constituency; my roots are here, my friends in the Labour Party are here and there is nowhere else I would want to stand"; wants Parliamentary procedures to be "more family friendly and easier for non-London MPs"; loyal Blairite reformer;
History: She joined the Labour Party at 28, '78; was elected to Trafford Borough Council May '86; she became Leader of Trafford's Labour Group May '92; when, for the first time, the Conservatives lost control to no overall control, she became Leader of the Council, with LibDem support May '95; Labour gained overall control of Trafford Council May '96; following the decision of Stretford's incumbent Labour MP, Tony Lloyd, to fight the safer Manchester Central seat, she was selected for new Stretford and Urmston, defeating another local councillor, David Actor, by 50% to 35% Mar '96; declared her intention to carry on as Leader until the general election: "there is still a job for me to do in Trafford and I have been asked to stay on by my colleagues" May '96; won the new seat with a majority of 13,640, on a pro-Labour swing of 9.9% May '97; in her Maiden deplored the decline of help for local housing during the Tory years and welcomed Labour's plans to ease improvements in house-building June '97; asked about NHS allocation of drug abuse funds June '97; co-sponsored motion congratulating Manchester on its its progress in rebuilding in the wake of the IRA bombing June '97; urged inclusion of child pornography and paedophile activity in Birmingham Summit June '97; backed review of procedures under which asylum seekers were detained July '97; asked about local hospital waiting lists July '97; asked about ending need to re-authorise deductions of union subscriptions every three years July '97; asked about inter-country adoption July '97; asked about interest on late payments to small businesses July '97; asked about qualifications for those writing wills July '97; urged debate on dangers of mixing leisure drugs July '97; asked about the appointment of a 'drug tsar' July '97; co-sponsored motion calling for a world class sports stadium July '97;
Born: 30 March 1950, Venezuela
Family: Daughter, of late Norman Hughes, materials supervisor, Shell UK, and Doris (Gillard); she is the eldest of eight children; m '73 Tom McDonald; 1s Michael '84, 2d Anna '79, Sarah '81;
Education: Ellesmere Port Grammar School; Manchester University (BSc Hons); Liverpool

University (Diploma in Applied Social Studies); Manchester University (MSc)
Occupation: Senior Lecturer, in Social Work '81-93 and Head of Department '94-96 at Manchester University (AUT); Research Associate, Manchester University '76-81; previouslyly a Probation Officer, Merseyside '71-76;
Traits: Medium-length reddish-blonde hair and fringe; specs; sharp chin; persistent ("I will not be barracked and I will finish my point!"); enjoys jazz, walking and family;
Address: House of Commons, Westminster, London SW1A 0AA; 39 Marlborough Road, Flixton, Manchester M41 1QP;
Telephone: 0171 219 3611 (H of C); 0161 748 1122 (constituency);

Mrs Joan (Jovanka) HUMBLE JP **Labour** **BLACKPOOL NORTH & FLEETWOOD '97-**

Majority: 8,946 over Conservative 5-way;
Description: A '95-new seat comprising the northern half of old Blackpool North and the urban coastal strip - Thornton Cleveleys and Fleetwood - from the dissected old Wyre seat; on '92 figures it was expected to produce a 3,000 Tory majority;
Position: Lancashire County Councillor (Chairman, Social Services '90-97) '85-97;
Outlook: A fulltime municipal politician identified with her targets: of nursery school places for all children in the year when they reach five and the networking of volunteers with social workers; a Christian Socialist; before her election she was ridiculed by the Tory tabloids and Tory MPs because, as Chairman of Lancashire's Social Services Committee, she had approved of investing £2,000 a week in sending a 17-year-old girl suffering from psychiatric problems associated with an eating disorder on a horse-riding holiday in Ireland and on a flight to Australia; this did not seem to damage her voter-appeal;
History: She joined the Labour Party at 27, '78; she was elected to Lancashire County Council May '85; was selected to contest the new Blackpool North and Fleetwood seat '96; she was attacked by Blackpool North's Conservative MP, Harold Elletson, and other local Conservative MPs in a debate on the overspend of the Social Services budget Nov '96; she replied: "the Social Services Committee maintains a continuing review of the arrangements for social care services in Lancashire, taking account of recommendations made and the guidance provided by the Department of Health and the Audit Commission; this will continue and a clear focus will be kept on the needs of the most vulnerable people in Lancashire's community" Nov '96; Labour MP Ann Coffey described the Tory MPs' concerted attacks as "using the Chamber to attack the Labour opponents of sitting Conservative MPs"; "I know that the hon Member for Blackpool South (Nick Hawkins) is off to the safer Surrey suburbs, leaving the hon Member for Blackpool North (Mr Elletson) to struggle to hold his seat against our excellent candidate, Joan Humble" Nov '96; won the new seat by 8,946 on a pro-Labour swing of 14.4% May '97; in her Maiden urged Foreign Secretary Robin Cook to concentrate on quota-hopping in looming EU fishing talks, to guarantee "that Fleetwood has a future as well as a past" June '97; asked about the employment possibilities of the tourist trade for the welfare-to-work programme June '97; backed banning of fox-hunting June '97; urged a

constructive solution to the fisheries crisis, in the interests of the Fleetwood fishermen July '97;
Born: 3 March 1951, Skipton, Yorkshire
Family: Daughter, of Jovo Piplica, bus driver, and Darinka (Kukic); is married to Paul Nugent-Humble, with two children;
Education: Greenhead Grammar School, Keighley; Lancaster University (BA Hons);
Occupation: Lancashire County Councilllor '85-97; ex: Civil Servant '72-77 in DHSS and Inland Revenue;
Traits: Dark; longish hair; admits her predecessor spoke better Russian than she does; did not mention any other Slavic language;
Address: House of Commons, Westminster, London SW1A 0AA; 11 Cromwell Road, Ribbleton, Preston PR2 6YB;
Telephone: 0171 219 3000 (H of C);

Alan (Arthur) HURST **Labour** **BRAINTREE '97-**

Majority: 1,451 over Conservative 6-way;
Description: A large seat in the geographical centre of Essex; made up of Braintree and 40 surrounding villages, including beautiful Finchingfield; some were medieval wool towns; it was thought by psephologists that Labour could win the '97 general election without overwhelming Tony Newton's '92 majority of 17,494;
Position: On Select Committee on Agriculture '97-; Essex County Councillor '93-; ex: Southend Borough Councillor (Deputy Leader '94-95) '80-96;
Outlook: One of the great surprises of the '97 election, a symptom of the Essex counter-revolution, the 21st least-expected Labour victor; a Southend-based councillor-solicitor who ended the Commons career of Tony Newton after 23 years in the seat;
History: He was elected to Southend Borough Council May '80; was elected to Essex County Council May '93; became Deputy Leader of Southend Borough Council May '94; was selected for Braintree against Tony Newton, Leader of the Commons Mar '95; campaigned on local issues: school transport, problems of local businesses, the battle against 4,500 new homes in Witham, accident black-spots, library services in rural areas, affordable housing for locals; won the seat on a notional swing of 12.9% after an ICM poll in the OBSERVER predicted, four days before the election, that he had 43% support, against 40% for Tony Newton, with the LibDem vote halved, an almost perfect prediction of what happened four days later May '97; in his Maiden, urged the survival of Black Notley Hospital May '97; co-sponsored a motion demanding the BBC's Director General apologise for allowing "a self-confessed paedophile to appear on a day-time entertainment show", 'Kilroy' June '97; suggested increasing the number of nominees for Parliamentary candidates to 1% of those eligible to vote June '97; co-sponsored motion paying tribute to cricket captain Graham Gooch on his retirement July '97; was named to the Agriculture Select Committee July '97;
Born: 2 September 1945,
Family: Married to Hilary; has three children;
Education: Westcliff High School, Westcliff-on-Sea; Liverpool Unversity (BA in History);

Occupation: Solicitor: Senior Partner, in Southend firm; Past President, of Southend Law Society;
Traits: Egg-shaped head; balding, with grey fringe; bird-watcher; local history buff; cricket-lover;
Address: House of Commons, Westminster, London SW1A 0AA; 28 Whitefriars Crescent, Westcliff-on-Sea, Essex SSO 8EU
Telephone: 0171 219 3000 (H of C); 01702 345313;

Dr Brian IDDON **Labour** **BOLTON SOUTH EAST '97-**

Majority: 21,311 over Conservative 5-way;
Description: Bolton's unaltered safest Labour seat, created in '83 by the incorporation of the Labour-voting outlying townships of Farnworth, an old mining community, and Kearsley; the former home of the Bolton Wanderers and of decimated engineering and textile factories and closed-down pits;
Position: Bolton Metropolitan District Coouncillor (Chairman, Housing '86-96) '77-
Outlook: A new crusader for a Royal Commission on drugs; a local Leftwing Old Labour Eurosceptic Chemistry Reader starting a new Commons career at 56; his political springboard has been as an innovative housing chairman, responsible for the creation of Bolton Community Homes Ltd (building 1,700 homes in three years), and Careline (home security for the old and disabled); also well-known as a crusader for better knowledge about science among school children and the general public; also believes in: regional government based on Manchester, complete reform of the judicial system, abolition of compulsory competitive tendering, elimination of private medicine in the NHS, a return to public ownership of the Post Office, water, gas, electricity, a full restoration of union rights, a Freedom of Information Act;
History: He joined the Labour Party at 34, '74; was elected to Bolton Metropolitan District Council as the first Labour councillor in the ward Aug '77; after ex-MP Frank White was eliminated, was selected for Bolton SE by beating, by 62.5% to 37.5%, the ageing and inactive incumbent, David Young; Iddon said a higher campaigning profile was needed, with a locally-based secretary, regular newsletters, reports back to branches and closer connections between MP and councillors; this was the first de-selection by OMOV (one-member one-vote) Nov '94; Iddon was photographed in TRIBUNE, protesting at W H Smith's refusal to stock the Leftwing periodical in its Bolton shop Apr '96; won the seat by a majority of 21,311 on the back of an 11.8% swing May '97; complained that because of delays by Child Support Agency, "many responsible fathers who have entered second relationships have suffered so badly that those relationships have also broken down, causing another group of children to suffer" June '97; backed ban on fox-hunting June '97; asked about Government's plans to "tackle one of the nation's most deadly killers" -smoking July '97; urged re-introduction of requirement for local councils to provide caravan sites July '97; co-congratulated Bolton for attracting an £8m Hitachi investment for production of engine control systems to make car exhaust emissions more environmentally friendly July '97; in the wake of the drugs-related killing of a five-year-old in Bolton, called for a Royal Commission on drugs: "I know this is a

very sensitive subject within the party, but now the election is out of the way, there are many new MPs who, like myself, feel the time is ripe for a rethink" Aug '97; was also involved in the vitamin B6 controversy Aug '97;
Born: 5 July 1940, Tarleton, Lancashire
Family: Son, of John Iddon, market gardener and butcher, and Violet (Stazicker), worker in family business; m 1st Merrilyn Ann (Muncaster); 2d Sally Jane '65, Sheena Helen '68; m 2nd '95 Eileen (Barker), former care assistant in residential home for elderly; 2 stepsons: Lee '70, Ian '74;
Education: Tarleton C of E Primary '45-51; failed 11-plus; Christ Church Boys' School, Southport '51-56; Southport Technical College '56-58; Hull University '58-64 (BSc Special Hons in Chemistry); PhD in Organic Chemisry; DSc '81 for "significant contributions to the study of heterocyclic compounds"; FRSC; C Chem;
Occupation: Reader in Organic Chemistry, Salford University '86-97; ex: Senior Lecturer '78-86, Lecturer '66-78, Temporary Lecturer/Senior Demonstrator, at Durham University (AUT) '64-66;
Traits: Oval face; balding with grey fringe; tinted glasses; serious-looking; enjoys not being "folletted" by the "luvvies"; meticulous; stamp collector;
Address: House of Commons, Westminster, London SW1A 0AA; 60 St George's Road, Bolton BL1 2DD (constituency office);
Telephone: 0171 219 4064/2653(Fax) (H of C); 01204 372202 (constituency);

Alan (Arthur) JOHNSON **Labour** **HULL WEST & HESSLE '97-**

Majority: 15,525 over Liberal Democrat 5-way;
Description: The city centre and fishing docks of this little-known, isolated east coast port - although the UK's largest distant-water port; it has long been a Labour stronghold; to equalise the numbers, the adjoining, politically-mixed town of Hessle, at the northern end of the Humber bridge, was added in '95;
Position: On the Select Committee on Trade and Industry '97-; on Labour's National Executive '95-; ex: Joint General Secretary, Communication Workers' Union '95-97; General Secretary, Union of Communication Workers '93-95; on TUC General Council '94-95;
Outlook: Moderate former leader of postmen's union who often sounds more Blairite than Tony Blair; an articulate spokesman, recently for Hull's trawlermen; "Tony Blair's favourite trade union leader" (FINANCIAL TIMES); he was rewarded with a safe seat three weeks before the election, secured by shoehorning out the previous MP, Stuart Randall, who was then paid off with a peerage; "immensely able and articulate" (Robin Cook MP); seen by Labour's hard-Left as the likely front man for Blair's attempt to reduce union influence in 'New Labour';
History: He joined the Union of Postal Workers (UPW) on becoming a postman '68; he joined the Labour Party '75; he became Chairman of the Slough branch of the UPW '76; was elected to the UPW's National Executive Council '81; was elected UPW's fulltime officer in charge of delivery postmen '87; following fellow moderate Alan Tuffin, was elected General Secretary of Union of Communications Workers '92; hired Sir Tim Bell, Thatcher's former

PRman/lobbyist to run the last three months of the UCW campaign against Michael Heseltine's Post Office privatisation plans '94; during '95, his union contributed £600,000 to Labour Party funds; was elected to Labour's National Executive Oct '95; at Labour's special conference, was the only union leader to speak out in favour of revising 'Clause IV' Dec '95; during postal strikes against Post Office management's attempt to alter working practices, had to give in to membership's demands for continued industrial action June '96; claimed that unions' new relationship with Labour meant "there is no special privileged position for trade union leaders" Sep '96; after incumbent MP, Stuart Randall, was persuaded to stand down "to spend more time with my family" and the promise of a peerage, was hurriedly selected for Hull West by a subcommittee of the NEC, with Hilary Benn and Bryan Davies MP also on the short-list Apr '97; declined to be interviewed by Sir David Frost when he discovered the main subject was the firemen's strike, since he was not their spokesman Apr '97; was elected by a majority of 15,525, on a swing of 3.2% from the LibDems and 9% from the Tories May '97; was one of three NEC members who investigated bribery charges against newly- elected Govan Labour MP Mohammed Sarwar May '97; opposed selling arms to Indonesia June '97; welcomed Nigerian Nobel Laureate Wole Soyinka for the Wilberforce lecture in the emancipator's birthplace of Hull July '97; was named to Select Committee on Trade and Industry July '97; in his Maiden heavily deplored the harsh treatment meted out to Hull's trawlermen July '97; defended Labour leadership's plans to curb influence of hardline activists in Labour's annual conferences Sep '97; wittily replied for the NEC at the Brighton annual conference Sep '97;
Born: 17 May 1950, London
Family: Son, of Stephen Arthur Johnson, painter and decorator, and Lillian May (Gibson), cleaner; m 1st '68 Judith Elizabeth (Cox); 1s, 2d; divorced; m 2nd '91 Laura Jane (Patient);
Education: Sloane Grammar School, Chelsea;
Occupation: Director, Unity Trust Bank Plc '93-; ex: Joint General Secretary, Communication Workers Union '95-97, General Secretary, Union of Communications Workers '93-95, UCW Officer in Charge of Delivery Postmen '87-92; Postman '68-87;
Traits: Oval-faced; heavy-lidded baggy eyes; fast-talking, in a London accent; neat, spruce, sleek, sharp-looking;
Address: House of Commons, Westminster, London SW1A 0AA;
Telephone: 0171 219 6637 (H of C);

Melanie JOHNSON JP **Labour** **WELWYN-HATFIELD '97-**

Majority: 5,595 over Conservative 5-way;
Description: Hertfordshire's volatile marginal seat made up of two new towns: Hatfield and Welwyn Garden City, centres of pharmaceuticals and, formerly, planebuilding; captured from Helen (now Baroness) Hayman by the Tory MP Christopher Murphy in '79 and, from '87, retained by extrovert Rightwing populist David Evans; it lost Tory-leaning Wheathampstead ward in '95;
Position: Cambridgeshire County Councillor '81-97;
Outlook: A Blairite county councillor and schools inspector who secured the candidacy in an all-woman selection contest and then won fame from the nasty comments of her foul-mouthed opponent, David

Evans, who symbolised the very male-dominated politics she has sought to correct; she believes more women MPs will make for "a different style of working, more geared to results than noise-making; women [are] more likely to use common sense and try to build a consensus"; in Greenpeace and formerly in CND;

History: She joined the Labour Party at 23, '78; she was elected to Cambridgeshire County Council May '81; led successful campaign to improve safety in school transport; contested the Cambridgeshire Euro-seat, coming within 2.2% - 35.4% to 37.6% -of her Conservative opponent June '94; was selected to contest Welwyn-Hatfield against David Evans from an all-woman short-list Mar '95; was attacked by David Evans in a talk with sixth-formers - which he did not know was being taped - as not having a chance of winning the seat as "a single girl, lives with her boy friend, three bastard children, lives in Cambridge, never done a proper job" Feb '97: she replied: "I am used to the hurly-burly of politics, but he has descended into the gutter; I am horrified he could attack my children with this foul word"; she also objected to Evans' jibe that being a schools inspector was "not a proper job"; Evans' outburst prompted a delegation of Labour women MPs to 10 Downing Street demanding Evans' de-selection; he refused to apologise, insisting: "whether you like it or not, they are bastards" Mar '97; she ousted Evans on a swing of 11%, securing a majority of 5,595 May '97; in her Maiden was kind to David Evans; she emphasised the need to redevelop the British Aerospace site in Hatfield May '97; asked, "does the Prime Minister not find it astonishing that some 100,000 children do not attend their schools in England and Wales each day? will he tell the House what the government intend to do about that?" June '97; she backed the abolition of fox-hunting June '97; probed the performance of insolvency practitioners July '97; with lots of pharmaceutical plants in Welwyn, she co-sponsored a motion supporting the Biotechnology Patenting Directive July '97;

Born: 5 February 1955, Ipswich

Family: Daughter, of David Johnson, civil engineer rtd, and Angela (Matthews); Partner, since '79, of William Jordan, civil servant; 1s Thomas '86, twin daughers: Melissa and Sarah '84; asked why they had never married, she replied: "we are happy as we are";

Education: Clifton High School for Girls, Bristol; University College, London (BA in Philosophy and Ancient Greek); King's College, Cambridge

Occupation: Schools Inspector, with OFSTED '93-97; Senior Manager, in Family Health Services Authority (UNISON) '90-91; Member Relations Officer, in Co-operative Society '81-88;

Traits: Dark hair; pretty, broad face;

Address: House of Commons, Westminster, London SW1A 0AA; 102 Richmond Road, Cambridge CB4 3PT;

Telephone: 0171 219 4119 (H of C);

Fiona JONES | **Labour** | **NEWARK '97-**

Majority: 3,016 over Conservative 4-way;
Description: An unaltered Nottinghampshire seat of twin market towns, Newark and Southwell, on the A1 trunk road; its passing into Tory hands in '79 seemed further confirmed by its loss of former mining communities in '83; had '92 been repeated, it would have provided the Tory incumbent with an 8,000 majority;
Position: On Select Committee on Agriculture '97-; ex: West Lindsey District Councillor '90-94;
Outlook: A low-profiled provincial journalist and councillor who thought MPs are "out of touch"; hoped to change Parliament from "a confrontational gentlemen's club"; an RC anti-abortionist (in Labour Life Group);
History: She joined the Labour Party at 17, '74; was elected to West Lindsey District Council May '90; wrote letter to GUARDIAN commenting on an unidentified NHS employee who had elicited from the then junior Health minister, Stephen Dorrell, that it had cost £127,000 for the NHS's Chief Executive, Duncan Nichol, to write to all NHS employees praising the new Conservative reforms; she commented: "what a sad state our Health Service is in when employees are afraid to speak out and the Government would sooner spend money on propaganda than on beds" Oct '91; fought hopeless Gainsborough & Horncastle, nearly doubling the Labour vote to 11,619 (20%) while still remaining in 3rd place Apr '92; was selected to contest Newark against Richard Alexander '95; captured the seat on a swing of 10.2%, achieving a majority of 3,016 May '97; co-urged cancellation of £780m Milliennium Exhibition, with money to be spent on health, education and transport June '97; appeared with Lord Longford at an anti-abortion fringe meeting sponsored by 'Labour Life Group' at the Brighton annual conference Oct '97;
Born: 27 February 1957, Liverpool
Family: She is married, with two children
Education: Mary's Help of Christians Convent Grammar School, Liverpool; attended colleges in Preston and Wirral (Media and Communications degree);
Occupation: Journalist; Chairman, Lincolnshire branch of NUJ '89-;
Traits: Shoulder-length tousled blonde hair; pretty; Roman Catholic; an uncommunicative journalist; enjoys photography;
Address: House of Commons, Westminster, London SW1A 0AA; 55 Church Road, Saxilby, Lincolnshire LN1 2HH;
Telephone: 0171 219 3000 (H of C); 01522 703685;

EXPLOSIONS:
Sometimes an explosion unveils those who rely on our volumes. After the 1994 explosion damaged the Israeli Embassy in London, an eagle-eyed Welsh fan of ours scanned one of the pictures of its damaged interior and spotted a set of these volumes. A similar photograph of the interiors of other embassies would often show the same - foreign diplomats have been among the most enthusiastic about our interest in the positions of MPs on crises abroad, such as the deep split in the Commons over former Yugoslavia.

Helen JONES **Labour** **WARRINGTON NORTH '97-**

Majority: 19,527 over Conservative 4-way;
Description: The inner-city portion of this industrial town north of the Mersey with terraced housing and a small ethnic minority; in '95 two wards were transferred to Warrington South; in '81 the undivided seat was the site of a tight confrontation between Roy Jenkins, as the candidate of the rising SDP, and Doug Hoyle, until '97 Labour's incumbent;
Position: On Commons Catering Committee '97-; on Labour's North West Regional Executive; ex: Chester City Councillor;
Outlook: Widnes-based moderate Leftwing solicitor; a veteran northwestern activist-candidate for two decades; became the focus of a revolt in Warrington North against the imposition of a Millbank candidate (Yvette Cooper) when unexpectedly dropped by the NEC into a short-list for a safe seat four weeks before the election;
History: She joined the Labour Party at 22, '76; contested the safe Conservative seat of Shropshire North against John Biffen, coming 3rd with 7,860 votes (14.7%) June '83; fought Euro-seat of Lancashire Central June '84; came close to winning Ellesmere Port and Neston, increasing Labour's share from 32.6% to 41.2%, on the largest pro-Labour swing in the northwest (5.1%), cutting the Tory majority to 1,853, June '87; as a 'Welsh' woman make-weight was short-listed for Newport East, after Roy Hughes was shoehorned out by the promise of a peerage; she came bottom in the selection with 18 votes and the selection went, as desired, to the Tory defector, Alan Howarth Mar '97; four weeks later she was rewarded at Warrington North where, after Doug Hoyle had been seduced upstairs into the Lords, she was short-listed with three other women, all locally considered "Londoners"; she called for a North West Development Agency, a minimum wage, job training, employment rights as in Europe and "properly funded" education; partly because she was a veteran northwestern activist and candidate - and not a favourite of the 'Millbank Tendency' - she won by 143 votes over Valerie Vaz (87) and Yvette Cooper (29) Mar '97; there were challenges, because of the exclusion of local candidates and voting irregularities Apr '97; she retained the seat with a pro-Labour swing of 9.9%, almost doubling the majority May '97; in her witty Maiden she indicated that, when she had not received the Labour Whip, she feared she was viewed with suspicion by the leadership: "I carefully scrutinised my election address and reviewed my whole campaign, and I can honestly say, unlike some hon Members, that the word 'socialism' did not get past my agent's eagle eye" June '97; opposed shutdown of Memory Lane Cakes in Warrington June '97; opposed sending of arms to Indonesia June '97; opposed cutback of customs officers as increasing the threat of illegal drugs imports July '97; sought reassurance that, if mines were used to protect British troops, "we would de-mine those areas after hostilities had ceased" July '97;
Born: 24 December 1954, Chester
Family: Daughter of Robert Jones, Shotton steelworker, and Mary (Scanlan) of Irish descent, who was a factory worker, then a school cook; is married to 'Mike' Vobe, who worked for a Widnes housing association and recently for Ben Chapman the MP who won the Wirral South by-election; 1s Chris '89;
Education: Chester College; University College, London; Liverpool University;

Occupation: Solicitor, specialising in personal and industrial injuries; ex: Justice and Peace Officer, Liverpool RC Archdiocese; Development Officer, of MIND; Teacher (NAS-UWT);
Traits: Dark; front-combed fringe; RC; of Welsh and Irish origins;
Address: House of Commons, Westminster, London SW1A 0AA; she lives in Widnes;
Telephone: 0171 219 3000 (H of C); 01925 2322480/232239 (Fax) (constituency)

'Jenny' (Jennifer) JONES Labour WOLVERHAMPTON SOUTH WEST '97-

Majority: 5,118 over Conservative 4-way;
Description: Traditionally the safely-Conservative seat in this West Midlands town long associated with Enoch Powell ('50-74) and his acolyte Nicholas Budgen ('74-97); in the past its fifth of pro-Labour non-whites in the town centre have been more than counter-balanced by the Tory-voting middle-class residential wards on its periphery;
Position: Wolverhampton Borough Councillor (Chairwoman its Labour Group '94-96) '91-97; on Wolverhampton Community Health Council '81-86;
Outlook: Training manager and local councillor who overthrew 47 years of Tory control from the springboard of an all-women selection contest; "independent-minded with Left credentials" (RED PEPPER); had a high profile locally for her '80s campaign against the high death-rate among local newly-born;
History: She joined the Labour Party at 31, '79; was named to the Wolverhampton Community Health Council '81; campaigned to reduce the high death-rate among the newly-born locally in '82-83; was elected to Wolverhampton Borough Council May '91; was selected from an all-women short-list to contest Wolverhampton South West against incumbent Tory MP Nicholas Budgen '95; her Tory opponent, Nick Budgen, campaigned against coloured immigration; she said: "he's desperate and that's why he has raised the race card" Apr '97; she ended Budgen's 23-year-long reign with a 9.9% swing which produced a majority "beyond my wildest dreams" (JJ) May '97; opposed fox-hunting June '97; opposed selling arms to Indonesia June '97; urged "improved training and qualifications in the tourist industry" June '97; asked about tax losses from illegally imported beer July '97; co-urged a "world-class sports stadium" within the Millennium Exhibition July '97; urged "measures to confiscate the assets of terrorist organisations to cut off their economic supply line" Oct '97;
Born: 8 February 1948, London
Family: She is married but refuses to "give information for publication on my family";
Education: Tom Hood Comprehensive, Leytonstone; Bradford University '68-72; Birmingham University '85-87; Wolverhampton University '94;
Occupation: Training Manager, Black Country CDH Ltd (giving start-up advice to small and medium-sized enterprises) (MSF); Social Worker; Housing Researcher; Member, Institute of Personnel and Development
Traits: Chubby; red hair; full-faced; adores Wolverhampton Wanderers; likes cats; enjoys swimming and gardening;
Address: House of Commons, Westminster, London SW1A 0AA; 56 Goldhawk Road, Wolverhampton WV2 4PN;
Telephone: 0171 219 4105 (H of C);

Sally KEEBLE **Labour** **NORTHAMPTON NORTH '97-**

Majority: 10,000 over Conservative 5-way;
Description: An old county town designated as a new town in '68; it contains some of the better residential districts and the headquarters of the Nationwide Building Society; won from Labour in '79, on '92 figures it was expected to provide Tony Marlow with a majority of 4,000 - on which he did not count;
Position: On Agriculture Select Committee '97-; Southwark Borough Councillor (Leader '90-94) '86-94
Outlook: One of the successful former council leaders, who froze the poll tax for three years running; in Walworth Road in the Kinnock years was "one of the 'New Realism' apparatchiks; was one of the first to move to the Right in the Inner London boroughs - part of the 'Margaret Hodge tendency'" (a former Lambeth councillor); recently a Blair loyalist and one of the new "shoulder-pad socialists" (TIMES); also a former union and party communicatins expert;
History: She joined the Labour Party in '83; was elected to Southwark Borough Council May '86; became Leader of Southwark Borough Council May '90; initiated court action against Health Secretary Virginia Bottomley over closure of Guy's Hospital; was selected from an all-women short-list to oust maverick Rightwing Europhobe and male chauvinist Tony Marlow from Northampton North Feb '95; at annual conference at Brighton, claimed Labour would build safer communities Oct '95; after the industrial tribunal decided against all-women short-lists, said it was "a surprising decision, but in seats such as mine they had all-woman shortlists by choice and there is whole-hearted support for it" Jan '96; won the seat on a swing of 13.3%, ousting Marlow by a majority of 10,000 May '97; co-sponsored motion on improved treatment of breast cancer June '97; in her Maiden attacked the attempted raid on the Nationwide Building Society, based in her constituency June '97; co-urged rape law review June '97; attacked racial harassment July '97; led motion complaining that only 10% of the 600,000 who had been mis-sold pensions had been compensated July '97; co-opposed opencast mining July '97; was named to Agriculture Select Committee July '97;
Born: 13 October 195l, Berlin
Family: Daughter of Sir Curtis Keeble GCMG, diplomat (Ambassador to Moscow '78-82 and GDR '74-76), and Margaret (Fraser); m lst '73 Chris Coetzee, university lecturer; divorced '79; m '2nd '90 Andrew Porter, financial consultant; 1s Lewis '96, 1d Eleanor '94;
Education: Cheltenham Ladies' College; St Hugh's College, Oxford University (BA in Theology); University of South Africa;
Occupation: Author: Conceiving Your Baby: How Medicine Can Help (Heinemann; 1995); Consultant, at Public Policy Unit '95-; ex: Journalist: on DURBAN DAILY NEWS (South Africa), BIRMINGHAM POST (NUJ); Head of Communications in GMB; Press Officer, Labour Party (NUJ);
Traits: Attractive in a horsey way; pageboy bob; streaky blonde; hooded eyes; high cheek bones; long nose; square jaw; strident tones; well-dressed mandarin's daughter; wealthy;
Address: House of Commons, Westminster, London SW1A 0AA; 7 Little Bournes, Alleyn Park, Dulwich, London SE21 8SD;
Telephone: 0171 219 3000 (H of C); 0181 670 4501 (home);

Mrs Ann (Lloyd) KEEN **Labour** **BRENTFORD & ISLEWORTH '97-**

Majority: 14,424 over Conservative 6-way;
Description: The previously marginal west London dormitory and industrial seat on the north bank of the Thames; it embraces the historic town of Isleworth, Osterley, Brentford and Chiswick, with their parks and sewage farm;
Position: On Select Committee on Health '97-; Chairman, Brentford Crime Prevention Panel '92-; on Labour Party's Health Advisory Panel;
Outlook: The third member of her family currently in the Commons, third-time-lucky in this same seat, with a vengeance; the former Kinnockite nurse, a younger, less restrained version of her sister, Sylvia Heal, who is back for Halesowen and Rowley Regis (after having won the '90 by-election for Mid-Staffordshire and then lost it to Michael Fabricant in '92); it was then that her husband, Alan Keen, won adjoining Feltham and Heston; "Mrs Keen is actually about as Labour Party as you can get" (Matthew Engel, GUARDIAN); a close friend of the Kinnocks; in the Socialist Health Associatiion, formerly in the Medical Campaign Against Nuclear Weapons;
History: She was born into a family of active socialists in North Wales, whose council house hosted party meetings, councillors' surgeries and election campaign teams; she joined CND at 14, the Labour party at 16, '65, attending her first conference at 17; was a council candidate in Clwyd; after moving South, was a council candidate in Spelthorne; was selected to contest Brentford and Isleworth against incumbent Tory MP Barney (later Lord) Hayhoe on the 4th ballot by 33 to 27, Nov '85; as Spelthorne's delegate to annual conference, she deplored the desperate shortage of nurses and chiropodists in the the NHS and the privatisation of hospital services; she also urged the nationalisation of the pharmaceutical industry Oct '86; she complained that "Parliament is too full of male lawyers and economists" Jan '87; contested Brentford & Isleworth, losing by 7,953, June '87; at annual conference fervently supported a composite urging the end of nuclear weapons, whether by unilateral, bilateral or multilateral means; "I believe that nuclear weapons are the greatest horror ever made by man; I believe that it is the duty of our generation to rid the world of all nuclear weapons, and because I believe that, this party should do everthing in its power to secure nuclear disarmament; for all these reasons, I joined CND some 20-odd years ago and I am still a member working for nuclear disarmament" Oct '88; tried for selection for marginal Delyn in her native North Wales Mar '90; was re-selected for Brentford and Isleworth Feb '91; in the general election, because she did not quite match the winning swing of her husband, Alan, she only reduced the majority of the new, Ceylon-born Tory candidate, Nirj Deva, to 1,675 Apr '92; was again selected for Brentford and Isleworth, this time from an all-women short-list Nov '95; she was listed as one of the 16 GMB members to be specially supported in the election Apr '97; she finally won the seat on a massive swing of 14.3%, which produced her Labour majority of 14,424 May '97; backed ban on fox-hunting June '97; expressed solidarity with a jailed Indonesian trade union leader June '97; co-sponsored motion applauding a £100m cut in NHS bureaucracy June '97; co-spponsored motion enthusing about increased breast cancer care June '97; in her Maiden expressed the hope that her decrepit local West Middlesex University Hospital, where she had worked, would soon be rebuilt July '97; she was named to the Select Committee on Health July '97;

Born: 26 November 1948, Buckley, North Wales
Family: Her grandfather was a Shotton steelworker; her father John Lloyd Fox, was also a Shotton steelworker and local Labour councillor; her mother, Ruby, was a Labour Party member from '36; her older sister, Sylvia, became MP for Mid-Staffordshire '90-92 and Halesowen & Rowley Regis '97-; in the wake of the '97 election, Ann disclosed that, like Clare Short, she too had given up her son for adoption, following a pregnancy when she was 17; she had been reunited with Mark Lloyd Fox after 28 years in '95; Ann married in '80, Alan Keen, who became MP for Feltham & Heston in '92; one steps, one stepd;
Education: Ewloe Green County Primary; failed the 11-plus, like her sister; Elfed Secondary Modern School (left school at 15); qualified as a State Enrolled Nurse at Spelthorne '76, State Registered Nurse at Ashford Hospital, Middlesex; then qualified as a District Nurse; Surrey University (a Certificate of Education in Community Nursing as a mature student); she then qualified as Senior Nursing Tutor;
Occupation: General Secretary, Community and District Nursing Association (CDNA)(GMB); ex: Head of Faculty for Advanced Nursing, Queen Charlotte's College, Hammersmith Hospital; District Nurse; State Registered Nurse, in training position with Hounslow and Spelthorne Health Authority; State Enrolled Nurse; Clerk, in the NHS; Worker, in Clwyd paper factory;
Traits: Very pretty; grey-blonde; blue eyes; gentle North Welsh lilt; "conveys an air of North Country warmth and concern" (Matthew Engel, GUARDIAN); Brentford Town supporter;
Address: House of Commons, Westminster, London SW1A 0AA; 38 Brook Road South, Brentford, Middx TW8 0NN;
Telephone: 0171 219 3000 (H of C); 0181 847 0987 (home);

Paul (Stuart) KEETCH **Liberal Democrat** **HEREFORD '97-**

Majority: 6,648 over Conservative 4-way;
Description: The perennial Conservative-Liberal Democrat marginal; half its voters are in the small and ancient city of bus-infested Hereford, with the other half in the many small villages of southern Herefordshire;
Position: On the LibDems' Health team '97-; ex: Hereford City Councillor '83-86;
Outlook: The first Liberal MP for Hereford since journalist Frank Owen ('29-31); a locally-born and locally-active campaigner who finally cashed in on two decades of hard work; a fighter for local cider and cattle; has worked as a consultant to the Electoral Reform Society on voting reforms in Eastern Europe; in LibDem Forum for the Countryside, Charter 88; his interest in defence may be related to the SAS base in Hereford;
History: He served as Parliamentary election agent in the general elections of '83, '87 and '92 (when the Welsh extrovert, Gwynoro Jones, lost a couple of thousand votes); at annual conference at Brighton rejected the call of the LibDem youth and student wing to abolish the monarchy at the end of the present Queen's reign; he argued that "with the empire gone, Britain no longer needed a large imperial family, but that does not mean the monarchy itself should be abolished" Sep '95; was one of two UK observers sent to observe the rigged

Albanian elections, finding them fundamentally flawed May '96; called for Albanian President Sali Berisha to resign or form an all-party coalition and call new elections, in a letter to the INDEPENDENT Mar '97; supported decision of LibDem-controlled South Herefordshire Council to defer planning permission for a British Gas pumping station at Treaddow; this followed action by the incumbent local Tory MP, Sir Colin Shepherd, who had written in May '96 to British Gas Chairman Richard Giordano to move a proposed pumping station from Bridstow, where his brother lived nearby; two months later Mr Giordano wrote to Sir Colin that the pumping station would be placed in Treaddow, spoiling its view of the Wye valley; Keetch supported the Treaddow protest: "it is going to be of no benefit to the local community; no jobs will be created" Mar '97; won the seat on a swing of 9.2%, giving him a majority of 6,648 over Sir Colin Shepherd May '97; in his Maiden expressed the fear that "the 616th mayor of the city [of Hereford] who was installed three weeks ago, could well be the last" without new legislation; also deplored the costly damage done to "the pure-bred herds of Hereford, fed solely on grass and with no history of BSE" June '97; asked about cleanliness of vehicles hauling possibly-infectious "specified bovine material" July '97; asked about Environment Agency taking over navigation authority for the rivers Wye and Lugg July '97; asked about alternatives to abandoned road projects July '97; urged rapid increase in computer training July '97; co-urged more ecumenical prayers in the Commons July '97;
Born: 21 May 1961, Hereford
Family: Is married to Claire; they have one son;
Education: Hereford High School for Boys; Hereford Sixth Form College;
Occupation: Director: of a computer company and a building company; Adviser: to two charities; Political and Corporate Affairs Consultant;
Traits: Dark; specs;
Address: House of Commons, Westminster, London SW1A 0AA;
Telephone: 0171 219 3000 (H of C);

Ruth KELLY **Labour** **BOLTON WEST '97-**

Majority: 7,072 over Conservative 5-way;
Description: A longtime Lancashire marginal including much of the town's best residential areas as well as British Aerospace Dynamics; it twice had its Conservative leanings stiffened: in '83 by adding posh residential areas and again in '95, by moving out the Asians in Halliwell ward; had the whole country not swung decisively to Labour, its able young Tory Minister, Tom Sackville, might have clung on, again;
Position: On Select Committee on the Treasury '97-; ex: Treasurer, Bethnal Green and Bow Constituency Labour Party '94-96;
Outlook: A thoughtful young Blairite moderniser and social democratic economist, formerly employed by the Bank of England; in the Fabian Society, the Employment Policy Institute, the Christian Socialist Movement; espouses 'feminism tempered by Catholicism'; "a doughty fighter" (John Prescott MP); "one of the stars to watch" (Barbara Follett, MAIL ON SUNDAY); "a high-flyer" (Matthew Brace, INDEPENDENT); believes a Labour Government "has to almost eradicate long-term unemployment, [and] get the young unemployed back to work because at

the moment the culture of work is almost disappearing"; is hostile to unregulated flexible labour markets because they are not effective in creating jobs; favours strong employee-employer relations and longer-term contracts to give job security, but believes the right to work should be balanced by responsibility to work; believes also that union rights should be balanced by responsibilities, as in Sweden, "where they are involved in running the unemployment system and therefore are aware that the more they press pay increases, the more unemployed they will have to look after";

History: She joined the Labour Party after university "because I was worried about the alienation of the unemployed" '90; was selected from an open short-list of six to contest Bolton West -where she had no connections - to oppose the attractive and able incumbent Minister, Tom Sackville Feb '96; became a member of the Criteria, a club for Left-leaning Eurosceptic intellectuals organised by Anne McElroy the Deputy Editor of SPECTATOR Sep '96; was attacked as a "typical yuppie-based New Labour candidate" by her Old Etonian opponent, Tom Sackville, son of the Earl De La Warr; asked by local journalist Andrew Grimes whether she was a socialist, she replied: "Socialism has many strands; if you mean, do I believe in society, yes I do"; asked whether she shared "Tony Blair's keenness to perpetuate the most repressive trade union laws in western Europe", she replied: "I certainly think that union policies were lax in the 1970s and did a great deal of damage to the country" Apr '97; won Bolton West on a swing of 11.3%, ousting Tom Sackville by a majority of 7,072 May '97; in her Maiden - a week before she gave birth - she emphasised the benefits Labour's minimum wage would bring to poorly paid Boltonians and the importance of employment for its jobless youth; she also promised to carry on Tom Sackville's fight for a Bolton University May '97; had her baby son Eamonn but hardly interrupted her questions June '97; co-sponsored motion urging an affordable creche in the Commons June '97; asked for the statistics of those on low pay in Bolton June '97; expressed solidarity with jailed Indonesian trade union leader June '97; elicited the response that the Bank of England would not, without drastic change, meet all the requirements for central bank independence in the Maastricht Treaty June '97; asked Harriet Harman about "a national child care strategy" June '97; asked about prescription fraud in Bolton July '97; led motion congratulating Bolton on securing £8m in investment from Hitachi July '97; led motion congratulating Bolton Wanderers on their promotion to the Premier League July '97; was named to the Select Committee on the Treasury July '97;

Born: 9 May 1968, Limavady, N Ireland

Family: Daughter of Bernard James Kelly, pharmacist, and Gertrude Anne (Murphy); m '96 Derek Gadd, an archaeologist working as a Labour Party constituency agent; 1c Eamonn '97;

Education: Millfield Junior School '79-81; Sutton High School for Girls '81-83; Holy Trinity School, Killeney, Dublin '83-84; Westminster School '84-86; The Queen's College, Oxford University '86-89 (BA Hons in PPE); London School of Economics '90-92 (MSc);

Occupation: Economist: for the Bank of England, where she was Deputy Head of the Inflation Report Division '94-97; Economic Journalist, on the GUARDIAN (where she set up the "seven wise women" panel of female economists) '90-94;

Traits: Blonde; pretty; young (among the youngest of the new Labour women intake); "svelte" with "the assured creamy drawl of the Sloane Ranger" (Andrew Grimes, MANCHESTER EVENING NEWS); diffident; personable; Irish; practicing Roman Catholic;

Address: House of Commons, Westminster, London SW1A 0AA; 2 Cloyster's Green, London E1 9LU;

Telephone: 0171 219 3496 (H of C); 01204 523920 (constituency); 0181 345 6789 880026 (pager);

Fraser KEMP **Labour** **HOUGHTON & WASHINGTON EAST '97-**

Majority: 26,555 over Conservative 4-way;
Description: The slightly altered ultra-safe Labour seat embracing Washington New Town and the former pit villages in the Houghton-le-Spring part of the former Durham coal field; the least urbanised of all the Tyne and Wear constituencies;
Position: The Labour Party's National Special Projects Officer '96-97; National General Election Co-ordinator '94-96; West Midlands Regional Secretary '86-94;
Outlook: A locally-born organiser-fixer of oustanding ability; part of Blair's 'Geordie Mafia' of northeasterners with direct access; but has wider roots in the old Black Country Labour Mafia, unions and Old Labour; is Centre-Left and intuitively libertarian; a regionalist favouring a Northern Regional Assembly; self-described as "a moderniser with traditional values" (FK); "is it not a great betrayal to deny power to the common people by sticking to old-fashioned ways which repel the voters of Middle England rather than modify these ways in order to gain power for the common good?" (FK); "people don't just want their MP to be angry about their problems; they want somebody who can help find and influence the solutions to these problems as well" (FK);
History: He joined the Labour Party at 15, '74; in succession became CLP Secretary, Political Education Officer, Executive Committee member and Election Agent for Giles Radice in Chester-le-Street May '79; was Election Agent for Roland Boyes in his successful bid for the Durham Euro-seat June '79; was appointed to Labour's East Midlands Region '81; became the youngest-ever regional organiser, for Birmingham '86; established his reputation as an organiser as agent for Sylvia Heal's capture of safe-Tory Mid Staffordshire in the by-election, winning on a swing of 21% Mar '90; iced the cake of his reputation in the by-election campaign for Dudley West, captured by Ian Pearson on a 29% swing, a 59-year record; a feature of this was Kemp's idea to have Tony Blair meet disillusioned Tories Dec '94; Kemp greeted this victory as "a positive endorsement of New Labour and in particular Tony Blair as Leader"; he received Blair's praise: "Fraser has a great flair and a great feel for political campaigning"; he cheekily applied for the job of Labour's General Secretary after Tony Blair had sacked Larry (later Lord) Whitty, though it was clear the job would go to Tom Sawyer; Sawyer admired his chutzpah and took him on as his deputy; he was brought to Labour headquarters at Walworth Road as National General Election Co-ordinator Jan '95; as Conference Arrangements Committee Secretary at Labour's Special Conference on Clause IV, ruled as inadmissible Arthur Scargill's motion to have the proceedings declared unconstitutional Apr '95; was responsible for sifting out motions hostile to the leadership, admitting: "we just want to ensure Labour projects a very positive image" Oct '95; was overwhelmingly selected on the first ballot, on the slogan "local roots, national experience", to replace the retiring, ailing (Alzheimer's), non-Blairite Roland Boyes, in his natal constituency, Houghton and Washington Aug '96; as an aide to Peter Mandelson, described as "ill-advised" Clare Short's slur on Mandelson as one of the people operating "in the dark" Aug '96; seeing the Conservative Party as likely to disintegrate if Labour won, said: "we must set the scene for a generation of Labour in government"; "if we fail to win, the future will look very bleak for the party, and there's one hell of a lot riding on us" Aug '96; was elected, on a swing of 9.1%,

achieving a majority of 26,555 May '97; was named to the prestigious Committee of Selection June '97; led a motion attacking the new Conservative Leader for diverting 'Short Money', assigned to supporting the Opposition in Parliament, to finance the Conservative Research Department, servicing the party at large July '97; urged an experimental introduction of the 'Florida Scheme' where drug users had to undergo legally enforceable rehabilitation July '97; led a motion urging the British Museum to return the Lindisfarne Gospels to Northumbria July '97; urged a pilot scheme to ensure the projected Regional Development Agencies had the necessary expertise and experience July '97;
Born: 1 September 1958, Washington, Co Durham
Family: Son, of 'Billy'/William Kemp, miner, and Mary (Smith) shopworker; m '89 Patricia (Byrne) Lecturer; 2s Matthew '92, Alex '95; 1d Kate '93;
Education: Biddick Primary School, Washington; Washington Comprehensive School;
Occupation: National Special Projects Officer '96-97; National General Election Co-ordinator '94-96; West Midlands Regional Secretary '86-94; Regional Officer, East Midlands '81-86; Civil Servant, '75-80;
Traits: Tall; dark; balding; egg-shaped face; affable; raconteur; convivial and gregarious beer-drinker; football-crazy; "a certain knowing self-mockery" (NORTHERN ECHO);
Address: House of Commons, Westminster, London SW1A 0AA; 23 Biddick Villas, Columbia Village, Washington, Tyne & Wear NE38 7DT;
Telephone: 0171 219 3000 (H of C); 0191 416 0599 (home & Fax)

David (Neil) KIDNEY **Labour** **STAFFORD '97-**

Majority: 4,314 over Conservative 5-way;
Description: Mostly the town of Stafford itself, shorn in '95 of its more rural and small-town Conservative bits, which have gone to Stone, along with vote-sensitive Bill Cash;
Position: Stafford Borough Councillor '87-97; ex: Staffordshire Moorlands Parish Councillor '84-87;
Outlook: Another of Labour's municipal politicians, this one a solicitor who believes in saving marriages; a moderate pro-European reformer; is in the Society of Labour Lawyers, Labour Party Rural Renewal, Labour Housing Group, the British Agencies for Adoption and Fostering,
History: He joined the Labour Party at 17, '72; was elected to Staffordshire Moorland Parish Council for Checkley May '84; was elected to Stafford Borough Council May '87; contested Stafford on its old boundaries, losing by 10,900 (17.6%) Apr '92; was re-selected for more-winnable Stafford May '95; one of the few Labour candidates who responded to a DAILY TELEGRAPH questionnaire: on the minimum wage, he said, "my judgement is that the figure will be just below £4"; on air traffic control privatisation: "my heart is not in it; I don't like the sound of it; I think we have had more than enough privatisation; I think it's got to the stage where it is harmful"; on the single European currency, said he was "fully in line with my party's policy" Apr '97; on a notional swing of 10.7%, he won altered Stafford with a majority of 4,314 over the Cash-replacement Tory candidate, David Cameron May '97; in his Maiden speech he paid tribute to his only Labour predecessor, the late Stephen Swingler, who represented Stafford '45-50 before moving on to

Newcastle-under-Lyme '51-69; his emphasis was on what the new Labour Government could do for children May '97; urged support for National Marriage Week June '97; urged replacement of PSBR by a "general Government financial deficit" June '97; urged abandoning the widening of the M6, spending the money on improving the West Coast Main Line railway June '97; he finished with a jingle when opposing the rushing through of the Plant Varieties Bill, which would force farmers to pay royalties even on farm-saved seeds June '97; asked about foreign language teaching in Staffordshire's schools June '97; co-sponsored motion opposing any merger of the Staffordshire Regiment June '97; asked the new Government to improve the claims scheme against the newly-privatised railways: "at Stafford in March 1996...two trains collided, two Royal Mail workers died, more than 20 were injured and one train left the track and struck a row of houses; all the licensed companies had to do was deny liability and the whole scheme collapsed; some 16 months later, no one has been helped" July '97; was hopeful that the new Office for the Supervision of Solicitors would better deal with complaints against the profession July '97; asked about the number of deaths from dangerous and drunken driving July '97; suggested the licensing of car boot sales July '97; urged a multi-agency approach to fitting smoke detectors into the homes of new-born babies July '97; asked how many had been imprisoned for non-payment of fines and council tax July '97;

Born: 21 March 1955, Stoke on Trent

Family: Son, of Neil Kidney, an Edinburgh-born clerk, and late Doris (Booth), flower-maker in the Potteries; he is married, with one son and one daughter;

Education: Longton High School; City of Stoke on Trent Sixth Form College; Bristol University (LLB)

Occupation: Solicitor, in private practice; he was a Trainee Solicitor '77-79, Assistant Solicitor '79-84, Partner '84-97 (MSF);

Traits: Dark, parted hair; specs; toothy; bridge and chess player; enjoys swimming and watching Rugby Union;

Address: House of Commons, Westminster, London SW1A 0AA;

Telephone: 0171 219 6472/0919(Fax) (H of C); 0785 41027 (home); 01785 241027/24471(Fax) (constituency);

'Andy' (Andrew) KING **Labour** **RUGBY & KENILWORTH '97-**

Majority: 495 over Conservative 4-way;

Description: An unaltered seat held by the Conservatives since its creation in '83, when Labour-leaning Rugby was linked unaccountably with unlike, Conservative-inclined affluent Kenilworth and villages;

Position: Warwickshire County Councillor (Chairman, Social Services '93-96) '89-; Rugby Borough Councillor '95-; Treasurer, Rugby and Kenilworth Constituency Labour Party '84-88;

Outlook: A loyal Scots-born former manual worker turned social work manager; managed one of Labour's least-expected victories on the back of his work as a local politician; still very much the reforming county councillor; not overly partisan;

History: He was elected Treasurer of the Rugby and Kenilworth Constituency Labour Party

'84; was elected to Warwickshire County Council May '89; became its Chairman of Social Services May '93; was elected to Rugby Borough Council May '95; was selected to contest "hopeless" Rugby and Kenilworth against its incumbent Tory MP James Pawsey July '95; on a swing of 10.6% unexpectedly took Rugby with the narrow majority of 495, ousting its veteran Tory incumbent; this made him the 29th least-expected Labour victor May '97; expressed solidarity with jailed Indonesian trade unionist June '97; urged Harriet Harman to simplify the social security system to speed justice for claimants July '97; co-sponsored motion urging that local community health services be protected against any financial short-falls July '97; in his Maiden stressed the painful reorganisation and regeneration of Warwickshire education and its need for an extra £2m July '97;
Born: 14 September 1948, Bellshill, Lanarkshire
Family: He is married to Semma; they have a daughter;
Education: St John the Baptist School, Uddington, Lanarkshire; Coatbridge Technical College; Nene College, Northamptonshire; Missionary Institute, London; Hatfield Polytechnic
Occupation: Social Work Manager, for Northamptonshire County Council (Unison) '87-97; ex: Labourer, Postal Worker, and Apprentice Motor Vehicle Mechanic;
Traits: Parted, retreating, dark hair; specs; thin moustache; has the appearance of an insurance clerk; RC by education; likes golf, dominoes, football;
Address: House of Commons, Westminster, London SW1A 0AA; 45 Julliet Drive, Rugby, Worcestershire CV22 6LY;
Telephone: 0171 219 3000 (H of C);

Oona KING **Labour** **BETHNAL GREEN & BOW '97-**

Majority: 11,285 over Conservative 9-way;
Description: An East End Labour fortress, briefly threatened in the '80s by the Liberals' capture of Tower Hamlets council; nearly two-fifths non-white, mostly Bengalis; altered in '95 to incorporate three mainly-white wards still controlled by the racism-tinged local LibDems;
Position: On the Select Committee on International Development '97-; Political Assistant, to Glenys Kinnock MEP '94-95, to Glyn Ford, Leader of Labour's MEPs '91-93;
Outlook: Labour's answer to Whoopy Goldberg: the half-black, half-Jewish successor to Peter (Lord) Shore; "I am honoured to be the second black woman to take up a seat in the Chamber"; an ambitious, pro-European moderniser and internationalist pursuing a childhood ambition; well-read, with a good sense of humour and sharp elbows; her priority target in her multi-ethnic seat is "to combat racism": "one side of my family were slaves, the other went through the Holocaust, so I am pretty well equipped to handle racism";
History: Her obsession with politics began when she was four or five years old: "I remember my mother crying about some famine she saw on the news and I thought there must be a way to stop this"; she gave up her plan to be an air hostess; she joined the Labour Party under-age at 14, '81; was the NUS' Black Rights Officer at York University '85-86; visited Nicaragua '86, El Salvador '89; travelled in her lunchbreak as a temporary civil servant from Vauxhall to Downing Street to greet Margaret Thatcher's resignation with a placard: "Bye Bye Maggie!;

I've Waited Half My Life To Say Goodbye" Nov '90; went to work in Brussels for Glyn Ford MEP, Leader of Labour's MEPs '91; transferred to staff of Glenys Kinnock MEP '94; unsuccessfully sought nomination in the re-selection contest in Hackney North and Stoke Newington against incumbent hard-Left black MP, Diane Abbott '93; with Bridget Prentice MP, wrote the Labour Party's draft policy document on careers Sep '96; was unexpectedly included in an NEC short-list of four (three non-white, one white) imposed on the embattled Bethnal Green and Bow CLP, in the wake of Peter Shore's announced retirement as MP; only Pola Uddin was Bengali; the leading Bengali, Councillor Rajan Uddin Jalal, was excluded for being linked to alleged multiple membership applications and involvement in a brawl outside a Whitechapel pub; she won the selection contest, defeating the favoured Claude Moraes, after a split in the Bengali and white vote Mar '97; she won the seat with a majority of 11,285 (down from 12,385) after a 5.9% swing to the Bengali Conservative candidate, Dr Kabir Choudhury May '97; introduced her Private Member's Bill, Local Authority Tenders, to allow local authorities to ease up on compulsory competitive tendering June '97; urged a timetable in phasing out tobacco advertising June '97; expressed solidarity with a jailed Indonesian trade union leader June '97; asked how many under-25s in East London were unemployed July '97; asked how many employers had been investigated under the Asylum and Immigration Act July '97; made her Maiden in debate on International Development, pointing out that the poorest 20% of the world "have seen their cake reduced to less than 2%" July '97; she was named to the Select Committee on International Development July '97;

Born: 22 October 1967, Sheffield

Family: Daughter of Professor Preston King, exiled Afro-American '60s civil rights activist from Georgia and political scientist, and Hazel (Stern) working-class Jewish teacher from Newcastle who "taught in inner London for more than 20 years"; "she'd teach all the kids who had been kicked out of other schools, the kids no one else was interested in"; her parents separated when she was 30 months old; she was brought up by her mother in North London; she has spent holidays with her father in Kenya and Australia; m '94 Tiberio Santomarco, Italian advertising man she met in the European Parliament;

Education: Haverstock Comprehensive, North London ("my school saw class sizes increase and teacher numbers cut" [OK]); York University (BA 1st in Politics);

Occupation: Regional Officer, Southern Region Race Relations Officer, GMB '95-97; Political Assistant: to Glenys Kinnock MEP '94-95, Glyn Ford '91-93; Researcher, with Socialist Group in the European Parliament '91; Civil Servant (temporary), with DHSS '90

Traits: Attractive oval face; "her sculpted face and waist-length hair make her instantly recognisable" (OBSERVER); coffee-coloured complexion; she caught the 'flu when Tony Blair kissed her; "some people call me a 'nigger', some black people call me a 'Yid'; many of both races sometimes call me a 'mongrel'; but I am proud of my heritage, and the bringing together of cultures is what we must aim at" (OK); "talented and personable" (Kim Sengupta, INDEPENDENT); "very sharp and very tough" (a supporter); multilingual (French and Italian);

Address: House of Commons, Westminster, London SW1A 0AA; 36 Penshurst Road, London E9 7DT;

Telephone: 0171 219 5020 (H of C); 0171 613 2274 (constituency):

We reach the uncovered parts of MPs the press no longer notice, because the correspondents leave the Press Gallery too early.

'Tess' (Teresa Jane) KINGHAM **Labour** **GLOUCESTER '97-**

Majority: 8,259 over Conservative 6-way;
Description: The new barometer seat, the city of Gloucester, which Labour had to win, allegedly, to secure a one-seat majority; in '70 Sally Oppenheim won it from Labour's Jack (later Lord) Diamond; Douglas French inherited a 12,000 majority in '87, but this was halved to 6,000 in '92; in '95 it lost 3,400 voters in suburban villages to Stroud;
Position: On the Select Committee on International Development '97-; Chairwoman, all-party Parliamentary Group on Western Sahara '97-; Secretary, all-party Parliamentary Group on Human Rights '97-; ex: on Home Offic Working Group on Youth Crime '92-94;
Outlook: A feminist campaigner, recently for compulsory sprinkler systems, but in the past largely a fund-raiser for charities and international causes: in Nicaraguan Solidarity, Western Sahara Campaign, Mozambique-Angola Committee, Egyptian Exploration Society, Campaign for Vietnam Cinema; a founder-member of CHANGE (Charities and Not-for-profit Groups' Europe);
History: She joined the Labour Party at 19, '82; contested the Cotswold Euro-seat held by Tory MEP Lord Plumb, cutting his majority to 2% or 4,000 votes in a total poll of 195,000 June '94; was selected for Gloucester from an open short-list Sep '95; after a fire engulfed the building housing the MFI superstore in Gloucester, she was horrified to find that a sprinkler system was not compulsory May '96; described the seat as "Labour's Basildon", or victory barometer Aug '96; hosted Tony Blair's visit to Gloucester Mar '97; won the seat on a swing of 11.5%, ousting its Tory incumbent MP Douglas French with a majority of 8,259 May '97; led motion congratulating new Labour Government on ending ban on trade unionists at GCHQ May '97; backed ban on fox-hunting June '97; expressed solidarity with jailed Indonesian union leader June '97; was an OSCE international observer at the Albanian elections June '97; asked about ban by privatised railways on disabled people's tricycles July '97; led motion calling for sprinkler systems for new supermarkets July '97; was named to Select Committee on International Development July '97; in her Maiden on an adjournment debate, urged sprinkler systems be made compulsory for all new warehouse-style single-storey buildings over 2,000 square feet used for commercial purposes; this would prevent fires getting out of control and limit stock damage by saturation July '97;
Born: 4 May 1963, Lewisham, South London
Family: Daughter of Roy Thomas Kingham, deeds clerk, and Patricia (Murphy) bakery assistant; m '91 Mark Luetchford, charity campaigner; 1d Rosa '95;
Education: Dartford Grammar School for Girls '75-81; Royal Holloway College, London University (BA Hons in German and Italian); East Anglia University (Post-Graduate Certificate of Education);
Occupation: Head of Appeals, War on Want '96-97; ex: Communications Executive, Oxfam '94-96; Editor, YOUTH EXPRESS (published by DAILY EXPRESS) '92-94; Marketing and Communicationsd Director, Blue Cross, (animal welfare charity) '90-92; National Appeals Officer, War on Want '86-90; Norfolk Liaison Officer with British Trust for Conservation Volunteers '85;
Traits: Heart-shaped face; short-cropped white-blonde hair; linguist; enjoys modern music,

art, archaeology, international food and foreign places;
Address: House of Commons, Westminster, London SW1A 0AA;
Telephone: 0171 219 4081 (H of C); 01452 311870;

Julie KIRKBRIDE **Conservative** **BROMSGROVE '97-**

Majority: 4,895 over Labour 5-way;
Description: An old market town, now largely a middle-class commuting constituency for people working in Birmingham and the Black Country; the only unaltered seat in the county of Hereford and Worcester;
Position: On Select Committee on Social Security '97-;
Outlook: The "poacher" as former TELEGRAPH Lobby correspondent turned backbench "gamekeeper"; "she has moved from a larger Conservative institution - the DAILY TELEGRAPH - to a smaller one, the Parliamentary Conservative Party" (Gordon Brown MP); a firm Eurosceptic Rightwinger, self-confessedly "strongly in favour of Michael Howard's reforms on law and order and keen on Peter Lilley's social security reforms" (JK); "one of Thatcher's children" (Michael White, GUARDIAN); a Northern daughter of the working class who rejected her background; talks of "Britain's once inept political culture - prosperity destroyed by the power of trade unions and the socialists seeking to consolidate their grip among the working class by making them dependent on them for their council houses and their state handouts"; "I have a personal reason to be allergic to Labour and the trade unions; I was brought up in the working-class North, in Halifax, in a terrace house on a cobbled street; my father was a lorry-driver who died when I was seven, and my mother raised us single-handedly by going out to work; I should be a natural Labour supporter, but while the local Labour council wanted me to know my place among life's victims, the Conservative Party offered me the opportunity to go to an excellent grammar school" (JK); is expected to be in a Tory Cabinet by 2020 (MAIL ON SUNDAY);
History: She joined the Conservative Party at 14, '74; was active in Halifax Young Conservatives over the next four years til "78; while at Girton College, Cambridge University, she became Vice President of the Cambridge Union, Lent '81; after working for Yorkshire TV and ITN, she worked for the DAILY TELEGRAPH and SUNDAY TELEGRAPH almost wholly on politics from '92 to '96; she was one of 150 applicants for safe-Tory Bromsgrove, denuded of its MP, Roy Thomason, by the threat of a bankruptcy only held at bay by the Royal Bank of Scotland; she gave a shrewdly-calculated performance, exploiting the needs of the moment: "the Tory hierarchy wants more women MPs, the grassroots want more Rightwing MPs" (Michael White, GUARDIAN); she won Nov '96; she refused to talk to the EVENING STANDARD about her former friendship with the late Lord Kagan Nov '96; she was listed in the DAILY TELEGRAPH as one of the prospective candidates who expected to rule out in their election addresses that Britain would enter a single European currency in the next Parliament Dec '96; retained Bromsgrove despite a 7% swing against the Tories, with a majority of 4,895 (down from 13,752) May '97; she opposed Labour's attempt to tighten gun control June '97; she was on the Hague campaign team June '97; co-sponsored motion

criticising Lord Simon of Highbury for not selling his £2m in BP shares July '97; asked Clare Short what support her department was giving to de-mining organisations July '97; in her Maiden, made without notes, paid tribute to her grammar school teachers who helped her to enter Cambridge; she admitted her mother thought her "mad" for trying to become an MP July '97;
Born: 5 June 1960, Halifax, Yorkshire
Family: Daughter, of Henry Raymond Kirkbride, lorry driver who died when she was 7, and Barbara (Bancroft), secretary at Rowntree Mackintosh; she has an elder brother and sister; m '97 Andrew MacKay, divorced MP for Bracknell and former Deputy Chief Whip; was formerly the girl-friend of the late Stephen Milligan MP about whose odd death she was among the first to be informed;
Education: Boothtown School, Halifax; Highlands Grammar School, Halifax '71-78; Girton College, Cambridge '78-81 (MA 2:1 in History and Economics): University of California's Graduate School of Journalism, Berkeley (on Yorkshire Area Rotary Club Scholarship) '82-83;
Occupation: Journalist: Social Affairs Editor, SUNDAY TELEGRAPH '96-97; Chief Political Correspondent, SUNDAY TELEGRAPH '96; Political Correspondent, DAILY TELEGRAPH '92-96; Producer, ITN '89-92; Programme Researcher, YORKSHIRE TV '83-86;
Traits: Schoolgirlish plain good looks; small, widely-spaced eyes; long blonde hair; "vivacious attractiveness - backed by whirlwind energy" (Stephan Harrison, BIRMINGHAM POST); "toothsome, buxom" (Paul Routledge, INDEPENDENT ON SUNDAY); "fiery, forthright and fetching" (MAIL ON SUNDAY); "plans to burn the black leather mini-skirt which made her such a hit with [male] MPs" (SUNDAY EXPRESS);
Address: House of Commons, Westminster, London SW1A 0AA; 118 Sinclair Road, London W14 0NP
Telephone: 0171 219 1011 (H of C); 0410 316862 (mobile);

Dr Ashok KUMAR **Labour** **MIDDLESBROUGH SOUTH & EAST CLEVELAND '97-**

Majority: 10,607 over Conservative 4-way;
Description: The unpronounceable former marginal Langbaurgh seat, only slightly altered, apart from its new long-winded name; contains an attractive coastal strip, a rural area plus the lovely 600-year-old town of Guisborough and conurbations south of the Tees; lots of dereliction from abandoned iron-ore mines, an iron industry that has run out of ore and unemployment from demanning by ICI and British Steel; economically bound to Teesside, it has strong emotional ties with Yorkshire and a reputation for disliking Geordies; its very marginal quality led it to go from Tory Richard Holt in '87, to Labour's Dr Ashok Kumar in the '91 by-election and back to the Tories' Michael Bates in '92, all on tiny majorities - until '97;
Former Seat: Langbaurgh '91-92
Position: On Select Committee on Science and Technology '97-; Middlesbrough Borough

Councillor '87-; ex: on Consolidation Bills Committee '91-92;

Outlook: A modernising Fabian British Steel research scientist returning in overwhelming triumph to the seat which he held for only five months; he was previously Labour's first Asian-born by-election victor in a Tory-held seat, selected by an all-white constituency Labour Party; was Vice Chairman of Teesside Fabian Society; is a believer in a Northern Development Agency; an Asian in an an overwhelmingly white seat, he has built his reputation mainly on his work as a local councillor, in setting up the Hemlington Skills Training Initiative in collaboration with the private sector; "I believe in opening doors for people"; he has moved from a soft-Left position in '91 to modernising Blairite in '97;

History: He arrived in the UK as a two-year-old; unemployed at 15, he started reading TRIBUNE, making Aneurin Bevin and Michael Foot his early heroes '71; joined the Birmingham Young Socialists '72 becoming Chairman of its Small Heath branch; he joined the Labour Party '76; having moved to Teesside to work for British Steel, he was elected to Middlesbrough Borough Council for Southfield May '87; with EETPU backing, was selected as Labour's candidate for marginal Langbaurgh from among 70 candidates, including Ben Pimlott, leading academic biographer and the TGWU-backed runner-up; this made Kumar the first non-white Labour candidate to be fielded in a marginal seat not held by Labour, selected by an all-white local party on the day Nelson Mandela was freed from prison Feb '90; he expressed sympathy for the Cheltenham black Tory barrister, John Taylor, for being "rejected by bigots" Dec '90; voiced concern over risk of cancer from power lines linking ICI's Wilton plant to the National Grid Feb '91; opposed "brazen favouritism" in higher funding for opted-out schools Feb '91; expressed fear over double threat from the greenhouse effect and over-intensive farming in the North Yorkshire moors May '91; on the death of Langbaurgh's incumbent Tory MP, Richard Holt, he was strongly backed by Leader Neil Kinnock Oct '91; was accused of "double standards" by his Tory opponent, Michael Bates, for having bought 500 BT shares while opposed to privatisation; he replied that he took "a pragmatic view of things, and if you want to influence things you have to take part" Oct '91; Michael Heseltine misleadingly suggested that, because he attended an anti-poll tax meeting he had not paid his poll tax Nov '91; a controversial LibDem leaflet said "You could vote for Ashok Kumar or a local man you can trust" Oct '91; his opponents called attention to his £9,000 expenses as local councillor and his attendance at 13 of 4l council meetings Oct '91; attacked Government plan to allow two local hospitals and the Cleveland ambulance service to opt for trust status Oct '91; he won the seat on a majority of 1,975, replacing the previous Tory majority of 2,088, after a race-tinged campaign that Roy Hattersley described as "the dirtiest I have known since Smethwick 27 years ago" Nov '91; in his Maiden speech called for the economic regeneration of the Cleveland area, based on a Northern Development Agency, to pull it out of "the vicious spiral of decline, dereliction and distress" and stressing Europe as the "most important trading bloc of the 21st century" Nov '91; called for a "regional renaissance" with strong local and regional government structures as in Europe; decried the creation of "two nations" under Mrs Thatcher, with 1.3m jobs created in the south and more than 100,000 lost in the northeast alone Dec '91; was said by the DAILY TELEGRAPH, together with Keith Vaz MP, to have "spelt out the electoral implications of a future Labour Government siding with Pakistan over Kashmir", since there were twice as many ex-Indians in the UK Jan '92; when he over-ran his time in a speech on poverty, was asked by front bench winder-up, Graham Allen, to "wrap it up" Jan '92; called for an end to "callous disregard for local government" Feb '92; attacked the Tory Government's Bill on Further and Higher Education as an illustration of the "hatred and contempt the government has for institutions that are locally controlled and managed" Feb '92; lost his seat after five months to his by-election opponent, Michael Bates, by a majority of 1,564 Apr '92; returning to his job at British Steel, said: "half a million people have lost their

jobs this year; I lost my [MP's] job but was able to get another one, so I can't complain" Jan '93; was re-selected to fight the slightly altered seat with the new name of Middlesbrough South and East Cleveland Sep '95; on the eve of annual conference, said union votes at conference "ought to be gradually reduced further" Sep '96; recaptured the seat on an 11.1% swing, with a majority of 10,607 May '97; backed ban on fox-hunting June '97; in his second Maiden, strongly supported the end of Assisted Places as the beginning of a "healing process" in education; Teesside had suffered particularly from the magnified class divisions of the Thatcher-Major years and "like the walking wounded of the Somme, the human casualties will be with us for many years to come" June '97; pressed for the minimum wage because "one in seven of [my constituents] is earning less than £3.50 an hour" July '97; pressed for increase in manufacturing investment because employment in manufacture in the Teesside had halved from '78 to '95, July '97; urged a new public-private bus network and a passenger transport authority to cover Teesside to end the isolation of many of his villages in the wake of bus deregulation July '97; urged Chancellor Brown to "end the cycle of boom and bust" July '97; co-sponsored motion on pensions mis-selling under the Conservatives July '97; was named to the Select Committee on Science and Technology July '97;
Born: 28 May 1956, Haridwar, Uttar Pradesh
Family: Son, of J R Saini, middle manager in industry, and Santosh (Kumari), who died during the Langbaurgh by-election;
Education: Rykneld School for Boys (leaving at 15 with 2 O-levels); he was persuaded to return to higher education, taking A-levels at 16; Aston University (BSc in Chemical Engineering '78, MSc '80 and PhD in Fluid Dynamics '82);
Occupation: Research Scientist, with British Steel (AEEU) '92-97, '85-91; Research Fellow, Imperial College of Science and Technology '82-85; Member of the Institute of Chemical Enginering, Institute of Energy, Steel and Industrial Managers Association;
Traits: Round face; enthusiastic, sensitive Fabian intellectual; an agnostic of Sikh origins; articulate (but long-winded); "dapper, hard-working" (NORTHERN ECHO); cricketer (Marton Cricket Club); also enjoys badminton and jazz;
Address: House of Commons, Westminster, London SW1A 0AA; 23 Canberra Road, Marton, Middlesbrough TS7 8ES;
Telephone: 0171 219 4650 (H of C); 01287 610878 (constituency);

Dr Stephen (John) LADYMAN  Labour THANET SOUTH '97-

Majority: 2,878 over Conservative 5-way;
Description: The formerly safe Tory Kentish coastal seat, previously graced by Jonathan Aitken and his 'Sword of Truth'; contains Broadstairs, birthplace of Edward Heath, the working ferry port of Ramsgate, the Cinque Port of Sandwich, with its Open championship golf course; three-quarters owner-occupiers; plenty of pensioners; high unemployment and social deprivation; on '92 figures was expected to produce an 11,000-plus Tory majority;
Position: Thanet District Councillor (Chairman of Labour Group and Finance '95-97) '95-; Research Assistant, to Labour's Science Spokesman, Dr Jeremy

Bray '86-97;

Outlook: Locally-employed computer scientist and councillor; has benefited from the plaudits of the District Auditor for his local reforms as Chairman of Finance and as a member of the 'Ramsgate Renaissance' team; a Fabian self-described as "Centre-Left"; pro-Brussels because of the structural and regional funds the EU provides to curb heavy local unemployment; has changed drastically since the bearded, bespectacled Leftist who fought Robert Jackson at Wantage in '87;

History: He stood for Labour in school elections from the age of 12, '64; joined the Labour Party in East Kilbride while taking his PhD at the University of Strathclyde '76; was selected as prospective candidate for hopeless Wantage, from a short-list of three men and one woman, by 9 votes to 3 to 1, Sep '85; was photographed with Lord Soper, the Leftwing pacifist Methodist leader, who was giving the Faringdon Memorial Lecture Sep '85; his candidacy was confirmed by the NEC Dec '85; he deplored the damage Tory monetarism was doing locally: in cuts in local housing, transport and the health service Dec '85; he criticised local people for taking part in the traditional Boxing Day fox-hunt, which he described as "this degrading, cruel and despicable pastime" Jan '86; warned that, unless Labour was elected, the arms race would escalate Jan 86; attacked the incumbent Conservative MP, Robert Jackson, who came back from South Africa saying "the unrest is awful" but opposed destabilising its Apartheid government; Ladyman insisted, "the violence will get worse and worse until the Government makes some real concessions" Feb '86; became the Research Assistant to Dr Jeremy Bray MP, Labour's Science Spokesman Mar '86; promised Labour would spend more on science, partly by transferring research from military projects Mar '86; he spearheaded new attempts to ban fox-hunting and hare-coursing on Oxfordshire County Council land May '86; warned that only the election of a Labour Goverment could stop the privatisation of British Leyland in whose Cowley plant many locals worked May '86; warned against "appalling consequences for local workers" if Harwell and Didcot Power Station were to be privatised June '86; at an annual conference fringe meeting, as a "radiation biologist" he cast doubt on the CEGB's reassurances on leukaemia clusters Sep '86; attacked Government plans to cut the subsidies to BR, which would increase rail charges Oct '86; backed the local Civil and Public Servants Association in their resistance to privatising mess catering at the Vauxhall Barracks, which he called a "disgrace" Nov '86; ran 3rd in the general election with 15.5%, after the incumbent Tory Robert Jackson (54%) and the SDP (30.5%) June '87; having changed jobs and moved to Ramsgate in '91, he did not contest the next general election Apr '92; he was elected to Thanet District Council, becoming Chairman of Finance May '95; was selected to stand against Jonathan Aitken for Thanet South Sep '95; in one of the bigger surprises of the general election, though not apparently to his opponent, he won Thanet South with a majority of 2,878 over Jonathan Aitken, on a swing of 15% (1% more than the swing in Thanet North); he became the first-ever Labour MP for Thanet South May '97; co-sponsored a motion criticising the Conservative-controlled Kent County Council for its moratorium on spending on school-building June '97; co-sponsored a motion warning of the dangers of using open lattice goods wagons in the Eurotunnel June '97; in his genial Maiden, underlined the high unemployment in Thanet and "the good things that the European Union is doing" by providing "structural and regional funds on which my constituency depends" June '97; asked about secondary health care services in East Kent July '97; led a motion deploring the "dishonourable and self-serving" decision of Inntrepreneur Pub Company to release all their tied public houses, breaking their agreements with their tenants July '97; secured an adjournment debate on 'Thanet Regeneration', needed because of the area's heavy unemployment and economic deprivation; spoke persuasively, as a local district councillor deeply involved, of progress in regeneration, with funds from the EU and central Government, but stressed the need for more,

to improve inadequate transport access to secure inward investors and retain those, like his former employer, Pfizer, who might be tempted to move to more accessible locations July '97;
Born: 6 November 1952, Ormskirk, Lancashire
Family: Son of Frank Ladyman, telephone engineer, and Winifred (Lunt), Inland Revenue clerk; m '75 Heather Margaret (Jones) laboratory technician; divorced '95; m '95 Janet (Baker) 1d '94; 2 steps '73, '84; 1 stepd '79;
Education: Our Lady of Walsingham, Netherton, Liverpool; Birkenhead Institute; Liverpool Polytechnic (BSc in Applied Biology); Strathclyde University (PhD in Natural Isotopes in the Soil);
Occupation: Computing Manager, for Pfizer Central Research. Sandwich (GMB) '90-97; Computer Scientist, at the Kennedy Institute of Rheumatology (arthritis and rheumatism research charity) (MSF) '83-90; Researcher, at Medical Research Council, Harwell '79-83;
Traits: Broad face; close cropped dark hair; clean-shaven (in contrast to the dark beard worn when fighting Wantage in '87; genial; clever; residual Lancashire accent; enjoys golf, football (manager of the Ramsgate under-13s):
Address: House of Commons, Westminster, London SW1A 0AA; Chilton Farmhouse, Chilton Lane, Ramsgate, Kent CT11 0LQ (home); Willson Hall, Willsons Road, Ramsgate CT11 9LZ (constituency);
Telephone: 0171 219 3000 (H of C); 01893 852696/852689(Fax) (constituency)

Mrs Eleanor LAING **Conservative** **EPPING FOREST '97-**

Majority: 5,252 over Labour 5-way;
Description: Top Essex residential areas around the ancient forest of Epping and in Buckhurst Hill, Theydon Bois and particularly Chigwell (its pre-'74 name); as Epping it was once Winston Churchill's seat; its largest town is Loughton; it had a bit of Harlow added in '95; its centre is where the M25 meets the M11; it is under the trees of Epping Forest that Elizabeth I was reputed to have had her famous liaison with the Earl of Essex, an inspiration to later 'Essex Girls';
Position: On Select Committee on Education and Employment '97-; Secretary, Conservative MPs' Environment, Transport and Regions Committee '97-; ex: on Conservative Central Office Executive '95-97; Special Adviser to John MacGregor when Cabinet Minister '89-94; Chairman, of Edinburgh South CPC '83-85;
Outlook: Very ideological, highly partisan, Rightwing Scots unionist loyalist; a fervent defender of grant maintained schools and an opponent of devolution, on which she insisted on being allowed to vote in the referendum; a former backrooom girl (to John MacGregor when Education Secretary, Leader of the Commons and Transport Secretary); a Tory Lobbyist (Sunday trading); an assiduous seat-chaser who lost at hopeless Paisley North in 1987 and 15 subsequent selection contests; an opponent of positive discrimination in favour of women candidates: "we are getting there and we did it fairly, so the men can't whinge";
History: "In my family, Winston Churchill was regarded as the greatest hero of all time"; "one of my earliest childhood memories is of being made to sit for several hours with the curtains closed, watching his funeral on television"; she started distributing Tory local

government leaftlets at 12, in support of her father who was a Renfrewshire councillor for 20 years '70; was the first woman to be elected President of the Students Union at Edinburgh University '80; contested hopeless Paisley North -where she had been born - against late Allen Adams MP, insisting that Labour voters would desert to the Tories because the scrapping of Trident would cost hundreds of jobs at the local Babcock and Wilcox plant; she regained second place for the Tories from the SDP with 16% of the vote, down from 21% in '83, June '87; when she went to work as Special Adviser to John McGregor, the post was classified as a civil service post, which barred her from becoming a candidate for '92; she worked for John MacGregor advising him on the Student Loans Act of '90, expanding grant-maintained schools and preparations for the privatising Railways Act; she received a presentation about Blue Circle's hopes for Ebbsfleet from Maureen Tomison, Chairman of the lobbying firm Decision Makers and also a Tory Scotswoman with Parliamentary aspirations; John MacGregor later told the Nolan Committee, "it is true that Decision Makers left some documents on the Ebbsfleet issue with my Special Adviser; she looked at them and did not pass them on to me because she said they contained nothing that was not already in the official representations that she had seen" July '93; as MacGregor's Special Adviser, she was even more enthusiastic than he was over rail privatisation; she applied for many winnable seats, including 15 before the end of '95; she came second to David Amess MP (by five votes) in Southend West and to David Prior at Norfolk North; she won Epping Forest after Steven Norris had announced his impending departure; one of 250 applicants, she won out in the final round over Caroline Spelman and Gary Ling Dec '95; with five other loyal Tory candidates, co-signed a letter to the DAILY TELEGRAPH backing John Major's wait-and-see policy on a single European currency Dec '96; retained Epping Forest by 5,252 votes (down from 21,182), after a pro-Labour swing of 13.6% May '97; with other new Tory partisans, defended the counter-devolutionary Labour MP Llew Smith from alleged threats from Welsh Secretary Ron Davies June '97; was on William Hague's campaign team June '97; attacked Labour's new Budget for its windfall tax and pension impost July '97; in her Maiden, compared the '97 Tory defeat to that of '45, recalling Churchill's words, "We shall not surrender!"; complained that the Budget's "cruel" stamp tax would hit people in "a fairly ordinary three-bedroomed house in Epping Forest [which] costs £250,000" July '97; demanded that all Scots who lived outside Scotland - like herself - should be allowed to vote in the referenda on devolution July '97; strongly defended grant-maintained schools July '97; raised a point of order about a Scottish Labour MP using Commons telephones to co-ordinate Labour canvassing in the Uxbridge by-election July '97; was named to Select Committee on Education and Training July '97;

Born: 1 February 1958, Paisley

Family: Daughter, of late Matthew Pritchard, master builder and Tory councillor, and Betsy (McFarlane); m '83, Alan Laing, solicitor and Director of the Oracle Corporation, one of the biggest software companies, specialising in databases;

Education: John Neilson School, Paisley; St Columba's School, Kilmacolm, Renfrewshire; Edinburgh University (BA LLB; President of the Students Union)

Occupation: Executive, in Conservative Central Office '95-97; Free-lance Public Relations Consultant, working with Laura Sandys and others '94-95; Special Adviser, to Transport Secretary John MacGregor '89-94; Lobbyist, on deregulating Sunday trading '87-89; Solicitor, in City of London '85-87; Trainee Solicitor, with W S Lindays in Edinburgh '83-85;

Traits: Reddish blonde; pleasant-looking; amiable; determined; enjoys golf, music, the theatre, gardening and travel;

Address: House of Commons, Westminster, London SW1A 0AA;

Telephone: 0171 219 4203/2086 (H of C);

Andrew Lansley CBE **Conservative** **CAMBRIDGESHIRE SOUTH '97-**

Majority: 8,712 over Liberal Democrat 6-way;
Description: A shire county seat including safe Tory wards from Cambridge and South West and South East Cambridgeshire; "combines natural beauty with economic and intellectual dynamism" (AL); on '92 figures it was expected to produce a Tory majority of about 19,000;
Position: On the Select Committee on Health '97-; on the Conservative National Union's Executive Committee and General Purposes Committee '90-; ex: Director, Conservative Research Department '90-95;
Outlook: The 'brain' behind John Major's 1992 electoral success now out of the backroom; highly-intelligent, well-informed and conspicuously active as a questioner and debater; has been tagged as a member of a Tory Cabinet by 2020 (MAIL ON SUNDAY); a loyal Eurosceptic opponent of a single European currency during this Parliament; a solid, almost stolid Rightwing loyalist, alternately quasi-informative and intensely partisan; has backed the use of immigration arguments against Tories' opponents;
History: He "might have been content to remain a Whitehall high-flyer but he was made Norman Tebbit's Private Secretary [in '84]; he was soon a convert in the Thatcherite cause, toning down some of his more Rightwing enthusiasms only when he reached the Research Department" [in '90] (James Landale, TIMES); head-hunted by Kenneth Baker, the then party Chairman, he was named Director of the Conservative Research Department '90; "he spent five years at Central Office perfecting Tory propaganda and helping John Major to win the ['92] election" (James Landale, TIMES); he decided in Oct '91 to hold the election the next April ['92], and to start a huge poster and press campaign from early January ['92]; he was credited with having been "the architect of the tax bombshell campaign" (SUNDAY TIMES) Jan-Apr '92; warned Tory Minsters on the eve of the Euro-election that the party's Euro-manifesto must not become a stepping stone to a federal Europe Mar '94; "he started applying seriously for seats" Mar '95; "he realised that candidates had to look the part so he shaved off his moustache, lost weight and bought a new suit" (James Landale, TIMES); was selected for Cambridgeshire South, in succession to retiring Sir Anthony Grant, in preference to James Arbuthnot, Defence Procurement Minister Sep '95; at Blackpool annual conference, insisted the party would recover swiftly from the shock of the desertion of Alan Howarth MP - a predecessor of his in Central Office - and could overcome the threat of Tony Blair's 30% lead in the opinion polls Oct '95; recalled that "immigration, an issue we raised successfully in 1992, and again in the 1994 Euro-elections campaign, played particularly well in the tabloids and had more potential to hurt" Labour Oct '95; received the CBE in the New Year's Honours List Jan '96; found that one in six of his seat's former Tory voters was doubtful about voting Conservative again Aug '96; in an article in the SUNDAY TIMES urged a defence of the "supremacy of Parliament with regard to European Union law"; also urged strengthening of select committees and election of local mayors Sep '96; with five other Tory loyalist candidates wrote to the DAILY TELEGRAPH that "only a Conservative government can be trusted to promote and protect Britain's interests in Europe" Dec '96; retained Cambridgeshire South by a majority of 8,712 after an anti-Tory swing of 8.7% May '97; in his Maiden, as "the grandson of Scots as well as the English" declared himself a unionist and an opponent of Labour's devolution plans and, immediately, of the form of its referenda May '97; urged the

Labour Government to "resist any extension of powers of co-decision for the European Parliament" June '97; backed Michael Howard for Leader June '97; congratulated the new Tory control of Cambridgeshire County Council for "increasing the delegation to schools by £3m" June '97; urged delay in Local Govenment Finance Bill in the absence of a spelling out of its full implications June '97; helped filibuster against abolition of Assisted Places Scheme June '97; with Unilever-owned Plant Breeding International in his constituency, supported the royalty-producing Plant Varieties Bill June '97; was critical of the closure of the Royal Greenwich Observatory July '97; asked a chain of questions about the Particle Physics and the Astronomy Research Council July '97; asked for "an assessment of the potential for misuse through biological warfare of the Human Genome Project on genetic engineering July '97; in an adjournment debate, took up the crusade of his predecessor, Sir Anthony Grant, that Cambridgeshire was short-changed in its revenue support grants July '97; was named to the Select Committee on Health July '97; was the campaign manager for John Randall, the successful Tory candidate in Uxbridge July '97;

Born: 11 December 1956, Hornchurch, Essex

Family: "I am a grandson of Scots as well as of English"; son, of Thomas Lansley OBE, medical laboratory scientist and former Chairman of the Institute of Medical Laboratory Scientists, and Irene (Sharp), secretary; m '85 Marilyn (Biggs) GP and school doctor; "she turned up to everything and was fantastic at saying that she supported me fully" (AL); 3d: Katherine '87, Sarah '89, Eleanor '89;

Education: Suttons Primary School, Hornchurch; Brentwood School (direct grant), Essex; Exeter University '75-79 (elected sabbatical President of Guild of Students '77-78; BA IIi in Politics '79);

Occupation: Author: 'Conservatives and the Constitution' (1997 with C R Wilson), 'A Private Route' (1988); Political Lobbyist, as a Director, of Public Policy Unit '95-97; Director, of Conservative Research Department '90-95; Deputy Director General, British Chambers of Commerce '87-90; Civil Servant in Trade and Industry '79-87, working as Principal Private Secretary of Norman Tebbit for three of them '84-87;

Traits: Rounded doughy face, with slight jowls; parted greying hair; slightly portly; active Anglican;

Address: House of Commons, Westminster, London SW1A 0AA; 37A High Street, Trumpington, Cambridge CB2 2HR;

Telephone: 0171 219 3000 (H of C); 01223 841380 (home);

Mrs 'Jackie' (Jacqueline) LAWRENCE Labour PRESELI-PEMBROKESHIRE '97-

Majority: 8,736 over Conservative 6-way;
Description: The bulk of the old marginal Pembroke constituency, based on Preseli District, with Fishguard, Haverfordwest and the oil-refining port of Milford Haven as its main towns; scenically very beautiful, but it suffers from low wages and poor employment for its young; on projections from '92 voting, this half was thought to be marginally Conservative;
Position: On the Select Committee on Welsh Affairs '97-; ex: Pembrokeshire County Councillor (Leader of Labour Group) '95-97; on Dyfed-Powys Police Authority '94-97; Dyfed County Councillor '93-95; Chairman, Secretary, Pembroke Ccnstituency Labour Party; on Pembrokeshire Coast National Park Committee '93-95;
Outlook: A locally-based thoughtful mainstreamer who has long worked with Nick Ainger, the current MP for Carmarthen West '97-and '92-97 for Pembroke, from which Preseli has been split off; has lived in Pembrokeshire for over 20 years; in the Christian Socialist Movement; favours electoral reform; initially had a fairly low profile in Westmister, preferring to strengthen her position locally; had tacit TGWU support;
History: She joined the Labour Party '72; she was Labour's election agent for Nick Ainger, when he won Pembroke Mar-Apr '92; was elected to Dyfed County Council May '93; with the implicit backing of the TGWU was selected for Preseli from an all-woman short-list, which had been opposed by some older male chauvinists among local activists Aug '95; derided as a "farce" the claim of Independents to hold the balance of power on the newly restored Pembrokeshire County Council, of which she was the Leader of the Labour Group Oct '95; she urged a wider membership for the Pembrokeshire National Park Committee Oct '95; denied the Labour Group wanted a witch-hunt of Freemasons; insisted its call for a Register of councillors' connections was in the interest of openness and accountablity Nov '95; visited Fishguard to underline fears about threat to its rail link arising from privatisaton Jan '96; at annual Labour conference made an impasssioned speech on law and order, citing local incidents Oct '96; launched local petition to ban combat knives Nov '96; at a candidates' meeting with the local NFU said that if the UK withdrew from the European Union, 3m jobs dependent on foreign investment could be lost Feb '97; said it was wrong in a bi-lingual area to limit candidates' descriptions to six words Apr '97; welcomed report that Department of Environment was considering prosecuting the Department of Transport for its handling of the 'Sea Empress' disaster: "there can be little doubt that the whole situation was appallingly mismanaged; what could have been a containable grounding became a major disaster because of the Government's failure to take the appropriate action and have the necessary equipment on hand"; she paid full credit to the local authorities and volunteers whose rapid clean-up had restored Preseli "to its full glory as one of the world's premier holiday destinations" Apr '97; won the new seat with an unexpectedly high majority of 8,736, on a notional swing of 11% May '97; announced she would be standing down from Pembrokeshire County Council May '97; one of her first priorities, she said, was to improve the train services on which she would be relying May '97; asked about freight facilities grants to firms in Wales June '97; in her Maiden during the Welsh Development Agency debate, emphasised that Pembrokeshire's

beauty hid the scarce employment possibilities for its young, who had to leave to find decently-paid work; she complained the Welsh Development Agency had previously neglected west Wales June '97; co-sponsored motion urging a review of the law on rape, to remove the defendant's right to cross-examine the victim June '97; expressed solidarity with jailed Indonesian trade union leader June '97; backed ban on fox-hunting June '97; was named to the Select Committee on Welsh Affairs July '97; pointed out that a Welsh Assembly would cost a third as much as the quangos which had been running Wales; recalled that John Redwood, when Welsh Secretary, had "returned £100m that was meant for Wales to the Treasury, to support his Rightwing credentials, rather than spending it on essential infrastructure and investment in Wales for the people of Wales" July '97; as a co-sponsor of the Bill to bar fox-hunting, objected to the emotions raised by Tories favouring it Oct '97;

Born: 9 August 1948, Birmingham

Family: Daughter, of Rita and Sidney Beale; m '68 David Lawrence, Local Government Officer (recently Acting Director of Development Control for Pembrokeshire); 2s Richard '71 a civil engineer, John '76 in a Welsh pop group, Gorky's Zygotic Mynci; 1d Amy '78 at Pembrokeshire College;

Education: Upperthorpe School, Darlington; Upperthorpe College, Darlington; Open University;

Occupation: Ex: Political Researcher for Nick Ainger, Labour MP for Pembroke '92-97; in Pembroke branch of TSB '87-92;

Traits: Large mop of dark hair; pretty chubby face, with cleft chin; beaky nose; specs; "thoughtful and thought-provoking" (Elfyn Llwyd MP); a Brummie by birth, brought up in the northeast, learned Welsh in order to help her children with their bilingual education; enjoys walking and viewing wildlife (in West Wales Naturalists Trust and RSPB);

Address: House of Commons, Westminster, London SW1A 0AA; Panteg, Vale Road, Houghton, Pembrokeshire SA73 1NW;

Telephone: 0171 219 3510/2757 (H of C); 01437 767470 (constituency);

'Bob' (Robert) LAXTON — Labour — DERBY NORTH '97-

Majority: 10,616 over Conservative 5-way;

Description: This long-standing marginal has most of the city's better residential areas, including new private housing estates; these helped the Tories' Greg Knight to take over from Labour's Phillip Whitehead in '83, and resist the rising Labour tide until '97; it has Rolls-Royce and had British Rail workshops;

Position: On Select Committee on Trade and Industry '97-; Derby City Councillor (Leader, of its Labour Group '86-97, Leader of the Council '86-88 and '94-) '79-; ex: Chairman, National Communications Union's District Council '84-87;

Outlook: A low-profiled mainstream local politician and trade unionist; Fabian; a supporter of local partnership with private industry; an opponent of smoking;

History: He joined the Labour Party '76; was elected to Derby City Council May '79; was elected Leader of Derby City Council's Labour Group, and of the Council itself May '86; played a key role in the city's major investment in improved public housing; was selected as

candidate for Derby North against Greg Knight Dec '89; lost by 4,453 to Greg Knight because of an inadequate (2%) swing to Labour, the lowest in the East Midlands Apr '92; again became Leader of the City Council May '94; was re-selected to fight Greg Knight '95; when justifying Derby City Council's ban on smoking, described the habit as "a filthy, dirty, unhealthy, bourgeois habit" Aug '95; at annual conference at Brighton stressed the importance of a partnership with industry Oct '85; at annual conference opposed the closure of hospitals, especially Derby's children's hospital Oct '96; took the seat, ousting Greg Knight by a majority of 10,615 on a massive swing of 13.2% May '97; co-sponsored motion urging the diversion of the £780m planned for the Millennium Exhibition in London to health, education and transport June '97; urged that bribery of MPs be made a criminal offence July '97; co-sponsored motion welcoming Professor Wole Soyinka, Nigerian Nobel Laureate, to his Wilberforce Lecture July '97; was named to the Select Committee on Trade and Industry July '97;
Born: 7 September 1944, Derby
Family: His father was unemployed; he himself was married and had one child but is now divorced;
Education: Allestree Woodlands Secondary; Derby College of Art and Technology;
Occupation: Ex: Telecommunications Engineer with BT (NCU/CWU);
Traits: Parted grey hair; grey beard; low square glasses; articulate; hill walker
Address: House of Commons, Westminster, London, SW1A 0AA; 62 Larges Street, Derby DE1 1DN;
Telephone: 0171 219 4096 (H of C); 01332 206699 (constituency); 01523 523 523/880040 (pagers)

David LEPPER **Labour & Co-operative** **BRIGHTON-PAVILION '97-**

Majority: 13,181 over Conservative 9-way;
Description: Seven-eighths of the more elegant western part of town plus one eighth comprising former Kemptown's Hanover ward to make it more marginal; was hit hard by recession; has a large gay community; on '92 voting projections was still expected to produce a small Tory majority
Position: On Select Committee on Broadcasting '97-; on new Brighton and Hove Unitary Authority '95-97; ex: Brighton District Councillor (Mayor '93-94, Leader '86-87, Deputy Leader '90-93) '80-97;
Outlook: The Blairite, formerly soft-Left, teacher-councillor who became the first Labour MP for this seat after having been the first Labour council Leader in Brighton's 150-year history; his capture of the seat was the climax of a 30-year love affair; he came to Brighton to study teacher-training at Sussex University and never left; formerly on the Left he gradually moderated into a classic 'New Labour' candidate; was formerly an NUT activist and a leading member of the National Council for Civil Liberties; is also in the Co-operative Party, Fabian Society, Socialist Education Association, Socialist Health Association, Labour Co-ordinating Committee, the former Anti-Apartheid Movement;
History: He joined the National Union of Teachers in '68, the Labour Party in '76; he was elected to Brighton District Council May '80; became Leader of the Labour Group on Brighton District Council May '84; was elected Brighton's first Labour Leader of Council May

'86; the next year he made way as Leader for Steve Bassam May '87; as Chairman of the Police Committee, set up a Community Crime Prevention Forum later recommended as a model by HM Inspectors of Constabulary '88; was selected to fight Brighton-Pavilion against Derek Spencer, who won by a majority of 3,675 despite a considerable, 6.4% swing to Labour Apr '92; became Mayor of Brighton '93; chaired Brighton's Economic Development Committee, which attracted £25m in Government funds to tackle local deprivation; was re-selected to contest the seat which was made more marginal by the addition of pro-Labour Hanover ward, formerly in Kemptown; said: "we are already moving in the direction of a victory next time; I think Tony Blair will help us to achieve that" July '94; as Membership Officer of the constituency party, saw the doubling of membership from 800 to 1,500 '94-96; gave up his teaching job to concentrate on winning the election '96; pledged to Brighton's large gay community that he would support 16 as the uniform age of consent Apr '97; on a near-record swing of 16%, won the seat with a majority of 13,181, ousting the Tory Solicitor General May '97; in his Maiden emphasised his constituency's heavy unemployment and low wages June '97; backed outlawing of fox-hunting June '97; expressed solidarity with jailed Indonesian trade union leader June '97; was named to the Select Committee on Broadcasting July '97;

Born: 15 August 1945, Richmond, Surrey

Family: Son of late Harry Lepper, lorry driver, and Maggie (Osborne); m '66 Jeane (Stroud), also a local councillor; 1s Joe,'72, 1d Eve '75; both were educated in local state schools;

Education: Gainsborough Road Secondary Modern, Richmond; Wimbledon County Secondary; University of Kent (BA Hons); Sussex University (PGCE); Polytechnic of Central London (Postgraduate Diploma in Film);

Occupation: Ex: Teacher of English and Media Studies in Falmer School (a state secondary school) (NUT) '68-96;

Traits: Balding; broad forehead; probably Huguenot by origin; enjoys cinema and music; a fan of professional cycling (secured Tour de France for Brighton in '94); works locally on behalf of Alzheimer's charities;

Address: House of Commons, Westminster, London SW1A 0AA;

Telephone: 0171 219 4421 (H of C); 01273 551532 (constituency);

Chris(topher) LESLIE **Labour** **SHIPLEY '97-**

Majority: 2,996 over Conservative 4-way;

Description: A seat based on the affluent suburbs and rural areas of Bradford, previously the only "safe" Tory seat in Bradford metropolitan borough and their safest in West Yorksahire; includes not only Shipley but the Tory-leaning small towns of Bingley and Baildon; also Saltaire, the town built by Sir Titus Salt, whose mill is now a designer art gallery housing Hockneys and a luxury flat complex; on '92 projections the seat was expected to give a 12,000 majority to Sir Marcus Fox, the Rightwing populist MP who was Chairman of the Conservative MPs' influential 1922 Committee;

Position: Bradford Metropolitan District Councillor '94-

Outlook: The Blairite 'Baby of the House'; the not-yet-25-year-old 'David' who shook the political world by toppling the tiny political 'Goliath', the not-quite-70-year-old "Shipley Strangler", Sir Marcus Fox; Leslie's campaigning slogan was "we need somebody with a bit of energy to give them a bit of a kick down in Westminster"; in fact, he was fairly restrained during his first Parliamentary months;

History: At 14, at Bingley Grammar School, he approached the visiting Education Secretary, Kenneth Baker, to ask him what he would do about their leaking roof: "the school roof was held together with chicken wire and I took the day off to see Baker on his walkabout and ask what he was going to do about it; I got a blase answer and was swiftly shouldered out of the way by the secret service lot who were surrounding him; I was really annoyed and decided straight away that I was going to join the Labour Party"; he did so, under-age, at 14, '86; "if there's one person to whom I particularly owe my thanks it is Michael Foot; I wrote to him...when I was starting a course in Parliamentary studies, asking him for suggestions on where to find a second hand copy of a book; by return of post came his own signed edition which I've been using ever since" '89; at not-yet-22, was the first-ever Labour winner of Bingley ward on Bradford Metropolitan Council May '93; at 23 was selected as Labour's candidate against Sir Marcus Fox for "hopeless" Shipley '95; defied Walworth Road by keeping his local activists in "unwinnable" Shipley, instead of letting them canvas in the winnable marginal of Keighley; "I told the voters that [Sir Marcus] had only spoken three times in the past five years in Parliament, yet he held six company directorships and three consultancies"; campaigned against Sir Marcus mainly on his failure to deliver the Shipley relief road by '96, demanding repeatedly "where's the road?"; was not believed when he told local newsmen that his own polls put him neck-and-neck with Sir Marcus; the Conservative YORKSHIRE POST insisted: "there is so much clear blue water between the two candidates you would need a swimming certificate to chart it" Apr '97; among many astonishing results, one of the most staggering was the toppling of Sir Marcus Fox by a young unknown who, on a swing of 13.8%, won a majority of 2,996, ending the 27-year reign of Sir Marcus, who made a very bitter speech on election night; this made Leslie Labour's 24th least-expected victor May '97; Sir Edward Heath urged him: "take your time, pace yourself" May '97; in his early Maiden mentioned that his elderly predecessor, Sir Marcus, had made his Maiden 18 months before he himself was born; "I'm sorry I missed it" May '97; his correspondence bag was inundated with requests for help with immigration problems, planning disputes and job requests to become his research assistant May '97; urged the Bingley relief road on the new Government June '97; asked about a local outbreak of cryptosporidium in Bingley's drinking water June '97;

Born: 28 June 1972, Keighley, West Yorkshire

Family: Son, of Michael Leslie, architect, and Dania (Kos), college lecturer, who warned: "he's got to beware of those blondes in the Central Lobby!";

Education: Bingley Grammar School; Leeds University (BA Hons in Parliamentary Studies; MA in Industrial and Labour Studies);

Occupation: Office Administrator for Bradford City Councillor and Bradford Labour Party (living on about £5,000) '94-97; Researcher, for Gordon Brown MP, Barry Seal MEP and US Congressman Bernie Sanders '93-94;

Traits: Close-cropped dark tonsure; long face with strong nose; nice smile; boyish look; "I'm young; I can't change that; there's nothing I can do about my age"; enjoys films, opera, art and travel;

Address: House of Commons, Westminster, London, SW1A 0AA; 7 Whitlam Street, Saltaire, Shipley BD18 4PE;

Telephone: 0171 219 3000 (H of C);

Dr Oliver LETWIN **Conservative** **DORSET WEST '97-**

Majority: 1,840 over Liberal Democrat 5-way;

Description: The most rural of Dorset seats, stretching to 103,000 hectares; Hardy country, including Dorchester (his 'Casterbridge'), Sherborne and the seaside resort of Lyme Regis; "the loveliest part of the loveliest county in England" (OL); its embracing of Tolpuddle does not vitiate its previously strong Tory leanings; the serious recent challenge has come from Liberal Democrats;

Position: Ex: in PM Margaret Thatcher's Policy Unit '83-86; Special Adviser, to Sir Keith Joseph at Department of Education and Science '82-83;

Outlook: An extremely sensitive, polite and civilised Rightwing intellectual and merchant banker bursting out of the Redwood mould; manages to combine representing farmers with beef and pigs threatened by BSE and Swine Fever with his sophisticated criticisms of Labour policies as an NM Rothschild merchant banker; "a post-Thatcher Conservative intellectual", "very brainy and rather dry", "fonder of balance sheets than people"; "it is said of Letwin that if he passed St Peter's Gate his first question would be: 'what is the exchange rate here'" (Sara Sands, EVENING STANDARD); self-described as a "radical Thatcherite, a devout admirer of the [former] Prime Minister and a believer in a very tight monetarist policy"; in the 'No Turning Back' Group; was a proud co-parent of the poll tax (which he defends as a "completely misunderstood phenomenon") as well as the Assisted Places Scheme; an N M Rothschild adviser to foreign governments on the privatisation of nationalised industries; "he is not crude enough to be a politician; Oliver speaks as though he was briefing a Cabinet Minister; he doesn't go for the cheap shots" (Stephen Games, his '92 Green Party opponent); "not only immensely clever, but also amazingly modest" (Peregrine Worsthorne, SUNDAY TELEGRAPH); one of the most unremitting opponents of Maastricht-style Euro-federalism, frequently displayed earlier in the SUNDAY TELEGRAPH; his manifesto said Britain should never join a single European currency; has threatened that he might quit the Conservative Party if it were led by a European federalist; a Hampstead Jewish intellectual in rural Dorset;

History: His family, immigrants from Chicago, was Thatcherite Conservative; he himself was a Conservative at Eton; he joined the Conservative Party at 26, '82; he served as Special Adviser to his parents' friend, Sir Keith Joseph, Education Secretary '82-83, helping to father the Assisted Places Scheme; survived the Grand Hotel bombing in Brighton Oct '84; in Mrs Thatcher's Policy Unit was a strong supporter of the poll tax after his boss in the Downing Street Policy Unit, John Redwood, asked him to evaluate it and report to Mrs Thatcher '86; warned against Labour's plans to make the police "democratically accountable" as leading to domination by the anti-police hard-Left; fought Diane Abbott in Hackney North and Stoke Newington; she threatened to sue when he reproduced her views as printed in Trotskyist publications; his office was incinerated by unknown arsonists; "I can only assume that this is the way the new Left fight elections"; he achieved a 2% swing to the Tories June '87; in a joint report with John Redwood for the Centre for Policy Studies, concluded the NHS was an "untameable monster" which should be converted into an independent trust, separated from the Department of Health and Social Security; more involvement of the private sector should follow, including competitive tendering for surgery; medicine could be financed by a "pill tax" Jan '88; warned against the Tories letting up in pursuit of radical policies, especially in NHS reforms and law and order May '88; was considered as a possible candidate for the Kensington by-election May '88; in his new book, Privatising the World, claimed that Britain had become a "net idea-exporter" by pioneering privatisation June '88; was said to be Mrs Thatcher's favourite to replace Leon Brittan in the by-election for Richmond, where local Tories preferred Yorkshireman William Hague Aug '88; as an NM Rothschild adviser, urged a "unified pool" to link regional electricity boards Jan '89; wrote a pamphlet against further federalising the European Community for the Centre for Policy Studies Nov '89; was selected to contest Hampstead and Highgate for the Conservatives Mar '90; insisted the protests against the poll tax he had co-fathered was a "song and dance about not much" Mar '90; urged a "quantum leap" in educational expenditure, involving billions of pounds, if education was to avoid a shocking decline Oct '90; backed Mrs Thatcher in her first-round contest against Michael Heseltine Nov '90; outlined ways in which Mrs Thatcher's defeat, despite the "speed and manner of whose departure" he deplored, could be turned to good use by the new PM, John Major Nov '90; John Major recalled his former agent Woods Thomson from retirement in Scotland to help Letwin in his Hampstead campaign Dec '90; Letwin welcomed John Major's arrival as making it possible to push out Tory frontiers into areas like road-pricing without relying on outdated Thatcherite "rhetoric" Dec '90; urged the abolition of mortgage tax relief and provision of vouchers for private tenants to ease the shortage of private rented properties Dec '90; said Tory policies were directed towards "helping ordinary people standing on their own two feet" May '91; derided road-pricing as "a piece of regulatory interference" June '91; deplored Ted Heath's anti-Thatcher outburst as not being helpful to achieve a workable political relationship with Europe June '91; deplored anti-homosexual verbiage of Conservative Family Campaign as being "over the top" Aug '91; as the local candidate, chided the Bursar of his old school, Eton, as freeholder of 700 properties in Hampstead, for not treating its tenants properly Aug '91; he insisted that "people of all sexual persuasions should refrain from displays which are offensive to other bathers" when swimming in Hampstead Heath's open air pools Sep '91; wrote: "it is obvious, but seldom remembered, that inheritance is the basis of society" DAILY TELEGRAPH Oct '91; co-signed with other Eurosceptic candidates, a warning against creeping federalism DAILY TELEGRAPH Nov '91; warned against giving "control to Strasbourg and Brussels over our army, our foreign affairs and other crucial points which make a country" Oct '91; while canvassing claimed he could usually tell in advance the political views of residents: "you can tell the Tories from the neatly clipped hedge, the litle pots of geraniums, from the fact that the front porch is tidily swept"; he rejected the proposal from Central Office to dig up dirt on Glenda Jackson, and his agent's proposal to publish a nude picture of his Labour opponent from her film, 'Women in Love', only partly because it might not lose her votes; at the very end of the campaign he said that immigration had to be strictly controlled to preserve the existing makeup of British society; "I don't want this society to be turned into a quite different society; if we don't want this society to be torn apart, we do have to have control" Mar '92; he confirmed that he still believed the NHS should be taken out of the hands of politicians Mar '92; although he predicted he would win by 100 votes, he lost the seat by 1,440 votes, after a 4% swing to Labour Apr '92; he blamed his defeat in Hampstead on the Liberal Democrats: "the Liberals collapsed and the bulk of them went to Labour" Why? "I don't know"; wrote: "the establishment of a [European] Union citizenship is part of a carefully-conceived, step-by-step approach to the creation of an increasingly direct relationship between the powers of European central government and the individual" SUNDAY TELEGRAPH Jan '93; warned against a federal Europe forming its own army Feb '93; warned that unless Britain also opted out of Maastricht's "Stage Three when the time comes, it will be goodbye to Westminster and all that so far as the economy is concerned" SUNDAY TELEGRAPH Feb '93; warned that Maastricht's pressure for a common European

Union foreign policy might mean Britain giving up its permanent place on the Security Council to Germany SUNDAY TELEGRAPH Mar '93; warned that "the Maastricht Treaty is not an end point but rather the beginning of a process" of federalisation SUNDAY TELEGRAPH June '93; after Sir Jim Spicer announced he would not stand again, was selected for very rural Dorset West Nov '94; in a reversal of what he had said as a Hampstead candidate, told Dorset squires that while he did not hunt himself, he had no rooted objection to others doing it Nov '95; told the DAILY TELEGRAPH that his manifesto would oppose Britain ever adopting a single European currency Dec '96; was among the 247 Tory candiidates who accepted campaign funds from businessman Paul Sykes for ruling out ever backing a single European currency Apr '97; narrowly won the seat with a 1,840 majority, after a 5.6% swing to the Liberal Democrats May '97; was on John Redwood's campaign team May '97; made his Maiden opposing the Education (Schools) Bill to undo the Assisted Places Scheme; as Sir Keith Joseph's Special Adviser, "I played a role in [its] creation" June '97; criticised fluoridation of water, ending of tax relief on pensioners' medical insurance premiums, exports of electric shock equipment June '97; asked about wild boar and swine fever in the southwest, and culling of cows from BSE-infected herds June '97; backed anti-rabies inoculations instead of quarantine June '97; warned about the increase in borrowing and spending on house-building by local authorities under the Local Government Finance Bill July '97; described Chancellor Brown's removal of Advanced Corporation Tax credits in the Budget as using "the language of managerial capitalism" but "without in the least understanding the way in which the capital markets in this country and around the world operate"; it would lead investment managers "to redirect their investment from this country's equity into fixed debt and equities overseas" July '97; asked about public funds for campaigning on Scottish devolution July '97; opposed cuts in payments for culled beef July '97; accused Social Security Secretary Harriet Harman of introducing a Treasury-driven measure on benefits for lone parents in which she did not believe, but the Tories did July '97;

Born: 19 May 1956, Hampstead, London

Family: Only son of William Letwin, Emeritus Professor of LSE, Senior Adviser to Putnam Hayes and Bartlett '88-, Director, FPL Financial Ltd '88-, and late Shirley (Robin) Chicago-born Thatcherite academic, writer and Director of Centre for Policy Studies; m '84 Isabel Grace (Davidson), solicitor;

Education: Hall School, Hampstead; Eton; Trinity College, Cambridge University (BA MA PhD - on 'The Philosophy of Emotion')

Occupation: Merchant Banker, with N M Rothschild, where he has headed the International Privatisation Unit, which he inherited from John Redwood '87-; Author: Ethics, Emotion and the Unity of the Self (1987), 'The Aims of Schooling' (1989), Britain's Biggest Enterprise; Ideas for Radical Reform of the NHS' (1988), Privatising the World (1988), Drift to Union (1990); Landlord; ex: Executive, in Prime Minister Thatcher's Policy Unit '83 -86; Special Adviser, to Sir Keith Joseph '82-83; Lecturer, in Philosophy at Cambridge and Princeton '80-82

Traits: Thin, sensitive, intellectual face; "has a shock of unruly black hair and casual clothes, his voice is light, and his laughter is high-pitched, he looks and sounds younger than his years" (SUNDAY TIMES); "immaculately polite" (Glenda Jackson); "complete with suit and stripy shirt and the sort of ruddy face which suggests a chap's been eating lots of cream and green vegetables" (SUNDAY TIMES); "as a balletomane, I dislike opera" (OL); has a tiny handwriting; "cerebral" (Julie Kirkbride, DAILY TELEGRAPH); oleaginous" (critics); Jewish ("the grandson of Jews who fled to the United States from the Russian Revolution; his parents moved to England" (SUNDAY TIMES))

Address: House of Commons, Westminster, London SW1A 0AA; 255 Kennington Road,

London SW1 6BY;
Telephone: 0171 219 3000 (H of C);

Tom LEVITT **Labour** **HIGH PEAK '97-**

Majority: 8,791 over Conservative 4-way;
Description: Northwest Derbyshire's beautiful, mountainous Peak District, on Manchester's doorstep; Britain's first national park; "the most beautiful seat in Britain" (TL); four-fifths of its voters are in five mill-based towns, which look as though they have been transported from Lancashire or Yorkshire; a marginal also won by rebellious Leftwinger Peter Jackson in the previous 1966 Labour high tide;
Position: On the Select Committee on Standards and Privileges '97-; Vice Chairman: Future of Europe Trust '97-, all-party Group on Charities and Voluntary Sector '97-, all-party Parliamentary Group on Poland '97-, all-party Parliamentary Group on Disablement '97-, all-party Parliamentary Group on Cricket '97-, PLP Committee on Education and Employment '97-; Derbyshire County Councillor (for Buxton North) '93-; ex: Stroud District Councllor '90-92; Cirencester Town Councillor '83-87; NUT Gloucestershire County President '85;
Outlook: A teacher-councillor, formerly soft-Left but recently a mainstream loyalist; a veteran local councillor and candidate, both Parliamentary and European; an ex-teacher who has been a strong supporter of David Blunkett's modernisation of Labour's education policy; "as a member of SERA I have worked for a greater 'green' aspect of Labour policies over a number of years"; recently a consultant on disability, particularly in facilitating the access of the disabled to local services; formerly linked with the Labour Co-ordinating Committee; a onetime contributor to TRIBUNE, formerly in CND and the Anti-Apartheid Movement;
History: He was born into a Labour family, with his teacher-mother serving as a Labour councillor from '62; joined the Labour Party '69; left the Labour Party as "too Rightwing" '72; rejoined the Labour Party '77; was elected branch secretary of Cirencester and Tewkesbury CLP '79; was elected Chairman of Cirencester and Tewkesbury CLP '80; in pre-OMOV days, was selected as candidate for Stroud by 20 votes against 6, 5 and three for his competitors Sep '85; warned Labour Party against ignoring the National Association of Local Councils, which took quite enlightened decisions, despite its depiction as "a beanfeast for the massed ranks of shire Tories" Nov '85; criticised his opponent, Anthony Kershaw MP, for a "paranoid and hysterical" Tory leaflet which claimed "Labour would come out of NATO and join the Warsaw Pact" if victorious; "as someone whose wife's family left their native Poland to escape tyranny, I find it particularly offensive" Mar '87; backed Gloucestershire County Council's plan for comprehensive education in Stroud May '87; he came third in Stroud with 18.5% of the vote, a marginal improvement over the previous election June '87; met Lech Walesa in Poland, from whence his wife's family had fled '88; as a Euro-candidate was responsible for an initiative on behalf of GCHQ trade unionists in European Parliament; unsuccessfully contested the Cotswold Euro-seat against incumbent Tory Lord Plumb June '89; was beaten by Sylvia Heal on the short-list for the Mid-Staffordshire by-election, later won by her Jan '90; he published a pamphlet, 'Breaking the Silence' a charter to make local authority services

accessible to the deaf '91; was selected for High Peak as an outsider, with no local candidates contesting; fought High Peak, halving the Tory majority Apr '92; Labour took overall control of High Peak Borough Council with 30 of 44 seats May '95; was re-selected for High Peak; the Labour Party targeted High Peak as their 53rd seat of the 55 needed to achieve an overall Commons majority; he derided incumbent Tory MP Charles Hendry's claim that British youth had never had it so good, pointing out that one in four of the unemployed in High Peak were under 25 Aug '96; his local party reached its 1000th member, more than double the number it had had at the previous election Jan '97; won the seat with a majority of 8,791, on an 11.7% swing May '97; in his Maiden chortled about his seat's having "a Labour borough council, a Labour county council, a Labour Member of the European Parliament and now a Labour Member of Parliament"; but, as a former teacher for 19 years, had a long catalogue of decrepit and overcrowded schools, because of Derbyshire's having for so long been deprived of adequate funds May '97; co-sponsored motion deploring "the escalating financial crisis in Britain's further education colleges" June '97; backed pilot "marriage support projects" June '97; pressed for strengthened laws against young people drinking in public June '97; urged restoration of national pay negotiations in the NHS July '97; backed comprehensives as providing "opportunity for all" as one "educated entirely in comprehensive schools and I taught in comprhensive schools for 19 years" July '97; backed better access for disabled people to polling stations July '97;

Born: 10 April 1954, Crewe

Family: Son of John Levitt, university lecturer, and Joan (Flood) teacher and Labour councillor for Staffordshire Moorlands '62-92; m '83 Teresa (Sledzieska), a translator of Polish origins; 1d Annie '83 musician;

Education: Westwood Road Primary, Leek, Staffs; Westwood High (Head Boy '71-72), Leek; Lancaster University '72-75 (BSc Hons); Oxford University '75-76 (PGCE);

Occupation: Consultant, on Access for Sensorily Impaired '93-97; Author: Sound Policies (1994), Sound Practice (1995), Clear Access (1997); ex: Teacher, of Biology and Science, in secondary schools and further education college, for 19 years '76-95;

Traits: Balding; grey-white ear-covering; concerned about the disabled; has a limited ability to use sign language; enjoys: cricket, theatre, travel;

Address: House of Commons, Westminster, London SW1AA; 42 Bath Road, Buxton, Derbyshire, SK17 6HJ; 20 Hurdwick Street, Buxton, Derbyshire SK17 6DH (constituency);

Telephone: 0171 219 6599 (H of C); 01298 22260; 01298 26366(Fax);

Ivan LEWIS | **Labour** | **BURY SOUTH '97-**

Majority: 12,433 over Conservative 4-way;
Description: The classic former marginal north of Manchester, "in the valley of the River Irwell, in the shadows of the Pennines, at the edge of the east Lancashire plain" (IL); middle-class commuter territory, including posh Prestwich (a largely Jewish suburb), and Whitefield plus the old Lancashire mill town of Radcliffe; it is the seat with the greatest proportion of Jewish voters outside of London; in '92 it stubbornly insisted on delaying its expected fall to Labour;
Position: Bury Borough Councillor (Chairman, Social Services '91-96) '90-;
Outlook: Youthful Blairite local councillor; a locally-born campaigner on educational standards in Bury; in Labour Friends of Israel; "keenly supportive of Israel" (JEWISH CHRONICLE);
History: He joined the Labour Party at 19, '86; was elected to Bury Borough Council at 23, May '90; became Chairman of Social Services May '91; was selected to contest this marginal against Tory MP David Sumberg Jan '96; when Peter Hain MP was sent to support his crucial campaign, they both had some difficulty explaining why they smelled so perfumed, after a factory visit to Fragrance Oils in Radcliffe Apr '97; won this marginal seat with the enormous majority of 12,433, on a swing of 13%; said: "not in my wildest dreams could I have foreseen a majority of over 12,000"; his witty opponent, David Sumberg, told of the scale of other Tories' defeats, quipped in his farewell speech that even if he had a held on again, "I don't think I'd have recognised anyone at the Commons" May '97; backed motion congratulating Manchester on its year-long progress in restoring the damage inflicted by the IRA bomb outrage June '97; expressed solidarity with a jailed Indonesian trade union leader June '97; co-sponsored motion noting "the escalating financial crisis in Britain's further education colleges" June '97; asked about the Government's plans to integrate "early-years education and child care" June '97; urged the removal of VAT from women's sanitary products June '97; expressed concern about the effective ban on the export of chickens from the USA to Europe June '97; in his Maiden complained that the abandoned M62 relief road had cost the taxpayer £25-30m, "blighted a once-pleasant residential area and exposed incompetence of the highest order in both the Department of Transport and the Highways Agency" July '97; expressed the hope that the Middle Eastern peace process could be "put back on track" July '97;
Born: 4 March 1967, Prestwich
Family: Son, of Joel Lewis, salesman, and Gloria (Goodwin); his sister, Naomi, is an actress who has appeared in 'Emmerdale Farm'; m Juliette (Fox), a Director of Rakusen's, the kosher food firm in Leeds; 2c;
Education: William Hulme's Grammar School; Stand Sixth Form College;
Occupation: Chief Executive, Greater Manchester Jewish Social Services (Manchester's major Jewish welfare organisation) (MSF) '92-97; founded and worked for Contact Community Care '89-92; "at the age of 18, I began my working life on a work-and-training programme for Outreach, a voluntary organisation in my constituency working with people with learning disabilities" '87-89;
Traits: Dark tonsure; rounded face with slight underchin; Jewish; a keen supporter of Manchester City ("a lifelong, passionate and traumatic relationship" (IL));

Address: House of Commons, Westminster, London SW1A 0AA; 513 Bury New Road, Prestwich, Manchester M25 (constituency);
Telephone: 0171 219 6404 (H of C); 0161 773 1529 (home); 0161 773 5500 (constituency);

Dr Julian (Murray) LEWIS **Conservative** **NEW FOREST EAST '97-**

Majority: 5,215 over Liberal Democrat 3-way;
Description: A safely-Tory new Hampshire seat running from the edge of Southampton to the southern end of Southampton Water: four-fifths Romsey and Waterside on the west bank of Southampton water, one-fifth old New Forest; has hosted a long line of boat-building, seaplane-building and special-operations training bases; includes Fawley, the country's biggest oil refinery;
Position: Joint Secretary, of Conservative MPs' Defence Committee '97-; Director of Policy Research Associates (PRA) '96- '85-90; ex: Deputy Director, Conservative Research Department '90-96; Founder-Director of Media Monitoring Unit '95-96, '85-90; Director, Coalition for Peace Through Security (CPS) '81-85;
Outlook: Has disappointed his advance billing by settling initially for trying to be a more-litigious, less-amusing Tory version of Dennis Skinner, starting with elbowing LibDems out of front-row seats; a hard-Right supporter of the nuclear deterrent; a Eurosceptic who refuses to contemplate a single European currency because it would "lead to a single European superstate which would then take over control of Britain's defence policy"; associated with the Freedom Association and Conservative Way Forward; formerly Central Office's most assiduous political dirt-digger: "its 'witch-finder general" (MAIL ON SUNDAY); "one of the biggest thorns in the side of the CND" (Tim Jones, TIMES); "a dogged political street-fighter of the old school", "one of the last of the great Cold Warriors" (DAILY TELEGRAPH) who saw CND and various Soviet 'peace' fronts as threatening to provide the former USSR with a monopoly of nuclear missiles; "he is the Tory who adopted the methods of the Far Left and beat them at their own game" (Gordon Greig, DAILY MAIL); "one-man scourge of the Beeb"; "when he spots an enemy, he goes right for the jugular" (Chris Blackhurst, INDEPENDENT); "a friend of the Rightwing 'Freedom Association'", is "the bane of CND, a former infiltrator of the Labour Party", "is against all things pacifist" (Andrew Pierce, TIMES); "darling of the Conservative party's hawks" (CITY LIMITS); "one of the Conservative Party's most effective campaigners" (Patrick Wintour, GUARDIAN); "a man with a long history of targeting opponents with unashamedly aggressive tactics"; "Lewis's association with some of the most virulent cold-war warriors of the '80s has placed him as a central figure in that network of Anglo-American pressure groups and think tanks - formerly seen as the lunatic fringe of the Right and with strong intelligence connections - which informed much of the Reagan-Thatcher political agenda" (Richard Norton-Taylor, David Pallister, GUARDIAN);
History: At Oxford, he became Treasurer of the Oxford University Conservative Association '71, Secretary of the Oxford Union '72; he first came into prominence when he joined the Newham North East Labour Party to fight the attempt of the Trotskyist 'Revolutionary Socialist League' (aka Militant Tendency) to de-select the local Rightwing Labour MP, Reg

Prentice, who later became a Tory and Tory Minister; writs, financed by the National Association for Freedom, flew as he exploited Labour's rule book to gain control of the constituency party Oct '76-77; "he was extremely successful on the doorstep with his winning, cheeky-chappie smile; the membership increased hugely in three key wards; we realised from the start what he was up to, although he lived in such a fantasy world he was difficult to understand" (Phil Bradbury, Chairman of Newham North East CLP); with Edward Leigh and Tony Kerpel - also prospective Conservative Parliamentary candidates - set up the Coalition for Peace Through Security (CPS) "to counter subversive [CND] propagandists in peacetime" '81; his organisation harassed the CND leader, Bruce Kent, on his American campaign tour; its members always arrived before Kent to brief local media about the "pro-Communist" priest and barracked his meetings '82; was briefly arrested, but not charged, for breach of the peace, while playing the national anthem over an anti-Falklands march headed by Tony Benn and Arthur Scargill '82; the court prevented the CND from barring his CPS from printing its leaflets with the Communist hammer-and-sickle overlaying the CND symbol Feb '83; Monsignor Bruce Kent refused to debate with him Mar '83; finished a confidential report on the 1982 CND conference showing its leadership was dominated by the Left, including Communists Jan '83; his analysis was the basis of the anti-CND speech made by Michael Heseltine Apr '83; his CPS flew a plane over a Greenham Common demonstration trailing the banner: "CND - KREMLIN'S APRIL FOOLS" Apr '83; attacked CND officials as "Communists, neutralists and defeatists" Apr '83; nearly unseated Alan Williams and won marginal Swansea West for the Tories, losing by 2,350 May '83; attacked the GUARDIAN for not reporting in its coverage of the Communist Party conference that Monsignor Bruce Kent had described Communists as his "partners in peace" Nov '83; nominated Lady Olga Maitland for £1,000 media peace prize of United Nations Association Jan '84; attacked the Trade Union Bill for its weakness in providng for ballots to be filled in at the workplace: "this is so open to manipulation and abuse that the Communist ballot-riggers of the old Electrical Trade Union would have been perfectly happy" Apr '84; failed to get Press Council to take up complaint against OBSERVER for describing his group as smearing distinguished former NATO officers when it attacked 'Generals for Peace' as linked to the Soviet-controlled World Peace Council May '84; with its loudspeakers belting out patriotic songs from the rooftops, his CPS had a banner, "PRESIDENT REAGAN IS OUR FRIEND", flying over a CND demonstration protesting 'Cruise' missiles June '84; with Lord Chalfont and Peter Blaker MP, attacked 'Generals for Peace', run in London by Brigadier Harbottle, as a puppet of the Soviet Politburo Sep '84; helped to wash out a CND meeting designed to attract Tory sympathisers of unilateralism with a flood of anti-CND activists Sep '84; attacked a Bradford University conference on peace studies as refusing to criticise the USSR as the main threat to peace Sep '84; at the Conservatives' annual conference, urged a ban on peace studies to avoid pro-CND, biased indoctrination Oct '84; was the driving force in founding the Media Monitoring Unit to investigate [anti-Conservative] media bias; it was originally financed by £25,000 to hire a Director, raised by CBI adviser Sir Peter Tennant and City friends; this provided Norman Tebbit with some of the ammunition for his fusillades against the BBC's "Leftwing bias" '85; Monsignor Bruce Kent again refused to debate with him Feb '85; in letter to the TIMES, insisted that his CPS researchers had been able to prove from the press that the CND's top organs had been dominated by socialists and Communists, without any help from MI5 Mar '85; with Tony Kerpel, attacked the Labour-controlled GLC's financial support for unilateralism Apr '85; in an article in CIA-financed ENCOUNTER treated the CND's campaigns against 'Polaris', 'Pershing II' and 'Cruise' missiles as designed to give the Soviets' SS20s an offensive monopoly July '85; congratulated Cecil Parkinson for having won the 1983 election without fudging his Rightwing principles or trying to attract floating voters Aug '85;

complained without success to Jenny Abramsky, then BBC Producer of "The World This Weekend", that Victor Marchetti had been introduced as a former CIA official, without adding that he had become one of its most virulent critics Sep '85; said: "Joe McCarthy has a lot to answer for, for giving anti-Communism a bad name" Dec '85; paid tribute to deceased Josef Josten, the Czech exile most feared by the Soviets Dec '85; showed that Dr William Howard, the National Co-ordinator of 'Freeze', had previously been the CND's full-time Financial Strategy Director Feb '86; Bruce Kent again refused to debate with him Feb '86; his CPS's effort to join the UN's International Year of Peace aroused opposition from "a combination of pacifists, unilateralists and even some pro-Soviet agitators" (JL) Mar '86; his PRA commissioned a poll backing a ban on political indoctrination in the schools May '86; CPS members armed with megaphones disrupted a CND ceremony marking the dropping of the atom bomb on Hiroshima Aug '86; his PRA, in collaboration with Conservative Party, polled 103 Labour candidates to show how Leftwing they were on public issues, including unilateralism Sep '86; in an open letter to Cardinal Hume in Roger Scruton's SALISBURY REVIEW, challenged the right of Bruce Kent to remain a Catholic Monsignor; this was decisive in persuading Kent to resign from his church post Oct '86; welcomed this resignation to devote full time as Vice Chairman of CND: "for the last six years Bruce Kent has been exploiting his clerical status to give unwarranted authority to his political campaigning" Feb '87; his PRA commissioned Gallup Poll which showed that 67% still backed the nuclear deterrent Apr '87; commissioned a photographic survey showing that only half as many marched with CND in a Hyde Park rally as the CND claimed Apr '87; claimed that multilateral disarmament was incompatible with unilateral disarmament Apr '87; his PRA protested that unions were not allowing the secret postal ballots required by law May '87; in letter to NEW STATESMAN dismissed allegations of CPS plots against CND on the authority of Piers Wooley as being the untrustworthy testimony of a mole at Conservative Central Office of Leftwing journalist Duncan Campbell June '87; on Jenny Abramsky's appointment as the BBC's Editor of News and Current Affairs, wrote letter to SUNDAY TELEGRAPH recounting her refusal in 1985 to correct her descripton of Victor Marchetti as a former CIA official, refusing to add that Marchetti was one of its most virulent critics, as he informed her at the time July '87; in letter to INDEPENDENT again defended the use of "strategiic nuclear weapons...to deter strategic nuclear aggression" against the arguments of Bruce Kent June '87; in a tortuous exchange of letters to the NEW STATESMAN, he denied claims from Duncan Campbell and David Leigh of the OBSERVER that anti-CND electoral propaganda had originated with MI5, insisting it had come from him June-Aug '87; Labour Research attributed to his PRA the Government's proposal to require postal ballots from unions Aug '87; wrote to DAILY TELEGRAPH warning against a bogus Soviet front attempting to entrap women Aug-Sep '87; failed in his attempt to succeed Mrs Thatcher in Finchley '89; was named Deputy Director of the Conservative Research Department, where "some of his new colleagues privately muttered he made Mrs Thatcher look Leftwing" (Andrew Pierce, TIMES); "his appointment by party Chairman Kenneth Baker was greeted with consternation in the Labour Party and total apoplexy in certain Conservative quarters" (Gordon Greig, DAILY MAIL); he insisted "I don't go in for smearing people"; "but I do show people how easily they can be hoodwinked by the devious minds of the Left" Jan '90; insisted that despite its leadership's rejection of unilateralism, Labour was still unilateralist at heart July '91; Conservative Central Office published his 259-page WHO'S LEFT, detailing the links of 207 Labour MPs to Left and ultra-Left causes, with its endorsement as "a serious and scholarly work" by party Chairman, Chris Patten Mar '92; the SUNDAY TELEGRAPH apologised for printing, the month before, the false allegation by the dismissed former Tory Agent for Hampstead and Highgate that Dr Lewis had urged the local party to "dig up the dirt" on the successful Labour candidate, Glenda Jackson Apr '92; the MAIL ON SUNDAY defamed him as having damaged Anglo-American relations by smearing President Clinton Dec '92; complained that Labour's one-member one-vote reform would weaken the influence of moderate trade unions; complained that "as long as the myth of conference 'sovereignty' is allowed to dominate its thinking, the Labour Party will remain in a state of constitutional crisis" Sep '93; he collected substantial damages from the MAIL ON SUNDAY after it had libelled him as having spread false allegations about President Bill Clinton Oct '93; attacked, with Edward Leigh and Tony Kerpel, the persistence of KGB-inspired "agents of influence"; in this letter to TIMES detailed that Labour MP Allan Rogers, just appointed to the new Parliamentary Intelligence and Security Committee, had shown sympathy to the World Peace Council and Marxist regimes in Grenada, Angola and Nicaragua Dec '94; warned distributors of SCALLYWAG that they would be liable for libel damages after the magazine had made false allegation against him, forcing it to close Jan '95; "I have always said my action is not against the existence of the magazine as such; it is to clear my name of defamatory charges made against me" Feb '95; wrote to Leftwing TRIBUNE to warn readers against helping SCALLYWAG which was financed by racist Ann Raynes who had claimed "London seems to have been taken over by black paramilitaries in a coup" Mar '95; Jonathan Aitken's attack on the BBC's alleged political bias was incorrectly attributed to Lewis's providing a dossier on the BBC to his friend, John Bercow, then Aitken's adviser Mar '95; his solicitor bought on his behalf documents abandoned by SCALLYWAG which, he said, yielded "fascinating insights into this despicable publication as well as its supporters" Apr '95; revived the Media Monitoring Unit to study alleged BBC political bias July '95; in a letter to the TIMES -co-signed with Norris McWhirter - about his controversy with the BBC about the Hiroshima bomb, repeated his insistence that it had been dropped to speed the end of the war with Japan Aug '95; the MAIL ON SUNDAY wrongly claimed his days were numbered at Central Office "as one of the few Thatcherites left in Smith Square" with the ascendancy of the new Research Director, Danny Finkelstein Aug '95; succeeded in being selected for safe New Forest East, against 178 other candidates Feb '96; denounced LibDem support for Labour as threatening to bring in "undemocratic" PR Mar '96; in a SPECTATOR letter denied that he had lacked access to his new boss, Danny Finkelstein, whom he credited with "burying the preposterous and counter-productive 'Coca-Cola' strategy favoured by some influential Conservative figures a few months ago; this was the notion that the party should acknowledge that Labour had become quasi-Conservative and that voters should thus be urged to support 'the real thing' rather than Tony Blair's cheap imitation"; he also denied that there was an anti-Semitic campaign against Finkelstein; "being Jewish has not prevented me from being selected as a prospective Parliamentary candidate for a distinctly winnable seat" July '96; claimed that unruly schools were a result of having banned the cane Sep '96; insisted that in September 1994 the Liberal Democrat conference had voted to decriminalise cannabis Sep '96; denounced the stifling of free debate on Europe at the Tory conference, with the exclusion of anti-EMU speakers like himself Oct '96; resigned as Deputy Director of the Conservative Research Department because he was put in an "anomolous position" by the Cabinet's decision to leave open the option of a single European currency; explained: "Conservative Central Office is constitutionally the office of the Leader of the Party; so I had to quit my job if I wanted to campaign against EMU" Dec '96; in a letter to DAILY TELEGRAPH warned that "a single currency would lead to a single European superstate which would then take over control of Britain's defence policy" Dec '96; insisted that a single European currency would mean "national suicide" Dec '96; won an apology, £39,500 in damages and costs in excess of £70,000 from magazine distributors of SCALLYWAG Feb '97; retained the new seat of New Forest East by a majority of 5,215, despite a pro-LibDem notional swing of 4.5% May '97; in his "non-controversial" Maiden, contrasted the Labour Government's Queen's Speech pledge to retain the nuclear deterrent with Foreign Secretary Robin Cook's 1982 plea to Labour's annual conference "to vote for unilateral nuclear disarmament" May '97; came 2nd in the lottery for Private Members' Bills May '97; was on John Redwood's campaign team May '97; in the first round of the Leadership campaign, when Redwood came 3rd, showed his pager message from Mr Redwood, "we're going all the way, JR" June '97; when Redwood was knocked out of the Leadership contest, said, "I am minded to abstain" June '97; did not vote in the 3rd ballot for Tory Leader July '97; introduced, as his Private Member's Bill, the Mental Health (Amendment) Bill, with all-party support, to provide greater access to hospital accommodation for mentally-ill people June '97; led motion deploring the alleged threats of Welsh Secretary Ron Davies against counter-devolutionary Welsh Labour MP Llew Smith June '97; paid ironic tribute to Labour's new Solicitor General, Lord Falconer, "an outstanding and gifted lawyer", known to PM Tony Blair "since their school days"; Lord Falconer had taken a slash in income from about £500,000 in private practice, to "a derisory £78,000; out of that he will still have to find the £21,000 that he apparently spends sending his four children to private schools" June '97; the MAIL ON SUNDAY claimed that, to annoy the LibDems, he was "sneaking into the Commons as early as 6 AM to bag their prized front-bench seats just below the gangway" June '97; asked what were the implications of the Treaty of Amsterdam for the future control of the British nuclear deterrent July '97; wrote to Cabinet Secretary Robin Butler drawing attention to apparent breaches in the rules laid down in 'Questions of Procedure for Ministers' arising from Lord Simon's failure to inform Margaret Beckett, President of the Board of Trade, about his continuing to hold over £2m in BP shares July '97; led motion defending John Redwood and his wife against the unfair and erroneous "slur" alleging that, while a Minister, he had influenced decisions relating to BA while his wife was employed by BA July '97; led amendment to a nuclear disarmament motion, recognising: "that general and complete nuclear disarmament must be accompanied by general and complete conventional disarmament if it is not simply to make the world safe, once again, for full-scale conventional warfare" July '97; asked about implications of the BSE cull July '97;

Born: 26 September 1951, Swansea

Family: Son, Samuel Lewis, tailor and designer, and late Hilda (Levitt);

Education: Dynevor Grammar School; Balliol College, Oxford University (MA in PPE '77); St Antony's (DPhil in Strategic Studies '81);

Occupation: Research Assistant: to Lord Orr-Ewing '85-; Founder-Director, of Policy Research Associates (Rightwing pressure group owned by him and Thomas Robinson, a prominent Freedom Association member; Patrons: Lord Chalfont, Edward Leigh MP, Norris McWhirter, founder of the Freedom Association) '85-; Author: Changing Direction: British Military Planning for Postwar Strategic Defence 1942-47 (1988), Who's Left? (1992), Labour's CND Cover-up (1992), The Liberal Democrats: the Character of Their Politics (1993); Who's Left in Europe (1994), What's Liberal: Liberal Democrat Quotations & Facts (1996); ex: Deputy Director, Conservative Research Department '90-96;

Traits: Tall ("5'11.5"); a "soft-spoken, baby-faced figure" (Chris Blackhurst, INDEPENDENT); chubby (but dieting); "has few interests outside politics, and [had] few friends at Central Office"; "a loner"; "thrives on conspiracy theories"; allegedly "shreds his newspapers so that no one will know what articles he has cut out"; "had security devices installed in his office, presumably to deter the enemies from within"; "drives to work on a powerful motorcycle" (Andrew Pierce, TIMES); his current bike is a 750cc BMW; "oddball" (MAIL ON SUNDAY): was a seaman in the HM Royal Naval Reserve '79-82; Jewish ("the Communists couldn't call me a Fascist because I just had to point out what happened to my family - five were left out of 50");

Address: House of Commons, Westminster, London SW1A 0AA| 13 The Parade, Southampton Road, Cadnam SO40 2NG;
Telephone: 0171 219 3000 (H of C); 01703 814905; 01703 814906 (Fax) (constituency);

Martin LINTON **Labour** **BATTERSEA '97-**

Majority: 5,360 over Conservative 6-way;
Description: Marginal, somewhat gentrified gateway to south London, with the southern end of six of its bridges, its former power station, its park, its dogs' home; part of inexpensively-run Conservative-controlled Wandsworth borough;
Position: On the Select Committee on Home Affairs '97-; Chairman, Battersea Arts Centre; ex: Wandsworth Borough Councillor (Chairman, Leisure and Amenities '71-77) '71-82;
Outlook: An awkward Fabian would-be reformer with the over-seriousness of a Scandinavian; "a promising new lickspittle" (Simon Hoggart, his former Press Gallery colleague on the GUARDIAN); despite inhabiting the Press Gallery for some years, seems to have little feel for the rules of the Commons; a psephologist supporting electoral reform (in Labour Campaign for Electoral Reform) and transparency in party funding;
History: He joined the Labour Party '68; was elected to Wandsworth Borough Council, becoming its Chairman of Leisure and Amenities May '71; in pursuit of the Labour selection for Brecon and Radnor, was the only candidate who did not wear a union badge Dec '91; opposed women-only short-lists in Battersea Jan '95; suggested Labour could emulate his natal Sweden's Labour Party by regularly revising its aims; after Labour's Clause Four conference he suggested relations with the unions could be improved by having union delegates elected as individuals, urging: "the delegates of one union might not all vote in the same way but they would reflect the views of the levy-payers who elected them and this represents the balance of opinion in the union" May '95; was selected for Battersea Mar '96; in a study of Clapham with Jane Mulholland for the local Labour Party, concluded there was chronic "area confusion": "people who live in the same street, often the same house, say they live in different places" - Clapham, Battersea or Wandsworth Sep '96; wrote that the SUN still had a "Tory mindset" and its "knee-jerk reaction was still to take the Tory line" Jan '97; was attacked by SUN Political Editor Trevor Kavanagh for his "breathtaking...naivety" in thinking that the SUN's scoops relied on Conservative Central Office handouts Jan '97; won his marginal seat on a 10.2% swing, with a majority of 5,360, ousting John Bowis, one of the Conservatives few able and popular Ministers May '97; in his "non-controversial" Maiden, in which he paid full tribute to his Tory predecessor, John Bowis, he launched a bitter attack on Wandsworth Council "who did their best to gerrymander Battersea into Conservative hands...by selling entire estates to private developers and, more insidiously, by selling vacant flats on the open market instead of renting them to people who they knew to be in acute housing need - unlawfully as the District Auditor has since found"; he also accused Tory leaders of "failure to stop the corruption of the political system through the growth of large secret donations to the Tory party, often from overseas"; honours had been awarded systematically to big donors; unprecedentedly, Tory MP Sir Michael Spicer interrupted him to ask the Deputy Speaker

whether Linton was "allowed to make such a controversial Maiden speech" May '97; trying to score points on the superiority of Labour's recent Leadership election system over that still operated by the Conservatives, had to be interrupted by Speaker Boothroyd twice to point out what he must have known from his first days in the Press Gallery, that "questions must be asked of the Prime Minister for which he has responsibility; he has no responsibility for what happens on the Conservative benches" June '97; expressed solidarity with jailed Indonesian trade union leader June '97; led a motion urging the Lord Chancellor recognise the work of law centres July '97; was named to the Select Committee on Home Affairs July '97;
Born: 11 August 1944, Stockholm
Family: Son, of Sydney Linton, Church of England clergyman, and Karin (of Swedish origins); m late Kathleen (Stanley); 2d Polly, '75, Essie '77;
Education: Christ's Hospital, Horsham; Universite de Lyon; Pembroke College, Oxford Unversity (MA in PPE);
Occupation: Author: Was It The Sun Wot Won It? (1995), Money and Votes (IPPR 1994), Labour's Road to Electoral Reform (1993), The GUARDIAN Election Guide (1992, 1977), 'The Swedish Road to Socialism' (Fabians 1984); ex: Political Journalist: on GUARDIAN '81-97; before that on DAILY STAR ("where he liked to blame the subs for his mistakes" - Trevor Kavanagh, SUN Political Editor) '79-81; LABOUR WEEKLY '71-79, FINANCIAL TIMES '71, DAILY MAIL '66-71 (NUJ);
Traits: Very tall; slim; blond; specs; over-serious; inhibited; multilingual (Swedish, French); plays the trumpet; a Fulham FC supporter; a slow writer who was ousted for this from his Press Gallery job by former GUARDIAN Political Editor Ian Aitken;
Address: House of Commons, Westminster, London SW1A 0AA;
Telephone: 0171 219 4619 (H of C); 0171 207 3060 (constituency);

Richard (Arthur Lloyd) LIVSEY CBE **Liberal Democrat** **BRECON & RADNORSHIRE '97-, '85-92;**

Majority: 5,097 over Conservative 5-way;
Description: Wales' largest seat - with 750,000 sprawling acres - and often its tightest cliffhangers; in '87 Richard Livsey held on by 56 votes, in '92 Tory Jonathan Evans retook it by 130; luckily they don't have to count the sheep, who outnumber people by 20 to one; has spectacular scenery as in the Brecon Beacons; its towns include Brecon, the spa Llandrindod Wells, Hay-on-Wye, Labour-voting Ystradgynlais (iron-working, coalmining, Lucas Industries); 10,000 voters in fringe mining villages were transferred out in '83;
Position: Spokesman on Wales '97-, '88-92; on Select Committee on Welsh Affairs '87-92; Leader of Welsh Liberal Democrats '88-92; Liberal Spokesman, on Water '88-89, on Agriculture '86-88;
Outlook: The return of a progressive Welsh Liberal Democrat; a champion of devolution to a Welsh Assembly; a caring, earnest, somewhat pedestrian, small-farmers' friend; technically knows most about the economics of farm management;
History: He joined the Liberal Party '60; contested Perth and East Perthshire - where he was a farm manager June '70; contested Pembroke against Welsh Secretary Nicholas Edwards,

losing his deposit June '79; contested Brecon and Radnor, coming 3rd May '83; was again selected to contest Brecon and Radnor on the death of its Tory incumbent, Tom Hooson May '85; apologised for the smears of his aide, Peter Chegwyn, that he was "the only major party candidate with a secure family background" to call attention to the Labour candidate "living in sin" and the bachelor status of the Tory candidate, Chris Butler (later an MP) July '85; accused Labour leaders of being "wolves in sheep's clothing" to keep the Scargill factor alive in the wake of the miners' strike; won by 559 votes after a last-minute Welsh-language telephone campaign to sheep farmers by Geraint (later Lord) Howells MP July '85; urged better use of NCB funds to keep open local marginal pits like St John's Maesteg Sep '85; criticised Government cuts in agricultural research Nov '85; backed demands for a Welsh Assembly Nov '85; called for severe action against salmon poachers Mar '86; called for adequate compensation for small farmers having to hold their lambs back from market because of Chernobyl contamination July '86; backed full sanctions against 'Apartheid' South Africa Aug '86; backed clause in Public Order Bill to prevent mass invasions of farm land Nov '86; retained Brecon and Radnor with Britain's joint smallest majority: 56, June '87; insisted in need to keep name 'Liberal' in merger with SDP Sep '87; with Alex Carlile, steered Liberal Assembly away from a motion banning export of live animals Sep '87; protested electricity privatisation Feb '88; the loss of more Welsh collieries was "intolerable" Feb '88; on the impending retirement of Geraint Howells, became Leader of the Welsh Liberal Democrats Mar '88; opposed David Alton's abortion-curbing Bill Mar '88; co-sponsored a motion enabling the use of Welsh in the Select Committee on Welsh Affairs Mar '88; Paddy Ashdown named him Spokesman on Wales and Water Sep '88; backed Geraint Howells' motion for a Welsh Assembly Nov '88; introduced amendment to Water Bill requiring a court order before water could be disconnected Jan '89; welcomed victory of "Liberal Democrats" over "Democrats" as name of merged party Oct '89; was confirmed as Welsh Spokesman, dropping Water Oct '89; supported Roy Hughes' Badgers Bill Dec '90; was defeated in the general election by Tory Jonathan Evans by 130 votes Apr '92; was again chosen as LibDems' candidate for Brecon and Radnor Jan '96; at annual conference complained bitterly about the weakening of Welsh local government and the stranglehold of the quangos Sep '96; the Brecon and Radnorshire result "was the 40th to be declared in Wales; I was the person who removed the last Conservative Member of Parliament from Wales", "on my birthday" with a majority of 5,097 on a swing of 6.1% May '97; in his second Maiden, said "we are now on the threshold of achieving a modest level of democratic accountability in Wales; at the moment there is a huge democratic deficit there" May '97; insisted that the Welsh Development Agency had largely neglected Mid-Wales June '97; opposed the cuts in payments for culled beef July '97; in an adjournment debate deplored the record of Powys ambulance service, whose area stretched for 135 miles July '97; strongly supported a Welsh Assembly - although he would prefer it to have more powers - because undevolved Wales had been "marginalised" by being controlled from London by the Tories or Tory-controlled quangos in Wales July '97;

Born: 2 May 1935, Manchester

Family: His family worked in the South Wales steel industry for three generations; one grandfather "went down a pit at the age of 14"; son of late Arthur Norman Livsey, master mariner who died when he was three, and Lillian Maisie (James), headmistress of Gweryfed School, Aberllynfi, at the time of the by-election; m '64 Irene Martin (Earsman); 1d 2s: David '70 (at UCW Aberystwyth did a BA in Modern Languages; was twice involved in inquests over a friend's involvement in pushing a man to his death off a bridge);

Education: Talgarth County Primary; Bedales School; Seale-Hayne Agricultural College, Devon; Reading University (BSc in Agricultural Management);

Occupation: Ex: Director, of Welsh Agriultural Training Board '92-97; Lecturer, in Farm

Management at the Welsh Agricultural College, Aberystwyth '71-86; Farmer, on 57 acres in Llanbon, Ceredigion, with 200 sheep and some cattle; Farm Manager, on 1,500-acre farm, Blairdrummond, Perthshire, '67-71; Development Officer/Agricutural Director ICI Northeastern Division, Hexham '61-67;
Traits: Tall; gangling; canny-looking; self-effacing; "an upright, grey, restrained rather old-fashioned man" (Simon Heffer, DAILY TELEGRAPH); "has a prim, rather hesitant air" (Oliver Pritchett, SUNDAY TELEGRAPH); "soporific in manner, but this may be well calculated to appeal to country reticence (George Hill, TIMES); "long on sincerity, short on charisma" (Adam Raphael, OBSERVER) "the personality of a cow-pat" (opponent Chris Butler); a fair Welsh-speaker (although born in Manchester, was brought up in Talgarth, in Breconshire); cricketer, angler and former Rugby player;
Address: House of Commons, Westminster, London SW1A 0AA; Llanon, Ceredigion,
Telephone: 0171 219 3000 (H of C); 01874 658445 (home);

David LOCK **Labour** **WYRE FOREST '97-**

Majority: 6,946 over Conservative 6-way;
Description: The northwestern corner of Worcestershire, with the carpet towns of Kidderminster and Stourport as well as as medieval Bewdley; an almost all-white owner-occupier constituency in the outer orbit of the West Midlands, with Conservative Anthony Coombs, a former Birmingham councillor, as its MP '87-97; although Labour won Kidderminster - then the seat's name - in '45, until recently the main challengers to the Tories were the Liberal Democrats; this changed in '92, when Labour came 2nd, and above all in the '97 general election, before which Coombs was expected to have a majority of roughly 10,000 if '92 voting was repeated;
Position: Wychavon District Councillor '95-;
Outlook: A Left-of-Centre Birmingham-based legal adviser to the Labour Party, with radical, anti-elitist views on education and health; Chairman of the West Midlands branch of the Society of Labour Lawyers;
History: He was elected to Wychavon District Council, becoming Chairman of Amenities, Economic Development and Leisure May '95; was selected to contest Wyre Forest against incumbent Tory MP Anthony Coombs '95; although it superficially seemed a longshot, Labour had already chalked up 53% of the local council election vote; the former LibDem challengers had faded with the division of their local voters between LibDems and Liberals; during the election campaign spoke to youngsters at Kidderminster's £3,885-a-year Holy Trinity School for Girls; he told them that the Assisted Places Scheme was helping to perpetuate an elitist society and private schooling was denying pupils from state schools their due places at universities and the best jobs; he later accepted, in discussions with the BIRMINGHAM POST that, in the heat of argument, he had gone beyond party policy in suggesting that private schooling could be "a cancer upon the British education system" Apr '97; he somewhat unexpectedly won the seat with a majority of 6,946, on a big swing of 13.7% May '97; in his Maiden, on NHS charges, urged national priorities, instead of the uneven patchwork which

was partly a result of the NHS"s "amoral" internal market June '97; expressed solidarity with a jailed Indonesian union leader June '97; urged exemption from court fees for those on benefit July '97; asked how much was paid out by NHS trusts for medical negligence July '97; urged "a fair crack of the whip in future schemes" for Lottery funds for those "outside the southeast" July '97; urged Education Secretary David Blunkett to improve the collaboration of education authorities and schools to provide the many with special educational needs instead of the past concentration on "an elitist educational system which benefits only the few" July '97;
Born: 2 May 1960, Woking, Surrey
Family: Son, of John Lock, research engineer, and Jeanette (Bridgwater) nurse; is married, with children;
Education: Surbiton Grammar School; St Peter's and Merrow Comprehensive; Woking Sixth Form College; Jesus College, Cambridge University (LLB); Central London Polytechnic; Inns of Court School of Law;
Occupation: Barrister, Inns of Court '86- Adviser to the Labour Party; his practice was based in Birmingham; (MSF);
Traits: Dark, parted hair; high forehead; specs; heart-shaped face; well-spoken; "appreciates the high arts" (DL); he lives in the village on which 'The Archers' is based;
Address: House of Commons, Westminster, London, SW1A 0AA; The Pumphouse, Hanbury, Worcestershire B60 4BX;
Telephone: 0171 219 3000 (H of C);

Tim(othy) LOUGHTON Conservative WORTHING EAST & SHOREHAM '97-

Majority: 5,098 over Liberal Democrat 5-way;
Description: The eastern wards of the borough of Worthing with Adur district from Shoreham, including its port; SmithKline Beecham is a large local employer; contains the country's highest percentage of pensioners; Liberal Democrats were the main challengers to Tory predominance;
Position: On Executive: of Selsdon Group '94-, of London Area Conservatives '93-; ex: Deputy Chairman, Battersea Conservative Association '95-96;
Outlook: Dynamic young Rightwinger with local (Lewes) roots; one of the most assiduous debaters among the new Tory MPs, willing to be thrown in by his Whips to fill time; can sound condescending about his "wooden top" opponents and his superior City knowledge, although specialist opponents can consider his viewpoints "complete and utter rubbish" (Labour MP Geraint Davies, former Marketing Manager of Colgate Palmolive); a Eurosceptic who insists on ruling out Britain joining a single European corrency; a successful City type (Director of Fleming Private Asset Management); "very social and garrulous in committee" (Paymaster General Geoffrey Robinson MP);
History: Joined the Young Conservatives at 15, '77; became Chairman of Lewes Young Conservatives at 16, '78; became Vice Chairman of Sussex Young Conservatives and Lewes Conservative Association at 17, '79; became Vice Chairman of South East Area Young Conservatives at 18, '80; became Secretary of Warwick University Conservative Association at 18, '81; joined Cambridge University Conservative Association '83; helped Tim Eggar in his

election contest June '87; unsuccessfully contested Wandsworth ward in local election, achieving the biggest local swing to the Tories May '90; was selected at 29 to contest hopeless Sheffield, Brightside against David Blunkett Jan '91; rejuvenated local party, increasing its membership six-fold; increased the Tory vote by 1% to 17% and cut Blunkett's huge majority by 2,000 to over 22,000 Apr '92; was made Life Vice President of Brightside Conservative Association Feb '93; was elected Chairman of Battersea Ward Conservative Association Feb '93; became a member of Conservatives' London Area Executive Committee Feb '93; was elected Deputy Chairman of Battersea Constituency Conservative Association Mar '94; was selected for Worthing East and Shoreham, instead of Shoreham's Tory MP, Michael Stephen, who wanted to inherit without a contest Nov '95; was one of 59 prospective Tory candidates planning to rule out Britain's entry into a single European currency Dec '96; won the new seat by a majority of 5,098, despite a notional swing of 3.9% to the LibDems; said he was "relieved and gobsmacked"; "in the light of safe seats around the country tumbling like ninepins, for us to come out with this majority was marvellous" May '97; joined William Hague's campaign team May '97; insisted Labour's windfall tax would not come from the utilities' "pot of gold" but from their borrowings May '97; urged the abolition of the Government Office of the South East, because it seemed set on pushing for more homebuilding in West Sussex than agreeable to local authorities there July '97; in opposing the Government's withdrawal of tax exemption on pensioners' BUPA subscriptions, said that he had "enjoyed a corporate BUPA subscription for some years" and paid tax on it as a benefit, but had only used the NHS July '97; co-sponsored Tory motion baiting Lord Simon on his retention of £2m in BP shares July '97; intervened "as an employee of the company (Fleming's) that floated Billiton's" to complain that the Budget changes had hurt its share price; Paymaster General Geoffrey Robinson countered that he had received "a personally-written letter that arrived on my desk" from the company "which showed that the negotiations that we conducted with Billiton and its advisers might well serve as a model for how Government and industry can work together" July '97;

Born: 30 May 1962, Lewes

Family: Son, Rev Michael Loughton, clergyman/teacher, and Pamela Dorothy (Brandon); m '92 Elizabeth (MacLauchlan); 1s Hector, 1d Freya;

Education: Priory School, Lewes; University of Warwick (BA lst Class Honours); Clare College, Cambridge University;

Occupation: Director '92-, Executive '84-92 Fleming Private Asset Management '92-;

Traits: Parted dark brown hair; specs; young; dynamic; good sense of humour; long-winded (often at the Tory Whips' request); enjoys skiing, tennis, hockey;

Address: House of Commons, Westminster, London SW1A 0AA;

Telephone: 0171 219 4471 (H of C);

ANOREXIA OR OBESITY

Profiles, like politicians, can be very slim or very full-bodied. This can depend on how varied and colourful is the past of the MP concerned, or the quality of the newspapers reporting them. Some politicians are paranoid about disclosing anything beyond the bare minimum and then complain if second-hand information beyond the bare essentials turns out to be less than accurate. Others turn to their libel lawyers as an expensive threat. We adhere to the quaint idea that if people have decided to plunge into the glass fishbowl of politics they are not entitled to wear wetsuits. After all, most wrongdoing has been exposed by the media's investigative journalists, very little by politicians themselves.

'Andy' (Andrew) LOVE **Labour & Co-operative** **EDMONTON '97-**

Majority: 13,472 over Conservative 6-way;
Description: Unaltered outer northeast London working-class seat tucked into the southeast corner of Enfield; one-fifth non-white, mainly Afro-Caribbean; voted Labour in local elections but backed a Tory for three elections before '97;
Position: Chairman, of the all-party Building Societies Parliamentary Group '97-; ex: Parliamentary Officer, of the Co-operative Party '94-97; Haringey Borough Councillor (Chairman: of Housing, Finance) '80-86; on Greater London Labour Party Executive (Chairman of its Policy Commission} '84-94; on North East Thames Regional Health Authority '86-89; Secretary, Political Committee of Co-operative Retail Society (CRS) '85-94; Acting Treasurer, British Peace Assembly '87-89; on World Disarmament Council '87-90;
Outlook: Centre-Left Scottish veteran of local government and the Co-operative Party and movement; for a decade has co-ordinated charity appeals through the CRS, raising tens of thousands of pounds for Oxfam, Save the Children, Lebanese refugees; was earlier attacked by hard-Right 'cold warriors' for administering some of the causes adopted by the fellow-travelling infiltrators of the Co-ops; a multi-cause groupie: Fabian Society, War on Want, Amnesty International, formerly the Labour Co-ordinating Committee, UK-Cuba Friendship Association, the Labour Euro-Safeguards Campaign;
History: He joined the Labour Party in '75; was elected a Haringey Councillor May '80; as Haringey's Chairman of Finance, forced through the setting of a legal rate, despite hard-Left protests '84-85; became acting Treasurer of British Peace Assembly, which supported the Soviet-backed regime in Afghanistan '87-89; (after he left, the British Peace Assembly lent its offices to the Committee to Stop the War in the Gulf which condemned the US-led military build-up in the Gulf Dec '90; was nominated to the World Disarmament Council '87-90; was selected to fight Edmonton, considered a Labour-Co-operative seat Mar '90; lost Edmonton to Dr Ian Twinn by 593 votes despite a high (7%) swing to Labour Apr '92; the local Labour Agent, Ted Hill, told the ENFIELD ADVERTISER he was taking legal advice about people being directed to wrong polling stations and about Tory leaflets claiming Love had opposed the Gulf War and supported unilateral disarmament May '92; complained that privatisation was stopping installation of closed-circuit TV cameras to curb crime and vandalism, co-funded initially by the local West Anglia Great Northern rail organisation and Enfield Borough Council; "rail privatisation has scuppered a very valuable initiative; local people are losing out" Apr '96; refused to answer an EVENING STANDARD telephone poll of candidates which was trying to place candidates in Labour's political spectrum July '96; was not happy about the electoral tactic of pledging not to increase income tax; "there's a lot of talk about the [Treasury] coffers being empty; God knows what the implications of that would be!" Mar '97; won the seat, on a near-record swing of 15.6%, achieving a majority of 13,472 May '97; urged the new Labour Government to restore support for co-operatives in developing nations June '97; co-sponsored a motion congratulating the Co-op societies for banning alcopop drinks June '97; welcomed Government's decision to compile a register of its assets July '97; as Chairman of the Commmons Building Society Parliamentary Group, asked for a debate on the threat to them July '97; headed a motion backing help to flood-damaged Poland July '97;

Born: 21 March 1949, Greenock
Family: Son, of James Love and Olive (Mills); m '83 Ruth (Rosenthal), Systems Manager with GRE Investments (major insurance company in the City);
Education: Greenock High School; Strathclyde University (BSc Hons in Physics; then trained as a teacher); completed two-year study programme of the Institute of Chartered Secretaries and Administrators '92-94 (ACIS);
Occupation: Trustee, of ICOF (revolving loan fund for workers' co-ops) '91-; ex: Parliamentary Officer of Co-operative Party '94-97; Political Secretary, Co-operative Retail Services Ltd '85-94; on Board of Directors, Greater London Enterprise '88-91; (NACO); Office Manager, in London '74-85; (TGWU)
Traits: Dark hair; high forehead; dark moustache; Scots burr; amiable; engaging; keen golfer (formerly a junior champion on his course);
Address: House of Commons, Westminster, London SW1A 0AA;
Telephone: 0171 219 5497/6623(Fax) (H of C); 0181 803 0574/5332(Fax) constituency;

'Steve' (Stephen) McCABE Labour BIRMINGHAM-HALL GREEN '97-

Majority: 8,420 over Conservative 4-way;
Description: One of two Birmingham seats which never fell to Labour before '97 (the other being Edgbaston); a tree-rich, largly middle-class residential constituency on the city's south and southeastern edge; its Sarehole Mill, where J R Tolkien spent his boyhood, was the inspiration for 'The Hobbit' and 'The Lord of the Rings'; most of its voters are owner-occupiers, with few council tenants; a tenth of its voters are non-white, half the proportion in Birmingham as a whole; Labour could not previously capture its wards even in the May '94 city council elections, when the Tories did very poorly;
Position: Birmingham City Councillor (Chairman, its Transport Committee '93-) '90-;
Outlook: The seat's first-ever Labour incumbent: a classic of new Labour entrants: a local councillor in public employment; "Left-inclined but cautious" (RED PEPPER); keeps a low profile; has called himself a "socialist Blairite"; favours electoral reform;
History: He joined the Labour Party in Scotland; was elected to Birmingham City Council May '90; was selected to fight "hopeless" Hall Green '95; toward the end of the campaign, the BIRMINGHAM POST printed a poll showing Labour leading in Birmingham by 13%, followed by a poll in the BIRMINGHAM EVENING MAIL showing Labour ahead by 6% even in never-before-won Edgbaston; the campaign was enlivened by an attack by Hall Green's incumbent Tory MP, Andrew Hargreaves, over a misprint in a Labour leaflet which wrongly described McCabe as the seat's MP already Apr '97; unexpectedly this misprint was corrected by his winning the seat, ousting Andrew Hargreaves by a majority of 8,420, a swing of 14% May '97; in his Maiden enthused about the abolition of the Tory-sponsored nursery vouchers, because it would have "diverted staff time from work with children" to "acting as little more than ticket collectors, chasing vouchers for children already in school"; he also welcomed the appointment of Birmingham City Council's Chief Education Officer, Professor Tim Brighouse, to the new standards task force June '97; backed outlawing of fox-hunting June '97;

co-sponsored motion urging water companies to provide a free repair service to householders whose supply pipes were leaking June '97; expressed solidarity with a jailed Indonesian trade union leader June '97;
Born: 4 August 1955, Scotland
Family: He does not disclose family details;
Education: Port Glasgow Senior Secondary School; Moray House College of Education, Edinburgh; Bradford University;
Occupation: Former Adviser to the Central Council for the Education and Training of Social Workers (MSF);
Traits: Parted greying hair; broad forehead; Marathon runner; climbed Himalayan peak to raise money for the Reiner Foundation;
Address: House of Commons, Westminster, London SW1A 0AA;
Telephone: 0171 219 3000 (H of C); 0121 444 8162 (home);

Chris(tine) McCAFFERTY **Labour** **CALDER VALLEY '97-**

Majority: 6,255 over Conservative 6-way;
Description: The affluent wool valleys of West Yorkshire surrounding Halifax, with many small factories; it follows the River Calder winding down from the Pennines from Todmorden 27 miles to Brighouse; created mainly from Sowerby in '83, it took in bits of Halifax and Brighouse and Spenborough, making it Sowerby - its former name - minus pro-Labour Sowerby Bridge plus pro-Tory Brighouse and Rastrick; it includes Hebden Bridge; its canny, tight-fisted inhabitants are three-quarters owner-occupiers and 98% white; until '97 it defied the pollsters' predictions, as Sir Donald Thompson kept repeating until May 1;
Position: Calderdale District Councillor '91-; on the West Yorkshire Police Authority '94-; a Director of Royd Regeneration Ltd; Chairman, of Calderdale Domestic Violence Forum;
Outlook: Low-profiled local councillor and social worker; a "notorious Blair groupie" (RED PEPPER); "the young must have training and jobs; it's hard for parents to watch their children sitting around with nothing to do" (CMcC); favours electoral reform;
History: She joined the Labour Party at 17, '65; she was elected to the Calderdale District Council for Luddenden Foot ward May '91; after the bruising rejection of its previous, male Labour candidate, David Chaytor, (who found solace in Bury North), she was selected from an all-women short-list to oust Sir Donald Thompson from marginal Calder Valley Feb '95; on the doorstep she did not find voters wanted to talk about the unpopular Calderdale Council: "people are concerned about education - class sizes - about unemployment and regeneration; people are terrified of losing their jobs"; her targeted marginal was visited by Lord (Richard) Attenborough, then by a busload of 20 Labour MPs Apr '97; she won the seat by a majority of 6,255, on a swing of 9.5%, ending Sir Donald Thompson's 18-year reign May '97; led a motion extolling the "substantial world-wide market opportunities available to British suppliers of environmental technologies and services in a world market worth £400b" July '97
Born: 14 October 1948, Manchester
Family: She is married, with one child;

Education: Whalley Range Grammar School for Girls; Footscray High School, Melbourne, Victoria, Australia;
Occupation: Project Manager, Calderdale Well-Women Centre (MSF) '89-97; Education Welfare Officer, with Manchester Education Committee '69-72; Welfare Officer for the Disabled, Community Health Service, Manchester '64-69;
Traits: Blonde, with bangs; prison lay visitor; enjoys swimming gardening, camping and caravanning; she took her caravan to the Brighton annual conference in '97;
Address: House of Commons, Westminster, London SW1A 0AA;
Telephone: 0171 219 3000 (H of C); 01422 843713 (home/Fax);

Siobhain McDONAGH **Labour** **MITCHAM & MORDEN '97-**

Majority: 13,741 over Conservative 9-way;
Description: Unaltered South London marginal in industrial Wandle valley in Merton borough; has pro-Labour St Helier council estate and other Labour-leaning wards; was captured by Tory MP Angela Rumbold in 1982 when its sitting Labour MP Bruce Douglas-Mann defected to the SDP and insisted on trying to secure his constituents' endorsement, thus splitting the non-Tory vote;
Position: On Select Committee on Social Security '97-; Merton Borough Councillor (Chairman of Housing '90-95) '82-;
Outlook: Matured former "child prodigy" who, at 27, was the youngest candidate in the 1987 general election; "once had a reputation herself as a bit of a Leftwing firebrand" (David McKie, GUARDIAN) but is now a Scargill-bashing Blairite moderniser; a "leading anti-Left witch-hunter; in [the] mid-'80s London Labour Party, [was] instrumental in action against Lambeth Council" (RED PEPPER); a long-standing advocate of membership ballots; a housing specialist who, as Merton's Chairman of Housing, set up one of the country's most successful public-private partnerships which demolished three tower blocks on a run-down estate and built 300 new homes and improved 300 other properties; a strong Catholic of Irish working-class origins; "I hope to see nation-wide one-stop breast cancer clinics that can offer women same-day test results";
History: She was born locally into an Irish working class family; joined the Labour Party at 16, '76; was elected at 22 to Merton Council for her natal ward, Colliers Wood, May '82; made her first speech at 23 as the youngest delegate at Labour's annual conference Oct '83; at 25 was selected as Labour's opponent to Tory MP Angela Rumbold Oct '85; won applause at annual conference by insisting crime was the most important issue for many women and elderly people in the constituency Oct '86; contested Mitcham and Morden, losing by 6,183 votes (12.9%), did only 1% better than Labour's previous '83 effort despite a 10% drop in support for the SDP candidate, Bruce Douglas-Mann - the constituency's previous Labour MP; his lost votes went equally to the Tories and Labour June '87; was re-selected for Mitcham and Morden Oct '89; came within 1,734 votes (3.4%) of unseating Angela Rumbold, by mopping up almost half the third-party vote with the disappearance of Bruce Douglas-Mann from the ballot paper Apr '92; at annual conference fiercely attacked Arthur Scargill's attempt to reopen the Clause Four debate, deriding him as "King Canute, wishing the

waves of time were not coming forward" Oct '95; with 17 other candidates, proclaimed Labour as a "united dynamic party" Oct '96; sounded very confident before her third contest: "we have lanced the problems that we did have"; "people will ask you how we are going to pay for our commitments, which we have real answers to" Jan '97; asked for her educational views, opted for rigorous streaming in comprehensives; "grammar schools failed a lot of children; comprehensives, when they work well, give greater opportunities for mobility" Mar '97; was listed as one of the 16 GMB member-candidates backed by the union Apr '97; won the seat, burying Dame Angela Rumbold with a majority of 13,741, on a swing of fully 16% May '97; expressed solidarity with jailed Indonesian trade union leader June '97; was named to the Select Committee on Social Security July '97;

Born: 20 February 1960, Colliers Wood, Merton

Family: Daughter of Cummin McDonagh, Irish building worker, and Brenda (Donogue) nurse; her younger sister, Margaret, the youngest Regional Organiser in the 1983 general election campaign, recently was Labour's key seats co-ordinator and was named Deputy General Secretary July '97;

Education: St Anselm's Primary, Colliers Wood, London; Holy Cross Secondary Modern, Colliers Wood; Essex University '81 (BA Hons in Government);

Occupation: Housing Adviser: Development Co-ordinator, Battersea Housing Trust (GMB) '88-; Catholic Housing Advice Service, Wandsworth; Homeless Person's Unit, Wandsworth Council (NALGO/UNISON);

Traits: Parted longish dark hair; full face; persuasive; articulate; RC; enjoys music and watching Wimbledon Football Club;

Address: House of Commons, Westminster, London SW1A 0AA; 147 Boundary Road, Colliers Wood, London SW19 2DE;

Telephone: 0171 219 3000 (H of C); 0181 542 3262 (home); 0181 542 4835 (CLP office); 0181 664 4014 (work);

John McDONNELL **Labour** **HAYES & HARLINGTON '97-**

Majority: 14,291 over Conservative 6-way;

Description: A virtually unaltered mixed West London area including most of Heathrow; until Labour MP Neville Sandelson's '81 defection to the SDP, was considered safely Labour; the '83-97 reign of the Rightwing populist Tory MP Terry Dicks showed Thatcherism's appeal for the working-class; has had a substantial inflow of Sikhs from neighbouring Southall;

Position: Secretary, of Association of London Government '95-; on Labour Party National Policy Forum '93-; Chairman: Labour Party Irish Society '80-, Britain and Ireland Human Rights Centre '92-; ex: Secretary, of Association of London Authorities '87-95; on Greater London Regional Executive Committee '82-87; Editor, LABOUR HERALD '85-88; Greater London Councillor (Deputy Leader '84-85, Chairman of Finance '82-85) '81-86;

Outlook: A slightly more subtle version of the veteran hard-Leftwinger of semi-Trotskyist hue (LABOUR HERALD, BRIEFING); recently a London Labour apparatchik, he would like to be involved in London planning by a Labour government; a hard campaigner but still of the Over-the-Top tendency (he made two expensive libellous attacks on his Tory opponent, Terry Dicks MP, in '92 and '94; these cost him and his sympathizers £20,000 in libel damages and £54,500 in costs); in GLC days thought Ken Livingstone a revisionist because he felt compelled to set a rate; of Liverpool Irish origins; in Labour Committee on Ireland, Labour Irish Society; remains sympathetic to Sinn Fein rather than SDLP in Northern Ireland; has empathy with Asians in the constituency;

History: Joined the Labour Party '73; was elected a GLC Councillor for Hayes and Harlington May '81; became Chairman of the GLC's Finance Committee '82; contested Hampstead and Highgate against Geoffrey Finsberg, losing by 3,370 votes June '83; became Deputy Leader of the GLC '84; fell out with GLC Leader Ken Livingstone over the latter's insistence on setting a rate, in compliance with government regulations '85; became Editor of the Trotskyist LABOUR HERALD, previously allegedly part-financed by the Libyans '85; was named Principal Policy Advisor to Camden Borough Council '85; was appointed Secretary of the Association of London Authorities '87; just before the Allies launched their attack on the Iraqi forces in Kuwait, alleged that his Tory opponent, Terry Dicks, was sympathetic to Saddam Hussein, having been the regime's guest in 1988, Jan '91; had to pay Terry Dicks £15,000 in libel damages and £55,000 in costs for having called him a sympathiser of Saddam Hussein and then refusing to apologise Mar '92; thought that he would win the seat because of economic conditions: "the rise in unemployment since early 1990, from around 3% to nearly 10% has been one of the fastest in Western Europe; about 75% of first-time buyers, who purchased their homes at the height of the Lawson boom in 1988, are now paying mortgages above their present value; Brentford Court has handled the second highest number of home repossession orders in the country; you see bailiffs' notices saying 'you are ordered to remove your goods and chattels by such-and-such a date' on the windows; I do a street stall every Saturday; you notice people getting poorer and poorer and problems building up; you notice privation of the sort we've never had in Hayes; it's as if the town's been bankrupted" Apr '92; narrowly lost to Terry Dicks, by 56 votes Apr '92; asked for contributions from 270 Labour MPs to help him with his libel costs to save him from having to sell his Hampstead flat May '92; "for the past two months, all of my time outside of working hours has been devoted to raising the needed cash, through car boot sales, dinner dances and jumble sales"; this was followed by a concert at the Hackney Empire, with bands offering their services free June '92; was named the member for Greater London of Labour's National Policy Forum '93; Labour made serious advances in council elections in Hayes May '94; called for return of rail, water, gas and electricity to public oownership July '96; won the seat on a near-record swing of 17.4%, by a majority of 14,291 May '97; joined the hard-Left Campaign Group May '97; in his Maiden could not praise his "Tory buffoon" predecessor, Terry Dicks who, he alleged, "brought shame on the political process of this country by his blatant espousal of racism and his various corrupt dealings"; he also defined the abolition of the GLC, of which he had been Deputy Leader, as "an act of malignant spite by a Prime Minister in the first demented throes of megalomania"; he criticised Labour's proposal of a directly-elected Mayor as "the result of enthusiasm from above" which "grates against my notion of democratic socialist practice" because it could lead to the "abuse of power and corruption" June '97; backed outlawing of fox-hunting June '97; asked for an inquiry into Freemasons in the Lord Chancellor's Department June '97; denied that he had been a supporter of the Migrant Training Company, a charity set up to train Irish immigrants, on whose behalf eight Labour councils were asked to repay almost £500,000 to the European Commission for false expenditure claims, as alleged by The OBSERVER July '97; led a motion criticising BA's "intimidatory tactics" against its striking staff July '97; co-sponsored motion opposing a 12-lane superhighway to provide

acccess to the proposed Terminal 5 at Heathrow July '97; was one of five Leftwing Labour MPs - including his old boss, Ken Livingstone - who abstained against the Government's capping of Oxfordshire and Somerset, after a speech in which he claimed capping was contrary to Labour policies, in "undermining" the "power of the community" July '97;
Born: 8 September 1951, Liverpool
Family: Son, of Robert McDonnell, docker/bus driver, and Elsie (Brunson); m 1st '71 Marilyn Jean (Cooper); 2d; divorced '87; lived with Julia Devote, Camden Councillor; m 2nd '95 Cynthia Marie (Pinto); 1s;
Education: Great Yarmouth Grammar; Burnley Technical College; Brunel University (BSc in Government); Birkbeck College, London University (MSc in Politics and Sociology);
Occupation: Secretary, Association of London Government '95-; Secretary of Association of London Authorities '87-95; Principal Policy Advisor, Camden Borough Council '85-87; (UNISON); fulltime GLC Councillor Hayes and Harlington '82-86; Research Assistant: TUC '78-82, NUM '76-78; Production Worker '68-72;
Traits: Greying dark hair; acquiline Celtic featurers; fit; enjoys gardening, cinema and the theatre;
Address: House of Commons, Westminster, London SW1A 0AA; 38 Clayton Road, Hayes, Middx UB3 1AZl
Telephone: 0171 219 6908 (H of C);

Martin McGUINNESS **Sinn Fein** **MID-ULSTER '97-**

Majority: 1,883 over DUP 6-way;
Description: The strife-torn west-central rural seat in Northern Ireland; despite its nationalist majority over unionists (69% to 31%), its electoral result has normally depended on whether a single candidate stands from one community, while more than one stands for the rival community; thus Bernadette Devlin (later McAliskey) could win as a 21-year-old in the '69 by-election as the Nationalist Unity candidate; in '83 Sinn Fein's Danny Morrison came within 78 votes of beating the DUP; incredibly, the extreme anti-Catholic DUP gospel-singer, Rev William McCrea, could hold on for 14 years ('83-97), so long as his two Catholic opponents -the moderate SDLP and the immoderate Sinn Fein - were evenly split; this has been undermined partly by the weakening of the SDLP in favour of the Sinn Fein, partly by Catholics believing a strengthened Sinn Fein vote could discourage the IRA's reliance on arms; Sinn Fein was also helped in '95 by the removal of large chunks from Mid-Ulster to create the new seat of West Tyrone and the addition of Coalisland;
Position: Vice President of Sinn Fein and its Senior Negotiator; on Sinn Fein's National Executive; ex: Northern Ireland Assemblyman '82-86;
Outlook: The born-again Sinn Fein leader, no longer seen only as the "hard man" of the top duo, more closely linked with the Provos' military wing; the "most significant republican leader in nearly 30 years of the troubles"; "while Mr Adams has been the figurehead of the movement, Mr McGuinness [in the past] worked in the background as a key strategist in his party's efforts to attract electoral support; he has been prominent at IRA funerals and

republican rallies" (DAILY TELEGRAPH);

History: He joined the Official IRA '70, then the recently-established Provisionals '71; was imprisoned for IRA membership '71; at 22 was flown secretly from Ulster with other imprisoned IRA leaders, including Gerry Adams, to negotiate with the Northern Ireland Secretary, William Whitelaw July '72; was convicted twice in the Republic for IRA membership '73 and '74; later denied allegations that he was an IRA leader in the '70s; he went along with Gerry Adams' conclusion that there could be no military victory for either the British Army or the IRA '80; was banned from entering Britain '82; was elected to the Northern Ireland Assembly Oct '82; contested Foyle, coming 3rd after John Hume with 20.3% June '83; denied that he was IRA Chief of Staff, insisting the allegation was part of a British plan to have him assassinated '85; again went along with Gerry Adams' conclusion that since the IRA wa unable to achieve its aim of a British withdrawal by military means, and Sinn Fein was unable to overtake the SDLP because of its link with the IRA, it was advisable to link up with the SDLP, Dublin and the USA's Irish lobby to offer a ceasefire in exchange for British withdrawal '86; again contested Foyle, coming 3rd with 17.9% June '87; was arrested by the police in 'Derry on two successive days, first because Mrs Thatcher was visiting and then because a suspect device was found during a football match Sep '89; he had three hours of conversations with a Foreign Office official in a Northern Ireland suburb which led to further meetings Oct '90; he allegedly informed the British Government that the military conflict was over, in effect, but wondered how it could be brought formally to a close Feb '93; an aide memoire from Sir Patrick Mayhew, was secretly and orally communicated to him, emphasising that the "peace process would be destroyed" by "acts of violence" and "a potentially historic opportunity...squandered" Mar '93; the IRA Bishopgate bomb exploded in the City Apr '93 but the talks with him allegedly continued until June '93; he and Gerry Adams carried the coffin of the IRA man who blew himself up while planting the Shankill Road bomb that killed nine Protestants Oct '93; he confirmed the authenticity of the March 1993 aide memoire to him from Sir Patrick Mayhew as disclosed by the anti-negotiations DUP MP Rev William McCrea; he also disclosed the conversations he had had in 1990 with a Foreign Office emissary of Mrs Thatcher Nov '93; he was one of the winners when Sinn Fein took a larger-than-expected share of the vote, winning 17 of the 110 seats in the Forum (15.4%), the party's best-ever result in an election in the Province, topping its previous high of 12.4% in '93; he said he would call for a new ceasefire if PM John Major gave an assurance that the talks would be meaningful and the Unionists would not be allowed a blocking veto May '96; after the disastrous failure of the Government's policing of the Portadown march, he addressed 5,000 demonstrators in 'Derry, urging the angry crowd to remain "united, calm, dignified" July '96; after the same day's Enniskillen bomb, said: "Sinn Fein still has a peace strategy and that strategy is still centered around the reality of what is required - peace negotiations without pre-conditions" July '96; Gerry Adams confirmed that Martin McGuinness would contest Mid-Ulster when there was a question of Roisin McAliskey contesting from prison the seat her mother had held '69-74 as Bernadette Devlin Mar '97; he hinted at a possible renewal of the ceasefire when he said that it was necessary to create a "peaceful atmosphere" before talks could go ahead; he hinted he thought Tony Blair would be much more amenable than John Major Mar '97; he spoke favourably after a meeting with Mo Mowlam, Labour's shadow Ulster Secretary: "she identified the need for confidence-building measures and specified prisoners, marching and the RUC; she also recognised that the status quo cannot be allowed to remain and the need to move forward decisively" Apr '97; he won Mid Ulster by a majority of 1,883 over the Rev McCrea on a notional swing of 10.3% May '97; he and Adams were not able to take their seats as MPs because they could not meet the stipulated condition of swearing allegiance to the Queen May '97; he and Adams were able to tell the Army Council

of the IRA that a ceasefire could secure Sinn Fein's entry to negotiations provided the IRA agreed to consider decommissioning of arms during the process of all-party negotiations July '97; a cease-fire went into effect, but he told Sky TV that "the IRA have said that they will not decommission a single bullet and I have not heard any statement from them saying they have changed their position on that" July '97; started legal action to challenge the legality of being denied a Commons seat for refusing to swear loyalty to the Queen Aug '97; after a slight adjustment of conditions, he and Gerry Adams entered the all-party talks, with the Ulster Unionists joining in Sep '97; in a speech to republicans in Coalisland, said he was taking part in the peace talks to "smash the Union" Oct '97;
Born: 23 May 1950, Bogside, 'Derry
Family: He is the oldest of seven children; m '74 'Bernie'/ Bernadette; 2s: Fiachra and Emmet; 3d: one daughter, Grainne '76, has become a model; Fionnuala '77 attended the '97 count at Mid-Ulster with him;
Education: Christian Brothers Technical College, Brow o' the Hill, 'Derry;
Occupation: Sinn Fein Organiser; ex: Butcher's Assistant;
Traits: Curly retreating hair; 'Derry accent; strongly Gaelic cultural preferences, including his children's names; "I have little time to go fishing but I relax with TROUT AND SALMON which transports me to the lakes, rivers and mountains where I feel most at peace"; reads Irish poetry and novels (Liam O'Flaherty, Walter Margen) rather than "dull" political biographies; in films enjoyed 'Braveheart' ("escapism peppered with a bit of history") and 'Into the West';
Address: Terraced home in 'Derry;

Mrs Anne McGUIRE **Labour** **STIRLING '97-**

Majority: 6,411 over Conservative 6-way;
Description: The virtually unaltered seat in West Perthshire and West Stirlingshire, formerly the fourth most marginal in Scotland, and one of its most historic; the pro-Labour town of Stirling is counter-balanced by 800 square miles of surrounding hills and lochs - including Loch Lomond; it includes Dunblane; this battleground was won by hundreds of votes by the formidable Michael Forsyth in '87 and '92;
Position: On the Executive of Scottish Labour Party, as the GMB's delegate (Chairman '92-93) '84-; a Director of the John Wheatley Centre (think tank) '90-; ex: Strathclyde Regional Councillor '80-82; Deputy Director, Scottish Council for Voluntary Organisations '93-97;
Outlook: The moderate, pro-European Scottish apparatchik modest about her role as the unseater of Michael Forsyth; an "able party apparatchik loyal to [the] leadership" (RED PEPPER); a member of the 'Network' of Scottish moderates anxious to keep the Leftish Scottish party in step with the new Centrist Blairite leadership; close to Rosemary McKenna and George Robertson;
History: She joined the Labour Party '67; she became the Election Agent for East Dumbartonshire Apr '79; she was elected for Blairdard ward to Strathclyde Regional Council May '80; became Election Agent for moderate Norman Hogg in Cumbernauld & Kilsyth May '83; again served as Election Agent for Norman Hogg in Cumbernauld & Kilsyth June '87; was

again Election Agent for Norman Hogg in Cumbernauld & Kilsyth when they lost 7,000 votes to the SNP Apr '92; became Chairman of the Scottish Labour Party, after eight years on its Executive '92; she was initially thought of as a likely successor to Labour's deceased Leader, John Smith, as the MP for Monklands East, partly because his death coincided with crisis over the under-representation of Scottish women in Parliament May '94; she was selected for marginal Stirling from an all-women short-list Sep '95; at annual conference spoke in support of Gavin Strang and his work in criticising the deplorable record of the Government on BSE; she was particularly critical of Government for alienating Europe, with whom she was anxious to collaborate Oct '96; she was reported in the SCOTSMAN as being one of the half-dozen prospectives lined up with others in the 'Network' organised in the autumn of 1996 to keep the Scottish party in step with the more Centrist Blairite leadership south of the Border Jan '97; apart from considerable national party support for her campaign, including a visit by Tony Blair, she was also one of 16 GMB members backed by the union Apr '97; was elected for Stirling on a swing of 7.7% by a majority of 6,411 over the incumbent, Scottish Secretary Michael Forsyth May '97; in her Maiden she strongly endorsed the Scottish Parliament May '97; with Dunblane in her constituency, she vigorously supported the new Government's ban on .22 calibre handguns June '97; asked about improved training for tourism June '97; co-sponsored a motion urging the installation of sprinklers in supermarkets and superstores July '97;

Born: 26 May 1949, Glasgow

Family: Daughter of late Albert Long, railway signalman, and late Nancy (Coney); m '72 Leonard McGuire, chartered accountant; 1s, Paul, at Glasgow University; 1d Sarah, at Strathclyde University;

Education: Our Lady of St Francis, Glasgow; Glasgow University (MA Hons in Politics with History '67-71; Diploma in Secondary Education '74-75)

Occupation: Deputy Director, Scottish Council for Voluntary Organisations, Edinburgh (GMB) '93-97; previously: Scottish National Officer, of Community Services Volunteers;

Traits: Dark brown hair with bangs; specs; stocky; RC-educated;

Address: House of Commons, Westminster, London SW1A 0AA; 25 Meadows View, Cumbernauld, Glasgow G67 2BY;

Telephone: 0171 219 5014 (H of C); 01786 446515 (constituency);

Anne McINTOSH MEP **Conservative** **VALE OF YORK '97-**

Majority: 9,721 over Labour 5-way;

Description: A new seat comprising the most Tory bits of Ryedale, Richmond, Harrogate and Skipton & Ripon; among the safest Tory seats in Yorkshire;

Position: MEP: for North Essex and South Suffolk (British Conservative Spokesman on European Parliament's Transport Committee '92-) '94-, for North East Essex '89-94;

Outlook: The second new Tory woman after Theresa May to win selection for a safe seat; a multilingual MEP who changed her mind after previously strongly favouring a federal Europe and a single European currency; a Scots lawyer specialising in European Law; "her appetite for politics is

insatiable" (Scottish Secretary Donald Dewar); "I'd like to introduce [to England and Wales] the Scottish law where any prisoner not brought to trial after 110 days is released" (AMcI);
History: Selected to contest Workington against Dale Campbell-Savours, she claimed Labour support was sagging there; she promised to keep Sellafield open and to extend it; she lost but achieved a swing to Tories of 0.1%, June '87; was elected Euro-MP for North East Essex with a majority of over 39,000 June '89; as someone born a Scot, she was asked by Scottish Secretary Malcolm Rifkind to be responsible for monitoring EC developments of direct interest to Scotland, since all Scottish Tory MEPs had been defeated Feb '90; she was one of the 22 Euro-federalist Tory MEPs who voted for a federal Europe in a motion calling for "a European union on a federal basis" and economic and monetary union, including a single currency; the motion also called for common foreign, security and defence policies with binding guidelines and noted the precedence of European law over national law July '90; the Mistley branch of her Euro-constituency was suspected of having been taken over by the British National Party after it staged hostile demonstrations at events she organised and demanded the resignation of John Major Feb '94; PM John Major was challenged to disown her and 15 other committed federalist Euro-candidates whose commitment to a federal Europe was at odds with the party's manifesto for the Euro-election May '94; was re-elected Euro-MP for North Essex and South Suffolk with a majority of 3,633 June '94; was elected to Bureau of EPP July '94; urged a Europe-wide transport infrastructure June '96; despite 149 other applicants, including Ken Clarke's Special Adviser, David Ruffley, won selection for the Vale of York, only the second new Tory woman to capture a safe seat nomination Nov '96; said that, if elected for the Vale of York, "I will continue to represent my Euro-seat until the elections in 1999; I will not seek re-election" Apr '97; after supporting field sports, was sent an envelope full of razor blades and an abusive message ("murdering bastard") by animal liberationists Apr '97; won the Vale of York by a majority of 9,721, despite a notional swing to Labour of 15.6% May '97; made her Maiden against the referenda on Welsh and Scottish devolution as "a Scot by birth and a Scottish advocate by profession" June '97; opposed "any further erosions of sovereignty or any moves toward federalism" in Europe June '97; wholly opposed the new Labour Government's European policies, especially its signing up to the EU's Social Chapter; also urged a revised timetable for EMU June '97; led a motion urging the National Grid to bury its power lines instead of building pylons across North Yorkshire July '97; urged better consumer protection against high pressure selling of home improvements July '97; was criticised for missing her Saturday surgeries in the Vale of York because of absences in Brussels Oct '97; introduced Bill to curb delays in trials Oct '97;
Born: 20 September 1954, Edinburgh
Family: In '92 she married John Harvey;
Education: Harrogate College '64-73; Edinburgh University '73-77 (LLB Hons); University of Aarhus, Denmark '77-78; trained at Scottish Bar '80-82; was admitted to the Faculty of Advocates, Edinburgh '82;
Occupation: MEP '89-; ex: Political Adviser, to European Democratic Group in European Parliament '83-89; Advocate with Eurpean Community Law Office, Belmont, Brusssels '82-83; Legal Adviser, with Didier & Associates, Brussels, '79-80; Trainee, in Competition Directorate of European Commission, Brussels '78-79;
Traits: Pretty blonde with dark roots; high forehead; intense expression; "a very lively style" and "a particularly distinctive Scottish accent...possibly the impact of Harrogate in earlier and better years" (Scottish Secretary Donald Dewar); has a cursory style of speaking; multilingual (speaks Danish, French, German, Spanish and Italian); enjoys swimming and cinema; used to enjoy beagling and fellwalking (when the candidate for Workington);
Address: House of Commons, Westminster, London SW1A 0AA; The Old Armoury, 3

Museum Street, Saffron Walden, Essex, CB10 1JN; European Parliament, rue Belliard 97, 1047 Brussels, Belgium;
Telephone: 0171 219 3000 (H of C); 44 1799 596349/523621(Fax); 00 322 284 5239/9239(Fax) (home);

Shona McISAAC **Labour** **CLEETHORPES '97-**

Majority: 9,176 over Conservative 4-way;
Description: The renamed former Brigg & Cleethorpes, minus the small Tory-leaning market town of Brigg; based on the traditional seaside resort town of Cleethorpes plus the booming deep-water industrial port of Immingham, with its oil refineries, electric power stations and chemical works; it also includes the market town of Barton-upon-Humber; the seat curls around Grimsby like a kidney; it is a low-pay area, with many part-time jobs;
Position: On Select Committees: on Standards and Privileges '97-, Education and Employment '97- and Northern Ireland '97-; Wandsworth Borough Councillor (Deputy Leader, its Labour Group '92-95) '90-;
Outlook: A women's magazine sub-editor and Blairite moderniser who emerged victorious from her first Parliamentary contest; her previous battles have been against "some of the most Rightwing Tories in the country" (SMcI) in Wandsworth borough and against more traditional 'Old Labour' types there; a Scots-born, Plymouth-educated, "economic migrant" to London;
History: She joined the Labour Party at 25, '85; was elected for Tooting to Wandsworth Borough Council May '90; realising that Labour was not speaking up on the issues that most concerned voters, persuaded her local party to listen to local voters, thus moving it toward 'New Labour'; became Deputy Leader of Labour Group on Wandsworth Borough Council May '92; was selected for Cleethorpes from an all-women short-list Apr '95; urged her opponent Michael Brown to support full disclosure of outside earnings Nov '95; Deputy Leader John Prescott visited the seaside constituency amidst a flurry of sticks of rock and whirly hats Aug '96; with other loyalist Labour candidates wrote to the INDEPENDENT that the Labour Party was "a united dynamic party ready to solve the problems this country faces" Oct '96; attacked Michael Brown as "arrogant" for pretending he did not have to declare the previously-concealed money received from corrupting lobbyist Ian Greer Oct '96; she fought against Michael Brown's effort to force an expensive name-change on the Humberside Police, as part of his "campaign to expunge the name of Humberside from the English language" Mar '97; he counter-attacked against her attacks on his corrupt activities, describing her as a "nobody" whose only policy was "to grin inanely all the way to polling day" Apr '97; he had to be adopted as the Tory election candidate in secret Apr '97; she won the seat by 9,176 on a notional swing of 15.1%, ousting Michael Brown after 14 years May '97; in her Maiden backed the scrapping of Assisted Places Scheme partly because her local education authority was practically at the bottom of the league for class sizes June '97; urged promotion of British seaside resorts June '97; backed ban on fox-hunting June '97; urged an end to "the practice of private slimming clinics prescribing slimming pills" June '97; urged "a national scheme for the grading of guest houses and hotels" June '97; urged the "tackling [of] levels of obesity and

obesity-related illnesses" June '97; urged compulsory swimming lessons June '97; urged action against "misleading nutritional information on food labels" July '97; was named to the Select Committee on Standards and Privileges; this appointment was challenged by Neil Hamilton's friend, retread MP Gerald Howarth, because she might have to judge the alleged misdeeds of her former opponent, Michael Brown July '97;
Born: 3 April 1960, Dunfermline
Family: Daughter, of Angus McIsaac, "my father was in the Forces" as a cook in the Royal Navy, and Isa (Nicol), shop assistant/school dinner lady; m '90 Peter Keith, Advertising Manager, Chartered Institute of Bankers;
Education: Attended Forces schools, including the Canadian Forces school at NATO headquarters in Brussels; Barne Barton Secondary Modern, Plymouth; Stoke Damerel High, Plymouth; Durham University (BSc in Geography) '78-81;
Occupation: Journalist: Sub-Editor on WOMAN, CHAT, BELLA and SLIMMER (NUJ) '86-95; Lifeguard in Tooting '85-86; employed on trade and specialist publications '81-85; Hospital Orderly '80;
Traits: Big head of curly red hair; enjoys cycling, archaeology of the UK, and jewellry design; as a qualified lifeguard, was involved in a number of rescues in Tooting Pool in the mid-'80s;
Address: House of Commons, Westminster, London SW1A 0AA;
Telephone: 0171 219 5801 (H of C); 0181 682 0424 (home);

Mrs Rose McKENNA CBE, JP **Labour** **CUMBERNAULD & KILSYTH '97-**

Majority: 11,128 over SNP 7-way;
Description: The new town of Cumbernauld 15 miles northeast of Glasgow, linked to the smaller, older town of Kilsyth across the river on the north bank of the river Kelvin; many of the new town houses have been bought by their occupiers, without helping the Tory vote; the SNP made the main advance in '92, helped by the counter-devolutionary stance of the then incumbent MP, Norman Hogg;
Position: On the Select Committee on Scottish Affairs '97-; on the European Union's Committee of the Regions '93-; ex: North Lanarkshire Councillor '95-97; on Cumbernauld Development Corporation '85-97; President, of the Convention of Scottish Local Authorities (COSLA) '94-96; in the Scottish Constitutional Convention til '92; on the Labour NEC's Local Government Committee '94-96; Cumbernauld and Kilsyth District Councillor (Provost '88-92, Leader '84-88) '84-96; Chairman, Cumbernauld CLP '79-85;
Outlook: Respected, strongly pro-devolution, pro-EU Blairite moderniser: "devolution for Scotland would change the UK from being the most centralised country in Europe" (RMcK); she "has worked hard on the [Scottish Parliament] project for a long time" (Scottish Secretary Donald Dewar, with whom she worked in the Scottish Constitutional Convention until '92); "a heavyweight of local government" "and a leading exponent of New Labour" (Jim McBeth, SCOTSMAN); the ninth woman MP in Scottish Labour's once male chauvinist ranks; co-founder, with Jim Murphy, new MP for Eastwood, of the 'Network' of local authority potentates anxious to move the Scottish Labour Party away from the Left and closer to the

Centrist national Labour leadership; also close to Anne McGuire, new MP for Stirling;
History: She joined the Labour Party on moving from Glasgow to Cumbernauld '66; campaigned for devolution '79; was elected Chairman of the Cumbernauld CLP '79; was elected to Cumbernauld and Kilsyth District Council May '84; became Leader of Cumbernauld and Kilsyth District Council May '88; became Provost of Cumbernauld and Kilsyth May '88; joined the multi-party Constitutional Convention to seek a consensus about a Scottish Parliament; became President of COSLA '94; was elected to North Lanarkshire Council in the unitary elections May '95; was elected to the Scottish Executive of the Labour Party '96 was selected, almost at the last minute, to replace the suddenly-retired incumbent, anti-devolution MP, Norman Hogg; "there were nine candidates, five of whom were men; the four best candidates happened to be women" (RMcK) Mar-Apr '97; during the campaign she was able to send volunteers to her friend Anne McGuire, fighting marginal Stirling Apr '96; she won the seat on a 2.9% swing from the SNP by a majority of 11,128 May '97; made her Maiden in the debate on the referenda on devolution to Wales and Scotland May '97; congratulated Scottish Secretary Donald Dewar on his White Paper, enthusing: "we are on the threshold of the most exciting change in the constitution of this country for at least 300 years"; asked him to accept that "thanks ar due to the Constitutional Convention of which I have been a member since the beginning" July '97; it was disclosed that she had attended 9 out of 10 meetings of the European [Union's] Committee of the Regions July '97; was named to the Select Committee on Scottish Affairs, the Joint Committee on Statutory Instruments July '97; gave up her post as North Lanarkshire Councillor Aug '97;
Born: 8 May 1941, Renfrewshire
Family: She is married, with four grown-up children;
Education: St Augustine's Comprehensive; Notre Dame College of Education (Diploma in Primary Education '74);
Occupation: Former Primary School Teacher '74-94 (gave up the job to become President of the Convention of Scottish Local Authorities in '94); previously had various secretarial positions in the private sector '58-65;
Traits: Grey/blonde curly hair; rounded face with slight underchin; square specs; slow-spoken style; Roman Catholic;
Address: House of Commons, Westminster, London SW1A 0AA; lives in Cumbernauld;
Telephone: 0171 219 3000 (H of C);

WELCOME WORDS

One of the MPs' bouquets most welcome among the occasional brickbats is the frequent refrain: "Thanks for recalling that speech! I had completely forgotten ever making it...."

PROSPECTIVES SATISFACTION

The 1 May 1997 general election increase in the number of Labour and Liberal Democrat MPs provided what might be called "archive satisfaction". In a fair number of cases we have been tracking such candidates as "possible" victors for as many as four or five contests, badgering them for information and writing up their profiles, just in case. In their cases - as in the case of the 17 'retreads' - there was the satisfaction of knowing that the previous efforts were not wasted.

'Tony' (Anthony) McNULTY **Labour** **HARROW EAST '97-**

Majority: 9,738 over Conservative 6-way;
Description: The down-the-hill, less-affluent part of the outer northwest London suburb; it includes Harrow town centre, Wealdstone, Harrow Weald, Kenton and Stanmore; it has a 30% ethnic minority, mostly middle-class Indians, but also strong Irish and Jewish contingents; in '92 it provided its longtime incumbent Tory MP, Hugh Dykes, with an 11,098 majority; in May '94 Labour won 14 council seats, the LibDems won 11 and the Tories 8, ending Conservative control;
Position: On European Standing Committee B '97-; Harrow Borough Councillor (Leader '96-, Deputy Leader '90-96, of its Labour Group) '86-; ex: on the Greater London Labour Executive '87-90;
Outlook: An almost wholly locally-focussed Blairite loyalist; a locally-raised former Poly lecturer besotted with education in Harrow; is probably the only MP who can have an orgasm over a White Paper on education; in the Socialist Education Association and the Fabian Society;
History: He joined the Labour Party at 20, '78; was elected to Harrow Borough Council May '86; became a member of the Greater London Labour Party Executive '87; became Deputy Leader of Harrow Council's minority Labour Group May '90; contested Harrow East against incumbent Hugh Dykes, increasing the Labour vote from 23.5% to 33.8% almost entirely at the expense of the LibDems Apr '92; was re-selected for Harrow East June '95; won the seat on a near-record swing of 18.1% - among the largest in the country -achieving a majority of 9,738, ending Hugh Dykes' 27-year reign May '97; was told by Health Minister Alan Milburn that, because of spending restraints, there was no chance of saving Edgware Hospital's Accident and Emergency facility, on which he had campaigned May '97; his Maiden, apart from a handsome tribute to his Tory predecessor, concentrated wholly on education in Harrow "which has emerged as one of the most effective and best-performing local education authorities in the country"; "Harrow is, without doubt, the best comprehensive education authority in the country" May '97; urged alteration in the performance league tables for schools to take into account "value-added data, the inclusion of absent and statemented [or mentally-retarded] pupils" June '97; asked PM Tony Blair to agree that "the repeated assurances of the previous Government that class sizes had no consequence on educational performance defied the instincts of all parents and common sense" June '97; urged reduction of waste in the NHS June '97; co-sponsored motion urging a public inquiry into the "many scandals" in Conservative-controlled Westminster Council June '97; co-sponsored motion attacking BA for its selling off of its catering division because of the "disproportionate effect" it "would have on the Asian community in west London" July '97; was wildly enthusiastic about David Blunkett's White Paper on schools, deploring the Tory Opposition's carping, unlike the Harrow Conservatives who, for eight of his eleven years on the local council, ran Harrow's state education on a non-partisan basis with "full support from the Labour Group of which I was the Leader, and the Liberal Democrats" July '97;
Born: 3 November 1958, Kensington, London
Family: Son, of James Anthony McNulty, self-employed builder from Donegal, and Eileen Anne (Dawson) from Kilburn;

Education: Salvatorian College, Wealdstone; Stanmore Sixth Form College; Liverpool University (BA Hons); Virginia Polytechnic Institute and State University (MA);
Occupation: Principal Lecturer, at The Business School, Polytechnic (now University) of North London (NATFHE) '83-97;
Traits: Short dark hair; specs; gets turned on about education; also enjoys cinema, Rugby, football and Gaelic games;
Address: House of Commons, Westminster, London SW1A 0AA;
Telephone: 0171 219 4108 (H of C); 0468 392882 (mobile);

Fiona (Margaret) MACTAGGART **Labour** **SLOUGH '97-**

Majority: 13,071 over Conservative 6-way;
Description: Betjeman-damned unglamorous but prosperous working-class town to the West of London; has Europe's largest industrial estate, substantial council housing and a population a third of which has immigrant origins; its middle-class pockets do not explain the success of Tory MP John Watts in winning three elections before he fled before '97, but not to safety;
Position: Founder-Director and Associate Editor of RENEWAL '93-; ex: Chairman, of Executive of LIBERTY '92-96; Wandsworth Borough Councillor (Leader of Opposition '88-90) '86-90; Director, of Joint Council for the Welfare of Immigrants '82-86; Vice President and National Secretary of National Union of Students '78-81;
Outlook: Very wealthy Fabian anti-racist who rejected her Conservative inheritance from both her parents; an assiduous, intelligent, well-researched questioner and debater; believes taxation is a tool which "should be spent efficiently, otherwise it is robbery"; is in favour of electoral reform, divergent forms of education; is very mildly Eurosceptic, partly dating from the childhood influences of her anti-European Tory father who "told me that if we went in, chocolate would turn pink and kippers would turn grey"; she is mainly anti-CAP; "ambitious, but may not be Blairite enough to fly high" (NEW STATESMAN); a former university lecturer and primary school teacher;
History: Her great grandfather, Sir John Mactaggart, was the Treasurer of the first-ever branch of the Labour Party under Keir Hardie; he left it to support Ramsay Macdonald in the National Government '31; her mother's father, Sir Herbert Williams Bt, was a Conservative MP; her baronet father was a Tory Parliamentary candidate '45, '70; he influenced her against the Common Market '71-72; she became Vice President '78-80 and National Secretary '80-81 of the National Union of Students; she attended the Youth Festival in Cuba '78; she joined the Labour Party '80; became the Director of the Joint Council for the Welfare of Immigrants '82; "I was associated with a series of cases that went to the European Court of Human Rights involving women whose foreign husbands were not allowed to join them under the immigration rules"; was elected a Wandsworth Councillor, for Shaftesbury Ward May '86; her father, a Rightwing Tory who was a member of the Monday Club (where he was associated with young Gerald Howarth), left her a fifth of his £6,465,367 estate '87; she was elected Leader of Wandsworth's Labour Group '88; was elected to Executive of LIBERTY '92; on the all-woman shortlist imposed on Slough, became the main challenger to Brenda Lopez,

Chairman of the Slough Borough Council's Housing Committee and wife of the previous Labour candidate in '87, Eddie Lopez, who had failed to retake the seat by 514 votes; although she had only two nominations initially, she defeated Mrs Lopez Sep '95; at annual conference at Blackpool made a strong attack on racism which, she claimed, was being fed by the Conservatives Oct '95; rejected a GUARDIAN correspondent's proposal to wipe out Slough, pointing to "our spectacular Richard-Rogers-designed Learning Resource Centre at Thames Valley University", "our 14th century manor house, Upton Court, the exquisite St Michael's Church and a host of other buildings" Dec '96; admitted she was mildly Eurosceptic: "I describe myself as a sceptic and would like to see us rid of the wasteful Common Agricultural Policy" Mar '97; won Slough on a 13.7% swing. chalking up a majority of 13,071 May '97; in her Maiden backed the winding up of the Assisted Places Scheme: "we have not heard about the degree to which most children who benefit from the scheme already have educational advantage within their families; more than two-thirds of those pupils' mothers have themselves received a private or selective education, and their mothers are four times as likely as members of the general population to have an A-level"; backed the use of the money saved to cut class sizes: "I have been a primary teacher and I remember how much more exhausted I was in the year in which my class numbers increased by five pupils over the previous year" June '97; urged a reassessment of local flood threats June '97; congratulated Government on its pledge of a public inquiry into abuse in residential homes of people with learning difficulties, but asked assurance that the report would be made public July '97; asked how many husbands, wives, fiances and fiancees - previously banned under the primary purpose rule -would now be admitted and when July '97; backed a motion urging limits on the number of asylum seekers detained July '97; asked how employment would be suited to the needs of the unemployed July '97; complained that visa computer failures in British consulate in Islamabad had blocked visits from her constituents' relatives Oct '97; applauded the Government's Special Immigration Appeals Commission Bill to accord better appeal rights for those threatened with deportation for suspected terrorism Oct '97;

Born: 12 September 1953, London

Family: Daughter, late Sir Ian Auld Mactaggart 3rd Bt, multi-millionaire Glasgow property developer and Tory candidate in '45 and '70, and Rosemary (Williams), daughter of Conservative MP Sir Herbert Williams 1st Bt; both parents were Conservative local councillors;

Education: Cheltenham Ladies' College; King's College, London (BA); Goldsmiths College (PGCE); Institute of Education, London (MA);

Occupation: Lecturer, in Primary Education, at Institute of Education (AUT) '92-97; ex: Primary School Teacher, Lyndhurst School, Camberwell (NUT) '87-92; General Secretary, Joint Council for the Welfare of Immigrants '82-86; Public Relations Officer, National Council for Voluntary Organisations '81;

Traits: Strapping; dark brown hair; strong chin; big specs; "I [was] a primary school teacher and I have a voice that children can hear at the other end of the playground" (FM); thoughtful; garrulous extrovert; enjoys watching Steve Bochco TV productions;

Address: House of Commons, Westminster London, SW1A 0AA; 29 Church Street, Slough, Berkshire SL1 1PL; 61 Taybridge Road, London SW11 5PX;

Telephone: 0171 219 3416 (H of C); 0171 228 4468; 01753 517207 (home); 01753 518161;

'Tony' (Anthony) McWALTER Labour-Co-operative HEMEL HEMPSTEAD '97-

Majority: 3,636 over Conservative 5-way;
Description: The Hertfordshire New Town, restored to its original name and core, having shed successive Tory-leaning affluent add-ons, the last being Tring; it still has 30% of local authority housing despite sales to occupiers; it has a broad economic base with relatively few manual workers and only a tiny (3%) non-white population;
Position: Treasurer, National Committee of Philosophy '94-; ex: North Hertfordshire District Councillor '79-83; Chairman, Hertfordshire North CLP '79;
Outlook: Possibly the first Kantian philosopher in the Commons; "I am very keen on Kant; I think people who don't know why they're in politics are less likely to do the public a service than those who have thought through how to live their lives; I don't apologise for having giving that protracted thought; I don't talk about Kant on the doorstep, but I hope we will one day have a Kantian ethic underpinning society; it infuses what I do; it's about respect for persons, universality and welfare for everyone"; a many-sided veteran candidate who has been fifth-time-lucky; a onetime lorry-driver who lectures on philosophy; has long been on the libertarian Left of the party; he is against intensive agriculture, has not believed that the Irish Border can be sustained without major bloodshed, is ambivalent about proportional representation; has given evidence on green issues at three public enquiries '80-86; a multi-cause groupie over the years: Amnesty International, Greenpeace, Friends of the Earth, SERA, League Against Cruel Sports, Socialist Countryside Group, World Development Movement, Compassion in World Farming, CND, formerly Anti-Apartheid
History: His family was vaguely Labour; at school he was vaguely Conservative; he joined the Labour Party at 28, '73; opposed Chancellor Denis Healey's economic "fix" at annual conference Oct '76; favoured the Bullock Report on industrial relations '77; at annual Labour conference opposed the block vote Oct '80; at annual conference moved the resolution that the EEC should be less market-orientated Oct '81; contested the Hertfordshire Euro-seat June '84; complained about the GUARDIAN's exaggerating Alliance political clout in St Albans, where he was the Parliamentary candidate; contested St Albans, coming 3rd with 11%, a third of the Alliance vote June '87; having been stigmatised as a CND member by Michael Heseltine, contested the Bedfordshire South Euro-seat June '89; contested Luton North against John Carlisle coming second with 32.9% Apr '92; was selected for Hemel Hempstead '95; unexpectedly won the changed seat on a notional swing of 12%, ending the 14-year reign of its incumbent Tory MP and Minister, Robert Jones May '97; complained of "punitive levels of settlement" under the Child Support Agency, citing a constituent earning £14,000 asked to pay £500 a month, after having left his ex-wife the family home May '97; in his noncontroversial Maiden urged a new road to make his strained local hospital more accessible June '97; co-sponsored motion backing cuts in NHS bureaucracy June '97; co-sponsored motion with Campaign Groupies criticising BA for "intimidatory tactics" toward its striking staff July '97; backed ban on arms exports to Indonesia July '97; enthused about White Paper, 'Excellence in Schools' as making it clear "that the system we have inherited is intolerable and must be changed"; his criticism was that it did not allow for enough moral enlightenment July '97;
Born: 20 March 1945, Worksop, Notts

Family: Son, of late Joe McWalter, painter and decorator, and late Ann (Murray), office cleaner; m 1st '78 Sue (Curtis), careers officer; divorced; m 2nd '91 Karry (Omer) lecturer; 1 stepson, Jack '84, 2d Sophie '91, Grace '94;
Education: Sacred Heart RC Primary, Ruislip; St Benedict's, Ealing; University College of Wales, Aberystwyth (BSc in Maths, BSc Class I Hons in Philosophy); McMaster University, Canada (MA); University College, Oxford University (BPhil, MLitt);
Occupation: Principal Lecturer, in Philosophy and Computing at Hatfield Polytechnic/University of Hertfordshire (NATFHE); its Branch Chairman '81-90) '74-97; Author: Kant and His Influence (Editor, 1990); ex: Teacher, at Cardinal Wiseman School, Greenford '63-64; Lorry Driver (TGWU) '63-64;
Traits: Balding, with greying fringe; specs; engaging manner; slightly puritanical (upbraided journalist Paul Routledge for swearing in Annie's Bar); Catholic-educated; enjoys squash, snooker, bridge (master ranking at contract), tennis and computing;
Address: House of Commons, Westminster, London SW1A 0AA; 5A Marlowes, Hemel Hempstead, Herts HP1 1LA;
Telephone: 0171 219 4547 (H of C); 01442 251251 (home);

Humfrey (Jonathan) MALINS CBE **Conservative** **WOKING '97-**

Majority: 5,678 over Liberal Democrat 7-way;
Description: Affluent Surrey's largest town, slimmed down almost to its Woking borough core in the '95 boundary revisions; it has working-class terraces and a council housing estate, but a repetition of '92-style voting figures in '97 would have yielded a Tory majority of 20,000;
Former Seat: Croydon North West '83-92
Position: On Select Committee on Home Affairs '97-; Chairman of Trustees, of the Immigration Advisory Service '93-; ex: Leading Advocate, for Conservative Party before Boundary Commissioners '93-94; Vice Chairman, Conservative MPs' Legal Committee '86-88; PPS: to Virginia Bottomley '89-91, to Tim Renton and Douglas Hogg, Home Office Ministers '87-89; on Select Committees: on Consolidation of Bills '83, on Broadcasting '89-92; Mole Valley District Councillor (Chairman of Housing) '73-83; Chairman, of Dorking Young Conservatives '70-73;
Outlook: One of the exceptions: the return as a 'retread' of an enlightened liberal 'One Nation' Tory; an independent-minded, socially-conscious but puritanical libertarian who favoured hanging and nuclear power but has also favoured proportional representation; tends to speak from his own professional experience; as a Recorder is a sensible reformer of court procedures and druggie criminals; has "a good record on raising [immigration] issues" (Labour Minister Mike O'Brien);
History: He was a slow starter in politics because both his grandfather and father were non-political clergymen; dabbled in the Oxford Union; was elected Chairman of the Dorking Young Conservatives '70; was elected to the Mole Valley District Council May '73; contested hopeless Toxteth, Liverpool Feb and Oct '74; fought Lewisham East May '79; was elected for Croydon North West, ousting the by-election-winning Liberal, Bill Pitt June '83; condemned miners' extra-Parliamentary opposition July '83; in Maiden criticised forced fingerprinting and

intimate body searches Nov '83; opposed Austin Mitchell's Bill to end the solicitors' conveyancing monopoly Dec '83; rebelled by abstaining on Rates (capping) Biill Jan '84; supported divorce reform Bill Feb '84; backed Rugby tour of South Africa Feb '84; introduced petition for proportional representation July '84; rebelled against Government's Education (Corporal Punishment) Bill, which allowed parents to permit caning Jan '85; complained of tremendous local abuse of bed-and-breakfast accommodation by unscrupulous hotel owners Apr '85; voted against deregulating Sunday trading May '85; voted aginst generous awards of Top Salaries Review Body July'85; complained of inadequate funding for urban programme in deprived areas of southern Croydon Nov '85; again voted against deregulating Sunday trading Apr '86; supported right of parents to withdraw their children from sex education classes Oct '86; welcomed initial contribution of Public Order Act to curbing hippy convoy invasions Nov '86; deplored lack of spiritual leadership among modern clergy Dec '86; backed Don Anderson's Bill to improve fire precautions for bedsits Feb '87; voted to restore capital punishment Apr '87; abstained from opposing Michael Mates' proposal to adjust poll tax to income Apr '88; urged an overhaul of legal aid May '88; co-sponsored Andrew Hunter's Control of Smoke Pollution Bill Dec '88; voted against allowing divorced men to be ordained July '89; because of Croydon's awful traffic levels, urged "a much more efficient, faster and cheaper transport system" June '91; in a housing magazine ROOF interview said that one of the reasons for home repossessions was over-extending on mortgages Dec '91; he was defeated in Croydon North West by one of the biggest swings in the London area Apr '92; he founded the new Immigrant Advisory Service; the Tory ex-MP, Keith Best, was appointed its £35,000-a-year Director Mar '93; he appeared as Leading Advocate for the Conservative Party before the Boundary Commisioners, when Labour's representatives were thought to have done much better '93-94; was selected for Woking, succeeding Sir Cranley Onslow Sep '95; held Woking, with a majority of 5,678 (down from 17,731) after a 10.4% notional swing to the Liberal Democrats May '97; joined William Hague's campaign team May '97; led motion urging the retention of tax relief on medical insurance for the over-60s May '97; said both the Tory and Labour curbs on shooters were "hasty" and punished "innocent sportsmen" June '97; pointed out that the Immigration Advisory Service which he had founded four years before was at the forefront of calls to set up a register of scrupulous immigration advisers June '97; was awarded a CBE for services to immigration policy June '97; asked a chain of connected questions on drug and alcohol abuse in prisons and how their importation could be halted July '97; urged cuts in legal aid costs July '97; was named to the Select Committee on Home Affairs July '97; urged raised requirements for teachers' training colleges entry July '97; warned about Somalis arriving by Eurostar at Waterloo claiming asylum and benefits although they had mostly come from safe third countries July '97; on the basis of his experience as a Recorder and former Stipendiary Magistrate, said courts could be speeded by limiting unnecessary delays July '97; insisted that his UK Immigration Advisory Service provided "extremely cost-effective legal advice" in comparison with providing legal aid to immigrants July '97; since half the crimes he had tried in court were drug-related, he urged stronger action against drug-smuggling into prisons and more rehabilitation of druggie prisoners July '97; urged "real power, real money and a real target" for the newly-appointed 'drugs tsar' Oct '97;

Born: 31 July 1945, Nuneaton

Family: Son, of Rev Peter Malins, Army Chaplain, and late Lilian (Dingley); m '79, Lynda Ann (Petman) who worked in Probation Service; 1s Harry '85, 1d Katherine '82;;

Education: St John's School, Leatherhead; Brasenose College, Oxford University (MA Hons in Law); College of Law, Guildford;

Occupation: Solicitor '67-, Partner '73- in Tuck and Mann (Dorking solicitors specialising in crime, matrimonial and criminal advocacy); Recorder '96-, Assistant Recorder '91-96, in

Kingston and Southwark Crown Courts; ex: Acting Metropolitan Stipendiary Magistrate '92-97
Traits: Oval face; parted hair; puritanical; sports enthusiast: golfer (former Secretary of Commons Golf Team, Captain of Commons Rugby Union team, previously played for Oxford, Richmond and South of Englaned against the New Zealand All Blacks in '72; "my father was a Cambridge Blue and both my brother [Julian] and I played for Oxford"; "my most terrifying moment was when I was picked to play for the University against the Australian touring team in 1967 at the tender age of 22"; "Ross Cullen, the Australian hooker was so frustrated that he tried to sink his teeth into my ear; that appendage was covered in Vaseline"; "thank God for Vaseline!";
Address: House of Commons, Westminster, London SW1A 0AA; Highbury, Westcott Street, Westcott, Dorking, Surrey RH4 3NU;
Telephone: 0171 219 4169 (H of C);

Judy MALLABER **Labour** **AMBER VALLEY '97-**

Majority: 11,613 over Conservative 4-way;
Description: A virtually-unaltered part-gritty, part-lovely East Midlands industrial seat in mid-Derbyshire, embracing Alfreton, Heanor, Ripley and Crich, the setting for TV's 'Peak Practice'; the site of the little-known Pentrich Rebellion of 1817; "we are north of Derby, south of Chesterfield and we are a gateway to the Peak District National Park" (JM); it lost its last pit in the '60s but has acquired a diverse industrial base; although cocky, wealthy Phillip Oppenheim - son of Sally - won it at 27 in '83, he expected to be defeated in '92, and, with the '95 local elections, was certain long before '97;
Position: On Select Committee on Education and Employment '97-; ex: Director, Local Government Information Unit '87-95; on Labour's Greater London Regional Executive '93-95-; Vice Chair and Chair, Hornsey and Wood Green Constituency Labour Party '93-96; Chair, Labour Research Department '73-75;
Outlook: The area's first woman MP, a highly-intelligent, fluent and witty speaker; recently "proud to be a part of Tony Blair's New Labour" but was initially in the Communist Party and Chair of Labour Research Department; most of her career as an Oxford-trained economist was as a researcher in NUPE; recently in Liberty (ex-NCCL), Socialist Education Association, Friends of the Earth, Amnesty, Action for Southern Africa (ex-Anti-Apartheid);
History: She joined the Communist Party '76; left the Communist Party '78; joined the Labour Party '80; as Vice Chair and Chair of Hornsey and Wood Green CLP, helped increase its membership to 2,000 '93-96; was selected for Amber Valley from an all-women short-list Apr '95; Labour took two-thirds of the vote in local council elections May '95; was elected for Amber Valley on a swing of 11.7%, winning 54.7% of the votes and achieving a majority of 11,613 over incumbent Tory MP and Minister Phillip Oppenheim May '97; described Westminster as looking like a "public schoolboys' feast" May '97; backed Chancellor Gordon Brown in his ceding to the Bank of England the right to set interest rates May '97; in her fluent, informed and witty Maiden emphasised a minimum wage as the path to a high-skill competitive economy, the need to avoid opencast mining and the need for skilling the young

May '97; backed ban on fox-hunting June '97; congratulated Northern Ireland Secretary Mo Mowlam on "her excellent start" in the "Northern Ireland peace process" June '97; co-sponsored motion urging a review of rape law to remove "the defendant's right to cross-examine the victim" June '97; co-sponsored motion urging a creche at affordable prices for all those working in the Palace of Westminster June '97; urged "quality jobs and training, not makeweight jobs" for her hopeful young unemployed July '97; was named to the Select Committee on Education and Employment July '97;

Born: 10 July 1951, Colindale, London

Family: Daughter, of Kenneth Mallaber and Margaret Joyce (Eddowes), both librarians;

Education: North London Collegiate, Edgware; St Anne's College, Oxford University (BA Hons in PPE);

Occupation: Research Fellow '95-96, Director '87-95, Deputy Director 85-87 of Local Government Information Unit (UNISON); Research Officer, NUPE '75-85; Lecturer in Economics;

Traits: Frizzy, curly, reddish mop of hair; heart-shaped face; small eyes; specs; confident; combative; fast-talking; enjoys cinema, theatre;

Address: House of Commons, Westminster, London, SW1A 0AA; EPOS House, 268 Heage Road, Ripley, Derbyshire;

Telephone: 0171 219 3428/0989(Fax) (H of C); 01773 745002 (constituency);

John MAPLES **Conservative** **STRATFORD-ON-AVON '97-**

Majority: 14.106 over Liberal Democrat 8-way;

Description: Shakespeare's home town, set amidst 120 villages in beautiful farming country in safely Conservative south Warwickshire, where the last witch-lynching took place in the '40s, and a Ku Klux Klan headquarters was unearthed in the '70s; it has suffered the resignations of John Profumo, Angus Maude and Alan Howarth; in '95 it lost 5,000 voters to Warwick and Leamington;

Former Seat: Lewisham West '83-92;

Position: Shadow Health Secretary '97-; ex: Deputy Chairman, Conservative Party '94-95; Economic Secretary to the Treasury '90-92; PPS, to Norman Lamont '87-90;

Outlook: Highly-intelligent, privately-objective retread barrister-businessman with plentiful private means who previously won fame as "a user-friendly face to make soothing noises" (Michael White, GUARDIAN); when he lost marginal Lewisham West in '92, he became Chairman and Chief Executive of Saatchi & Saatchi Government Relations Worldwide; was then also named the Conservative Party's Deputy Chairman in '94 because he "was seen as politically astute and financially sound", "the professional pair of hands" (Alice Thompson, TIMES); after his '97 return for Stratford-on-Avon was rewarded by Hague with the Shadow Health Secretary job after playing the unlikely role of a simple-minded Rightwing partisan in this field; this may have been an effort to overcome his disadvantage in an even more Rightwing Tory Parliamentary party of having been, in the '80s, "a wealthy businessman with Tory 'wet' credentials" (Michael White, GUARDIAN); but it reversed his famous private internal warning in '94 for Tories to stay off this subject; before his '92 defeat he was seen as the "Treasury's rising star", "adroit at striking a balance, demonstrating a political sensitivity" (Philip Stephens, FINANCIAL TIMES); is more Rightwing in economics than in social matters;

History: After working abroad '67-78, "I became actively involved in politics in the mid-1970s because I was concerned at the direction our country was taking; above all, I wanted to see the re-establishment of a free-enterprise economy"; contested Vauxhall by-election for GLC Feb '80; won marginal Lewisham West from Labour, unseating Chris Price June '83; urged Government to sign Protocol Six of European Convention to abolish the death penalty July '83; in his Maiden, urged an "extensive reform of local government finance and of the rating system" July '83; backed the right of Jews to leave the USSR July '83; backed free bus travel for pensioners Oct '83; backed the abolition of GLC so London ratepayers would not have to pay for its "financial excesses" Nov '83; rebelled to support the House Buyers Bill to break the solicitors' conveyancing monopoly Dec '83; gave 13 reasons for taking London Transport away from the GLC July '84; welcomed ratecapping of Lewisham Council Aug '84; with Nigel Forman produced 'Work to be Done', a pamphlet urging cuts in unemployment Feb '95; urged a radical shift in personal taxation to cut rates and allowances Apr '85; urged relaxation of rent controls on flats to help solve homelessness June '85; complained about refusal of Ulster politicians to make any compromises June '85; urged probationary licenses for new council tenants to prove they could be good neighbours Nov '85; urged retention of jury trials, even in complex fraud trials Jan '86; urged curb on credit, to help channel more into productive investment Feb '86; urged decentralisation of business from London June '86; attacked banks for aggressive lending on property and personal spending Dec '86; explaining he did "some work for a company that manages a Business Expansion Scheme", urged a better carry-over of tax relief Apr '87; increased his majority by 1,000 after a campaign attacking the "extravagant, inefficient, loony-Left excesses of Lewisham Council" June '87; was named PPS to Norman Lamont, Chief Secretary to the Treasury July '87; opposed uprating of child benefit, insisting the principle of universal benefits was a recipe for high taxation July '87; voted against 2nd Reading of David Alton's abortion-curbing Bill Jan '88; backed televising of Commons Feb '88; backed a 26-week ceiling for abortion May '88; welcomed refusal to refer the takeover of Rowntree by Nestle, despite the "whingeing " of MPs who probably did not know until two months before that Nestle was Swiss May '88; voted against restoring capital punishment June '88; said, "many of us think it is wrong that the Inland Renue is allowed to take £4.5b from husbands so that the Department of Social Security can give it back to their wives" in child benefit Oct '88; wittily seconded the Loyal Address Nov '88; defended rate-capping for Lewisham because of the "outrageous waste, inefficiency and extraordinarily distorted sense of priorities" of its local Labour councillors, including their tolerance of rent arrears Feb '89; said child benefit should be concentrated on the most needy July '89; opposed any more motorways being driven through the middle of London; improving public transport was the answer Nov '89; insisted the student loan Bill was the only way of expanding the number of students in higher education Dec '89; backed the Consumer Guarantee Bill to prevent consumers from being "ripped off and sold shoddy goods" Jan '90; was not sure the Sexual Offences Bill would curb kerb-crawling Feb '90; was named Economic Secretary to the Treasury July '90; was thought to have voted for Michael Heseltine rather than Mrs Thatcher in the 1st round of the Leadership contest Nov '90; told Channel 4: "I think you are not going to see significant growth until next year" July '91; was very open in declaring his former involvement in Lloyd's Oct '91; was considered to have engineered the Keynesian suspension of stamp duty to get the housing market going Dec '91; lost his Lewisham West seat on a 6.2% swing to Labour, from the tactical voting of LibDems in southeast London Apr '92; was named Chairman and Chief Executive of Saatchi and

Saatchi Government Communications Worldwide July '92; sought nomination for the Newbury by-election but failed to get it Mar '93; wrote the famous leaked Maples Memorandum after interviewing 80 former Tory voters: said they thought the Major Government was weak, divided, clumsy, lacking in direction and responsible for the recession still going on; to recover these disenchanted Tories, he suggested silence on the NHS, using Tory backbench "yobbos" to bruise Tony Blair, repeating endlessly "killer facts" (like 1m more treated annually through NHS reforms); since living standards would fall for two years, he urged delaying increases in VAT on fuel and backed increased taxes on fat cats' perks Sep '94; his leaked proposals to use Tory backbench "yobbos" to put Tony Blair off his stroke was deprecated by Speaker Boothroyd Nov '94; told BBC: "it is perfectly clear to me that most Labour councillors do not have their hands in the till" Mar '95; blamed the party's terrible results in council elections on disenchantment with the economy May '95; was short-listed for Hampshire North East, with Nick St Aubyn, John Bercow, Hugh Summerson, Keith Simpson and James Arbuthnot (who won) Sep '95; was short-listed for Kensington and Chelsea Oct '95; defeating Desmond Swayne and Hugh Summerson, was selected from a short-list of three for Stratford-on-Avon, whose former Tory MP, Alan Howarth, had defected to Labour Dec '95; retained Stratford with a majority of 14,106 (down from Alan Howarth's 22,892), after a 5.2% swing to the LibDems May '97; became a member of William Hague's campaign team, because he fulfilled the "five Maples rules": an ability to unite the party, to perform well in the Commons, rebuild policy, rebuild the party base, and to have voter appeal May '97; staunchly defended fundholding as "one of the great successes of the NHS" July '97; after Hague's victory in the leadership campaign, was named Shadow Health Secretary in a Right-dominated Shadow Cabinet July '97;

Born: 22 April 1943, Hampshire

Family: Son, Thomas Cradock Maples, director of wine company (Bushell Maples), and Hazel Mary (Olive); m 1st '?? ????? (?Maiden?) divorced '81; m 2nd '86, Jane (Corbin) award-winning TV investigative journalist; 1s Tom '89, 1d Rose '92;

Education: Marlborough College; Downing College, Cambridge University (2:1 in Law); Harvard Business School; Inns of Court (passed 21st out of 650 in Bar Finals); foreign language schools in Spain and France;

Occupation: Chairman and Chief Executive, Saatchi & Saatchi Government Communications Worldwide '92-; Barrister '65-; Shareholder: Formby Maples and Company '87-90, SEP Industrial Holdings PLc '88-; ex: Name in Lloyd's '83-89; unusually, made an estimated profit of £20,000 after underwriting £250,000 in '88; Consultant, with Alexander Stenhouse Group '84-90; Shareholder: Medisport International Ltd '79-87, Hewhand Ltd '80-86, Leopard Investments '74-84, Dolphin Investments Ltd '80-84; placed "on behalf of a BES fund, a modest £5m in 20 or so firms over five years" (Michael White, GUARDIAN); worked abroad '67-78

Traits: Tall; grey, parted wavy hair; handsome; persuasive; moderate-sounding; sardonic; "a quiet, if occasionally laconic, style" (Philip Stephens, FINANCIAL TIMES); "urbane good looks and smooth television performances" (David Graves and Julie Kirkbride, DAILY TELEGRAPH); enjoys sailing, skiing, cricket (his XI beat that of his then neighbour, Colin Moynihan, in '91);

Address: House of Commons, Westminster, London SW1 0AA;

Telephone: 0171 219 5495 (H o C); 01789 292723 (constituency);

Gordon MARSDEN **Labour** **BLACKPOOL SOUTH '97-**

Majority: 11,616 over Conservative 3-way;
Description: Three-quarters of old Blackpool South, extended to embrace one-quarter of old Blackpool North; although Blackpool is the premier northern working-class resort, many of its voters are seaside landladies, whose grey heads used to provide massed support for Tory conferences there;
Position: On Select Committee on Deregulation '97-; Secretary, PLP Education and Employment Committee '97-; Treasurer, all-party Arts and Heritage Parliamentary Group '97-; Chairman, Fabian Society's Programme Committee '96-; on Fabian National Executive; on Board of Institute of Historical Research '93-; Vice President, British Resorts Association;
Outlook: Pro-European Fabian academic; an "intellectual Rightwing moderniser" (RED PEPPER); says: "on privatisation, everything is up for review; it doesn't matter if a cat is black or white, if it catches mice"; succeeded the second time, after having urged Labour in '92 to imitate Clinton's success in "driving modest programmes with radical rhetoric"; his previous Tory opponent, Nick Hawkins, fled the field; is an exception among the '97 wave of OMOV-chosen Labour candidates, who are often local councillors: a Manchester-born, Oxford-educated, Brighton-based editor of HISTORY TODAY, published from London; is in the Christian Socialist Movement; in his early months in Parliament asked mainly blunt-pointed questions;
History: He joined the Labour Party in Hazel Grove at 18, '71; became Secretary of Childs Hill Labour Party and Political Education Officer of Hendon South CLP '76-78; was in the East European Solidarity campaign in the late '70s; was against Militant and the far-Left in the NUS and as Fabian representative on the British Youth Council; was selected for Blackpool South '90; debated sea and beach pollution at annual conference Oct '90; the local elections gave Labour a majority on Blackpool Council for the first-time ever May '91; said he dreamt of creating a "silicon coast" of hi-tech industries Mar '92; despite adding 9% to his party's vote, narrowly lost the count by 1,667 votes Apr '92; the boundary changes made the seat more winnable, since three of the four wards added had Labour majorities '95; wrote to TRIBUNE that the Baring scandal strengthened the case "for a powerful European central bank" - "but how to place it under democratic control is another matter"; "the Bank of England proved inadequate to paper over the cracks; this questions its ability to act as the long-stop of control it has always claimed to be"; "more fundamentally, we need a new Bretton-Woods-style settlement of international finance, which has been allowed to spiral out of control via new technology since the late eighties"; "it is up to Labour, 'new' or 'old' to urgently seek partners on a European or global basis and start providing at least a figleaf" Mar '95; with a score of other Blairite candidates wrote to INDEPENDENT to proclaim "the Labour Party is a united dynamic party ready to solve the problems this country faces" Oct '96; was one of its 16 member-candidates endorsed by the GMB Apr '97; won the marginal seat by a majority of 11,616 on a notional swing of 11.6% May '97; expressed solidarity with jailed Indonesian union leader June '97; urged modification of licensing laws to suit seaside tourist towns July '97; urged alterations to the jobseeker's allowance for local people in seasonal unemployment July '97;

Born: 28 November 1953, Manchester
Family: Son of George Henry Marsden, refrigeration engineer, and Joyce (Young);
Education: St Andrew's C of E Primary '58-60; Romiley County Primary '60-65; Stockport Grammar School '65-73; New College, Oxford University (BA in Modern History, 1st Class Hons; MA) '73-76; Warburg Institute, London University '76-80; Harvard University (John Kennedy Scholar) '78-79;
Occupation: Editor of HISTORY TODAY (GMB) '85-97; Author: Victorian Values (editor; 1990, 1998); ex: Chief Public Affairs Adviser, to English Heritage '84-85; Open University Staff Tutor '77-97; Consultant Editor, of NEW SOCIALIST '89-90;
Traits: Very short blond hair; long face; "matinee-idol features" (GUARDIAN); elegant; soft-spoken; discerning; cerebral; very sociable partygoer; self-absorbed; enjoys swimming, world culture, medieval music;
Address: House of Commons, Westminster, London SW1A 0AA; 132 Highfield Road, Blackpool FY4 2HH; 46 Egremont Place, Brighton BN2 2GB;
Telephone: 0171 218 4166 (H of C); 01253 344940 (constituency);

Paul MARSDEN **Labour** **SHREWSBURY & ATCHAM '97-**

Majority: 1,670 over Conservative 7-way;
Description: Dominated by Shropshire's medieval county town, with its famous public school, agricultural show and 15th century black-and-white Tudor housing; it also includes rural areas stretching west to the Welsh border; it is the birth-place of Charles Darwin; partly because the '92 results showed Labour and the LibDems neck-and-neck both over 10,000 votes behind the incumbent Tory MP, he was thought to be safe for '97;
Position: On Select Committee on Agriculture '97-; on National Executive of Young Fabians '90-;
Outlook: The first-ever Labour MP for Shrewsbury, a young quality control manager who managed it "against all the odds" (PM); he picked up 5,000 votes, mostly from ex-Tories, leaping from 3rd place to lst; one of the youngest of Labour's new entrants, he confesses to being more afraid of his wife than of the Whips;
History: His father, Tom, was to become a Labour councillor; he himself joined the Young Fabians, then the Labour Party '83; was elected to the National Council of the Young Fabians '90; was selected to contest the "hopeless" seat of Shrewsbury against Derek Conway '95; because Labour had been a few hundred votes behind the second-place LibDems in '92, both with over 15,000 votes to the Tories' 26,000-plus, it was seen that they would first have to overtake the LibDems and show Labour as the main contender; he said later "against all the odds, we won the seat but we also won the argument; it was Labour, not the Liberal Democrats, who fought the Conservatives"; completely unexpectedly, on a swing of 11.4%, won the seat by a majority of 1,670 over the Tory incumbent, Derek Conway; this made him the 36th least-expected Labour victor May '97; in his Maiden, promised to try to "play a part in bringing more investment to the town and surrounding areas; I hope that our Challenge 2000 bid to try to create a new business venture in the north of Shrewsbury, which will bring up to 2,500 much-needed jobs to the town, will be successful; youth unemployment is

especially bad in some deprived areas of Shrewsbury" May '97; backed outlawing of fox-hunting June '97; was named to the Select Committee on Agriculture July '97;
Born: 18 March 1968, Frodsham, Cheshire
Family: He is the son of Tom Marsden, Labour Councillor in Frodsham; is married to Shelly; 1s Alexander '95; (he brought him as an 18-month-old to show him the Palace of Westminster; "I had to explain that the television [monitors] around the House cannot yet be tuned to 'Postman Pat' or the 'Teletubbies'"; "my son is so young that he did not know the ways of this great Palace; when he could not get his own way, he decided to lay prostrate in the corridors of power, kicking and screaming; I was a little embarrassed until I found that that was not too unusual in the Commons";
Education: Helsby High School; Mid-Cheshire College; Teesside Polytechnic; Open University (Diploma in Management);
Occupation: Quality Assurance Manager in a bank (BIFU); ex: Civil Engineer (UCATT); Member: Institute of Management, American Society of Quality Control;
Traits: Dark hair; high widow's peak; specs; good sense of humour; enjoys cross-country-running, researching local history and gardening; in Shropshire Wildlife Trust;
Address: House of Commons, Westminster, London, SW1A 0AA;
Telephone: 0171 219 3000 (H of C); 01743 884691 (home);

Robert MARSHALL-ANDREWS QC **Labour** **MEDWAY '97-**

Majority: 5,354 over Conservative 5-way;
Description: The Labour-leaning town of Rochester, the dockyard of Chatham plus Strood and some 20,000 voters in the Tory-leaning villages and suburbs in the flatlands on the north side of the Medway; Dame Peggy Fenner's almost-9,000 majority in '92 was thought safe by psephologist-soothsayers, but not by her in the last weeks leading up to May '97;
Position: Former Chairman, of Richmond Constituency Labour Party '73-75
Outlook: Distinguished QC and Recorder, second-time-lucky in this seat; is in the Society of Labour Lawyers; has set as his target to make Medway an industrial and cultural gateway to Europe; "Rochester is proud to be a European city; it lies at the gateway to Europe and, with a new council and unitary authority in place, we look forward to addressing some of the problems that have beset the Medway towns in the past 20 years; we lost no less than 70% of our manufacturing base in that time and we are the largest conurbation in Europe without its own university; during my stewardship, one of my principal aims will be to see the laying of the foundation stone of a new academic institution - possibly the first university of Europe - in that area";
History: He joined the Labour Party at 27, '71; he contested hopeless Richmond-on-Thames Oct '74; brought up in the Darent Valley, was selected for Medway '89; while slightly improving the Labour vote, lost Medway to Dame Peggy Fenner by 8,786 votes Apr '92; was re-selected for Medway '95; challenged Dame Peggy Fenner to a debate on the local NHS, complaining that under-funding had left Medway hospitals dangerously short of staff and resources; "for instance, we have one orthopaedic surgeon per 90,000 members of the

population; in Dartford, this improves nearly 50%" Jan '96; said, "the past 15 years have not been happy for the industrial towns of North Kent and the surrounding countryside; Government indifference and neglect have ensured record levels of unemployment and poverty with all the related problems for commerce and services; worse still we have been regarded as a convenient dumping ground for the region's waste and an area which will bear the worst rail and road network with the maximum of pollution and the minimum of benefit; this unfairness can be tolerated no longer; what is required is nothing less than a comprehensive plan of regional renewal to rebuild within a decade the prosperity and identity of the Towns" Sep '96; won the seat on a swing of 14.9%, by a majority of 5,354 over Dame Peggy; this made him the 47th least-expected Labour victor May '97; made his Maiden on the Firearms (Amendment) Bill, disclosing his wife was Chairman of the Gun Control Network, and spoke powerfully in favour of total gun control as the only way to diminish the chance of another Dunblane June '97; asked Government's plans for compensating haemophiliacs infected with Hepatitis C June '97; backed a motion expressing concern about Iraq's sanction-busting July '97;

Born: 10 April 1944, London

Family: Son, of Robin Marshall-Andrews, printer, and late Eileen Nora; m '68 Gillian Diana (Elliott), Chairman of the Gun Control Network; 1s Tom '73, 1d Laura '71;

Education: Mill Hill School; Bristol University (LLB); winner of OBSERVER Mace in National Debating Competition); Gray's Inn;

Occupation: Barrister '67-; QC '87-; Recorder of the Crown Court '82-; Author: The Palace of Wisdom (novel; 1990)

Traits: Parted, retreating light brown hair; laugh wrinkles; witty; bombastic; enjoys Rugby and cricket; interested in wildlife (Trustee of the George Adamson Wildlife Trust); holidays in Broadhaven, Pembrokeshire;

Address: House of Commons, Westminster, London SW1A 0AA; 4 Paper Buildings, Temple EC4Y 7EX; lives in constituency at Castle Hill, Rochester

Telephone: 0171 219 5188 (H of C); 0171 353 3366 (chambers)

Rt Hon Francis (Anthony Aylmer) MAUDE Conservative HORSHAM '97-

Majority: 14,862 over Liberal Democrat 6-way;

Description: At its core is the comfortable market town of Horsham, with affluent commuter villages like Nuthurst and Billingshurst; in '95 it acquired seven Tory-leaning wards from Crawley and Chichester and lost 30,000 voters to Arundel and South Downs; it is the second safest seat in West Sussex, previously an almost wholly safe-Tory area; only in the '93 county council elections did the Conservatives lose control there;

Former Seat: Warwickshire North '83-92

Position: Shadow National Heritage Secretary '97-; ex: Financial Secretary to the Treasury '90-92; Minister of State, Foreign Office '89-90; Under Secretary, Corporate and Consumer Affairs, DTI '87-89; Asssistant Whip '85-87; PPS, to Peter Morrison '84-85;

Outlook: The return as a retread of one of the brightest, hard-working and deft and, mostly, reasonable-sounding of the Thatcherite Rightwing radicals; a Eurosceptic who wants to water down the Maastricht Treaty he negotiiated and signed; although in the Thatcherite 'No Turning Back' group, lacks the staring-eyed fanaticism of some of his fellow zealots; has "the forensic skills" of a former "criminal barrister"; "what makes him formidable is that he is a workaholic as well as extremely clever" (Donald Macintyre, SUNDAY CORRESPONDENT); "like his father [Angus Maude], he is as sharp as a needle"; "has an uncluttered mind and a relentless prosecuting intellect; his grasp of principle is unerring" (Matthew Parris, TIMES]]; has "loyalty and purity" (Michael Brown); his climb up the greasy pole was interrupted by the electorate in '92; is said to be willing to sit out this and the next Parliament before emerging as Chancellor of the Exchequer;

History: His journalist father, Angus, was a Conservative MP and Minister; his own first affiliation was at Cambridge, where he was not active; was elected to Westminster City Council at 25, May '78; after missing out on two other short-listings, was selected for the Labour-held marginal Warwickshire North Apr '83; was elected with a 2,529 majority June '83; sponsored motion condemning union blacking of a BUPA gift of a kidney-stone machine to St Thomas' Hospital June '83; supported death penalty for murder by terrorists, by shooting or in furtherance of theft July '83; condemned Arthur Scargill's call for extra-Parliamentary opposition to the elected Government July '83; called for denationalisation of coal, rail, post and electricity July '83; backed relating MPs' pay to an agreed outside salary to avoid the need of barristers like himself to moonlight July '83; favoured Commons reform, including use of County Hall by MPs, serviced by a minibus shuttle, with electronic counters for voting Aug '83; urged a more efficient NHS, with cottage hospitals providing care on a human scale Oct '83; became PPS to Peter Morrison Jan '84; urged concentration on the most economic mines Mar '84; warned against a third motorway through West Midlands Dec '84; urged end to coal subsidies May '85; introduced 10-minute-rule Bill to deregulate rents which lost by one vote (but was later adopted by the Government) July '85; urged reduced taxes July '85; backed abolition of Property Services Agency Sep '85; was named Assistant Whip, making him the youngest member of Mrs Thatcher's Government at 32 Oct '85; co-authored 'No Turning Back', the pamphlet urging the extension of the Thatcherite revolution Nov '85; backed hanging for child murderers Jan '87; voted for restoration of capital punishment Apr '87; was re-elected with 3% larger share of the ballot June '87; was promoted Under Secretary at Trade and Industry, as 'Minister for Corporate and Consumer Affairs', "the most surprising leap to prominence" (James Naughtie, GUARDIAN) June '87; claimed that opposition to sale of TODAY derived from Labour MPs' hatred of Rupert Murdoch July '87; opposed early ban on polyurethane foam, which had "many excellent qualities" July '87; after refusing to study Film Finance Ltd and Gresham Trust Plc, was accused by Labour MPs Brian Sedgemore and Dennis Skinner of "investigating cases of fraud on a selective and unlawful basis" Oct '87; insisted, in private, that Nigel Lawson could not become Foreign Secretary "as a Jew" Dec '87; after a number of fatal fires and pressure from Chief Fire Officers, reduced time to bar polyurethane in furniture from three years to 14 months, which was hailed by opponent Tony Blair as as "profound and justified a climbdown as has ever been made in consumer safety" Jan '88; was deprived of his Consumer Affairs portfolio and limited to Corporate Affairs Feb '88; controversially insisted that video recordings had to be wiped after 28 days May '88; admitted his department had renewed the license of Barlow Clowes, fraudulent fund managers, after beginning to investigate its affairs June '88; was initially distraught and "tearful", looking "puffy around the eyes" (Alan Clark, DIARIES) at being passed over in the reshuffle: "I thought that at least I might have some recognition for all my work in the Financial Services" July '88; admitted the Government had agreed to EEC demands to phase out the mile, the pint, pounds and ounces Feb '89; warned that economic and monetary union as envisaged by Delors implied political union Mar '89; was promoted Minister of State at the Foreign Office by Mrs Thatcher, replacing pro-European Lynda Chalker as No 2, July '89; was alleged by Lord O'Hagan to have misrepresented Tory MEPs as becoming more sympathetic to the Thatcherite view of the European Community Dec '89; voted against trying elderly East European immigrants for alleged war crimes, despite Mrs Thatcher's enthusiasm for the trials Dec '89; had sharp confrontation with Norman Tebbit in the Commons tearoom over whether it was excessive to allow as many as 150,000 Hongkong Chinese UK passport holders to settle in the UK Dec '89; described the east European revolution of 1989 "as profound as those of 1789 and 1848" Jan '90; backed deregulation of motorway restaurants June '90; was appointed Financial Secretary to the Treasury with responsibility for privatisation and taxation and European Community financial matters July '90; was an early supporter of John Major's Leadership bid; told Alan Clark that Major had a better chance than generally thought, but would not make a move while Mrs Thatcher was in the field Nov '90; was a signatory to the Maastricht Treaty Dec '91; lost marginal Warwickshire North to Labour's Mike O'Brien by 1,454 votes on a swing of 3.7% Apr '92; joined Salomon Brothers as head of their privatisation unit June '92; was made a Privy Councillor July '92; became a Director of ASDA Group Plc July '92; became Chairman of Public Policy Unit Ltd Aug '92; declined to fight the impending Newbury by-election Mar '93; withdrew from contest to head the No 10 Policy Unit, claiming it would be impossible to combine it with fighting a seat in the next general election Dec '94; showed such arrogance at Witney, where Douglas Hurd had announced he was stepping down, that he did not even make he short-list '95; was selected to fight Horsham after Sir Peter Hordern announced his impending retirement Nov '95; insisted that Britain's status in the EU had to be redefined to enable it to stay in without tensions; the European Court had to be "reined in", majority voting had not to be extended, the CAP abandoned and the Common Fisheries Policy renegotiated DAILY TELEGRAPH June '96; urged more tax cuts, more deregulation, decentralisation, a total "new settlement" SUNDAY TIMES Sep '96; retained Horsham, with a majority of 14,862 (down from 25,072) after an 6.8% notional swing to LibDems May '97; joined the campaign team of Michael Howard May '97; tried to insist the Bill on referenda in Scotland and Wales was a constitutional measure which had to be taken on the floor of the House June '97; as the unpaid Chairman of the Governors of his old school, Abingdon - formerly direct grant but now independent and operating the Assisted Places Scheme - fiercely attacked the abolition of the Scheme which would "damage the education of tens of thousands of children" June '97; co-opposed Government's Bill to further control handguns June '97; protested the Government's reported intention of ending the contract of Sir Michael Bishop, Chairman of Channel 4, on the basis that he was a Conservative supporter July '97; effectively twitted Heritage Secretary Chris Smith on becoming a convert to the success of the National Lottery July '97; was much more cautious in criticising the Millennium Dome than desired by some Tory Mandelson-bashers Oct '97;

Born: 4 July 1953, Oxford

Family: Son, of late Angus (later Lord) Maude, Paymaster General, and Barbara (Sutcliffe); m '84 Christina (Hadfield) an architect by training who became his secretary; 2s, including Henry '90; 3d including Julia '86, Cecily '88;

Education: Cranbrook School, Sydney; Petworth Primary; Audley House Prep, Bicester; Abingdon School, Berkshire '66-71; Corpus Christi College, Cambridge University '72-76 (BA Hons in History; Hulse Prize, Avory Studentship); Inns of Court School of Law '76-77 (Forster Boulton Prize); Inner Temple College of Law;

Occupation: Managing Director, Morgan Stanley (£200,000 a year as head of its privatisation unit) '93-; Director: ASDA Group Plc '92-, Benfield Reinsurance Ltd '92-, Sportfact Ltd; ex: Chairman, HM Government Deregulation Task Force '94-97; Barrister '77-

initially practiced at the Criminal Bar '77-85; ex: Salomon Brothers '92-93;
Traits: Slim; brown, parted, retreating hair; boyish; diffident manner; "has the voice of a stage villain and the mien of the Mekon in the EAGLE comic" (Matthew Parris, TIMES); "sensible and quiet [as a PPS], but with a good mind and a sense of humour"; but could turn crybaby if denied justified promotion (Alan Clark, DIARIES); enjoys: music, opera, cricket ("a cricket fanatic, and a useful if rather stolid batsman at club level" Donald Macintyre, SUNDAY CORRESPONDENT);
Address: House of Commons, Westminster, London SW1A 0AA; Dial Post, nr Horsham, West Sussex; 25 Cabot Square, London E14 4QA;
Telephone: 0171 219 3000 (H of C); 0171 425 5010 (work); 0385 361 588 (mobile); 0171 582 2665 (home);

Mrs Theresa MAY **Conservative** **MAIDENHEAD '97-**

Majority: 11,981 over Liberal Democrat 7-way;
Description: New, safely-Tory Thamesside seat made up three-quarters of old Windsor and Maidenhead, one-quarter of Wokingham; dominated by affluent Maidenhead but its Berkshire village hinterland stretches almost to Reading; it is host to the Henley Regatta; Liberal Democrats have made inroads in council elections;
Position: On the Select Committee on Education and Employment '97-; ex: Merton Borough Councillor (Deputy Leader its Conservative Group '92-94) '86-94; on Merton Community Health Council '86-88;
Outlook: Very bright, articulate and witty new eager-beaver; the first new Tory woman to be selected for a safe Tory seat, after a six-year search; a Rightwing Eurosceptic who is a darling of the Tory Whips for her willingness to repeat, with some freshness, propaganda lines against Labour legislation; "I congratulate the hon Lady on her assiduous repetition of propaganda from Central Office" (Labour's Scottish Secretary, Donald Dewar); in the British Field Sports Society, is a defender of field sports, including fox-hunting; an opponent of opencast mining near homes; a highly-skilled City professional (was in inter-bank payment clearances); she is an opponent of all-women short-lists: "I'm totally opposed to Labour's idea of all-women short-lists and I think they are an insult to women; I've competed equally with men in my career, and I have been happy to do so in politics too";
History: She cut her political teeth as a teenager stuffing envelopes for the Tories in Oxfordshire; at 17, stood as a Tory in her school's mock general election Feb '74; she was active in Tory politics at Oxford University, where she met her husband, Philip; was elected to Merton Borough Council May '86, where she favoured concentrating on "basics" like rubbish collection; was re-elected to Merton Borough Council with a swing to the Tories in a marginal seat May '90; supported locally-negotiated pay for teachers, based on appraisal, at Tories' Local Government Conference '90; was selected as Tory candidate for hopeless Durham North West; in general election came second to Labour's Hilary Armstrong, with 28% of the vote, almost identical with the '87 vote of her Tory predecessor Apr '92; continuing her interest in Durham North West, she accused the Labour Party there of trying to establish

control over the police Apr '93; having been selected to contest hopeless Barking against Margaret Hodge in the by-election, stood down as a Merton Borough Councillor May '94; was pushed into third place with 1,976 votes, 10.4% of the total; in '92 the Tory candidate had come second with 11,956 votes (33.9%); Margaret Hodge defeated the second-place 22-year-old Liberal Democrat by 11,414 votes, nearly double the 1992 Labour majority, but on a lower turnout June '94; was through to the final selection at Ashford Dec '94; was the runner-up in the candidate selection for Tewkesbury Sep '95; was short-listed for Chatham and Aylesford Oct '95; after having missed out on five previous tries, was chosen for Maidenhead over Sir George Young (whose family had lived in Maidenhead for 200 years), Sir Paul Beresford, John Watts and Eric Forth, all Ministers on the "chicken run"; in the final round she beat Nick St Aubyn and Philip Hammond Nov '95; after her selection, the TIMES Diary was sickened by "goo-goo press releases" issued on her behalf, including one: "Life begins at 40 and Theresa May...got her birthday off to a good start on September 27 [four days before her birthday] when the Prime Minister [John Major] helped her celebrate and blow out the candles on her cake" Nov '96; her neighbour, John Redwood, spoke for her during the election campaign Apr '97; won the seat with a majority of 11,981 despite a notional swing of 4.1% to the LibDems May '97; refused to join any of the Leadership campaign teams May '97; used her witty Maiden and a number of later speeches to help delay the abolition of the Assisted Places Scheme, claiming: "Socialism is about levelling down, Conservatism is about levelling up" June '97; attacked abolition of Tories' nursery voucher scheme before putting alternative arrangements in place June '97; urged the Highways Agency to plant trees that turned red in autumn June '97; urged Government to ensure BNFL did not transport radioactive material by plane to Sellafield until the safety of such flights had been assessed June '97; attacked the Budget, including its windfall tax, explaining Southern Electricity had its headquarters in her constituency July '97; asked all Government departments about their current payments of debts July '97; led motions deploring attacks by Consumers Affairs Under Secretary, Nigel Griffiths, on cartel arrangements in the travel industry on which he would have to sit in judgement July '97; was named to the Select Committee on Education and Employment July '97; asked Sports Minister Tony Banks, eight weeks in the job, why he was taking so long to locate the British Academy of Sport July '97; asked for the timetable to complete the European internal market July '97; complained that the Labour Government's proposed welfare-to-work proposals were "likely to be expensive and unnecessary" compared with the previous Tory Government's workfare trials July '97;

Born: 1 October 1956, Eastbourne

Family: Daughter, of Rev Hubert Brasier, Anglican cleric, and Zaidee (Barnes); m '80 Philip May, City investment manager and ex-Chairman, Wimbledon Tories, then Treasurer, Tories' London SW Euro-constituency;

Education: Heythrop C of E Primary; St Juliana's, Begbroke, Oxon; Wheatley Park Comprehensive, Oxon; St Hughes College, Oxford University (MA in Geography); FRGS;

Occupation: Senior Adviser '96-97, Head of European Affairs Unit '85-96, Association for Payment Clearing Services; Consultant, for the Inter-Bank Research Organisation '83-85; Shareholder: in the Prudential Corporation; ex: Executive Officer, Bank of England '77-83;

Traits: Attractive; auburn hair with natural grey splashes; can speak without notes, well and wittily; "an image of professionalism" (Michael Evans, TIMES); since her name is Theresa, proposed wearing a badge, "No, I am the other one"; is anxious to observe best Commons codes of polite behaviour; had an over-enthusiastic pre-election publicist; a practicing Anglican (her father's daughter);

Address: House of Commons, Westminster, London SW!A 0AA;

Telephone: 0171 219 5206/1145(Fax) (H of C); 0181 969 9530 (home);

Gillian MERRON **Labour** **LINCOLN '97-**

Majority: 11,130 over Conservative 5-way;
Description: The isolated, somewhat industrialised county town, now deprived of 13,000 voters, mainly in Tory-leaning suburbs; its Left-of-Centre local political supporters were split for a dozen years by the 1973 defection to his own pro-European, social democratic Democratic Labour Party of its former Labour MP, Dick [recently Lord] Taverne, a LibDem peer;
Position: On the Select Committee on Trade and Industry '97-;
Outlook: A former Centre-Left mainstreamer, turned Blairite loyalist, who has developed a tendency to feed Labour Ministers stooge questions; was one of the new young women graduates who became trade union organisers; her UNISON background makes her sensitive to low pay; a multi-cause groupie: Greenpeace, Amnesty International, Action for Southern Africa and the National Campaign for Nursery Education;
History: She joined the Labour Party at 24, '83; became Labour's Regional Key Campaign Schedules Co-ordinator for its Central Region Mar-Apr '92; did the same job in the Euro-election May-June '94; on the UNISON Parliamentary Panel, was selected from an all-women short-list for Lincoln, whose boundary changes again made it winnable by Labour (with the sitting MP Ken Carlisle retiring early) Mar '95; at annual conference spoke on the prevalence of poverty wages Oct '96; explaining why she was a candidate, said: "I have a responsibility; if women like me don't enter, nothing will change"; "a third of the under-25s in Lincoln are out of work; it's a terrible waste; I want to give young people realistic hope" Apr '97; on a notional swing of 11% won the seat by a majority of 11,130 May '97; complained her constituents earned £40 a week less than the national average May '97; backed outlawing of fox-hunting June '97; supported Government's review of detention for asylum seekers June '97; urged the useful role of the voluntary sector and environmental task forces for finding employment for the young July '97; told Paymaster General Geoffrey Robinson that "in my constituency of Lincoln we have a first-rate example of public-private partnership in the presence of the new University of Lincolnshire and Humberside, which is the first purpose-bult university in the country for many decades" July '97; gushed loyally about the Budget as "a breath of fresh air for the whole nation" July '97; told Home Secretary Jack Straw that in her constituency, "many people are kept prisoners in their homes" since "their fear of crime is one of the most insidious features of our current lives" July '97;
Born: 12 April 1959, Ilford, Essex
Family: She is unmarried;
Education: Wanstead High School, London E11; Lancaster University (BSc Hons in Management Science);
Occupation: Senior Regional Officer of UNISON for Lincolnshire and East Midlands, with responsibilities for gas, electricity and transport til '97; previously NUPE Area Officer from '87; Business Adviser to Worker Co-operatves; Welfare Rights Officer for Derbyshire County Council;
Traits: Dark brown hair; pretty; long face with strong chin; is vulnerable to Tory barracking when she reads out questions; enjoys swimming, films and the performing arts;
Address: House of Commons, Westminster, London SW1A 0AA; 24 Dale Road, Derby

DE23 6QW;
Telephone: 0171 219 4031 (H of C); 01332 762887 (home); 01522 529322/567836(Fax) (constituency office);

Laura (Jean) MOFFATT **Labour** **CRAWLEY '97-**

Majority: 11,707 over Conservative 6-way;
Description: The borough of Crawley, the north-of-Brighton London overspill New Town, finally denuded in '95 of its typically-Sussex Tory hinterland, causing the flight to safer Mid-Sussex of its former Tory MP, Nicholas Soames; the town has lots of modern light industries, skilled workers and social housing;
Position: On Select Committee on Defence '97-; ex: Crawley Borough Councillor (Mayor '89-90, Chairman, its Environmental Services '87-89) '84-96
Outlook: A London-born Leftwing nurse graduated from local government; active in local charities: Founder of Crawley Furnaid (to provide furniture for the needy; granted £140,000 by the National Lottery); a thin-skinned feminist; cause groupie in Socialist Health Association and CND;
History: She joined COHSE '72, the Labour Party '79; was elected to Crawley Borough Council May '84; was selected to contest Crawley June '90; contested Crawley, losing by 7,765 votes, despite a swing to Labour of 4%, Apr '92; was re-selected from an all-women short-list to contest Crawley May '95; at Brighton annual Labour conference complained that NHS workers were having to sacrifice themselves to shield patients from Tory cuts Oct '95; told annual conference that she hated the 2.4% pay increase after 12-hour shifts had been imposed; pledged that nursing staff were determined to make the NHS recover "under Tony Blair and New Labour" Oct '96; took Crawley after a notional swing of 13.4% by a majority of 11,707; this made her one of Labour's unprecedented five-strong Sussex intake May '97; showed concern that women from Crawley's one-tenth of ethnic minorities might not take up the enhanced breast-screening programme unless addressed in their own languages June '97; co-sponsored motion to abolish fox-hunting June '97; co-sponsored motion asking for a review of rape law, including "the removal of the defendant's right to cross-examine the victim" June '97; backed proposed ban on tobacco advertising June '97; argued that NHS "should not be broken up and commercialised", that it "cannot be run like a supermarket chain"; called for restoration of national pay bargaining in NHS June '97; was named to the Select Committee on Defence July '97;
Born: 9 April 1954, London
Family: Daughter of Stanley Field, retired toolmaker, and Barbara Amy (Bastable), retired office manager; m '75 Colin Moffatt, who has done shift-work at Gatwick for 20 years; 3s: Russell '77, Alistair '79, Edward '82;
Education: Pound Hill Infants and Junior School; Hazelwick Comprehensive; Crawley College of Technology (pre-nursing);
Occupation: State-Registered General Nurse for 23 years (UNISON);
Traits: Parted auburn hair; pretty oval face; combative; enjoys swimming, canoeing, caravanning, boating, water skiing;

Address: House of Commons, Westminster, London SW1A 0AA; 9 Adrian Court, Chadwick Close, Broadfield, Crawley RH11 9LQ;
Telephone: 0171 219 3619 (H of C); 01293 530585 (home); 01293 526005 (constituency);

Michael (Kevin) MOORE **Liberal Democrat** **TWEEDDALE, ETTRICK & LAUDERDALE '97-**

Majority: 1,489 over Labour 7-way;
Description: A Border seat, dependent economically on agriculture, textiles and electronics; it still retains the market towns of Galashiels, Selkirk and Peebles; it has been made more marginal by taking in the Midlothian town of Labour-leaning Penicuik and the departure of Sir David Steel to the House of Lords;
Position: On the Select Committee for Scottish Affairs '97-, on the LibDem Scottish Team (its Commons Spokesman on the Economy and Health) '97-; in Scotland, LibDems' Spokesman on Business and Employment '95-;
Outlook: Young successor to Sir David (recently Lord) Steel who spent two years successfuly introducing him to the constituency; one son of the Manse succeeding another; has repeated Sir David's achievement 32 years earlier, despite boundary changes which helped Labour; came into the Liberal Democrats via the Social Democrats; considers the need for a "Scottish Parliament based on proportional representation" a "major priority" (MM);
History: He was co-founder of the short-lived Jedburgh Youth Politics Society, which concentrated on supporting Polish Solidarity; joined the SDP '83; moved to Liberal Party '86; joined the staff of Liberal Democrat MP Archy Kirkwood '87; his selection for Tweeddale, was described by predecessor Sir David Steel as an "exciting choice" Apr '95; retained the seat with a majority of 1,489 despite a notional swing of 7.4% to Labour May '97; in his Maiden, which withdrew LibDem opposition to a referendum on a desired Scottish Parliament, he pleaded for a new transport infrastructure for the Borders as well as investment and training to avoid the young having to leave for work, as he had June '97; asked about financial crises of Borders NHS trusts June '87; backed proposal for ecumenical Commons prayers July '97; asked about help for a failed firm in Selkirk July '97; was named to Select Committee on Scottish Affairs July '97; he spoke there on the Budget's impact on Scotland July '97;
Born: 3 June 1965, Dundonald, Northern Ireland
Family: Son, of Rev (William) Haisley Moore, Church of Scotland Minister, and Geraldine Ann /"Jill" (Moorehead), physiotherapist;
Education: Wishaw Academy Primary School; Strathallan School (a public school) '77-82; Jedburgh Grammar School (comprehensive) '82-83; Edinburgh University '83-87 (BA 2:1 Hons in Politics and Modern History);
Occupation: Chartered Accountant '91-: Manager in Corporate Finance Practice of Coopers & Lybrand '93-97; ex: Research Assistant, to Archy Kirwood '87-88;
Traits: Parted brown hair; long triangular face; young-looking; Celtic-handsome (when Lady Steel was introducing him as "my husband's successor", a local farmer asked: "your toy-boy?"; enjoys jazz (former presenter of jazz programme on hospital radio), films, music, hill-walking and golf;

Address: House of Commons, Westminster, London SW1A 0AA; Wells Brae Cottage, Innerleithen, Peeblesshire EH44 6HR
Telephone: 0171 219 2236 (H of C); 01896 830597 (home);

Margaret MORAN **Labour** **LUTON SOUTH '97-**

Majority: 11,319 over Conservative 7-way;
Description: Old marginal Luton South with one neutral ward removed in '95 to Luton North; contains the Vauxhall car works, Luton Airport and the huge Arndale Shopping Centre;
Position: On Labour's National Policy Forum '94-, its Economic Policy Commission '94- and NEC's Local Government Committee '94-; Lewisham Councillor (ex: Leader '93-95, former Chairman of Housing, Direct Services) '84-; Deputy Chairman, of AMA '94-95, Chairman, of AMA Housing Committee '94-; Chairman, of London Housing Unit '90-; is in City 2020 Forum on Urban Regeneration; ex: National President, Housing Associations Branch of NALGO;
Outlook: A highly-rated dynamo from local government: formerly a "dynamic, hard-working Leader of a model borough with a reputation for toughness" (MUNICIPAL JOURNAL); "earned her stripes in local government; she took over the chaotic, wasteful and divided Lewisham Council in southeast London, saw off the hard-Left and turned it into a modern operation" (Clare Longrigg, GUARDIAN); pro-European, "soft-Left feminist" (NEW STATESMAN); is in Labour's Women's Network but does not like to be considered one of the "Shoulder Pad Tendency" or the "Glamorous Tendency" of the New Labour power-dressers; of Irish origins, is in Labour Party Irish Society;
History: She joined the Labour Party at 26, '81; was elected to Lewisham Borough Council May '84; was selected for hopeless Carshalton and Wallington Mar '92; came third in Carshalton, after the Liberal Democrat, with 17.7% of the vote Apr '92; became Leader of Lewisham Council, the first woman in this post May '93; was involved in setting up 16 neighbourhood community forums, with videoboxes for community feedback, citizens' juries; secured EC funding for a TV-democracy project to secure young people's views; was selected from an all-women's short-list for marginal Luton South Apr '95; ceased being Leader of Lewisham Council May '95; expressed regret when all-women's short-lists were declared illegal: "most of us are very disappointed and very surprised by the decision; I think that the party will be looking at an appeal, because we took legal advice and had the agreement of the Equal Opportunities Commission; but I don't think that it is going to be a major setback" Jan '96; joined with other loyalist candidates in joint letter to INDEPENDENT, proclaiming Labour was "a united dynamic party ready to solve the problems this country faces" Oct '96; won the seat on a notional swing of 12.3%, ending the 14-year reign of John Major's former PPS, Sir Graham Bright by a majority of 11,319 May '97; co-sponsored motion attacking the London Docklands Development Corporation for selling to luxury flat developers the land planned for a memorial to local people killed in the wartime bombing of London May '97; asked about targets for training in IT skills May '97; co-sponsored motion backing improved breast cancer treatment June '97; co-sponsored motion urging action against prescription fraud

June '97; complained of "slow and inefficient" benefit services, especially on appeals June '97; contradicting a Tory spokesman, forcefully berated the former Government for curbing local authorities' ability to finance house-building while more than doubling the national debt; backed the new Labour Government's Bill to enable local authorities to borrow to build July '97; welcomed the IRA ceasefire; supported the efforts of Northern Ireland Secretary Mo Mowlam despite "violence and disruption" July '97;
Born: 24 April 1955, London
Family: Daughter, of late 'Jack'/John Patrick Moran, caretaker, and Mary (Murphy) home help, both Irish;
Education: St Ursula's Convent School, Greenwich; St Mary's College of Education, Twickenham; Birmingham University (BSocSc Hons in Geography and Sociology);
Occupation: Director, of Housing for Women (housing association; in this capacity, she led the refurbishment of a tough inner-city estate in partnership with government and the private sector; this included training and provided construction jobs for 100 local young people);
Traits: Dark hair; pretty rounded face; Irish-looking; "dynamic", "hard-working", "a reputation for toughness" (MUNICIPAL JOURNAL): classless cockneyfied speech; Roman Catholic; enjoys cinema and visiting sites of historic interest;
Address: House of Commons, Westminster, London SW1A 0AA; 4 Ilfracombe Road, Downham, Bromley, Kent BR1 5HD;
Telephone: 0171 219 5049 (H of C); 01582 735365 (home); 01582 31882; 0850 693713 (mobile); 0850 693713-880069 (pager)

Alasdair MORGAN Scottish National GALLOWAY & UPPER NITHSDALE '97-

Majority: 5,624 over Conservative 7-way;
Description: The little-changed seat in remote southwestern rural Scotland, the old counties of Kirkcudbright and Wigtown, with their mountains, glens, lochs and forests and equally beautiful place-names; was first captured by the SNP '74-79, then retaken by Ian Lang '79-97, becoming Scottish Secretary '90-95, then President of the Board of Trade '95-97;
Position: On the Select Committee on Trade and Industry '97-; National Secretary of the SNP '92-; Secretary of the SNP's Scottish 'Cabinet' '91-; ex: SNP Senior Vice Convener '90-91, National Treasurer '83-90,
Outlook: The low-profile veteran SNP candidate, officer and organiser who administered the "final push" to retake Ian Lang's former seat in which Morgan once taught school before becoming a computer consultant;
History: Without any previous political involvement, he joined the SNP '74; contested North Tayside against Tory MP Bill Walker, coming second, 26.8% behind May '83; contested Dundee West against Labour incumbent Ernie Ross, coming 3rd with 15.3% June '87; was named Defence Spokesman by the new SNP Leader, Alex Salmond Oct '90; was named the General Election Campaign Director Oct '91; also contested Dumfries, coming third with 14.3% Apr '92; was the SNP's preference for the Perth and Kinross by-election selection contest won by Roseanna Cunningham May '95; was selected to contest Galloway against Ian

Lang, who had won in '92 by a 5.5% majority over the previous SNP candidate Oct '95; announced that 370,000 people in Scotland had been made redundant since '92 and 260,000 businesses had failed and 3,700 homes had been repossessed Feb '97; retook Galloway on a notional swing of 9.5%, ending Ian Lang's 18-year reign with a majority of 5,624 May '97; complained to Speaker Boothroyd about reported plans of Tory MPs' 1922 Committee to adopt constituencies like his that the Tories had lost June '97; urged the up-grading of local roads June '97; unsuccessfully asked Scottish Secretary Donald Dewar for an independent inquiry into the offshore dumping of radioactive waste in Beaufort Dyke July '97; asked about local low-flying and the cost of cleaning up after the crash of a Harrier jet July '97; complained about the local shortage of community care beds July '97; urged the abolition of milk quotas July '97; complained that the Scottish part of the Dearing Report on higher education was not available July '97; was named to the Select Committee on Trade and Industry July '97; at the SNP conference opposed the call for the abolition of the monarchy in an independent Scotland by his Parliamentary colleague, Roseanna Cunningham MP Sep '97;
Born: 21 April 1945, Aberfeldy
Family: Son, of Alexander Morgan, insurance superintendent, and Emily (Wood); m Anne (Gilfillan); 2d: Gillian, Fiona;
Education: Downfield Primary, Dundee; Breadalbane Academy, Aberfeldy; Glasgow University (MA Hons in Maths and Political Economy) '68; Moray House College of Education; Open University (BA Hons in History) '90;
Occupation: Computer Systems Team Leader, with West Lothian Council and its predecessor Lothian Regional Council '86-97; previously with Fife Regional Council '84-86, US GEC '80-84, Shell '74-80; a Teacher of Maths, at Douglas Ewart High School, Newton Stewart (in the constituency) '73-74;
Traits: Retreating blond hair; angular features; "steady but dull"; has shown a strong aesthetic sense; enjoys hill-walking;
Address: House of Commons, Westminster, London SW1A 0AA;
Telephone: 0171 219 3174 (H of C);

Mrs Julie MORGAN **Labour** **CARDIFF NORTH '97-**

Majority: 8,126 over Conservative 5-way;
Description: The most middle-class residential part of its capital and of Wales as a whole; inhabited by many of Cardiff's professionals, many of them in the public sector; under different boundaries, it fell once before to Ted Rowlands, in Labour's '66 high tide;
Position: On Welsh Affairs Select Committee '97-, Cardiff Unitary Authority '95-; ex: South Glamorgan County Councillor (Chairman, Women's Committee) '??-95;
Outlook: A low-profile former social worker and stalwart of the South Wales Labour establishment, married to Cardiff West's MP, Rhodri Morgan; close to Ann Clwyd in her overseas attitudes; on domestic affairs, her early Parliamentary activity resembled that of a local councillor and social worker: "I'd like a universal system for childcare for parents who need it"; is strongly pro-devolution; was active in the Anti-Apartheid and Nicaragua Solidarity Campaign; a feminist and supporter

of the Campaign Against Pornography, saying: "Page Three and girlie magazines create a climate in which woman are perceived as sex objects instead of human beings with intelligence and talents";

History: She joined the Labour Party in the '60s; contested Cardiff North, losing to Conservative Gwilym Jones by 2,969 votes (6.2%) after achieving a 6.2% swing to Labour Apr '92; was again selected, this time from an all-women short-list '95; won the seat on an 11.5% swing, unseating Welsh Under Secretary Gwilym Jones by a majority of 8,126; she was the first woman MP for the seat and the first in Cardiff May '97; in her Maiden speech in favour of Welsh devolution ("devolution is about people-friendly, women-friendly policies"), indirectly attributed her victory to the "job insecurity" of its professionals, caused by "the privatisation, contractorisation and short-term contracts that have become commonplace in public service" May '97; asked about council tax for students in full-time higher education June '97; asked about car-parking charges at the University Hospital of Wales June '97; urged the reform of the administration of the Social Fund June '97; backed a bar on fox-hunting June '97; asked about decontamination of Army's closed former Atomic Weapons Establishment site at Llanishen in Cardiff June '97; backed motion expressing solidarity with a jailed Indonesian trade union leader June '97; co-sponsored motion opposing export of arms to Indonesia July '97; pressed for replacement of radiotherapy machines in Velindre hospital July '97; was named to Welsh Affairs Select Committee July '97; asked about NIREX and its long-term storage of low and intermediate radioactive nuclear waste July '97; co-sponsored motion expressing concern about Iraq's sanctions-busting July '97; asked about toxic effects of mercury tooth-fillings July '97; urged discouragement of smoking among the young in Wales July '97; asked about the outside interests of those on the Spongiform Encephalopathy Advisory Committee July '97; chaired British Council fringe meeting on women's rights at Brighton annual conference Oct '97;

Born: 2 November 1944, Cardiff

Family: Her maiden name was Edwards; m '67 Rhodri Morgan, MP for Cardiff West ("our life has always been rosettes rather than roses"); two daughters: Mari '68, Siani '69; and one adopted son, Stuart '68 who was charged with living off immoral earnings '88, burglary '89, with possessing and supplying cannabis '90 and jailed for three months for beating up his girlfriend in a jealous rage June '97;

Education: Howell's School, Llandaff; University of London (BA Hons); Manchester University (Postgraduate Diploma in Social Administration); Cardiff University (Certificate of Qualification in Social Work);

Occupation: Assistant Director for Child Care at Barnardo's headquarters in Cardiff til '97; ex: Principal Social Services Officer for West Glamorgan; Social Worker;

Traits: Centre-parted brown hair; pleasant-plain face; enjoys swimming;

Address: House of Commons, Westminster, London SW1A 0AA; Cardiff North BCLP, Lower House, Michaelstone-le-Pit, Dinas Powys, South Glamorgan;

Telephone: 0171 219 3000 (H of C); 01222 514262 (home); 01222 623661 (constituency);

DOORSTEPPING JOURNALISTS

We accept that one of the weaknesses in this volume is paucity of information about the parents of politicians. We find it valuable to know whether the father of an MP is a multi-millionaire property developer or a plumber. But some MPs claim that their parents fear press intrusion. Any pressman with experience of doorstepping journalists or aggressive photographers can understand some trepidation. But our jury is still out on whether this is the main reason for withholding such information.

Kali MOUNTFORD **Labour** **COLNE VALLEY '97-**

Majority: 4,840 over Conservative 7-way;

Description: The unaltered West Yorkshire scenic seat recently popular as the site of 'Last of the Summer Wine'; it has twin valleys: the industrial Colne Valley and the scenic Holme Valley; its historic interest for Labour is as the birthplace of Harold Wilson and in its past MPs: Victor Grayson, the first socialist MP, and Philip Snowden, the defecting Chancellor; long basically a three-way marginal which only seemed a Lib-Lab marginal: it was held intermittently between '66 and '87 by Liberal Richard Wainwright, with tacit support from Tory voters; it was then won in '87 by Rightwing Tory Graham ('Cash for Questions') Riddick; this was largely a result of the '83 addition of pro-Tory wards from western Huddersfield; it ceased to be a true marginal in '92, when heavy tactical voting by anti-Labour LibDem voters gave Riddick a majority of 7,225;

Position: Sheffield City Councillor (Chairman of Finance and Personnel, Deputy Chairman of Economic Development '92-97) '92-;

Outlook: The articulate and very northern-shrewd first woman MP for a historic seat; a former civil servant and trade unionist in Employment, she learned how to adapt Labour's message to hard-headed local Yorkshire folk; a strenuous campaigner for a simplified, more just social security system;

History: The daughter of a train driver and school dinner lady, she was brought up on a council estate; she first "became interested at 14" in politics, inspired by two sister-teachers of history, government and citizenship at Crewe Grammar School for Girls '68; she joined the Labour Party at 22 (after becoming a civil service clerk in Employment) '76; during time out from the civil service to raise two children, she took a degree; was elected to Sheffield City Council May '92; as Chairman of Sheffield City Council's Finance Committee introduced new IT systems and financial management which save £11m in one year; also discovered £3m lying unused in council trusts; was selected from an all-women short-list for Colne Valley Mar '95; told annual conference, "I feel socialism in my bones" Oct '95; was forced to resign from the civil service as a candidate, although she claimed she had been granted "political permission" '96; campaigned in constituency to keep open a threatened hospital, to improve rural bus services and to curb Yorkshire Water's price increases '96-97; while she was canvassing, "I visited two of my constituents in January"; "these people had worked hard throughout their lives and had made savings, but were having some difficulties; they showed me into their best room because they wanted to show themselves at their very best, and certainly provided me with a cup of tea; I became blue with cold in that room because they could not put on their heating" Jan '97; "I spoke in person to more than 1,000 people in my constituency...in particular, on VAT on fuel"; she found local voters preferred plain speaking: "what did they like about Margaret Thatcher?" "people liked the simplicity of her message; she appealed to many women who liked practical arguments rather than the academic; she talked in terms of how policies would affect them, their sons and daughters, their shopping baskets; these are people who do not think in terms of, say, internal markets and Thatcher [knew] that; and, it has to be said, they disliked Kinnock - whether it was because he was Welsh, or even because he had red hair, there are many theories; but he was sold to them through the press as a windbag who made mistakes - which I don't agree with"; "then there was this fear of trade unions; people who have not been in unions tend to demonise them, afraid that they really are hot-beds of Communists waiting to control the Labour Party; anyone involved in unions these days would bark a bitter, hollow laugh at such suggestions, but for those outside the trade union movement, such myths are strong"; "Tony Blair is delivering them the clarity that Thatcher once appeared to have, although she ultimately failed them; Tony Blair's talk about building communities means more to them than grand socialist dreams"; Blair's saying that privatising air traffic control could not be ruled out appealed to Yorkshire people as "simply checking whether the public's money is being wisely spent" Apr '97; she took the seat on a 10.4% swing, unseating incumbent Tory MP Graham Riddick by a majority of 4,840 May '97; in her Maiden extolled the local public-private partnership which had converted a former mill into 122 new homes, adding: "if we were able to release the £30m of housing capital receipts now held for Kirklees Council, imagine how we could spend that money to invigorate our local economy"; she also wanted to use the windfall levy to finance "a new environmental task force" to renovate "its canals, rivers and dry stone walls" May '97; co-sponsored motion celebrating restoration of union rights at GCHQ May '97; urged "long-term spending plans for public spending priorities" June '97; asked for speeded appeals procedures for social security benefits June '97; expressed solidarity with jailed Indonesian union leader June '97; complained that three-quarters of small businesses closing in Colne Valley had done so due to lack of investment July '97; pointed out that a constituent had been mis-sold a personal pension plan and "lost nearly £7,000 of his savings; he used to be a Tory voter, but he was so disappointed by what happened with his personal pension plan that he reverted to the Labour Party" July '97; asked new Government to assess why 1,150 pensioners in her constituency did not take up their available pensions July '97; pointed out that, on four monthly occasions, the former Chancellor, Kenneth Clarke, had declined to put up interest rates, although warned about the danger of missing the inflation target July '97; urged a review of the sporting events reserved for terrestrial TV July '97; said she had received only one letter in favour of retaining tax relief on pensioners' private medical insurance fees July '97; urged a reform of the compensation recovery scheme, whereby injured workers who received benefit while unemployed, had much of the benefit recovered once they received compensation awards for their injuries July '97; speaking on the Social Security Bill, disclosed she had been for 20 years a civil servant in the Benefit Service; originally clerks had to calculate benefits in their heads and were not allowed to use calculators; when computers were introduced they resented them, because they thought them a threat to their jobs and believed they were "more humane and more caring"; then the system improved and "people got decisions more quickly and the decisions were more accurate" July '97; urged action against employers who withheld their employees NIS payments on July '97;

Born: 12 January 1954, Crewe

Family: Her father is a retired train driver, her mother a retired dinner lady; she is married to Ian Leedham; they have a son and a daughter and three grandchildren;

Education: Crewe Grammar School for Girls (had to leave at 16); Crewe and Alsager College (BA Hons in Philosophy, Psychology and Sociology; graduated at 35);

Occupation: Civil Servant, in Department of Employment (CPSA) '75-96; "in 1975, I joined the Benefits Service as a young and inexperienced clerk"; had to resign in '96, after having been selected, "I was unemployed for a year before the election" (KM);

Traits: A big head of reddish-blonde hair; full-faced; chubby; persistent; enjoys "reading anything she's told not to";

Address: House of Commons, Westminster, London SW1A 0AA; 16 Hilltop Fold, Slaithwaite, Huddersfield HD7 5EQ;

Telephone: 0171 219 4507 (H of C); 01484 841471 (home); 01484 841473/841471(Fax) (constituency);

Dennis MURPHY **Labour** **WANSBECK '97-**

Majority: 22,367 over Liberal Democrat 5-way;
Description: An unaltered Northumberland seat based on the lovely market town of Morpeth, after which it was named until '83; northeast of Newcastle, squeezed between the Blyth Valley and Berwick-upon-Tweed, it embraces as well the major former coalmining town of Ashington - the home of Jackie Milburn and Bobby and Jackie Charlton; it includes Bedlington, home of the Northumbrian (bag)pipes, and the quiet seaside town of Newbiggin, which is also industrial: Alcan aluminium, chemicals and pharmaceuticals; the seat also houses affluent commuters from Newcastle;
Position: Wansbeck District Councillor (its Leader '94-) '90-;
Outlook: The "Newish Labour" (NEW STATESMAN) former mines electrician who "will probably be the last miners' Member of Parliament to represent my constituency" because of the "near closure of the mining industry" there (DM); one of only 12 NUM members in a PLP of 418 and the only new one;
History: He joined the NUM, then the Labour Party; as an NUM-sponsored candidate, was elected to Wansbeck District Council May '90; became Leader of Wansbeck District Council May '94; on the announced retirement of Jack Thompson, was selected as his successor Nov '96; his selection was endorsed by the NEC Jan '97; the decimated NUM was not able to contribute to his election funds Apr '97; retained the seat on a 2.5% swing from the Liberal Democrats, with a majority up by over 4,000 to 22,387; Tories sank into third place May '97; in his Maiden, admitted he was probably the last miners' MP from Wansbeck because of the death of coalmining; "our people however have not sat back and whinged; they have worked in partnership with local government and the private sector to expand and broaden the base of the local economy" June '97;
Born: 2 November 1948, Ashington
Family: He is married, with two children;
Education: St Cuthbert's Grammar School, Newcastle-upon-Tyne; Northumberland College;
Occupation: General Secretary, of the Association for Colliery Mechanics '94-; Mines Electrician, in Ashington Colliery '65-94; "I was made redundant three years ago [in '94]; I...signed on the dole along with many colleagues with whom I had worked for more than 25 years"; "part of the team with which I had worked...are still out of work" in '97; "what a terrible human waste" (DM);
Traits: Parted greying dark hair; specs; articulate;
Address: House of Commons, Westminster, London SW1A 0AA; 87 Ariel Street, Ashington, Northumberland NE63 9EB;
Telephone: 0171 219 3000 (H of C);

'Jim' (James) MURPHY **Labour** **EASTWOOD '97-**

Majority: 3,236 over Conservative 7-way;
Description: The renamed middle-class suburban seat southwest of Glasgow, formerly called East Renfrewshire; it was the Scottish Tories' safest seat, despite its pro-Labour "blemish", industrial Barrhead, where the WC was invented;
Position: Projects Manager, Scottish Labour Party '96-97; ex: President, National Union of Students '94-96; President, National Union of Students (Scotland) '92-94; on Scottish Executive of Labour Party '91-92;
Outlook: The first Labour MP for Eastwood for 73 years; one of four former NUS Presidents in Labour's '97 intake; wrote the first policy documents for the 'Network' of Scottish moderates wishing to pull the Leftish Scottish Labour Party into alignment with the centrist Labour leadership nationally; an "impeccable Blairite...fixer with good London contacts" (NEW STATESMAN); "an affable [Scottish] version of Mandelson, working behind [the] scenes to get loyalists into position" (RED PEPPER); an eager-beaver 'New Labour' super-loyalist, always willing to go to bat against Tories in the Commons, even without being tickled by the Whips; in the Fabians and Labour Friends of Israel;
History: After spending his teens in South Africa, "witnesssing the evil of Apartheid" (JM), returned determined to view the British political process as a "source of opportunities, not problems"; was elected Chairman of Scottish Labour Students; was elected President of Scottish NUS '92; was elected President of the national NUS on a platform endorsing free higher education '94; as President of the NUS, changed it into a charity, and persuaded it to back post-graduate repayments of fees '96; was selected to fight Scottish Tories' safest seat of Eastwood '96; won the seat on a swing of 14.3% by a majority of 3,236 May '97; made his Maiden as "the first Labour MP for Eastwood for nearly three-quarters of a century" July '97; asked about the settlement of the contracts with Norwegian arms company negotiated by the fraudster Gordon Foxley July '97; co-sponsored motion on pensions mis-selling under the Tories July '97; in the debate on the Finance Bill disclosed that almost 40% of the young in his middle-class constituency were unemployed July '97; his letter trying to organise Labour MPs' visits to the Uxbridge by-election, on Commons stationery, was discovered by Scottish emigre Tory MP Eleanor Laing July '97;
Born: 23 August 1967, Glasgow
Family: He is "the son of a plumber and a dinner lady who [returned] from South Africa" (PRIVATE EYE);
Education: Bellarmine Secondary School, Glasgow; Milnerton High School, Cape Town, South Africa; Strathclyde University (Law and Politics);
Occupation: President, of National Union of Students '94-96, Director of Endsleigh Insurance (its insurance company) '94-96;
Traits: Thin; dark; centre-parted hair; beaky; ambitious; voluble-articulate; enjoys football, horseracing;
Address: House of Commons, Westminster, London SW1A 0AA; 52 Albert Avenue, Glasgow G42 8RE;
Telephone: 0171 219 3000 (H of C); 0181 802 4309 (home);

Dr (John) Doug(las) NAYSMITH FRSM **Labour-Co-operative** **BRISTOL NORTH WEST '97-**

Majority: 11,382 over Conservative 8-way;
Description: Altered seat made up seven-eighths of old marginal Bristol NW, one-eighth of Northavon wards; has lost an ultra-Tory ward, Westbury-on-Trym, and gained three Labour-leaning wards in Patchway; two-thirds owner-occupiers, one-third council tenants; still has Filton (British Aerospace aircraft and Rolls-Royce engines) and Avonmouth Port; has long been a "barometer seat" (BRISTOL EVENING POST);
Position: Delegate to Council of Europe and WEU '97-; Vice Chairman, PLP Health Committee '97-; Bristol City Councillor (Labour Group Whip '88-97, Chairman Docks Committee '86-91) '81-; ex: National President, Socialist Health Association '90-97; Bristol Council Director on Board of Bristol Port Company '91-95; on NEC Co-operative Party '93-97; Chairman, Bristol District Labour Party '78-81, President, Bristol AUT '85-87;
Outlook: Veteran Labour candidate who has struck it lucky the fourth time; an active AUT trade unionist and former CND supporter; a crusading President of the Socialist Health Association and a life-long supporter of the Co-operative movement into which he was born; supports Amnesty International, World Development Movement and Bristol and Bath Wildlife Trust; a "pragmatic Leftwinger with a strong commitment to the NHS" (NEW STATESMAN); a Scot who, as a longtime Bristol University medical lecturer and local councillor is deeply rooted in local politics; one of the oldest of the '97 Labour intake;
History: His parents and most relatives were Labour Party members: initially his father paid his party subscriptions; he joined the Labour Party, paying his own subscriptions at 25, '66; a resident of Bristol since '72, was elected Chairman of the Bristol District Labour Party '78; contested Bristol in Euro-elections June '79; was selected for hopeless Cirencester and Tewkesbury '86; in reply to Nicholas Ridley, who claimed that Labour councils like Bristol were as repressive as East Germany and Poland, said: "people are fearful in [Cirencester], but the kinds of things they are frightened of are losing their jobs, not being able to get a house and, thanks to Mr Ridley, of finding their bus services disrupted by the Government" Nov '86; criticised inequality under the poll tax, claiming the rich - including Ridley - would save thousands a year at the expense of the poor May '87; came third in Cirencester and Tewkesbury behind Nicholas Ridley and the second-place Liberal, with only 8% of the vote, like his 1983 predecessor, June '87; became Labour Whip on Bristol City Council '88; was selected for Bristol North West over ex-MP Terry Walker and Dr Sarah Palmer, daughter of a former Bristol MP; his candidacy was thought to be helped by his wife being a local GP in Southmead and his daughter Catherine in the sixth form at Henbury; said it would be a "tough fight" to overcome the 6,952 majority of the incumbent Tory MP, Michael Stern Jan '90; he missed taking the seat by 45 votes, after achieving a 6% swing Apr '92; was re-selected to contest Bristol North West '95; won the seat on a notional swing of 7.12%, ousting the incumbent Tory MP Michael Stern by a majority of 11,382 May '97; asked about benzodiazepine addiction July '97; asked about improved relations between the prison and probation services July '97;
Born: 1 April 1941, Musselburgh, Midlothian

Family: Son, of James Chalmers Naysmith, charge hand in Co-op grocery, and Wilhelmina (Vass), manageress of Co-op hardware department; m '66 Margaret Caroline (Hill), GP; 1s, Stephen '68; 1d Catherine '73; separated;
Education: Musselburgh Burgh School; George Heriot's School; Edinburgh University (BSc, PhD); Yale University (Post-Doctoral Fellowship); FRSM, MI Biol, CR Biol, PR D;
Occupation: Scientist-Administrator, Bristol University '81-97; Lecturer in Pathology, Bristol University Medical School (AUT -has been President, and Secretary and Treasurer of its Bristol branch) '72-81 ; ex: Open University Tutor '73-79; Medical Scientist with Beecham Research Laboratories '69-72; Medical Technician in Civil Service '58-61;
Traits: Front-falling grey hair; grey beard; specs; active in the Paddle Steamer Preservation Society; enjoys films, swimming and watching football;
Address: House of Commons, Westminster, London SW1A 0AA; 2 St Mary's Road, Shirehampton, Bristol BS11 9RN;
Telephone: 0171 219 4187 (H of C); 0117 938 0804 (home & Fax);

'Archie' (Archibald John) NORMAN Conservative TUNBRIDGE WELLS '97-

Majority: 7,506 over Liberal Democrat 6-way;
Description: Kent's fourth safest Tory seat: an elegant and affluent inland spa with an old tradition and a prosperous hinterland; this has been reduced by the cutting away of Cranbrook and Sissinghurst as part of the Boundary Commission's effort to provide Kent with a seventeeth constituency;
Position: Vice Chairman, of the Conservative Party '97-; ex: Patron, North East Bow Group; on Council of Federation of Conservative Students '75-76;
Outlook: An outspoken graduate of the "McKinsey Mafia" like the new Conservative Leader; the first FT-SE Chairman to enter the Commons for over three decades; with a first-class track record in improving large organisations, believes in a bottom-up managerial revolution, admittedly often on the basis of borrowed ideas: "I never have any good ideas"; "in retailing it is not essential to have original ideas; it is essential to be good at copying other people's"; was "one of the few prominent representatives" among Tory candidates "coming from business and manufacturing" (James Blitz, FINANCIAL TIMES); wants to instill excitement and motivation into a defeated Tory Party after having predicted: "it's possible we may lose the next general election; well, it's not just possible"; "I'm not going in as a political careerist; I'm going in as a businessman"; "I am prepared to be tough; [in ASDA] we made 5,000 people redundant; I hope we did it with care and concern, but that's business"; a pro-European and anti-federalist, he believes a single European currency should be off the agenda for the next decade; he has long had close links with Francis Maude, a Director of ASDA; "the youngest chief executive yet of a FT-SE 100 company", he led the revival of ASDA through US-style staff involvement - the "Tell Archie" campaign - and union-shrinking" (Neil Buckley, FINANCIAL TIMES): his turn-around of ASDA made him the City's pin-up; his next task: the Conservative Party;
History: He helped Charles Morrison MP in Devizes Feb '74, David Lane MP in Cambridge Oct '74; became Chairman of Cambridge University Conservative Association '75, Chairman of Eastern Region Federation of Conservative Students '75; unsuccessully contested

Southwark Council seats '83 and '86; campaigned for Iain Sproat in his unsuccessful contest against Archie Kirkwood in Roxburgh and Berwickshire June '83; campaigned successfully to provide tax relief on share options for low-paid employees, including 30,000 in ASDA Nov '95; campaigned successfully to end the price-fixing Net Book Agreement Nov '95; banned foreign beef from shelves of ASDA May '96; was selected for super-safe Tunbridge Wells in the wake of retiring Sir Patrick Mayhew, beating Sarah Whitehouse, barrister, and Professor Philip Treleaven, a former MEP candidate, Andrew Tyrie and Alan Clark Nov '96; in a NEW STATESMAN interview said the Tories would possibly lose the looming general election Nov '96; was one of 59 Tory prospective candidates who favoured ruling out in their election addresses Britain's entry into a single European currency during the next Parliament Dec '96; said that he would remain a part-time Chairman of ASDA because "being a backbench MP is not a full-time occupation" Dec '96; opposed hostile takeover of Kent Water by its French-owned neighbours, South East Water and Folkestone & Dover Dec '96; retained Tunbridge Wells with a majority of 7,506 (down from 13,146) despite a notional swing of 5% to the LibDems May '97; joined the campaign team of William Hague, a fellow member of the "McKinsey Mafia" May '97; he was named a Vice Chairman and asked to recommend changes to reform and reorganise the Conservative Party by its new Leader, William Hague June '97; his Maiden was a comprehensive attack on Labour's first Budget, particularly the minimum wage, the windfall tax on the privatised utilities and the end of subsidies on pensioners' private medical insurance ("short-sighted, mean-spirited and economically insignificant") July '97; caught the mood of the Tory annual conference at Blackpool in urging serious party reform Oct '97;

Born: 1 May 1954, London

Family: Son, of Archibald Percie Norman MBE, MD FRCP, and Aleida Elisabeth (Bisschop) Doctor; m '92, Vanessa (Peet) publisher; 1d Florence '84. formerly at Newbury boarding school;

Education: Charterhouse; University of Minnesota; Emmanuel College, Cambridge University (BA Hons in Economics; MA); Harvard Business School (MBA);

Occupation: Chairman '96-, Group Chief Executive '91-96, ASDA Group Plc (Britain's 3rd biggest grocers, with £6.5b in sales; in '96 he picked up a total of £2.2m from his ASDA job, mostly from cashing in share options; in '95 he earned £3.69m in pay and options); Director: Railtrack Plc '94-, of DTI Deregulation Task Force '94-; Hill Farmer in Scotland: a 700-acre family farm on Arran off the West Coast; ex: Group Finance Director, Kingfisher Plc (Britain's largest retailer with £3b in sales) '86-91; Director, Geest Plc '87-91; on British Railways Board '92-94; Partner (its youngest), in McKinsey & Company Inc (management consultants) '79-86; Account Manager, in Corporate Financing, Citibank NA '75-77;

Traits: Youthful-looking; brown, front-falling parted hair; boxer's nose; "tall, lean and fresh-faced, he is earnest and reserved, apt to lapse into the consultant-speak learned through a Harvard MBA and seven years with McKinsey" (Neil Buckley, FINANCIAL TIMES); "flamboyant" (NEW STATESMAN); inclined to "populist rhetoric" Rogert Cowe, GUARDIAN); "is both direct and intractable, condemned - always anonymously - as a cold fish; a figure who is held in overwhelming deference, despite his jolly exterior"; "only Monday evenings are sacrosanct, reserved for soccer (he plays midfield in the office team) and pizza to follow" (Mary Riddell, NEW STATESMAN); enjoys opera, tennis, ski-ing; practicing member of Church of England;

Address: House of Commons, Westminster, London SW1A 0AA; Park House Farm, Ribston Park, Little Ribston, nr Wetherby, North Yorkshire LS22 4EZ;

Telephone: 0171 219 3000 (H of C); 01892 522 581; 01892 522 582 (Fax); 0113 243 5435 (work);

Dan NORRIS **Labour** **WANSDYKE '97-**

Majority: 4,799 over Conservative 7-way;
Description: The successor to the old North Somerset constituency, extended in '95 to take in the Chew Valley; centered on Keynsham, between Bristol and Bath, it has lots of affluent commuter villages and a defunct coalfield; was considered a Conservative stronghold and, had '97 been like '92, its Tory candidate was entitled to expect an 11,000-plus majority; the only hint of a possible looming change was when Labour overtook the LibDems, taking second place in '92;
Position: Bristol City Councillor '95-97, '89-92; ex: Avon County Councillor '94-96;
Outlook: Third-time-lucky surprise winner, initially very low-profiled except locally; "the acceptable face of socialism: undogmatic, thoughtful, interested" (BRISTOL EVENING POST); another of Labour's many local councillors with experience of the public sector, as a child-protection social worker and previously a teacher; in the Socialist Education Association, League Against Cruel Sports, formerly Anti-Apartheid;
History: The son of an active Labour-supporter and feminist mother, later a Labour councillor and Parliamentary candidate, he joined the Labour Party at 18, '78; he supported his mother June, as Labour's candidate for Northavon May-June '83; he was selected as her successor as candidate '85; after campaigning strongly against cuts in local bus lines and hospital services and secrecy about the local nuclear power stations, he came 3rd as Tory MP John Cope's opponent, with 13.9% of the vote June '87; he was elected to Bristol City Council May '89; was elected to Avon County Council May '94; selected for difficult Wansdyke, he increased the Labour vote from 23.3% in '87 to 27.7%, pushing the LibDems into 3rd place, but still trailing 13,341 votes behind the incumbent Tory MP, Jack Aspinwall Apr '92; was re-selected for the still difficult seat, despite the expected retirement of its spine-injured incumbent Tory MP '95; his victory was predicted in the WESTERN DAILY PRESS and DAILY MIRROR Jan '97; when candidates were invited to a public meeting in Keynsham and he was unable to come "for personal reasons", he was represented instead by his mother, also a Labour councillor and former Parliamentary candidate Apr '97; won the seat on a notional swing of 14.4% ousting the new Tory candidate by a majority of 4,799 May '97; co-sponsored motion deploring the problems of employees with legitimate compensation claims whose former employers have gone into liquidation July '97;
Born: 28 January 1960, London
Family: Son, of David Norris, social worker, formerly rates manager, and June (Allen), a feminist (in 300 Group) and Labour candidate for Northavon '83 and later a Labour councillor on Avon Council;
Education: State primaries and comprehensives in Avon; Sussex University (MSW)
Occupation: Researcher and Trainer in Prevention and Reduction of Violence (GMB/APEX) '92-97; Honorary Fellow, of the School of Cultural and Community Studies, University of Sussex '89-; Author, 'Violence Against Social Workers' (1990); ex: Child Protection Social Worker (NUPE/NALGO) '86-92; Residential Social Worker '85-86; Teacher (NAS-UWT) '84-85;
Traits: Dark upstanding hair; long oval face with strong, dimpled chin; "his style is the quiet, caring listener, not surprising from a social worker specialising in child abuse cases"

(BRISTOL EVENING POST); enjoys swimming and photography;
Address: House of Commons, Westminster, London SW1A 0AA;
Telephone: 0171 219 3000 (H of C); 0117 985 4856 (office);

Mark OATEN **Liberal Democrat** **WINCHESTER '97-**

Majority: 2 over Conservative 8-way;
Description: The most affluent of constituencies, with its sumptuous cathedral, prestigious Winchester College and well-heeled and almost fully-employed inhabitants; in '95 its geographic epicentre shifted to the south, with the loss of 20,000 voters from its northeast, around Alton, to redrawn Hampshire East; in compensation it gained 15,000 voters on its southern flank from Fareham; this was nothing compared to the shift in its political epicentre to midway between the Tories and the LibDems, according to the challenged ballot of May '97;
Position: On the LibDem Social Security team '97-; ex: Watford Borough Councillor (Leader its Liberal Democrat Group) '86-94;
Outlook: A young lobbyist, formerly in the SDP, in real politics as a Liberal Democratic MP, by a hairsbreath; played a very low-profile national role initially while awaiting the outcome of the court challenge from his opponent, Gerald Malone and the court's decision for a rematch;
History: Joined the Social Democrats '83; was elected to Watford Borough Council as a Social Democrat at 22, one of the country's youngest councillors May '86; joined the merged Liberal Democrats '88; became the Leader of the LibDems on Watford Council '90; selected to contest Watford agains incumbent Tristan Garel-Jones, came 3rd with 17.2% (3,000 less votes than the SDP had registered in '87, which had gone back to Labour) Apr '92; was selected for Winchester June '95; at the annual LibDem conference claimed William Beveridge had "set up the Health Service" Sep '96; after a count and two recounts lasting 19 hours - making it the last result to be declared - was proclaimed to have won Winchester by 2 votes over incumbent, Health Minister Gerald Malone; there was also a rogue candidate Richard Huggett (the '94 "Literal Democrat"), who polled 640 votes at Winchester as the "Liberal Democrat Top Choice" May '97; expressed himself as "astonished" that Gerald Malone had mounted a legal challenge to overturn the result, saying "this is a touch of sour grapes; he should have accepted defeat honourably" May '97; asked about suicides in Winchester Prison May '97; in his Maiden urged a radical reform of the Commons and a ban on copycat candidates; led motion calling on MPs to deliver an annual report to every constituent July '97; asked about responsibility for pupils' safety on buses July '97; voted against Labour's Budget, against its ban on handguns June-July '97; it was suggested he would have to face a re-run of his disputed election for Winchester Aug-Sep '97; the court ordered a repeat poll Oct '97;
Born: 8 March 1964, Watford
Family: Son, of Condell Oaten, rtd teacher, and Audrey (Matthews), Director of a computer firm; m '92. Belinda (Fordham); 1d Alice '96;
Education: Greens Secondary Modern, Watford; Hatfield Polytechnic (later Hertfordshire University);
Occupation: Managing Director, of Westminster Public Relations (public relations

consultancy, with the Audit Commission as one of its main clients) '94-; Director, of Oasis Radio;
Traits: Parted blond retreating hair; longish face; youthful looking; enjoys swimming and gardening; confessed to TODAY in '86 that he had been "a love rat", leaving a girl stranded in a pub while he left her for another, saying "I'm a local councillor...I had been called out at the last minute";
Address: House of Commons, Westminster, London SW1A 0AA;
Telephone: 0171 219 6232 (H of C); 01962 779997 (home); 0171 222 0666 (Westminster Public Relations);

Lembit OPIK **Liberal Democrat** **MONTGOMERYSHIRE '97-**

Majority: 6,303 over Conservative 6-way;
Description: Rural Welsh marginal county with more sheep than people, a fifth of whom speak Welsh; once had Laura Ashley as a new industry before its decline; has had an almost-unbroken Liberal tradition for a century, although its recent spokesmen have been somewhat exotic imports;
Position: Spokesman on Northern Ireland '97- and Youth '97-; on LibDems' Parliamentary Welsh team '97-; Newcastle City Councillor '92-; on Federal Executive of Liberal Democrats '91-; ex: on LibDems Parliamentary Education team May-July '97; Deputy Chairman, Northern Region Liberal Democrats '91-96; Vice Chairman, Newcastle Liberal Democrats '92-93;
Outlook: One of the most sensibly assiduous of the LibDem new boys; a shrewd questioner, he is sinking his Welsh roots while applying the skills learned at Procter and Gamble and on Newcastle Council; an exotic, soft-spoken, political gypsy: Ulster-born of Estonian refugee parents, Bristol-educated but recently Newcastle-based as a Procter & Gamble executive; was widely-travelled in that multinational job;
History: Became President of the Bristol University Student Union '85; joined the National Executive of the NUS Apr '87; stood as an independent for the President of the NUS '88; was elected to Federal Executive of Liberal Democrats Oct '91; contested Newcastle-upon-Tyne Central against Jim Cousins, coming 3rd with 14% of the vote, 2% down on his '87 predecessor Apr '92; was elected to Newcastle City Council May '92; contested Northumbria in Euro-election June '94; in the wake of Alex Carlile's announced imminent retirement, was selected quite unexpectedly for Montgomeryshire, exchanging one ethnic exotic for another Sep '96; in a speech to Liberal Democrats' annual conference, described John Major as a "useless git" Sep '96; in the election campaign emphasised the perilous state of the local NHS, adding: "only the Liberal Democrats have the courage and honesty to say not only how we would protect the Health Service, but also how we would pay for it" Apr '97; retained Montgomershire with an enhanced 6,303 majority, on a 2% swing to the LibDems May '97; was initially (and briefly) named to the LibDems' Parliamentary Education team May '97; in his Maiden, strongly supported devolution to a Welsh Assembly and the end of the stultifying "quango culture" while conceding Labour was "timid" to require a referendum May '97; warned that the problem with New-York-style "zero tolerance is that many people involved

with tackling youth crime tend to feel that it leads to zero understanding of why young people become involved in crime in the first place" June '97; on behalf of the LibDems, supported Labour's abolition of the Assisted Places Scheme, but wanted "local authorities to have some limited flexibility" to provide students with special educational opportunities June '97; urged the Government to provide the BBC World Service with "funding intentions for five years" June '97; urged more investment in training June '97; co-sponsored motion deploring cut in payment to beef farmers July '97; was named Spokesman on Ulster and Youth and placed on the LibDems' Welsh team, being dropped from the Education team July '97; welcomed the Welsh Assembly, although it was not fully proportional in its election July '97; urged a modification of rules on the marching season in Ulster, the land of his birth July '97;
Born: 2 March 1965, Bangor, County Down, Northern Ireland
Family: His grandfather, Ernest Opik, was an astronomer; son, of Uono Opik, Lecturer in Physics and Maths, and Liivi (Redo); the name Opik (with an umlaut over the O) is very unusual, even in Estonia; his parents left Estonia separately in wartime, to avoid the invading Russians, meeting up in the UK and settling in Ulster, where he was born; he has a girl-friend called Samantha Parrish, school teacher;
Education: Royal Belfast Academical Institution; Bristol University (BA Hons in Philosophy);
Occupation: Procter & Gamble Executive '88-97: Global Human Resources Manager '96-97, Corporate Training and Organisation Development Manager '91-96, Assistant Brand Manager '89-91, Brand Assistant '88-89;
Traits: Young; tall; brown hair; long thin face and long chin; has the look of a graduate student; slightly twists his mouth when speaking; specs; humorous; soft-spoken; Ulster intonation; points out that his name is an anagram of "I like to b MP" or "I kil to be MP"; has often been called "Lemsip" or "Optic"; a Lutheran; has two motorcycles and a pilot's licence; a conjurer; also enjoys paragliding and windsurfing;
Address: House of Commons, Westminster, London SW1A 0AA; Tynyreithin Hall, Newtown, Powys SY163JZ;
Telephone: 0171 219 1144 (H of C); 0973 891365 (mobile); 01686 625527 (constituency office); 01665 574383 (political officer);

Mrs Diana ORGAN **Labour** **FOREST OF DEAN '97-**

Majority: 6,343 over Conservative 7-way;
Description: The scenic ancient forest of the former West Gloucestershire seat between the Wye Valley and the Severn, stripped of 17,000 pro-Tory voters in suburban towns around Gloucester; this brings it back, in name and fact, to the former traditionally pro-Labour area of the Forest of Dean, whose loyalties depended on small towns and villages clustered around tiny coalmines, now longsince worked out; it has a separate dialect and identity;
Position: On the Select Committees: on Agriculturre '97-, and the Joint Committee on Statutory Instruments '97-; Chairman, of the PLP Committee for Culture, Media and Sport '97-; ex: on Labour's South West Regional Executive '90-91; on South West Women's Committee '87-90; on

Political Advisory Board of Television South West '88-90; Assistant Secretary, Somerton and Frome CLP '87-90;

Outlook: The former Deputy Head of a primary school and a specialist in special-needs teaching; has campaigned hard for neglected rural communities, both in '92 and '97; succeeded after the Boundary Commission helped make her second bite of the cherry more tasty without Gloucester's Tory suburbs; a feminist in the 300 Group who thinks women candidates and MPs will alter the public's perception of Labour as no longer made up of "working-class, middle-aged men"; a "fiery campaigner...strong on women's issues" (NEW STATESMAN); wants "an end to poverty pay"

History: She joined the Labour Party '70, left it in '73, rejoined it in '82; was selected to contest the Euro-constituency of Somerset and Dorset West against Tory MEP Margaret Daly; while narrowing her difference over Europe with her pro-European Tory opponent, she also campaigned on the dangers to single-industry towns of the South West in further European unification June '89; refused to pay poll tax but opposed a campaign for mass non-payment Apr '90; was selected to contest West Gloucestershire '90; at a candidates' conference confessed that on the doorstep, she kept being asked, "Why don't you get rid of that man Kinnock? Then I might vote Labour" Oct '91; in the general election increased the Labour vote by almost 7,000, more than halving the majority of incumbent Tory MP Paul Marland Apr '92; was re-selected from an all-women short-list to fight the restored seat of Forest of Dean Mar '95; said: "Labour used to be so biased towards their favoured sons it was risible; seats were kept warm for working-class middle-aged men; when it comes to an election, no one will remember the infighting; they will just see a modern-looking party" May '95; she changed her tune when the women-only short-list was ruled illegal: "it puts us in a bit of a mess; I'm a bit annoyed that the Labour Party went ahead with it when it was likely to be against the Sex Discrimination Act; potentially, in some seats we could have more men who feel disgruntled and think 'this is my chance'" Jan '96; was accused by Paul Marland of falsely foisting on Chancellor Kenneth Clarke the intention of imposing VAT on Severn Bridge tolls Jan '97; said, "I want to make the state system [of education] so good that the public [school] system withers on the vine" Mar '97; won the seat on a notional swing of 5.6% ousting incumbent Tory MP Paul Marland by a majority of 6,343 May '97; welcomed the end of nursery vouchers as having caused "huge amounts of unnecessary work" in the Forest of Dean "while not extending provision" May '97; urged "an equal and fair share of lottery funding" for rural areas like the Forest of Dean May '97; co-sponsored motion celebrating the return of union rights at GCHQ May '97; in her Maiden insisted her 18 years as a teacher, mainly of children with learning difficulties, had convinced her of the importance of "first-time good [teaching] practice in smaller classes" June '97; led motion endorsing Millennium celebrations June '97; expressed solidarity with imprisoned Indonesian union leader June '97; said her local pensioners would be delighted with the reduced VAT on fuel June '97; deploring the "appalling" standards previously reached in English by 11-year-olds, urged improved teaching methods "at key stage 2" June '97; expressed doubts about the monitoring of educational standards, particularly about Ofsted's Chief Inspector, Christopher Woodhead July '97; was named to the Select Committee on Agriculture and the Joint Committee of the Select Committee on Statutory Instruments July '97; urged policies to "develop and sustain rural areas" but not including "large-scale private housing developments" July '97;

Born: 21 February 1952, West Bromwich

Family: Daughter, of Jack Pugh, Finance Comptroller of GKN, and Vera; m Richard Organ, Managing Director (Manufacturing) of Jaeger; 2d: Lucy '82, Daisy '86;

Education: Edgbaston Church of England School for Girls; St Hugh's College, Oxford University (BA Hons in Geography); University of Bath School of Education; Bristol

Polytechnic (Diploma in Special Education);
Occupation: Researcher, for Labour Group on Oxfordshire County Council (UNISON) '93-95; Head of Special Education Unit, Somerset '79-82; Deputy Head, of St Germans VC Primary School, Cornwall (NUT) '77-79; Special Needs Teacher '79-82, 86-92;
Traits: Light blonde hair in a short tonsure; attractive-featured triangular face; "articulate and lively" (Kate Ironside, BRISTOL EVENING POST); enjoys sailing, gardening, swimming, cinema and travelling;
Address: House of Commons, Westminster, London SW1A 0AA; 4 Elsfield Road, Old Marston, Oxford OX3 0PR;
Telephone: 0171 219 5498 (H of C); 01865 243312 (home); 01594 516097 (FoD);

Sandra OSBORNE **Labour** **AYR '97-**

Majority: 6,543 over Conservative 5-way;
Description: The birthplace of Robert Burns; formerly the Conservatives' most vulnerable Scottish seat, it narrowly avoided being lost to them in '92; in '95 it had strong Tory wards removed; it still includes Prestwick, home to British Aerospace, and Troon, with its championship golf course and Ailsa Shipbuilding, and 17 miles of sandy beaches;
Position: On the Select Committee on Information '97-; South Ayrshire Councillor (Secretary of Labour Group, Convenor of Community Services, Housing and Social Work) '95-; ex: Kyle and Carrick District Councillor '91-96; on Scottish Women's Committee; Secretary of Ayr CLP '86-90;
Outlook: The first-ever Labour MP and first woman for this constituency; also one of the rare women to follow their living husbands as candidates; a community worker with victims of domestic violence (Kilmarnock Women's Aid); was a finalist for 'Scottish Woman of the Year' '97; a homeruler: "my priority is a Scottish Parliament; it will give women a greater input, especially for health and education"; a Blairite moderniser: "New Labour believes that people should progress through merit and hard work";
History: She joined the Labour Party '77; became Secretary of Ayr CLP '86; was elected to Kyle and Carrick District Council May '91; her husband Alistair fought the Ayr constituency, losing by only 85 votes Apr '92; she later commented: "I had to convert Alistair from the SNP; then he went on to do so well"; she became a South Ayrshire Councillor May '95; was selected for Ayr from an all-women's short-list, her husband, Alistair - the '92 candidate - having been ruled out Sep '95; she later commented: "I make no excuses for having been involved in such a controversial exercise and indeed I think it should have been continued; there is no doubt that we need more women in Parliament"; said her husband "will be supporting me in the coming weeks and I plan to go one better than him, although I freely admit that it will not be easy" Apr '97; was elected on a notional swing of 5.2%, ousting the incumbent Tory MP Phil Gallie by a majority of 6,543 May '97; made her graceful Maiden in the fishing debate, calling attention to the low morale in the industry and in fish processing in her constituency July '97;
Born: 23 February 1956, Paisley
Family: Married to Alistair Osborne, community worker, former Church of Scotland minister and the '92 candidate for this seat; they have two children;

Education: Camphill Senior Secondary School, Paisley; Anniesland College; Jordanhill College (Diploma in Community Education); Strathclyde University (MSc);
Occupation: Kilmarnock Women's Aid Worker (TGWU) '83-97; ex: Glasgow Community Worker '76-80;
Traits: Parted reddish-brown hair with bangs; specs; has a sense of humour (asked why she had become an MP, said she was too short and too old to become a fire-fighter);
Address: House of Commons, Westminster, London SW1A 0AA; 57 Brewlands Drive, Symington, Ayrshire KA1 5RQ. less than five minutes from Prestwick airport;
Telephone: 0171 219 3000 (H of C); 01292 476000 (home);

Dr 'Nick' (Nicholas) PALMER  **Labour** **BROXTOWE '97-**

Majority: 5,575 over Conservative 4-way;
Description: One of Nottingham's three main middle-class residential suburbs, together with Gedling and Rushcliffe (the only survivor of the '97 Labour floodtide); it embraces Beeston (Boots headquarters), after which it was named until '83, and a number of suburban communities curving around the western fringe of Nottingham; these house overwhelmingly white middle-class voters; its ultimate destiny was indicated in '92, when its longtime incumbent, 'One Nation' Tory MP Jim Lester, had his majority cut from 16,651 to 9,971;
Outlook: A multilingual, foreign-educated computer scientist, one of half a dozen senior scientists recruited by Labour; he unseated another internationalist he much respected, Sir James Lester; his early months in Parliament gave little indication as to how his formidable skills will adapt to domestic politics; so far it has been limited to applying TQM (Top Quality Managment) techniques from business, like same-day acknowledgements for all letters, one day to help constituents with crisis requests, three days for non-urgent inquiries; a hero of the Cleft Palate Association; in Labour Finance and Industry Group, Compasion in World Farming, Labour Animal Welfare Society, World Development Movement;
History: He joined the Labour Party at 21, '71; he contested hopeless Chelsea against Nick Scott, coming 3rd with 12.8% June '83; he contested equally hopeless East Sussex and South Kent in the Euro-election, coming 3rd with 16.4% June '94; was selected for Broxtowe, then outside Labour's target area Dec '95; he spent the 18 months leading up to the election flying back from his Ciba-Geigy job in Switzerland almost every weekend to listen to 10,000 voters, culminating in 14 special-interest leaflets; on a swing of 12.9% unexpectedly unseated Sir Jim Lester after 23 years by a majority of 5,575 May '97; led a motion urging the spending of the £780m scheduled for the Millennium Exhibition on more important health, education and transport June '97; in his Maiden, hailed his predecessor as possibly a better man, for never bending to the prevailing winds; like Sir Jim, urged more for overseas aid; at home, said that the British people looked to Parliament to "provide underlying security...at least a minimum income, a roof over their head, a tolerable environment, decent health care and decent education for their children" and "protection against arbitrary disaster"; only with such essential security could Britons become "flexible" July '97; in debating the new Bill on radio spectrum management warned that pledges to hold down prices to that necessary for its

managtement was "undesirable in principle and illusory in practice"; "we will have to put up prices to the market level to get an orderly market" Oct '97;
Born: 5 February 1950, London
Family: Son, of Reginald Palmer, translator/editor, and Irma (Markin), language teacher;
Education: International Schools, Copenhagen and Vienna; Copenhagen University (MSc); Birkbeck College, London University (PhD in Mathematics);
Occupation: Computer Scientist, ultimately head of Novartis Internet Service, with the Swiss firm Ciba-Geigy, later merged into Novartis (multinational pharmaceutical company) '85-97; Author, two books on conflict simulation games; ex: Developer, of COMPACT, doctors' clinical trials package, for Medical Research Council (MSF) '82-85; Clinical Trials Computing, with Ciba-Geigy '77-82; Researcher, into Artificial Intelligence (language translation), Copenhagen '75-77;
Traits: Parted greying brown hair; egg-shaped face; speaks six languages, including Danish, German, French; probably the first modern MP to have overcome a cleft palate;
Address: House of Commons, Westminster, London SW1A 0AA; 19 Oriental Place, Brighton BN1 2LL; 54 Main Road, Watnall, Nottingham;
Telephone: 0171 219 4197 (H of C); 0115 938 3281 (Nottingham home); 0115 943 0721 (constituency office);

Owen (William) PATERSON **Conservative** **SHROPSHIRE NORTH '97-**

Majority: 2,195 over Labour 4-way;
Description: An overwhelmingly agricultural seat on the Welsh border, with some light industry; its biggest town, Oswestry, gave the seat its name before '83; it has had 14,000 voters removed to give the county an additional seat, without changing its basic loyalty;
Position: On the Select Committee on Welsh Affairs '97-;
Outlook: A well-married - to Viscount Ridley's daughter -youngish local businessman trying to replace retired John (now Lord) Biffen; as Eurosceptic as his predecessor and more Rightwing, beneath a charming veneer; pro: free trade, privatisation, low taxation; against: state regulation, closed markets; from a prosperous local tanning and farming family, has previously devoted most of his effort to rising to managing director in the leather trade;
History: Joined the Conservative Party '80; served as personal assistant to John Biffen, the incumbent MP for Shropshire North, in the general election June '87; campaigned to save Ellesmere Cottage Hospital '88-89; helped Christopher Prout in campaign for Euro-constituency of Shropshire and Stafford June '89; selected as Tory candidate for Wrexham, campaigned to save the Royal Welch Fusiliers '91; was socked in the jaw by "Labour bully boys" who tried to take flags from his campaign vehicle Mar '92; in the general election gained an added 122 votes but lost .4% of Tory vote in comparison with '87, while Labour vote was increased by 4.4%; he later claimed to have "increased Conservative vote to 18,114, beating the national swing" because the swing in Wrexham was 2.4% from Labour and the swing in Wales was 2.7%, May '92; supported local Tories in council elections in

Wrexham May '93; again helped Sir Christopher Prout in Euro-campaign for Shropshire and Herefordshire June '94; again helped local Tories, this time contesting Oswestry council election May '95; on the announced imminent retirement of John Biffen was selected from a wide field, including Mrs Biffen Sep '95; was one of 59 Tory candidates who told the DAILY TELEGRAPH that his election address would pledge him to ruling out Britain's entry into a single European currency during the next Parliament Dec '96; won the seat with a majority of 2,195, despite a swing to Labour of 11.8% May '97; in his Maiden speech defended field sports, dismissed Labour's Budget as unnecessary, "bad" and sending out "dreadful signals to the outside world" July '97; was named to the Select Committee on Welsh Affairs July '97; he complained about beef prices hitting a "16-year low" and told the Agriculture Minister "he cannot keep hiding behind the actions of the previous Government", Dr Cunningham said he was "living in cloud cuckoo land" if he thought that "in seven weeks the [Labour] Government could have undone the untold damage inflicted by previous Conservative Ministers" July '97;
Born: 24 June 1956, Whitchurch
Family: Son, of Alfred Dobell Paterson, chairman of family tanning business, and Cynthia Marian (Owen); m '80 Hon Rose Emily (Ridley), picture valuer and journalist, daughter of Viscount Ridley and niece of late Nicholas Ridley and eight prior generations of MPs, including "the worst Home Secretary in the 19th Century" (OP); 2s: Felix Charles '86, Edward Owen '88; 1d Evelyn Rose '92;
Education: Abberley Hall; Radley College, Berkshire (4 A-grade A-levels) '69-74; Corpus Christi College, Cambridge University '75-78; National Leathersellers College, Northampton '78-79;
Occupation: Managing Director '93-, Sales Director '83-93, the British Leather Company; he joined the company in '79;
Traits: Tall; good-looking; dark brown, forward-falling hair; articulate (speaks without notes); charming; good-humoured; displays middle-class politeness; energetic; fluent French and German;
Address: House of Commons, Westminster, London SW1A 0AA; Shellbrook Hill, Ellesmere, Shropshire SY12 9EW; The British Leather Company, Hawthorne Tannery, Bootle, Merseyside L20 6JR (business);
Telephone: 0171 219 5185 (H of C); 019787 710667 (home);

Linda PERHAM **Labour** **ILFORD NORTH '97-**

Majority: 3,224 over Conservative 4-way;
Description: The more Conservative of the two Ilford seats; this leaning was reinforced in '95 by wards from Wanstead and Woodford; Ilford is an Essex-bordering dormitory town for London; it has a large housing estate at Hainault, an 18% concentration of Jews in Gants Hill (including many taxi drivers); its voters are three-quarters owner-occupiers; even the unbolstered seat was only once held by Labour, by Millie Miller ('74-77) after whose death the '78 by-election exposed the electorate's shift to the Right; Vivian Bendall, a Rightwing Tory estate agent, thereafter held the seat - in '92 by 14,049 votes - right up to the May '97

Labour flood;
Position: On Select Committee on Accomodation and Works '97-; Redbridge Councillor (Mayor '94-95; Chairman: Highways '95-96, Leisure '96-97) '89-97; Redbridge Community Health Councillor '84-88; Secretary, Ilford North CLP '87-91;
Outlook: "New Labour" (NEW STATESMAN) local councillor and ex-Mayor; wants NHS improvements above all: "I want to see improved conditions at our local hospitals and shorter waiting lists; Labour has pledged to cut waiting for cancer surgery"; an ex-GLC librarian, she favours a new strategic London authority; in Socialist Education Association, Labour Friends of Israel and Co-operative Party; Joint Vice Chairman, Consumer Safety International;
History: She joined the Labour Party '79, was elected Secretary of the Ilford North CLP '87; was elected to Redbridge Borough Council May '89; "in May 1994, when Labour took minority control of the London borough of Redbridge for the first time in 30 years, I was elected as the first woman Labour mayor of that council and the first Labour mayor for 26 years" May '94; as Mayor, first met Tony Blair when he attended the local annual meeting of Jewish Care Nov '94; was selected for safe-Tory Ilford North Dec '95; having served on the local Community Health Council for four years, campaigned heavily on the NHS Apr '97; was elected on a notional swing of 17.3% - overcoming the eighth biggest Tory lead in the country - unseating Vivian Bendall after 19 years by a majority of 3,224 May '97; led a motion and introduced a Private Member's Bill to ban age discrimination in advertisements June '97; in her Maiden speech, recalled her work in the Research Library of the GLC a quarter century before and strongly endorsed a restoration of a "desperately needed" "strategic London authority" June '97; asked Health Secretary Frank Dobson what he was doing to end prescription fraud, which would give "each health authority...an extra £1m" to spend "on 145 heart by-pass operations" June '97; her attempt to introduce a Private Member's Bill to bar ageist advertisements was discouraged by the Labour Whips Oct '97; worried about the impact of Government's new regulations for the radio spectrum on her radio-controlled cabby constituents Oct '97;
Born: 29 June 1947, Camberwell, London
Family: Daughter, of George Sidney Conroy, statistics clerk at the SE London Gas Board, previously a bus and tramcar driver and Edith Louisa (Overton), shop assistant; m '72 Raymond John Perham, Director of Surveying and Engineering, Metropolitan Police; 2d Caroline '79, Sarah '80;
Education: Mary Datchelor Girls' School, Camberwell; Leicester University (BA Hons in Classics) Ealing Technical College (Postgraduate Diploma in Librarianship); ALA;
Occupation: Bibliographical Librarian: Epping Forest College (UNISON) '85-97, previously in Fawcett Library, City of London Polytechnic '81-92; Staff Development Librarian, City of London Polytechnic '76-78; Archives and Publications Librarian '72-76; Information Officer, GLC Research Library '71-72;
Traits: Big mop of dark hair; enjoys cinema, theatre, art, history and setting and participating in quizzes;
Address: House of Commons, Westminster, London SW1A 0AA;
Telephone: 0171 219 1161 (H of C); 0181 500 7291 (home);

WE'RE GETTING FATTER
MPs profiles tend to get fatter, like the papier mache masks we made in our youth by adding to a clay portrait model soggy strips of newsprint soaked in flour and water. Just as you can build up a strong papier mache mask, so too we hope we have transformed a dimly lit outline form into sharp features plus a few warts.

James PLASKITT **Labour** **WARWICK & LEAMINGTON '97-**

Majority: 3,398 over Conservative 8-way;
Description: For 34 years Sir Anthony Eden's scenic former Midlands seat: Royal Leamington Spa plus Warwick minus Kenilworth, which went to Rugby in '83; a thriving area, with Ford, Volvo and Automotive Products; has a big Asian minority (7,000 Sikhs) in South Leamington; contains 19,000 pensioners, many in its residential homes for the elderly; in '95 a few thousand voters were taken in from affluent villages in Stratford-upon-Avon; had the constituency voted in '97 as in '92, Sir Dudley Smith could have expected a majority of over 11,000;
Position: Oxfordshire County Councillor (Leader of Labour Group '90-96) '85-; on Labour's International Policy Commission '94-; Chairman, Oxford East CLP '88-90;
Outlook: A pro-European moderniser, Centrist on economic and business policy, Left on social and constitutional issues; favours electoral reform (in Labour Campaign for Electoral Reform); also in Fabians, Charter 88, Liberty (ex-NCCL), Labour Committee on Ireland, Co-operative Party;
History: He joined the Labour Party '70; was elected to Oxfordshire County Council May '85; was elected Chairman of the Oxford East CLP '88; became Leader of the Labour Group on Oxfordshire County Council May '90; contested Witney against Douglas Hurd, coming second with 21.3% - overtaking the LibDems -but still 22,568 behind Apr '92; he thought Warwick and Leamington, which had a base of almost 20,000 Labour voters, could be be made winnable; was selected for Warwick and Leamington against Sir Dudley Smith (whose majority had been halved to 8,935 in '92) '95; "our telephone canvassing showed us some months before the poll that we were on target to win"; won the seat on a notional swing of 12%, ending the 29-year-long reign of Sir Dudley Smith May '97; expressed solidarity with jailed Indonesian union leader June '97; in his Maiden, loyally supported all aspects of Gordon Brown's Budget and welcomed closer, constructive relations with the EU, including the completion of the internal market and acceptance of the Social Chapter July '97; welcomed review of handling of asylum-seekers July '97; co-sponsored motion opposing further live export of farm animals July '97; criticised capping of Oxfordshire July '97;
Born: 23 June 1954, Grimsby
Family: Son, of late Ronald Plaskitt, headmaster and Methodist pastor, and Phyllis, retired teacher;
Education: Pilgrim School, Bedford; University College, Oxford University (MA, MPhil;
Occupation: Business Consultant, with Oxford Analytica (its Director '93-95) (MSF) '85-; ex: Lecturer, in Politics at Oxford University '83-86, '77-79 and in Government at Brunel University '79-83;
Traits: Greying tonsure; thin moustache; a nice line in irony; enjoys swimming, used to run;
Address: House of Commons, Westminster, London SW1A 0AA; Elstow, 22 Kenilworth Rd, Leamington Spa, Warwickshire CV32 6JB;
Telephone: 0171 219 6207 (H of C); 01926 831151 (constituency); 01865 261600 (work)

Kerry POLLARD **Labour** **ST ALBANS '97-**

Majority: 4,459 over Conservative 6-way;
Description: The old town of St Albans and the more middle-class and Tory town of Harpenden; the '94 boundary changes shifted the seat to the south; 29,000 northern voters, mainly in Harpenden were lost, replaced by importing 18,000 from the south, mostly from Watford; psephologists, but not Peter Lilley, thought he was safe; they also thought the main threat came from the LibDems, who had done well in local councils in '93 and '94;
Position: Chairman, 'Homes for Homeless People' '93-; ex: St Albans District Councillor '82-97; Hertfordshire County Councillor '89-97;
Outlook: A "slightly Left of New Labour" (self-description), potentially rebellious former local councillor, both district and county; he stormed past the LibDems to victory over the Lilley-replacement on very local issues; was endorsed as "hard-working and experienced", "with his feet on the ground" by the former Conservative Mayor, Ken Davies; the former LibDem Leader of the Council, Geoff Bliss, also urged his election to defeat the Tory candidate; he says he is willing to rebel if his party does not meet its pledge on cutting hospital waiting lists; he also wants abolition of the Greenwich ruling, which means that local secondary schools have to admit pupils from outside the district; he also wants the Child Support Agency "kicked into touch"; he wants too the county council to be able to increase its taxes to pay for threatened services; "there comes a time when you stand up and fight for what you believe is right; my first loyalty is to the people who elected me" (KP); is in the Christian Socialist Movement;
History: He joined the Labour Party '73; he was elected to St Albans District Council May '82; was elected to Hertfordshire County Council May '89; selected to fight St Albans, came 3rd after the LibDem with 19.4% of the vote (7.9% more than the previous election, thanks to the return to Labour of SDPers) Apr '92; was again selected to fight "hopeless" St Albans, where Labour had previously come third '95; Labour became the 2nd party in local elections May '95; Labour became the largest local party within the altered boundaries, registering 40% of the vote in local council elections May '96; a University of Hertfordshire poll showed Labour on 41%, the Tories with 22% and the LibDems with 15% in the constituency Jan '97; he campaigned against the loss of the Accident and Emergency Services at City Hospital, capitalising on local feeling that the outgoing Tory Cabinet Minister, Peter Lilley, had let people down; also attacked the bus pass cuts introduced by the LibDems on the local council Apr '97; unexpectedly won the seat on a notional swing of 14.7%, a majority of 4,459 over the Lilley-replacement, David Rutley, ending 47 years of local Tory domination May '97;
Born: 27 April 1944, Pinner
Family: Son, of Patrick Pollard, publican, and Betty (Wadham); m Maralyn (Murphy); 5s: Mark '67, Adam '69, Jamie '71, Daniel '74, Ben '80; 2d: Sally '76, Elizabeth '85;
Education: Thornleigh Grammar School; Thornleigh College, Bolton (HNC, BA)
Occupation: Director, of Cherry Tree Housing Association (housing former patients of mental hospitals and people with learning disabilities) (NALGO) '93-97; ex: Process Engineer, with British Gas (MSF) '60-92;
Traits: Greying tonsure and beard, with darker eyebrows and moustache; his forename is Irish, meaning "firm of purpose, generous and kind of spirit"; because it can seem a girl's

name, "until I was about 12 years old, I regularly had to drop my trousers to show that I was a male" (KP); enjoys swimming; Roman Catholic;
Address: House of Commons, Westminster, London SW1A 0AA;
Telephone: 0171 219 3000 (H of C); 01727 761031/761032(Fax) (constituency); 015232 523523 St Albans (mobile);

Chris[topher]] POND **Labour** **GRAVESHAM '97-**

Majority: 5,779 over Conservative 6-way;
Description: Unaltered North Kent bellwether seat, in which Labour voters in Gravesend and other workaday Thamesside towns have been counter-balanced by Tory commuters to its pretty inland villages like Meophan; 'Chinese' Gordon built its fort; Charles Dickens lived there; Pocahontas died there of a broken heart;
Position: On the Select Committee on Social Security '97-; Director, Low Pay Unit '80-97; former Co-opted member: of Labour NEC's Employment Subcommittee, of joint PLP-NEC Committee on Poverty, Taxation and Social Security;
Outlook: Labour's leading expert on low pay and a persistent campaigner for a minimum wage and more progressive tax and social security policies; formerly a youngish Fabian redistributionist, mainstream Centre-Left, in CND, Amnesty and Anti-Apartheid Movement; after selection for marginal Gravesham he became a fervent Blairite who said, "you can't solve the problem of poverty by throwing money at it" and "Tony Blair's New Labour offers solutions"; he "could be either an asset to a Blair Government or a thorn in its side" (close colleague); he was initially a very low-profile MP, not living up to his advance billing as a prolific letter-writer to the GUARDIAN;
History: He joined the Labour Club at Sussex Unversity '71; he joined the Labour Party '78; was selected as the candidate for Welwyn-Hatfield '85; in the wake of the local council elections, it appeared he could take the seat May '86; in the event he came third, with 26.4% after Tory David Evans and SDPer Linsay Granshaw June '87; wrote to the INDEPENDENT to correct Mrs Thatcher's claim there was no North-South divide: "according to official figures", "household incomes in the northern region are now lower than those in any other part of the UK, including Northern Ireland" Jan '88; explained that leaked draft proposals for a minimum wage were not yet official Labour Party policy Oct '91; warned that Tory plans to abolish Wages Councils would cost the lowest-paid £300m for every 10p an hour cut from wages Feb '92; although he made it to the short-list, failed to secure the Nottingham East candidacy Feb '92; wrote in the GUARDIAN: "official statistics show that the gap between the highest and the lowest paid is now wider than at any time since 1896, when the figures were first collected" Dec '94; warned: "all the Job Seeker's Allowance will do is to force people on to Income Support and make any savings illusory" May '96; wrote that Peter Lilley's "department figures tell us that the numbers on low income, measured by a European definition, have increased from five million in 1979 to 14 million today; yet he and other senior ministers continue to deny the very existence of a problem" June '96; was selected for the Tory-held marginal Gravesham (originally designated for all-women selection) July '96; warned Austin Mitchell against sneering at the Blair leadership; "the Labour Party has offered

a number of key pledges to improve the health service, create employment and provide a nimimum wage, which would enhance the quality of life for millions; under Tony Blair's leadership, the likelihood of achieving such change is greater than at any time in the past two decades; I, like many others in front-line marginal constituencies, will be fighting hard to make that change a reality" Sep '96; with other Blairite loyalist candidates, wrote to the INDEPENDENT insisting that the "Labour Party is a united dynamic party ready to solve the problems this country faces" Oct '96; at Labour's annual conference pointed out that it was the Tories who had created the dependency culture Oct '96; sharply criticised North London University report blaming poor school results on mums absent working; blamed it on the "pitiful level of childcare provision" Feb '97; won Gravesham on a 10% swing, ousting incumbent Tory MP Jacques Arnold by a majority of 5,779 May '97; in his Maiden wound up with an endorsement of the minimum wage, after having underlined his constituents' problems with crime and NHS inadequacies May '97; introduced a Private Member's Bill restricting the hours that children could work June '97; urged restoration of the World Service's three-year funding programme June '97; elicited the information that £557m had not been paid in maintenance by absent fathers - in contrast to the £400m paid - despite full maintenance assessments July '97; defended his support for the Social Security Bill as contributing to "the creation of a social security system that will give people back their self-respect" July '97; was named to the Select Committee on Social Security July '97;

Born: 25 September 1952, London

Family: Son, of Charles A Pond, Co-op milkman and later shop manager, and Doris Violet, shop manageress; m '90 Carole Tongue MEP; 1d;

Education: Hazelwood School, Palmers Green; Minchenden School, Southgate; Sussex University (BA Hons Economics);

Occupation: Author: To Him Who Hath (with Frank Field and Michael Meacher (Penguin 1977), Taxation and Social Policy (with C Sandbird & R Walker; Heinemann 1980), The Poverty Trap (Open University 1978), 'Low Pay: Labour's Answer' (Fabian Tract 488), 'Tracing Pay Inequalities' (Fabian Tract 466); ex: National Director, Low Pay Unit '80-97; Visiting Professor, Middlesex University '95-97; ex: Consultant, Open University '91-92, '87-88; Visiting Research Fellow, Surrey University '84-86; Visiting Lecturer in Economics, Kent University '83-84; Lecturer, in Economics, Civil Service College, Sunningdale '78-79; Research Officer, Low Pay Unit '75-78; Research Assistant in Economics, Birkbeck College, '74-75;

Traits: Parted retreating brown hair, worn in a quiffy style; articulate; long-distance runner (seven Marathons; in London Road Runners Club);

Address: House of Commons, Westminster, London SW1A 0AA; 27-29 Amwell Street, London EC1R 1UN (work); 123 Richmond Avenue, Islington N1 0RL (home);

Telephone: 0171 219 3000 (H of C); 0171 700 1090 (home); 0171 713 7616(work)

Stephen POUND **Labour** **EALING NORTH '97-**

Majority: 9,160 over Conservative 5-way;
Description: A formerly marginal residential and light-industrial seat straddling the London end of the A40; it has a mixture of affluent middle-class homes, council houses and a sixth of non-whites; it was kept tingling in Parliamentary ears by the endless constituency questions of Harry Greenway, its former Tory MP, whose second love was horses; although once Labour-held, during his 18-year reign he pushed the Tory majority as high as 15,000 - in the wake of the rate increases by a Labour-controlled council; he even secured over 9,000 in '92; his hold was thought to be strengthened by the '95 addition of strongly-Tory Pitshanger ward from Acton;
Position: Ealing Borough Councillor (Mayor '95-96) '82-
Outlook: The former local Mayor whom Harry Greenway could not demonise adequately, apparently forgeting he was a student union leader when at LSE; in the Fabian Society, Co-operative Party and Catholic charitable groups;
History: He joined the Labour Party '72; was elected to Ealing Borough Council May '82; was a student union leader while a mature student at LSE '79-84; became Ealing's Mayor May '95; was selected to stand in Ealing North against Harry Greenway July '95; unexpectedly won the seat on a notional swing of fully 16%, ousting Harry Greenway after 18 years May '97; was congratulated by Tony Banks for "freeing the House from the Ealing One" May '97; urged Tony Banks to "redouble his efforts to secure the World Cup [for England] in 2006" May '97; backed the outlawing of fox-hunting June '97; co-sponsored motion deploring BA's selling off of its catering division, with its "disproportionate effect" "on the Asian community in West London" July '97; co-sponsored motion opposing a 12-lane superhighway to Heathrow in favour of better rail connections, after a public inquiry July '97;
Born: 3 July 1948, Hammersmith
Family: Son of Pelham Pound, journalist (one of the 'Old Codgers' of the DAILY MIRROR), and Dominica (James) teacher; m '76 Maggie RGN; 1s Pelham '90, 1d Emily Frances '88;
Education: Hertford Grammar School; TUC Postal Studies Course; LSE '79-84 (Diploma in Industrial Relations, BSc Econ);
Occupation: Area Housing Manager, of Paddington Churches Housing Association (TGWU) '90-97; previously Housing Officer '84-90; Hospital Porter '70-79;
Traits: Balding; is often mistaken locally for Neil Kinnock; a lay reader at RC church; enjoys watching Fulham Football Club, collecting comics;
Address: House of Commons, Westminster, London SW1A 0AA; 115 Milton Road, London W7 1LG;
Telephone: 0171 219 1140 (H of C); 0181 933 0308 (home);

With all the destabilizing constituency changes, we think it necessary to try to have accurate seat descriptions. Some newspapers (like the SCOTSMAN and GLASGOW HERALD), some MPs, and especially The Almanac of British Politics by Robert Waller and Byron Criddle (Routledge), have been particularly helpful.

David PRIOR **Conservatve** **NORFOLK NORTH '97-**

Majority: 1,293 over Liberal Democrat 4-way;
Description: An unaltered agricultural seat which includes a coastal strip with part of the Broads and resort towns like Cromer and Sheringham; "Britain's last remaining feudal state" (DAILY TELEGRAPH): its formerly well-organised farm workers underpinned a Labour MP from 1945 until ousted in 1970 by Sir Ralph Howell, who retired in 1997;
Position: On Select Committee on Trade and Industry '97-; ex: Chairman, Norfolk Conservative Association; on Trade and Industry Advisory Group helping the former Prime Minister and his President of the Board of Trade on the Election Manifesto '94-97
Outlook: Jim Prior's more Rightwing son: more hostile to unions, state intervention and European integration; his 20 years with British Steel convinced him that its "fantastic" improvement in "competitiveness and efficiency" came about "through deregulation, tax reduction, vastly improved industrial relations, privatisation and much less government" under the Tories; on Lord Prior's shrewd advice, is not rushing into the fray too early;
History: He helped his father, Jim Prior, when MP for Waveney until '74; became Chairman of the Cambridge University Conservative Association '74; was elected Treasurer of his local Conservative Association in a Hammersmith ward '88; contested the Norfolk District Council elections May '95; was selected as prospective candidate for Norfolk North to replace retiring Sir Ralph Howell Sep '95; at annual conference in Bournemouth told fellow Conservatives that there had been a second industrial revolution in Britain, and that it was necessary to remain competitive by continuing to curb strikes and attract inward investment Oct '96; was one of 59 Tory candidates who told the DAILY TELEGRAPH that he favoured his election manifesto saying that Britain's entry into a single European currency should be ruled out for the ensuing Parliament Dec '96; narrowly retained the seat by a majority of 1,293 (down by nine-tenths from 12,445) after a 9.3% swing to the LibDems May '97; supported William Hague's Leadership bid May-June '97; in his Maiden, said he deplored "the awful waste of long-term unemployment" but "I do not believe that welfare-to-work, based on Government subsidy, is the right way to cure the problem"; it was an "illusion" that Government could "create jobs; in fact, only competitive and strong companies and businesses can create jobs; jobs built on short-term subsidies will have no security" July '97; said that "the withdrawal of Advance Corporation Tax credit ha[d] come as a complete bombshell to my constituents"; it was not in the Labour manifesto; "it is bad for investment, for jobs, for competitivenss, for the public finances, for pensioners and for future pensioners" July '97; co-sponsored amendment to nuclear disarmament motion, insisting on recognising that "general and complete nuclear disarmament must be accompanied by general and complete conventional disarmament, if it is not simply to make the world safe once again for full-scale conventional warfare" July '97; was named to the Trade and Industry Select Committee July '97;
Born: 3 December 1954, Halesworth, Suffolk
Family: Son, of Lord (Jim) Prior, former Conservative MP '59-87, Chairman of GEC and Northern Ireland Secretary, and Jane (Lywood); m '87 Caroline (Holmes), concert agency organiser; twins: Nicholas '88, Helena '88;
Education: Charterhouse '66-71 (10 O-levels, 3 A-levels, 2 S-levels); Pembroke College,

Cambridge University '72-75 (MA in Law [Exhibition]); qualified as Barrister '76, but did not go into practice;
Occupation: Chairman: Lurmark Ltd (which manufactures a range of plastic and metal components for agricultural and industrial spraying); Director, GEI Plc (engineering and manufacturing); involved in small family boat business on the Norfolk Broads; ex: Executive, for 20 years with British Steel, including being its Commercial Director for seven years;
Traits: Bald; specs; triangular face;
Address: House of Commons, Westminster, London SW1A 0AA; Swannington Manor, Swannington, Norwich NR9 5NR; Lurmark Ltd, Station Road, Longstanton, Cambridge CB4 5DS;
Telephone: 0171 219 3000 (H of C); 01954 260097 (business); 01603 851560 (home); 01603 260834 (Fax)

Gwyn PROSSER **Labour** **DOVER '97-**

Majority: 11,739 over Conservative 5-way;
Description: Southeast England's major ferry port, whose nearby white cliffs acquired a wartime patriotic significance; an '80s site of ferry rivalry, recently Dover ferries have been threatened by the competition of the Channel Tunnel; remnants of Labour militance have also survived from the now-dead nearby Kent coalfield; it also has Tory-leaning seaside resorts but was deprived of safely-Tory Sandwich, which went to Thanet South; a traditional marginal, it was expected to be the first Kent seat to revert to Labour control, when there were no expectations of seven others;
Position: Dover District Councillor (Vice Chairman, Labour Group) '87-; Kent County Councillor (Chairman, Economic Development) '89-; Executive Councillor, NUMAST '85-;
Outlook: Although he won wider fame as the terminator of the career of the controversial Conservative, David Shaw, is basically an active local district and county councillor preoccupied with economic regeneration in an unemployment-troubled area; has turned to London and Brussels for redevelopment money: "I am pro-Europe, but also a realist; I want us at the heart of Europe along with the single currency, but not at the expense of huge job losses"; he earlier fought against undermanning on local ferries and against the Channel Tunnel; has supported Greenpeace, Socialist Educational Association, Fabian Society and Co-operative Party;
History: He joined his ferry officers' union, NUMAST '62; he joined the local Labour Party '83; was elected to Executive Council of NUMAST '85; became co-ordinator of local opposition groups against Channel Tunnel Bill '85; was Parliamentary Agent for petitioners against Channel Tunnel Bill before select commmittees of House of Commons and House of Lords '86; was elected to Dover District Council May '87; was elected for Dover South to Kent County Council May '89; was selected as Labour's candidate for Dover, against incumbent David Shaw '89; with Joan Walley MP promised a future Labour government would demand: safer standards for cross channel roll-on roll-off ferries and act to restore safe manning levels on British ships July '91; cut Tory majority of 6,541 to 833 in general election

contest won by David Shaw Apr '92; as Chairman of Economic Development on Kent County Council, spearheaded the campaign for Assisted Area status to mop up the unemployment created by the shutdown of the Kent coalfield and demanning on the ferries; was re-selected as candidate '96; talking about the union-Labour relationship, said, "there will always be a bond; there has already been a shift; I wouldn't want any further separation" Mar '97; won the seat on a swing of 11.6%, ousting David Shaw by a majority of 11,739 May '97; joined in attack on Channel Tunnel's inadequate fire safety, saying: "we should be looking at the fundamental safety of the Tunnel; there is a need to segregate pasengers from their vehicles" May '97; led motion urging safer, closed wagons for Channel Tunnel trains June '97; co-sponsored motion attacking Conservative-controlled Kent County Council for its moratorium on school capital expenditures June '97; backed end of fox-hunting June '97;
Born: 27 April 1943, Swansea
Family: Is married with three children;
Education: Dunvant Secondary Modern School; Swansea Secondary Technical School; Swansea College of Technology; Member of Institute of Marine Engineers;
Occupation: On Executive Council of NUMAST '92-; ex: unemployed '91-92; Chartered Marine Engineer: Chief Engineering Officer with Sealink '79-91;
Traits: Dark; trim-bearded (resisted pressure from Labour's media consultants to shave it); parted hair; no neck; pedestrian speaker; Welsh lilt; enjoys: hill walking, sub aqua diving, Rugby Union;
Address: House of Commons, Westminster, London SW1A 0AA; 3 Cowper Road, River, Dover, Kent CT17 OPF;
Telephone: 0171 219 3000 (H of C); 01304 823457 (home); 01904 705513

'Lawrie' (Lawrence) QUINN **Labour** **SCARBOROUGH & WHITBY '97-**

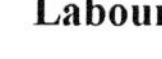

Majority: 5,124 over Conservative 4-way;
Description: North Yorkshire's lovely seaside resorts - where "the classic British seaside holiday was invented" (LQ) - fishing ports, the dramatic coast stretching between them and the agricultural hinterland; one of the largest, most lightly-populated seats in the land; had its voters been frozen in their '92 attitude, John Sykes could have repeated a Tory victory by a margin of 10,000-plus votes;
Position: North Yorkshire County Councillor '89-93; on Labour Party's Yorkshire Regional Executive '87-; ex: Secretary, York CLP '93-96
Outlook: One of the totally unexpected arrivals who tried to co-found "The Unlikely Lads and Lasses Club" for those who reached the Commons on outsized swings like his (14.7%), which made him the seat's first Labour MP; a rail transport buff, professionally - "I have spent most of my life building bridges" - and politically (in Transport 2000, SERA, the Permanent Way Institute); a loyalist in the "Ain't Misbehaving Tendency" (Paul Routledge, INDEPENDENT ON SUNDAY); supports electoral reform (Labour Electoral Reform Society); also in the Fabian Society;
History: He joined the Labour Party '72; was elected to North Yorkshire County Council May '89; was selected for "hopeless" Scarborough and Whitby Aug '95; unexpectedly won the

seat on a swing of 14.7%, ousting its Rightwing Tory incumbent, John Sykes by a majority of 5,124 May '97; asked the Home Secretary "what plans he has to improve" the UK's "record on human rights" May '97; urged "a national concessionary travel scheme for pensioners and the disabled" June '94; in his Maiden, noted the increase in suicides among farmers June '97; asked about quota-hopping June '97; co-sponsored motion deploring Australian mistreatment of 100,000 aboriginal children June '97; expressed solidarity with jailed Indonesian union leader June '97; had an Adjournment debate on the inadequacies of the North Yorkshire Ambulance Trust June '97; co-sponsored motion on pensions mis-selling under the Tories July '97; urged a "value for money" second pension so elderly "can have a proper standard of living and afford a proper existence in retirement" July '97; was concerned that the new Bill to police the radio spectrum would serve the police and farmers in his large constituency Oct '97; as the son of a locomotive driver, urged the extradition of Ronald Biggs Oct '97;

Born: 25 December 1956, Carlisle

Family: Son, of Jimmy Quinn, locomotive driver, and Sheila (Richardson); m '82 Ann (Eames);

Education: Harraby School, Carlisle; Hatfield Polytechnic (BSc in Civil Engineering); Institution of Civil Engineers; Engineering Council;

Occupation: Chartered Engineer: Planning and Development Engineer, with Railtrack London North Eastern '94-97, with British Rail '79-94;

Traits: Parted dark brown tonsure; enjoys biographies, cooking, theatre, surfing the Internet; a long-distance fan of Carlisle United; hopes to visit all the European countries by rail by the end of the century;

Address: House of Commons, Westminster, London SW1A 0AA; 36 Aberdeen Walk, Scarborough;

Telephone: 0171 219 3000 (H of C); 01723 507000 (constituency);

'Bill' (William} RAMMELL **Labour** **HARLOW '97-**

Majority: 10,514 over Conservative 6-way;

Description: A slightly-changed postwar new town in northwest Essex which has grown on the back of industries both large (BP, Standard Telephones) and small; its lost traditional industries have been replaced by research-based firms, including pharmaceuticals (SmithKline Beecham, and Merck, Sharp & Dohme); it was initially Labour but, like most new towns, went Conservative in the '80s, with Jerry Hayes as its entertaining MP '83-97; in '95 it lost a Tory-leaning ward;

Position: Harlow District Councillor (its Deputy Leader) '85-; Chairman: Harlow Community Safety Panel, Harlow Health Services Monitoring Group; on West Essex Community Health Council; ex: President of Cardiff's University College Student Union '82-83;

Outlook: Pro-European soft-Left graduate of the student union movement; "egalitarian, privately sceptical of Blair though publicly supportive" (RED PEPPER); "oily" (Simon Hoggart, GUARDIAN) in his loyalism; proud of "an ordinary working-class background", the sort of people who "my party lost contact with in the 1980s"; a fervent pro-European ("I strongly believe in a deepening and growing European Union, a Europe that I am certain will, in time, develop a single currency"); supporter of electoral reform (in Labour Campaign for Electoral Reform);

History: He joined the Labour Party '79; was elected President of Cardiff's University College Student Union '82; was elected to Harlow District Council at 26, May '85; was selected as Labour candidate for Harlow '90; despite a 2.7% swing from the Conservatives to Labour, was defeated by Tory incumbent Jerry Hayes by 2,940 votes Apr '92; re-selected for the seat '95, helped push up party membership from 500 to 800 in two years; claimed: "the Tories have ruined Britain's transport system, forcing through privatisation against the wishes of the people; the Tories deregulated bus services, causing 'bus wars' between operators; the only loser was the travelling public; Labour will create an effficient transport system improving services for all" '96; said: educational "selection is a British disease; it will always benefit 20% of children at the expense of 80%" Mar '97; captured the seat on a notional swing of 12.6%, ousting Jerry Hayes by a majority of 10,514 May '97; in his Maiden, strongly supported closer ties with the European Union: "the idea that Britain could remain outside a single currency for a long time without enormous damage to our economy is fool's gold"; also said that "Harlow's innovative approach to training and job creation in the past year alone has brought in almost £1m of European funds" June '97; insisted that "to get secure long-term employment" for young people "training to at least NVQ3 level is necessary" and urged "that the release of council receipts will be tied in some way to training provision and NVQ qualifications" June '97; co-sponsored a motion urging the need for a Parliamentary creche June '97; led a motion expressing shock at the BBC's interviewing on 'Kilroy' a "self-confessed paedophile...on a day-time entertainment show" June '97; co-sponsored motion urging "a world-class sports stadium" at the Millennium Exhibition July '97; urged a bar on "universities charging top-up tuition fees" July '97; told Prime Minister Blair that "comprehensive schools in my constituency of Harlow have been successfully streaming pupils by ability for decades" and "there is all the difference in the world between that kind of successful streaming by ability in the same school and selection at the age of 11, which condemns four out of five children to permanent failure" July '97; told Social Security Secretary Harriet Harman that in Harlow "60% of lone parents were unemployed" "because of the inadequacy of child-care support" July '97; urged a "European code of conduct on arms sales to ensure uniformity of policy across the European Union" Oct '97;

Born: 10 October 1959, North London

Family: Is married with a son and a daughter;

Education: Burnt Hill Comprehensive, Harlow; University College, University of Wales, Cardiff (BA Hons in French and Politics);

Occupation: Commercial and General Manager, of University of London Union (the University of London's student union, with an annual budget of £5m and a new conference and entertainment complex a-building; (MSF); ex: General Manager, of Student Services at King's College, London (MSF);

Traits: Light brown thinning hair; burly; "looks as if he is the manager of a Sunday football team", "sounds as if he ought to be straight out of The Ragged Trousered Philanthropist" (Paul Routledge, INDEPENDENT ON SUNDAY); he enjoys cricket and football; Glen Hoddle "was a classroom contemporary" (WR);

Address: House of Commons, Westminster, London SW1A 0AA; 9 Orchard Croft, Harlow Essex CM20 l3BA;

Telephone: 0171 219 3000 (H of C); 01279 439706 (home);

John RANDALL **Conservative** **UXBRIDGE '97-**

Majority: 3,766 over Labour 4-way;
Description: One of three Hillingdon seats, stretching north and south, adjoining Heathrow; over 70% of its voters are owner-occupiers, only 7% are in social housing; although west of London, its voters feel an identity separate from west London, as shown in the by-election of July '97, after the death of Sir Michael Shersby, its Tory incumbent '72-97, only seven days after he narrowly survived the May '97 Labour landslide; the Tories' retention of the seat in the by-election was partly attributed to Labour's insensitive imposition of an 'outside' candidate from west London, while Conservatives shrewdly picked a man from a long-standing local family;
Position: Chairman, Uxbridge Consrvative Association '94-
Outlook: A winning local shop-owning mainstreamer who scored in the by-election by conducting a deliberately parochial campaign on his home turf; he did this despite his exotic outside interests: a degree in Serbo-Croat and birdwatching in Cuba;
History: He joined the Conservative Party '75; became President of the London University Students Union '75-76; active locally throughout his adult life, he served as Election Agent in Uxbridge to Sir Michael Shersby Apr-May '97; he was selected to contest the Uxbridge by-election in the wake of the death of Sir Michael seven days after he survived the general election by a margin of 724 votes ; Labour's candidate, Andrew Slaughter, was the Leader of Hammersmith Council, replacing local Uxbridge Council's Deputy Leader, David Williams, who had almost beaten Sir Michael June '97; in the by-election campaign Randall campaigned largely on local issues, highlighting the unpopular push by Labour-controlled Uxbridge Council to develop green-belt land, which Sir Michael had opposed; he concentrated on former Tory voters who had defected to Labour, as well as the 5,000 or so disillusioned Tory voters who had not turned out to vote; also played the local-boy angle: "the last thing we want in Uxbridge is someone who only knows where it is because he fell asleep on the Tube and forgot to get off at Hammersmith" July '97; retained the seat with a majority over Labour of 3,766 - 3,000 more than Sir Michael's majority in May - the first Conservative to win a by-election since his new Leader, William Hague, retained Richmond in 1989, July '97;
Born: 5 August 1955, Uxbridge
Family: Son, of Alec Randall, the hereditary Director of his family's Uxbridge departmental store, Randalls, founded by his great grandfather in 1891, and Joyce (Gove); m '86 Kate (Gray), ex-teacher; 2s: Peter '89, David '94; 1d Elizabeth '95;
Education: Rutland House School, Hillingdon; Merchant Taylor's School, Northwood; School of Slavonic and East European Studies, London University (BA in Serbo-Croat);
Occupation: Managing Director, of his family's local departmental store, Randall's '92-, Director '80-88; Tour Leader for Birdquest Ltd and Limosa Holidays as specialist ornithologist '86-;
Traits: Light brown hair; reddish beard; "his beard makes him look like a scaled-up verson of the gnomes which adorn a number of gardens in Uxbridge, and he has the air of a man who drinks beer in preference to wine; he makes jolly, self-deprecating jokes" (Valentine Low, EVENING STANDARD); "affable" (Rebecca Smithers, GUARDIAN); "charmingly disarming", "a simple Forrest Gump, the straw-sucking hometown man" (John Dodd,

OBSERVER); an ornithologist (the first person to lead a British bird-watching tour of Cuba); studied Russian as well as Serbo-Croat; also enjoys the piano and local history: "in particular the story of Randall's shop over the last hundred years" (JR);
Address: House of Commons, Westminster, London SW1A 0AA; 13 Church Road, Cowley, Uxbridge, Middx UB8 3NB;
Telephone: 0171 219 6885 (H of C); 01895 234374 (home); 01895 239465 (constituency);

Syd(ney) RAPSON BEM **Labour** **PORTSMOUTH NORTH '97-**

Majority: 4,323 over Conservative 6-way;
Description: Portsmouth north of the dockyard and city centre; mostly owner-occupied but with some council estates, like Paulsgrove; for 18 years it was a safe berth for the one-time 'Parliamentary leper', Peter Griffiths; in '95 two pro-Tory wards were returned to Havant, from which they had come in '83; on the basis of the '92 split in the votes, this was only expected to reduce the Tory majority to 8,000-plus;
Position: On Select Committee on Accommodation and Works '97-; Portsmouth City Councillor (Deputy Leader '94-95, Leader of its Labour Group) '79-; District President, of the AEEU; President, Portsmouth Athletics Club; ex: Lord Mayor of Portsmouth '90-91; Hampshire County Councillor '73-77; Portsmouth Borough Councillor '71-78;
Outlook: An unusual combination for New Labour: a homegrown skilled working class fitter, senior local trade unionist and veteran municipal politician who has specialised in sports, including those for the disabled; apart from his Maiden on the Special Olympics for the mentally disabled and asking Defence questions, he displayed a low profile in his early days in Parliament;
History: He joined the AEU '60, the Labour Party '68; after contesting wards in '69 and '70, was elected for Buckland to Portsmouth Borough Council May '71; was elected to Hampshire County Council May '73; was elected to Portsmouth City Council May '79; became Lord Mayor of Portsmouth May '90; delayed the Portsmouth Docks being privatised by using his casting vote; oversaw the enlargement of the Continental Ferryport to take the new super-ferries; became Deputy Lord Mayor of Portsmouth May '91; came 3rd in the election for Portsmouth South with 14.6% of the vote Apr '92; was selected for Portsmouth North '95; won the seat on a notional swing of 13.5%, ending Peter Griffiths' 18-year reign by 4,323 votes May '97; in his Maiden, gave publicity to the Special Olympics - for people with learning difficulties - being hosted by Portsmouth June '97; showed solidarity with jailed Indonesian union leader June '97; backed ban on fox-hunting June '97; co-sponsored motion deploring lack of insurance cover for injured workers in companies in liquidation July '97; asked Foreign Secretary Cook about the ban on the export of electro-shock weapons July '97;
Born: 17 April 1942, Isle of Wight
Family: Is married to Phyllis, a Portsmouth City Councillor and Chairman of Portsmouth Labour Party; 1s John '76, 1d Sydna '74, who is married to Lieut Ian Taylor RN;
Education: Southsea Modern, Portsmouth; Paulsgrove Secondary Modern, Portsmouth; Portsmouth Dockyard College;

Occupation: Senior Craftsman Aircraft Fitter, at local Ministry of Defence establishment, Royal Navy Aviation Yard (AEU Works Convenor '79-) '63-97; Apprentice Aircraft Fitter '58-63;
Traits: Bald; heavyweight ("the highlight of my career as Chairman of a leisure committee was when we rearranged the Tour de France leg for Great Britain and [Robert Key] and I were in Trafalgar Square trying to straddle a bicycle; it was hilarious, given the size of us both"); "not at all the sharp-suited figure of New Labour" (Francis Hardy, DAILY MAIL); Freeman of City of London; enjoys swimming and gardening;
Address: House of Commons, Westminster, London SW1A 0AA; 79 Washbrook Road, Paulsgrove, Portsmouth PO6 3SB;
Telephone: 0171 219 3000 (H of C); 01705 389494 (home)

'Andy' (Andrew) REED Labour & Co-operative LOUGHBOROUGH '97-

Majority: 5,712 over Conservative 4-way;
Description: A constituency changed enough to make Stephen Dorrell flee it after the middle-class suburbs of the Soar Valley, with its 20,000 Tory-leaning voters, were removed; partly-industrial Loughborough, which remains the seat's core, has been thought marginal; it has 11,000 students in Loughborough University and 6,000 Asians;
Position: Charnwood Borough Councillor (Chairman of Economic Development) '95-; ex: Birstall Parish Councillor '87-91;
Outlook: A locally-rooted Blair loyalist and Christian Socialist; "as much a pragmatist as an idealist" (INDEPENDENT ON SUNDAY); "thought to be soft-Left" (NEW STATESMAN); "well-presented and behaved and good with the media, no politics whatsoever...the smarmy image of Tony Blair" (RED PEPPER); belongs to every organisation in town; favours proportional representation (in Labour Campaign for Electoral Reform); also in Nicaragua Solidarity Campaign, Greenpeace, formerly in Anti-Apartheid;
History: He joined the Labour Party, "driven initially by Third World poverty, unemployment and inequality" '83; served as constituency press officer for five years; was elected a Birstall Parish Councillor May '87; became Parliamentary assistant to Keith Vaz '87; became Chairman of his Constituency Labour Party '88; won selection for Loughborough on the third ballot, with 44% of the vote Nov '90; despite a pro-Labour swing of 5.9%, lost Loughborough to Stephen Dorrell by 10,883 votes Apr '92; in Labour's Leadership campaign, after it had nominated Bryan Gould, persuaded the Loughborough party to back John Smith June-July '92; backed the Blair leadership on watering down Clause IV '94; the Boundary Commission removed 20,000 voters, mostly in the Tory-leaning Soar Valley '94; was elected a Charnwood Borough Councillor May '95; "ran a successful year-long lobbying campaign persuading the European Commission to grant £5m in regional economic aid to the former Leicestershire coalfield"; was re-selected as Labour's candidate for this now-marginal seat (its incumbent Tory MP Stephen Dorrell, decamping to safer Charnwood) '96; said the NHS was the Labour achievement he most admired: "it encapsulates all that I believe in - a socialist principle that works" Mar '97; in the last stages of the campaign, had the advantage that his actual Tory

opponent was little-known, with many thinking Stephen Dorrell was still the candidate Apr '97; won the seat on a notional swing of 8.9%, with a majority of 5,712 May '97; in his Maiden jokingly deplored the absence of Labour legislation against "nuisance neighbours" like his in Rushcliffe (Kenneth Clarke) and Charnwood (Stephen Dorrell, who was also his constituent as a local councillor); said he wanted to revive the local engineering and textile industries which had declined June '97; with other local MPs, co-sponsored a motion extolling Leicester's National Space Science Centre June '97; urged the new Government to accord Leicestershire the status required to receive EU funds July '97; urged PFI funding to provide a new general hospital for Loughborough July '97; was tagged "stooge of the week" by the INDEPENDENT after he asked PM Tony Blair to allow "the best-known and well-loved East Midlands" to have its own regional assembly like Scotland and Wales July '97;
Born: 17 September 1964, Kettering
Family: Son, of Don Reed, electrician, and Margaret (Thrall); m '92 Sarah Elizabeth (Chester);
Education: Riverside Infants and Junior School, Birstall '69-76; Stonehill High School, Birstall '76-79; Longslade Community College '79-81; Leicester Polytechnic '83-87 (BA IIi Hons in Public Administration);
Occupation: European Affairs Advisor '94-96, Employment Initiatives Officer '90-94, with Leicestershire County Council (UNISON/NALGO: Union Convenor of the Planning and Transport Department of Leicestershire County Council) '90-96);
Traits: Dark, close-cropped hair; humorous; has been accused of "reeding"; enjoys running, volleyball, tennis, badminton and Rugby (represented Leicestershire County);
Address: House of Commons, Westminster, London SW1A 0AA; 3 Newbold Close, Sileby, Loughborough LE12 7PB; Loughborough CLP, 4 Hawthorn Avenue, Birstall, Leicester LE4 4HJ;
Telephone: 0171 219 3529 (H of C); 01509 261226 (constituency);

Laurence (Anthony) ROBERTSON **Conservative** **TEWKESBURY '97-**

Majority: 9,234 over Liberal Democrat 3-way;
Description: The very altered Gloucestershire seat cobbled together from the town of Tewkesbury and the Gloucester-Cheltenham suburbs; on the basis of 1992 voting, these new boundaries were expected to produce a Conservative majority of almost 10,000;
Position: Chairman, Grindleford Conservative Association '91-93; on Conservative National Advisory Committee on Education '89-91; Treasurer, of Bolton SE Conservative Association '85-86;
Outlook: A bright Redwood-supporting hard-line Eurosceptic; a strong opponent of a single European currency; also an anti-devolutionist: "I have a great passion for the United Kingdom"; the son of a colliery electrician who sees himself as part of a determined "new breed" taking over the Conservative Party from the "landed gentry";
History: He joined the Conservative Party '81; selected for hopeless Makerfield to oppose Labour's Ian McCartney, he lost by 15,558 after a 3.8% swing to Labour June 1987; served as Agent in Merseyside East in Euro-election June '89; was selected for hopeless Ashfield, to

oppose Geoff Hoon; was one of 24 Tory candidates who wrote to the DAILY TELEGRAPH opposing a single European currency or European political union Nov '91; lost by 12,987 after a 7.1% swing to Labour Apr '92; a self-proclaimed supporter of Redwood, he said: "obviously the Conservative Party has changed - and not before time - in the years since Margaret Thatcher took over; there is a new breed of people coming in which is different to the old landed gentry; I admire John Redwood because he has clarity of thought, which I feel we have been missing - that is why we have been drifting; he was willing to resign his position and give something up to fight last summer - I feel you can trust him on the big issues; I'm not convinced that Michael Portillo would resign over something like the single currency" Aug '96; was one of the 59 Tory candidates who told the DAILY TELEGRAPH that their election addresses would pledge them never to support Britain's entry to a single European currency Dec '96; he fought both against Euro-federalism and devolution Apr '97; won the seat by a majority of 9,234 with a derisory 0.5% notional swing to the Liberal Democrats May '97; in the Leadership contest, joined the Redwood campaign team May '97; in his Maiden, complained about rushing through the pro-devolution legislation May '97; asked about charging to see GPs or for hospital stays June '97; asked about Royal Commission into care for the elderly June '97; asked about compensation for faulty radiotherapy treatment June '97; asked about council tax for people in mobile homes July '97; asked about identity cards for the young purchasing alcohol July '97; urged that "companies in the construction industry do not gain an unfair advantage by classing employed labour as self-employed" July '97; warned PM Tony Blair that "building on green fields as opposed to brown-field sights will cause great alarm" in Gloucestershire July '97;

Born: 29 March 1958, Bolton

Family: Son, of James Robertson, colliery electrician, and Jean Christine (Larkin), former office worker; m '89 Susan (Lees), who was elected to Gloucestershire County Council on the same day he was elected to the Commons; 2 stepdaughters: Sarah Victoria Nichols '73; Jemma Diane Nichols '81 a YC;

Education: Farnworth Grammar School;

Occupation: Director: L A Robertson (Public Relations) '89-, Philip Gore (Bolton) Ltd (general trading); Self-Employed Fund-Raiser for charities (claims to have worked for 80 organisations and raised over £1m for charities, organising large-scale high-profile events at Lambeth Palace, St James's Palace, Chatsworth and 10 Downing Street) '92-; ex: Public Relations Consultant '89-92: Industrial Consultant '82-89; Work Study Engineer '76-82;

Traits: Pleasant-looking; parted light brown hair; rising forehead; sharp chin; has completed six Marathons;

Address: House of Commons, Westminster, London SW1A 0AA; Tewkesbury Conservative Association, Lloyds Bank Chambers, Abbey Terrace, Winchcombe, Glos GL54 5LL;

Telephone: 0171 219 3000 (H of C); 01242 602388/602288 (Fax) (constituency); 01242 603428;

CHECKING DRAFTS

We submit drafts of our profiles to MPs to minimise errors and reduce the threat of libel actions. It sometimes produces amusing insights. One MP, whose daughter was reported as having been arrested for prostitution, set us straight. She had gone to Bristol to procure drugs. When arrested, she claimed she was offering sexual favours, knowing it would incur a much lighter sentence.

Frank ROY **Labour** **MOTHERWELL & WISHAW '97-**

Majority: 12,791 over SNP 6-way;
Description: Central Scotland's again-renamed version of old Motherwell South with almost 3,000 extra voters from Motherwell North; an engineering and steel seat, formerly dominated by the shut and blasted Ravenscraig; a safe-Labour working class seat that is overwhelmingly dominated by council housing;
Position: On Select Committee on Social Security '97-; ex: Personal Assistant to Helen Liddell '94-97;
Outlook: A "politically astute" (Ken Smith, GLASGOW HERALD) ex-steelworker replacing highbrow Dr Jeremy Bray in his own home town; a pro-Blair moderate in the 'Network' (SCOTSMAN); takes a tough line on education standards ("poor teachers and poor teaching methods cannot be tolerated"); knows first-hand the problems of Ravenscraig's closure, which cost him his job after 13 years there; "a classic case of fighting back from adversity; he took British Steel's help after Ravenscraig closed to go to college, then on to university - all the while supporting his wife and two children with evening shifts in pubs" (Ken Smith, GLASGOW HERALD);
History: He joined the Labour Party '79; served as Election Agent to Dr Jeremy Bray in Motherwell South '87 and '92; he volunteered to work for Helen Liddell in the bitterly-fought Monklands East by-election, becoming a member of her team June '94; victorious Helen Liddell "saw his potential and hired him to work full-time in the constituency as her Personal Assistant - in reality her trusted eyes and ears to ensure she is always informed of what is happening in Airdrie while in Westminster" (Ken Smith, GLASGOW HERALD); he decided he too would like to become an MP; was selected for his home constituency of Motherwell and Wishaw, on the announced imminent retirement of veteran Labour MP Dr Jeremy Bray Aug '95; decided to set up his constituency office in Wishaw, to counter any hint of preference for his home town of Motherwell; was described as part of the pro-Blair 'Network' (SCOTSMAN) Jan '97; won the seat by a majority of 12,791, on a derisory notional swing to the SNP of .1% May '97; expressed solidarity with jailed Indonesian union leader June '97; was named to the Select Committee on Social Security July '97;
Born: 29 August 1958, Motherwell
Family: Son, late James Roy, settler manager, and Esther (McMahon) retired homehelp; m '77 Ellen (Foy); 1s: Brian '80, 1d Kelly-Anne '82;
Education: St Joseph's and Our Lady's High Schools, Motherwell; Glasgow Caledonian University (BA in Consumer Management Studies '92-94)
Occupation: Ex: Personal Assistant, to Helen Liddell, MP for Monklands East (GMB) '94-97; Barman, during period at Glasgow Caledonian University '92-94; Steelworker, at Ravenscraig '78-91;
Traits: Dark; jowly chubby face; snub-nosed; sculptured, mouth-encircling beard; RC; enjoys football, gardening and music;
Address: House of Commons, Westminster, London, SW1A 0AA;
Telephone: 0171 219 6467 (H of C);

Chris(topher) RUANE **Labour** **VALE OF CLWYD '97-**

Majority: 8,955 over Conservative 6-way;
Description: The new marginal seat in the county of Clwyd, centred on the River Clywd and based on the down-market resort of Rhyl plus Prestatyn to the east, with the tiny cathedral city of St Asaph and its castle; it was the Welsh Tories' 5th most marginal seat;
Position: Rhyl Town Councillor '88-; ex: Chairman, of West Clwyd NUT '89-90; former Chairman, founder-member and press officer of the Rhyl Anti-Apartheid Movement and Rhyl Environment Association;
Outlook: The locally-born Centre-Left local councillor and Deputy Head of a local primary school; a local activist, he campaigned against nursery vouchers, to clear up the River Clywd, to set up a network of community centres in Rhyl; he previously fought Rod Richards for Clwyd North West last time, halving his majority;
History: He joined the Labour Party '86; was elected a Rhyl Town Councillor May '88; became Chairman of the West Clwyd NUT '89; selected to fight hopeless Clwyd North West, was defeated by Rod Richards by 6,050 votes (11.4%) despite a 6% swing from the Conservatives, which halved the majority Apr '92; was selected for new marginal seat of Vale of Clwyd '95; criticised Government proposals to introduce cadets into schools: "I could think of many more focussed ways to spend the money than teaching young people to march around a square with a gun" Jan '97; won the seat by a majority of 8,955 on a notional swing of 13.9% - the biggest in Wales May '97; asked which Welsh local councils had installed smoke detectors in their housing stock June '97; expressed solidarity with jailed Indonesian union leader June '97; the strong point in his Maiden was his tirade against the "quango state in Wales" July '97;
Born: 18 July 1958, St Asaph
Family: Son, of late Michael Ruane, navvy, and Esther (Roberts); he is married, with a daughter, Seren;
Education: Blessed Edward Jones High School, Rhyl; University College of Wales, Aberystwyth (BSc Econ); Liverpool University (Teaching Certificate); South Wales Poly (Diploma in Media Education);
Occupation: Deputy Head, of Ysgol Mair Primary School (NUT) '82-97;
Traits: Front-combed retreating grey hair; round face; enjoys cooking; Roman Catholic;
Address: House of Commons, Westminster, London SW1A 0AA; 33 Grange Road, Rhyl, LL18 4RD;
Telephone: 0171 219 3000 (H of C); 01745 354626 (home);

David RUFFLEY **Conservative** **BURY ST EDMUNDS '97-**

Majority: 368 over Labour 5-way;

Description: Despite its retained name, this is largely a new seat, with only 33,000 of its voters from the town which gives it its name; fully 36,000 were formerly in Suffolk Central; it was expected, on a '92-style voting division, to provide a 10,000 majority for its new Tory candidate;

Position: Ex: Special Adviser to Kenneth Clarke '91-96;

Outlook: The former self-styled "Rightwing conscience" of Ken Clarke, having served him as Special Adviser at Education, the Home Office and the Treasury; "pragmatic" (FINANCIAL TIMES); "whizz political adviser" (DAILY EXPRESS); "super-bright" (NEW STATESMAN); prides himself as a communicator, which Conservative Central Office exploited half-time until the election; "clever and assertive" (DAILY MAIL); "displays a distrust of mandarin pieties, a cool, sceptical intelligence and civilised taste" (Michael Gove); "by all accounts the coming man" (MAIL ON SUNDAY), tagged to be in a Conservative Cabinet by 2015; previously a "buttoned-down corporate lawyer from the City";

History: He joined the Young Conservatives in Bolton West '79; became an officer of the Cambridge University Conservative Association '81; at Cambridge, like Michael Portillo, came under the influence of the high-Tory don Maurice Cowling; he displayed the "distrust of mandarin pieties, the relish for intrigue, the cool, sceptical intelligence and civilised taste for grown-up relations that mark out Cowling's pupils" (Michael Gove); while working as a solicitor in the City, served as a part-time research assistant to Bolton MP Tom Sackville for five years from '85; after he joined Kenneth Clarke's staff at Education, later claimed to have fought for "simpler testing of the National Curriculum and school league tables" '91; organised the election campaign for Kenneth Clarke Apr '92; at the Home Office, later claimed to have "successfully fought for legislation to crack down on bail bandits, to give courts greater powers to pass custodial sentences and to overhaul the unit fines system" '92-93; was on the short-list of three, compressed from 150 candidates for Harrogate; as the runner-up, luckily lost out to Norman Lamont by three votes in the selection contest Jan '96; failed in the contest for Buckingham, where he was confused with David Rutley, also a short-haired Treasury Special Adviser Feb '96; was selected as the Conservative candidate for changed Bury St Edmunds Mar '96; resigned from the Civil Service as Kenneth Clarke's Special Adviser Mar '96; said he would refuse to replace the pound with a single European currency Apr '97; barely retained Bury St Edmunds by 368 votes after "two nail-biting recounts" after a 9.6% notional swing to Labour - one of the lowest in East Anglia May '97; joined William Hague's campaign team in the Leadership contest May '97; in his graceful Maiden, dismissed the Budget of Chancellor Gordon Brown as "cunning" but not "wise" for the usual City Tory reasons July '97; tried unsuccessfully to get Cabinet Secretary Sir Robin Butler to investigate Charles Whelan's briefings on a single European currency Oct '97;

Born: 18 April 1962, Bolton

Family: Son, of Jack Laurie Ruffley, solicitor and the Town Clerk of Darwen, and Yvonne Grace (Harris);

Education: Bolton School; Exhibitioner and Foundation Scholar of Queen's College, Cambridge Unversity (1st Class Hons in Historical Tripos Part I '83, BA Law '85);

Occupation: Consultant: to Grant-Maintained Schools Foundation '91-; ex: Economics Consultant, to Conservative Central Office '96-97; Special Adviser ("responsible for policy advice, speech-writing and handling media relations"), to Kenneth Clarke, at Education, the Home Office and Treasury '91-96; Solicitor, with Clifford Chance (leading City commercial practice) '85-91;
Traits: Full open face; short hair; articulate; "rarely at a loss for words" (INDEPENDENT ON SUNDAY); known to the press as "'Treat Me' Ruffley"; "a keen golfer and Manchester United supporter" (INDEPENDENT); also enjoys cinema;
Address: House of Commons, Westminster, London SW1A 0AA;
Telephone: 0171 219 3000 (H of C);

Christine RUSSELL **Labour** **CITY OF CHESTER '97-**

Majority: 10,553 over Conservative 6-way;
Description: The historic market town and cathedral city, with its Roman walls, mock-Tudor buildings and Georgian squares; despite two Tory-leaning wards added from Ellesmere Port, in '97 it could not resist the pull of the Left-moving urban northwest;
Position: Chester Borough Councillor '80-; Sheriff of Chester '92-93;
Outlook: The historic city's first-ever Labour MP and first-ever woman MP; a local librarian-magistrate who is more into silk blouses than the colourful pullovers displayed by her noisy Tory predecessor, Giles Brandreth; "I care passionately about international development" (CR); is also interested in transport, urban regeneration and crime (a member of the Magistrates' Association); is active in the Women's Hostel Association and the Citizen's Advice Bureau;
History: She joined the Labour Party '67; became Labour's Election Agent '86-87; resigned as Election Agent, hoping to be selected as Chester's Labour candidate '95; her selection from an all-women short-list was under way when the industrial tribunal ruled such selections illegal Jan '96; she was re-selected from an open short-list Feb '96; her victory was predicted in a LIVERPOOL DAILY POST poll Apr '97; won the seat for Labour for the first time, on a notional swing of 11.4%, ousting Giles Brandreth by a majority of 10,553 May '97; asked Deputy PM John Prescott what impact the Government's release of capital receipts would have on the availability of affordable housing units in Chester May '97; in her Maiden, urged the new Government to show its attitude toward 3rd world development by enabling the universities to revert to their old habit of providing scholarships for overseas students July '97; asked about anti-personnel mines July '97; "as one who has been a magistrate for the past 17 years" complained that "the current system is costly and not very effective"; "it is not at all unknown for a young offender who has been arrested at Christmas not to arrive in court until the summer holidays" July '97; called attention to breast cancer campaign Oct '97;
Born: 25 March 1945, Holbeach, Lincolnshire
Family: She was married and subsequently divorced; she has a son and a daughter, who is a graduate of Sussex University;
Education: Spalding High School; North West London Poly;
Occupation: Librarian, ALA: recently worked as Co-ordinator of Chester and Ellesmere Port

Advocacy Project for MIND (GMB) '94-97; Press Officer, for Brian Simpson MEP '92-94; **Traits:** Dark; pageboy bob with bangs; pretty; broad of beam; "sensible"; "she hates jumpers; she's more into silk blouses" (an aide); enjoys art, architecture and the cinema (an organiser of the Chester Film Society);
Address: House of Commons, Westminster, London SW1A 0AA; 59 Cheyney Road, Chester CH1 4BS;
Telephone: 0171 219 3000 (H of C); 01244 390686 (home);

'Bob' (Robert Edward) RUSSELL **Liberal Democrat** **COLCHESTER '97-**

Majority: 1,581 over Conservative 5-way;
Description: The urban wards of Roman-founded Colchester - Britain's oldest recorded town - reunited in a single marginal seat; although its rural hinterland has been Tory, the LibDems took 10 of the town's 13 wards in '92, and 12 of them in '94; in the past, its political ambivalence has lain in the tendency of the LibDems to under-perform in Parliamentary contests;
Position: On LibDems' Home and Legal Affairs team '97-; Colchester Borough Councillor (Mayor '86-87, Leader of Council '87-91, Chairman of Policy, Arts and Leisure) '71-
Outlook: The veteran local councillor and Parliamentary candidate, "a local man to his toenails" (John Sweeney, OBSERVER); succeeded in overtaking the favoured Tory candidate by heavily emphasising the LibDems' strong commitment to greater education spending; a member of the tactical voting lobby, GROT (Get Rid Of Tories), he was especially interested in attracting Labour voters to back him as a former Labour Parliamentary candidate twice over, and an SDPer at heart; "eccentric" (Jack Straw MP);
History: He joined the Labour Party, contesting Sudbury and Woodbridge as Labour's candidate Oct '74; contested Colchester as Labour's candidate against Antony Buck May '79; left Labour for the Social Democrats '81; joined the merged Liberal Democrats '88; strongly defended local teachers against Conservative criticism: "it is a wonder that anyone wants to go into teaching, or remain in teaching in the face of such unfounded comments; what local Tories are trying to do is to divert attenton from the real problem: the general under-funding of education at all levels from nursery through schools to adult education; all who have a genuine interst in education know full well that the Tories have made cuts after cuts in education; Labour is now following the Tory line; 'New' Labour is not offering any 'new' money for education; they are more interested in trying to outbid the Tories on the question of tax; the Liberal Democrats are the only party pledged to invest more in education, about £2b every year, and if this means putting 1p more on income tax, then we believe it is in the local and national interest" (letter to EAST ANGLIA DAILY TIMES) Mar '97; concentrated on wooing small and medium local businesses, pointing out the out-of-town super-markets paid lower rates and small shops paid more than departmental stores Apr '97; won the seat by a majority of 1,581, after a notional swing of 6.2%, defeating the exotic Tory Stephan 'Shakespeare' May '97; in his Maiden recalled how his "generous, co-operative and constructive letter" requesting financial help to buy security cameras had received "an extremely rude, arrogant and dismissive" reply from Tory Home Office Minister David

Maclean; he also complained that Colchester had been "lumbered" with a punishment bootcamp, "a very expensive gimmick", because the Tory Home Secretary Michael Howard wanted to make a dramatic proposal to the annual Tory conference May '97; led motion congratulating Neighbourhood Watch on its 15th anniversary June '97; expressed solidarity with jailed Indonesian union leader June '97; asked about increasing pensioners' £10 Christmas bonus July '97; led motion congratulating cricket captain Graham Gooch on his retirement July '97; co-sponsored motion advocating annual report by MPs to their constituents July '97; urged more road safety measures for Colchester High Street July '97; insisted that "being an MP should be a full-time job" Aug '97;
Born: 31 March 1946, Colchester
Family: He is married with two sons and two daughters (one deceased);
Education: Myland Primary, Colchester; St Helena Secondary School, Colchester; North East Essex Technical College; National Council for Training of Journalists;
Occupation: Journalist and Press Officer (NUJ): Reporter, ESSEX COUNTY STANDARD '63-66, News Editor, BRAINTREE & WITHAM TIMES '66-68, Editor of MALDON AND BURNHAM STANDARD (the youngest in the country) '68-69; Sub-Editor on LONDON EVENING NEWS and EVENING STANDARD '69-73; Press/Publicity Officer: BT (Eastern Region), GPO Telecommunications '73-85, University of Essex '86-97;
Traits: Front-combed grey hair; big specs; high cheekbones; nice smile; "Worzel Gummidge lookalike" (John Sweeney, OBSERVER); local historian; fastest MP-typist (75 wpm); Colchester United fan;
Address: House of Commons, Westminster, London SW1A 0AA; 10 North Hill, Colchester CO1 1DZ (LibDem offices);
Telephone: 0171 219 3000 (H of C); 01206 45200 (home); 01206 500009; 01206 710172 (LibDem HQ); 01206 710184 (Fax);

Joan RYAN Labour ENFIELD NORTH '97-

Majority: 6,822 over Conservative 6-way;
Description: London's most northern seat, where Greater London meets the Hertfordshire countryside; it stretches from the Tory-leaning green belt in the west to the Labour-voting tower blocks and industrial areas - which gave birth to the Lee Enfield rifle - in the east; Enfield Town and beautiful Enfield Chase have been Tory and Ponders End - birthplace of Norman Tebbit - and Enfield Wash have been Labour, with Enfield Lock marginal; the seat was taken from Labour's Bryan Davies in '79 by Tim Eggar, who built his majority up to 14,000 in '87, declining to 9,430 in '92;
Position: Barnet Councillor (its Deputy Leader and Chairman of Policy and Resources Committee '94-) '90-;
Outlook: Enfield North's first woman MP: another example of a Labour teacher and Deputy Leader of a council; has strong professional feelings: "I'm a teacher and I want to see our target for literacy in 11-year-olds met, and the school-home partnership improved"; but she is cautious with Lord Rothermere's minions on the EVENING STANDARD as to where she stands in he Labour Party; in Greenpeace, SERA, Socialist Education Association and the

Labour Women's Network;
History: She joined the Labour Party '83; was elected to Barnet Borough Council May '90; was elected Chairman of North London Euro-CLP '92; was named as one of the first eleven women aspirants to receive support from 'Emily's List' Mar '94; was elected Deputy Leader of Barnet Council May '94; was selected for Enfield North Sep '95; at Labour's annual conference at Brighton, said that the first priority of a Labour Government should be the creation of jobs Oct '95; declined to tell Rothermere's EVENING STANDARD whether she was Leftwing or Rightwing, saying: "as a member of the Labour Party, I do not see any divisions"; asked whether she wanted to see the gas, water and BR back in public hands, said: "it is a case of if and when allowed" July '96; unexpectedly won the seat on a 16.1% swing, a majority of 6,822 over her Conservative opponent; this made her the 46th least-expected Labour victor May '97; with Dr Rudi Vis, decided to keep her seat on Barnet Council May '97; pushed for abolition of admission fees to museums June '97; co-sponsored motion attacking prescription fraud June '97; led motion welcoming improved breast cancer treatment June '97; urged Education Secretary David Blunkett to persuade parents to play their full part in education, along with teachers and pupils July '97; in her Maiden complained of the heavy unemployment among the young in Enfield North: 47% among the 18-24 category, with more among blacks and Bangladeshis; she welcomed the plan of Ford to invest £40m in Enfield and to expand its youth training July '97;
Born: 8 September 1955, Warrington
Family: Daughter, of Michael Joseph Ryan, painter and decorator, and Delores Marie (Joyce), cook; she is married with two children;
Education: Hurlingham and Chelsea Secondary School; Hawksmoor Sixth Form College; William Morris Academy; City of Liverpool College of Higher Education (BA Hons in Sociology and History); South Bank Polytechnic (MSc in Sociology);
Occupation: Ex: Teacher and Free-Lance Researcher;
Traits: Reddish-blonde; long oval face; good smile showing even teeth;
Address: House of Commons, Westminster, London SW1A 0AA;
Telephone: 0171 219 6502 (H of C); 0181 444 6400 (home);

'Nick' (Nicholas Francis) ST AUBYN **Conservative** **GUILDFORD '97-**

Majority: 4,791 over Liberal Democrat 6-way;
Description: The virtually-unaltered county town which, pre-'97, was the least safely-Tory of all the 11 Conservative seats in Surrey; it is partly a commuting city but big enough to be a commercial centre on its own and the home of Surrey University; a middle-class seat with a high proportion of professionals; its only change in '95 was the shift of a village into neighbouring Surrey Heath; if '97 voting had followed the '92 pattern, it should have produced a majority of 13,000 for the Tory victor;
Position: On Select Committee on Education and Employment '97-; President, of the Conservative Cornwall & Plymouth East Euro-Association '95-; ex: Westminster City Councillor (Chairman of New Technology) '82-86;
Outlook: A rarity from a recently endangered species - an Old Etonian Tory MP (one of only

three in the '97 intake) - belatedly rewarded with a safe seat after three struggles to retake marginal Truro from the Liberals and LibDems in '87 (twice) and '92; a Cornish aristocrat with 10 Cornish MPs in his family "the 11th generation of my family to be elected" (NStA); a symbol of the abandonment by the southwest of top-class Tory candidates; a Cornwall-based manufacturer who claims to know and understand the problems of small business and its employees;

History: He was a Liberal at Oxford, Secretary of its Liberal Society '75; joined the Conservative Party at the instigation of his new mother-in-law '80; became branch Chairman of the Conservative Association in Little Venice, Paddington '81; successfully challenged a Labour-held seat, Little Venice, on Westminster Council, securing the biggest swing in London May '82; was selected as the Tory candidate for Truro, in the hope of retaking the only non-Tory seat of the five in Cornwall from Liberal David Penhaligon July '86; the death of Penhaligon in Dec '86 faced him with Penhaligon's 24-year-old researcher, Matthew Taylor; he emphasised the Treasury's willingness to spend £25m on a package to keep alive the Cornish tin industry as showing Tories could be caring Jan '87; St Aubyn defended the Conservative Government, which had dealt harshly with the county's need for more finances; he insisted Mrs Thatcher had had to be "tough" when she took over in '79; "what I always hoped would happen - and what is starting to happen - is that when the time was right we would be able to show that we are caring spenders and effective spenders" Feb '87; at St Aubyn's adoption meeting for the by-election, Norman Tebbit said: "this is a seat we can now win" Feb '87; David Steel, recalling St Aubyn's great-grandfather had been the MP for Truro, commented: "even for a Tory, that's taking the hereditary principle a bit far..." Mar '87; he came out for capital punishment, but not in the case of domestic disputes; said: "it was the '60s generation which now accounts for most of the criminal class; they were brought up in the permissive society" Mar '87; predicted victory: "we are closing the gap and I maintain we will win" Mar '87; was engulfed by the 14,517-majority of the young Liberal, Matthew Taylor, who increased Penhaligon's previous majority by a third Mar '87; re-contested the seat at the general election, cutting Taylor's majority to 4,753, helped by the enlarged Labour vote and a record increase in the Tory vote June '87; at annual conference promised to take Truro next time, with the help of a full-time agent; opposed excessive deregulation, urging it be left to local councils Oct '87; at annual conference said it would have been better to save a few jobs in Cornwall's English China Clay than lose all 1,000 jobs Oct '87; was formally adopted as Truro's Tory candidate Feb '90; criticised Cornwall's county council's proposed charge of £10 a week to transport mentally disabled to training centres Oct '91; at annual conference in Blackpool urged Regional Assistance for Cornwall: "Cornwall can compete is today's market, but we must have the same range of investment incentives for manufacturing business as other regions, such a Scotland, Wales and other parts of Europe" Oct '91; attacked the "self-serving complacency" of Liberal Democrats on local councils for failing to secure funds available to their localities Nov '91; his selection as the candidate for Truro was welcomed by local Conservatives because "he came from a local family which had been involved in the life of the [Cornish] area for generations" Mar '92; saw Matthew Taylor's majority rise to 7,570 Apr '92; was on the three-person short-list for Hampshire North East Sep '95; came second in Witney Oct '95, Maidenhead (won by Theresa May) Oct '95, and Mole Valley Nov '95, before being selected for Guildford Mar '96; wrote against a single European currency in the DAILY TELEGRAPH Aug '96; was one of the 59 Tory prospectives whose election addresses would oppose Britain's entry into a single European currency in the next Parliament Dec '96; co-signed letter to DAILY TELEGRAPH by a dozen Tory prospectives, in which they complained that Labour MEPs were unreconstructed "old Labour" socialists Feb '97; asked by the SUNDAY TIMES who would succeed John Major in the event of a defeat, said: "if we lost, we would look for a different type of leader, we would go back to first principles" Mar '97; retained the seat with a majority of 4,791 after a notional swing of 7.1% to his Liberal Democrat opponent May '97; complained about the impact of the abolition of the Assisted Places Scheme would have on local pupils and schools June '97; urged more privatisation of council housing June '97; said Labour's new Solictor General, who had suffered a pay cut on assuming office, should take no pay at all because no extra pay had been found for Joan Ruddock June '97; baited Welsh Secretary on powers for Welsh Assembly July '97; opposed abolition of tax relief on pensioners' private health insurance premiums as hurting 5,000 in his constituency July '97; was named to Select Committee on Education and Employment July '97;

Born: 19 November 1955, London

Family: The family came to Cornwall 700 years ago as Breton crusaders; "from one of the oldest land-holding families in Cornwall; his uncle is [Lord St Levan], one of Cornwall's biggest landowners, with an ancestral home on St Michael's Mount" (Ewen MacAskill, SCOTSMAN); his 18th century ancestor, Sir John St Aubyn Bt, was MP for Cornwall for 25 years; nine of his other ancestors were Cornish MPs; his elder brother, James, the heir to St Michael's Mount, was also at Kleinwort Benson before going into business in Plymouth, and was a Social Democrat in the '80s; son, of Hon Piers St Aubyn, second son of 3rd Baron St Levan and Mary (Bailey) of Olierhoutpost, South Africa;; m '80 Jane (Brooks) "a jolly blonde Tory", "pretty, with no side" (Alan Watkins, OBSERVER); 5c: Henry '81, Kitty '83, Alice '86, Camilla '90, Edward '95;

Education: St Peter's School, Seaford; Eton College; Trinity College, Oxford University (Open Exhibition; MA Hons in PPE);

Occupation: Owner and Director, of Fitzroy Joinery, the southwest's biggest specialist manufacturer '93-; previously ran "his own manufacturing business...Gemini Clothes Care Ltd (a company in Redruth with 20 employees, established to develop and manufacture a new product)... on the Cardrew Industrial Estate, Redruth '88-93; was Vice President for Financial Products of AIG '87-89; after coming down from Oxford, he worked as a merchant banker in the City '77-87, latterly as an Assistant Director of Kleinwort Benson - their expert on currency swaps and capital markets '86-87; previously was an Executive, of J P Morgan, after training in their London and New York offices in banking and capital markets '77-86

Traits: Dark; slim; long face; parted dark hair falling over his right eye; contact lenses; still somewhat boyish; in 1987 had "all the qualities expected of a Tory in this [Cornish] part of the world: the vowels of Eton and Oxford, a Range Rover and a duvet waistcoat, a career in merchant banking, with a little farming on the side in Cornwall" (Ewen MacAskill, SCOTSMAN); "affects an aristocratic negligence of dress; he wears a check sports coat, a high-necked navy pullover and, for outside engagements, one of those waterproof [waxed] coats that are always being advertised in the colour supplements" (Alan Watkins, OBSERVER '87); enjoys playing ragtime and Gershwin and Porter on the piano; "urbane" (SUNDAY TELEGRAPH); "is an easy-going and affable fellow, relaxed in tweeds and very much a cuddly Conservative of the old-fashioned, paternalist kind" (Mark Rosselli, INDENDENT); CofE;

Address: House of Commons, Westminster, London SW1A 0AA; Keepers, Gate Street, Bramley, Surrey GU5 0LR; 7 Queen Anne's Gate, London SW1;

Telephone: 0171 219 3000 (H of C); 01483 893637 (home); 01752 562542 (work);

Martin SALTER **Labour** **READING WEST '97-**

Majority: 2,997 over Conservative 6-way;

Description: Reading is considered a British version of 'Middletown', a microcosm of the nation: partly industrial, but also a university town, with a mixture of council estates and middle-class suburbs; Reading West was considered to be rather too skewed to the Right to be a political weather-vane, with its affluent Thames-side villages like Pangbourne and Purley; in his last, '92 contest, its popular Rightwing Tory MP, Sir Anthony Durant, clocked up a 13,298 majority, which caused would-be inheritors to flock for selection; former Pembroke Tory MP Nicholas Bennett even married to qualify for what turned out to be the short straw;

Position: Former: Reading Borough Councillor (Deputy Leader, Chairman its Leisure Committee), Berkshire County Councillor;

Outlook: A former Deputy Leader of Reading Borough Council who was one of the surprise victors of May '97, the 19th least-expected Labour winner; a former demonstrator for CND and the miners, recently a crusader for "a new politics, new political structures and a political system that connects with the public and their aspirations"; although an acknowledged "tribalist", accepts that "the two-party system has had its day" as "confrontational, absurd and often irrelevant"; a longtime advocate of Lib-Lab collaboration from "the days when it was unfashionable" (NEW STATESMAN), he cashed in this time, by securing a crucial third of the LibDem vote; but he later boasted that "we're smothering them"; he made a slow start in the Commons, concentrating initially on locally-raised issues; a keen angler who detests fox-hunting;

History: He joined the Labour Party, participating in CND demos; having moved to Reading in '80, he was elected to Reading Borough Council May '84, becoming its Deputy Leader; participated in demonstrations for striking miners '84-85; he was also elected to Berkshire County Council; he became Leader of the Labour Group on Reading Borough Council; was selected for Reading East by a vote of 24 to 9 to 2, Nov '85, endorsed by Labour's NEC Dec '85; contested Reading East against Sir Gerard Vaughan, coming 3rd with 21.5% of the vote June '87; decided to contest Reading West after his popular Tory predecessor, Tony Durant, announced he would not stand again; was selected for Reading West '95; received the endorsement of Janet Bond the former Liberal Democrat Mayor of Reading: "this time we have to vote tactically at the general election" Feb '97; completely unexpectedly, won Reading West on a 15% notional swing, defeating Nick Bennett by a majority of 2,997; this was 141st on Labour's list of seats to win May '97; urged a much higher number of nominators in Parliamentary contests, insisting "it is a nonsense that only 10 signatures are required on a ballot paper when someone is seeking to represent 70,000 people within a Parliamentary constituency, whereas the same number of signatures is required to represent 2,000 people at parish council level" June '97; complained that Reading people were "outraged" by the sale of alcoholic freezerpops which "have caused illness in children as young as two" June '97; pointed out that "replica pistols, which are exact copies of those used in gun clubs are openly and lawfully on sale to young children in Reading...and can and have been used in armed robberies" June '97; co-sponsored motion attacking prescription fraud June '97; took up the case of a Thames water bailiff in his constituency being threatened by an unruly gang of

anglers June '97; an angler, he urged more active culling of cormorants to save fish from their predation July '97; co-sponsored motion urging the protection of water meadows July '97; led motion urging "a world-class sports stadium" at the Millennium Exhibition July '97; in his brilliant Maiden - which included attacks on former opponent Nick Bennett - he criticised the Commons' procedural arrangements, including its working hours, voting in person, lack of seating, involvement of Whips in appointments to select committees; he urged electoral reform, but not by cutting the constituency link July '97; at a Brighton fringe meeting derided the LibDems as as "an opportunistic party" while admitting he had been elected on their tactical votes Sep '97; spoke as a "keen angler" who had "witnesed at first hand the brutality and depravity of a fox-hunt kill" Oct '97;
Born: 19 April 1954, Hampton, Middlesex
Family: He is single and does not disclose family details;
Education: Hampton Grammar School; Sussex University '72-75;
Occupation: Regional Manager, Co-operative Home Services housing association (TGWU) til '97; ex: Co-Ordinator, Reading Centre for the Unemployed;
Traits: Front-combed grey, curly, collar-length hair; matey; jokey; has a market-trader style; estuarial speech; enjoys angling and therefore hates the pollution of the rivers Thames and Kennet;
Address: House of Commons, Westminster, London SW1A 0AA; 144 Elgar Road, Reading RG2 0BN;
Telephone: 0171 219 3000 (H of C);

Adrian SANDERS **Liberal Democrat** **TORBAY '97-**

Majority: 12 over Conservative 6-way;
Description: The unaltered, bustling, popular south Devon coastal resorts of Torquay and Paignton, sometimes uprated to 'the English Riviera'; long a Tory stronghold because, until '97 the Liberal Democrat challenge was successful only at local, county and - except for the intervention of a 'Literal Democrat' - at European levels;
Position: On the LibDem Parliamentary team on Local Government (specialising in Housing) '97-; ex: Torbay Borough Councillor '84-86; Vice President, National League of Young Liberals '84-85;
Outlook: A former Ashdown aide, successful on his third effort, including the Euro-contest; experienced and sensible on local government; has an old-fashioned moralistic approach; "forceful and energetic" (George Parker, WESTERN MORNING NEWS)
History: Joined the Liberal Party '79; was elected to Torbay Borough Council May '84; was elected Vice President of the National League of Young Liberals '84; secured a 3.2% swing from the Tories to the Liberal Democrats, but lost Torbay to Rupert Allason by 5,787 votes Apr '92; in the election to the European Parliament was cheated out of winning Devon and East Plymouth by the intervention of Richard Huggett, a 'Literal Democrat', who won 10,203 votes from careless or sloppy Liberal Democrat voters, thus enabling his Tory rival, Giles Chichester, to win by 700 votes June '94; failed in legal attempt to reverse the result in the election to the European Parliament Nov '94; with Richard Younger-Ross, the LibDem

candidate for Teignbridge, unveiled plans for a South Devon Railway to link the area to the Channel Tunnel June '96; in the campaign urged regional development agencies plus a 2% tax on the water companies to pay for a clean-up of the beaches by better sewage treatment Apr '97; won Torbay, on a 5.1% swing, ousting the incumbent Tory MP Rupert Allason by the second narrowest margin of 12 votes, ending 73 years of Conservative rule May '97; in his widely-admired extemporaneous or memorised Maiden speech urged better sewage treatment as well as clean-up of ballot papers, to prevent being blocked again by a "Literal Democrat" May '97; led motion urging pen needles be supplied to insulin-dependent diabetics, like himself May '97; asked about taxes on bed and breakfast accommodation May '97; asked about asthma levels in Torbay June '97; urged simple changes in Parliamentary elections, like not listing candidates from the beginning of the alphabet, to block the efforts of "pre-emptive spoilers" June '97; urged the protection of allotments against developers June '97; co-congratulated Neighbourhood Watch on its 15th anniversary June '97; elicited the information that 36% of local workers earned under £4.50 an hour, 26% under £4, 16% under £3.50 and 6.5% under £3 an hour June '97; urged settlement of claims of servicemen harmed by the fall-out from British nuclear tests in the Pacific June '97; led motion urging the setting of lower council tax bands to cover mobile homes July '97; publicised the English Riviera Film Festival July '97; complained that the Government's Bill about capital receipts was really about giving councils permission to borrow someone else's money rather than spend their own July '97; tried to amend the Local Government Finance (Supplementary Credit Approvals) Bill July '97;
Born: 25 April 1959, Paignton, Devon
Family: Son, of John Reeve Sanders, insurance official, and Helen Mary (Wilmot), nurse; m '92 Alison Claire (Nortcliffe), for four years the secretary to Paddy Ashdown '86-90;
Education: Kirkstead College, Torquay; Torquay Boys' Grammar;
Occupation: European Grant Advisor to Voluntary Sector Organisations and Local Government Researcher '93-97; ex: Political Assistant, to Paddy Ashdown, organising his 'Beyond Westminster' tours '92-93; Parliamentary Officer, for Lib-Dem Whips '89-90; Political Secretary, to the Devon and Cornwall Regional Liberal Party '83-85;
Traits: Dark brown hair; chubby dimpled face; a "powerful" (Tory MP Michael Ancram) speaker when extemporaneous (or memorised); not so impressive when reading a speech; "Sanders of the [English] Riviera"; an insulin-dependent diabetic since '91;
Address: House of Commons, Westminster, London SW1A 0AA; 9B Laura Avenue, Paignton, Devon;
Telephone: 0171 219 6304 (H of C); 01803 555615 (home);

Mohammed SARWAR **Labour** **Glasgow-GOVAN '97-**

Majority: 2,914 over SNP 10-way;

Description: Radically altered seat now made up two-fifths from old Govan, a third from old Pollok, a fifth from Glasgow Central and a sixteenth from old Cathcart; it has Glasgow Rangers' ground; the Orangeman leanings of its Protestant working class makes it vulnerable to the SNP, as shown in the by-election victories of Jim Sillars and his wife Margo Macdonald; still normally a safe Labour seat; has 15,000 residents of Pakistani origins;

Position: Glasgow District Councillor '92-; on Labour's Scottish Executive Committee '94-; Director, Ethnic Minority Enterprise Centre, UK Overseas Pakistan Chamber of Commerce; ex: Chairman: Pollokshields Development Association, Council for Human Rights; Secretary: Islamic Centre, Glasgow Central Mosque;

Outlook: The first Muslim to win a safe Labour seat, from which he was quickly suspended by the Parliamentary Labour Party; is fiercely ambitious behind a bland exterior; "is prepared to use every legitimate weapon at his disposal, to sail as close to the wind as he has to" (Magnus Linklater, SUNDAY TIMES); a Blair-supporting Rightwinger who is also close to Leftwinger George Galloway; a selfmade Pakistan-born cash-and-carry millionaire who successfully fought a selection contest, initially rigged against him; his reputation was destroyed, and the Labour Whip suspended when he admitted to "lending" £5,000 to a rival candidate;

History: He was politically active initially in Pakistan, joining the Bhuttos' Pakistan People's Party, becoming President of its students' organisation; was able tp emigrate to Scotland at 26 as a result of an arranged marriage to his cousin '78; joined the Labour Party '84; won Pollokshields seat on Glasgow District Council May '92; was elected to Labour Party's Scottish Executive Committee '94; supported Tony Blair's succession and the revision of Clause Four '94-95; Mike Watson could have succeeded at the new Govan constituency without a contest as the former MP for one of its constituent parts, Glasgow Central; this was torpedoed by the unexpected entry of the late James Dunnachie, 64-year-old MP for Pollok, who was expected to retire in the wake of boundary changes; it was suspected by Watson that Sarwar had persuaded Dunnachie to enter the contest, to enable Sarwar to fight for selection as well; initially Sarwar was allegedly defeated 237 to 236 by Mike Watson, after 52 postal votes were declared invalid, forty of which were in Sarwar's favour; "Sarwar was cheated at the last minute," claimed his strongest supporter, Leftwing Labour MP George Galloway; Sarwar complained to Tom Sawyer, Labour's General Secretary, promising to resign all his political offices if any of his postal voters were dead, as alleged by his critics Dec '95; Labour's National Executive voted against accepting Mike Watson as the approved candidate for Govan Feb '96; Mike Watson lost his court action to stop a rerun of the vote; in the rerun, Sarwar won by 279 to 197 for Mike Watson June '96; his idea of a second referendum on taxing powers for a Scottish Assembly was accepted by the Labour leadership after the Scottish Executive was deadlocked at Stirling Sep '96; the SNP accused him of abusing Glasgow's Labour Party machine to build a power-base in the constituency Nov '96; the SNP candidate, Nicola Sturgeon, claimed that Adil Bhatti, one of Sarwar's former supporters - who claimed to have recruited Sarwar to the Labour Party - had defected to the SNP Feb '97;

Sarwar won the seat, despite a 3.2% swing to the SNP, by a majority of 2,914 May '97; he took his seat, swearing allegiance on the Koran May '97; after a NEWS OF THE WORLD exposure, with photographs of his paying £5,000 to rival candidate, Badar Islam, to "ease off" in his campaign, Labour's NEC set up a three-man investigation May '97; he admitted having handed over £5,000 as a "loan" but announced he was suing the NEWS OF THE WORLD for libel May '97; as a result of Labour's NEC inquiry, he was criticised for "action grossly detrimental to the party" and "unbecoming and totally inappropriate for a Labour MP" and suspended from the Parliamentary Labour Party while police investigations were continuing June '97;
Born: 18 August 1952, Saleempur, Faselabad, Pakistan;
Family: Son, of a Pakistan-born Rothesay pedlar; m '76 Perveen, his beautiful cousin; 3s: Athif '78, Asim '82, Anas '83; 1d: Faiza '77;
Education: University of Faselebad, Pakistan (BA in Political Science, English and Urdu);
Occupation: Owner, of United Grocers, United Homestores and United Wholesale, with a turnover of £100m; began his business life in Glasgow selling eggs from a barrow;
Traits: Bald; trim moustache; "he is good at winning friends; he gets on well with people, sometimes too well" (Bashir Maan); "hockey and swimming are more my thing, but I look forward to attending a [football] match when I am an MP";
Address: House of Commons, Westminster, London SW1A 0AA; Maxwell Park, Pollokshields, Glasgow; 5 Glencairn Drive, Glasgow G41 4LN;
Telephone: 0171 219 3000 (H of C); 0141 423 6542 (home); 0141 429 3299 (work);

Malcolm (Kemp) SAVIDGE Labour ABERDEEN NORTH '97-

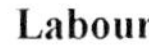

Majority: 10,010 over SNP 5-way;
Description: An altered seat thought less safe for Labour; now made up of over half of old Aberdeen North, two-fifths of old Gordon and a tiny bit of old Aberdeen South; comprises the Labour-leaning council estates of Northfield and Mastrick and private suburban housing estates which lean to the Liberal Democrats;
Position: Aberdeen City Councillor (Deputy Group Leader '92-96) '80-96; on Labour's Scottish Executive; ex: on National Council of Education Institute of Scotland '89-90, '80-86;
Outlook: Veteran candidate who finally made it despite his Surrey origins and a dull speaking style; at the '91 Kincardine by-election it was said he "would seem to have been put up to prove that the Mogadon Man factor lives" (DAILY MAIL); "dull party loyalist" (RED PEPPER); a cause groupie: Medical Aid for Palestine, World Disarmament Campaign, SERA, the Co-Operative Party; UNA, Scientists for Global Responsibility, formerly CND;
History: He joined the Labour Party '72; was elected to the Management Committee and Executive Committee of the Aberdeen North CLP '77; won the Willowpark ward from the SNP to become an Aberdeen City Councillor May '80; became a deputy member of the Scottish Constitutional Convention '89; was chosen by the Kincardine and Deeside CLP to fight the next general election May '91; with the death of the respected Tory incumbent, Alick Buchanan-Smith, contested Kincardine and Deeside in the by-election where Labour had

previously come third; the seat was won by the Liberal Democrat, Nicol Stephen, with Labour finishing fourth behind the SNP Nov '91; again contested Kincardine and Deeside, again coming fourth after the Tory, LibDem and SNP Apr '92; invited Mikhail Gorbachev to deliver peace lecture Dec '93; became a full Member of the Scottish Constitutional Convention '94; was selected to fight Aberdeen North '95; won the seat with a swing from the SNP of 6.7% by a majority of 10,010 May '97; in his Maiden, urged all parties to back devolution to a Scottish Parliament since all Scottish MPs had been elected on pro-devolution manifestos May '97; urged the "western peripheral road" for Aberdeen "to help us to fulfil our ecological responsibilities" July '97; co-sponsored motion berating AIR UK for requiring disabled people to present a humiliating medical declaration July '97;
Born: 9 May 1946, Redhill, Surrey
Family: "...a certain Sir Arnold Savidge held the position of Speaker on at least two and possibly three occasions" in the 1400s (MS); single; "I am half-English, half-Scots";
Education: Wallington County Grammar School for Boys; Aberdeen University '65-70 (MA Hons); Aberdeen College of Education '71-72 (Teaching Certificate);
Occupation: Ex: Teacher of Mathematics at Kincorth Academy, Aberdeen (EIS) '73-97, Peterhead Academy '72-73, Greenwood Dale Secondary School, Nottingham '71; Production and Stock Control and Computer Assistant, at Bryans' Electronics '70-71;
Traits: Dark, parted hair; square face; specs; Cheshire Cat smile; "Savidge by name, not by nature" (local by-election joke); "a tongue-tied pedant who has had a personality bypass" (Bruce Anderson, SUNDAY EXPRESS); "a nervous-looking local maths teacher with a long record of local service, he has a tendency to nod at everything and lapse into his subject; he says 'in percentage terms' more than anyone" (Robert Hardman, DAILY TELEGRAPH); a "curious parson's voice" (GUARDIAN); "you could feel sorry for him but nobody dislikes him" (local activist); appeared on 'University Challenge';
Address: House of Commons, Westminster, London SW1A 0AA; 13F Belmont Road, Aberdeen AB2 3SR;
Telephone: 0171 219 3000 (H of C); 01224 632369;

Phil(ip) SAWFORD **Labour** **KETTERING '97-**

Majority: 189 over Conservative 5-way;
Description: Mainly agricultural but lightly industrialised old Kettering, changed in '95 only by adding a tiny slice of rural and commuting villages from Daventry; after a 12,000-plus majority in '92, its former Tory MP and Cabinet Minister, Roger Freeman, felt safe enough to devote the '97 election campaign to designated East Midlands marginals, but not to his own seat;
Position: On the Select Committee on Information '97-; Kettering Borough Councillor (Leader '91-97) '86-97, '79-83; Desborough Town Councillor '77-97; Chairman, Kettering Centre for the Unemployed;
Outlook: One of the more unexpected Labour victors in the East Midlands, the 27th least-expected Labour win in the country, by its second-smallest margin; a former council Leader, a locally-born onetime carpenter and steelworker who re-educated himself as a training specialist, after his own redundancy from

the Corby steelworks; Left-of-Centre: in the Co-operative Party, League Against Cruel Sports, CND;

History: He joined the Labour Party '71; was elected to Desborough Town Council Oct '77; was elected to Kettering Borough Council May '79; as a steelworker in the threatened Corby plant, fought closure there in '79-80; after completing his education at Leicester University, was again elected to Kettering Borough Council May '86; selected to contest Wellingborough, increased Labour vote there by almost 6,000 votes, mostly at the expense of the Liberal Democrats Apr '92; was selected for Kettering, the constituency in which he was born Oct '96; as a member he was backed by the GMB during the election campaign Apr '97; he unexpectedly won the seat, on a notional swing of 10.6%, by a slender 189 votes, Labour's second smallest majority May '97; backed outlawing of fox-hunting June '97; expressed solidarity with jailed Indonesian union leader June '97; co-sponsored motion urging more care in extraction of aggregates July '97; in his Maiden loyally backed the Chancellor's Budget July '97; was criticised by the local District Auditor for not declaring an "indirect pecuniary interest" when four payments were made to his Kettering Centre for the Unemployed by Kettering Council of which he was Leader and then to the Phoenix Training Company, by which he was employed; he claimed it was a "technicality" and "my record is as clean as a whistle" Aug '97;

Born: 26 June 1950, Loddington, Kettering

Family: Son, of John Sawford, construction worker, and Audrey (Coleman); m '74, Rosemary (Stokes); 2s Lee '74, Andrew '76;

Education: Kettering Grammar School '61-66; Ruskin College '80-82; Leicester University (BA Hons in Sociology) '82-85; MIPD;

Occupation: Ex: General Manager, of Phoenix, a Wellingborough training organisation, dealing mainly with the unemployed (GMB)'85-97; Steelworker, at Corby steelworks '77-80; Carpenter and Joiner, in the construction industry;

Traits: Dark brown, centre-parted, tonsured hair; full face; plays guitar; enjoys music, juggling;

Address: House of Commons, Westminster, London SW1A 0AA; 1A Meadlands, Kettering, Northamptonshire NN16 7ER;

Telephone: 0171 219 6213 (H of C); 01536 411900/410742(Fax) (constituency); 0966 205 729 (mobile);

Jonathan SAYEED **Conservative** **BEDFORDSHIRE-MID '97-**

Majority: 7,090 over Labour 5-way;
Description: An almost wholly restructured and shrunken - but still Tory -seat made up largely of farmland, interspersed with brickfields; it retains Ampthill but, in '95, acquired Flitwick and Toddington from Luton North in part-exchange for lost Biggleswade and Sandy;
Former Seat: Bristol East '83-92
Position: On Select Committee on Broadcasting '97-; ex: PPS to Lord Belstead '91-92, to Michael Mates '91-92; on Select Committees: on Defence '88-91, on Environment '87-92; Chairman '91-92, Vice Chairman '85-91, Secretary '83-85, Conservative MPs' Shipping and Shipbuilding Committee, Deputy Chairman '87-92, Secretary '84-87, all-party Maritime Group;
Outlook: "I am one of those biological improbabilities - twice a maiden" (JS); the quiet relocation of a Rightish Eurosceptic retread; a man of varying and variable judgement; unlike the Labour half-blacks opposite, has never exploited his half-Indian origins; "his reputation with colleagues has improved over the years" (Tory colleague); he clung to his marginal Bristol East seat - which he won from Tony Benn - partly by generating stories in the BRISTOL EVENING POST; after the seat's loss in '92, he turned his skills into his own lobbying organisation, Ranelagh; a former RN engineering officer, he has little outlet for his enthusiasm for the shrinking merchant marine in the middle of Bedfordshire; has remained somewhat Left of Centre on racism and social matters, but is anti-abortion and anti-gipsy; has moved Rightward on Defence, Europe and fiscal prudence;
History: He unsuccessfully contested GLC seats in Lewisham East '78 and North Islington '82; unexpectedly ousted Tony Benn from Bristol East June '83; urged immediate action against 'video nasties' June '83; opposed sale of local INMOS at "bucket shop prices" to "asset-strippers" June '84; visited St Helena Oct '84; after his second visit to South Africa - the first was in the Royal Navy - said that the "monstrous" Apartheid regime had to be eradicated Nov '84; voted against Enoch Powell's Unborn Children (Protection) Bill Feb '85; voted against Government's Bill to liberalise Sunday trading May '85; opposed big salary rises for Top People July '85; backed nuclear power Mar '86; although anti-Apartheid, opposed sanctions against South Africa as helping its far-Right June '86; assailed teachers' strike as "disgraceful" Oct '86; in election campaign boasted "only the Conservatives are against a gipsy camp" in Bristol May '87; strongly supported David Alton's abortion-curbing Bill Jan-May '88; backed compulsory identity cards Jan '89; defended poll tax Apr '89; backed equal treatment for all war widows Nov '89; warned of "tensions" if Wrens were allowed to sail with the fleet Feb '90; backed restoration of caning in schools June '90; after its invasion of Kuwait, urged a "surgical air strike" against Iraq to prevent its acquiring a nuclear capability Sep '90; backed registration of dogs Oct '90; was a major organiser of a behind-the-scenes lobby for tax help for the merchant marine '90-91; lost his Bristol East seat to Labour's Jean Corston on a swing of 6.8% Apr '92; was narrowly chosen over Sir Nicholas Lyell for Bedfordshire-Mid, with migratory Sir Nicholas finding refuge in Bedfordshire North East the next night Sep '95; was one of the 59 Tory candidates who promised to oppose a single European currency during the next Parliament Dec '96; retained Bedfordshire-Mid with majority of 7,090, despite a notional swing to Labour of 13.9% May '97; asked how many jobs were being lost by interest rate

increases, since "it is estimated that every 1% increase in interest rates costs about 250,000 export jobs" May '97; urged a single Boundary Commission for the whole UK, since Bedfordshire-Mid had 68,000 voters and the average Scottish constituency only 55,000 May '97; joined the campaign team of William Hague, offering him his Victoria office May '97; asked the new Home Minister whether, since Mr al-Fayed had been offering inducements to MPs, he thought him "a fit and proper person to receive British citizenship" July '97; complained that the Budget had "increased the cost of pensions by more than 15%" July '97; attacked the "malignant detail" of Scottish devolution July '97;

Born: 20 March 1948, London

Family: His grandfather, was an Indian doctor, his uncle an Indian admiral; son, of Indian-born electrical engineer M M Sayeed and English-born Lorna (Perls); m '80 Nicola Anne (Parkes Power), nurse and counsellor; 2s Edward Charles '85, Richard Athol '88;

Education: Christchurch, Hampstead; George Eliot Primary, Swiss Cottage; Wolverstone Hall, Suffolk (3 A-levels; 10 O-levels); Britannia Royal Naval College, Dartmouth; Royal Naval Engineering College, Manadon (BSc in Electrical and Electronic Engineering);

Occupation: Ex: Chairman: Training Division, of Corporate Services Group Plc '96-97, Ranelagh Ltd (his PR company) '92-96; Director, Love Lane Investments (holding company) '92-96; Chairman and Chief Executive, of Calmedy Insurance Services Ltd '82-83; Founder-Director, of Wade Emerson & Co Ltd (shipping company) '74-82; Management Trainee, Marks & Spencer '73-74; Royal Navy: rating, engineering apprentice and officer '65-72

Traits: Dark black, greying wavy hair; cafe-au-lait complexion; thickset; half-Indian; "relentlessly elegant" (Michael Lord, BRISTOL EVENING POST); "pleasant and easy to get on with" (Tory colleague); generously polite; motor cyclist; plays squash, tennis, golf; a horseman; takes his sons to football;

Address: House of Commons, Westminster, London SW1A 0AA; 1 Love Lane EC1V 7JJ;

Telephone: 0171 219 2335 (H of C);

Jonathan SHAW — Labour — CHATHAM & AYLESFORD '97-

Majority: 2,790 over Conservative 6-way;

Description: A new seat combining Chatham, a tough working-class town long linked with its Royal Navy dockyard, formerly a site of nuclear sub refitting (taken from Kent-Mid), and much smaller Aylesford, with its surrounding villages (taken from Tonbridge & Malling); it was estimated as likely, on '92 projections, to provide a Tory majority of 13,000-plus;

Position: On Select Committees on Environment '97-, Audit '97-; Secretary: PLP Kent Group '97-, all-party Child Migrants Parliament Group '97-; Rochester Councillor (Chairman, Community Development) '93-98;

Outlook: A youthful Centre-Left hereditary social worker who achieved the 14th least-expected win; another local councillor working in public service; is concerned about cancer deaths from nuclear refitting in Chatham's former RN dockyard; backs electoral reform but not PR; in the Fabian Society and Co-operative Party;

History: He joined the Labour Party at 18, '84; was elected to Rochester Council at 26, May '93; after the death of his friend Councillor Tim Robson, a former dockyard worker, was selected for "hopeless" Chatham and Aylesford Dec '95; quite unexpectedly won Chatham and Aylesford on a notional swing of 15.1%, registering a majority of 2,790 over his favoured Tory opponent, Richard Knox-Johnston May '97; backed ban on fox-hunting June '97; asked about the maximum level of radiation workers could safely be exposed to when the Royal Navy took delivery of the nuclear reactor for the HMS Dreadnought June '97; welcomed the Ministry of Defence's offer of health counselling for Chatham Dockyard workers who might have suffered radiation injuries while refitting nuclear submarines; he said he knew more than 100 people who were keen to take up the offer as a start toward compensation June '97; co-sponsored motion attacking Kent County Council, newly under Tory control again, for its moratorium on capital spending on schools June '97; backed motion expressing concern about fire safety in the Euro-Tunnel June '97; co-sponsored motion urging better protection of water meadows July '97; made his Maiden in the Defence debate, concentrating on Chatham's former royal dockyard's many casualties from refitting nuclear submarines Oct '97;
Born: 3 June 1966, Aylesford, Kent
Family: Son, of Alan Shaw, social worker rtd, and Les (John); his brother "served in the Blues and Royals Regiment for 18 years" (JS);
Education: Vintners' Boys School, Maidstone; West Kent College of Further Education; Bromley College of Further and Higher Education;
Occupation: Social Worker, in Kent til '97 (UNISON shop steward);
Traits: Egg-shaped face; balding with dark fringe;
Address: House of Commons, Westminster, London SW1A 0AA; 8 Kellaway Road, Walderslade, Chatham, Kent ME5 8BY;
Telephone: 0171 219 6919 (H of C); 01634 811573 (home);

Debra SHIPLEY **Labour** **STOURBRIDGE '97-**

Majority: 5,645 over Conservative 4-way;
Description: A new marginal seat based on the town of its name in the Metropolitan Borough of Dudley in the West Midlands conurbation; in inherits three-fifths of its voters from old Halesowen and Stourbridge, one-fifth each from Dudley West and Dudley East; if voters had voted in '97 on '92 lines, the Tory incumbent MP, Warren Hawksley, should have been re-elected with a 5,000-plus majority;
Position: Delegate to Council of Europe and WEU '97-; on Executive, of Socialist Environmental Research Association (SERA);
Outlook: One of Labour's most successful front-line women warriors who won in a marginal; an enthusiastic environmental crusader who wants her constituency and the world to be saved from choking on harmful traffic fumes; a loyal Blairite writer, formerly a university lecturer; is interested also in education and health: "I'd like better labelling of food; we need to improve our diet and health, and the Government needs to lead us on this"; is in the Fabian Society and the Co-operative Party;
History: She joined the Labour Party '89; was on the final short-list for the Eastleigh

by-election, initially nominated by Eastleigh CLP's Women's Section Mar '94; was selected for marginal Stourbridge from an all-women's short-list Sep '95; co-signed letter to INDEPENDENT of loyalist Labour prospectives insisting Labour was "a united dynamic party ready to solve the problems this country faces" Oct '96; told the INDFEPENDENT's Fran Abrams she used Tony Blair's five promises all the time: "I can get them over very clearly" Jan '97; she was one of 16 members the GMB backed in key seats Apr '97; somewhat unexpectedly won Stourbridge - Labour's 70th target seat - on a notional swing of 11%, ousting Warren Hawksley by a majority of 5,645 May '97; in her Maiden in the Earth Summit 2 debate, said that Stourbridge's roads were "choked with traffic fumes" which increased asthma; she hailed a new cycle path and the role of "new environmental task forces" in opening "more facilities, rejuvenating our parks and turn[ing] some of our neglected and vandalised cemeteries into wildlife havens" June '97; backed ban on fox-hunting June '97; led the motion urging a review of the law on rape, insisting on "the removal of the defendant's right to cross-examine the victim" June '97; asked Foreign Secretary Robin Cook whether he realised that Britain, in contrast to France, Germany and Italy, was experiencing "a fall in its share of exports to the 'tiger economies' [of Asia] and in its share of total world exports" June '97; co-sponsored motion backing comprehensive education "as the foremost and most efficient way to provide secondary education" June '97; pressed for the establishment of a Food Standards Agency July '97;
Born: 22 June 1957, Shrewsbury
Family: Daughter of a factory worker and an office worker;
Education: Kidderminster High School; Oxford Polytechnic (BA); Unversity of London (MA);
Occupation: Author: of books on travel, history and cookery; ex: Development Manager, for new courses, at University of Central England, Birmingham (GMB); Consultant, on Architecture, to Arts Council of Great Britain; Organiser, of Voluntary Action, in Camden for three years); FRSA;
Traits: Dark hair; pretty; strong-willed; "immaculately groomed, politically and sartorially" (Fran Abrams, INDEPENDENT); enjoys theatre, cinema, travel and cooking;
Address: House of Commons, Westminster, London SW1A 0AA;
Telephone: 0171 219 3053 (House of Commons);

Keith SIMPSON **Conservative** **NORFOLK MID '97-**

Majority: 1,336 over Labour 6-way;
Description: The seat almost surrounding Norwich on the west, north and east, like a large banana; it was changed in '95 only by the loss of 9,000 voters to Norwich North; it includes part of the Broads and a stretch of Tory-leaning small towns in Norfolk's interior, including East Dereham; if voting had followed '92 lines, it would have provided a Tory majority of almost 17,000 in '97;
Position: Secretary, Conservative MPs' Defence Committee '97-; ex: Special Adviser, to Defence Secretaries George Younger and Tom King, '88-90;
Outlook: Fun-loving but shrewd, assiduous and hard-hitting former Sandhurst lecturer, Central Office

apparatchik and Tom King hatchetman; backed Kenneth Clarke in the Leadership contest; a hardworking questioner on defence, where he does not believe Labour can be trusted - not even George Robertson; in debate, favours the use of heavy irony, ridicule and well-honed historical quotations in attacking his Labour opponents from the Right; after a lengthy pursuit of safe seats, he finally struck it lucky in Richard Ryder's abandoned seat in his natal county;

History: He joined the Conservative Party at 17, '66; he became National Vice Chairman of the Federation of Conservative Students '72; his contemporaries in the FCS included Andrew Neil, Stephen Dorrell and David Davis; after 13 years of lecturing at Sandhurst, became Head of the Overseas and Defence Section at the Conservative Research Department '86; was selected as Tory candidate for Plymouth-Devonport Feb '91; spoke in the defence debate on the "Labour can't be trusted on defence" theme at Conservative annual conference at Blackpool, although the debate centred on the amalgamation of Scottish regiments and his would-be constituency's interests were naval; wrote afterward that "the conference has always reminded me of the travelling court of a medieval king with intrigue and jollificaton taking place on the fringe" Oct '91; was defeated at Plymouth-Devonport by Labour's David Jamieson, after a 7.6% swing from the Tories to Labour Apr '92; was short-listed for Aldershot but was not selected, despite being "fondly remembered by a generation of Sandhurst cadets for his War Studies talks" (EVENING STANDARD) June '93; was short-listed for Hampshire North East but was not selected Sep '95; was selected for Norfolk Mid after the retirement of Richard Ryder, due to ill health; in the DAILY TELEGRAPH poll of candidates, was one of 104 who loyally supported the Major Government's "wait and see" policy on a single European currency Dec '96; with 11 other loyal candidates wrote to the DAILY TELEGRAPH to deplore the 'old Labour' Leftwing anti-racist antics of Labour MEPs in Brussels Feb '97; retained Norfolk Mid by 1,336 (down nine-tenths, from 16,994) after a 13.1% notional swing to Labour May '97; joined Kenneth Clarke's campaign team in the Leadership contest May '97; asked 20 questions on Defence on one day June '97; attacked the abolition of the Assisted Places Scheme as "nasty and selfish", "shot through with hypocrisy", "a dog's breakfast" June '97; stigmatised the Government's Local Government Finance Bill as the "bailing out of Labour local authorities Bill" June '97; urged a continuation of compulsory competitive tendering in the NHS June '97; in Budget debate said the Labour Government was "unclear on how they will deliver their contradictory promise of not raising personal taxes while keeping to the previous Government's departmental spending ceilings"; he added, "the Budget resembles an Arthur Daley deal; we must look beyond the Chancellor's extra-large print and read the small print; many people are beginning to realise that the Budget is a time-bomb" July '97; asked about impact on Scottish local authorities if they had to pay a £4 an hour minimum wage July '97; asked about the number of senior officers in the Forces from the ethnic minorities July '97; asked how many military personnel had been discharged for homosexuality July '97;

Born: 29 March 1949, Norwich

Family: Son, of Harry Simpson, cost clerk, and Jean Betty (Day); married to Pepita, a former Army officer; they have a son George '91;

Education: Thorpe Grammar School, Norfolk; Hull University; King's College, London University;

Occupation: Military Historian and Defence Consultant; ex: Co-Director, Cranfield Security Studies Institute, Royal Military College of Science, Shrivenham '90-97; Special Adviser, to George Younger and Tom King, Defence Secretaries, '88-90; Head of Overseas and Defence Section, Conservative Central Office '86-88; Senior Lecturer in War Studies and International Affairs, Royal Military Academy, Sandhurst '73-86;

Traits: Rounded face, with full under-chin; greying parted hair; bushy moustache; specs;

jovial; a Sandhurst-lecturer-style Rightwing wit; enjoys telling historical anecdotes and drinking malt whiskey (was in the Highlands and Islands Malt Whiskey Club);
Address: House of Commons, Westminster, London SW1A 0AA; Glebe House, Norwich Road, Reepham, Norwich NR10 4NH (home); The Stable, Church Farm, Attlebridge, Norwich, Norfolk NR9 5ST (constituency);
Telephone: 0171 219 4053/0975(Fax) (H of C); 01603 873335/873335(Fax) (home); 0411 088503 (mobile); 01603 261594/261794(Fax) (constituency);

Marsha SINGH **Labour** **BRADFORD WEST '97-**

Majority: 3,877 over Conservative 8-way;
Description: An unaltered seat containing the University, Bradford Grammar School and middle-class residential areas plus the worst inner-city areas of a declining textile town; a third of its populace is Asian, most of them Muslims, giving it Britain's largest populace of former Pakistanis (mostly from Mirpur) and Kashmiris, as well the ethnic rivalries which bedevil its politics; the troubled, heavily-Asian Manningham area saw disturbances in '95;
Position: On Select Committee on Home Affairs '97-; Chairman, Bradford West Constituency Labour Party '95-97, '86-92;
Outlook: The unexpected Leftish Sikh who won narrowly in a seat where Muslims are the largest ethnic minority; "a secular socialist, Mr Singh is opposed to privatisation and in favour of redistributive taxation; he also voted with his local constituency party against the abolition of Clause IV" (Job Rabkin, INDEPENDENT); "is not an advocate of Sikh politics"; "his background, as the founder in the early 1980s of the Asian Youth Movement, is in a secular and expansive kind of politics; he seeks to include, not to exclude" (John Yates, YORKSHIRE POST); he deplored "ethnic factionalism" in Labour's ranks and insisted on campaigning "as a Bradfordian"; "to judge people by their background is racist"; "I aim to represent everyone in the constituency"; "the problems around here are crime, unemployment and bad housing and that's true for both Asians and whites"; the difficulty was that he could not persuade a lot of local Muslims who normally supported Labour; as an MP he made a slow, low-profile start until he won a relatively low place in the ballot for Private Members' Bills and introduced one to restrict the amount of a person's capital which may be taken into account by a local authority in determining whether he should be provided with residental accommodation under the National Assistance Act;
History: He joined the Labour Party at 20, '74; was a founder of the Asian Youth Movement in the early '80s; was elected Chairman of the Bradford West Constituency Labour Party '86; opposed the watering down of Clause IV, as urged by Tony Blair '94-95; the 1996-97 selection process was dogged by controversy; Max Madden, the 55-year-old hard-Left sitting Labour MP, had initially decided not to stand again, expecting a Muslim Labour successor; he then re-entered the contest because he feared the seat would be won by a Muslim Tory candidate; he failed to find a ward nomination, allegedly because of an "Islamic pact" to veto non-Muslim candidates; Madden made the short-list after Labour's NEC took over the selection contest after complaints about irregularities; after Madden was knocked out, Singh

won the selection process, narrowly beating by 56% a Muslim trade unionist, Mohammed Taj, although Muslims are five times as numerous as Sikhs in the constituency Feb '97; Madden warned Tom Sawyer, the Labour Party's General Secretary, that the seat would be at risk because the Tories, who had a Muslim candidate (a defector from Labour), would claim that Labour was anti-Muslim Mar '97; Singh retained the seat with a majority of 3,877 over the Conservative, with an unusual swing of 5.45% from Labour to the Muslim Conservative (Mohammed Riaz), due to a 7,000-plus drop in the Labour vote May '97; he made a slow start as an MP, not rushing his Maiden speech; he co-sponsored a motion urging the Indian Government to protect human rights in Kashmir May '97; asked the Deputy Prime Minister, John Prescott, "how he intends to take forward the Government's commitments to develop an integrated transport policy to fight congestion and pollution" June '97; expressed shock about the "utter waste" of the previous Government in spending £37m in consultancy fees on the PFI schemes June '97; made his first big splash, having won a place in the ballot for a Private Member's Bill, by introducing a Bill with all-party support to "restrict the amount of a person's capital which may be taken into account by a local authority in determining whether he should be provided with residential accommodation" "under Part III of the National Assistance Act 1948" June '97; expressed solidarity with jailed Indonesian union leader June '97; was named to the Home Affairs Select Committee July '97; co-sponsored motion urging self-determination for Kashmir July '97; asked about mixed wards in psycyhiatric hospitals, with particular regard to the concerns of ethnic minorities July '97; asked about treatment of emotionally disturbed children in adult wards July '97;

Born: 11 October 1954, Punjab, India

Family: Son, of Harbans Singh, foundry worker, and Kartar (Kaur);

Education: Green Lane Primary School; Frizing Hall Junior High; Bellevue Boys Upper School; University of Loughborough (BA in the Language, Politics and Economies of Modern Europe);

Occupation: Health Service Manager (UNISON) '90-97; Principal Education Officer, in Bradford's Local Education Authority '83-90; Bradford Law Centre '80-83; Bradford Community Relations Council '79-80; Trainee Manager, Lloyds Bank '70-79;

Traits: Tonsured greying hair and beard, with darker moustache; rounded face; cafe-au-lait complexion; radiates confidence;

Address: House of Commons, Westminster, London SW1A 0AA; 15 Middlebrook Drive, Bradford, Yorkshire, BD8 0EU;

Telephone: 0171 219 3000 (H of C); 01244 11274 402220 (constituency);

KEEPING PARLIAMENTARY SECRETS

A rueful MP claimed, with some truth, that the best way to keep something secret is to make a speech about it in the Palace of Westminster. He was commenting on the emptiness of the Press Gallery (except for HANSARD writers and the Press Association). Long gone are the days when serious newspapers carried a full or half-page summarising Parliamentary debate. Of late, Westminster has been used as a source of news stories. In our old-fashioned way, we read HANSARD daily and watch the Commons and Lords on the Parliamentary Channel. Parliamentary debaters are very self-revealing in debate. And we don't mean only Kerry Pollard MP, in whose Maiden he disclosed that until 12 he had to drop his trousers regularly to prove that Kerry was not a girl's name.

Angela SMITH **Labour & Co-operative** **BASILDON '97-**

Majority: 13,280 over Conservative 4-way;
Description: The altered alleged weathervane seat which, because it reported its results early, was taken to be the confirmation of John Major's hold on power in '92; it was supposedly strengthened in its Tory leanings in '95 by the addition of 10,000 net East Thurrock voters from its more-Conservative neighbour, Billericay; but local Tories could not win a single seat on Basildon Council in '95, which they had swept three years before; this was enough to cause its sitting Tory MP, David ("I Love Basildon") Amess, to do a runner to safer Southend West; he did not believe the psephologists who claimed that, if '92 was repeated, he could still win in Basildon by some 2,500 votes;
Position: Essex County Councillor (Chief Whip '93-96) '89-97;
Outlook: Open, friendly, dynamic Centre-Left activist; she has inherited the fierce local pride of her predecessor, because she too was a child-migrant to Basildon from East London; a multi-cause groupie: Amnesty International, Vegetarian Society, Action Aid, War on Want; was close to TRIBUNE, the Leftwing weekly, for which she organised fund-raising prize raffles, and was a regular contributor to its letter pages and fighting fund;
History: She joined the Labour Party at 20, '79, the Co-op Party in '80; selected for Southend West, she came a poor third, with 7.6% of the vote, unchanged from the previous election June '87; she was elected to Essex County Council for Basildon-Pitsea May '89; she won selection for Basildon from an all-women short-list Sep '95; she explained the halving of Tory support in Basildon in a MORI Poll for the SUN: "there is a theme of betrayal: a lot of people trusted the Tories on tax, crime and youth unemployment and their hopes have been dashed" Dec '96; she was surprised by the extent to which she swept the general election vote with a notional swing of 14.7%, scoring a majority of 13,280 over the Tory Amess-substitute May '97; in her Maiden, backed the Government's Bill to ban handguns; she also approved of the SUN's and DAILY TELEGRAPH's approving descriptions of Basildon, in contrast to that of the GUARDIAN, insisting Basildon had "a lively, ambitious and energetic population" June '97; as the former head campaigner for the League Against Cruel Sports, she spearheaded the motion to ban fox-hunting June '97; she led the motion congratulating the Co-ops for banning alcopops June '97;
Born: 7 January 1959, East London
Family: Daughter, of Patrick Evans, machine operator at Ford's, Basildon, and Emily (Russell), pre-school supervisor; m '78 Nigel Smith, author, teacher-councillor and Labour's '97 candidate for Rochford and Southend East;
Education: Chalvedon School, Pitsea, Basildon; Leicester Polytechnic (BA Hons in Public Administration};
Occupation: Researcher, for Alun Michael MP '95-97; ex: Head of Public and Political Relations, League Against Cruel Sports (TGWU) '83-95;
Traits: Young-looking; light red curly centre-parted hair; open and friendly; "Angie"; "pretty, dresses with business-like chic and has a smile her Leader might envy"; is "relaxed and articulate" (DAILY TELEGRAPH); enjoys watching 'Coronation Street';
Address: House of Commons, Westminster, London SW1A 0AA; 45 Sandown Avenue,

Westcliff-on-Sea, Essex SS0 9YA;
Telephone: 0171 219 6273/0926(Fax) (H of C); 01268 464120/464050(Fax) (constituency);

Geraldine SMITH **Labour** **MORECAMBE & LUNESDALE '97-**

Majority: 5,965 over Conservative 5-way;
Description: The seaside town of Morecambe, separated in '83 from Lonsdale (now in Cumbria) but linked instead with similar-sounding Lunesdale in Lancashire; it includes Heysham, with its nuclear power station and ferry terminal, as well as the old railway town of Carnforth, where Lord Parkinson was born; in '95 it took in three Skerton wards from Lancaster; although strongly pro-Labour, they were not thought to be enough to reduce the Tory majority below 10,000, if the voters stuck to the '92 pattern;
Position: Morecambe Borough Councillor '91-; Chairman, Morecambe Constituency Labour Party;
Outlook: Left of Centre local councillor and former postal clerk whose heart thrills to the beauties of her constituency but bleeds for its deprived; an enthusiastic campaigner, formerly in CND, she sees the new Government as offering new opportunities; "I'm happy to see money from the Lottery will be used to set up health and education projects";
History: She joined the Labour Party at 18, '79; she progressed up the local party ladder, becoming branch secretary, branch chairman, constituency secretary, constituency chairman; was elected to Morecambe Borough Council May '91; was chosen, from an all-women short-list '95; joined the local campaign against the Prison Service's attempt to convert an abandoned Pontins holiday camp at Heysham into a prison facility: "the beach is packed out in summer; how are parents going to feel at letting their children play freely, with prisoners just a few yards away?" Jan '97; quite unexpectedly, on a notional pro-Labour swing of 16%, she captured the seat with a majority of 5,965, ending the 18-year Commons career of Sir Mark Lennox-Boyd; this made her the 36th least-expected Labour victor May '97; in her Maiden she contrasted the beauties of her constituency ("one of the most important sites in Europe for migrating birds and harbours more curlew, oyster catcher, turnstone and migrant waders than any other site in Britain") with its social problems ("some parts of it host the highest rates of unemployment in Lancashire", "large number of people live in appalling accommodation", in such areas "poverty, ill-health, anti-social behaviour, drug and alcohol abuse and crime abound"; a regeneration process was under way, but much more had to be done to renew the infrastructure of such resorts and eliminate mass unemployment July '97;
Born: 29 August 1961, Belfast
Family: She does not disclose any family details;
Education: Morecambe High School; Morecambe and Lancaster College;
Occupation: Ex: Clerk, with Royal Mail (CWU) til '97;
Traits: Dark hair in pageboy bob with bangs; pretty; tends to read her Parliamentary speeches; enjoys chess, campaigning;
Address: House of Commons, Westminster, London SW1A 0AA;
Telephone: 0171 219 3000 (H of C); 01524 425680 (home); 0802 924866 (mobile);

Jacqui SMITH **Labour** **REDDITCH '97-**

Majority: 6,125 over Conservative 5-way;

Description: This new seat is based on the West Midlands overspill new town of Redditch, largely carved out of Mid-Worcestershire; since Labour had been winning most of its wards, it is understandable that Eric Forth did a runner to Bromley from his former seat of Mid-Worcestershire - which he won by almost 10,000 in 1992 - once 27,000 rural, Tory-leaning voters were stripped out by the boundary commissioners and Peter Luff moved in; all this despite the projection that, on the '92 voting pattern, a Tory candidate could still win Redditch by 3,000-plus;

Position: Redditch Borough Councillor (Chairman of Development) '91-; on Labour Party's West Midlands Regional Executive '96-; ex: Chairman, Redditch Education Forum '94-97; Vice Chairman, Redditch CLP '94-96; Secretary, National Association of Labour Students '84-85;

Outlook: The first MP for a newly-created seat: a "Blairite moderniser" (NEW STATESMAN) and experienced activist and candidate, mixing her former roles of teacher and local councillor as is typical of the new wave of Labour MPs; a combative debater; says she would like to see "the decentralisation of power to a more local level"; also: "I'd like to see class sizes reduced and nursery provision expanded; I have a 3-year-old myself and know this will improve standards"; and: "what is important is that a woman's perspective is put to all our policies"; a cause groupie: in Labour Women's Network, the Socialist Educational Association and, formerly, the Anti-Apartheid Movment;

History: She has been politically active since the age of seven, when she forced a local councillor to back down on a decision to prohibit school children from cycling on the pavement '69; joined the Labour Party at 16, '79; she was active in the National Association of Labour Students, becoming its Secretary '84; she was elected to Redditch Borough Council May '91; she contested Mid-Worcestershire against Eric Forth, improving the Labour vote percentage by 7.8%, a 4.9% swing from the Conservatives Apr '92; was one of the first 11 beneficiaries of 'Emily's List' Mar '94; in the wake of the death of Tory MP John Blackburn, she was short-listed for the Dudley West by-election; in the final run-off, she was defeated by 69 votes to 42 by Ian Pearson, who then captured the seat for Labour Nov '94; with some backing from 'Emily's List', was selected for Redditch from an all-women short-list May '95; her old employer, Terry Davis MP, who had won a seat in the area in '71, campaigned for her; so did Tony Blair, allegedly because she was a "well-known Blairite" (Job Rabkin, INDEPENDENT); as a member, she also had GMB support Apr '97; she took the seat on a notional swing of 10.2%, giving her a 6,125 majority over her Tory lady opponent May '97; backed ban on fox-hunting June '97; made her Maiden in full support of the Budget; later in the Budget debate, challenged its Tory critics: "is there not a certain illogicality in proposing that a tax subsidy in the housing market to promote home ownership is effective while arguing that a subsidy in the labour market to promote employment is ineffective?" July '97; co-sponsored motion backing compulsory fire sprinklers for superstores July '97; strenuously defended Government's ending of tax relief on pensioners' medical insurance premiums July '97;

Born: 3 November 1962, London

Family: Daughter, of Michael Smith, headteacher rtd, and Jill, a retired teacher minding a village Post Office; is married to Richard Timney, civil engineer; 1 s James '93;
Education: Dyson Perrins C of E High School, Malvern; Hertford College, Oxford University (BA Hons in PPE); Worcester College of Higher Education (PGCE);
Occupation: Ex: Head of Economic and Business Studies, at Haybridge High School (NUT) '90-97; Political Researcher for Labour MP Terry Davis (GMB) '84-85
Traits: Dark tonsured hair; a Harriet Harman lookalike who sounds slightly Cockney; fast-talking; energetic; bird-like; enjoys playing badminton; an Aston Villa season ticket-holder;
Address: House of Commons, Westminster, London SW1A 0AA;
Telephone: 0171 219 5845 (H of C); 01527 63497 (home);

John (William Patrick) SMITH Labour VALE OF GLAMORGAN '97-, '89-92

Majority: 10,532 over Conservative 4-way;
Description: The most marginal seat of '92, taken back into Tory hands by 19 votes; its Labour vote comes from the old industrial port of Barry, formerly the biggest coal exporter, which gave the seat its previous name; its Tory support, which kept the late Sir Raymond Gower in the Commons for 38 years, comes from the Vale's soft and affluent farming land centered around Cowbridge and from middle-class commuters to Cardiff; it lost Penarth and some Tory villages in '83, while adding rural and coastal terrain from Pontypridd and agricultural land around Cowbridge; this time only a couple of hundred voters have been added from Cardiff West;
Position: PPS to John Reid '97-; Delegate to North Atlantic Assembly '97-; ex: on Select Committees on Welsh Affairs '90-92, Broadcasting '91-92; PPS to Roy Hattersley '90-92; Co-Chairman, Parliamentary Adisory Council for Transport Safety '90-92; Vale of Glamorgan Borough Councillor (Leader of its Labour Group '83-88) '79-90; Chairman, Welsh Labour Party '88-89; Chairman, of Wales Anti-Apartheid '87-95;
Outlook: The return as a retread of the ambitious, fast-moving soft-Left South Wales politician; the '89 by-election winner, whose hopes were set back by his narrow loss in '92; "has had a distinguished careeer in furthering the economic development of Gwent before he re-entered the House" (Welsh Secretary Ron Davies); was "the kind of solid, straight-forward socialist the [former] Labour Leader [Neil Kinnock] hope[d would] make the party respectable again with the mass of working-class voters" (Colin Brown, INDEPENDENT); "safe rather than inspired", "a good platform speaker" (David Millward, DAILY TELEGRAPH); a former unilateralist who went mute on the subject during the '89 by-election; a quick starter (agreed to contest the NEC only days after first becoming an MP in '89);
History: He joined the Labour Party '72; was elected to Vale of Glamorgan Borough Council May '79; became Leader of the Labour Group on Vale of Glamorgan Borough Council '83; was selected as candidate for the Vale of Glamorgan, on the second round, by 27 votes to 26 Nov '85; contested the Vale of Glamorgan against the incumbent Tory MP, Sir Raymond Gower, increasing Labour's vote by almost 9% June '87; wrote an article about the need to raise Labour's profile in Wales in the MORNING STAR which described him as "a

supporter...for twenty years" Aug '88; the death of the widely popular sitting Conservative MP for 38 years, Sir Raymond Gower, precipitated a by-election Feb '89; Smith attacked the Government for rushing the abolition of the National Dock Labour Scheme without consultation Apr '89; was again selected, from a short-list of five May '89; captured the seat, which had been Tory for 38 years, by a majority of 6,028 over the Welsh-language broadcaster, Rod Richards, with a swing of 12.35%, the biggest since Labour took Toxteth in '35, May '89; welcomed Neil Kinnock's departure from unilateralism May '89; received 72,000 votes in constituency section of NEC Oct '89; flew back from Cyprus to vote in abortion debate, in favour of ceilings of 24, 26 or 28 weeks Apr '90; congratulated BA on creating 1,200 skilled engineering jobs at its new maintenance base at Cardiff Airport June '90; backed continuation of Lome Convention which would have allowed West Indian bananas to land still in Barry Port July '90; welcomed more money for Development Board for Rural Wales and inward investment of £1.1b in his constituency Nov '90; with Tory MP Stephen Day backed speed-checking cameras Dec '90; lost his seat by 19 votes, after three recounts, to Tory Walter Sweeney; he was dismayed to discover how many of his supporters had not bothered to vote Apr '92; was re-selected to contest the Vale of Glamorgan Oct '95; was elected with a majority of 10,532, a 9.8% swing to Labour May '97; urged that imported beef comply with the same standards as domestic beef June '97; complained that in local Cowbridge market "finished cattle prices were lower than they were 14 years ago" June '97; strongly defended the week's delay in the votes on devolution between Scotland and Wales and their different powers of home rule: "two-thirds of all investment in Wales is predominantly English and we depend on it"; however, while "Wales has done well in attracting direct foreign investment, in fact double the UK average", "Wales under-performs" "when it comes to the share of UK investment" July '97;

Born: 17 March 1951, Penarth

Family: Son of John Henry Smith, self-employed businessman, and Margaret Mary (Collins); m '71 'Kathy'/Kathleen (Mulvaney); 2s Nathan '74, Theo '79, 1d Melanie '71;

Education: Fairfield Primary; Penarth County School; Gwent College of Higher Education (Diploma in Industrial Relations); University College, University of Wales Cardiff (BSc Hons Econ);

Occupation: Chief Executive, Gwent Image Partnership (a company encouraging inward investment) (MSF) '92-; ex: Senior Lecturer, in Business Studies, at West Glamorgan Institute of Higher Education, Swansea '85-89; Tutor, at University College, Cardiff '83-85; Joiner '71-76; Cook in RAF '67-71; Building Worker '66-68;

Traits: Parted brown hair; "one of nature's NCOs who bears a striking resemblance to Windsor Davies, the sergeant major in 'It Ain't Half Hot Mum' (Colin Brown, INDEPENDENT); "rugged"; "rather stolid and glum", with "authentic working-class roots" (George Hill, TIMES); part-Irish; has "a love for our country's national sport, Rugby, but I also love soccer" (JWPS);

Address: House of Commons, Westminster, London SW1A 0AA; 75 Colcot Road, Barry, South Glamorgan CF62 8HL;

Telephone: 0171 219 3000 (H of C); 01446 743769 (home);

Sir Robert ('Bob') SMITH Bt **Liberal Democrat** **ABERDEENSHIRE WEST & KINCARDINE '97-**

Majority: 2,662 over Conservative 5-way;
Description: A newly reconstituted Tory-LibDem marginal in Scotland's Grampian or northeast region; includes the rural hinterland of the previous Kincardine and Deeside seat and a sizeable chunk of Gordon; its component parts have changed loyalty intermittently for three decades;
Position: On LibDems' Parliamentary team on Transport '97-; Aberdeenshire Councillor (Vice Chairman, Grampian Police Board) '95-; Education Spokesman of the Liberal Democrats in Scotland '95-; ex: Grampian Area representative on Scottish and national councils of the SDP '82-87;
Outlook: The pragmatic 3rd baronet-landowner, formerly the leading SDPer in the area, who succeeded in ousting Tory junior Scottish Minister George Kynoch; a Europhile (in the European Movement);
History: He campaigned, while an Aberdeen University student, for Lord Mackie, the Liberal candidate in the Euro-election, June '79; was a local founder-member of the SDP Feb '81; inherited the baronetcy '83; contested the Grampian Regional Council for the SDP May '86; as an SDPer, contested Aberdeen North against Bob Hughes, coming third with 17.8% of the vote, a swing to Labour of 7.3% June '87; as one of the speakers against a pact with Labour at the LibDems' annual conference, said: "the problem when you come to dealing with the Labour Party is that there are individual members of Labour at all levels who understand and accept the need for constitutional reform and reform in Scotland; but when it comes to dealing with Labour as an institution, it is committed to one thing and one thing only: trying to get its hands on power for no other reason than to get its hands on power" Sep '92; was elected to Aberdeenshire County Council for Upper Donside May '95; was selected to fight Aberdeenshire West and Kincardine '95; having played heavily on the need for tactical voting, was elected for Aberdeenshire West on a notional swing of 8.3%, by a majority of 2,662 over George Kynoch, former Scottish Under Secretary May '97; in his Maiden on the devolution referenda, was very impatient about the setting up of a Scottish Parliament not dominated by Strathclyde socialists May '97; urged the electrification of the East Coast Main Line to Aberdeen, which would "greatly increase the chance of piggyback freight" June '97; urged a review of the police widows' pension regulations July '97; backed more ecumenical Commons Prayers July '97;
Born: 15 April 1958, London
Family: Grandson, of Sir William Smith MP, lst Baronet, Conservative MP for Central Aberdeenshire and Kincardine '24-45; son of Sir (William) Gordon Smith 2nd Baronet, VRD and Diana (Goodchild); is related, as "a double second cousin' to the late Tory MP for Kincardine & Deeside, Alick Buchanan-Smith; m '93 Fiona Anne (Cormack) BBC radio journalist; 1d Helen '94;
Education: Merchant Taylor's School, Northwood; Aberdeen University (MA in Mathematics);
Occupation: Manager, of his family's estate at Chapel of Garioch in Inverurie, Aberdeenshire; ex: Rector's Assessor (Assistant to student-elected Rector), Aberdeen University '86-89;

Traits: Tall; burly; dark hair, short-back-and-sides; chubby face; specs; boyish-looking; affable; diffident-seeming; canny; enjoys hill-walking, DIY, sailing (in Royal Yacht Assocation);
Address: House of Commons, Westminster, London SW1A 0AA; Crowmallie House, Pitcaple, Inverurie AB51 5HR;
Telephone: 0171 219 3000 (H of C); 01467 6811595/681464(Fax) (home);

Helen SOUTHWORTH **Labour** **WARRINGTON SOUTH '97-**

Majority: 10,807 over Conservative 5-way;
Description: An altered seat, whose leaning towards the Conservatives was increased by the removal of a Labour stronghold in Halton to the new Weaver Vale constituency; the remaining seat's middle-class population is centred in private housing estates in suburbs south of the Manchester Ship Canal; a crossroads since the bronze age, it was developed by the Romans; now it is midway between Manchester and Liverpool, at the junction of the M6 and M62;
Position: St Helens Metropolitan Borough Councillor (Chairman of Leisure '95-96) '94-; ex: Director, of Age Concern in St Helens '86-97; Director, of St Helens and Knowsley Health Authority '94-97; St Helens and Knowsley Community Health Councillor '88-94;
Outlook: Centre-Left Labour activist in caring organisations; preoccupied with social cohesion and care for the elderly and disabled;
History: She joined the Labour Party at 23, '79; contested Wirral South against the late Barry Porter, securing a 3% swing to Labour but losing by 8,000 votes Apr '92; she was elected to St Helens Metropolitan Borough Council May '94; one of the first eleven aspirant women politicos to acquire the backing of Emily's List, was selected for the altered, thought marginally-Tory seat of Warrington South, after its sitting Labour MP, Mike Hall, did a runner to neighbouring, safer Weaver Vale; she was chosen from an all-woman short-list of four, after rejecting two men, including Councillor Mike Hannon, the former Mayor of Warrington Nov '95; at Labour's annual conference, she spoke up for the disabled Oct '96; she was attacked by anti-abortionist Tory women MPs for pledging her support for a woman's right to choose in exchange for support from the Emily's List lobby to encourage more women MPs Mar '97; was elected on a notional swing of 12.3%, with a majority of 10,807 over her Tory opponent May '97; made her Maiden in the debate on RAF Burtonwood, the former US supply depot that the Conservative Government, without local consultation, had leased as a storage depot used by heavy vehicles, although surrounded by high-quality suburban homes; she urged the local authority be allowed to develop it into an "urban village" June '97; she backed ban on fox-hunting June '97; urged a review of Parliamentary privilege June '97; urged action to curb drugs July '97; asked about discussions with US officials about reducing emissions of carbon dioxide July '97; urged a debate on the sale of alcopops to children July '97; urged health initiatives to curb ill health costing the country £12b a year July '97;
Born: 13 November 1956, Preston, Lancashire
Family: In '76 she married Edmund Southworth, museum curator; 1s '79; she does not disclose information about her parents;

Education: Larkhill Convent, Preston; Lancaster University (BA Hons);
Occupation: Director, of Grosvenor Housing Association (1,500 homes in Warrington); ex: Chief Executive, Age Concern in St Helens (project leader of a new £2m leisure and cultural centre for the elderly) '86-97; Communty Development Worker '79-86 (MSF);
Traits: Brown pageboy bob; full set of smiling teeth; lived-in face; in the photograph of Labour's 101 women MPs, she was the one sticking out her tongue May '97; she enjoys walking the family dog, gardening, painting and restoring the Sankey canal;
Address: House of Commons, Westminster, London SW1A 0AA; Town Hill, Warrington WA1 2NG;
Telephone: 0171 219 3000 (H of C); 01925 240002 (constituency); email: Heln.Southworth@geo2.poptel.org.uk;

Mrs Caroline SPELMAN **Conservative** **MERIDEN '97-**

Majority: 582 over Labour 4-way;
Description: A marginal which has changed six times in the last 30 years; it combines two leanings: the Labour-leaning voters of the Birmingham overspill estate of Chelmsley Wood, between the Birmingham city boundary and the M6 motorway, plus the rural areas around Solihull; it also contains the National Exhibition Centre, Birmingham International station and Birmingham airport; if '97 had reproduced '92 voting patterns, a Tory could have been assured of a 14,000-plus majority;
Position: On Select Committee on Science and Technology '97-; on Food from Britain Export Council;
Outlook: An internationally-experienced new Tory businesswoman, one of only five new Tory women MPs; a defender of the 'Meriden Gap' green belt and its farmers; a former spokeswoman for the European beet-growers, she resists the concreting-over of Meriden's farms because of new CAP "reforms" that may give subsidised advantage to European competitors;
History: She joined the Conservative Party; was a delegate to the GATT talks on behalf of the European Farming Union, speaking for the International Confederation of European Beet-Growers '84-89; selected for hopeless Bassetlaw against Joe Ashton MP, garnered 35% of the vote, down 2.5% from the previous Tory effort Apr '92; was selected late for Meriden following the death of Tory MP Iain Mills Feb '97; her election address opposed a single European currency; during the campaign said, "I'd like to see introduced a tax-break for non-working spouses; it recognises the sacrifices many make to care for relatives" Apr '97; retained the seat by the narrow majority of 582, after a swing of 11.6% to her Labour opponent May '97; in her Maiden worried that the wrong sort of CAP reform "could result in Meriden's farms going under concrete forever"; CAP reform would be even trickier if the EU was extended eastward, to embrace "the vast collectivised farms of eastern Europe" with "the competitive advantage that they would enjoy with their economies of scale and low wage costs" June '97; urged a programme to encourage more extensive sports among schoolgirls, to encourage fitness and avoid obesity, by providing more role models of sportswomen June '97; asked about the retention of the green belt area known as the "'Meriden Gap' between

Coventry and Birmingham" July '97; she was named to the Science and Technology Select Committee July '97; asked about the future of Solihull Hospital July '97;
Born: 4 May 1958, Bishops Stortford
Family: Daughter, of Marshall Cormack, banker, and Helen (Greenfield) ex-BBC; a mother of three, she is or was married to a Mr Spelman, about whom she discloses nothing;
Education: Hertfordshire and Essex Girls' Grammar School; Queen Mary's College, London University;
Occupation: Commercial Negotiator, specialising in purchase contracts for foods and pharmaceuticals '89-; Broker, of commercial disputes '89-; Free-Lance Consultant on Agricultural Affairs '89-: ex: Research Fellow, at Wye College '89-93; Deputy Director, International Confederation of European Beet-growers '84-89; Administrative Secretary, to National Farmers' Union's Sugar Beet Committee '80-84;
Traits: Dark, front-combed tonsured brown hair; a long oval face; enthusiastic traditionalist with an old-fashioned manner; was Lay Assistant and member of the Choir of St Michael's Church, Paris '87-89;
Address: House of Commons, Westminster, London SW1A 0AA;
Telephone: 0171 219 4189 (H of C);

Dr Phyllis (Margaret) STARKEY Labour MILTON KEYNES SOUTH WEST '97-

Majority: 10,292 over Conservative 4-way;
Description: Previously the more marginal of MK's two seats, partly because it includes Wolverton, an old railway town; it also has Bletchley where in wartime the gigantic 'Colossus' computer broke the Nazis' 'Enigma' codes; the accepted wisdom before the May '97 election was that if this seat went Labour, it would mean a Blair Government; it did;
Position: On the Select Committee on Modernisation of the House of Commons '97-; Vice Chairman, PLP Health Committee '97-; Oxford City Councillor (Leader '90-93, Deputy Leader '88-90) '83-; ex: Chairman, of Local Government Information Unit '95-97; on Labour NEC's Local Government Committee '95-97; on Labour's National Policy Forum '95-97;
Outlook: Among the most obsessively dynamic and cerebral of Labour's new women MPs; an internationally-recognised biochemical research scientist, she is also a widely-experienced and networked councillor; always looking for new challenges, she does not like to see opportunities unexploited; she is a confident and articulate spokeswoman for the scores of incoming Labour councillors and council leaders; "genteel but strong advocate of greater local authority involvement in the party" (NEW STATESMAN); "we have been trying to get the message across that for the past 15 years it is Labour councillors who have been developing the party's policies and practices because they're the only people who have had recent experience of actually governing; that experience needs to be used by the party at large" (PS); a cause groupie also in CPAG, Greenpeace, Fabians, Liberty, Labour Co-ordinating Committee, World Development Movement, CND, formerly in Anti-Apartheid in Cambridge;
History: Her Welsh parents were never Labour but "instilled in me feelings that you should have principles and you have responsibilities for society at large"; she joined the Labour Party

at Cambridge, becoming Vice Chairman of her branch '74; she first became involved with the Co-operative Society there as part of a campaign to persuade it not to sell goods from South Africa '75-78; was elected with Co-op support to Oxford City Council May '83; joined the Co-operative Party '85; was elected Deputy Leader of Oxford City Council May '88; was elected Leader of Oxford City Council May '90; helped form the 'Network of Labour Councils in the South' to exchange good practice and inform Labour policy development '91; was elected Chairman of the Local Government Information Unit Nov '92; relinquished her post as Leader of Oxford City Council under Oxford's three-year rule, which coincided with her job taking her to Swindon Feb '93; was an unsuccessful candidate for the NEC in the constituency section as the only councillor to stand; she secured 15,522 votes, beating four MP-contestants Oct '94; after the death of the Tory MP, Dr John Blackburn, was one of the four on Labour's short-list for Dudley West, from which Ian Pearson was selected, handsomely winning the subsequent by-election for Labour Nov '94; was selected from an all-women short-list to contest marginal Milton Keynes South West Feb '95; was elected to the NEC's Local Government Committee by the Association of Labour Councillors Oct '95; was elected to the National Policy Forum Oct '95; defended the women-only short-list system: "the old system was a disaster for women; we need this quick boost and then we can return to a more equitable system" Jan '96; with 17 other loyal Labour candidates wrote to the INDEPENDENT that Labour was a "united dynamic party ready to solve the problems this country faces" Oct '95; on a 14.7% swing won Milton Keynes South West by a majority of 10,292, ousting Barry Legg May '97; in her elegant Maiden, urged the modernisation of Commons procedures so that it did not again spawn hopeless bodies like the Child Support Agency May '97; led motion supporting comprehensive education as the "most efficient way to provide secondary education" June '97; congratulated Clare Short on her initiatives in banning land-mines June '97; urged Tessa Jowell to see that research was properly disseminated to ensure that clinicians took the right decisions on treating breast cancer June '97; expressed solidarity with jailed Indonesian union leader June '97; was named to the Select Committee on the Modernisation of the Commons June '97; co-sponsored a motion to retain 'Yesterday in Parliament' July '97; co-sponsored motion attacking mis-selling of pensions under the Tories July '97; co-sponsored motion backing genetic patenting July '97; urged guidance on the cost effectiveness of homeopathic versus conventional treatments for food allergies July '97; in the wake of her trip to Gaza and the West Bank, complained of 65% unemployment among Palestinian Arabs as a result of Israeli border closures Oct '97;

Born: 14 Jan 1947, Ipswich

Family: Her grandfather, who hated the Co-op, had a grocer's shop in the Welsh district of Liverpool; daughter of John Williams, food chemist, and Catherine (Hooson Owen); m '69 Hugh Starkey, Assistant Director, Centre for Modern Languages, at Open University; 2d: Laura Miriam '74, Claire Catherine '77; when her daughters were born she only took off nine months, because there was no maternity pay then and because she did not like being away from her research work: "I just was not happy at home all the time and it therefore wasn't doing a favour to the family";

Education: Perse School for Girls, Cambridge '58-65; Lady Margaret Hall, Oxford University (BA Hons in Biochemistry Class II, Distinction in Pharmacology) '66-70; Clare Hall, Cambridge University (PhD in Biochemistry) '84;

Occupation: Head of Assessment Branch, Biotechnology and Biological Sciences Research Council (MSF) '93-97; ex: Research Fellow, Somerville College, Oxford University '87-93; University Lecturer, Nuffield Department of Obstetrics and Gynaecology, John Radcliffe Hospital, Oxford (AUT) '84-93; Post-Doctoral Fellow, Sir William Dunn School of Pathology, Oxford University '81-84; Post-Doctoral Fellow and Deputy Head of Biochemistry

Department, Strangeways Laboratory, Cambridge '79-81; Editor of JOURNAL OF PHYSIOLGOY, Cambridge '77-78; Post-Doctoral Fellow, Strangeways Laboratory, Cambridge '75-77; Research Assistant, then Research Student, Strangeways Laboratory, Cambridge '70-74;
Traits: Parted dark blonde hair; long oval face; Welsh by origin; "ready laughter and a musical voice"; soft-spoken but her husband tells her she addresses him as if he was a public meeting" (Janet Barber, LOCAL GOVERNMENT CHRONICLE); "we used to go to the Congregationalist Church in Cambridge, but though I've grown away from it, I suppose I would still count myself as a believer at root"; "if I see something that should be done, I want to do it if nobody else is doing it; I can't leave a stone unturned; I'm the perennial activist; I feel very strongly that if you don't do things, the enemy will win; I believe very strongly that for evil to triumph it is only necessary for the good to do nothing"; "it's just an obsessive feeling that if you can see something you can do, then you must do it; you shouldn't just hope that somebody else will do it"; "gardening is my one relaxation"; Founder, of the local Woodcraft Folk group; the Starkeys did not own a car for several years in the early '90s;
Address: House of Commons, Westminster, London SW1A 0AA;
Telephone: 0171 219 6427 (H of C); 01908 225522 (constituency); 0402 370032 (mobile);

David STEWART **Labour** **INVERNESS EAST, NAIRN & LOCHABER '97-**

Majority: 2,339 over SNP 7-way;
Description: The vast Scottish Highlands seat, the UK's second largest, with the nation's highest mountains, deepest lochs and most famous monster, in Loch Ness; for psephologists, it provided a four-way marginal result in '92, with less than four percentage points between the lot;
Position: On the Select Committee on Scottish Affairs '97-; Inverness District Councillor (Deputy Leader, of the Labour Group '88-96) '88-; ex: Chairman, Highland Labour Party '93-95; on Labour Party's Scottish Executive '85-95; Dumfries District Councillor '84-86;
Outlook: The third-time-lucky first Labour MP for Inverness who added the largest blob of red to Labour's election map; thought to be Left-of-Centre; "the SNP likes to paint him as a man who would slavishly follow the party line regardless of the constituency interest" (David Ross, Glasgow HERALD); in Labour Campaign for Electoral Reform, Tribune Group;
History: He joined the Labour Party '80; contested Inverness, Nairn & Lochaber, coming second with 25.3% June '87; contested Inverness, Nairn & Lochaber again, coming within 458 votes of unseating Sir Russell Johnston Apr '92; Robin Cook and others in the Shadow Cabinet campaigned for him Apr '97; captured the seat with a majority of 2,339, a notional swing from SNP to Labour of 3.4% - seeing off a strong challenge from Fergus Ewing - and a swing from the LibDems in excess of 10% May '97; in his Maiden in the devolution referendum debate, he was fervent for a Scottish Parliament; he also said he would "campaign for a reduction in the price of petrol and diesel, which is extortionate in the Highlands and Islands" May '97; was named to the Select Committee on Scottish Affairs July '97; co-complained against British Airways complicity in the disintegration of transport policy Oct

'97;
Born: 5 May 1956, Inverness
Family: Son, of John Stewart, postal executive, and Alice (McKenzie); m '82 Linda (Macdonald), college lecturer; 2s: Andrew '87, Liam '90 (dcd '91), 1d Kirsty '93;
Education: Inverness High; Paisley College (BA Hons); Stirling University (Diploma in Social Work, Certificate of Qualification in Social Work); Open University (Diploma in Management);
Occupation: Social Work Team Manager in Social Work Department of Highland Regional Council '87-97; previously Social Worker, in Dumfries and Dingwall '81-87; Lecturer, on Community Care, at Esk Valley College '81;
Traits: Dark, close-cropped hair; long face; long nose; no longer bearded; humorous (recommended to the Tories the Scottish game of shinty, because it had "replaced clan warfare as a way to settle internal disputes"); enjoys swimming, hill-walking, and music;
Address: House of Commons, Westminster, London SW1A 0AA; 37 Burn Brae, Westhill, Inverness IV1 2RH;
Telephone: 0171 219 3586 (H of C); 01463 793213 (home); 01463 237441 (constituency); (

Ian STEWART **Labour** **ECCLES '97-**

Majority: 21,916 over Conservative 4-way;
Description: A slightly-altered safe-Labour working-class and industrial seat along the banks of the Manchester Ship Canal, in the middle of Manchester's metropolitan borough of Salford; in '95 it had two strongly Labour wards added from the Worsley constituency;
Position: Chairman, Salford District Labour Party; Vice Chairman, Manchester West Euro CLP; Vice Chairman, Eccles CLP; Director, of Salford Business Education Partnership;
Outlook: Joan Lestor's much less committed successor: "I have known Ian for twenty years and I have no idea where he stands on anything; he will adapt easily to the Blair leadership" (close political colleague); a behind-the-scenes union fixer; slightly paranoid about publicity, even resisting the efforts of a MANCHESTER EVENING NEWS columnist to write up his fascination for information technology; pro-European (Founder, of European Foundation for Social Partnership and Continuing Training Initiatives);
History: After the announcement of Eccles' former MP, Joan Lestor, that she was standing down, he came up from nowhere; with the help of the local TGWU infrastructure, he managed to secure most of the postal votes, overtaking the larger number of votes garnered in the selection conference itself by Bryan Davies, the veteran Labour MP for Oldham East Nov '96; won the seat on a 10.7% swing, with a majority of 21,916 May '97; expressed solidarity with a jailed Indonesian union leader June '97;
Born: 28 August 1950, Blantyre, Scotland
Family: He is married with three children;
Education: Calder Street Secondary; Irlam High School; Stretford Technical College; Manchester Metropolitan University;
Occupation: TGWU Northwest Regional Officer '78-97; ex: Chemical Plant Operator

'73-78; Apprentice Electrician;
Traits: Dark; balding; bearded; oval face; secretive; enjoys: walking, running, reading, painting; Tai Chi, physical training; an IT freak;
Address: House of Commons, Westminster, London SW1A 0AA;
Telephone: 0171 219 3000 (H of C); 0161 775 9589 (home); 0161 237 2402 (TGWU);

Paul (David) STINCHCOMBE **Labour** **WELLINGBOROUGH '97-**

Majority: 187 over Conservative 5-way;
Description: An old Northamptonshire industrial area - tanning, shoemaking and iron foundries - to which new service and light industries have been added; since '83 it has been based on the towns of Rushden, Wellingborough and historic Higham Ferrers; Wellingborough town has a strong Asian and Afro-Caribbean presence; although the seat was sporadically Labour-held from 1918 - if not between '69 and '97 - pundits writing before the '97 Labour landslide claimed that Labour could "never win it back", "even if they win the next general election, even with an overall majority" because "the 10% swing needed for Labour to take it would be almost unprecedented in a general election"; actually, 9.9% was enough;
Position: Former Camden Borough Councillor (Chairman of its Labour Group '92-94) '90-94;
Outlook: A highly idealistic young Christian Socialist internationalist and committed environmentalist, whose idealism survived a stint on Camden Council; "passionate, committed and well-informed" (Professor Steve Webb MP); in the Society of Labour Lawyers, Lawyers for Liberty, Amnesty, Friends of the Earth;
History: He joined the Labour Party at 17 '79, on returning from Kenya where he had worked as a voluntary teacher; at 28 he won the Brunswick ward on Camden Borough Council from the Leader of its Tory Group May '90; became Chairman of the Labour Group on Camden Council '92; was selected for "hopeless" Wellingborough July '95; on an unexpected pro-Labour swing of 9.9%, narrowly won the seat by a scant 187 votes (0.3%) - the smallest Labour majority of the election; this was less than the votes of the fourth and fifth parties in the contest, but enough to oust the Tory incumbent, Sir Peter Fry, after 28 years May '97; was passionately idealistic in his Maiden, but accepted the nasty realities of the well-intentioned Child Support Agency, which provided "the overwhelming bulk of complaints in my postbag and surgeries"; he cited a local family which had broken up because of a letter from the CSA falsely claiming the husband had fathered a child by another woman, although the CSA then admitted the real father had another name, address and date of birth; this was followed by a letter offering £100 in compensation, together with a disclaimer of liability; Stinchcombe proposed an independent appeals machinery, a proper and expeditious enforcement mechanism, an elimination of evasion and fraud, and giving priority to those most in need June '97; expressed solidarity with a jailed Indonesian union leader June '97; co-sponsored a motion welcoming the visit to Britain to give the Wilberforce Lecture of the Nigerian Nobel laureate, Professor Wole Soyinka July '97; led a motion urging more care in the extraction of aggregates July '97;

Born: 25 April 1962, Haslemere
Family: Son, of Lionel Stinchcombe, local government officer, and Pauline (Hawkins) factory accounts clerk; m '90 Suzanne (Gardiner) 2s: '92, '94, 1d '91;
Education: High Wycombe Royal Grammar School; Trinity College, Cambridge University (MA Double First in Law); Harvard Law School (LLM)
Occupation: Barrister '85- (specialising in judicial review, local governmernt and environmental law) (MSF and GMB);
Traits: Dark brown hair in tight curls; rounded boyish face; no longer has a moustache; articulate; as a Christian Socialist can sound like a lay preacher; enjoys the visual arts, modern literature, and all sports - especially football, cricket, boxing, golf;
Address: House of Commons, Westminster, London SW1A 0AA; Middle Barn, Gloy Hill Farm, Woodburn Green Lane, Beaconsfield, Bucks HP 1HX;
Telephone: 0171 219 3000 (H of C);

Dr Howard (Geoffrey) STOATE **Labour** **DARTFORD '97-**

Majority: 4,328 over Conservative 6-way;
Description: The Kentish seat closest to southeast London, radiating from the Dartford Tunnel and the bridge carrying the M25; its role linking London and the Kent Coast has lasted since Roman times; 40% of its voters are commuters; it has some industry: cement, paper-making, pharmaceuticals (Glaxo Wellcome) and engineering; it was fought by Mrs Thatcher in '50 and '51, in its previous, more marginal shape; captured for the Tories by Bob Dunn in '79, it became safely Tory in '83 with the addition of 10,000 voters from Sevenoaks district; in '95, 5,000 such voters were subtracted; had the '97 voting pattern repeated that of '92, the incumbent Tory MP, Bob Dunn, should have been safe with an 8,000 majority;
Position: On Select Committee on Health '97-; Dartford Borough Councillor (Chairman, of Finance '94-) '89-; on South Thames Regional Graduate Medical Board '95-; ex: Chairman, Dartford Fabian Society '84-90, on National Executive of Fabians '91-92; Vice Chairman, Dartford CLP '84-87; Chairman, of Ethics Committee, of Bexley Health Authority '94-97;
Outlook: The area's senior GP, Fabian and local councillor; also in the Socialist Health Association, Greenpeace, Friends of the Earth and Amnesty International; one of the cohesive group of new Kentish Labour MPs;
History: His parents were Labour Party members; he was pro-Labour at school; joined the Young Socialists at 14, '68; joined the Labour Party at 16, '70; was elected Vice Chairman of the Dartford CLP '84; fought Old Bexley and Sidcup against Edward Heath coming third with 17.3% of the vote June '87; was elected to Dartford Borough Council for Littlebrook ward May '89; contested Dartford against Bob Dunn, coming second with 34.7% of the votes, losing by 10,314 votes, but knocking 5,000 off the Tory majority Apr '92; became Chairman of Finance on Dartford Council when Labour took control May '94; on his selection again for Dartford, said: "much has happened since 1992; we have a Labour Kent [County] Council, a Labour MEP and Dartford has a Labour Council; we also have a new leader, Tony Blair, who I feel confident will be leading a Labour Government" Sep '95; agreed with his political

opponent, Bob Dunn, that Dartford should be a unitary authority, with decisions taken locally rather than in Maidstone by the Kent County Council; he opposed merging Dartford with Gravesham, as urged by the Local Government Commission Oct '95; as one of eight sweeping Labour gains in Kent, won Dartford on a notional swing of 11.5% by a majority of 4,328, ending Bob Dunn's 18-year reign May '97; in his Maiden urged a review of "outdated and inconsistent" payments for prescriptions, citing two former asthmatic patients: one developed hypothyroidism and was exempt from both prescription charges, the other developed hyperthyroidism and had to pay double prescription charges; he complained that prescription charges, at £5.65, would be only 60p if they had risen at the rate of inflation May '97; co-sponsored a motion attacking the Kent County Council, again Tory-controlled, for its moratorium on capital spending for schools June '97; co-sponsored motion criticising Eurotunnel for its potentially dangerous use of open lattice goods wagons June '97; welcomed the Bill to clear the obstacles to building hospitals under the Private Finance Initiative, in the hope that the long-delayed Dartford and Gravesham hospital would finally be started; but he worried about the extent that private contractors might be involved in providing clinical services: "I do not want a takeover of health care by stealth" July '97; was named to the Select Committee on Health July '97; co-sponsored motion criticising Port of London's reduced use of pilots July '97; criticised fundholding for GPs July '97;
Born: 14 April 1954, Weymouth, Dorset
Family: Son, Alvan Stoate, engineer, and May (Russell) teacher; m '79 Deborah (Dunkerley) teacher, who also became a Dartford councillor; 2s: Thomas Henry '84, George Timothy '87;
Education: Danesfield School, Walton-on-Thames; Kingston Grammar; King's College, London University (MBBS '77, DRCOG '79, MRCGP '81); London University (MSc);
Occupation: General Practitioner (non-fundholding) '82-; Tutor, in General Practice: at London University '89-, at Queen Mary's Hospital, Sidcup; Fellow and Examiner, of Royal College of GPs '94- (BMA; MPU; MSF); Medical Journalist, for PULSE, FINANCIAL PULSE, MEDICAL MONITOR, MIMMS MAGAZINE '89-
Traits: Retreating blond hair; long, thin oval face; an eager fast-talker; has a charming smile;
Address: House of Commons, Westminster, London SW1A 0AA; 36 Heathclose Road, Dartford, Kent DA1 2PU;
Telephone: 0171 219 4571 (H of C); 01322 343234 (constituency);

Graham STRINGER **Labour** **MANCHESTER-BLACKLEY '97-**

Majority: 19,588 over Conservative 4-way;
Description: North Manchester's mixed but very safe Labour seat; since '95 it stretches further into central Manchester, including Strangeways Prison; varies from middle-class Heaton Park to multi-cultural Cheetham Hill, once a Jewish ghetto but recently a third non-white, mostly Asian; its industrial base has contracted, with the bankruptcy of Ferranti and the contraction of British Aerospace and ICI-Zeneca;
Position: On Select Committtee on Environment, Transport and Regional Affairs '97-; ex: Chairman, of Manchester Airport Plc til '97; Manchester City Councillor (its Leader '84-96) '80-96;

Outlook: "Dour Leftwinger turned dour Blairite" (NEW STATESMAN); "outstanding in terms of talent", "his attachment to Blair" "should see him rise quickly in government" (Michael Gove, SPECTATOR); favours an elected mayor for Manchester but opposes a Northwest Regional Assembly; Manchester's most controversial changeling, who swung from being a hard-Left headbanger to an Armani-suited world-travelling airport manager; "made the transformation from bolshie Bennite to Town Hall tyrant" (Trotskyist LABOUR BRIEFING}; in the '80s, in tandem with Sir Robert Scott, he helped Manchester emerge "as one of the most positive and pushy cities in Britain, constantly striving for improvements in all fields and particularly in sport"; "so convincing was their performance that, in partnership with private companies, they achieved an unparalleled range of sporting facilities including the Nynex Arena, the National Cycling Centre and the promise of a stadium for east Manchester that's at least big enough for the 2002 Commonwealth Games; ironically, considering Mr Stringer's original confrontation with the Government, the sporting programme has brought the city more Government grants than anywhere else in the country" (Janine Watson, MANCHESTER EVENING NEWS); more recently, as the Chairman of Manchester airport, he carried its case successfully through a 101-day inquiry, by claiming that it would provide tens of thousands of jobs for the northwest's many unemployed and promised to more than make up for any environmental damage; this display was a new example of his flexibility in changing policies while staying on target; this was shown during his twelve-year reign as City Council Leader; at its end he admitted readily in a 1996 interview that "his economic policies have moved to the Right in recent years; with ever-tightening restrictions on council spending powers, town halls would be mad to refuse to enter the current popular partnership arrangements with [the] private sector and Europe; but the [former] city Leader is proud there has been no shift in his social policies, and, if anything, he feels even more strongly today about making real improvements in the lives of disabled people, women and black people; although the number of city council employees has been reduced by 12,000 from when he took over in 1984, it's an achievement he rates highly that not one employeee has been forced to take compulsory redundancy despite a constant cash squeeze on the town hall"; "when he's good, he's very very good; and when he wants to be bad, he can be horribly determined" (Janine Watson, MANCHESTER EVENING NEWS);

History: He joined the Labour Party '74; "in 1979, he was instrumental in forcing [the] former Labour Minister, [ailing] Harold Lever to stand down from his Manchester Central seat; the next year, at the age of 30, he became Chair[man] of the then Leftwing Manchester City Labour Party and was elected a Councillor; over the following four years he was centrally involved in a struggle which led to him being expelled from the Labour Group, along with other Lefties, in 1980, '81...and '83 -on the last occasion [expelled sine die] following his voting against the official Labour Budget in full council; in 1984, following Left gains in local elections, Eric Heffer, then Chair[man] of the national [Labour] Party, intervened to unite the divided Manchester Labour Group; Stringer was elected Leader on the Left slate" (Trotskyist LABOUR BRIEFING); he became Leader of Manchester City Council at 34, in what amounted to virtually a coup by the young hard-Left May '84; "so radical were his policies in those days that he had already been politically banished on more than one occasion by Labour's old guard"; "with long-time allies like Pat Karney, Jack Flanagan and Val Dunn, traditions like the Lord Mayor were rapidly dumped; the Manchester United fanatic and his colleagues produced a range of initiatives as red as his favourite football team, including the controversial lease-back of many of the city's famous buildings; wrapped up in long woolly scarves and long political arguments, the new Leader was a frequent companion of other Leftwing city bosses like Liverpool's Derek Hatton and London's Ken Livingstone and Islington's Margaret Hodge" (Janine Watson, MANCHESTER EVENING NEWS); "having hedged his way through the rate-imposing climbdown of 1985, he gradually moved to the Right, making the final break with his former Left allies in 1987, when he pushed a cuts package through the Council"; "he proved himself an assiduous collector of the poll tax and willing jailor of nonpayers"; "he...played the familiar divide-and-rule game with the unions, using the GMB as a political base and castigating NALGO and other unions which [made] any attempt to resist cuts, privatisation or job losses"; "in the late '80s, Stringer formed a close political relationship with his old enemy, Gerald Kaufman [MP]; whatever, their differences, the two men found they were bound together by a shared loathing of the Left; increasingly, Stringer...intervened in the internal affairs of local Constituency Labour Parties, though the strings [were] pulled behind the scenes as they [were] on the Council; he [used] the local press to bounce and manipulate the Labour Group and...regularly leaked Labour Party documents to journalists in order to put pressure on his opponents within the Party"; he attacked Minister Tim Sainsbury for removing Manchester's Assisted Area status and "adding insult to injury by suggesting that cities should stop promoting themselves abroad" Oct '93; after 12 years, he decided to step down as Leader of Manchester City Council May '96; in the wake of the announcement of the veteran Labour MP for Blackley, Ken Eastham, that he would not stand again, Stringer was selected, to Eastham's dismay; Stringer promised that every precaution would be taken to secure the airport against protesters against a second runway, which had the support of most people in the northwest Jan '97; as an 'April fool' stunt, Daniel 'Swampy' Hooper, the tunneler leading the protest against a second Manchester Airport runway, pretended he would stand against Stringer in the general election; "I feel quite outraged that people who don't come from the area, who have not participated in the democratic process come and say they know better"; "it makes me very angry that young southerners come and stop people [in the northwest] getting off the dole queue"; a MORI Poll backed Stringer's claim that most local people wanted a second runway Apr '97; won the seat by a majority of 19,588, a notional swing to Labour of 9.3%, the second largest in Manchester May '97; answered tree protester in GUARDIAN that in the inquiry into the second runway over 100 objectors had spoken up out of a total of 180 witnesses, with 3,100 objecting letters outweighed by 11,600 supporters May '97; wrote to GUARDIAN: "the trespassers at Manchester Airport come from the same political tradition as Mussolini and Pol Pot in rejecting the ballot box in favour of direct action and violence" May '97; claimed airport expansion would create 50,000 jobs; his term as Chairman of Manchester Airport ended June '97; co-sponsored motion congratulating Manchester on its progress in rebuilding the city after the IRA bomb June '97; in his Maiden explained why Manchester has decided to include shooting in the 2002 Commonwealth Games there June '97; while agreeing with Ken Livingstone's "basic analysis", backed Chancellor Brown's Budget as a start to overcoming the problems of his inner-city constituents who had been hard-hit by 18 years of adverse Tory legislation: the poll tax, forced council rent rises, wage cuts forced by compulsory competitive tendering July '97; agreed with the Chancellor that control of inflation was the best way to avoid the negative equity that had afflicted millions in the late '80s July '97; in the NEW STATESMAN urged Labour to "embrace competition for public money" because "done properly, it works": "the redevelopment of places such as inner-city Hulme under City Challenge has been far more successful than spending twice as much money in the traditional local government way" July '97; was named to the Select Committee on Environment, Transport and Regional Affairs Juy '97;

Born: 17 February 1950, Beswick, Manchester

Family: Son, of Albert Stringer, railway clerk, and Brenda, proprietor of a small corner shop in Beswick, Manchester,

Education: Christchurch Primary; Merton Brock High School; Sheffield University (BSc

[Hons] in Chemistry;
Occupation: Chairman, Manchester Airport Plc til '97; ex: Leader of Manchester City Council '84-96; Employee, of a housing association '82-84; Analytical Chemist in plastics industry from which he was made redundant '81;
Traits: Burly; with parted flat hair; straight-faced; recently well-dressed; enjoys high-living and late-night nightclubbing; has "an upfront, aggressive approach" (Martin Wainwright, GUARDIAN); "dour" (Dr Adam Tickell); "humourless" (PRIVATE EYE); fanatical supporter of Manchester United;
Address: House of Commons, Westminster, London SW1A 0AA; 65 Polefield Road, Manchester M9 7EN;
Telephone: 0171 219 5335 (H of C); 0161 740 2528 (home);

Gisela STUART **Labour** **BIRMINGHAM-EDGBASTON '97-**

Majority: 4,842 over Conservative 5-way;
Description: The city's most middle-class constituency, which has never before been represented by Labour; it was altered in '95 to include Tory-leaning Bartley Green ward from old Northfield; a centre for education and broadcasting: Birmingham University, King Edward's Grammar School and the BBC's Pebble Mill; it also contains the Warwickshire County Cricket Club; Dame Jill Knight retired in '97 despite pundits' promises that she could still have a 5,000 majority, providing the voters stuck to '92 voting patterns;
Position: On the Select Committee on Social Security '97-;
Outlook: A Bavarian-born success story for the Labour Women's Network; the first-ever Labour MP for this middle-class seat; the announcement of her victory on a 10% swing - the first gain to be announced on election night - sounded the Tories' deathknell; a law lecturer who will crusade on pensions, particularly for excluded women; believes in constitutional reform, preferring the Additional Member system to STV PR; thinks the "critical mass" of women Labour MPs will make a difference; in the Labour Campaign for Electoral Reform, the Fabian Society and Charter 88;
History: She came to England to do business studies and law in '74; she did not become active in politics until the late '80s; she was 'politicised' when, with her legal hat on, she was shocked to see large companies legitimately switching millions of pounds out of their pension funds - followed by the Maxwell scandal; "it made me me realise that you can do all sorts of work behind the scenes, but if you want to make real changes, you have to be on the inside, at the heart of legislation"; she joined the Labour Party '89; "in November 1992 I was not eligible for any elected office in the UK; however, once Maastricht was ratified I could be elected to the European Parliament and I could participate in local elections; I arrived in the UK without ever having stood for election; the day spent [in '94] at the L[abour] W[omen's] N[etwork] training day was one of the most useful in my life"; "I met a number of women who have continued to cross my path who have remained supportive; I was introduced to 'Uphill All The Way' which is compulsive reading, and my picture was taken; the ratification of the Maastricht Treaty turned into something of a Westminster farce since the NEC would not allow me to be

selected as a candidate, subject to ratification; as far as I was concerned, I had missed the opportunity to take part in the 1994 Euro-elections; then three things happened in quick succession: Maastricht was ratified, some new European constituencies were created, and on the eve of nomination, the candidate who had been selected to fight Worcester and South Warwickshire withdrew; emergency procedures came into operation and we had six weeks to select a new candidacy; a friend rang and said 'go for it', your branch will nominate you; I was only familiar with one of the seven constituencies which formed the Euro-seat; I had only ever been to one selection meeting and I only had six weeks to get my act together; as I was the only woman interested in the seat, those constituenies who had selection meetings had to invite me; I had to find the places on the map first and certainly there was no time to find out about the constituencies; but I did have L[abour] W[omen's] N[etwork]; I rang up and was given a list of women who were within my patch; I talked to them and they gave me a thumbnail sketch of who was who, what were the main issues and what to watch out for; I did not have to go to any meeting without having had the opportunity of a friendly chat beforehand; Jacqui Smith [later an MP] in particular proved to be a supportive friend; she gave me tips on selection, looked at my draft speeches and gave general advice; once I had actually met her - at a selection meeting - she made useful comments on delivery, body language and general presentation; I was selected! the election would be eight weeks later;...on 9th June I lost by 0.54% [despite using my maiden name of Gschaider] - and that in a constituency which comprised seven safe Tory seats" June '94; was selected from an all-women's short-list for Edgbaston June '95; won the seat - the 67th on Labour's target list and the first Labour gain to be announced on election night - by a majority of 4,842 on a notional swing of 10% May '97; in her Maiden, she promised to concentrate her efforts on improving the lot of state pensioners, particularly women: "even today, only one woman in five is in receipt of a basic state pension in her own right" May '97; backed proposed ban on fox-hunting June '97; had a local problem of kerb-crawling in Balsall Heath June '97; was named to the Select Committee on Social Security July '97; showed concern about growth of smoking among young girls July '97; said the Social Security system was "universally hated" as a "worst-compromise scenario" July '97;

Born: 26 November 1955, Velden Vis, Bavaria

Family: Daughter, of Martin Gschaider, farmer, and Liane (Krompholz) farmer; m '80 Richard Scott Stuart, technologist; 2s '83, '86;

Education: Staat Realschule Vilsbiburg; Manchester Polytechnic (Business Studies); London University (LLB Law);

Occupation: Law Lecturer, at Worcester College (NATHFE); Researcher, on Pensions at Birmingham University '93-; ex: Deputy Director, London Book Fair (MSF) '82; Academic Bookseller '73-80;

Traits: Dark hair; short tonsure; intelligent-pretty face; sharp nose; in '79 represented Britain at fencing while at university;

Address: House of Commons, Westminster, London SW1A 0AA; 7 Tudor Eaves, Harborne Park Road, Birmingham P17 0DE (constituency flat);

Telephone: 0171 219 5051 (H of C); 0121 427 9399 (constituency flat and office);

Andrew STUNELL OBE **Liberal Democrat** **HAZEL GROVE '97-**

Majority: 11,814 over Conservative 6-way;
Description: Unaltered Greater Manchester suburban marginal in the southeast of Stockport, stretching from the centre of Stockport to the boundary of Peak District National Park; recently a commuter district for Greater Manchester; its former Tory MP, Sir Tom Arnold, unexpectedly held on for five contests, four of them by the skin of his teeth; it was held twice by the late Liberal Dr Michael [Lord] Winstanley;
Position: Deputy Chief Whip '97-; on Select Committees: on Broadcasting '97-, on the Modernisation of the House of Commons '97-; Stockport Borough Councillor '94-; Political Secretary, of the Association of Liberal Democratic Councillors '87-96; Cheshire County Councillor (Deputy Leader '82-)'81-; Chester City Councillor '79-90; Chairman: Cheshire Liberal Party '77-81, Vice Chairman, Association of County Councillors '85-91;
Outlook: A highly-intelligent practical reformer with an "un-Liberal intolerance of incompetence" (LIBERATOR); a victor who succeeded after a near-miss in retaking the seat held as Cheadle in '66 and as Hazel Grove in '74 by the late Liberal MP Michael Winstanley; an experienced veteran who could become a force for national as well as local government reform; believes that "those of us who have tackled these problems of changing public authorities in real life on balanced and [Liberal]-controlled councils have some practical ideas about how to prepare the way for changes needed nationally"; in coalition with the Tories on Cheshire Council, achieved a first-rate record for better services and higher efficiency, without budget increases; this gave him a misleadingly Rightwing impression; one of the most cautious of LibDem veterans, has long urged "when in doubt, do nowt"; "Liberals believe that dogma and greed make for very bad goverment"; as a councillor he "built up a strong grass-roots band of supporters" and was "known for his tremendous energy in tackling electors' problems" (MANCHESTER EVENING NEWS); "likely to be hostile to deals with Labour" (NEW STATESMAN); his power as the political chief of all the LibDem councillors had swollen greatly before he reached Parliament;
History: He joined the Liberal Party because it was the only one to fight for the admission of East African British passport holders '68; was selected as prospective candidate for Chester '77; was elected Chairman of the Cheshire Liberals '77; unsuccessfully contested Chester, polling 14%, May '79; was elected to Chester City Council May '79; was elected to Cheshire County Council May '81; urged a more fair system of apportioning local revenue; this might require a different banking system Sep '82; after long negotiations, his 7 Liberal councillors on Cheshire County Council went into coalition with its 29 Tories depriving its 34 Labour councillors of control Nov '82; spearheaded opposition to new C of E secondary school in Chester '83; again contested Chester, coming 3rd but increasing his vote to 24.7%; warned against tailoring Liberal changes to what they thought Labour or Tories would vote for; local government finance had to fit together and therefore required great care in making changes Sep '86; again contested Chester, coming 3rd with 19.5% of the vote, down from 24.7%, as a result of Labour's soaring into a stronger second place June '87; was selected to contest the Hazel Grove marginal against Tom Arnold Aug '87; was elected one of the 8 members of the Liberal negotiating team with the SDP Sep '87; urged government funding to finance

implementation of homelessness laws for councils like overwhelmed, Liberal-controlled Tower Hamlets Oct '87; at their special conference, said that, despite flaws in the SDP-Liberal merger package, he would vote for the merger Jan '88; complained that Labour-controlled councils were among the worst in refusing fair shares to Liberals as school governors Aug '88; at annual assembly, claimed that LibDems could boast about practical actions "in councils from Scotland to Land's End", but for Tories the slogan on the environment was "money first"; "they are fickle, they are shallow, they are deceitful"; Labour at best were "complacent and dosy" Sep '89; warned that Britain's economy and political and social structures were weak and would not stand up to a "big bang" solution; improvements would have to proceed slowly, from the bottom up, on the basis of consultation, not from the top down Sep '90; urged a reversal of the Tories' "nanny-knows-best" centralising policies: "we actually need local democracy, where people can get their voices through, change the system and change the policies" Apr '91; urged opponents of local Hazel Grove bypass to get technical advice to underpin their opposition Mar '92; warned that Tory promises of a tax cut were a cruel illusion, because, among other things they were imposing a surcharge of £150 on every family whose poll tax had not been collected Mar '92; narrowly lost Hazel Grove to Sir Tom Arnold by 929 votes Apr '92; in wake of the LibDems having won 873 council seats, urged them to put their agreed policies into effect May '93; was elected to Stockport Borough Council May '94; was awarded the OBE Jan '95;in a leaked analysis on the eve of local elections, warned LibDem councillors that the "Blair effect could prevent us making gains" because dissident Tories were transfering support to Labour instead of going to LibDems even when they were in second place Apr '95; urged a cap of £1m for Lottery prizes Aug '95; denying it was a "killjoys' charter", sponsored successful motion to ban National Lottery scratch cards and put a cap on prizes Sep '95; predicted LibDems could gain 50 to 100 seats and add 4 more councils to the 51 they already controlled Apr '96; Sir Tom Arnold announced he was standing down for health reasons Sep '96; Stunell took Hazel Grove by a majority of 11,814 on a swing of 12.8% May '97; urged free prescriptions for sufferers from cystic fibrosis June '97; was named to the Select Committee on the Modernisation of the House of Commons June '97; urged planning preference for the regeneration of town centre as against out-of-town and greenfield sites June '97; complained that anti-dumping duties had halved employment in one his local textile firms July '97; urged more help for closed circuit TV in shopping centres July '97; opposed time-tabling the Budget debate because the Budget was more complex than predicted and contained flaws like the windfall tax and the pension tax July '97; co-sponsored motion to introduce another, lower band of council tax to cover mobile homes July '97;

Born: 24 November 1942, Sutton, Surrey

Family: Son, of late Robert George Stunell, Chartered Mechanical Engineer, and Trixie (Thompson); m '67 Gillian (Chorley) musician, teacher; 3s: Peter '73, Mark '74, Daniel '79; 2d: Judith '69, Kari '70;

Education: Malden Parochial School, Worcester Park, Surrey; Surbiton Grammar; Kingston Polytechnic; Manchester University (architecture); Liverpool Polytechnic;

Occupation: Vice Chairman '85-91, Political Secretary '89-96, Special Projects Officer '96-97, Association of Liberal Democratic Councillors; Author: 'Open, Active and Effective' (1994), 'Budgeting for Real' (1992), 'Success in Balanced Councils' (1985); ex: Cheshire County Councillor '82-84; Chester City Councillor '79-80; Senior Architectural Assistant, Runcorn New Town (NALGO) '67-81, CWS Manchester '65-67; UNA Executive in refugee rehousing '59-64;

Traits: Grey, parted long frizzy hair; blue eyes; high forehead; specs; pale; long, sharp face; benign features; Baptist lay preacher; a former pullover man who has gone over to collars, ties and suits; has "an excellent, precise mind" plus compassion: "he used his architectural

skills...for refugees, helping the homeless in Germany and Austria, then Greece, Turkey and Yugoslavia, where he worked after the Skopje earthquake" (LIBERATOR);
Address: House of Commons, Westminster, London SW1A 0AA; 84 Lyme Grove, Romiley, Stockport SK6 4DJ
Telephone: 0171 219 5223/2302(Fax) (H of C); 0161 406 7070 (constituency); 0161 430 6739 (home & Fax);

Desmond (Angus) SWAYNE **Conservative** **NEW FOREST WEST '97-**

Majority: 11,332 over Liberal Democrat 5-way;
Description: New seat in the remnants of the hunting preserves of 11th century monarchs; its 64,000 voters were taken in '95 wholly from among the 75,000 in old New Forest; it embraces Ringwood, the port of Lymington, Fordingbridge and relatively populous New Milton;
Position: On Select Committee on Scottish Affairs '97-; ex: President, St Andrews University Conservative Association '77-79;
Outlook: An assiduous debater with his own style; a former student actor doing a new-boy parody of Nick Winterton; a long-standing Rightwing Eurosceptic; a former member of the far-Right Monday Club; a muscular Christian (in Prayer Book Society); "simplistic" (Commons Leader Ann Taylor); "virtually everything is a mystery to him" (PM Tony Blair);
History: At 18, he voted to withdraw from EEC June '75; became President of the St Andrews Conservative Association '77; helped to organise opposition to home rule in Eastern Scotland in the referendum '78; toured US lecturing on the 'Thatcher Revolution' '84; fought hopeless Pontypridd, coming second but losing over 3% of the Tory percentage June '87; contested West Bromwich West against Betty Boothroyd, losing by 7,830 Apr '92; was short-listed for the Stratford-upon-Avon seat abandoned by Alan Howarth, but was beaten by John Maples Dec '95; succeeded in winning selection for New Forest West Mar '96; insisted that Tory prospectives had to proclaim themselves against the single European currency in advance of the election: "it will be very difficult in an election if we are still trying to fudge the issue; to ask people to wait while we make up our minds is extraordinary" Aug '96; retained the seat by a majority of 11,332, despite a 3.2% notional swing to the LibDems May '97; a prison visitor to Wormwood Scrubs, he confided in his Maiden that a "murderer friend" had bristled when he mentioned he was backing Michael Howard for the Tory leadership May '97; as a Redwood supporter he opposed the Clarke-Redwood alliance June '97; he deplored the phasing out of Assisted Places Scheme, particularly where it prevented siblings from attending the same school, recalling how his older brother had helped support him at school June '97; perhaps because he attended St Andrews, and his middle name is Angus, was named to the Select Committee on Scottish Affairs July '97; told constituent: "I will never be bound by your opinions, especially if they conflict with mine" July '97; said the Government's "decision not to replace 'Britannia' is deeply regrettable" and due to "political posturing"; opposed women in the infantry, quoting St Bernard as saying, "to be always with a woman and not to have intercourse is more difficult than to raise the dead" Oct '97;
Born: 20 August 1956, Berne

Family: Son, of George Joseph Swayne, diplomat, and Elizabeth (McAlister Gibson); m '87 Moira Cecily (Teek), former Tory ward chairman; 1s Albert '89, 1d Judith '92;
Education: Drumley House, Ayrshire; Bedford School; St Andrews University (MA; he was a contemporary of Alex Salmond);
Occupation: Computer Systems Manager, Royal Bank of Scotland '88-96; ex: Teacher of Economics, at Wrekin College and Charterhouse '80-87; Director of Brick Sculptures Company Ltd;
Traits: Shock of swept-back, centre-parted grey hair; wide-spaced eyes; self-parodying; talks politics like a knockabout comedian; "with his floppy hair, floppy ties and oddly protuberant upper lip, Mr Swayne is, I suspect, a BBC stunt: he is actually one of Harry Enfield's much-loved characters, Tory Boy 10 years on"; suffers from "Swayne Fever" (Simon Hoggart, GUARDIAN); an active athlete: Rugby, fencing, boxing, swimming (440 yards daily in the Serpentine), cycling (12 miles daily); former student amateur actor; Terrier; prison visitor at Wormwood Scrubs;
Address: House of Commons, Westminster, London SW1A 0AA; 56 St Quintin Avenue, London W10 6PN;
Telephone: 0171 219 4886 (H of C);

John SWINNEY **Scottish National** **TAYSIDE NORTH '97-**

Majority: 4,160 over Conservative 4-way;
Description: A huge, largely-rural constituency of over 2,000 square miles, put together in '83 from the northern parts of old Perthshire and Angus; Forfar is its only sizeable town; Brechin, a small cathedral city, was added from Angus East in '95; "the most beautiful seat in Scotland, from the ruggedness of the Rannoch moor to the agricultural abundance of Strathmore" (JS); it was in this area that the Highland clearances began; it is probably the largest berry-producing area in the country; it also has the Bell whisky plant;
Position: Treasury Spokesman in SNP 'Cabinet' '95-; SNP Vice Convenor for Publicity '92-; ex: SNP National Secretary '86-92;
Outlook: An impressive new-boy, the second SNP MP, after Douglas Crawford '74-79, to sit for Highland Perthshire -formerly represented by Sir Alec Douglas-Home; "smart, politically deft, ambitious, Christian, family-orientated, a future PM of Scotland" (GUARDIAN); "another of the SNP's rising stars", "a close ally of Alex Salmond" (SCOTSMAN);
History: He joined the SNP at 15, '79; stood for election as SNP's National Secretary despite being only 21 and having finals in four months; beat an older and more experienced activist; he became the SNP's youngest-ever National Secretary at 22, '86; he contested Tayside North against its Tory incumbent, kilt-sporting Bill Walker, coming second 3,439 behind Apr '92; at the SNP's Perth conference, as National Secretary put forward a resolution abandoning its controversial "free by '93" slogan; his re-nationalisation resolution came under attack from the SNP's Leftwing Sep '92; at annual SNP conference, claimed an independent Scotland could generate another 100,000 jobs Sep '96; as the SNP's Treasury spokesman, proposed dropping the lower rate of income tax from 20% to 15% and lifting the upper limit of National

Insurance Nov '96; selected again, he won the seat by 4,160 votes, on a notional swing of 8.4%, ousting Bill Walker after 18 years there May '97; asked PM Tony Blair whether he would "argue for a zonal lifting of the European beef ban" May '97; asked about research into food poisoning June '97; accepted the Labour Government's proposal for the Scottish Grand Committee, including a cut in its sitting days June '97; urged speedier resolution of the "quagmire of decisions" by the Benefits Agency June '97; in his Maiden, in the European Union debate, insisted that in the beef ban negotiations the Conservative Government had sacrificed the interests of Scotland and Northern Ireland, which were almost BSE-free for those of England, with its much greater incidence of BSE June '97; described the Conservative criticism of Labour's handling of the European beef ban as "bare-faced cheek"; added: "the Scottish suckler beef industry produces the finest beef in the world; why should quality produce be eliminated" by "our European partners fixated on a drive simply to cut production" June '97; insisted that the Budget assumptions - despite having Scots as Chancellor, Chief Secretary and Economic Secretary - were irrelevant for Scotland because its economy was not overheating; moreover the petrol price increase would hurt more in Scotland because of its bigger distances; the changes in Advance Corporation Tax would hurt the Scottish pension industry July '97; co-opposed spending an additional £250m on the "increasingly expensive and irrelevant Greenwich Project" July '97; tried to amend the Finance Bill to reduce petrol tax for those in rural areas July '97;
Born: 13 April 1964, Edinburgh
Family: Son, of Kenneth Swinney, rtd garage manager, and Nancy (Hunter); m Loran Ann (King); 1s Stuart 96, 1d Judith '94;
Education: Forrester High School, Edinburgh; Edinburgh University (MA Hons in Politics);
Occupation: Strategic Planning Principal, with Scottish Amicable '92-97; previously Researcher, on Scottish coal industry;
Traits: Long thin face with a dark retreating hairline; specs; cerebral-looking; a "slick performer" (NEW STATESMAN); enjoys hill-walking;
Address: House of Commons, Westminster, London SW1A 0AA;
Telephone: 0171 219 6581 (H of C);

Robert SYMS **Conservative** **POOLE '97-**

Majority: 5,298 over Liberal Democrat 6-way;
Description: Half of this untidily expanding Dorset port town - "the second largest natural harbour in the world" (RS) - with one ward returned in '95 from Bournemouth next door;
Position: On the Select Committee on Health '97-; Wiltshire County Councillor '85-; Founder-Director, Calne Development Project Trust '86-; ex: on Wessex Regional Health Authority '88-90; North Wiltshire District Councillor (Chairman '84-87) '83-87; Chairman, North Wiltshire Conservative Association '84-86;
Outlook: Orthodox Rightwing Eurosceptic loyalist; a contractor in plant hire and Wiltshire councillor; a former Portillo supporter who has switched to Peter Lilley; in both the Bow Group and the Freedom Association;

History: He comes from a family of Tory local councillors; he joined the Conservative Party at 19, '75; won a seat on North Wiltshire District Council, becoming its Tory Whip May '83; became Leader of the North Wiltshire District Council, making him the youngest Conservative District Council Leader in the country '84; won a seat on Wiltshire County Council May '85; was re-elected to Wiltshire County Council May '89; selected as prospective candidate for Walsall North, contested it against David Winnick, losing it to a doubled Labour majority Apr '92; was re-elected to Wiltshire County Council May '93; was selected as prospective candidate for Poole in wake of John Ward's announced retirement Dec '94; urged a more Eurosceptic line to keep Conservatives more in touch with public opinion; "I'm a supporter of John Major, but if he was not around I would vote for Michael Portillo; I don't see [John] Redwood as a future Prime Minister and Portillo is more experienced in government; if we had a long period of Opposition he would be a good foil to what Tony Blair's Labour Party was offering" Aug '94; was one of 59 Tory prospectives who told the DAILY TELEGRAPH that their manifestos would favour ruling out Britain's entry into a single European currency during the next Parliament Dec '96; retained the seat by a majority of 5,298, a notional swing to the LibDems of 7.2% May '97; joined the Leadership campaign team of Peter Lilley May-June '97; in his Maiden, welcomed Poole's acquiring unitary status and promised to back a new bridge over Holes Bay June '97; co-sponsored motions denouncing Nigel Griffiths, Labour's Consumer Minister, for remarks about the travel industry which pre-empted an investigation by the Monopolies and Mergers Commission July '97; in his criticism of Labour's first Budget, did not deviate an iota from the standard Tory line July '97; was named to the Select Committee on Health July '97;
Born: 15 August 1956, Chippenham, Wiltshire
Family: Son, of Raymond Syms, building contractor and plant hirer, and Mary (Brain) school teacher and college lecturer; m '91 'Nicky'/Nicola (Guy), her husband's private secretary;
Education: Colston's Prep School '61-70; Colston's School, Bristol, '70-75 (2 A-levels, History and Economics); Road Haulage Managers' Certificate (CPC);
Occupation: Managing Director, of Saltersford Plant Ltd (family building and plant hire firm employing 75 people) in Chippenham, Wilts; Director: Marden Investments Ltd (property company), C Syms & Sons Ltd;
Traits: Dark, parted hair; pudgy blunt round face; hatchet-face; enjoys tennis, swimming and foreign travel;
Address: House of Commons, Westminster, London SW1A 0AA; 10 Sunridge Shades, Belle Vue Road, Poole BH14 8TW;
Telephone: 0171 219 4601 (H of C); 01202 718078 (home); 0249 650401 (business);

AN EXTENSION OF MPS
MPs have developed an added dimension, called researchers. Until recently only more sophisticated MPs used them. Or were used by them. One former Northwest MP, suddenly seemed fascinated with by Trans-Pacific trade, according to questions in his name. These were planted by his research assistant, an American PhD-aspirant, writing his dissertation with the help of answers provided by UK civil servants. Recently the number of questions has increased by a third, as researchers vie with lobbyists and cause groupies. One now has to distinguish between MPs' questions and those planted on them. Our monitoring does so.

Dari (Jean) TAYLOR **Labour** **STOCKTON SOUTH '97-**

Majority: 11,585 over Conservative 4-way;
Description: A slightly-altered, increasingly middle-class Teesside marginal, 'til '45 represented by Harold Macmillan; recently, it has experiencecd "awful changes" as a result of the contraction of its industrial base: "in some parts 50% of the residential area has no one in work" (DT); once called Thornaby, a former Labour MP turned SDPer, Ian Wrigglesworth, cast a long shadow; he was followed by Irish Tory barrister Tim Devlin, '87-97;
Position: On the Select Committee on Defence '97-; Sunderland City Counciillor '86-; Chairman, Domestic Violence Multi-Agency Forum '92-; on Northern Arts Board '92-, Wearside Women in Need '88-;
Outlook: Energetic Left-of-Centre Fabian ex-CNDer; as a "committed trade unionist, [is] not wholly reliable from [the Labour] leadership's point of view" (RED PEPPER); won her key seat with the help of the GMB, by whom she has been employed since '90; during the election she committed herself to giving priority to the renationalisation of the water industry; the Welsh-born daughter of late Dan Jones, former Labour MP for Burnley; a former further education teacher and lecturer, recently in charge of the GMB's regional education and equality programmes;
History: She grew up in the family of a Welsh miner, Dan Jones, who became an MP when she was 15, '59; she attended the Commons to hear her father and the PM, Harold Macmillan, until '45 the MP for Stockton; she joined the Labour Party '60; became Secretary for Abbey Ward party in Nottingham West '70; she supported the foundation, in Washington New Town, of the 'Bridge' training project to facilitate the entry of young women into college '84; was elected to Sunderland City Council May '86; she was active in regenerating her ward in Sunderland, in which 160 sub-standard houses were knocked down; with the money generated from sales of land to the private sector and in partnership with a housing association, 90 new and affordable private homes were built and housing improvements were carried out over a three-year period '90-93; she was selected from an all-women's short-list which the Stockton South party originally resented Feb '95; she later admitted that she had faced "a level of anger and opposition" at first; but "once the procedures began, it went through remarkably smoothly because it was party and conference policy" Apr '95; she started with an electorate of which a quarter were undecided; she soon had her Tory opponent on the run by proposing better school funding and, more controversially, by opposing a water sports centre on the Tees; she was one of 16 Labour candidates with express support from the GMB; during the campaign told the INDEPENDENT that public trust in politicians was at a low level: "people won't change their opinions; I know that; we politicians are going to have to prove that they can trust us; winning the election is going to be the easy part" Apr '97; talking to local sixth formers at Conyers Comprehensive, she was asked whether Labour would spend more on education; she replied: "people always ask us for more money and I'd like to promise more money for schools but other people are asking me for money for renationalisation of water and railways and they would be my priorities; there are many varied and competing priorities -sadly there is limited finance for any of these" Apr '97; she won the seat, on a notional swing of 15.8% by 11,585, ousting Tim Devlin after 10 years May '97; questioned Defence Secretary

George Robertson on the banning of anti-personnel mines June '97; co-sponsored motion applauding the promised improvement in breast cancer treatment June '97; co-sponsored motion attacking prescription fraud June '97; was named to the Select Committee on Defence July '97; in her Maiden urged the utilities to bury their lines, instead of spoiling her constituents' visual outlook with their invasive pylons July '97; ridiculed the idea that women were not strong enough for the services, pointing out that her five-foot-tall mother had worked as a nurse for 15 years, "lifting very heavy dead weights" Oct '97;
Born: 13 December 1944, Rhondda, South Wales
Family: Daughter, of late Dan Jones, former miner and Labour MP for Burnley '59-83, and Phyllis (Williams), nurse; m '70, Dr David Taylor, Metallury Lecturer and Acting Director, of the School of Engineering and Advanced Technology at Sunderland University; 1d Philippa '80;
Education: Ynyshir Girls' School, Rhondda; Burnley Municipal College; Nottingham University, '67-70 where she met her husband; (BA Hons in Politics); Durham University '88-90 (MA in Social Policy);
Occupation: Regional Education Officer, GMB '90-97; previously: Lecturer, in Nottingham Further Education College '86-90, '71-80;
Traits: Dark; specs; full head of hair, recently restyled; plain, school-mistressy look; "she has a new hairdo and wears suits" (former opponent, ex-MP Tim Devlin); "relaxed and friendly" (Steve Hilton, NORTHERN ECHO); had council estate youngsters singing, "We love you Dari, we do"; "workaholic" (close observers quoted by her husband); generous (offered colleague a bed or floor space in the Pimlico flat she was hoping to take over from former Labour MP Jack Thompson)
Address: House of Commons, Westminster, London SW1A 0AA; the family lived in Houghton-le-Spring but moved to Stockton South: 46 Yarm Road, Stockton-on-Tees TS18 3NG;
Telephone: 0171 219 4608 (H of C); 0191 584 1164 (home); 0370 482142 (mobile); 01426 200876 (pager); 01642 760965 (constituency);

David TAYLOR Labour & Co-operative LEICESTERSHIRE NORTH WEST '97-

Majority: 13,219 over Conservative 4-way;
Description: A largely unaltered East Midlands marginal astride the M1, beside the East Midlands airport; it is based on a district in the moderate former Leicestershire coalfield, its largest town is Coalville; it also contains fascinating-sounding Ashby-de-la-Zouch, the setting of 'Ivanhoe'; the constituency's greatest excitement in '94-95 was the exposure by the SUNDAY TIMES and the subsequent libel action against it by its hardworking incumbent Tory MP, David Ashby, over the allegation that he was a practicing homosexual; when his libel action failed, his local party de-selected him;
Position: Press Secretary of the North West Leicestershire TUC '93-97; Heather Parish Councillor '87-97; ex: Northwest Leicestershire District Councillor '92-95, '81-87;
Outlook: A local Christian Socialist, second-time lucky, with the help of the SUNDAY

TIMES; an "independent-minded, forward-looking Leftist," "well-regarded locally" (RED PEPPER); he is a local lay magistrate and churchwarden, a computer-manager, accountant and councillor; is in Greenpeace, Labour Rural Revival, Labour Campaign for Electoral Reform and CPRE;

History: He joined the Labour Party at 24, '70; he was elected to the Northwest Leicestershire District Council May '81; was elected to Heather Parish Council May '87; was selected to contest Leicestershire North West against its Tory incumbent, barrister David Ashby Dec '89; achieving a 5.9% swing, reduced the Tory majority by 7,000 to 979 Apr '92; was again elected to the District Council May '92; was again selected to contest Leicestershire North West Mar '95; Labour won control of the district with the same boundaries as the Parliamentary constituency May '95; won the seat on a 13.5% notional swing, defeating the replacement Tory candidate by a majority of 13,219 May '97; one of his first congratulations came from his former opponent, David Ashby May '97; in his Maiden, praised local initiatives to involve young people in tackling the roots of crime May '97; co-congratulated Leicester for its Space Science Centre June '97; co-congratulated the Co-ops for banning alcopops June '97; expressed solidarity with jailed Indonesian union leader June '97; urged a minimum wage because, with the collapse of local coalmining, "the void left by thousands of lost jobs has often been filled by the arrival of firms paying poverty wages"; "nearly 4,000 people in my area are paid less than £3 an hour", which was "an indictment of the party of exploitation - the Conservative Party" July '97; co-welcomed the arrival of the Nobel Laureate, the Nigerian writer, Professor Wole Soyinka, to give the annual Wilberforce Lecture July '97; backed curbs on open-cast mining July '97; told BBC TV he was unhappy about proposed increased debt burdens on undergraduates, particularly those from poorer homes Sep '97;

Born: 22 August 1946, Ashby-de-la-Zouch

Family: Son, of Leslie Taylor, civil servant, and Eileen (Foukes) postal worker; m '69 Pamela (Caunt); 4d: Rachel '74, Sarah '76, Jessica '79, Catherine '82; 1s David dcd '97;

Education: Heather County Primary; Ashby Boys' Grammar; Leicester Polytechnic; Lanchester Polytechnic; Open University (BA in Maths and Computing); qualified as Accountant; is an Associate of Chartered Institute of Public Finance and Accountancy (AIPFA);

Occupation: Computer Applications Manager, at Leicestershire County Council (NALGO/UNISON: Departmental Convenor in '70s) '77-97; ex: Lecturer, at Charles Keene College, Leicester, and Open University in '70s and '80s;

Traits: Forward-combed thinning hair; crumpled face; specs; enjoys cricket, jogging and marathons;

Address: House of Commons, Westminster, London SW1A 0AA; 14 Main Street, Heather, Coalville, Leicester LE67 2GP;

Telephone: 0171 219 4567 (H of C); 01530 261386 (home); 01530 814372 (constituency);

EXPLOSIONS:

Sometimes an explosion unveils those who rely on our volumes. After the 1994 explosion damaged the Israeli Embassy in London, an eagle-eyed Welsh fan of ours scanned one of the pictures of its damaged interior and spotted a set of these volumes. A similar photograph of the interiors of other embassies would often show the same - foreign diplomats have been among the most enthusiastic about our interest in the positions of MPs on crises abroad, such as the deep split in the Commons over former Yugoslavia.

Gareth THOMAS **Labour** **CLWYD WEST '97-**

Majority: 1,848 over Conservative 6-way;
Description: Contains north Wales' coastal belt from Rhos-on-Sea and Colwyn Bay to the outskirts of Rhyl, including Abergele, Towyn and Kinmel Bay, plus their large but sparsely-populated rural hinterland, stretching as far as the Llyn Brenig reservoir and town of Ruthin, associated with the figure of Owain Glyndwr; it has the most elderly population in Wales, hence the tag 'Costa Geriatrica'; if its vote had followed the '92 pattern, it was expected to go Tory by 7,000;
Position: On the Select Committee on Welsh Affairs '97-; Flintshire County Councillor '95-;
Outlook: The loyalist Liverpool Welsh barrister who ousted Rod Richards, expected to be the last remaining Tory MP in Wales; an enthusiast for Welsh and regional devolution and local economic regeneration; a cause groupie in the Fabians, Amnesty, SERA, Society of Labour Lawyers, Co-operative Party;
History: He joined the Labour Party '86; was elected to Flintshire County Council May '95; was selected for Clwyd West Jan '96; was urged by his LibDem opponent Gwyn Williams to stand down to avoid splitting the anti-Tory vote; Williams said that it was absurd for two candidates supporting constitutional reform to oppose each other Apr '97; Thomas later recalled: "I fought the election on a strongly pro-devolution platform, in contrast to my Conservative opponent [Rod Richards], who maintained an implacable hostility to any concept of devolution" Apr '97; unexpectedly ousted, by a majority of 1,846 on a swing of 11.10%, the controversial incumbent Tory MP - who had resigned as a Minister over a sexual pecadillo - despite strong votes for Plaid Cymru (13.47%) and the LibDems (12.8%) May '97; in his early Maiden speech emphasised the importance of devolution to a Welsh Assembly and to north Wales, and the need for economic regeneration locally, including electrification of the North Wales Coast line May '97; asked for funds to restore Colwyn Bay's Victorian pier May '97; urged local expansion of closed-circuit TV June '97; urged an end to "unnecessary bureaucracy" in the Crown Prosecution Service in the hope of increasing the number of convictions from one in 50, June '97; opposed Plaid's proposal for a multi-option referendum as engendering confusion June '97; opposed repression in Indonesia June '97; accused Tory spokesman David Heathcoat Amory of "extraordinary effrontery" for claiming the Tories were the "pensioners' champions" in view of their imposition of VAT on domestic fuel July '97; loyally supported Labour's first Budget for its "long-termism" and "judicious" backing of environmental protection July '97; was named to Select Commmittee on Welsh Affairs July '97; said the anti-devolution MP Llew Smith represented "a very small minority in the Welsh Labour Party" July '97; urged a "strong and effective European Court of Justice" as "essential to the interests of British industry if it is to take advantage of the Single Market" July '97; was congratulated by Welsh Secretary Ron Davies for "enthusiastically campaigning in north Wales" for a Welsh Assembly July '97;
Born: 25 September 1954, Bangor
Family: Son, late William Thomas, toolmaker, and Megan (Humphreys); m Sioned Wyn (Jones); 1s: '92, 1d '90;
Education: Rock Ferry High School, Birkenhead; University College of Wales, Aberystwyth; Council of Legal Education;

Occupation: Barrister '86-; previously, an International Insurance Loss Adjuster (MSF) '78-86; Associate of Chartered Insurance Institute;
Traits: Parted flat dark-brown hair; specs; a Welsh-speaker, but is not Welsh-accented;
Address: House of Commons, Westminster, London, SW1A 0AA; 3 Fford Trem Y Foel, Mold, Clwyd CH7 1NG;
Telephone: 0171 219 3000 (H of C);

Gareth (Richard) THOMAS **Labour** **HARROW WEST '97-**

Majority: 1,240 over Conservative 4-way;
Description: One of the fashionable middle-class seats least expected to go Labour; an unchanged seat in the outer suburbs of northwest London, mainly middle-class housing occupied by people with middle class jobs; it contains Harrow-on-the-Hill, with its public school, Pinner and Hatch End, what John Betjeman called "the serried avenues of Harrow's garden villages"; it has only 10% of council housing; its fifth of ethnic minorities are mainly Indian entrepreneurs; if voting had repeated '92 patterns, it should have produced a Tory majority of almost 18,000; it was 196th on Labour's target list;
Position: Harrow Borough Councillor (Labour Group Whip '95-97) '90-; Vice Chairman, Association of Local Government Social Services Committees;
Outlook: A record-breaking Labour success story, a locally-born youthful teacher-councillor who achieved an almost 18% swing, overcoming a Tory lead of 32.7%; this made him statistically the least-expected of all new Labour MPs; a multi-cause groupie: in the Fabian Society, Co-operative Party, SERA;
History: He joined the Labour Party at 16, '83; was elected to Harrow Borough Council at 22, May '90; was elected Whip of the Labour Group on Harrow Borough Council at 28, '95; was selected as Labour's candidate for "hopeless" Harrow West against incumbent Tory MP, Robert Hughes, who in '92 had chalked up a majority of 17,890, '95; campaigned on the deterioration of Harrow under the Conservatives: with 14,000 crimes locally in 1996, and a growth of local homelessness and hospital waiting lists Apr '97; unexpectedly ousted incumbent Tory MP Bob Hughes by a majority of 1,240, on an almost record-beaking swing of 17.52%; he captured a seat which was 196th on Labour's target list May '97; with four other local Labour MPs, met Health Minister Alan Milburn to try to save the Accident and Emergency department of Edgware Hospital; they were told they had no hope because there was not enough money May '97; suggested to PM Tony Blair that only collaboration between the Government and industry could "get our young people off the dole and into work" June '97; in Maiden emphasised how job insecurity and bad housing had destabilised local communities, hindering children's development at school, gnawing away at family relationships and fostered social tensions" June '97; backed attack on prescription fraud June '97; joined in congratulating London's Peabody Trust for installing solar power in Docklands housing association scheme June '97; urged more training of teachers in information technology July '97;
Born: 15 July 1967, Harrow, London

Family: Son of Sue and Howard Thomas, teacher;
Education: Pinner Park First and Middle Primary; Hatch End High School; University College of Wales, Aberystwyth (BSc Hons Econ; PGCE); King's College, London (MA in Imperial and Commonwealth History);
Occupation: Teacher, at Willesden High School (NUT) '92-96;
Traits: Dark hair; specs; heart-shaped face; of Welsh origins; enjoys canoeing, running and theatre;
Address: House of Commons, Westminster, London SW1A 00A; 1 Church Drive, North Harrow, Middx HA2 7NP;
Telephone: 0171 219 3000 (H of C); 0181 866 2253/2738 (Fax) (constituency office);

William ('Willie') THOMPSON **Ulster Unionist** **TYRONE WEST '97-;**

Majority: 1,161 over SDLP 6-way;
Description: Northern Ireland's additional new seat: a rural, predominantly Catholic seat in the west, made up of the handsome town of Omagh and less-handsome Strabane; three-quarters has been taken from Mid-Ulster, with the area around the town of Strabane coming from Foyle; it was rated a three-way marginal between the UUP-SDLP-Sinn Fein on the basis of the vote in this area in the Forum election of '96; this showed the SDLP slightly ahead of Sinn Fein, both on 28%, with the UUP trailing a poor third with 18%, and the DUP in fourth place;
Position: On the Executive of Ulster Unionists; ex: Chairman, of Mid-Ulster Ulster Unionists; Northern Ireland Assemblyman (Chairman of Finance '82-84) '82-86, '73-74; in the Northern Ireland Convention '75-76; Omagh Town Councillor;
Outlook: The hard-line old local Ulster Unionist warhorse, with 30 years of political experience, who has become an opponent of more flexible David Trimble; he managed to squeak in between the battling, evenly-matched SDLP and Sinn Fein in a Catholic-majority seat; he was helped by the DUP pulling out, thus avoiding splitting the Protestant/Unionist minority vote; "if elected to Westminster he will surely realise it might be prudent not to take out a lease on a London flat for any longer than five years" (Michal Simpson, BELFAST TELEGRAPH); a strong supporter of the Orange Order ("I make no apology for belonging...to the Orange Institution"); "everyone knows Willie Thompson and thinks he is decent" (Matthew Engel, GUARDIAN);
History: He joined the Ulster Unionist Party; he was elected to Omagh Town Council; he was elected to the Northern Ireland Assembly May '73; he was elected to the Northern Ireland Convention May '75; he was again elected to the Northern Ireland Assembly May '82; he was selected by the Ulster Unionists to contest the new seat of West Tyrone Mar '97; the Rev Ian Paisley pulled out his DUP candidate from West Tyrone, Oliver Gibson, "to help defeat the Sinn Fein", since the combined Unionist vote in West Tyrone was 34% and each of the Catholic parties had had 28% in the previous year's Forum election Apr '97; after the DUP pulled out, Thompson was able to attract Protestant/Unionist support by campaigning on the slogan, "Stop Sinn Fein - Vote Thompson" Apr '97; he won the seat by a majority of 1,161, 34.5% of the votes, with the SDLP and Sinn Fein splitting the 63% Catholic/Nationalist votes

almost evenly May '97; asked when the Labour Government would "extend democratic local government in Northern Ireland and reduce the number of non-elected quangos" May '97; asked PM Tony Blair that, since he basked in Labour's mandate, had "he noticed the proportionately greater mandate received by the [Ulster] Unionist Party in Northern Ireland, where we received 13 seats out of 18 and more than 50% of the vote?" June '97; in his Maiden said he had never expected to become an MP until a new seat was created in the area in which he had lived "all my life" June '97; complained about the EU rejection of an end to the beef ban because Northern Ireland exported "a greater percentage of its meat than does any other part of the United Kingdom" and its cattle had "enhanced computer traceabililty" June '97; defended the Orange Order tactics on parades when complaining that Labour's new Public Order (Northern Ireland) Bill required 21 days' notice of such parades, unlike the situation on the mainland; the Orange Order, he insisted, included "some of the best people", "some of the most honest and most respectable", who had "played a noble part in two world wars of 1914-18 and 1939-45"; he insisted that the Orange Order "does not march though Roman Catholic estates", only on the public highway, which might go alongside such estates; "because of changing population", alterations had had to take place; but now the IRA had "discovered that if they gather a crowd and threaten to sit down in the road, the police, rather than allowing the parade to go ahead, will stop it," thus conniving at a "direct attack on our Protestant ethos and culture" June '97; said, "I don't believe the UUP should sit with any paramilitary organisation which has guns" Aug '97; attacked UUP Leader David Trimble for his "absolutely ridiculous" and "bizarre" tactics leading to joining negotiations with the Sinn Fein Sep '97; complained that Sinn Fein was objecting to Remembrance Day parades Oct '97;
Born: 26 October 1939, Omagh
Family: No family details have been disclosed;
Education: Omagh Academy;
Occupation: Proprietor of a local radio-TV firm: "rents TVs from his village just outside Omagh, and has done so for 30 years" (Matthew Engel, GUARDIAN);
Traits: Grey retreating flat hair; specs; Ulster country accent; semi-articulate; tends to cock his head when speaking; Methodist lay preacher;
Address: House of Commons, Westminster, London SW1A 0AA;
Telephone: 0171 219 3000 (H of C);

Mark TODD — Labour — DERBYSHIRE SOUTH '97-

Majority: 13,967 over Conservative 5-way;
Description: The seat best known for its celebrity MPs: recently Edwina Currie and, under its previous name of Belper, George Brown; it covers a large area to the south and west of Derby; it is centred on Swadlincote, formerly a mining town and the centre of the south Derbyshire coalfield; many of its workers are now employed in the new £700m Toyota plant located there; in '95 it lost a middle-class residential ward to Derby South; Mrs Currie knew long in advance she had little chance of surviving '97;
Position: On Select Committee on Agriculture '97-; ex: Cambridge City Councillor (Leader '87-90, Deputy Leader '82-87) '80-92;

Outlook: Thoughtful, Cambridge-based Centre-Left former publishing executive; now a publishing consultant capable of cross-examining ministers about the payroll management systems purchased; a sensible would-be reformer of the CAP and CSA; allegedly "a known Blairite" (Job Rabkin, INDEPENDENT); grandson of a Tory MP; in Labour Finance and Industry Group, Fabian Society, Labour Co-ordinating Committee, Labour Campaign for Electoral Reform, Labour Party Rural Revival, Co-operative Party, Greenpeace;

History: He joined the Labour Party at 19, '74; he joined MSF in '77; was elected to Cambridge City Council May '80; became Deputy Leader of Cambridge City Council May '82; Leader of Cambridge City Council May '87; was selected to contest Derbyshire South against Edwina Currie May '90; fought the campaign as a loyal Kinnockite Mar '92; lost Derbyshire South by 4,658 but more than halved Edwina Currie's majority from 10,311 on a swing of 4.6% Apr '92; was re-selected for Derbyshire South Aug '95; kissed Edwina Currie on the cheek when he won the seat on a notional swing of 13.2%, by a majority of 13,967, ending her 14-year reign May '97; in his Maiden, he urged making the Commons more "family-friendly" because his grandfather had been an MP and this had impinged on his son; he wanted to see as much of his own four-year-old as possible; he complained that his constituency had many part-timers, who would be helped by a minimum wage; he also argued for more resources for the local police May '97; urged "a free market in agricultural products throughout the world" as "greatly favoured by many south Derbyshire farmers and other progressive farmers in this country" June '97; asked when capping of the budgets of local authorities would end June '97; co-sponsored motion backing an updating of laws on gays and lesbians July '97; urged improved 'phone access to Child Support Agency July '97; co-urged Government to be tougher on "road crime" July '97; was named to the Select Committee on Agriculture July '97; urged reform of Derby criminal courts, to separate witnesses from criminals and their friends July '97;

Born: 29 December 1954, Dorchester, Dorset

Family: His grandfather, Capt Alfred Todd, was the Conservative MP for Berwick-upon-Tweed '29-35; son, of Matthew Todd, RN officer then civil servant, and Vivienne (Tetlow) ex-Wren; m '79 Sarah (Dawson), Director of a medical communications business; 1s Peter '92;

Education: Sherborne School; Emmanuel College, Cambridge University (BA 2:1 in History) where he started the Cambridge Rock Music Competition;

Occupation: Consultant on publishing '97-; ex: UK Operations Manager, for Longmans (large international publishers for whom he managed warehousing, computing, customer services and building management; previously responsible for new business development) (MSF) '77-96; ex: Director, of the Cambridge and District Co-operative Society '86-89;

Traits: Dark brown, backswept hair; grey-brown moustache; bags under eyes; "rumpled", "pensive", "listens", "expounds Labour policy with friendly gravitas" (Hugh O'Shaughnesy, OBSERVER); a rock music enthusiast; enjoyed squash;

Address: House of Commons, Westminster, London SW1A 0AA; 30 Park Close, Linton, Swadlincote, Derbyshire DE12 6QB; East Barn, 40A South Street, Comberton, Cambridge CB3 7DU;

Telephone: 0171 219 3549 (H of C); 01223 264236 (home); 01283 761102; 01283 551573 (constituency);

Dr Jenny TONGE **Liberal Democrat** **RICHMOND PARK '97-**

Majority: 2,951 over Conservative 7-way;

Description: The renamed and more Tory-leaning version of the old Tory-Liberal marginal: historic, green and affluent Richmond and Barnes; for the new seat, one-third (26,000 voters) has been added from equally middle-class north Kingston, whose erasure sent Norman Lamont scuttling, finally and fatally, to Harrogate; in its previous form, the seat was the most dramatic demonstration of a highly-educated and well-heeled electorate preferring LibDems for local government services while voting narrowly for Conservative central government for low taxes; '97 changed that;

Position: Select Committee on International Development '97-; LibDem Spokesman on International Development '97-; ex: Richmond and Barnes Councillor (Chairman of Social Services '83-87) '81-90;

Outlook: A veteran local community health doctor and local councillor who has made it the second time round; "a Leftwinger" (Tory ex-MP Jeremy Hanley) on the LibDems' social-democratic wing; fervently pro-NHS; one of the early and outspoken supporters of tactical voting; "one of Ashdown's favourite women" (TIMES); practical: "the essence of giving women choice is childcare - we need a national strategy" (JT); in Friends of Earth, Amnesty International, RSPB;

History: She joined the Liberal Party at university '59; was elected for Kew to Richmond Borough Council May '81; became Chairman of Richmond Council's Social Services Committee May '83; was selected for Richmond and Barnes, a top LibDem target seat '89; successfully moved a motion at annual LibDem conference calling for the introduction of basic forms of investment tuition into the education curriculum Sep '91; favoured child care vouchers Mar '92; lost Richmond to Jeremy Hanley by 3,869 votes, a swing from LibDems to Tories of 2.3% Apr '92; at the LibDem conference at Harrogate after her defeat, publicly thanked Green and Labour voters for "for setting aside their party allegiances" enabling her to squeeze Labour's vote to the lowest in the country; LibDems had to be prepared to do the same to oust Tories Sep '92; she was short-listed to contest the Eastleigh by-election as "one of Ashdown's favourite women" Mar '94; she was re-selected to contest the altered seat of Richmond Park, with additional Tory voters coming in from dismantled Kingston Feb '95; reiterating her enthusiasm for the NHS, for which she had worked for 30 years, pointed out that her "lovely" husband had been saved by it the winter before Sep '96: insisted that "people are not confident about the economy" Mar '97; in her campaign literature, again tried squeezing the Labour vote with bar graphs and the exhortation "It's a two-horse race"; she also warned: "NHS funding has been squeezed in recent years; locally, Queen Mary's Hospital is once again under threat and Kingston Hospital is stretched; the Liberal Democrats want patients put before profits" Apr '97; won the seat on a notional swing of 9.7% by a majority of 2,951 over the popular Tory, Jeremy Hanley, its MP for 14 years May '97; in her Maiden worried about local hospital services, noise and air pollution, especially the proposed 5th Heathrow terminal June '97; urged a "no-fault medical accident compensation scheme" instead of huge medical negligence payments June '97; co-sponsored motion attacking organophosphates June '97; expressed support for jailed Indonesian union leader June '97; criticised Chinese repression in Tibet June '97; urged help to Afghan women June '97; opposed charging school parties for museum entry June '97; as the new LibDem spokesman on International Development urged the new Labour Government to tackle poverty first July '97; co-sponsored all-party motion urging an updating of laws on gay men and lesbians July '97; co-sponsored all-party motion opposing a 12-lane superhighway to proposed Terminal 5 at Heathrow July '97; warned against "a slide to privatisation" in clinical health care through PFI building of hospitals July '97; prodded new Labour Government on arms exports to Indonesia July '97; was named to the Select Committee on International Development July '97; co-sponsored motion urging more ecumenical prayers in Commons July '97; urged full British citizenship for inhabitants of Montserrat Aug '97;

Born: 19 February 1941, Walsall, Staffs

Family: Daughter, of Sidney Smith, schoolmaster, and Violet Louise (Williams); m '64 Keith Angus Tonge, Consultant Neuro-Radiologist at St Thomas' Hospital ("we met over a corpse on a dissecting table"); 2s David '68, Richard '76, 1d Mary '70;

Education: Princes End Primary, Tipton, Staffs; Dudley Girls' High School; University College, London University, and UCH Medical School (MB, BS '64, MFCH '90; MFFP '94);

Occupation: Ex: Clinical Medical Officer, (family planning) Brandon Centre NW5 '88-91; Senior Clinical Medical Officer, (Women's Services) Ealing Health Authority '83-88; in the NHS '64-97;

Traits: Red-brown, straight hair; pleasant, intelligent, lived-in face; thin mouth; quick-witted; articulate; sultry voice; middle-class speech; when she was first selected, admitted she "had to abandon my clinic clothes and sort out my untidy hair"; objects to importing Continental-style kissing, preferring handshakes: "a handshake is far more personal as you look at the person when you shake their hand"; an "old bruiser" (ex-MP Jeremy Hanley);

Address: House of Commons, Westminster, London SW1A 0AA; 28 Kew Gardens Road, Richmond TW9 3HD, Surrey;

Telephone: 0171 219 4596 (H of C); 0181 948 1649 (home); 0181 332 7919 (LibDem HQ); 0589 276988 (mobile); 0181 832 7919 (Fax);

Paul (Anthony) TRUSWELL | Labour | PUDSEY '97-

Majority: 6,207 over Conservative 4-way;

Description: Unaltered West Yorkshire middle-class dormitory seat on the edge of Leeds, on the Bradford side; the gateway to Ilkley Moor and the Yorkshire dales, it is the birthplace of many famous Yorkshire cricketers, including Len Hutton and Ray Illingworth; its exports are Silver Cross prams and Harry Ramsden's fish and chips; it was held by Conservatives from '22, the last six times by its genial, shrewd little former Tory MP, Sir Giles Shaw; the decline of Conservative support was thought to threaten to return it to its 1974 status as a three-way marginal;

Position: Leeds City Councillor (Chairman, its Community Benefits and Rights Committee, Secretary its Labour Group '94-97) '82-; ex: on Family Health Services Authority '92-96, Community Health Council '90-92, Leeds Health Authority '82-90;

Outlook: The local ex-journalist and crusader for health and environment improvements and

freedom of information who ended 75 years of Conservative reign; the son of a steelworker and cleaner; a "widely-respected principled Leftwinger and canny politician who will choose his moment to assert his independence" (RED PEPPER): a supporter of Liberty, SERA and the Socialist Health Association; "my flights of independence and martyrdom have largely been at local level" (PT)
History: He was born into a Labour-leaning family; he joined the Labour Party at 22, '77; was elected to Leeds City Council at 26, May '82; as Chairman of the Leeds City Council's Freedom of Information Committee was instrumental in Leeds' securing the National Freedom of Information Campaign Award '86; was Yorkshire Regional Press Officer in the general election Mar-Apr '92; as Chairman of the Leeds Green Strategy Group, helped Leeds' designation as the Environment City '92; was selected to contest Pudsey Jan '95; won Pudsey on a swing of 13.2% by a majority of 6,207, ending a 75-year reign by Conservatives May '97; in his Maiden, he disclosed that he had been brought up in a council house and that Leeds, which had built 1,200 council houses in '79-80, was no longer able to build any; "about £750m is needed by Leeds to put its housing stock in order" June '97; urged strategic planning of further education, especially where colleges were in competition June '97; urged access to "high-quality" jobs for his long-term unemployed, instead of the "the ragbag of often Mickey Mouse schemes" previously offered by the Tories July '97;
Born: 17 November 1955, Sheffield
Family: Son, of John Truswell, retired steelworker, and Olive (Turner) retired cleaner; m '81 Suzanne (Evans) civil servant; 2s: Richard '89, Michael '92;
Education: Ecclesfield County Primary; Firth Park Comprehensive; Leeds University (BA Hons in History);
Occupation: Local Government Officer: Principal Planning Manager, Social Services Department, on Wakefield Metropolitan District Council (UNISON '95-97/NUPE '88-95) '88-97; ex: Journalist, on YORKSHIRE POST (NUJ) '77-88; Labourer, in Firth Brown Steelworks '74;
Traits: Brown retreating hair; tall; witty; refreshingly modest (does not keep his own press cuttings, only "those on my opponents; perhaps the conceit required will come with practice"); thinks himself unexciting; enjoys gardening, photography and sports - when dragooned by his children;
Address: House of Commons, Westminster, London SW1A 0AA;
Telephone: 0171 219 3504 (H of C);

Des(mond) TURNER **Labour** **BRIGHTON-KEMPTOWN '97-**

Majority: 3,534 over Conservative 9-way;
Description: The plebeian east end of Brighton, afflicted with very heavy unemployment and homelessness; within its former boundaries it was the only Sussex marginal ever taken by Labour, in '64 and '66; it was thought immunised by the '95 boundary changes; these brought in neighbouring Tory-leaning coastal towns of Saltdean and Peacehaven from the Lewes constituency; this may have been counterbalanced by the 'sleaze' allegations which overlay the election campaign against the incumbent Tory MP, Sir Andrew Bowden '70-97;
Position: On the Select Committee on Science and Technology '97-; East Sussex County Councillor '85-; Brighton Borough Councillor '94-, Brighton and Hove Unitary Councillor '96-;
Outlook: The biochemist who is the first Labour MP to represent Kemptown since the late Dennis Hobden ('64-70); because of his professional background, he is preoccupied with health questions; he is enterprising enough to have started a brewery when research funds dried up; in the Fabian Society and Co-operative Party;
History: He joined the Labour Party at '76; contested hopeless Mid-Sssex against Tim Renton, coming 3rd with 15.5% of the vote May '79; he was elected to East Sussex County Council May '85, where he concentrated on social services; he was elected to Brighton Borough Council May '94; was selected for Kemptown Nov '95; he was elected to Brighton and Hove Unitary Authority May '96; the campaign was overlain by accusations that his opponent, Sir Andrew Bowden, had accepted money from Mohammed al-Fayed via lobbyist Ian Greer Mar-Apr '97; Turner captured Kemptown on a 13.9% swing by 3,534 votes, ending Sir Andrew Bowden's 27-year reign; Sir Andrew said he could not have held the seat in a Labour landslide May '97; in his Maiden, Turner claimed the election of a Labour Government and its Queen's Speech had given great hope to his constituents, very many of whom were unemployed and homeless; "we must go back to building low-cost accommodation that people can afford; if we are to take people off the streets, we must have somewhere to put them" May '97; asked about progress in clearing up bathing water on the coast June '97; expressed solidarity with jailed Indonesian union leader June '97; backed ban on fox-hunting June '97; urged tackling the problems of the Child Support Agency with the "greatest urgency" because its problems preoccupied so many MPs; he thought Peter Lilley had shown "outrageous impudence" to expect the new Labour Government to clear up within weeks the mess he had left after presiding "over the first five years of the Child Support Agency"; he was "agnostic" about how to sort out the mess, whether to reform it within its existing framework or tear it up and start from scratch; he was sure its staff should not be cut and payments to parents with care should be guaranteed; the abolition of penalties should be considered because "that does not penalise the parents but the children" June '97; was named to the Select Committee on Science and Technology July '97; led a motion urging no-fault compensation for road accidents Oct '97;
Born: 17 July 1939, Southampton
Family: Son, of Stanley Turner, aircraft engineer, and Elsie (Morris); m 1st Lynette (Gwyn-Jones), a Brighton and Hove Councillor); 1d Olivia '69; divorced '87; m 2nd '97 Lynn (Rogers), formerly his partner;

Education: Luton Grammar School, Luton; Imperial College (BSc), University College, London University (MSc PhD); Brighton University (PGCE); ARICS:
Occupation: Biochemist: Free-lance Researcher, Writer and Supply Teacher (MSF) '78-97; Medical Research Scientist (as a Fellow at Sussex University did research on diabetes and obesity) '64-78; Owner, of a small brewery in Brighton (when funding grew scarce for his research);
Traits: Parted grey hair; rounded face; specs; "fluent" (Tory MP Piers Merchant); enjoys fencing, dinghy-racing, music and tripping to Dieppe;
Address: House of Commons, Westminster, London SW1A 0AA; 49 Queen's Park Terrace, Brighton BN2 2TB;
Telephone: 0171 219 4024 (H of C); 01273 330610;

George TURNER **Labour** **NORFOLK NORTH WEST '97-**

Majority: 1,339 over Conservative 4-way;
Description: An unaltered, largely-agricultural seat, with some light industry in King's Lynn; under that last name it was held by Labour when in office '45-51 and '64-70; since it was taken by the Tories it has had a peculiar history, particularly when Christopher Brocklebank-Fowler became the only Tory MP to defect to the new Social Democrats in '81; standing for the SDP he was heavily defeated by Henry Bellingham in '83, but held the Labour vote down to 3rd place; it only began to come up in '92, when Labour resumed 2nd place, but was then still over 11,000 votes behind;
Position: Norfolk County Councillor (Leader, Labour Group '85-90) 77-; on the Norfolk Police Authority;
Outlook: Another unexpected Labour newcomer, elected with the help of the Referendum Party; despite this, he is trying to get better roads to the East Coast Channel ports; a dispassionate analyst of facts, not inclined to emotional excesses; a county councillor and university lecturer in electronic engineering; in the Socialist Educational Association and the Co-operative Party;
History: He joined the Labour Party at 20, '60; he was elected to Norfolk County Council May '77; became Labour's spokesman on Education on Norfolk Council May '79; became Leader of the Labour Group on Norfolk Council May '85; stopped being Leader of the Labour Group and resumed his role as Education Spokesman on Norfolk Council May '90; was first selected to contest Norfolk North West '90; on election day he pushed the Liberal Democrat into 3rd place, but remained 11,564 behind the Tory incumbent, Henry Bellingham Apr '92; was re-selected for Norfolk North West, which ranked 107th on Labour's target list '95; in the election campaign kept his head down - "a quiet figure" according to Jonathan Hartley of the LYNN NEWS - while the well-financed local Referendum Party was busy seducing mainly Tory voters; with the help of 2,923 predominantly-Tory voters defecting to the Referendum Party, Turner unexpectedly captured Norfolk North West by a majority of 1,339 on a swing of 10.4%, ousting Henry Bellingham after 14 years May '97; as the former Chairman of Norfolk's Education Committee welcomed the abandonment of the Tories' wasteful nursery voucher scheme which had been tested in Norfolk May '97; asked Education Secretary David Blunkett

what resources would be offered for schools to produce their development plans July '97; asked Northern Ireland Secretary Mo Mowlam "the basis on which she is looking for the removal of illegal weapons from Northern Ireland" July '97; complained that industries in Kings Lynn and East Anglia ports - as well as endangered pedestrians - were suffering badly from the role of the area as the "Cinderella" of the country's transport development July '97; was encouraged by Home Secretary Jack Straw's determination to punish anti-social behaviour, but concerned about securing witnesses "when they can so readily be threatened by those among whom they live" July '97; said his pro-hunting constituents were divided on why it was necessary and exaggerating wildly the impact of a ban on fox-hunting Oct '97;
Born: 9 August 1940, Corby, Northants
Family: He was married and divorced; they had two children;
Education: Laxton Grammar School, Oundle; Imperial College, London University (BSc); Caius College, Cambridge University (PhD in Physics);
Occupation: Lecturer, in Electronic Engineering, at East Anglia University (AUT) til '97;
Traits: Parted white hair, with dark eyebrows; has a dynamic manner when speaking; enjoys swimming (a qualified swimming judge) and watching cricket and football;
Address: House of Commons, Westminster, London SW1A 0AA; 78 Chapel Street, Kings Lynn PE30 1EF (constituency); 278 Unthank Road, Norwich NR2 2AJ (home);
Telephone: 0171 219 3000 (H of C);

(John) Derek TWIGG **Labour** **HALTON '97-**

Majority: 23,650 over Conservative 6-way;
Description: The slightly-altered union of older Widnes and newer Runcorn, linked by the bridge over the Mersey and dominated by the chemical industry, particularly ICI-Zeneca; demanning has created heavy unemployment, especially among the young; now Labour's safest seat in Cheshire, it was previously in Lancashire;
Position: Halton Borough Councillor (Education Spokesman '96-, Finance Chairman '93-96, Housing Chairman, '87-93) '83-; ex: Cheshire County Councillor '81-85;
Outlook: A wholly-local big frog on Halton Borough Council who inherited the place vacated in the bigger Westminster pond by Gordon Oakes; recently a union consultant, but long a local civil servant in Employment;
History: He joined the Labour Party '79; was elected to Cheshire County Council May '81; was elected to Halton Borough Council May '83; was elected Chairman of Housing on Halton Council May '87; was elected Chairman of Finance on Halton Borough Council May '93; after the announced retirement of Halton's veteran Labour MP, Gordon Oakes, was selected as his successor Jan '96; was the Education spokesman in the bid for a Halton Unitary Authority '95; won Halton on a notional swing of 11.9% by a majority of 23,650, almost twice that of the previous election May '97; in his Maiden spoke of the "massive land contamination" left by his seat's dominating chemical industry; "through the fantastic efforts of the borough council and the local community, that situation has been transformed by a large land reclamation programme over the past 20 years; where once were the most polluted tracts of land in the

country, we now have a superb shopping centre, a golf course, open spaces and parkland"; he pleaded for a second bridge over the Mersey and more skills-training to mop up 24% adult unemployment and 40% youth unemployment June '97; welcomed the windfall tax on utilities because "in my constituency, 44% of young people do not have a job and are not in training or at college" July '97;

Born: 9 July 1959, Widnes

Family: Son, of Kenneth Twigg, rtd chemical process worker, and Irene (Gallagher) rtd school dinner lady; he is married with two children;

Education: Bankfield High School, Widnes; Halton College of Further Education, Widnes;

Occupation: Political Consultant, to the Public Services, Tax and Commerce Union (PST) '95-; ex: Civil Servant, in Department of Education and Employment (resigned when he was selected as a candidate) (GMB and PTC) '74-95;

Traits: Dark, parted hair; shaved off his moustache in '95; is a Liverpool Football Club supporter; enjoys walking, sports and reading history;

Address: House of Commons, Westminster, London SW1A 0AA; 76 Victoria Road, Widnes, Cheshir WA8 7RA (constituency); 14 Shetland Close, Widnes, Cheshire WA8 3YJ; (home);

Telephone: 0171 219 3554 (H of C); 0151 424 7030/495 3800(Fax) constituency); 0151 423 2505 (home);

Stephen TWIGG **Labour** **ENFIELD-SOUTHGATE '97-**

Majority: 1,433 over Conservative 6-way;

Description: Enfield's most middle-class suburb in the west, on London's border with the Hertfordshire's green belt; it ranges from urban Palmers Greeen to rural Hadley Wood and is composed three-quarters of privately-owned homes, peopled two-thirds by middle-class commuters; this area remained loyal to the Conservatives even in May '94, when Labour took control of the borough of Enfield; even three years later its 15,545 majority was considered so safe by its incumbent Tory MP, Michael Portillo, that he sent his cadres to help in "more-threatened" nearby seats;

Position: Islington Borough Councillor (Deputy Leader '96, Chief Whip '95-96) '92-97; ex: General Secretary of Fabian Society '96-97; President, of the National Union of Students '90-92;

Outlook: The Portillo-Terminator; the young, openly gay and very talented Blairite Fabian 'wunderkind'; he arrived unexpectedly early by defeating Michael Portillo in one of London's safest Tory seats; a supporter of PR for the proposed Greater London authority as well as the Commons; a former protege of Margaret Hodge on Islington Council; "very New Labour", "one to watch" (NEW STATESMAN); "his drive and ambition are legendary" (RED PEPPER); one of the few new Blairite MPs about whom almost everyone he has touched - except the hard-Left, especially TRIBUNE - has only nice things to say; the hard-Left is the exception because he covertly orchestrated the NEC's dumping as candidate for Leeds North East of Islington's semi-Trotskist Liz Davies; in Stonewall, Amnesty, Labour Campaign for Electoral Reform;

History: He came from a Communist family, who brought "me up to believe in tolerance, solidarity and equality" (ST); "I have happy memories of them protesting during the Vietnam war"; he joined the Labour Party at 15, '81; became Secretary of his local branch at 17, '83; at Southgate Comprehensive ran a "vaguely Leftwing school newspaper, PEN & INK" (PRIVATE EYE) and clashed with the new local MP Michael Portillo '84; at 17 was the Enfield delegate to annual conference Oct '84; "Chris Smith's coming out in 1984 helped give me the confidence to come out soon after"; "in 1985, the failure of the miners' strike and the anti-ratecapping campaign convinced me that the hard-Left was politically bankrupt"; while at Balliol on a scholarship, he debated against Edwina Currie MP at the Oxford Union on a motion that the Labour Party was irrelevant to the '90s, winning by two-to-one '87; became the first openly gay President of the National Union of Students '90; opposed student loans; under his leadership the NUS declared that anti-Zionism was often a "cloak" for anti-Semitism; he also pledged support for the campaign on behalf of Soviet Jewry; was elected to Islington Council at a by-election '92; became Research Assistant to Margaret Hodge MP July '94; became Chief Whip of Islington Council '95; "earned much credit with the Labour leadership when he slapped Athur Scargill down at the...Clause IV conference" (EVENING STANDARD) Apr '95; was praised by Tony Blair as one of the party's rising stars '95; admitted he had "expressed an interest" in fighting Michael Portillo; "Enfield-Southgate is my home seat; I still know a lot of people there; my sister is a party member" May '95; unsuccessfully sought election to the Fabian Executive, not mentioning his "involvement with ultra-modernising outfit, Labour 2000" (TRIBUNE) Oct '95; made a scorching counter-attack on a TRIBUNE article "riddled with misrepresentations and inaccuracies" by John Cryer - later his Parliamentary colleague -about his role as Chief Whip on Islington Council; he flatly denied that he had leaked to a Tory MP a report on Islington's educational inadequacies: "indeed, the suggestion that I would have leaked anything to a Tory is laughable and ludicrous; the fact is that Islington's 1995 GCSE results were very poor"; "what matters is that firm action is taken to improve achievements in Islington schools; I am sick to death of hearing the argument that because of their home backgrounds children in inner city areas such as Islington are bound to fail; this dangerous thinking has for too long let down working class children" Feb '96; was in a three-way contest for the Leadership of Islington Council, which he lost to Alan Clinton by one vote, after "a very unpleasant bitter battle" (ST) Apr '96; sought selection for winnable Derbyshire South against Edwina Currie, claiming "I'm getting quite close to being selected" Apr '96; took over as General Secretary of the Fabian Society Aug '96; became Deputy Leader of Islington Council Sep '96; despite becoming its General Secretary, failed to win a place on the Fabian Executive, to the delight of hard-Left TRIBUNE Nov '96; in the GUARDIAN, defended the Blair changes to Labour as in line with those of other democratic socialist parties in western Europe, including the Italian ex-Communists Nov '96; was selected to contest "hopeless" Enfield-Southgate against Michael Portillo Dec '96; wrote to the TIMES: "surely we have progressed beyond the point where serious political opinion can suggest that it is unacceptable for someone to be an MP simply because they are openly gay" Dec '96; predicted a Blair government would be more pro-European than the Tories Jan '97; the Jewish vote in Southgate moved in his favour, according to the JEWISH CHRONICLE, because of his abandonment of anti-Zionism as NUS President; his first intimations of possible victory came when three local secondary schools voted Labour by overwhelming majorities Apr '97; in an astonishing electoral coup - televised nationally - won his home seat, Enfield-Southgate on a notional swing of 17.4% by a majority of 1,433, ending the local Parliamentary career of Michael Portillo May '97; in his Maiden urged proportional representation for the new Greater London authority May '97; asked PM Tony Blair whether he was aware of public concern over the five-fold increase in the number of drug offences May '97; in the GUARDIAN urged PR for local government as well: "the rotten borough undermines local democracy" May '97; backed ban on fox-hunting June '97; expressed solidarity with jailed Indonesian union leader June '97; led motion attacking loss of £100m annually through prescription fraud June '97; co-sponsored motion urging a public inquiry into Westminster Council June '97; co-sponsored motion acclaiming promise of better breast cancer treatment June '97; declined to join "The Unlikely Lads", a club proposed for those new Labour MPs whose elections were wholly unexpected; he said he might join a club with a "serious purpose", "and if it is serious, it shouldn't have a name like that" July '97; at Brighton annual conference backed the party's constitutional changes: "we must show that winning seats like Southgate and Wimbledon was not a flash in the pan but the beginning of a new era" Sep '97;

Born: 25 December 1966, Southgate, Enfield

Family: Son, of Jean and Ian Twigg, insurance clerk. both Communists; he has a younger sister, Paula;

Education: Southgate Comprehensive (Head Boy); Balliol College, Oxford University (Scholarship; BA in PPE);

Occupation: Ex: General Secretary of Fabian Society '96-97; PRman-Lobbyist, in Rowland, Sallingbury, Casey '96-97; Research Assistant, to Margaret Hodge MP '94-95; Political Lobbyist, for Amnesty International and National Council for Volunary Organisations '92-94; President, NUS '90-92, its Vice President '89-90;

Traits: Tall; dark; parted front-falling hair; boyish-looking; sallow complexion; charming; uncynical air; prissy; pays his researchers more adequately than most MPs; "an absolute charmer, an excellent student, the sort of person who's always in school uniform" (his former Southgate headmaster, Peter Targett); enjoys swimming, cinema, TV soaps (especially 'Eastenders');

Address: House of Commons, Westminster, London SW1A 0AA;

Telephone: 0171 219 6554 (H of C);

Andrew TYRIE Conservative CHICHESTER '97-

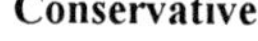

Majority: 9,734 over Liberal Democrat 5-way;

Description: Slightly-altered ultra-safe Conservative seat on West Sussex's border with Hampshire; a basically rural seat rolling down from the South Downs; it includes Midhurst (Cowdray Park), Petworth House, Goodwood, charming Chichester - which makes up a fourth of its population - and many affluent villages;

Position: On the Public Accounts Commission '97-; Secretary, City of London Conservatives '92-; on the Council of Social Market Foundation; ex: Special Adviser: to John Major '89-92, Nigel Lawson '86-89), to Patrick Jenkin and Richard Luce '86-86; Vice Chairman, City of London Conservatives '88-90;

Outlook: "An intellectual with clout and contacts" (NEW STATESMAN); a pro-European who wants a looser, more competitive EU extended well to the east; a self-professed minor Machiavelli who has finally come out of the back rooms into the light of Parliamentary day; a small businessman's Rightwing crusading son who wants: "much less government interference in people's lives, much lower taxes, less regulation from Brussels, tougher action on crime"; as a super-monetarist and former Special Adviser claims to have been innoculating a Prime Minister, successive Chancellors and other Ministers; has finally been rewarded for twenty years of nudging Ministers and Tory activism in pursuit of these views with one of their safest - and most aristocratic - of seats;

History: "I grew up in rural Essex, the son of a furniture retailer; my early experience with the family business helped form many of my political beliefs; I saw my father's business nearly destroyed by socialist legislation in the 1970s"; started as a Tory activist in '75; "briefed Prime Minister Margaret Thatcher personally before all her press conferences during the campaign and wrote the briefings for her"; was "Joint Editor of the 300-page Campaign Handbook" '83; was "co-ordinator of the 1984 European election campaign [at] Central Office"; was "Head of the Economic Team [in the] Research Department, [at] Conservative Central Office, 1983-1984"; was "Special Adviser to Rt Hon Patrick Jenkin MP, Secretary of State for the Environment, [and to] Richard Luce, Minister for Arts 1985-86"; "devised and helped execute the Conservative Party's successful attacks on Labour's tax and spending plans during the 1987 General Election"; was "full-time Adviser to successive Chancellors of the Exchequers, Rt Hon John Major MP and before him, Rt Hon Nigel Lawson MP"; "worked closely with them in the Treasury, giving advice on reducing taxes, particularly income tax, privatisation, encouraging enterprise and cutting red tape 1986-90"; he chaired the press conference that launched John Major's successful Leadership bid Nov '90; learned the inside motives for Continentals wanting EMU when trying to sell John Major's "hard Ecu": over lunch in Paris, a French official told him: "Look, Andrew, we need EMU because that is the only way we can control the Germans; we must get our hands on the Bundesbank and Britain must help us" '91; over lunch in Rome he was told: "You must understand, Andrew, that government in Rome is little short of a disaster; even government from Brussels is better than this" '91: in a pamphlet for the Centre for Policy Studies, urged a closer relationship with Germany and monetary union Mar '91; remained unofficial adviser and speechwriter for John Major until Apr '92; selected to contest hopeless Houghton and Washington against incumbent Labour MP Roland Boyes, claimed that investment had come into the northeast from abroad because "the Conservative Government took the tough decisions Labour had shirked in the 1970s" Jan '92; he managed to keep the Labour majority at 20,000 Apr '92; became Senior Economist at the EBRD (European Bank for Reconstruction and Development, set up to rebuild capitalism in East Europe) '92; was "runner-up for selection of Parliamentary candidate in Suffolk West and Arundel, Spring 1996"; was beaten for selection at West Worthing by Peter Bottomley MP July '96; was finally selected for Chichester - beating David Harris MP and Martin Howe QC - after Tony Nelson belatedly decided to give it up Feb '97; retained the seat with a halved majority of 9,734 over his LibDem challenger after a 7.6% swing to them May '97; in the contest for the Tory Leadership joined the Peter Lilley team May-June '97; in his Maiden insisted on the continued need for reform of the European Union, which had to restore its competitiveness and be extended in a looser form to the east; he also pledged himself to resist most housing developments in his seat June '97; asked about Labour's appointments of political advisers June '97; asked for verbatim minutes of Bank of England's Monetary Committee June '97; urged cut in UK's net contribution to EU June '97; was named to Public Accounts Commission June '97; asked about the admission of Slovenia to NATO July '97; criticised the Budget as political, rushed, and unnecessary July '97; complained about the "massive increase" in UK contribution to the EU budget July '97;

Born: 15 January 1957, Southend-on-Sea, Essex

Family: Son, of a furniture retailer; unmarried

Education: Felsted School, Essex; Trinity College, Oxford University '75-79 (MA in PPE); College of Europe, Bruges '79-80 (Diploma in Economics); Wolfson College, Cambridge

University '80-81 (MPhil in International Relations); Woodrow Wilson Scholar, Smithsonian, Washington '90; Fellow, Nuffield College, Oxford '90-91;
Occupation: Author: 'Prospects for Public Spending' (Social Market Foundation, 1997), 'A Cautionary Tale of EMU' (Centre for Policy Studies 1991), 'Subsidiarity' (Institute for Economic Affairs 1991); Senior Economist, at EBRD '92-97; ex: Consultant to BBC World Service on radio series to explain capitalism to East Europe '92-93; Special Adviser: to John Major '89-92, to Nigel Lawson '86-89, to Patrick Jenkin and Richard Luce '85-86; Head of Economic Team in Research Department of Conservative Central Office '84-86; Trainee, then Group Head Office Press Spokesman of BP '81-83;
Traits: Thin; his high forehead is extended by encroaching baldness; specs; thin nose; protruding chin; gentle and persuasive; golfer (ex-holder of HM Treasury Challenge Cup);
Address: House of Commons, Westminster, London SW1A 0AA; 92 Thomas More House, Barbican, London EC2; also lives in Bosham;
Telephone: 0171 219 3000 (H of C); 0171 638 8051 (Barbican flat);

Dr 'Rudi' (Rudolf Jan) VIS Labour FINCHLEY & GOLDERS GREEN '97-

Majority: 3,189 over Conservative 6-way;
Description: This seat represents the addition in '95 of three wards - strongly-Conservative Golders Green, strongly-Conservative [Hampstead] Garden Suburb and marginal Child's Hill - to Finchley, formerly held by Mrs Thatcher; since this made it an affluent northwest London suburb with a high proportion of Jews, it was thought to be completely safe for John Marshall, the Rightwing Scots Conservative who had made a speciality of doing the bidding of local Zionists and Orthodox Jews; on the basis of the '92 division of votes, he was expected to chalk up a Tory majority of 12,000-plus;
Position: Barnet Borough Councillor (Chairman of Finance '94-97) '86-; ex: Treasurer, Finchley CLP '82-86;
Outlook: Among the most surprised and reluctant of the new Labour 'virgins': the one who initially announced he preferred to keep lecturing in economics to becoming an MP; in the Socialist Education Association '86-; formerly in the Fabians and CND;
History: "I was born in the Netherlands in a town called Alkmaar at the beginning of the war; we were not Jewish, but my father spent most of the war assisting Jews in finding safehouses and farms"; while working in Washington before starting his studies at the University of Maryland, "at the weekends I was outside the Pentagon shouting and protesting against Vietnam"; "I worked for Cesar Chaves, the world-renowned Mexican-American union leader who was battling to improved the lot of the stateless Mexican-Americans"; he came to the UK to study at LSE '70; having been in the Dutch Labour Party, he joined the Labour Party in Harrow on the Hill '71; became Treasurer of the Finchley Constituency Labour Party '82; having been naturalised, he was elected to Barnet Borough Council May '86; on Barnet Council's Planning Committee, he was unsure about the 'Eruv', the self-segregating cordoning-off scheme pushed by some Orthodox Jews in Golders Green, and supported by the constituency's Tory MP, John Marshall; was selected to contest the new "hopeless" seat of Finchley and Golders Green against John Marshall; "we did not give ourselves a hope in hell"

Mar '96; he told local LibDems: "a vote for the Liberal Democrats here, where Golders Green and Hampstead Garden Suburb are traditionally Conservative, is a wasted vote", urging them to vote tactically for him: "we may just beat the Tories in this constituency", pointing to Labour's pledge of a referendum on a different voting system Apr '97; to his surprise and initial dismay, he gained the seat on a notional swing of 15.1% by a majority of 3,189 over John Marshall; he protested: "I have 200 students waiting for me on Tuesday"; he decided to finish his 12 hours of lecturing plus a number of tutorials May '97; he did not think he could resign from Barnet Council, in which there was no overall control: "another Labour Councillor (Joan Ryan, the new MP for Enfield North) is in the same position and if we both resign we would have a minority"; pressed by the Orthodox, the Zionists and the JEWISH CHRONICLE as to whether he would take up their baton, knocked out of John Marshall's hand, he said he was "pro-Israel" though he had not visited it, but would prefer it to be run by its Labour Party, which was more genuinely interested in peace with the Arabs May '97; with other victorious local Labour MPs, who had all campaigned on the issue, was told by Health Minister Alan Milburn that there was no hope of saving the Accident and Emergency department at Edgeware Hospital because of accepted limits in NHS spending May '97; launched a free school milk scheme in a school in Child's Hill, 26 years after the seat's former MP, Margaret Thatcher, had earned the tag of "milk snatcher" June '97; backed a ban on fox-hunting June '97; expressed solidarity with a jailed Indonesian union leader June '97; asked about postal thefts July '97; refused to join "The Unlikely Lads", a club for new Labour MPs unexpectedly elected outside the target seats: "this would be an insult to the many activists in my constituency party who worked so very hard to get me elected and truly believed, despite all the odds, that they could deliver the seat for Labour" July '97;

Born: 4 April 1941, Alkmaar, Netherlands

Family: Son, of Laurens Vis, insurance broker, and Helena (Kraan); m 1st Joan (Hanin) American he met at the University of Madrid; 1s Bram '69, a tax consultant who suffered from dwarfism as a child; divorced '82; his Partner of ten years, Jacqui (Suffling) was the Labour candidate for the Child's Hill council seat; their twin sons, Pip and Tog, were born prematurely in '94 after years of attempts at In Vitro fertilisation;

Education: Primary school, Alkmaar; High School, Alkmaar til '60; University of Maryland (BSc Econ 1st Class Hons) '70; LSE (MSc Econ) '72; Brunel University (PhD Econ) '76;

Occupation: Principal Lecturer '71-97 in Economics, at the University of East London (formerly North East London Poly) (NATFHE '71-94/ MSF '95-97); was "an Assistant Manager of Fox Language Institute" in Washington; "I worked as a Night Manager in a hotel in the red light district of Amsterdam"; was "a civilian worker in an American Air Force near Madrid";

Traits: Grey parted hair with whiter beard; cannot read his speeches without his specs; his surname in Dutch means 'fish'; has a dog called Sophie; he did his National Service in the Dutch Army as an airborne artillery spotter;

Address: House of Commons, Westminster, London SW1A 0AA;

Telephone: 0171 219 4956 (H of C);

BULGING EX-MP FILES

Because of the unprecedented retirements before the 1 May 1997 election and the major massacre of Conservative MPs on the day, our computer and paper files on former MPs are bulging to an unprecedented degree. These are kept up to date, partly because defeated ex-MPs may come back. We also update these files as the base of the obituaries in at least two of the broadsheets.

Robert WALTER **Conservative** **DORSET NORTH '97-**

Majority: 2,746 over Liberal Democrat 5-way;
Description: The north of the spectacularly scenic county made famous by novelists Thomas Hardy and John Fowles, made more rural by being stripped of the commuter suburbs north of Bournemouth in '83; its voters are centred in old market towns like Shaftesbury and Blandford Forum; in '95, it gained two wards from Christchurch and lost two to Mid-Dorset, a net loss of 11,000 voters; its central political conundrum, after the LibDem advance to 55% of the poll in the '93 county council election, was whether this would be carried forward in a general election;
Position: Vice President '95-, Chairman '92-95, Conservative Group for Europe; ex: Chairman: of the European Democrat Forum, Foreign Affairs Forum, Vice Chairman, Westbury CPC Committee;
Outlook: A moderately pro-European international banker and adviser on foreign currency reserves who is also a Devon sheep farmer; one of Ken Clarke's few new recruits to the Commons but is mainly a loyal partisan who happily joins in many Whip-endorsed motions attacking Labour ministers for real or contrived failings;
History: He joined the Conservative Party '66; was elected Chairman of his constituency's Young Conservatives; was elected Chairman of the Aston University Conservative Association; contested hopeless Bedwellty against Neil Kinnock, taking 20.7% of the vote, up from 11.8% May '79; was elected Chairman of the Conservative Group for Europe '92; sat on the Kingsdown Inquiry into Britain and the Single Currency '95; was selected to contest Dorset North on the retirement of its ailing incumbent Tory MP, the late Sir Nicholas Baker '96; retained Dorset North by a substantially decreased majority of 2,746 after a swing to the LibDems of 6.9% May '97; in the Leadership contest joined Kenneth Clarke's campaign team May-June '97; in his Maiden, emphasised the growing industrial implants in his agricultural constituency, but mainly delimited the extent of his pro-Europeanism; he reiterated his belief in "Britain's engagement with our European partners" but opposed Labour's acceptance of the Social Chapter and totally rejected "the concept of a centralised European super-state" June '97; supported the outgoing Tory Government's voucher scheme for nursery schools but, as chairman of governors of a state nursery school in Westminster, complained about the "confusing and bureaucratic" instructions to the local education authorities involved June '97; criticised Labour's first Budget as unnecessary, attacking the windfall tax and, in particular, the "very mean measure", the further reduction in mortgage tax relief as a "burden on home owners" July '97; urged an end to gender discrimination in bereavement benefit July '97;
Born: 3 May 1948,
Family: He is a widower with two sons, Charles, who was reading Geography at King's College, London, and Alexander, who completed his A-levels in '96; his daughter, Elizabeth, studied medicine at Guy's Hospital;
Education: Colston's School, Bristol; Weymouth School, Warminster; Aston University;
Occupation: Director and Vice President, of Aubrey G Lanston & Co; Adviser, on the management of their foreign currency reserves, to a number of governments; Sheep-Farmer, in Devon; ex: Investment Manager of an insurance company;
Traits: Parted, slightly greying dark hair; square face with jutting chin;

Address: House of Commons, Westminster, London SW1A 0AA; Staddon, South Brent, Devon TQ10 9EG;
Telephone: 0171 219 3000 (H of C);

Claire WARD **Labour** **WATFORD '97-**

Majority: 5,792 over Conservative 5-way;
Description: An old Hertfordshire market town industrialised in the 19th century but overtaken in growth by the county's new towns after World War II; it may make its comeback as Britain's Hollywood; it was initially held postwar by Labour's John Freeman, then Raphael Tuck; it was held by a Tory, F W Farey-Jones '55-64; in '79 it was captured by Tory Tristan Garel-Jones, defeating Tony Banks; the '83 addition of rural hinterland buttressed Tristan Garel-Jones; in the '95 boundary changes 10,000 voters left for St Albans but 8,000 were brought in from Hertfordshire SW; Garel-Jones' announced withdrawal before '97 shrewdly anticipated Labour's tidal wave;
Position: On the Select Committee on Culture, the Media and Sport '97-; Boreham Wood Town Councillor (Mayor '96-97) '94-; on the London Region CRS Political Committee '93-; ex: Youth Representative, on Labour's NEC '91-95;
Outlook: Labour's youngest winning woman MP at just under 25; "the archetypal Blair babe" (a close colleague); the "modernisers' answer to persistently Left-voting Young Socialists", "widely reviled as a 'stooge' of the leaderhip" (RED PEPPER); these assessments from the Left clearly imply a reaction against the influence of her parents, Clydeside Leftwingers, or ignore her ties to the TGWU; a Hertfordshire-educated product born on the Tyne of Clydeside parents; a 'wunderkind' who has simultaneously climbed the Labour, Co-operative and TGWU ladders since the age of 15;
History: Her father, a Leftwing Labour Party member and initially a Clydeside shipwright, had become Works Manager for Islington Borough Council, a Hertsmere councillor and Labour's candidate in Hertsmere against Cecil Parkinson; she recalls first being stimulated politically, at 12, by the '84-85 miners' strike with her parents in miners' support groups; she began taking time off from school - under protest from the nuns - for the weeks of the TUC and Labour Party conferences; she joined the TGWU, the Cooperative Party and the Labour Party at 15, '87; she won the South East TUC Mike Perkins Memorial Prize for Young Trade Unionists at 17, '89; she won the TGWU National Youth Award at 18 '90; she became Chairman of Boreham Wood Labour Party branch, delegate to the TGWU biennial delegate conference, and Youth Representative on Labour's NEC at 19, with the responsibility for changing the Trotskyist-dominated Young Socialists into acceptable Young Labour '91; she was elected Chairman of Hertsmere CLP at 20, '92; she worked fulltime at Labour headquarters during the general election Mar-Apr '92; at 21 she became a member of Labour's Central Region Executive Committee '93; was elected to her local Elstree and Boreham Wood Town Council May '94; was a member of the NEC's inquiry team which investigated allegations of intimidation and attempted vote-rigging in the Leicester East constituency party of Keith Vaz MP; she and the inquiry found evidence of interference in council business and

bullying of council members on behalf of Vaz's mother, but found it difficult to get the NEC to act '95; was selected for Watford July '95; the question of Keith Vaz's interference rose again, partly because of a new investigation by Labour's Central Region executive and a 'Dispatches' TV programme on Channel 4; she admitted she had written to Roy Maddox, Secretary of the Central Region telling him that she had tried to raise complaints with Vaz personally but he had torn up the letter; she told the GUARDIAN: "I am very disappointed with the manner in which the Labour Party has dealt with the Leicester inquiry" Nov '95; she won Watford on a notional swing of 12.3% by a majority of 5,792, ending a Tory reign of 18 years, making her the youngest woman MP and second youngest Labour MP by a month May '97; in her Maiden she emphasised the sports side of Watford, but threw in the hope that the Watford area - including Elstree -would become "Britain's Hollywood" June '97; successfully asked Tom Clarke to visit the Leavesden film studio in her constituency June '97;

Born: 9 May 1972, North Shields, Tyne & Wear

Family: Daughter of Frank Ward, free-lance Manager/Surveyor and Labour's '87 candidate against Cecil Parkinson in Hertsmere; her mother, Catherine (McClure) was a former sewing machinist; both her parents are Scottish and Hertsmere Councillors;

Education: Loreto College (nun-run RC girls' school), St Albans '83-90; University of Hertfordshire (LLB Hons) '90-93; Brunel University (MA in Britain and the European Union) '94-95; Legal Practice Course, College of Law, London;

Occupation: Trainee Solicitor '95-97; Part-time Personal Assistant, to Labour Group on Hertsmere Borough Council '92-95; Part-time Secretary-Receptionist, at Clarendon House Business Centre '89-92; Temporary Acounts Clerk, Hertsmere Borough Council '88; Part-time Secretary, Graham Aitken & Associates (building surveyors) '85-88;

Traits: Short; long black hair; chubby face; snub nose; good-humoured; "she is friendly but distant", "a curious mixture of sophisticated crispness with the odd hint of of something altogether more interesting" (Annalisa Barbieri, INDEPENDENT ON SUNDAY); Roman Catholic by education; enjoys films (especially Tom Cruise), soft pop (Celine Dion, Bryam Adams) and occasional gymnastics;

Address: House of Commons, Westminster, London SW1A 0AA; 7 Mildred Avenue, Boreham Wood, Herts WD6 1ET (home);

Telephone: 0171 219 3000 (H of C); 0468 901606;

David WATTS **Labour** **ST HELENS NORTH '97-**

Majority: 23,417 over Conservative 6-way;

Description: The northern part of the industrial town on the Merseyside fringe, dominated by Pilkinton's, coal, chemicals and pharmaceuticals (Beecham' powders); its former nuclear establishments are now just outside; it embraces peripheral areas like the old railway town of Newton-le-Willows, which gave its predecessor seat its name; long a safe Labour seat, it was previously held for 23 years - if you include Newton - by John Evans, the crusty former AEU-MP shoehorned into the Lords in '97;

Position: St Helens Borough Councillor (Leader '93-97) '81-

Outlook: John Evans' friend and former Research Assistant locally, self-described as "middle-of-the-road" Labour; has a local councillor's approach to Westminster problems; was the last-minute beneficiary of John Evans' being shoehorned out of St Helens into the Lords as an anti-Blairite trade unionist largely because of a clash over the frustrated candidacy of an AEU man in Swindon North in favour of a middle-class Blairite;

History: He joined the Labour Party '79; was elected to St Helens Borough Council May '81; became the local Research Assistant to John Evans '93; became Leader of St Helens Borough Council May '93; when John Evans was urged belatedly to give up his seat for one in the Lords, Watts won selection Apr '97; on a swing of 9.1% won the seat by an enhanced majority of 23,417 May '97; acclaiming the "historic" Labour victory nationally, admitted that he was inclined to continue on St Helens Council: "there is a precedent; I haven't ruled anything out yet" May '97; his Maiden, including tributes to John Evans and to his town's efforts to clear dereliction and improve education, welcomed the new Government's phased release of capital receipts from sold council houses; but it concentrated on a fierce attack on the "unfair" distribution of the previous Government's grants: "St Helens and Westminster have the same population; St Helens receives £583 of grant per person, whereas Westminster receives £995 per person; each Westminster secondary child receives £983 more grant than each St Helens child receives" June '97; claimed that many pensioners were deterred from taking up income-support benefits to which they were entitled by the stigma attached to means-tested benefits June '97; co-sponsored a motion defending the 500-strong workforce of Memory Lane Cakes against closure in Warrington June '97; challenged a Tory Spokesman, the retread Christopher Chope, on the cost of bed-and-breakfast housing benefit to the taxpayer during the 18-year period of Tory rule July '97; backed the Budget's windfall tax since the incompetent previous Conservative Government had under-valued utilities when selling them; "if there were any justice in the world, the Conservative Ministers involved would be facing a surcharge for losing such large amounts of taxpayers' money" July '97; urged the Social Security Department "do more to ensure that people take up the benefits to which they are entitled" July '97;

Born: 26 August 1951, St Helens

Family: Son, of Leonard Watts, storekeeper, and Sarah (Rowe);

Education: Seel Road Secondary Modern, Huyton;

Occupation: Leader, of St Helens Borough Council '93-97; Research Assistant, to John Evans MP '93-97; ex: Labour's Regional Organiser for the Northwest in the 1992 general election;

Traits: Brown, parted hair, retreating forehead;

Address: House of Commons, Westminster, London SW1A 0AA; Ann Ward House, 1 Mill Street, St Helen's, Merseyside (constituency);

Telephone: 0171 219 6325 (H of C); 01744 623416/623417(Fax) (constituency);

LAW OF UNEVEN DEVELOPMENT

One cannot impose pure egalitarian standards on MPs' profiles. One MP's file will be anorexia-slim, another's as overstuffed as that of former MP Sir Cyril Smith. This is not merely a difference of talent or attainment. A rent-a-quote backbencher with a flow of vivid views can mop up more publicity than a squad of Parliamentary Secretaries answering boring questions with more boring answers. Some MPs retire from controversy into being chairmen of committees. Others go into the Whips' Office, where they tear off strips in private. These strain our effort at equal treatment.

Professor 'Steve' (Steven) WEBB **Liberal Democrat** **NORTHAVON '97-**

Majority: 2,137 over Conservative 4-way;
Description: The former South Gloucestershire seat - once held by Anthony Crosland - renamed Northavon in '83, after the now-abolished Avon county had been created; it runs from the Severn Bridge in the west to Badminton in the east; it is a mixure of agricultural areas and middle-class suburban commuter towns looking to Bristol; it has not had Filton (Concorde), Stoke Gifford and Berkeley (nuclear power) since '83, and Patchway was lost to Bristol NW in '95; it still has the Oldbury nuclear power station, the Beaufort foxhounds and 50 lovely villages; its domination by prosperous commuting towns was thought, until May '97, to make it safe for its Tory MP, Sir John Cope, by a majority of 10,000-plus if its voters reverted to their '92 voting pattern;
Position: On the LibDems' Social Security team '97-, on the Commission for Social Justice;
Outlook: A young professor of social policy who has been influential in shaping LibDem policy on tax and benefits; an economist whose Christian beliefs led him to challenge "the ethos of greed and selfishness which has been the hallmark of the Conservatives in the 1980s"; is respected by Labour Ministers: "he has a long and distinguished record of work on social security and welfare reform" (Harriet Harman MP); "even Frank Field thinks that Steve is sharp" (Labour MP); he is in Amnesty International, World Development Movement, CPRE;
History: He joined the Liberal Democrats and was selected for Northavon; at annual conference complained that a local LibDem-administered authority had to close old peoples' homes Sep '96; unexpectedly captured Northavon on a notional swing of 10.4%, unseating Sir John Cope after 23 years May '97; in his Maiden, urged the outright abolition of the Child Support Agency and its replacement by a more flexible system of family courts capable of assessing circumstances and ensuring that maintenance was paid, but with "more efficiency and humanity than the CSA" June '97; tried to persuade Social Security Secretary Harriet Harman that "investment in affordable, quality child care is the only way to reduce the number of lone parents on income support, and that the spare change from the midweek Lottery does not constitute such an investment" June '97; complained about the use of the Jobseeker's Allowance to pressure a constituent to give up his education to take a "dead-end job" June '97; complained that the Budget had not addressed the problem of the low-income house buyer who lost his job and no longer had access to mortgage-payment benefit July '97; opposed the Social Security Bill because too much of it, particulary its discrimination against lone parents, had been inherited from the Tories July '97; said the LibDems would be urging an extra £5 a week for the over-80s, which "would be a better use of money than restoring the earnings link for everybody" Aug '97;
Born: 18 July 1965,
Family: He is married to Helen, Anglican Chaplain at Southmead Hospital; they have a daughter;
Education: Dartmouth High School, Birmingham; Hertford College, Oxford University;
Occupation: Professor of Social Policy, Bath University '95-97; ex: Economist, working on the effects of the personal tax and benefits system for the Institute for Fiscal Studies '86-95;
Traits: Light brown parted hair; broad, high retreating forehead; triangular face with longish

chin; "Five Brains"; "makes Willetts look like a thicko" (EVENING STANDARD); rather too proud of his recently-acquired title of 'Professor' which he initially insisted on having carried over into the Commons; plays oboe, piano and church organ; a fan of West Bromwich Albion FC;
Address: House of Commons, Westminster, London SW1A 0AA;
Telephone: 0171 219 3000 (H of C); 01454 615827 (home & Fax); 0976 313358 (mobile);

Brian WHITE **Labour** **MILTON KEYNES NORTH EAST '97-**

Majority: 240 over Conservative 6-way;
Description: The unaltered, more Tory-leaning of the two MK seats, which includes the Open University; its New Town wards are more middle-class, with fewer council houses; it is also tilted to the Right by rural villages (including pancake-racing Olney), the old borough of Newton Pagnell, and the affluent golfing commuters of Woburn Sands in north Buckinghamshire; under previous names, guises and shapes, the area was won for Labour by Aidan Crawley and Robert Maxwell; but in its present shape, if it had reverted to '92 voting patterns it was expected to give its engaging incumbent Tory MP, Peter Butler, another majority of around 14,000;
Position: Milton Keynes Town Councillor (Deputy Leader) '87-; Secretary, of Association of Labour Councillors; ex: Buckinghamshire County Councillor (on its Education Committee);
Outlook: Another victorious deputy leader of a local council; a "New Labour" (NEW STATESMAN) veteran computer systems analyst; a supporter of electoral reform and freedom of information;
History: He was elected to Milton Keynes Council May '87; was elected to Buckinghamshire County Counil; became Deputy Leader of MK Council; was selected to contest "hopeless" MK NE against the popular Peter Butler '95; campaigned in favour of a local comprehensive school instead of the grammar school desired by the Conservatives; he also opposed nursery vouchers Apr '97; with the help of over 2,000 tactical votes from the local LibDems, he quite unexpectedly won MK NE on a 14.2% swing, ousting the attractive incumbent Tory MP Peter Butler by a narrow 240 votes (less than the 576 that went to the Green candidate and much less than the 1,492 that went to the Referendum Party) May '97; in his Maiden enthused about Labour's education plans, and the need to deliver on them May '97; backed ban on fox-hunting June '97; co-sponsored motion backing Milton Keynes Council against the body seeking a grammar school there June '97; co-sponsored motion endorsing Labour's plan to redirect to patients the £100m cut from NHS bureaucracy June '97; pointed out to LibDem MPs protesting Labour's council capping that "those of us who set budgets in this year's local authority round knew the consequences of going above the cap; most of us took that into account when setting the budgets" July '97; welcomed the abandonment of "outdated dogma" in the new Bill to manage the radio spectrum; backed the Nordic example of public bodies competing with private companies Oct '97;
Born: 5 May 1957, Isleworth, Middlesex
Family: He is married with two stepsons;

Education: Methodist College, Belfast;
Occupation: Systems Analyst, designing computing systems for Abbey National (MSF) til '97; ex: Civil Servant, in HM Customs and Excise; "before I came to the House, I spent 20 years in information technology as an assistant analyst designing systems" (BW)
Traits: Parted dark hair and beard; heart-shaped face; beaky; pragmatic realist; enjoys ten-pin bowling;
Address: House of Commons, Westminster, London SW1A 0AA;
Telephone: 0171 219 3000 (H of C); 01908 313474 (home);

Dr Alan (Patrick Vincent) WHITEHEAD Labour SOUTHAMPTON-TEST '97-

Majority: 13,684 over Conservative 8-way;
Description: The western part of the south coast's leading port city; has vandalism-troubled council estates and middle-class residential areas; this seat was a classic marginal touchstone, but was tipped over to a Labour-leaning marginal by the loss of pro-Conservative Bassett ward to Romsey, and the acquisition of pro-Labour St Lukes from Itchen in '95;
Position: On Select Committee on Environment, Transport and Regional Affairs '97-; ex: on Labour's Regional Policy Commission '95-96; Advisor, to Labour's Local Government Policy Drafting Committee '94; Southampton City Councillor (Leader '84-92) '80-92
Outlook: A very bright, fourth-time-lucky local luminary; almost the political twin of his friend and neighbour, John Denham, now a Minister; has moved from being a semi-hard Leftwinger 20 years ago to a soft-Leftist now; in the interim has concentrated on reforming Southampton as its council Leader; he spearheaded the successful drive to save Southampton's Mayflower Theatre, now the best on the south coast; he was frustrated in his effort to provide Southampton with its own light railway; he tried three previous times to capture Test; in Labour Co-ordinating Committee, Fabian Society, SERA, Greenpeace and formerly in CND;
History: He joined the Labour Party '73; at Labour's Southern Region conference, urged the need for democratic local government May '77; selected to contest hopeless New Forest against Patrick McNair-Wilson, he came 3rd with 19.7% of the vote May '79; at Labour's annual conference rejected as "electoralism" Denis Healey's post-defeat call to restore Labour as a mainstream party with 11.5m voters; instead he called for Labour to be made into a campaigning party with a mass membership, like his constituency party: "quite honestly, comrades, our party is about as well designed for campaigning as [tiny, slender] Frank Allaun is for all-in wrestling"; "our party...must be a campaigning organisation that can actually win the allegiance of people in tenants' groups, in pressure groups all over the country; until we can actually convert our party to be able to react swiftly to events, to make people loyal to the party throughout the time in between elections...we are condemning ourselves just to being a party of Parliamentarians" Oct '79; was elected to Southampton City Council May '80; was selected to contest Test Nov '80; with other, then semi-hard and hard-Left candidates - Peter Hain, Harriet Harman, Kate Hoey, Peter Tatchell - supported "extra-Parliamentary activity" to keep Parliamentarians in touch with "the people they represent" Feb '82; Labour took 7 of 15

seats on Southampton City Council May '82; in a letter to the GUARDIAN insisted that the Southampton Labour Party was "a radical socialist party" and not "Militant-controlled" Aug '82; with others in the pro-Arab 'Labour Middle East Council' urged "support for the inalienable right of the Palestinian people to self-determination" and "recognition of the PLO as the legitimate representative of the Palestinian people" Apr '83; denied the accusation by witch-hunter Douglas Eden of belonging to "a Trotskyist organisation [SOCIALIST ORGANISER] which is now co-operating with [Ken] Livingstone's group" May '83; fought Test against James Hill, losing by 9,346 votes (17.1%) June '83; was elected Leader of Southampton City Council May '84; was again selected for Test by 42 to 33 on the 2nd ballot, from a short-list of four Dec '85; contested Test against James Hill, reducing his majority to 6,954 (12.3%) June '87; was again selected for Test Mar '90; his plan for a light railway for Southampton was defeated in the Commons, where the opposition to the private Bill required was organised by his longstanding Tory opponent, James Hill, on behalf of junior Minister Christopher Chope, through whose constituency the light railway would run Jan '91; was more narrowly defeated by James Hill, by 585 votes (1%) Apr '92; the boundary changes, including the loss of a pro-Tory ward and the acquisition of a pro-Labour ward made his seat winnable even without a national swing to Labour '94-95; was re-selected to contest the seat on an OMOV vote of 168 to 18 in '95; won Test on a notional swing of 10.5%, by the massive majority of 13,684 May '97; urged the introduction of a California-style ordinance to compel large companies to plan car-sharing among their employees May '97; in his Maiden enthused about abolishing the Assisted Places Scheme for "the unleashing of the potential of the many", rather than the few June '97; became the sponsor of the Southampton International Boat Show Bill frustrated in the previous session June '97; urged the introduction of a standard pint for beer June '97; complained about South West Trains' plan to limit space for carrying bicycles June '97; backed ban on fox-hunting June '97; was named to Select Committee on Environment, Transport and Regional Affairs July '97; in an adjournment debate called for safeguards on the operation of Higher Education Institutions, partly because of "the flawed system of governance in the new universities" July '97;

Born: 15 September 1950, Isleworth

Family: "My parents have led perfectly ordinary middle-class lives"; he married Sophie in '79; 1s Patrick '80, 1d Isabel '83; both "attend the comprehensive school that is nearest to my home" (AW))

Education: Isleworth Grammar School; Southampton University (BA Hons in Philosophy and Politics; PhD in Political Science);

Occupation: Professor of Public Policy, Southampton Institute (UNISON) '92-; Visiting Fellow, in Department of Politics, Southampton University '90-; ex: Director, of British Institute of Industrial Therapy '84-92; Director, of OUTSET '79-83; Deputy Director of OUTSET (charity assisting the disabled) '76-78;

Traits: Parted light brown hair and moustache (no longer his '70s beard); intelligent, earnest; is football mad: still plays ("is this wise at my age?") and has a season ticket to Southampton Football Club, which "generously lets in goals to visitors the length and breadth of the UK, although it sometimes scores itself" (AW); wore denims, and had a beard and long, light-brown hair in the '70s;

Address: House of Commons, Westminster, London SW1A 0AA; 32-36 Henry Road, Freemantle, Southampton SO15 3HA (constituency);

Telephone: 0171 219 6338 (H of C); 01703 577759 (constituency); 01703 556084 (home/Fax);

Mrs Betty WILLIAMS **Labour** **CONWY '97-**

Majority: 1,596 over Liberal Democrat 7-way;

Description: The unaltered northwest Wales three-way marginal containing the northern half of old Caernarvonshire, the seaside holiday resort of Llandudno, the university town of Bangor and the castle town of Conwy itself; the dualling of the A55 has increased the number of English immigrants into Bangor and Conwy; Welsh-speakers are in a shrinking minority but were influential in keeping in office the preceding Tory MP, Welsh-speaking Sir Wyn Roberts, who made many contributions to Welsh linguistic cultural survival - including the heavily subsidised Welsh-language TV channel;

Position: On the Select Committee on Welsh Affairs '97-; ex: Gwynedd County Councillor (Chairman, Social Services Committee '81-88) '76-94, Arfon Borough Councillor (Mayor '90-91) '74-91; Gwyrfai Rural District Councillor '70-74; Llanillyfni Community Councillor '67-83;

Outlook: A veteran northwest Wales councillor and repeat candidate who finally made the leap from third place to first; a Leftish feminist-devolutionist who previously collected brownie points for her special work for those handicapped like her son; a longtime advocate of the Welsh Assembly, believing it important as a practical way of solving Wales' education and health problems; believes that socialism, not nationalism, is the answer to Welsh problems;

History: She recalls that her dream of a Welsh Assembly took shape in the '60s; joined the Labour Party '64; contested Caernarfon coming 3rd with 19.4% June '83; was selected for Conwy, endorsed by NEC Jan '86; urged support for license-free TV for pensioners Jan '87; came 3rd with 22.3% of the vote June '87; demanded to know what was holding up the Conwy tunnel, which Sir Wyn Roberts described as a "magnificent engineering achievement" Sep '90; acknowledged the £250,000 contributed by the Welsh Development Agency to her Arfon valley, but still insisted that "there are more losers in Wales than gainers" Apr '91; complained that cyclists were not allowed to use the new Penmaenbach Tunnel Mar '92; again contested Conwy, coming 3rd with 25.8% Apr '92; was chosen again, from an all-women short-list '95; at annual conference in Brighton, spoke up for the disabled Oct '95; was attacked by anti-abortion Tory women MPs Ann Winterton and Elizabeth Peacock for accepting money from 'Emily's List', thus supporting a woman's right to choose Mar '97; received the support of SDLP Leader John Hume Apr '97; won the seat finally, as the first woman MP for Conwy, by a majority of 1,596 over the LibDem runner-up, the five-tries veteran LibDem candidate Rev Roger Roberts May '97; in her Maiden enthused about the looming campaign for devolution and "made Llandudno sound like Eden" (Matthew Parris, TIMES) June '97; co-sponsored motion urging a review of the law on rape, to ban cross-examination of the victim by the accused June '97; backed a ban on arms exports to Indonesia July '97; asked for a statement on the Welsh film industry July '97; was named to the Select Committee on Welsh Affairs July '97;

Born: 31 July 1944, Bangor

Family: Daughter of a slate quarryman; is married with two children; she has to push her disabled son in a wheelchair;

Education: Dyffryn Nantlle Secondary, Penygroes; Normal College, Bangor '92-95(BA Hons 2-1 in Communications as a mature student);

Occupation: Free-lance journalist and researcher; ex: secretary;
Traits: Dark; prettyish; Welsh-speaker, with a soft Welsh lilt in English; "more eloquent than she pretend[s]" (Matthew Parris, TIMES) in English; reticent about names of father, husband and son; won National Eisteddford prize for video about a Welsh heroine; former Chairman of National Eisteddfod Finance Committee; Deacon of Seion Congregational Church, Talysarn (one of the first two women so elected);
Address: House of Commons, Westminster, London SW1A 0AA; Ardwyn, Station Road, Talysarn, Caernarfon, Gwynedd LL54 6HL (constituency office)
Telephone: 0171 219 3000 (House of Commons); 01286 (Penygroes) 8806214 (home);

(George) Phil(ip) WILLIS **Liberal Democrat** **HARROGATE & KNARESBOROUGH '97-**

Majority: 6,236 over Conservative 4-way;
Description: The elegant spa town north of Leeds, recently a major conference centre; the '95 boundary change restricted its outer boundaries -shedding a solidly Tory hinterland - but retaining the beautiful and prosperous neighbouring town of Knaresborough; long safely Tory, it was therefore attractive to displaced Norman Lamont; the Liberal Democrats had increasingly predominated on its local council; this left open the question of whether they could translate this into Parliamentary votes;
Position: Higher and Further Education Spokesman on LibDems' Education team '97-; Harrogate and Knaresborough District Councillor (Leader '90-) '88-; North Yorkshire County Councillor (Deputy Group Leader '93-97) '93-; Chairman, Harrogate International Centre, '92-;
Outlook: The Lamont-Terminator: the first Liberal MP for Harrogate since 1906; from the social-democratic wing of his party, he initially maintained sympathetic pressure on Labour as a strong supporter of the state education system and an opponent of selection and the Assisted Places Scheme; at the LibDem Eastbourne conference of '97, he was suddenly transformed into a sharp critic of Labour's education spending, as a key part of the party's plan to distinguish itself from Labour; a former Leeds headmaster with a national reputation in 'inclusive education'; has also established a local reputation as a charismatic politician; "a sharp and effective operator" (Matthew Engel, GUARDIAN);
History: His family in Burnley were Labour supporters; he initially joined the Liberal Party '85;; was elected to Harrogate and Knaresborough District Council May '88; became its Leader when LibDems became the largest party in a hung council May '90; after the de-selection of David Ridgway, was on the short-list for Harrogate with three others, from which fellow Councillor Tim Hurren was selected Sep '91; stayed as Leader when LibDems won overall majority on Harrogate Council May '92; was elected to North Yorkshire County Council, becoming Deputy Group Leader May '93; was selected as the LibDem candidate for Harrogate Feb '95; said he was "delighted" when Harrogate was selected as one of seven conference centres which could become sites for casinos under new, more relaxed rules on gambling Nov '96; had to apologise to Norman Lamont for a LibDem leaflet falsely alleging Lamont had not been cleared in an interim report on "cash for questions" by Sir Gordon

Downey; in the campaign he pitched heavily for tactical Labour votes, saying: "if you want to see Lamont beaten, lend us your vote" Apr '97; with the help of about 2,500 tactical Labour votes, won Harrogate on a notional swing of fully 15.7%, defeating Norman Lamont by a majority of 6,236 May '97; in his witty Maiden, he quoted Norman Lamont's pro-European Maiden of '72; he also backed a minimum wage and attacked "slave wages"; but mainly he concentrated on demands that local government have restored to it the powers stripped from it by the Tories, especially the ability to borrow to build in Harrogate a new exhibition hall to buttress the town's economy as "Europe's finest conference and exhibition centre" May '97; urged compensation for women damaged by excessive radiotherapy after breast cancer operations June '97; pressed Health Secretary Frank Dobson about sexual abuse by a local psychiatrist June '97; complained that Labour's plans to educate all four-year-olds were not adequately funded June '97; while fully supporting Labour's plan to end the Assisted Places Scheme, he backed a Tory amendment to allow those in it to continue until 13, where necessary June '97; co-sponsored motion attacking the export of 1m live animals July '97; in his debut on LibDems' Education team, welcomed Labour's education White Paper as putting teaching "at the heart of our education system's future", but asked Education Secretary David Blunkett: "does he believe that he can deliver all the promises and commitments in the White Paper on the resources that he has been allocated?" July '97; a week later he was more critical of Labour's student loans Bill as "cobbled together by the previous [Tory] Administration" July '97; at the LibDems' Eastbourne conference he was one of the sharpest critics of Labour's inadequate funding of education and the post-Dearing costs of higher education Sep '97;

Born: 30 November 1941, Burnley

Family: Son, of George Willis, postman, and Hannah (Gillespie) nurse; m '74 Heather (Sellars) teacher; 1s Michael '80; 1d Rachel '76;

Education: Rosehill Primary, Burnley; Burnley Grammar; City of Leeds and Carnegie College (teaching certificate); Birmingham University (BPhil);

Occupation: Headteacher, John Smeaton Community High School, Leeds '83-97; Headteacher, Ormesby School, Cleveland (one of the youngest headteachers in the country) '78-83; Teacher '62-78;

Traits: Curly white front-combed hair; dark eyebrows; pebble specs; witty; "an assertive, gregarious manner" (Sarah Neville, YORKSHIRE POST); "charismatic" (ex-Liberal MP Clement Freud); enjoys theatre, music and dance, especially ballet; is a season ticket holder of Leeds United;

Address: House of Commons, Westminster, London SW1A 0AA; 75 Pimfold House, Wetherby Road, Rufforth, Yorks YD2 3QB; Station Parade, Harrogate HG1 1ST (LibDem HQ);

Telephone: 0171 219 5709 (H of C); 0113 2930484; 001904 738334 019043 736267 (Fax evenings); 01904 738334 (home); 01423 528888 (LibDem HQ); 01423 505700 (Fax);

PROFILERS AS BARBERS

When we started illustrating our volumes, we never anticipated outdated MPs' photographs would force us to double as barbers. In every volume ever published we have incurred cries of "I no longer have a moustache!" or "I have shaved my beard" or "I haven't worn my hair that long for five years". There is nothing more dismaying than telling your artist how good his sketch was and then seeing the woman MP portrayed with hair five inches shorter two hours later.

Michael WILLS **Labour** **SWINDON NORTH '97-**

Majority: 7,688 over Conservative 5-way;
Description: A new seat dividing up the former railway engineering town, recently an expanding base for new industries including Rover, Honda, GEC-Plessey; this new seat is made up of wards from Swindon north of the railway track, together with the northern wards of Thamesdown, formerly in Devizes, plus Cricklade from North Wiltshire; as such it is a mixture of built-up and rural areas; it was considered to be marginally Labour-leaning, perhaps by 1,000 votes or less, on the '92 division of its votes;
Position: Formerly in Peter Mandelson's Shadow Communications Agency;
Outlook: One of Peter Mandelson's and Gordon Brown's very bright (Double First) but surprisingly quiet friends; a TV producer and former policy adviser to Gordon Brown on utility 'fat cats' and VAT on fuel; a badly bruised but eventually successful product of the unpleasant class-clash between a friend of the Blairites and the Blair-loyal AEEU over his allegedly controversial selection; was battered by his exposure to the 'old Labour' culture of local union bossism and the reluctance of the 'New Labour' leadership to tackle such behaviour head-on; the leadership's fears were proved by the AEEU's withholding of its £250,000 contribution in punishment for the exclusion of its candidates in Swindon North and elsewhere;
History: He joined the Labour Party at 16, '68; after the election of '92, he spent two years getting himself known in Swindon; the '92 candidate, Jim D'Avila, the AEEU union convenor at the local Rover plant and a Swindon councillor for 20 years, who had come within 2,800 votes of winning the seat in '92, wanted to fight again; after a selection conference attended by 160 members, Wills won by 114 votes to 84, with 10% of his own votes coming from postal ballots and 75% of Jim D'Avila's Sep '95; D'Avila immediately challenged the result, complaining of irregularities in the opening and counting of postal votes; this was strenuously denied by local party officials; D'Avila and his union supporters applied for an injunction to stop the NEC endorsing Wills' candidature; this provoked a bitter row in Swindon, with the constituency splitting into opposing pro-D'Avila and pro-Wills camps; faced with this, the NEC voted that the selection should now be decided by a special NEC panel; this was opposed by both D'Avila, who wanted the contest re-run in Swindon, and by Wills, who believed he was entitled to be endorsed; nevertheless, the NEC decided by 14 (including Blair) to 10 (including Prescott) to set up the panel; D'Avila and the AEEU then returned to court to try to prevent the party doing this; although the judge was uneasy about the NEC's proposal, in the end he reluctantly conceded that they were within their rights to use the panel; the NEC panel of five - three trade unionists and two politicians (both of whom had previously taken the AEEU side) finally voted by 4 to 1 that Wills should be the candidate May '96; he only agreed to accept if the local party officials were cleared officially of D'Avila's charges of ballot-rigging; he won the seat on a notional swing of 7.1% by a majority of 7,688 May '97; made his Maiden in an adjournment debate on Swindon's crisis-ridden hopital facilities, due to the Tories' closing of the RAF's Princess Alexandra Hospital - "a bad decision taken in haste" - and the failure to repair and update the over-strained Princess Margaret Hospital, with its "£28m maintenance backlog" May '97; asked about monitoring of complaints against GPs June '97; urged a review of the law on surrogacy June '97; co-sponsored motion urging

locally-based Nationwide to remain a building society June '97; the AEEU decided to withhold a payment to Labour funds because of the exclusion of its candidates in Swindon North, Dudley North and Kilmarnock Sep '97;
Born: 20 May 1952, London
Family: Son, of Stephen Wills, civil servant and Austrian Jewish refugee, and Eileen (McKeown), a New Zealand Irish Catholic; m Jill (Freeman), former Producer on the 'South Bank Show' ; 3s Thomas '85, Joe '87, Nicholas '94; 1d Sarah '89;
Education: Haberdashers' Aske's, Elstree; Clare College, Cambridge University (BA in History, Double First);
Occupation: TV Producer: on LWT (where he was Peter Mandelson's boss on 'Weekend World') (TGWU) '80-97; Founder, of Juniper Productions (his own independent production company, making period drama for BBC and documentaries and current affairs programmes for Channel 4); ex: in HM Diplomatic Service '76-80;
Traits: Dark brown, curly mop of hair; pleasant-looking; square chin; half-Jewish half-Catholic by origins; "his problem: he's not a Christian" (RED PEPPER);
Address: House of Commons, Westminster, London SW1A 0AA;
Telephone: 0171 219 4399 (H of C); 01271 586 7456 (home);

'Rosie' (Rosalie) WINTERTON **Labour** **DONCASTER CENTRAL '97-**

Majority: 17,856 over Conservative 7-way;
Description: Unaltered communications hub housing varied industries: it was formerly at the centre of modern and productive coalfields; previously a marginal, held '51-64 by Tory MP Anthony [later Lord] Barber, it was won by Labour's Harold Walker in '64;
Position: Office Chief, to John Prescott, '94-96, '80-86
Outlook: A John Prescott protege, self-described as "Centre-Left"; a locally-educated woman, whose headmaster father was a Doncaster Labour councillor; she takes over from Sir Harold Walker; her initial activities were as an enthusiastic cheer-leader for the Blair Government;
History: Her family background was Labour, her father becoming a Labour councillor in Doncaster; her first political work was canvassing for her father there; unsuccessfully challenged the veteran hard-Left Eurosceptic Labour MEP Richard Balfe for his London South Inner seat, proclaiming that Labour could no longer send to Strasbourg people who would just say 'no' to everything Apr '93; worked on John Prescott's Leadership and Deputy Leadership bids May-July '94; was backed by John Prescott in her campaign to win selection for Doncaster Central, from which Sir Harold Walker was retiring; her main opponent was Mark Walker, of the RMT, who had worked on his selection for two years; another rival was a local councillor, Bev Marshall; John Prescott, who supported her by visits to Doncaster, clashed with Jimmy Knapp, RMT's leader, over backing her against the RMT nominee May '96; she was selected Nov '96; she won the seat on a swing of 10.1% by an enhanced majority of 17,856 May '97; in her Maiden enthused about the ability of the Local Government Finance Bill to provide local employment and help the "more than 5,000 people in my constituency

alone are victims of Tory neglect, waiting for homes and worried about accommodation for themselves and their families" June '97; led motion enthusing about Labour Government's promise to benefit patients by cutting £100m from NHS bureaucracy June '97; expressed solidarity with jailed Indonesian union leader June '97; complained that "free-lance clampers are regarded as litle more than modern-day highway robbers" July '97;
Born: 10 August 1958, Leicester
Family: Daughter, of Gordon Winterton, headmaster and Doncaster councillor, and Valerie (Drake), nursery school teacher;
Education: Park School; Wheatley High; Ackworth School; Doncaster Grammar; Hull University;
Occupation: Office Chief, to John Prescott '94-96, '80-86; ex: Managing Director, Connect Public Affairs '90-94; Parliamentary Officer of the Royal College of Nurses '88-90; Local Authority Officer, '86-88;
Traits: Blonde; extrovert; "irrepressible" (GUARDIAN); an "elfin blonde" who has been called "the Barbara Windsor of the House of Commons" (Paul Routledge, INDEPENDENT ON SUNDAY);
Address: House of Commons, Westminster, London SW1A 0AA; 25 Town Moor Avenue, Doncaster DN2 6BW; also lives in Kennington;
Telephone: 0171 219 0925 (H of C); 01302 735241 (constituency);

'Mike' (Michael) WOOD **Labour** **BATLEY & SPEN '97-**

Majority: 6,141 over Conservative 6-way;
Description: A hard-fought, largely working-class West Yorkshire marginal which lost Heckmondwike to Dewsbury in '95; Batley is a pro-Labour town with a large minority of Asians by origin; the Spen remainder of the seat is white and more Tory-leaning; the seat remained in Tory hands longer than expected because of the efforts of its hardworking former MP, Mrs Elizabeth Peacock, a rebel populist against her party's poll tax and pit closures;
Position: On Select Committee on Broadcasting '97-; ex: Kirklees Municipal District Councillor (Chairman, of Housing and Social Services, Deputy Leader '86-87) '80-88;
Outlook: An "Old Labour" (NEW STATESMAN) Leftwing former social worker and Kirklees Councillor; was GMB-backed in the election; is a founder-member of two workers' cooperative; belongs to SERA, SEA, Full Employment Forum, and to CND; a Campaign Groupie;
History: He joined the Labour party at 19, '65; was elected to Kirklees Municipal District Council May '80; was selected for hopeless Hexham June '86; his agent in his campaign against Alan Amos was Corrine Mulley, a local lecturer and the daughter of Lord (Fred) Mulley Oct '86; had a record nine pictures on his four-page election leaflet June '87; came third with 18% of the vote June '87; was selected for Batley and Spen July '95; was one of the 16 GMB members targeted for union support in the election Apr '97; insisted that his Tory opponent, Mrs Peacock, had not been as loyal to local miners as she claimed, since she had voted for electricity privatisation; "she is not prepared to accept the logic of her actions; we intend to

put her on the spot about this" Apr '97; won the seat on a notional swing of 7.4% by a majority of 6,141, ousting Mrs Peacock after 14 years May '97; was one of the few new Labour MPs to join the hard-Left Campaign Group May '97; co-sponsored motion criticising the BBC for interviewing a "self-confessed paedophile" on 'Kilroy' June '97;
Born: 3 March 1946, Crewe, Cheshire
Family: Son of Roland Wood, foundry worker, and Laura (Bailey), a school cleaner; he is divorced, with two adult children;
Education: Nantwich & Acton Grammar School, Nantwich, Cheshire; Southampton University (Certificate in Theology); Leeds University (Certificate of Qualification in Social Work); Leeds Metropolitan University (BA);
Occupation: Social Worker, in many places (GMB, UNISON) til '97; trained as a probation officer;
Traits: Greying, parted hair; dark beard; enjoys: ornithology, sport, reading, driving. music;
Address: House of Commons, Westminster, London SW1A 0AA; 2 Transvaal Terrace, Batley, West Yorkshire WF17 0AA;
Telephone: 0171 219 3000 (H of C); 01274 335233/335235(Fax);

Shaun (Anthony) WOODWARD **Conservative** **WITNEY '97-**

Majority: 7,028 over Labour 6-way;
Description: Solidly Conservative Witney (previously Mid Oxfordshire), in the heart of West Oxfordshire, which was for 23 years Douglas Hurd's well-upholstered seat; the suburban dormitory of Kidlington -just north of Oxford - was removed before the '97 election; within its new boundaries, with a '92-style division of the vote, it was expected to give its new Tory a 20,000-plus majority;
Position: On Select Committees: on Broadcasting '97-, European Legislation '97-; Director, English National Opera '94-; ex: Communications Director, Conservative Central Office '90-92;
Outlook: A Tory 'Golden Boy', with a safe seat, a beautiful and costly home and a Sainsbury heiress for a wife; "bright, ambitious and very well connected" (NEW STATESMAN); "one of life's strivers" ('Peterborough' DAILY TELEGRAPH); close to Chris Patten, Kenneth Clarke, Douglas Hurd; "I would put him firmly on the Left" (Dr Adrian Rogers, former Exeter Tory candidate); from his initial Commons outings, although he showed himself a supporter of Ken Clarke and Chris Patten on Europe, he displayed a Rightwing attitude on economics and a sneering and bitterly partisan attitude to Labour, which new Labour MPs found provocative;
History: He was on the short-list for Woodspring, where he was pipped by Dr Liam Fox '88; was head-hunted by party chairman Chris Patten, to be the party's new Director of Communications Jan '91; brought Saatchi & Saatchi back from the wilderness after their '87 falling out with the Tory leadership; together they planned the 'Labour Tax Bombshell' campaign Oct-Nov '91; unsuccessfully contested Avondale ward, Kensington May '94; on the short-list for Witney, from which Douglas Hurd was retiring, clashed with local authorities over his unauthorised alterations to his Wren-style home, Sarsden House: "we don't want another Teresa Gorman here" a local was quoted as saying Sep '95; was selected for Witney,

defeating ex-Minister Francis Maude Oct '95; co-signed a loyalist letter to DAILY TELEGRAPH with five other candidates, backing John Major's negotiations as putting Briain's interests first but warning that "if economic and monetary union is based on unsound economic foundations, it will fail, with potentially disastrous consequences both for those inside and outside a single currency" Dec '96; he retained Witney, despite a notional swing to Labour of 13.6%, by a majority of 7,028, down by two-thirds May '97; in the Tory Leadership contest, initially backed Stephen Dorrell, then joined Kenneth Clarke's campaign team; at the Vincent Square home of his father-in-law, Sir Tim Sainsbury, he played host to two Clarke-Redwood meetings to do a deal to stop Hague May-June '97; backed an attempt to kill the Government's Bill to further ban handguns June '97; in his Maiden, in addition to tributes to his predecessors in Witney, he paid homage to the Hongkong reign of his friend, Chris Patten; he emphasised the rural basis of his constituency, attacking as "ill-considered" the "recent moves in the name of progress and reform to prohibit the legitimate pursuit of country sports"; "I do not hunt, but I have become aware of the role that hunting plays in the life of the people of West Oxfordshire"; he wound up by suggesting that Budget leaks had come from the Treasury but, unlike Hugh Dalton, no apologies would be forthcoming July '97; asked Chancellor Gordon Brown why, since he "justified his breathtaking 17 tax rises on the need to curb the consumer boom" how he explained "£5b of his £6b tax rises were taken from the corporate sector?" July '97; attacked the Budget as "totally incoherent", as part of an attempt to mislead observers; "it proves, first and foremost that Labour's first instinct is always to tax, and to raise taxes, again and again" July '97; he again attacked Labour's damage to pension funds July '97;

Born: 26 Oct 1958, Bristol

Family: Son, of Dennis George Woodward, retired furniture retailer, and Joan Lillian (Nunn); m '87, Camilla Sainsbury, daughter of ex-MP Sir Tim Sainsbury; 1s: Tom '89; 3d: Ella '91, Olivia '93, Kate '96;

Education: Bristol Grammar School '65-77; Jesus College, Oxford University (MA; Double First in English Literature);

Occupation: Author: Tranquilisers (with Ron Lacey; 1983), Ben: The Story of Ben Hardwick (with Esther Rantzen; 1984), Drugwatch (with Sarah Caplin; 1985); Director, English National Opera '94-; Professorial Fellow, in Communication Studies, at Queen Mary and Westfield College '92-; ex: Fellow, Institute of Politics, Kennedy School, Harvard University '94-95; Communications Director, Conservative Central Office '90-92; Producer, of BBC's 'That's Life' '89-90; Director: Jerusalem Productions (promoting Christian broadcasting) '89-96; Senior Producer, 'Panorama' '87-89; Reporter/Producer, 'Newsnight' '85-87; Researcher, 'That's Life' '82-85; Parliamentary Affairs Director, National Consumer Council '81-82;

Traits: Long face; high, retreating forehead; an eager networker; a ravenous book-buyer; shows a sneering attitude toward Labour;

Address: House of Commons, Westminster, London SW1A 0AA; Sarsden House, nr Chipping Norton, Oxfordshire OX7 6PW;

Telephone: 0171 219 2680 (H of C); 01608 659223;

Phil[ip] WOOLAS **Labour** **OLDHAM EAST & SADDLEWORTH '97-**

Majority: 3,389 over Liberal Democrat 6-way;
Description: A new Lib-Lab marginal in the Pennines dividing Lancashire from Yorkshire: a disparate conglomerate made up two-thirds of old Littleborough and Saddleworth and one-third of old Oldham Central and Royton; this means it stretches from the pro-Labour decaying council houses of inner-city Oldham to the pro-Liberal affluent commuters in the desirable terraced hills of Saddleworth; in its previous, Littleworth and Saddleworth days, it was long the fiefdom of the late Rightwing populist Tory MP Geoffrey Dickens; on his death after a long struggle against cancer, it was the site of a bitter battle between the successful longtime LibDem contender, Chris Davies, and the dirty-fighting 'New Labour' machine spearheaded by Peter Mandelson;
Position: Chairman, of TRIBUNE Publications '97-; on Research and Publications Committee of Fabian Society '93-; ex: Communications Director of the GMB '91-97; President of the National Union of Students '84-86;
Outlook: An infinitely flexible and ambitious young politico; "one of those Labour men who seems capable of endless self-reinvention" (INDEPENDENT); now a "Rightwing fixer" (NEW STATESMAN); "in a previous incarnation, he was...a democratic socialist and a distinguished ambassador for his employer, the GMB, putting full employment and a minimum wage to the fore" (TRIBUNE): John Edmonds' longtime media-fixer who kept close links with the Labour Left, as the GMB's designated Director of TRIBUNE; a "consumate political animal" (a close colleague from NUS days); "modern, media-friendly, Blairite and never says anything foolish" (Andy McSmith, OBSERVER); not really 'New Labour', although, during the '95 by-election campaign, Tony Blair described him as "a stong supporter of mine over Clause IV"; "perhaps too Kinnockite to be entirely trusted by the [Labour] leadership" (RED PEPPER);
History: He joined the Labour Party at 16, '76; after fighting Sir Keith Joseph's plans to secure extra parental contributions for university tuition, was elected President of the NUS at 24, '84; was a "member of the soft-Marxist grouping 'Clause IV' (RED PEPPER); supported Scargill's miners' strike with an NUS contribution '84; in a GUARDIAN article about student radicalism, wrote: "propagate the new wave of student radicalism; if it takes a phone call to get something done - use a phone; if it takes a flour bomb - well use one" '85; co-authored Fabian pamphlet, 'Labour and Youth', calling for the replacement of Trotskyist-dominated Young Socialists by a more docile Young Labour Oct '86; backed vote for one-member, one-vote at Labour's annual conference Oct '93; was selected to contest Littleborough and Saddleworth by-election following the death of Tory MP Geoffrey Dickens May '95; the Mandelson-led 'New Labour' team used ruthless tactics to try to destroy his LibDem opponent, Chris Davies, as a weirdo, accusing him of being pro-raves, soft on drugs and high taxation and hell-bent on independence for the northwest, all only partly true; an attempt was made to repackage Woolas for local Methodists as a practicing Anglican, a regular churchgoer who "believes in strong family values and responsible, disciplined upbringing for the young" also only partly true; although Scunthorpe-born and Burnley-raised, he was presented as having been a Young Farmer in the Pennine village of Worsthorne just outside the constiituency, who wanted to "come home to speak up for local people in the corridors of

power" July '95; he dismissed his Tory opponent as a "local do-gooder" and the LibDem as "a flaky Liberal"; "they don't have the experience to fight on the national scene"; when accused of having supported John Edmonds in his '93 resistance to one-member one-vote, Woolas said that John Edmonds had been his employer but that he himself had voted for OMOV, and that Blair was his Leader - a line that had got him into difficulties with members of the GMB executive July '95; in a LibDem leaflet, he was accused of not being a Blair supporter, which Blair denied, insisting he had been "a strong supporter of mine over Clause IV"; other party sources said he had been an architect of recasting the block vote July '95; he came within 1,993 votes of winning the by-election, with the Tory coming a poor 3rd, after Labour had started out in 3rd place July '95; his result - a 14% increase in Labour's share of the poll -was considered by Deputy Leader John Prescott to have been the party's best result in a seat where Labour moved from third place to a close second Aug '95; with the backing of John Prescott, replied to Labour Party criticisms of his "dirty tricks" campaign in accusing the LibDem candidate of being soft on drugs and higher taxes: "we said that we would not increase taxes for low and middle-income families; now that is the whole basis of Gordon Brown's strategy for the past two years; anyone who criticises that is criticising the whole of Labour's policy" Aug '95; as a member of the Research and Publications Committee of the Fabian Society, stopped its Research Director, Stephen Pollard, from writing a pamphlet advocating support for selective education: "you can say things in the Fabians that you can't say anywhere else; but when it came to Stephen Pollard's proposal, it was beyond the pale; we wanted a serious debate about education, and this paper would have detracted from others we wanted to produce" Sep '95; the Liberal Democrats complained that a pro-Woolas issue of the DAILY MIRROR, distributed free on polling day, should have been counted as an election expense; he said: "what papers do is nothing to do with the Labour Party; we didn't spend more than we were allowed" Nov '95; was re-selected for the altered seat of Oldham East and Saddleworth '96; with 17 other loyal candidates, complained to the INDEPENDENT about being cross-examined to find divisions, insisting "the Labour Party is a united dynamic party ready to solve the problems this country faces" Oct '96; his was one of the key 16 seats in which GMB members were standing with union support Mar '97; warned that a Labour Government could not avoid pressure for better pay, particularly from public service workers: "reality will come crashing through the door of Labour Ministers" Mar '97; won the altered seat on a notional swing of 5.2%, by a majority over Chris Davies of 3,389 May '97; was forced to apologise to Dr Brian Mawhinney for taking his photograph eating alone on the Commons Terrace without his permission, a photo which turned up in the DAILY MIRROR May '97; urged Minister Tony Banks to visit Saddleworth's museum June '97; backed ban on fox-hunting June '97; in a letter to the INDEPENDENT played down the enhanced role of Rupert Murdoch through the award of the digital franchise to British Digital Broadcasting; insisted it might bring an investment of £300m and create 125,000 British jobs July '97; suggested there would not be enough university-trained candidates for digital broadcasting July '97; in his Maiden paid tribute to his seat's beautiful hills and "satanic mills" and the heavy unemployment in its worst patches; he also used the occasion to pledge: "I shall oppose any move to release Myra Hindley and Ian Bradley", perhaps because he anticipated it would be only bit that would be reported locally July '97; spoke effectively at Labour's annual conference Oct '97;

Born: 11 December 1959, Scunthorpe

Family: During the '95 by-election, when his Pennine origins were in dispute, the SCUNTHORPE EVENING TELEGRAPH tracked down his grandmother, Madge, his aunt Ann and "the rest of the Woolas clan" locally; son, of Dennis Woolas, industrial radiographer, and Maureen (White); is happily married to Tracey (Allen), head of Business at Millbank Tower Media Centre; 1s Joshua '93;

Education: Nelson Grammar (later Walton Lane High, a comprehensive); Manchester University (BA Hons in Philosophy);
Occupation: Chairman '97-, Director '92- of TRIBUNE (as GMB's representative); Communications Director, of the GMB (the inventor in '95 of 'Cedric the Pig' in the campaign against British Gas directors' perks) '91-97; ex: TV Producer: for BBC's 'Newsnight' and Channel 4 News (on the team which won the Royal Television Society Award for political coverage) '88-90; Fundraiser, for War on Want '86; President of the NUS '84-86;
Traits: Dark rumpled hair, with a quiff; retreating forehead; specs; short; "handsome in a raffish Italianate kind of way" (Paul Routledge, INDEPENDENT ON SUNDAY); "Mr Woolly Arse" (ex-Liberal MP Sir Cyril Smith); a member of Groucho Club, where he entertains contacts; he enjoys football, photography and watching cricket (member of Lancashire County Cricket Club);
Address: House of Commons, Westminster, London SW1A 0AA; 2 Dunham Street, Lees Oldham OL4 3NF; 16 Church Walk, Upper Butts, Brentford, Middx TW8 8DB;
Telephone: 0171 219 3000 (H of C); 0161 624 7671 (Manchester-area home);

'Tony' (Anthony) WRIGHT **Labour** **GREAT YARMOUTH '97-**

Majority: 8,668 over Conservative 3-way;
Description: Norfolk's largest working port and holiday resort town, unaltered by the boundary commissioners; the town itself is strongly Labour, but the seat has previously fallen into Tory hands because of the strength of Conservative voting in its rural hinterland and fringe seaside resorts; this may have been curtailed as much by the unpredictable behaviour of former Tory MP Michael Carttiss as by the Tory government's unpopularity;
Position: Great Yarmouth Borough Councillor (Leader '95-) '80-; Chairman, of the Great Yarmouth Marketing Initiative '95-97;
Outlook: A "Left-Centre" (NEW STATESMAN) locally-born, GMB-backed local council Leader; was so busy extricating himself from hometown involvements, that he had a low profile initially in the Commons; was a Mechanical Engineer before becoming a fulltime Labour Party Organiser;
History: Joined the Labour Party at 19, '73; was elected to Great Yarmouth Borough Council May '80; became the Agent-Secretary of the Great Yarmouth Constituency Labour Party '83; became Chairman of the Great Yarmouth Initiative, a public-private organisation '95; was selected to contest Great Yarmouth against the Tory incumbent, Michael Carttiss Apr '96; he was one of 16 GMB members listed for election support by the union Apr '97; won the seat on a swing of 13.9%, ousting Michael Carttiss by a majority of 8,668 May '97; expressed solidarity with jailed Indonesian union leader June '97; co-sponsored motion backing patenting of genetic advances July '97;
Born: 12 August 1954, Great Yarmouth
Family: Son, of Jean and late Arthur Wright; married, with a son, Carl '79, a daughter Emily '76, a stepdaughter Lisa '73;
Education: Secondary Modern hospital school;
Occupation: Director, Great Yarmouth Tourist Initiative '95-97; Chairman: Great Yarmouth

Marketing Initiative (a public-private partnership) '95-97, European Transport Project (which established a "private port authority to develop trade links and environmentally sound transport to Russia, Denmark, Scandinavia, Holland and Germany") '95-96; Labour Party Organiser (GMB) '83-97; Mechanical Engineer for electronic and oil companies (AEEU) '69-83;
Traits: Dark, parted hair with forelock; slight jowls; enjoys all sports, recently as a spectator;
Address: House of Commons, Westminster, London SW1A 0AA; 145 Burgh Road, Great Yarmouth, Norfolk NR31 8AZ
Telephone: 0171 219 3447 (H of C); 01493 662835 (home); 01493 851286 (constituency);

Derek WYATT **Labour** **SITTINGBOURNE & SHEPPEY '97-**

Majority: 1,929 over Conservative 6-way;
Description: The renamed old Faversham seat on the north Kent coast, stripped of 20,000 voters around Faversham, who have been transfered to Faversham and Mid-Kent; it is named after its two centres, Sittingbourne, on the A2, with 40,000 electors, the other the bridge-needing industrialised Isle of Sheppey, with its port of Sheerness; with its 70% of owner-occupiers and commuters, if the '92 pattern had still held, seven-time-winner Sir Roger Moate was expected to hold the seat by a majority of 11,000-plus;
Position: On the Select Committee on Culture, Media and Sports '97-; Chairman: all-party Parliamentary Groups on the Internet, Rugby Union and Mexico '97-; ex: Haringey Councillor '94-96; Chairman, of its Alexandra Palace Trust '94-96;
Outlook: Thrilled to be in the Commons as "one of the 80 or so unlikely lads and lasses who won on 1 May"; he was, in fact, the 13th least-expected new Labour MP; a radical thinker on sport and digital broadcasting; a former Director of BSkyB's Computer Channel, he is an advocate of a Labour-BT partnership to spearhead the digital revolution; he once asssaulted Tory press barons - and the GUARDIAN group - as slow-moving "old farts" "who have come to loathe the power and muscle of Rupert Murdoch's Newscorp" although "they have all had his chances and they have all had and paid for a bevy of consultants to advise them how to move their empires out of newspapers into something else"; also a crusader in sports, having helped found the Women's Sports Foundation; "as a supporter of Rugby Union" "he played" an "honourable role in bringing about a modicum of decency" (David Hinchliffe MP); a former asthmatic, he is a battler against tobacco sponsorship; in Amnesty International, Greenpeace, Charter '88;
History: He formed the Women's Sports Foundation in his office '84; he worked with the African National Congress for a decade, from '84: "I am most proud of launching the 'Campaign for Fair Play' in 1985, which was designed to stop the Lions' tour to South Africa"; he joined the Labour Party '88; he proposed an Academy of Sport to Sports Minister Iain Sproat, inviting him to visit the National Institute of Sport in Canberra '93; was elected, for Archway, to Haringey Council May '94; as the Chairman of its Alexandra Palace Trust, made a bid for £50m from the National Lottery to transform that debt-ridden structure into a TV museum and library Mar '95; was selected for "hopeless" Sittingbourne and Sheppey Apr '95;

in a major article in TRIBUNE - which did not disclose his BSKyB connection - urged a future Labour government to "seek a 50% partnership deal with BT so that there is public control and public accountability"; "we need to unleash the giant of BT today, not in 2001 or 2003", instead of allowing the cabling up of the country by US cable companies; "do we want to give away control of the new highways on an 0800 number that originates in New York? I think not; BT should cable the country; it should give 50 cables over to the US [cable companies] and anyone else for that matter; it should sell on, to companies like Murdoch, access at a commercial rate; but it should share ownership of the black digital box with us"; "we have a chance to recreate the essential backbone of the new community [of the future] if we back plans for a public information highway" July '95; unexpectedly won the Sittingbourne and Sheppey seat on a notional swing of 14.5%, unseating Sir Roger Moate after 27 years; this made him the 13th least-expected new Labour MP May '97; in his Maiden attacked the "shambolic" organisation of sports; he also said: "tobacco sponsorship of sport is a disgrace; it is disgusting; we should have no truck with it; the suggestion that there will be a shortage of money for sports sponsorships shows how unaware people are of the number of organisations that are queuing up to sponsor it" June '97; led a motion attacking the Kent County Council, again Tory-led, for its capital moratorium on schools June '97; co-sponsored motion expressing concern about fire safety in the Eurotunnel June '97; was named to the National Heritage Select Committee July '97; was a founder-member of the "Unlikely Lads and Lasses Club" for Labour MPs who had won despite not fighting target seats July '97; co-sponsored motion to protect water meadows July '97; opposed reduction of pilots in Port of London July '97;

Born: 4 December 1949, London

Family: Son, of Reginald Wyatt, accountant, and Margaret (Holmden); is married to Joanna Willett, drama producer (BAFTA award '96); 1s Jack '92; 1d Daisy '89;

Education: Colchester Royal Grammar School; St Luke's College, Exeter; Research, at St Catherine's College, Oxford University; Open University (BA Hons);

Occupation: Author: of five books, four on Rugby, one on films; Director, of Computer Channel, BSkyB '95-97; Head of Programmes at Wire TV '94-95; a Publisher and Director, at William Heinemann '85-88;

Traits: Bald/balding ("I now have three!"); egg-shaped head; specs; relaxed about clothes and appearance: "I'm not going to grow a beard or grow my hair long but I'm not overly concerned with what I look like; I'm not a suit man; I only have one"; "between the ages of 12 and 26 I was asthmatic", which he blames on smoke inhalation: "both my parents smoked between 40 and 60 cigarettes a day"; "if it were not for the brilliance of Bart's Hospital in London I would not be here, because its staff saved my life"; played Rugby for Bedford, Bath, Oxford (a Blue at 32 in '81), Barbarians and England;

Address: House of Commons, Westminster, London SW1A 0AA; 47 Mount Pleasant Villas, London N4 4HA;

Telephone: 0171 219 3000 (H of C);

